The
Hispanization of the
Philippines

Illustration from Gaspar de San Agustín's *Conquistas de las islas Philipinas* (Madrid, 1698), depicting the complementary nature of the spiritual and the temporal conquest of the islands.

From a copy in the Newberry Library.

The
Hispanization of the
Philippines

Spanish Aims
and
Filipino Responses
1565–1700

JOHN LEDDY PHELAN

The
University of Wisconsin
Press

Madison, Milwaukee, and London, 1967

Published by the University of Wisconsin Press
Madison, Milwaukee, and London
U.S.A.: Box 1379, Madison, Wisconsin 53701
U.K.: 26–28 Hallam Street, London W.1

Second printing 1967

Printed in the United States of America
Library of Congress Catalog Card Number 59–8602

For my parents

Preface

In the average Philippine community today three kinds of buildings are apt to capture the attention of a visitor. One is the Filipinos' homes, which are elevated on thick timbers and constructed with bamboo walls and nipa palm leaf roofs. This is the style in which Filipinos have been building their homes since time immemorial. Neither the advent of the Spaniards in the late sixteenth century nor the arrival of the Americans in the twentieth century has changed the style of Philippine folk architecture, which responds to the needs of that hot and humid climate. A second type of building also stands out. It is the Catholic church, frequently an ornate, baroque structure built under the direction of Spanish missionaries centuries ago. And the third building is the schoolhouse, constructed in the twentieth century under the auspices of the American regime. These buildings are visible expressions of the three movements that have shaped Philippine civilization over the course of the centuries—indigenous culture, Spanish culture, and more recently the influence of the United States. This book concerns itself with the meeting of indigenous society with Spanish culture.

The Spanish program in the Philippines envisaged a radical transformation of native Philippine society. Inspired by their previous experience in Mexico, the Spaniards launched a sweeping social reform in the islands, a reform which was religious, political, and economic in scope. To determine the nature of the Spanish program and to assess its permanent results are the basic aims of this book. In this ambitious design to reorganize Philippine society, Spanish successes were striking. So were some of their failures. The Filipinos were no mere passive recipients of the cultural stimulus created by the Spanish conquest. Circumstances gave them considerable freedom in selecting their responses to Hispanization. Their responses varied all the way from acceptance to indifference and rejection. The capacity of the Filipinos for creative social adjustment is attested by the manner in which they adapted many Hispanic features to their own indigenous culture. Preconquest society was not swept away by the advent of the Spanish regime. Rather, indigenous culture was transformed during the seventeenth century, in some cases profoundly so and in other cases only superficially. Significant though these changes were, a substantial degree of continuity between the preconquest and the Hispanic regimes was preserved. The principal aim of this study is to analyze how this result came about—in particular, to assess the role of the Spaniards as innovators and the complementary role of the Filipinos in adapting themselves to changes introduced by the Spaniards.

Since in this study I attempt to reconstruct the history of the Philippine people in the early Spanish period, Spanish historical materials constitute the principal sources. I have not, however, employed the historical method exclusively but rather have made an effort to combine sound historical practices with some anthropological techniques. Such an approach, already successfully applied by Ralph Roys, Charles Gibson, George Kubler, John Rowe, Howard Cline, and others, now has a designation of its own,

namely, "ethnohistory."* One of the major objectives of the
Philippine Studies Program directed by Professor Fred Eggan,
under whose auspices the research for this book was completed,
was to bring the disciplines of history and anthropology into closer
collaboration, and my study of Philippine society in the seventeenth
century is, therefore, oriented to a significant extent toward ethno-
history.

I have placed considerable attention on the religious aspect of
Hispanization. Events themselves suggest such a stress. The Spaniards put a heavy emphasis on Christianization as the most effective
means of incorporating the Filipinos into Spanish culture, and the
Filipinos themselves responded enthusiastically to the multiform
appeal of the new religion. Although it is abundantly clear that
Spain left its deepest imprint on the Philippines through the
agency of Catholicism, the economic, the political, and the social
aspects of Hispanization produced enduring consequences. Their
importance has not always been appreciated.

Spanish colonization in the Philippines cannot be viewed in a
vacuum. The islands constituted the Oriental outpost of a colonial
empire that stretched halfway around the globe. Spanish policy in
the Philippines was largely shaped in terms of previous experience
in North and in South America. Since this imperial perspective cannot be ignored, I have made a concerted effort in this book to draw
systematic comparisons between the intentions and the results of
Spanish policy in the Philippines, Mexico, and to a lesser extent
Peru.

The terminal date of 1700 was selected on the grounds that
the principal characteristics of Spanish influence had made themselves evident by the end of the Habsburg era. On the whole, this
working hypothesis has fitted the facts. In those cases, however,
where the terminal date has proved arbitrary or cumbersome, I
have not hesitated to carry the story into the eighteenth and nine-

* See Howard F. Cline, "Problems of Mexican Ethno-History: The
Ancient Chinantla," *Hispanic American Historical Review*, XXXVII (August,
1957), 273–95.

teenth centuries. The nature of the source material also suggested
1700 as a convenient terminal date. A substantial number of the
seventeenth century sources in Seville at the *Archivo General de
Indias* have already been published, and four months in Spain enabled me to examine many of the unpublished sources of that
period. But for the eighteenth century the situation is quite the reverse. The printed sources represent only an infinitesimal fraction
of the vast archival resources available to scholars, and until these
sources are examined, it will not be possible to make any firm conclusions about the eighteenth century. It is to be hoped that this
study dealing primarily with the seventeenth century will in time
be followed by monographs of other scholars dealing with the later
period.

This book was prepared under favorable circumstances. I spent
two and one-half years in Chicago as a Fellow in Philippine Studies
at the Newberry Library. This fellowship was a part of the Philippine Studies Program operated jointly by the Newberry, the Anthropology Department of the University of Chicago, and the Chicago Natural History Museum under a grant from the Carnegie
Corporation of New York. To the Carnegie Corporation and to
the trustees of the Newberry Library I should like to acknowledge
an abiding debt of gratitude. Two committees are in charge of the
program: a policy committee headed by Fred Eggan, of the University of Chicago, whose membership also includes Evett D.
Hester, Sol Tax, Harvey Perloff, of the University of Chicago,
Stanley Pargellis, Librarian of the Newberry, and Ruth Lapham
Butler, Custodian of the Ayer Collection at the Newberry. An
advisory committee presently consists of Fay-Cooper Cole, Felix
Keesing, H. H. Bartlett, Paul Russell and Leopold Ruiz. I am
deeply grateful to Mr. Eggan, Mr. Hester, Mr. Pargellis, and Mrs.
Butler, all of whom have been unfailingly generous with their
knowledge and their encouragement. The completion of this book
was facilitated by a summer grant provided by the research committee of the Graduate School of the University of Wisconsin.

I am particularly grateful to Professor C. R. Boxer of the University of London and to the Newberry Library for their joint permission to reproduce some of the illustrations in his manuscript of an early Philippine codex, a photostat copy of which is in the Newberry Library. For a complete description of the document see: C. R. Boxer, "A Late Sixteenth Century Manila MS.," *Journal of the Royal Asiastic Society* (April, 1950), pp. 37–39.

I would also like to express my appreciation to the directors and to the staffs of the *Archivo General de Indias* in Seville, the Library of the *Palacio de Oriente* in Madrid, the Bancroft Library of the University of California, the Knights of Columbus Foundation for the Preservation of Historic Documents at the Vatican Library of St. Louis University, and the Library of Congress for many helpful and courteous services rendered. I would also like to extend my warmest appreciation to all my good friends on the staff of the Newberry, who have aided me in countless ways. In addition I wish to acknowledge my indebtedness to the following persons who have helped me in the preparation of this volume: Woodrow Borah, John Donoghue, Robert Fox, Charles Kaut, Benjamin Keen, Paul Lietz, Francis Lynch, S.J., Stella Paluskas McPherron, Melvin Mednick, John Parry, Randall D. Sale (cartographer) Willis Siebley, Lesley Bryd Simpson, George Smith, Lutie Mae Springer, and Doris Varner Welsh.

J.L.P.

Milwaukee, Wisconsin
January, 1958

Contents

xiii

xiv   *Contents*

List of
Illustrations

THE TWO

PEOPLES

Chapter 1

The Spaniards

Few revolutions in history have enjoyed the good fortune of an immaculate conception, least of all, the Spanish conquest of America. In the conquest the whole range of human emotions found ample room in which to express themselves. Christian charity, humanitarian zeal, sadistic cruelty, and gross perfidy all had their personifications, and sometimes in the same man. There was more to the conquest than the sanguinary conquistador enshrined in the popular stereotype and the equally conventional image of the selfless missionary dedicated to saving the soul of the Indian. Conquistadores sought riches not only in the form of precious metals but also in the exploitation of native labor, for the latter was the traditional reward for those who had fought infidels in the Moorish wars in the peninsula. Many conquistadores were as desirous of fame as they were of riches. The heirs of medieval civilization, they were also men of the Renaissance who yearned for immortality in this world by having their deeds recorded for posterity.

Wanton destruction in abundance there was. The sanguinary character of the conquest cannot be minimized, but it should not

3

obscure the more constructive aspect of Spanish colonization, which was partially an outgrowth of Spain's historical development prior to 1492. Spanish expansion overseas retained many of the characteristics of the centuries-long *reconquista* of Spain from the Moors. Both enterprises were essentially military in character, Christian proselytizing, and territorially acquisitive. The military subjugation of infidels—be they Moors, Indians, or Asiatics—and the imposition of Christianity form one continuous temporal and spatial sequence in Spanish history, stretching from the Cave of Covadonga in the eighth century to the conquest of the Philippines in the late sixteenth century, from the Pyrenees to the Pacific. In both America and the Orient the *reconquista* tradition of suppressing paganism was supplemented by a Christian humanist ideal of Renaissance inspiration. The Indians were to be Hispanized as well as Christianized. The natives were to be resettled in compact villages and taught to live and to work as European laborers. The more enlightened members of the Spanish regular clergy envisaged in positive terms a harmonious synthesis of some elements of primitive society with certain features of Spanish culture.

Spaniards of all classes during the sixteenth century were inspired by an almost limitless faith in their nation's power and prestige. The Spanish race appeared to them as God's new Chosen People, destined to execute the plans of Providence. Spain's mission was to forge the spiritual unity of all mankind by crushing the Protestants in the Old World, defending Christendom against the onslaughts of the Turks, and spreading the gospel among the infidels of America and Asia.

To those of mystical inclinations, Spain's task of uniting mankind under "one faith, one pastor, and one flock" seemed like the fulfillment of the prophecies of the Apocalypse. The millennial kingdom would be established under Spanish auspices before the second coming of Christ and the Last Judgment. Many of the early missionaries in the Philippines, for example, regarded the islands merely as a convenient doorway to the fabled lands of China and Japan, just as the Antilles had previously served as the base of operations for the conquest of the American mainland. With the conversion of the peoples of Asia all the races of mankind would be brought into the fold of Christianity, an event which some interpreted as foreshadowing the approaching end of the world. Not all the Spaniards were apocalyptical mystics. Most of them, however, were inspired by a truculent faith in themselves, and this exuberant self-confidence helps to explain how the Spaniards were able, during the course of the sixteenth century, to spread their culture halfway around the globe.[1]

Were the Spaniards colossal hypocrites? None of them proposed to undo the conquest, yet they argued endlessly about the moral and the legal basis of their authority over their overseas possessions. These wordy disputes, however, cannot be dismissed as elaborate rationalizations of a *fait accompli*. All Spaniards shared the belief that Castilian jurisdiction in the Indies depended upon the fulfillment of the commitment to convert the Indians to Christianity. This unshakable conviction explains why no Spaniard ever proposed to repudiate the fact of the conquest, much though many deplored some methods by which it had been implemented. To this extent the Spaniards were rationalizing what to them was an irrevocable fact.

The most influential minds of the age—jurists, theologians and bureaucrats—agreed that the evangelical enterprise provided their compatriots with no license to trample over the legitimate rights of the natives. In the forefront were the spokesmen of the regular clergy defending the cause of the Indians. The colonists, on the other hand, vigorously expressed their conviction that colonizing must be made profitable for them. That meant, of course, some form of exploitation of native labor. The dilemma facing the governments of Charles V and Philip II was how to work out a humane and realistic compromise which would take into account the legitimate economic interests of the colonists without abandoning the Indians to ruthless exploitation. It is to the credit of the Spanish Crown that it stubbornly refused to consider the possibility that the interests of colonists and Indians might be irreconcilable.[2]

A striking feature of Spanish imperialism was the inseparable union of the Church and the state. Although both retained a vigorous amount of autonomy, the two institutions were inextricably interdependent. In a series of concessions the Holy See granted to the Spanish monarchs sweeping powers over the administration of the Church's revenues and the deciding voice in the selection of ecclesiastical personnel. In return for the patronage of the Church of the Indies, the Crown undertook the task of supervising the conversion of the Indians to Christianity. The new colonial church, vigorously supported by the military and financial power of the state, responded enthusiastically to this unique missionary opportunity. The religious conquest in turn did much to consolidate the political control of the Spanish Crown over the conquered race. In dealing with the indigenous population, Church and state usually shared a common set of objectives. Conflict, however, could be acrimonious over the choice of methods.

Spanish imperialism was not only theocratic; it was also profoundly bureaucratic. Only at the top was the imperial bureaucracy highly centralized in the persons of the king and the royal Council of the Indies. The latter exercised by royal delegation supreme jurisdiction over all phases of colonial life. There were four administrative hierarchies in the colonies, namely, the viceroys and governors, the Audiencias, the ecclesiastical, and the fiscal authorities. In spite of the nominal centralization of power in the hands of the viceroys and governors, the three other hierarchies retained a substantial amount of autonomous power. Hence there was an endless series of clashes among the various magistrates. Motivating the Crown was an abiding distrust of its officers overseas. Fearful that colonial magistrates might prove disloyal or mendacious given the long distances and the slow communications with Spain, the Crown deliberately played one administrative hierarchy against the other. Several agencies exercised the same powers, and all of them were directly responsible to the Council of the Indies.

Since authority was in practice multiplex, there was some room for decentralized decision-making on the part of colonial magistrates. The celebrated "I obey but do not execute" formula, by which the enforcement of legislation could be postponed until fresh instructions arrived from Spain, was a standard administrative procedure. This device served to apprise the central authorities of local conditions about which they might be ignorant as well as to enable colonial bureaucrats to influence the formulation of policy directives emanating from Spain.[3]

The Spanish bureaucratic system did provide for some kind of balance between centrifugal authority and centripetal flexibility. The colonial bureaucracy was not fast-moving, nor was it outstandingly efficient in the short run. Yet it was effective in achieving some of the ultimate objectives of imperial policy. Spain did preserve her empire for three centuries without heavy dependence on military coercion. Strenuous and often successful efforts were made to protect the native population. Thirdly, colonizing was made profitable, if not for all the colonists, for at least a significant minority. None of these goals was fully realized, but substantial progress toward these ends was registered. In bringing about this result, the imperial bureaucracy made a decisive contribution, rivaled in magnitude only by that of the Church.

Such are some of the principal features of Spanish expansion overseas. In the Philippines—the remote, Oriental outpost of this far-flung empire—the shape and pattern of Spanish activity differed in some respects from that of the Spanish empire in America. The contrasts are striking. So are the parallels.

Three objectives encouraged the Spaniards to colonize the Philippines. One was to secure a share in the lucrative spice trade, which heretofore had been a Portuguese monopoly. Another was to establish direct contacts with China and Japan, which might pave the way for their conversion to Christianity. And the third goal was to Christianize the inhabitants of the archipelago. Of the three objectives only the third proved realizable. The intervention of the Dutch ultimately dashed to pieces Spanish dreams in the Spice Islands, and the "spiritual conquest" of Japan and China was to prove a chimera.

Perhaps the most significant fact about the Spanish occupation of the Philippines is its date. Permanent occupation of the islands began in 1565 with the arrival of the Legazpi expedition. By that date the influence of the Muslims over the central and northern Philippines was still superficial enough not to present an insurmountable obstacle to the Spaniards. In the southern Philippines, however, the Muslims were sufficiently well entrenched to repulse Spanish penetration for 250 years. If Mohammedization had been allowed to spread unchecked throughout the islands for a few more decades after 1565, Filipino resistance might have been of such a hostile character as to discourage Spanish colonization. Secondly, their arrival in 1565 allowed the Spaniards forty years in which to consolidate themselves in the islands before the Dutch intervened in the area. Even this period of preparation barely sufficed, as the Dutch nearly ousted the Spaniards from the Philippines during the first half of the seventeenth century. Thirdly, by 1565 the subjugation of the American mainland had been consummated for many decades. The Spaniards had a secure base of operations from which to launch expansion into the Orient, and they had already acquired a varied fund of experience in dealing with conquered peoples.

The government of Philip II regarded the Philippines as a challenging opportunity to avoid a repetition of the sanguinary conquests of Mexico and Peru. In his written instructions for the *Adelantado* Legazpi, who commanded the expedition, Philip II envisaged a bloodless pacification of the archipelago. This extraordinary document could have been lifted almost verbatim from the lectures of the Dominican theologian, Francisco de Vitoria, delivered at the University of Salamanca. The King instructed Legazpi to inform the natives that the Spaniards had come to do no harm to their persons or to their property. The Spaniards intended to live among them in peace and in friendship and "to explain to them the law of Jesus Christ by which they will be saved."[4] Although the Spanish expedition could defend themselves if attacked, the royal instructions admonished the commander to commit no aggressive act which might arouse native hostility.

Philip II's project of a peaceful occupation of the Philippines was an outgrowth of that Dominican-led movement whose outstanding spokesmen were Vitoria and Las Casas. The Dominicans sought to outlaw bellicose methods. In this task they found in the philosophy of Thomas Aquinas a veritable arsenal of arguments. Both Vitoria and Las Casas stressed Aquinas' conviction that pagan peoples do not, as St. Augustine had seemed to imply, lose their social, political, and economic rights merely by coming in contact with a Christian people. The rights which all peoples enjoy by virtue of natural law and the law of nations must be taken into account by a Christian nation seeking to spread the gospel among the infidels.[5]

The adoption by the Spanish court of the Dominican-inspired ideal of pacification coincided with the founding of the Philippine colony. In fact, the Oriental archipelago became a testing ground for the new policy. In Legazpi, Philip II had a lieutenant with the patience and the skill necessary to execute such an arduous commission. Legazpi had to contend with firebrands in his own expedition, like Andrés de Mirandaola, who favored a conquest by fire and sword. The latter assailed the Filipinos as a "very vicious and treacherous race who are full of evil manners."[6] Nor did Legazpi's conciliatory aims always evoke the desired response from the Filipinos. They were often suspicious if not positively hostile to the initial overtures of the Spaniards. In a number of localities the Spaniards met some armed resistance, but this was the exception rather than the rule. In a boldly executed and relatively bloodless campaign Legazpi's youthful and dexterous grandson, Juan de Salcedo, pacified a substantial portion of the maritime provinces of Luzon.

Legazpi's task was facilitated by the geographical particularism and political decentralization of Philippine society. Small kinship units known as barangays were independent of, if not hostile to, each other. Hence armed resistance to the Spaniards on anything but a local scale was impossible. After testing the striking power and the determination of the invaders, the prevailing Filipino reaction was a prudent attitude of outwardly accepting the fact of Spanish hegemony.

The initial phase of the conquest under the leadership of Legazpi, who died on August 20, 1572, was not executed without some bloodshed. Neither can it be called sanguinary. Legazpi's achievement may not be as spectacular as Cortés' or Pizarro's, but it was a remarkable accomplishment. To the conqueror of the Philippines must be given the credit in large measure for realizing substantially but not completely Philip II's ideal of a pacific occupation.

Although the completion of the military conquest was swift and relatively bloodless, subsequent economic dislocations were more prolonged. An acute rice shortage in the 1570's and the early 1580's threatened the precarious existence of the new colony. Philippine agriculture was of the subsistence variety. The sudden descent of two groups of nonproductive consumers—the Spaniards and in much larger numbers the Chinese—created a severe food shortage.

The intensity of the economic crisis aggravated a virulent conflict between the clergy and the colonists over the exploitation of native labor. Following the Spanish custom in America most of the Filipino population was distributed among the colonists under the encomienda system. In return for the payment of an annual tribute, the encomendero was obligated to protect his wards and to indoctrinate them in the rudiments of the Christian doctrine. That the encomenderos abused their trust in a wide variety of illegal exactions is evident. The clergy, ably led from 1579 onward by the aged but energetic Bishop Salazar, caustically exposed these abuses to the authorities in Spain. From the pulpits zealous friars hurled threats of excommunication at those encomenderos who would not heed their strictures. Thus the encomenderos were confronted with a grim choice between the threat of external damnation in the next world and starvation in this world.[7]

Two developments may have been more effective in relieving pressure on the Filipinos than the vigorous defense of their rights waged by Bishop Salazar and the missionary prelates. By the mid-1580's rice production had expanded to meet the increased demand. The stabilization of the trade with China—the exchange of Chinese silks for Mexican silver—created a solid base of prosperity for the Spanish community.[8]

For two centuries the Manila galleon plying between Manila and Acapulco was the economic lifeline of the Spanish colony in the Philippines. In Mexico there was an almost limitless demand for Chinese silks, and Chinese merchants had an equally insatiable appetite for Mexican silver.[9] Like a magnet, the profits of the silver and silk trade kept most Spaniards in and around Manila. The Spanish colonists, never numbering more than a few thousand in the seventeenth century, had little incentive to settle in the provinces and to carve out for themselves large landed estates operated by cheap native labor. The religious along with a handful of civil bureaucrats bore most of the burden of maintaining Spanish authority over the 500,000 Filipinos under Spanish control.

To the galleon trade must be ascribed the beginning and the continuance of Chinese immigration, which has substantially altered the ethnic composition of the Philippines. So large was the Chinese colony that in the early 1580's it was assigned a separate quarter, the Parian, located within range of the guns of Manila's fortress. The Parian, meaning market place in Chinese, became the nerve center of the capital's commercial life. In its colorful bazaars could be purchased all the goods and products of East and West. The Chinese soon acquired a virtual monopoly of the retail business. They dominated the craft trades, and their agricultural skills eventually did much to increase productivity.

Sullen suspicion and mutual hostility characterized Sino-Spanish relations, exploding periodically into bloody massacres in which the wooden buildings of the Parian were committed to flames and the Chinese inhabitants slaughtered. Such anti-Chinese riots occurred in 1603, 1639, 1662, 1686, and 1762. In spite of deep-rooted racial antagonisms, neither the Spaniards nor the Chinese could get along without the other. After the smoke and fire of each riot had faded away the meaning of this fundamental interdependence asserted itself. These Sino-Spanish clashes sprang from the Spaniards' fear that the much larger Chinese colony was planning a revolt. The fear in fact was groundless, but a wave of panic and insecurity periodically seized Spanish officialdom. The Chinese merchants realized that their own prosperity depended upon a continuance of the Spanish regime—only a Spanish governor in Manila could secure that annual supply of Mexican silver which was the lifeblood of Sino-Philippine trade.[10]

Another fateful consequence of the galleon trade was to convert Manila into the undisputed metropolis of the whole archipelago. That position of predominance has never been seriously challenged from early Spanish times to the present day. Its excellent harbor facilities as well as its location adjacent to the "rice basket" of central Luzon made Manila an inviting headquarters for the new colony. The shortage of food production in the Bisayan island group compelled the Spaniards by the early 1570's to transfer the principal center of their activity to the more populous island of Luzon. By 1650 the approximate population of the Spanish walled city and the suburbs inhabited by the Chinese and the Filipinos was 42,000 people.[11] Containing the bulk of the Spanish population and the largest single concentration of Chinese and Filipinos, Manila was the only functional city in the Philippines.

The economic crisis following in the wake of the conquest was resolved by the mid–1580's. Pressure on the Filipinos lightened during the two decades between 1586 and 1609. Their lot certainly was not enviable, but it was tolerable in comparison to conditions before and after these dates. The relative economic equilibrium was shattered after the arrival of Governor Juan de Silva in June of 1609. Hispano-Dutch rivalry in the Old World spread to the Orient, which became a critical theater of operations in that global conflict. The Dutch originally went to the Far East to dispute the

Hispano-Portuguese monopoly of spices located in the Moluccas and the Celebes islands. What the Dutch eventually came to desire was Manila itself, whose geopolitical location and whose excellent harbor facilities made it the natural emporium for commerce in both spices and silks. The Spaniards lost the "war of the cloves," but in the face of severe odds they managed to hold on to the Philippines until the treaty of Münster (1648), in which Spain formally recognized Dutch independence, lifted the threat of Dutch conquest.[12]

The Filipinos themselves had to bear a great deal of the burden of defending the archipelago, which also served as a base of operations for the Spanish offensive in the Spice Islands. Without the ruthless exploitation of their labor services and the quasi-expropriation of their products Manila surely would have fallen to the Dutch. The period of the Dutch war was one of the decisive chapters in the development of Philippine society. As we shall see in Chapters VII and VIII, the Dutch war had much to do with shaping the permanent character of land tenure and labor. A large portion of the long-range program of economic Hispanization had to be sacrificed to the immediate need of mobilizing the human and material resources of the land for the war effort. In the face of official Spanish hostility the pre-Hispanic system of debt peonage and sharecropping was solidified, although modified under the stress of the prolonged war emergency.

During the decades following the conclusion of the peace of Münster, pressure on the natives lightened considerably. The main outlines of the semi-Hispanized society came into sharp focus by 1700, when the change of dynasties from the Habsburgs to the Bourbons inaugurated a new period in the history of the Spanish empire.

In conclusion, the occupation of the Philippines was essentially a missionary enterprise. Although the small merchant oligarchy of Manila reaped handsome profits, the colonial government itself produced an annual deficit fluctuating between 85,000 pesos and 338,832 pesos. The treasury of Mexico paid this deficit with sil-

ver bullion, most of which found its way into the coffers of the
Chinese merchants.[13] Three different proposals to abandon the
Philippines were debated at the Spanish court. These suggestions
were inspired by the merchants of Seville, who enjoyed a monopoly
of the trans-Atlantic carrying trade, and by the textile interests of
Andalucia. Both powerful vested interests were fearful that their
monopolistic privileges would be threatened if Mexico and Peru
were flooded with cheap Chinese silks. The Seville commercial
monoploy and the Andalucian textile industry secured their
minimum objectives to restrict Philippine commerce to the Manila-
Acapulco line and to abolish trade between Mexico and Peru.
The Crown limited the total value of goods which could be shipped
from Manila to Acapulco to 250,000 pesos annually, an amount
sufficient to maintain the Philippine colony and yet small enough
to be used up in Mexico. In practice, however, the annual value
of merchandise imported on the Manila galleon came closer to
2,000,000 pesos. The quantity of goods came to be determined not
by royal fiat but by the amount of shipping space available on the
galleons.[14]

What the enemies of the Philippine colony never could secure
was Spanish withdrawal from the archipelago. The representatives
of the missionary orders at the Spanish court reminded the sov-
ereigns in forceful language that their promise to convert the
Filipinos and to preserve the Faith in the islands was a solemn
commitment which in good conscience could not be liquidated.
Withdrawal from the archipelago, the religious spokesmen argued,
would result in either the return of the Filipinos to paganism or
the conquest of the islands by the Protestant Dutch. Its fiscal
deficit notwithstanding, the Philippines must be kept for their
spiritual value, in the words of one chronicler, as an "arsenal and
warehouse of the Faith," upon whose preservation rested the
cause of Catholicism in the Orient.[15]

More than any other single factor a religious and missionary
commitment kept the Spanish state in the economically profitless
colony of the Philippines.

Chapter 11

The Filipinos

Although the Spaniards were the conquerors and the Filipinos were the conquered, the meeting of these two cultures was not a one-sided process in which the Spaniards remade Filipino society into an exclusively Hispanic image. Much of preconquest culture survived the conquest. Indispensable to an understanding of how this result came about is an awareness of the way of life of the Filipinos on the eve of the arrival of the Spaniards.[1]

As we observed in Chapter I, the conquest was facilitated by the fragmentation of Philippine society. The only form of political and social organization was small kinship units known as barangays, a name derived from the sailboats which brought the early Malay immigrants to the Philippines. The barangays usually consisted of from 30 to 100 families. A few barangays, such as the ones of Manila, Vigan, and Cebu, contained as may as 2,000 people. In the barangay complex there were four distinct classes, with several gradations inside each one: (1) the chieftains, called *datus*, and their families, (2) *maharlika* or the nobles, (3) the freemen called *timagua*, and (4) the servile, dependent class whom the Spaniards misleadingly called slaves.

The precise nature of interbarangay relations is not always easy to determine. Frequently it was unmitigated hostility, which in the Philippines took the form of headhunting expeditions. There are also examples of interbarangay coöperation. Whether such cases deserve to be called confederations in which one *datu* was recognized as the overlord of a regional grouping of barangays is a moot question. In their understandable desire to ennoble the remote history of their land, some nationalist-minded Philippine historians have referred to the kings of pre-Hispanic times.[2] According to this opinion, the jurisdiction of the native leader Humabon extended over the whole island of Cebu at the time of Magellan and in 1570 all the barangays of central Luzon acknowledged the authority of one Soliman. Although some of the early Spanish chroniclers referred to the *reyezuelos* of Cebu and Manila, that title of kinglet was evidently synonomous for the *datu* of a large barangay.[3]

The following passage from Pigafetta, the chronicler of the Magellan expedition, suggests that the Spaniards did not find kinglets in the islands; hence they tried to create them.

The captain [Magellan] told the king [Humabon, the local chieftain] through the interpreter that he thanked God for inspiring him to become a Christian; and that now he would more easily conquer his enemies than before. The king replied that he wished to become a Christian, but some of his chiefs did not wish to obey, because they said that they were as good men as he. Then our captain had all the chiefs of the king called, and told them that unless they obeyed the king as their king, he would have them killed, and would give their possessions to the king. They replied that they would obey him.[4]

Pigafetta's account indicates that Humabon was nothing more than the *datu* of a large barangay. Magellan's policy was to promote him to the status of a kinglet subordinate to Magellan.

The introduction into the central and northern Philippines of a suprabarangay concept of political organization may have occurred as a result of Muslim influence during those very decades between Magellan's death in 1521 and Legazpi's arrival in 1565. Muslim traders from the islands of Malaysia introduced this notion into the southern Philippines sometime after 1450. In the sixteenth century Mohammedization advanced slowly northward, eventually reaching the bay of Manila. The communities that the Spaniards encountered in both Cebu and in Manila in the 1560's were superficially Islamized, but the principle of suprabarangay leadership apparently had not progressed beyond the embryonic stage.

The example of Mindanao, the largest island of the southern Philippines, is significant in that Mohammedization was allowed to unfold there without being checked by the Spaniards. A suprabarangay form of political organization, the *rajah* of Muslim origin, did emerge there. The same development probably would have occurred in the central and northern Philippines if the Spaniards had not halted the Muslim advance. Equally suggestive is the case of the mountain province of northwestern Luzon, which for three centuries was scarcely touched by either Spanish or Muslim influence. There no suprabarangay units developed.

The conquest did not destroy the "kinglets" of pre-Hispanic times, but merely arrested their rise. What did survive the shock of the conquest was the barangay. The Spaniards adroitly refashioned this patriarchal kinship unit into the cornerstone of local government. How they did will be examined in some detail in Chapter IX.

Geography does much to explain this state of political decentralization. The fact that the Philippines are an archipelago of more than 7,000 islands, each one varying in size from substantial land masses to uninhabited dots of land, obviously discouraged the formation of transinsular political units. Only eleven of the islands are as large as 1,000 square miles apiece. Mountain barriers in many cases made for intrainsular isolation. In the narrow valleys and along the rivers small clusters of population settled. In the mountains dwelt the fierce Negritos, perhaps the original inhabitants of the islands. They were driven into the highlands by the Malay invaders, who were in possession of the maritime lowlands when the Spaniards arrived.

Riparian geography in addition to the prevalence of mountain barriers made for geographical particularism and political decentralization. The latter in turn encouraged linguistic diversity. Although all the Philippine tongues go back to a common Malayo-Polynesian root form, the Filipinos spoke a bewildering variety of languages. On the island of Luzon there are six major languages, many minor ones, and a host of dialects. The Tagalogs of central Luzon where Manila is located formed the largest single linguistic group. In the Bisayan group of islands in the central Philippines there are three principal languages in addition to a confusing variety of minor languages and dialects. And the southern Philippines formed yet another Babel of languages.[5]

The Filipinos had an alphabet of their own consisting of seventeen letters, three of which were vowels and the rest consonants. The Tagalog text of the *Doctrina* of 1593, the first book printed in the Philippines, was printed in both the Latin and Philippine alphabets. Although the Philippine languages survived the conquest, not so the pre-Hispanic alphabet. The Philippine tongues were soon transliterated into the Latin alphabet. Pre-Hispanic literature, however, was scant. Only a few historical fragments have come down to us, and there is little evidence to suggest that the Spaniards deliberately destroyed Philippine manuscripts. The Filipinos had an alphabet, but they did not often use it for literary purposes, according to Chirino.[6] Their literature was largely oral.

Political decentralization and linguistic diversity notwithstanding, the cultures of the maritime provinces were sufficiently similar among themselves to justify our making some generalizations about the pattern of preconquest society. Philippine social organization did not extend beyond the immediate family and the extended family or kinship unit. Polygamy was not widespread among the Filipinos. Its practice was confined to the Bisayan islands of Samar, Leyte, and Cebu in the central Philippines. Probably introduced by Mohammedan traders from Borneo, it was a costly custom in which only the wealthy chieftains could afford to indulge. Divorce and remarriage, on the other hand, were more common. The failure to have children, a prolonged illness, or an opportunity to make a more advantageous marriage were sufficient causes to secure a divorce. Divorce was socially acceptable under certain conditions, but it was still the exception.

The marriage pattern was relatively stable. Parents negotiated the marriages of their children, with a view to cementing kinship alliances and property arrangements. The custom was for the groom, not the bride, to provide the dowry. Furthermore, the groom had to pay his future father-in-law "bride-price" or to perform "bride-service." The young man either paid his father-in-law a sum in gold (*bigay haya*) or he worked gratis for a period of time in his father-in-law's house (*maninirbihan*).[7] The engaged couple living under the same roof evidently had opportunities to indulge in premarital sexual relations. Circumstantial evidence suggests that for the Filipinos the authenticity of a marriage depended upon the birth of children. The final ceremonial formalities of the marriage might be postponed until after the bride gave evidence of her ability to become a mother.

The rationale underlying the Philippine customs of bride-price and bride-service never has been adequately explained. To fill this vacuum a few tentative hypotheses may be suggested. It may have been thought that the bride's father should be compensated for the expenses involved in rearing a daughter. Perhaps a more basic explanation is that with the bride-money obtained from his daughter's marriage a father could then provide for his son's marriage and thus insure the perpetuation of the kinship unit. Since the bride-gift was provided by the groom's kinfolk, the latter acquired a vested interest in the stability of the marriage. In case of divorce the bride-gift was not returned if the husband was the guilty party. Hence the husband's kinsmen were a potent force in stabilizing marriage.

The Spanish sources provide only a few clues about the precise nature of kinship ties other than to indicate in general terms their central importance. The only political unit in Philippine society, the barangay, was kinship-oriented. On Luzon patrilocal residence was the rule; in the Bisayas, however, there was a strong tendency toward matrilocal residence. Everywhere there was bilateral kinship descent with some emphasis placed on the paternal side. In this respect the Philippine custom did not differ substantially from that of the Spaniards.

In preconquest times landowning was communal in character, with the actual title vested in the barangay. Wealth was determined by how many dependents a chieftain could muster to cultivate the communally owned lands. Essentially a self-sufficient agrarian economy in which commerce with one's neighbors played only a minor role, Philippine agriculture was based upon the cultivation of rice and root crops and was supplemented by fishing and the raising of swine and fowl.

To call the pre-Hispanic system of labor organization slavery, as the Spaniards invariably did, is misleading. The whole arrangement had much more in common with debt peonage and sharecropping than it did with the European conception of chattel slavery. The term "dependent" is a more accurate designation of this class. Among the Filipinos many judicial sentences took the form of fines. This custom offers a partial explanation for the existence of a large group among the dependent class, the debt peons. Those who were unable to pay judicial fines or who found themselves in stringent circumstances could secure loans only at a usurious rate of interest. Loans were payable at each harvest season at 100 per cent interest. In addition to debtors the dependent population was swelled by those captured in raids on neighboring villages, those convicted of poaching on a *datu's* land, or those guilty of committing adultery with the wives or concubines of the *datus*.

The dependent population was divided into two principal categories. Among the Tagalogs the *mamamahay* could own property, and they could marry without their superior's consent. As compensation they usually received one-half of the harvest. The *tumaranpuh* was the Bisayan version of the Tagalog *mamamahay*. Enjoying the freedom of their persons, including the right to acquire and dispose of property, their obligation was to work for their superior one day out of every four. Both the Tagalog *mamamahay* and the Bisayan *tumaranpuh* were sharecroppers rather than chattel slaves.

The second division among the dependent population, known as the *guiguilir* in Tagalog, were not precisely chattels. To be sure they could not marry without the consent of their superiors. If they were not household servants, they could be sold. They did receive some compensation for their labor services, but their share of the crop was much less than that of the *mamamahay*. The Bisayan *ayuey* corresponded to the Tagalog *guiguilir*. The *ayuey*'s obligation was to work gratis three out of every four days. Nor could they contract matrimony without the consent of their superior. Yet they could own and dispose of property. The *guiguilir-ayuey* resembled to some extent debt peons.

The Spanish administration recognized the difference between the two classes among the dependent population. The more prosperous *mamamahay-tumaranpuh* were responsible for paying their own tribute. The tribute of the *guiguilir-ayuey*, on the other hand, was paid by their superiors.[8]

Dependent status was hereditary. There were two alternatives, differing according to local usage. Either the individual children of a free man and a dependent woman were half free and half dependent, and their descendants became progressively one-fourth, one-eighth or one-sixteenth dependent, etc., or the children might be divided, with half of them free and the other half of dependent status. An indication of the bewildering complexity of the system is the fact that the labor services of one dependent might be distributed among ten or twelve superiors.[9] Part-dependents but not whole-dependents enjoyed the privilege of purchasing their manumission at a set price. Before the conquest the price of manumission for a Bisayan *tumaranpuh* was the equivalent of twelve Spanish pesos. By 1635 it varied between sixteen and twenty pesos. When the number of dependents was already on the decline, in 1660, the price of manumission fluctuated between thirty-two and forty pesos.[10] Although the Filipinos could buy their way out of dependent status, it was far easier for them to sink into that class by borrowing at a usurious rate of interest.

Although the Spaniards misleadingly called this institution *esclavitud*, knowledgeable Spanish observers candidly recognized that the "peculiar institution" of the Philippines lacked the harshness and brutality of European slavery. In a system combining features of sharecropping and debt peonage, the dependents were linked to their superiors not only by the obligation to perform certain labor services but also, in many cases, by close ties of consanguinity.

The refinements in, and the evident expansion of, the dependent class might suggest at first glance that kinship ties were being replaced by social and economic differences by the eve of the conquest. Although no certain answer is available, the evidence seems to point to the conclusion that kinship ties were not disintergrating. On the island of Mindanao the Spanish conquest did not take place, and Muslim influence resulted in the emergence of quasi-political states in which kinship ties remained very strong. In the last analysis, kinship ties rather than political and economic differences remained paramount in that region.

At the top of the social pyramid were the chieftains and their families. Underneath them were the *maharlika* class, those born of noble blood, who served their chieftains in war and provided them with counsel in peace. There was also a numerous class of free men who possessed neither the privileges of the chieftains and nobles nor the obligations of the dependents. At the bottom of the ladder was the dependent population with a bewildering number of subdivisions. Each barangay, consisting of these three groups, was bound together in a kinship system of mutual dependence essentially patriarchal in character. Outside the umbrella of mutual security provided by the barangay, war of every man against every man was apt to prevail.

Of all aspects of preconquest culture the one that most aroused the curiosity of the Spaniards was the religion of the Filipinos, or to be more precise their religious rituals. The Philippine cults were a blending of monotheism and polytheism, with the latter tending to predominate. They had some conception of a Supreme Being, the creator of the universe and the ruler of men. In Tagalog he was called *Bathala* and in Bisayan *Laon* or *Abba*. This remote supreme deity was relegated to the background by a pantheon of gods and goddesses who were the specific protectors for all the activities in which men engaged.

The spirit world in Philippine religion was densely inhabited. The spirits were called *anitos* or *diwatas*. The good spirits were those of the Filipinos' ancestors and the bad spirits were those of their enemies. In order to placate their wrath and to acquire their good will, the Filipinos offered up prayers and sacrifices to them. The Spanish sources are full of detailed accounts of these ceremonies.

Many rituals concentrated on the cure of illness. Other ceremonies, in which ritual drinking was an integral part, stressed the need to propitiate the gods. The Filipinos drank copious libations of rice wine on certain ceremonial occasions, notably at betrothals, weddings, and funerals. Although these ceremonies might last as long as three days, they were not unadulterated alchoholic orgies. A Spanish worthy whose name has been lost to posterity put it succinctly when he wrote: "Although they are drunk, they do not entirely lose their senses, and I have never seen any of them fall down because he was drunk."[11] Alcina reported that the Bisayans might take as many as twelve cups of wine without losing their judgment or their senses. He did add that their color was "somewhat altered."[12] The duty of providing wine and food for the guests cast many a chieftain into the depths of poverty, but such largesse was periodically expected from those of that class. *Noblesse oblige*, Philippine version. Ritual drinking was more popular with the men than with the women, who drank separately from the men. The Ilokanos, the Tagalogs, and the Bisayans were the strongest imbibers. The Pampangans enjoyed a reputation for relative temperance.

Like the ancient Egyptians and the Assyrians, the Filipinos worshipped nature. They rendered divine honors to the sun, the moon, the rainbow, the rivers, the plants, the caves, the mountains, and the trees. They adored certain animals such as crows, sharks, and crocodiles. Perhaps as a reflection of Chinese influence the Filipinos were also ancestor-worshippers. Some of the spirits, or the *anitos*, were regarded as intermediaries between the living and the dead. To commemorate their ancestors they carved idols in stone, ivory, and wood. The Filipinos did have a conception of the afterlife, in which the good were rewarded with a heaven (in (Tagalog, *kalualhatian*, and in Bisayan, *ologan*) and the wicked in this life were punished by being committed to an inferno (*kasamaan* in Tagalog and *solad* in Bisayan). Interwoven into their religious beliefs were whole strands of magical practices and superstitions.

Some of the earliest Spanish observers expressed doubt as to whether there was a professional priestly class. Friar Juan de Plasencia's study of Tagalog customs (1589) settled this question affirmatively. Ritual sacrifices were performed by persons known as the *babaylan* or the *katalonan*. They were usually elderly women, the few men who practiced this priestly function ordinarily being transvestites.

What the Filipinos lacked were temples or buildings reserved for the exclusive use of religious functions. This situation puzzled some Spaniards, who seldom took note of the fact that as nature worshippers the Filipinos had a host of sacred groves and sacred caves which took the place of temples. There was no fixed calendar of religious celebrations. Functions occurred as specific occasions warranted. Although the majority of religious rituals consisted of offerings to the spirits, these sacrifices did not involve human beings. In Filipino mythology there was no conviction that the gods had to be nourished and propitiated by the constant flow of that most precious commodity, human blood. The Spaniards might dismiss these religious convictions and ceremonies as unadulterated superstition, but the Filipino pagan cults never aroused the degree of indignation that the sanguinary rituals of the Aztecs usually did.

Such are some of the principal features of the Filipino society which the Spaniards set out to remodel. They made a serious effort to acquire a moderately objective grasp of the character of pre-Hispanic culture, but the Spaniards also attached value judgments to the data they collected. Two of these value judgments merit special attention. One was that the religion of the Filipinos constituted the tyrannical enslavement of the devil over a pagan people; therefore, in spreading Christianity the Spaniards were "liberating" the Filipinos from the oppressive sway of the devil. The other value judgment was that the preconquest system of sharecropping and debt peonage based on usury was an unjust and tyrannical form of social organization. In conquering the islands the Spaniards were "liberating" the lower classes from the oppressive bondage of their chieftains. By this semantic exercise the Spaniards transformed themselves from "conquerors" into "liberators."

This concept owes its origin to the Valladolid debate between Las Casas and Sepúlveda (1550–51). In answer to the thesis of Las Casas about the illegitimacy of the conquest, Sepúlveda rejoined that the licitness of the conquest could be founded on the alleged injustices and tyrannies of the pre-Hispanic regimes. The viceroy of Peru, Francisco de Toledo (1569–81), authorized an elaborate historical investigation of Inca society in order to substantiate this thesis. In the Philippines, Spanish opinion, both ecclesiastical and lay, accepted this principle.

In various provinces of the Philippines native chieftains and freemen were assembled during the year 1599 in order to "elect" the Castilian king as their natural lord and sovereign. These election ceremonies were organized upon the urging of a royal cedula from Spain. The Filipinos based their voluntary submission on the contractual promise that the king and his new subjects would render each other certain services. In these documents the conquest was interpreted as a "liberation." The Spaniards were said to have liberated the Filipinos from the enslavement of the devil as well as freed them from unjust social abuses. The positive benefits that the king promised to render were religious instruction, the administration of justice, and protection against their enemies (Japanese, Chinese, and Mohammedan pirates, and hostile infidel neighbors).[13]

The amount of real freedom of choice that these Filipinos did have under these circumstances was probably negligible. Yet it would not be unreasonable to assume that some Filipinos accepted voluntarily the theory underlying this ceremony. This formula does illustrate one significant argument by which the Spaniards justified the conquest to themselves and to the Filipinos, and this argument was based upon a Spanish interpretation of preconquest society.

However the Spaniards may have interpreted the world of the conquered in order to rationalize their own actions, this indigenous culture was deeply embedded in the islands. Hence significant elements of the old culture blended into the new society emerging under Spanish auspices, and in many cases took forms contrary to the wishes of the new regime. The Filipinos were and still are tough and flexible, able to absorb new cultural influences without losing their own identity. They survived the "shock" of the conquest with far less psychological and material damage to themselves than did many native races of the Americas. Although partially Hispanized, they never lost that Malaysian stratum which to this day remains the foundation of their culture.

In this connection it is tempting to compare preconquest Philippine society with the civilized Indian peoples of America, in particular the Aztecs of Mexico and the Incas of Peru, and to examine the Spanish role in these different areas. The most obvious distinction is, of course, the fact that in America the Spaniards came in contact with civilizations that had developed in complete separation from the mainstream of Eurasian culture, while in the Philippines they encountered a culture long in contact with that mainstream, owing to the archipelago's proximity to China and Malaysia. While, therefore, in some respects the Filipinos were distinctly inferior to the Aztecs and to the Incas, in other areas the reverse is true. The American peoples had progressed far beyond the level reached by the Filipinos in political organization, and in science and art. The Incas, and to a lesser extent the Aztecs, had developed a political state, whereas the Filipinos were just emerging from the kinship stage. The artistic accomplishments of the Filipinos were aesthetically meager alongside the impressive temples and the magnificent sculptures of the New World. Yet one cannot avoid the impression that indigenous America was fossilized as a consequence of its isolation. These peoples lacked an alphabet, the use of metals, and, with the exception of the Incas, beasts of burden. Among the Aztecs, human sacrifice was practiced on a massive scale and cannibalism was not unknown. Here the advent of the Spaniards broke down the isolation and connected the New World with the Old.

In the Philippines, however, the Spaniards played no such role. The Philippine contact with Eurasian culture accounts for the existence of a system of writing in the islands, the use of metals, the prevalence of beasts of burden, and the absence of human sacrifice and cannibalism among the maritime peoples of the archipelago. All of this might suggest that the Filipinos were more capable of an independent cultural growth, without European influence, than were the Aztecs and the Incas.

This alternative existed, but its possibilities ought not to be exaggerated. That the Spaniards did not interrupt in the Philippines the flowering of a sophisticated and an advanced civilization of the same high quality as that of Japan or China may be seen by studying the case of the Moros. In the southern Philippines the Moros, who successfully resisted Spanish penetration for three centuries, were left to develop free from Spanish influence. Their cultural achievements were solid and modest but scarcely sophisticated or advanced. There are few grounds for assuming that the central and northern Philippines would, if left independent, have made much more progress than did the south. In fact, it was probably inevitable that the Philippines fall under some form of European domination. In contrast to Japan and China their society was not sufficiently well organized either politically or militarily to resist aggression, and the archipelago constituted an inviting prey to any European power anxious to secure a base of operations from which to extend its influence over the neighboring peoples of the Orient.

THE SPREAD

OF

CATHOLICISM

Chapter III

The Spanish
Missionaries

In the meeting of Philippine and Spanish cultures the regular clergy of the Spanish Church were leading protagonists. In order to evaluate their role, one must first understand the rather complex relations of the regular clergy with the episcopacy and the civil authorities. A clear and precise comprehension of the theocratic elements in Spanish imperialism is a necessary ingredient to any understanding of the impact of Spanish culture on Philippine society.

The Papacy transferred to the Spanish Crown the administration of the new Church of the Indies, and the Crown in turn entrusted to the regular clergy the specific task of Christianizing the natives. Taking perpetual vows of chastity, obedience, and poverty, the regulars lived according to a community rule (*regula*) under the jurisdiction of elected superiors. The religious of the regular orders, with their higher standards of discipline and asceticism, were better prepared for missionary work than were the members of the secular clergy. The latter, whose superiors were the bishops, formed the parish clergy in established Christian communities. Those regular orders who participated in the con-

version of the Filipinos were the Augustinians (1565), the Discalced Franciscans (1578), the Jesuits (1581), the Dominicans
(1587), and the Augustinian Recollects (1606).

The regulars received a generous grant of authority in the
omnimoda bull of Pope Adrian VI (May 9, 1522) to administer
the sacraments to the Indians and to perform the duties of parish
priests independently of the local bishop. This arrangement, convenient though it was for the missionaries in the New World,
violated one of the key reforms of the Council of Trent, which
declared no priest might exercise care of souls over laymen without being subject to episcopal authority. Philip II secured from
Pope Pius V the brief, *Exponi nobis* (March 24, 1567), in which
the Pontiff gave the Crown discretionary power in enforcing this
Trentine canon in the Indies. The canon was immediately applied
to Peru. The same action was taken in 1583 for the viceroyalty
of Mexico, to which the Philippines was nominally attached.[1] The
cedula of December 7, 1583, gave the secular clergy outright
preferential treatment for vacant benefices and made the regulars,
in the capacity as parish priests, subject to episcopal visitation.
The Crown looked with misgivings upon the regulars' disregard
for episcopal jurisdiction as an implicit denial of many of the
privileges the Crown enjoyed by virtue of its patronage over the
colonial church.

Two issues were at stake. One was tenure of benefices by the
regulars. The other was the claim of the bishops to supervise the
conduct of regulars in their role as parish clergy, i.e., the right of
ecclesiastical visitation. In most regions of the empire where well-
organized Indian parishes emerged the secular clergy replaced the
regulars. The latter often retired after an acrimonious rearguard
action. The Philippines is an outstanding exception to this trend.
Down to 1898 the regulars continued to hold the majority of
benefices, and episcopal visitation was a hollow claim. Various
archbishops of Manila met persistent failure in their attempts to
enforce visitation. The most notable incidents in this long controversy were those involving Bishop Salazar (1581) and the

Zambales.

Natives of the Zambal province.

*This and the following illustrations from a manuscript circa 1590
in the library of C. R. Boxer.*

Natives of the Cagayan province.

Natives of the Bisayan islands.

Natives from the Tagalog provinces.

archbishops Vásquez de Mercado (1612), García Serrano (1621), Poblete (1654–56), Camacho (1697), and Sancho de Santa Justa y Rufina (1767–76).[2]

The opposition of the religious to visitation would have been as futile in the islands as it had been in Mexico, if certain conditions peculiar to the Philippines had not prevailed. The regulars in the islands were irreplaceable. They knew it, and they took pains to make everyone else aware of the fact. In 1655 there were not more than sixty secular priests in the whole archipelago, in contrast to 254 regulars.[3] The secular priests in most cases did not speak the Philippine languages, and the Filipinos did not speak Spanish. In every serious attempt to enforce visitation the religious resigned their parishes or threatened to do so and retired to their convents in Manila. A restoration of the old arrangement always ensued. The civil authorities hesitated to take the drastic step of ousting the regulars from their benefices. Every responsible officer of the Crown realized that the continuation of Spanish hegemony in the provinces largely depended upon the authority and prestige that the religious exercised over their parishioners.

Archbishop Sancho de Santa Justa y Rufina (1767–76) sought to break the deadlock by the novel expedient of replacing the recalcitrant regulars with Filipino clergymen. These ill-trained priests, many of whom were hastily granted holy orders by the determined Archbishop, rendered a lamentable account of themselves.[4] The only result was to deal a crippling blow to the growth of a native clergy.

A genuine fear on the part of the religious was that episcopal visitation would endanger their corporate unity and might compel them to violate their vow of obedience to their superiors. Regulars serving as parish priests would thus be subject to two equal and coördinate jurisdictions—the bishop and the provincial superior—either one of which might issue conflicting orders. In addition the obligation imposed on the provincial superior to present a list of three candidates (the *nómina*) to the vice-patron (the governor) for every vacant benefice might jeopardize the freedom to assign his subjects. Another infringement of the provincial superior's freedom of action was to compel him to indicate to the vice-patron his reasons for removing or transferring a subject. The *nómina* itself, the regulars asserted, was unenforceable in the Philippines. In view of the diversity of tongues a superior was in-deed fortunate to have one priest familar with the language of a particular parish. If such confusion and limitation of freedom were allowed to prevail, religious in Spain might be discouraged from coming to the Philippines.

According to another argument of the religious, the Philip-pines was still an active mission, *en viva conquista espiritual*, as one missionary spokesman put it.[5] Only the maritime peoples had been converted, while the mountain peoples remained pagan. Even in the lowlands Christianization had been only partially completed. Scarcity of missionary personnel as well as the dispersal of the population was responsible. The missionary orders argued that under these circumstances the Filipinos were not yet ready to be turned over to the secular clergy.

The episcopacy and the secular clergy tacitly admitted the partial validity of the argument of the religious. The suffragan sees of Cagayan, the Camarines, and Cebu were indeed missionary fields. With only a handful of secular priests there was also an acute shortage of regulars in these dioceses. The serious attempts to enforce episcopal visitation were usually confined to the arch-bishopric of Manila, containing the largest concentration of people along with the best organized and the best indoctrinated parishes. What the secular clergy wanted to take over were the lucrative benefices of the metropolitan see, leaving the rest of the archi-pelago to the regulars. That kind of compromise the religious re-fused to make. They claimed that the resources of the more profitable parishes of the archbishopric were needed to support the less lucrative parishes of the outlying suffragan sees.

The jurisdictional conflicts between the archbishops and the religious orders produced periodic states of turmoil with demoraliz-ing consequences for all parties involved. But the religious did derive one indirect benefit from this tension. In defense of their common privileges the various orders retained an unusual degree of unity of purpose among themselves. Differences between the orders were kept at a minimum in the face of the common threat posed by the issue of episcopal visitation.

If the regulars could make a solid case for their opposition to visitation, the archbishops could also cogently justify its need. One of their pertinent arguments was that some external authority was required to investigate whether the regulars were performing their parish duties satisfactorily. An investigation conducted by Archbishop Camacho in December and January of 1697 and 1698 uncovered a whole series of irregularities requiring correction. Delays in baptizing the newborn, the refusal of the regulars to administer the last rites to the dying in their homes, excessive sacramental fees, inadequate indoctrination in the catechism, and undue pressure exercised by the regulars in extracting alms from their parishioners were some of the glaring abuses which the investigation documented.[6]

A justification for the episcopal contention that the regulars were unable to discipline themselves can be found in the demoralization which overtook the Augustinian Order. An episcopal inquest in 1593 unearthed evidence that some Augustinians were engaged in profitable mercantile operations at the expense of their parishioners. Nine Augustinians, including the then provincial superior, Juan de Valderrama, were charged with repeated violations of clerical celibacy.[7] The Augustinians split into two factions—the peninsular friars, who took their vows in Spain, and the creole friars, who entered the Order in the Indies. The specific bone of contention was the battle over which group was to get the lion's share of the offices and benefices which were voted upon in the triennial chapter meeting. The creole faction gained control during the second administration of Friar Lorenzo de León.[8] The provincial superior was accused of acting like a "public merchant" and failing to take disciplinary action against some of his subordinates' misdeeds, ranging from several amorous

adventures to the wholesale theft of church property. So scanda-
lous was this administration that under intense pressure from both
lay and ecclesiastical authorities the Augustinians took the drastic
step of deposing Lorenzo de León on January 7, 1607, midway in
his triennium. Upon being informed of this precedent-shattering
action, the king and the Augustinian superiors in Rome approved
the decision.[9]

The disciplinary crisis reached its nadir under the administration of Friar Vicente de Sepúlveda. As provincial superior,
Sepúlveda was driven by a single-minded purpose to remake the
Augustinian Order in his own ascetic image. His vigorous, but
unfortunately tactless, efforts to root out abuses drove his creole
opponents to desperation, and a cabal of these friars murdered
Sepúlveda in his cell on the night of June 31, 1617.[10] The atrocious
character of the Sepúlveda murder did result in some momentary
relaxation of the tension between the creoles and the peninsular
factions. But the conflict exploded again during the chapter meetings
of 1623, 1626, and 1629. The presence of some civil authorities
re-enforced by armed soldiers was considered necessary to maintain order during those turbulent chapter meetings.[11]

A study of the parish map of 1655 throws added light on the
underlying causes of the Augustinian crisis. That order was over-
extended in its commitments. The Augustinians held more
parishes than any other single religious community. They were
the first order to come to the islands, for five Augustinian friars
accompanied the original expedition of Legazpi. The remarkable
navigator of the fleet and its spiritual leader, Friar Andrés de
Urdaneta, had taken the Augustinian habit in middle age. His
crucial role in the expedition probably had much to do with
Viceroy Luís de Velasco's decision to dispatch the Augustinians.
As a consequence of their head start, the Augustinians acquired a
large number of the populous and lucrative parishes in the Tagalog
and Pampangan country. In order to staff these missions Mexican
creoles had to be imported. Some of these creoles had a dubious
religious vocation and were ill-trained. Hence a rapid decline in
discipline set in.

Although the feud between the Castilian and creole friars abated with the definitive victory of the former, the underlying issue posed by the conflict was never resolved. It is apparent that the inability of the orders to discipline themselves on occasion resulted from the decentralized character of their government. Provincial superiors and the definitors (the governing council), who held office for a three-year period, were often loath to take vigorous measures against malfeasance, since they themselves would soon return to the status of subjects. The inspection system, in which a visitor from Mexico or Spain was vested with broad powers of investigation and correction, did not prove very effective in rooting out abuses. The Franciscan visitors, for example, provoked considerable resentment in the Philippines, since they usually came from the Observant branch of the Order established in Mexico. The Philippine Franciscans were of the Discalced branch of the Order, and there was often ill-feeling between the two.[12] The power of the superiors in Rome was limited. The governmental structure of the mendicant orders goes back to the thirteenth century when the federal principle in ecclesiastical polity was in vogue.

Most observers exempted the Jesuits from the charge of ill-discipline. The Jesuits were more selective in choosing personnel, and they received a more rigorous training than did the friars of the mendicant orders. Furthermore the government of the Society was highly centralized. Rome appointed the provincial superiors, in contrast to the mendicants, who elected their superiors. Given the authoritarian character of the Jesuit organization, Rome could intervene in any province before abuses got out of hand. In the case of the mendicant orders Rome could step in only after the scandals had been publicly exposed.

Yet even among the Jesuits the maintenance of discipline posed serious difficulties. Alcina admitted that during his residence of twenty-six years in the Bisayas in the mid-seventeenth century fourteen Jesuits were expelled from the Society. Not all of these expulsions were caused by violations of chastity, but obviously the infractions of discipline provoking this action were serious.

In order to meet the deficit of their Bisayan missions, the Jesuits in that region engaged extensively in the beeswax trade. Their parishioners gathered from forests large quantities of beeswax, which in turn was shipped to and sold in Manila. While all the evidence suggests that the profits of the beeswax trade went exclusively to cover the deficit of the Bisayan parishes, Alcina noted a consequent decline in morale. Many of his confreres, he suspected, were giving too much attention to the administration of this enterprise at the expense of the more important business of Christianizing the Bisayans. He eloquently pleaded for a rededication to missionary enthusiasm.[13] Alcina's comments illustrate the kind of obstacles that the Jesuits constantly had to surmount in order to maintain as high standards as they usually managed to do.

The nature of the impasse is unmistakable. The regulars needed some external supervision of their parish work, but episcopal visitation probably would have destroyed their morale and their discipline as corporate entities.

Among the other mendicant orders there was no prolonged disciplinary crisis comparable to the one that demoralized the Augustinians. Yet the other orders were not entirely blameless. According to Salvador Gómez de Espinosa, a member of the Audiencia, abuses among all the regular orders were sufficiently widespread to arouse serious concern among the civil authorities. In his *Discurso parenético*, published in Manila in 1657, he meticulously documented these abuses in which the Augustinians were the most notable offenders. The book was suppressed and all known copies were destroyed. The reason for this drastic action was political. The author, a respected jurist and trusted bureaucrat, was never accused of publishing false or libelous information, but the Manila authorities feared that the very factualness of the account would provide to Spain's Protestant enemies ammunition with which to ridicule and to discredit the whole Catholic missionary enterprise.[14] Although abuses among all the orders cannot be glossed aside, neither should they be exaggerated. The majority of the religious apparently performed their duties conscientiously. The spectacular vices of the minority ought not to obscure the less dramatic virtues of the majority.

The important question is what effect this type of malfeasance had on the Spanish clergy and their Filipino parishioners. To the latter, sacerdotal celibacy was an innovation of the Spaniards. The pagan priests ordinarily were elderly women or effeminate men, and the average Filipino was probably not shocked at observing any violations of clerical celibacy. There is some evidence to indicate that parents may even have encouraged their daughters to make liaisons with the clergy.[15] Any children born of such a union would probably be well provided for in that a parish priest had potential sources of wealth far in excess of anything to which a Filipino could aspire. The conduct of erring friars, however, scarcely contributed anything to raising the moral tone of society. Such *donjuanismo*, in fact, created another obstacle in the realization of one major goal of the missionary enterprise, namely to make the Filipinos adhere more strictly to standards of premarital chastity and marital fidelity. From the point of view of the Spanish clergy the consequences of clerical laxity were even more serious. Flagrant violations of the monastic vow of chastity obviously set a demoralizing example to the rest of the regular clergy. The result was to diminish corporate morale.

Infractions of the vow of poverty, infractions in which some friars acted like public merchants with goods acquired from their parishioners for little or nothing, may not have provoked bursts of indignation among the Filipinos, who may in fact have thought it fitting that the clergy should profit materially from their elevated station. But here again such mercantile activities on the part of some religious acted as a source of discouragement to the rest of their brethren.

Throughout the Middle Ages the maintenance of ecclesiastical discipline posed a grave problem to the Church. Traditionally the monastic and conventual orders sought to resolve this difficulty by living together in a community. The safeguards and incentives of community life tended to fortify high standards of asceticism. Even so, communal controls were not always effective, as the history of medieval monasticism amply attests. In the Philippines the only effectively organized monasteries were in Manila itself. As we shall observe in greater detail in the following chapter, the vast majority of the religious were scattered in parishes all over the archipelago. In most of the parishes there were usually not more than two priests, and one of them was often travelling around the parish. The Spanish clergy set out to Christianize the Filipinos, but in so doing they ran the danger of "de-christianizing" themselves. Isolated from most social contacts with their own Christian culture and surrounded by temptation created by the power and the prestige of their sacerdotal status, only the strong-willed and the inflexibly dedicated could maintain the high standards of their calling. It was in the nature of things that some should go astray. The unusual fact in these circumstances is that more did not do so.

The clergy recognized the dangers inherent in their cultural isolation. Mid-triennial and triennial chapter meetings provided an opportunity to restore disciplinary fervor by the performance of community spiritual exercises. In their Bisayan missions the Jesuits congregated four times annually for this purpose.[16] Yet most of the time the regulars were isolated culturally and physically in their scattered parishes, and this condition had significant consequences for sacerdotal discipline.

The religious in the Philippines enjoyed a generous amount of autonomy. Unlike their colleagues in Mexico and Peru, they were never subject to episcopal supervision, nor were they ousted from their parishes by the secular clergy. In spite of these favorable circumstances the success of the regulars was limited. The explanation must be sought in the geographic and ethnic character of the Philippines.

The "Spiritual" Geography of the Philippines

If the missionaries were leading protagonists in the story of Spain's efforts to remodel Philippine society, geography was a major antagonist in the drama. A powerful negative factor, geography played a major part in determining what the Spaniards could and could not do. Transoceanic geography determined to a large extent the number of Spanish religious who could be transported to the Philippines. Intra-Philippine geography played an equally significant role in shaping the ultimate effectiveness of the work of the religious.

The principal handicap of the missionary enterprise was the constant shortage of personnel. The number of ecclesiastics administering to the Filipinos varied between 254 and 400 priests. This number was pitifully inadequate. Most of the regular clergy came from Spain. The small Spanish colony in the islands could only supply a few candidates for the priesthood, and they were apt to join the secular clergy occupying the benefices of the cathedral of Manila. The overpopulated monasteries in Mexico could have furnished a substantial number of priests, but the Mexican regulars were predominately creoles, and the bitter dissensions between the creole and Castilian friars among the Philippine Augustinians dis-

couraged the other orders from accepting more than a controllable
minority of Mexican creoles in their ranks. Nor did the regular
clergy favor the growth of a native Filipino priesthood, as we shall
see in Chapter VI. Hence the monasteries in Spain had to provide
the distant Philippine missions with the bulk of their personnel.

The fabled Manila Galleon was both the economic and the
spiritual life-line of the Spanish colony. The galleons, which plied
between Manila and Acapulco, brought the sinews with which to
maintain Spanish power in the distant archipelago—silver and
friars. Mexican silver was exchanged in Manila for Chinese silks—
the trade which spelled either prosperity or ruin for the Spanish
colonists. Mexican silver also provided the subsidy, the *situado*,
which covered the chronic deficit in the annual budget of the Manila
government. The loss of one single galleon spelled ruin for the
merchants and bankruptcy for the government. Without the constant reinforcements of clergy, whom the galleons transported,
the Spanish commitment to maintain and to spread the Faith in
the islands could not be met.

To supply the Philippines by using the route around the tip of
Africa was not feasible in the seventeenth century. For one thing,
it was Mexico and not Spain which had the surplus silver to export.
Spain's silver came from the New World. Secondly, the line of
demarcation laid down by Pope Alexander VI and modified in
Portugal's favor by the treaty of Tordesillas (1494) established
that remarkable partition of the world between the two Iberian
nations. The whole of Africa and India belonged to the Portuguese
sphere of influence. Spain scrupulously respected this treaty commitment long after it had become outmoded by the colonial expansion into Asia of the Dutch, the English, and the French. Even during the period when the Habsburg kings wore the crowns of both
Spain and Portugal (1580–1640), Spain observed the prohibitions
of the treaty of Tordesillas. It was not until the late eighteenth
century that the Spaniards began to use the Cape of Good Hope
route. In the sixteenth and seventeenth centuries the use of the
Cape route could not have modified the extreme isolation of the

Philippines from Spain. No matter what route was followed, nothing could have altered the fact that the Philippines were situated at the other end of the world from Spain. Furthermore, the hazards and hardships of navigating the tip of Africa were just as perilous as the trans-Atlantic and the trans-Pacific crossings.

It was a formidable problem in missionary logistics to transport Spanish clergymen from Spain to the Philippines. All the expenses incurred in the voyage as well as a complete clerical wardrobe were provided by the royal treasury, and the deepening bankruptcy overwhelming the Spanish state during the course of the seventeenth century further complicated the task. Although the actual amount of time for the trans-Atlantic and the trans-Pacific crossing was approximately eight months, the journey seldom took less than two years. Long delays at the terminal points of Seville and Acapulco were inevitable. The rigors of oceanic travel, including squalid living conditions breeding epidemic diseases, required that trans–Atlantic arrivals recuperate for at least six months in Mexico before undertaking the perilous crossing from Acapulco to Manila.[1] Death, illness, and discouragement meant that many priests originally assigned to the Philippines never reached their destination. Many remained in Mexico in violation of repeated royal ordinances to the contrary.[2]

Once these missionaries had survived all the hazards involved in reaching the Philippines, the problem was how to keep them in the islands. Nature itself was the first obstacle. The hot and humid climate evidently took a heavy toll among the new arrivals. The roster of invalids was usually numerous. In addition the Philippines seemed to many new arrivals a barren missionary field in contrast to the glittering prize that the ancient and fabled civilizations of China and Japan offered. Many of the early missionaries regarded the Philippines merely as a convenient resting station before setting out for Japan or China. Vigorous measures on the part of the authorities in Manila failed to stop the exodus.[3] What eventually did, within a few decades, was the adamant hostility of the Chinese and Japanese authorities to the spread of Christianity in their lands.[4]

Villages and Parishes

If isolation from Spain created a serious handicap for the Spanish clergy, the geographical particularism of the islands offered them an equally formidable obstacle. This particularism, which had facilitated the military phase of the conquest, proved a barrier to the consolidation of the "spiritual conquest." How could a few hundred Spanish priests hope to reach 500,000 Filipinos scattered in tiny clusters adjacent to their rice paddies. There was only one feasible means of overcoming this difficulty. The Filipinos must be "congregated" or "reduced," to use the official terminology, into compact villages varying in size between 2,400 and 5,000 people. In Mexico and in Peru the Church and the state had acquired a wealth of experience in resettling the Indians.[5] These lessons could be profitably applied in the Orient. But the problem in the Philippines was even more arduous in view of the greater dispersal of the population. Inspiring the resettlement policies of the Spanish regime in all parts of the Indies was a common set of objectives. It was generally recognized that the natives could not be adequately indoctrinated in the Christian faith, nor could the Spanish program of societal reorganization be implemented or the material resources of the land be efficiently exploited unless the Indians were congregated into large villages.

The decentralization of Philippine society clashed with one tradition deeply rooted in Spanish culture. As the heirs of Greco-Roman urbanism, the Spaniards instinctively identified civilization with the city, whose origins go back to the *polis* of ancient Greece. For the Spaniards, man was not only a rational animal gifted with the capacity to receive grace. He was also a social animal living in communion with his fellow men. It was only through this daily social contact with other men that he might hope to achieve a measure of his potentiality. The Spanish chroniclers endlessly repeated that the Filipinos lived without polity, *sin policía*, and for them that term was a synonym for barbarism.[6]

An ambitious program of resettling the Filipinos into compact villages similar to those already organized in Mexico and in Peru was laid out in the 1580's and 1590's.[7] Progress toward reaching this goal was slow. By the end of the seventeenth century there were not twenty villages in the whole archipelago (excluding the suburban villages of Greater Manila) with a population of over 2,000 people.[8]

The Filipinos tenaciously resisted resettlement. Sentimental ties kept them close to their rice fields. Archbishop García Serrano observed in 1622:

Although it is impossible to deny that the natives would be better instructed and would live in more orderly ways if the small villages [barrios] were to be reduced to the capital [*cabecera* or población], making one or two settlements of each benefice, they consider it such an affliction to leave their little houses where they were born and have been reared, their fields, and their other comforts of life, that it could only be attained with difficulty, and little fruit would result therefrom. Thus has the experience of assembling the people into communities in Nueva España proved, and so has what little of it has been attempted here. However, in the visit that I shall make in this archbishopric, I shall try to reduce them to as few settlements as possible.[9]

In face of native hostility even the clergy, who had the most to benefit from rural resettlement, faltered. Furthermore, the traditional rice economy provided no compelling material inducement to move into the new settlements that the clergy were seeking to organize around the parish churches. The Filipinos were subsistence and not surplus farmers. Their traditional adaption to their environment required that they live adjacent to the land they cultivated. In addition, fishing and hunting were important sources of food, and the transfer to compact villages threatened to destroy the whole ecological balance of existence, a fact which does much to explain the hostility of most Filipinos to the resettlement policy of the Spaniards.

In the Bisayan islands the Moro raids created another obstacle. Several new villages were destroyed by Moro depredations. Bisayans were discouraged from moving into these new communities sponsored by the clergy, since these riparian and coastal villages were exposed to Moro raids. Furthermore, the encomenderos in the Bisayas were often hostile to the regrouping of the population. Resettlement meant that some encomiendas would lose tributes, which were collected on a territorial basis.

Only military coercion could overcome resistance to resettlement, and the Spaniards rarely exerted this kind of compulsion except in cases of extreme provocation. An outstanding example is the case of the Sambals. In 1680, in retaliation against frequent raids by the fierce Sambals on the villages of the fertile and loyally pro-Spanish province of Pampanga, a Spanish expedition of some three hundred soldiers pulled thousands of Sambals from their caves and huts in the mountains. They were resettled in three lowland villages, which some Dominican friars had laid out. The friars hired some neighbors to teach the Sambals the methods of sedentary rice agriculture. The whole project cost the Dominicans 10,000 pesos.[10] The case of the Sambals is unusual. Not all the Filipinos were so fierce that coercion seemed the only alternative. Nor was Spanish military strength so great that compulsion could be employed on a large scale.

Of all the regions in the Philippines the Bisayan islands proved least responsive to resettlement.[11] The Sambal country and the province of Cagayan in northwestern Luzon also lagged. A contributory cause for the unrest in Cagayan during the last years of the sixteenth century was native resistance to resettlement. The Dominicans, who administered the province, were compelled to abandon their ambitious plans to relocate the Ibanag people into large villages.[12] By the end of the eighteenth century the Franciscan parishes in the Camarines and Laguna de Bay were moderately successful examples of resettlement.[13] In the provinces of the central plain of Luzon the Tagalogs were more compactly settled than were peoples of other regions, and they were more subject to Hispanic influences radiating from Manila. Yet by Spanish standards population patterns left much to be desired. In 1768 the energetic *fiscal* of the Audiencia, Francisco de Viana, vainly proposed that the civil authorities, in coöperation with the clergy, undertake a wholesale uprooting of the inhabitants of the populous Tondo province and their resettlement into larger villages.[14]

Since most Filipinos could not be coerced into the new villages, they had to be enticed. And the principal inducement was the colorful ritual of the Church. The Filipinos did flock to the churches for such ceremonial occasions as Holy Week, the feast of Corpus Christi or the patronal fiesta of the locality. They might even build houses near the church, but these were "Sunday houses," vacated as soon as the religious celebrations ended. Many of these communities were intermittent rather than constant, forming and dissolving in response to the performance of certain rituals fixed by the Church. The *cabecera* was the capital of the parish and was designed to be the location of a compact village. Since the Filipinos were reluctant to move into these settlements in large numbers, every parish had a whole series of *visita* chapels. The latter were visited periodically by nonresident clergy whose headquarters were at the *cabecera*.

The *cabecera-visita* complex, whose origins go back to the early missionary enterprise in Mexico, gradually became the prevailing pattern of rural settlement in the Philippines. In 1583 Bishop Salazar could write Philip II: "Your islands are not like Nueva España [Mexico] where there is a chief village and many others subject to it. Here [the Philippines] all are small villages and each one its own head."[15] During the course of the seventeenth century a gradual but remorseless change occurred. The Mexican system, in which a string of subordinate clusters of population were attached to a principal village, took root in the Philippines. No chapels were built in the numerous sitios, which were units of usually not more than ten families. The inhabitants of the sitios attended religious services at the nearest *visita* chapel. The *cabecera-visita* system was a compromise, inadequate in many ways, but the only feasible alternative, given the shortage of ecclesiastical personnel and the scattered distribution of the population.

This compromise was destined to leave an enduring mark on the patterns of rural settlement in the Philippines. The modern pobla-

ción grew out of the early *cabeceras*. Many *cabecera* churches indicated on the 1655 map can be found on a modern map as the location of a población. The prototype of the contemporary rural barrio
can be traced back to the *visita* chapel of the early missionaries. The
change from *cabecera* to población and from *visita* to barrio is
largely a shift from an ecclesiastical to a civil nomenclature.[16]

The *cabeceras* were usually established in the lowlands adjacent
to the coasts and rivers. The *visitas* were apt to be located upvalley
and in the foothills. The area beyond the *visitas* formed a kind of
buffer zone separating the quasi-Hispanized peoples of the maritime lowlands from the pagan Negritos of the mountains. The
people of the buffer zone were only half-Christian. In the late
seventeenth century the regular clergy sought to stabilize the
frontier by founding in these areas what were called *misiones vivas*.
Staffed with small garrisons of soldiers, these "active missions"
provided some kind of defense in depth, protecting the Christian
peoples of the lowlands from raids of the pagan peoples in the
mountains.[17]

The physical layout of the *cabecera* villages usually followed a
gridiron pattern with a central plaza and rectangular street blocks.
Of Greco-Roman origins, the gridiron was revived as the ideal
urban layout by some Italian Renaissance theorists. Adopted
throughout the Spanish empire, the gridiron plan provided a feasible and simple masterplan for the multitude of new communities
founded by the Spaniards.[18] But in the Philippines this layout of
compactly situated houses was a distinct fire hazard, since native
dwellings were wooden frames with bamboo walls and palm tree
roofs. In Mexico, on the other hand, Indian houses made of adobe
were not highly inflammable. In the eighteenth century the wisdom of the compact, rectangular plan was questioned in favor of a
more decentralized grouping of houses. One of Governor Raón's
ordinances read: "They [the *alcaldes mayores*] shall not allow any
house to be more than one-half league [approximately one and one
third miles] from a church; and, on the other hand, shall not allow
them to be built so close together than there is danger of fire."[19] A

similar ordinance was issued for the province of Cagayan in 1739.[20] Edicts were probably issued for other provinces. The fire hazard provides a partial explanation for the slogan, seldom used before the eighteenth century, that the Filipinos should be resettled *bajo de campana*, that is, within hearing of the church bells.

These ordinances represent an admission of the failure of the seventeenth-century program of rural resettlement. The Manila government apparently sought a compromise between its traditional objective of bringing the Filipinos into direct contact with Spanish culture, institutionalized in the local church, and the profound unwillingness of the Filipinos to abandon their isolated dwellings. How effective was this modified resettlement program? No satisfactory answer can emerge until the archives for the eighteenth century are carefully studied.

Although the early Spanish town planners fell far short of their goal, their efforts did initiate a gradual transformation of settlement patterns in the direction of concentration in larger villages. The results certainly were not as sweeping as the missionaries wanted, but preconquest decentralization was sufficiently reduced so that Filipinos were brought into some social contact with Hispanic culture.

Geoethnic Distribution of the Missionary Foundations

Given the triple handicaps of a shortage of ecclesiastical personnel, the scattered distribution of the population, and linguistic diversity, the geographical apportionment of the missionary foundations required careful advance planning; the lack of such foresight, prior to 1594, had led to the abandonment of several missions. But on April 27, 1594, the Council of the Indies in Spain instructed the governor and the bishop to divide up the Philippines into contiguous areas among the four religious orders. The resulting partition rigorously followed geoethnic lines. All the orders received some parishes in the Tagalog country, but the bulk of these parishes went to the Augustinians and the Franciscans, who were strongly entrenched there prior to 1594. A much smaller Tagalog area was given the Jesuits. The Dominicans assumed responsibility for the Chinese community, most of whom lived in the Parian of Manila.

In addition to their extensive holdings in the Tagalog country, the Augustinians received the provinces of Pampanga and Ilokos, the former being one of the most fertile and populous provinces in the archipelago. The Franciscans took charge of Bikol-speaking province of the Camarines. Hence the Augustinians and secondly the Franciscans administered the most populous and best organized parishes in the islands. Dominican territory included the provinces of Pangasinan and Cagayan. The Bisayan islands were divided along linguistic and geographical lines between the Augustinians and the Jesuits. The parishes of the Dominicans and the Jesuits were much less populous and lucrative than were the holdings of the Augustinians and the Franciscans. The Augustinian Recollects, as the last order to arrive in the islands, staffed only a small string of parishes widely scattered over the archipelago.

From the viewpoint of the Crown, this partition contained some disadvantages. A settled royal policy was not to allow any one religious corporation to dominate a large, contiguous, ethnic-territorial area. A notable exception to this policy was the Seven Missions of Paraguay organized by the Jesuits after 1630. The Crown allowed this territorial concentration of power because those missions acted as an effective barrier against further Portuguese penetration from Brazil toward the silver mines of Upper Peru. Standard policy was to build up the power of the episcopacy and the secular clergy and to balance one missionary order against the other in order to create a situation in which the Crown held the ultimate balance of power. The geographical distribution of the Philippine missions violated this principle, but the geoethnic diversity of the archipelago offered no feasible alternative.[21]

The outstanding practical advantage resulting from this partition was that it enabled each order to concentrate its linguistic studies in not more than four different languages. Only thus could the religious hope to train sufficiently competent linguists in the wide variety of Philippine languages, for a maxim of Spanish missionary policy was that converts should be indoctrinated in their own tongues. It was thought that the natives would respond more readily if the Faith were not preached in an alien language.

The four printing presses in the islands published approximately one hundred books during the course of the seventeenth century. Since all the printing presses were operated by the religious orders, the bulk of the Philippine imprints were bilingual catechisms, dictionaries, grammars, and confessionals. In addition to these printed works, many linguistic manuscripts circulated.[22] The linguistic studies of the missionaries were a laborious undertaking, but in many languages the research done was inadequate. Of all the native tongues Tagalog was the most rigorously studied. The Tagalogs were the largest single ethnic group, and these provinces formed the citadel of Spanish power. Bikol studies undertaken by the Franciscans were extensive. But only the minimum was done in the Bisayan tongues and in the other major languages of Luzon (Pampanga, Pangasinan, and Ilokos). Nothing was published in the Ibanag language of Cagayan, although some Ibanag manuscripts circulated in the Dominican convents. Little systematic research was done in the various languages of Mindanao, where effective Spanish control was confined to a few coastal areas.

These linguistic studies were of a utilitarian character. The religious did just enough research to prepare them to discharge their sacerdotal obligations, and in some cases they even fell short of this goal. Yet the majority of the Spanish clergy managed to speak the tongues of their parishioners with fluency sufficient to deliver an occasional "canned" sermon or to hear confessions.[23] How deeply they penetrated the linguistic barrier separating them from their flocks is a moot question. Some religious undoubtedly did, others much less so.

It is apparent that geoethnic factors had much to do with delimiting the impact of Spanish culture on the Filipinos. Isolation and consequent poor communications with Spain prevented the Church from adequately staffing its Philippine missions. Rural decentralization, which the Spaniards could only partially change, gave the Filipinos more freedom in selecting their responses to Hispanization than they would have had if they had been congregated into large, compact villages under the daily supervision of the religious. As we observed in the last chapter, the very effectiveness of the clergy was sometimes vitiated by the cultural isolation in which they spent most of their time. The dispersal of clergy, necessitated by the settlement patterns of their parishioners, sometimes contributed to a relaxation of sacerdotal discipline. Yet the work of the missionaries was not totally ineffective, as subsequent chapters will indicate. What success the religious did achieve may be ascribed in large part to the realistic adjustment they made to the limitations that geoethnic factors imposed on their activity.

Chapter v

The Imposition
of Christianity

Spanish missionaries viewed themselves as soldiers of Christ waging with spiritual weapons a war to overthrow the devil's tyranny over pagan peoples. They envisaged their work as a "spiritual conquest" of the minds and hearts of the natives, a supplement to, and the ultimate justification for, the military conquest. A superb iconographical expression of the Spanish view of the complementary nature of the temporal and the spiritual conquests can be found in Friar Gaspar de San Agustín's chronicle of 1698, a reproduction of which serves as the frontispiece of this book.

Christianity was presented to the infidels not as a more perfect expression of their pagan beliefs but as something entirely new. Any resemblance between the two religions was dismissed as a diabolical conspiracy in which the devil deceived unbelievers by mimicking the rituals and the beliefs of Christianity. The policy of breaking abruptly with the pagan past explains the vigor with which temples and idols were destroyed. The Spanish missionaries have been much criticized for this practice. Yet the religious were not modern archaeologists. In their eyes pagan artifacts were but the visible symbols of the devil's tyrannical dominion, and hence they merited destruction.

In the Philippines there were no temples to demolish. But sacred groves were cut down by zealous Spanish religious who were determined to break the magic sway such groves exercised over the Filipinos. And pagan idols by the thousands were committed to the flames by iconoclastic religious in the presence of bewildered and fascinated Filipinos.[1] The dismantling of outward pagan observances was but the first step in the introduction of Christianity.

Baptism

In most cases the missionaries were preceded by the encomenderos. The latter were supposed to teach their wards the rudiments of the Christian religion and to build chapels. That most encomenderos poorly performed their quasi-missionary responsibility is abundantly clear. Their principal concern was to pacify their wards in order to collect tribute taxes from them. The religious, fearing that the conquered would be repelled by the religion of the conquerors, often decried the forceful methods with which the encomenderos went about their task. Such fears, although plausible, proved in fact groundless. Actually by their very blood and fire methods the encomenderos rendered a service to the religious by breaking the backbone of native resistance. The indigenous peoples with whom the Spaniards came in contact seldom showed any desire to abandon voluntarily their own religious values. Compulsion of some sort had to be employed. Given their Christian humanitarianism, the clergy usually protested against the use of force; but without coercion, or the threat of it, the natives in many cases would have rejected the appeals of the religious to discard paganism.

Sullen distrust but not armed defiance usually greeted the newly arrived missionary. More than one friar woke up in the morning to a deathly silence only to discover that his would-be flock had stolen away to the mountains during the night. One Augustinian not only had his hut burned but also suffered from attempts to poison his drinking water. In some localities the distrustful inhabitants refused to supply the clergy with the necessities of life.

Wherever the religious met morose distrust, they did not attempt to impose themselves on the elders of the community. What the religious usually requested was that some of the children be committed to their care. The chieftains might shun the monastery for some time, but out of a combination of curiosity and fear they would hand over some of their children to be educated by the religious. Evangelization followed a standard pattern. The children of the chieftains were first indoctrinated, and then the chieftains themselves were persuaded. With the conversion of the leaders of the community, the baptism of their followers came as a matter of course. Although the indoctrination of ex-pagan adults was conscientiously pursued, it was realized that their adjustment to Christianity would be incomplete. Special attention, therefore, was concentrated on the children. The children proved enthusiastic and effective auxiliaries of the religious in winning over the parents to the new religion, reporting clandestine pagan rituals, and in catechizing the older generation.

A substantial aid to the early missionaries in removing the barrier of distrust was the impression which rapidly gained currency among the Filipinos that baptism not only wiped away the sins of the soul but also helped to cure the ailments of the body. The ecclesiastical chronicles are full of accounts of ill people who made "miraculous" recoveries after receiving baptism and cases of converts who "miraculously" avoided catching a local epidemic. Since their pagan cults had stressed the cures of illness, the popular conviction that baptism was corporeally efficacious did much to attract the Filipinos to the new religion.

The missionary enterprise in Mexico provided the Philippine clergy with a wealth of experience upon which to draw. Baptism without benefit of some preliminary instruction was seldom performed in the Philippines except in cases of serious illness. The early Franciscans in Mexico had been sharply criticized for administering baptism without benefit of prior instruction. From this controversy emerged an ideal definition of the content of prebaptismal instruction. Converts were expected to repudiate paganism and to affirm their belief in the efficacy of the sacrament. The marriage of a convert was required to be monogamous. Adult converts were supposed to be able to recite by memory the *Pater Noster*, the *Credo*, the *Ave Maria*, and the Ten Commandments. Finally, some idea of the meaning of the other sacraments and an awareness of the principal obligations of a Catholic (attendance at Mass on Sundays and holydays and mandatory annual confession) were considered desirable baptismal conditions. These standards were not always observed in the Philippines, but they did provide a yardstick which was often enforced.

The missionary enterprise got off to a very slow start between 1565 and 1578. During the first five years there were not more than one hundred baptisms. In 1576 there were only thirteen Augustinian friars, and their baptisms had been confined mostly to children. Linguistic ignorance, paucity of priests, and the missionary interest in China account for this lack of progress. The coming of the Franciscans in 1578 and the arrival of large contingents of Augustinians and Franciscans after 1578 produced a change in the scope and tempo of evangelical operations. The Franciscans were soon followed by the Dominicans and the Jesuits. The decisive decade was the one between 1576 and 1586. During this period the number of missionaries rose from 13 to 94, and by 1594 there were 267 regulars. The number of baptisms rose proportionately to the increase in missionary personnel, as the following approximate figures suggest:[2]

1583...................	100,000 baptisms
1586...................	170,000 "
1594...................	286,000 "
1612...................	322,400 "
1622...................	500,000 "

Thus it took some fifty years of intensive missionary activity to lay the foundation of Philippine Christianity.

The sacrament was seldom granted to anyone who expressed strong antipathy to the new religion. According to Catholic doctrine, the efficacy of the sacrament depended upon a sincere act of repentance on the part of the convert. Many indifferent Filipinos probably were, however, swept along in the baptismal current, which flowed swiftly during the 1580's and 1590's. Although there are some examples of obdurate natives refusing baptism, such cases were rare. Most religious held that infidels could be compelled only to listen to the preaching of the gospel. Las Casas rejected even this proposition, but his opinion was shared by few missionaries. No responsible Spaniard argued that pagans could be compelled to believe.

The religious may have respected the ultimately voluntary nature of baptism, but they did exert various forms of individual and social pressure which few Filipinos were able to resist. As one Jesuit observed in 1604: "It seems to me that the road to the conversion of these natives is now smooth and open with the conversion of the chiefs and the majority of the people, for the excuse which they formerly had saying, 'I will become a Christian as soon as the rest do' has now become their incentive toward conversion and they now say, 'We desire to become Christians because all the rest are Christians.' "[3] With the achievement of a Christian majority, serious outward opposition vanished.

The Catechism

The effectiveness of prebaptismal instruction depended upon subsequent indoctrination in the catechism. The Christian doctrine taught to the Filipinos was dogmatic Catholicism reduced to its essential minimum. The Tagalog-Christian *Doctrina* of 1593, the first book printed in the Philippines, included the following: *Pater Noster*, the *Ave Maria*, the *Credo*, the *Salve Maria*, the fourteen articles of the Faith, the seven sacraments, the seven capital sins, the fourteen works of mercy, the Ten Commandments, the five commandments of the Church and the act of general confession.[4]

The *Doctrina* of 1593 closely followed the Nahuatl catechisms previously compiled for the Mexican Indians. In the seventeenth century, however, the majority of the Philippine *doctrinas* were adaptations or translations of the much used *Dottrina Cristiana*

(1597) edited by the prominent Jesuit theologian, Robert Cardinal Bellarmine. The overwhelming popularity of the Bellarmine catechism in the Philippines is an indication of the success of the Holy See in standardizing catechismal instruction throughout the Catholic world.[5]

The catechisms published in the various Philippine languages were not meant to be distributed to the Filipinos themselves, although they possessed a long tradition of literacy. The high costs of printing and the use of fragile rice paper ruled out the feasibility of instruction by means of written materials. Indoctrination was oral, and the catechisms were for the Spanish clergy, who required accurate translations into heretofore unfamiliar languages of complex doctrinal concepts which medieval theologians had taken centuries to define. In conformity with the policy of deliberate rupture with the pagan past, the key concepts of Christianity were never translated into the Philippine tongues. Lest the converts confuse or identify the Christian with the pagan, such terms were ordinarily left in the Spanish form. Sometimes the Latin term was used.[6]

The religious organized and instructed the first catechismal classes. They were usually held on Sundays in the *cabecera* villages and in the outlying *visitas* at whatever time the itinerant priest happened to be there. In response to the shortage of priests, all the orders devised some system in which the brighter students taught the less advanced. In this method the Spanish religious foreshadowed by three centuries the Lancastrian system of instruction. The Jesuits, for example, cast the prayers, the Creed, and the commandments into Bisayan verse adapted to the traditional planting and rowing chants of the region.[7]

The sons of the chieftains might board for a few years at the parish residence, called the *convento* in the Philippines, where they were given a more intensive training in the doctrine. Reading, writing, and music as well as Spanish were also on the curriculum. In contrast to the practice in Mexico, the Filipinos were seldom taught Latin. The aim of these monastic schools was to train an elite class who could act as intermediaries between the Spaniards and the Filipino masses. Although primary schools were founded by all the orders, the Franciscan institutions were the most effective. Such had previously been the case in Mexico. Primary education flourished from the 1580's onwards, but after the intensification of the Dutch war, from 1609 onward, the quality of instruction fell off noticeably.[8]

During the seventeenth century the burden of organizing and supervising catechismal instruction fell increasingly on the *fiscales*. An important personage in the community, the *fiscal* was more than a sacristan. He was the intermediary between the clergy and their parishioners. Among his other duties were those of organizing the village's patronal fiesta, arranging for the ornamentation of the church, and cajoling if not compelling, his scattered charges to attend Mass and catechismal classes.

The *fiscales* were brought to the Philippines from Mexico, where they were sometimes called *mandones*. The role of the *fiscal* reflects the inalterable conviction of the Spanish clergy that the Filipinos required external disciple to compel them to perform their religious obligations. As one Jesuit observed: "They [the Filipinos] readily receive our religion. Their meager intelligence does not permit them to sound the depths of its mysteries. They also have little care in the fulfillment of their duties to the Christianity which they have adopted; and it is necessary to constrain them by fear of punishment and to govern them like school children."[9]

Informed observers agreed that most Filipinos had memorized, parrot-like, the catechism and the prayers. Reflective missionaries sometimes expressed doubts about the degree of the natives' comprehension. Alcina, for example, was discouraged in the face of his repeated failure to explain to his Bisayan parishioners the meaning of paradise. The brighter ones, he wrote, were willing to grant the plausibility of a heaven for the Spaniards, but they refused to believe that the Bisayans would be allowed to share it with the Spaniards. The Christian notion that worldly differences of race, wealth, and education did not exist in the sight of the Almighty shocked the earthy realism of the Bisayans. For them the inequalities of this

world would be perpetuated in the next. Alcina confessed that after
sixty years of missionary activity in the Bisayas very few of the
converts had acquired a clear comprehension of the basic mysteries
of the Catholic creed. Other thoughtful missionaries expressed
equally searching doubts.[10]

The degree to which the Filipinos understood the meaning of
the doctrine was often in proportion to the density of population.
The inhabitants of the maritime provinces of Luzon were settled
in larger units and were cared for by a greater number of priests
than were those of the Bisayan islands. Hence the former tended
to be better indoctrinated than the latter. On Luzon itself the Tagalog provinces, Pampanga and the Camarines, were better instructed
than the outlying provinces of Ilokos, Pangasinan, and Cagayan.
Natives living nearer the *cabecera* church, where there was a resident
priest, usually acquired a firmer grasp of the doctrine than those
living in the vicinity of the outlying *visita*, serviced only by an
itinerant priest.

Although the methods of indoctrination varied considerably
from order to order, these variations were not always exactly reflected in the quality of instruction in particular areas. The Augustinians, for example, were the least effective teachers of the doctrine, a fact which may be ascribed to the prolonged disciplinary
crisis in that order. Yet the level of instruction in their Tagalog
and Pamgangan parishes was not appreciably inferior to that in the
parishes administered by the other orders. These Augustinian
parishes were some of the most compactly settled in the archipelago.
The Augustinian parishes in Ilokos and the Bisayas, however, were
probably the worst instructed in the islands, for in addition to the
mediocre quality of the clergy there was widespread rural decentralization. Of all the orders the Jesuits had developed the sound-
est pedagogical methods. Nevertheless, the scattered population of
their Bisayan parishes were no more intensively indoctrinated than
the Tagalog and Pampangan parishes of the Augustinians. Not
more, and often fewer, than thirty itinerant Jesuit priests administered to between 50,000 and 70,000 Bisayans.[11] Where Jesuit

pedagogical skill did produce impressive results, however, was in their residences of Antipolo and Silan adjacent to Manila, where there was considerable density of population. The Dominicans in their parishes in Cagayan and in Pangasinan faced the same handicaps of rural decentralization confronting the Jesuits in the Bisayas. Given the obstacles, the sustained zeal of the Dominicans achieved maximum results with the limited means available. Instruction in the Franciscan parishes was of the highest quality in the islands. Not only did the Franciscans retain a respectable degree of discipline among themselves, but also they enjoyed the good fortune of holding a series of populous and compactly organized parishes in the Tagalog and Bikol country. All of which suggests that the level of instruction depended not so much on the quality of the clergy as it did on the density of the population. Given the difficulties involved in maintaining ecclesiastical discipline, and the decentralized character of settlement patterns, catechismal instruction could only meet minimum standards. But this result was remarkable in view of the internal and external obstacles confronting the clergy.

The Sacraments

By virtue of baptism the Filipinos entered the Church. Instruction in the catechism gave them a modicum of knowledge about the doctrine of their new religion. The reception of three other sacraments was necessary before the Filipinos could become practicing Catholics. They were matrimony (for the married ones), penance, and Holy Eucharist.

Polygamy and the prevalence of divorce among the Filipinos were obstacles to the introduction of the Catholic sacrament of matrimony. Both customs were the prerogatives of chieftains. And both traditions created hindrances to the spread of Christianity in that missionary policy was to concentrate initially on the conversion of the chieftains. Since polygamy was a custom derived from recent Muslim influence in the Bisayas (Samar, Leyte, and Cebu), it was easily liquidated.[12] More formidable, however, was the task of the missionaries to teach the Christian doctrine of the indissolubility of marriage to the members of a society accustomed to the principle of divorce.

The first problem confronting the missionaries was to Christianize those marriages already performed according to pagan usages. Recognizing the existence of natural marriages among the Indians, Pope Paul III in his bull, *Altitudo divini consilii* (1537), declared that the legitimate wife was the first woman that a man had espoused. In case of doubt as to which one was the first, the Indian might chose any one of his wives and be married to her *in facie ecclesiae*.[13] The Holy See's dictum had as one aim to prevent natives from becoming Christians in order to exchange an older wife for a younger one.

The papal solution proved unworkable in the Philippines, and some of its provisions were quietly disregarded. Converts were allowed to chose for a Christian spouse any one of their present or former wives. In practice, this meant the present wife and her children. Hence few Filipinos were compelled to exchange a younger wife for an older one and thus leave the children of the younger wife fatherless and destitute. The Philippine religious flexibly interpreted canonical principles in order to avoid undue economic and emotional hardships on the neophytes.[14] Later on in the seventeenth century, after the majority of Filipinos had become Christian, a more literal interpretation of Paul III's bull prevailed. The right of choice could be exercised only in cases where the first pagan wife had disappeared or had refused baptism.[15]

The penchant of the Filipinos for divorce was a habit not easily suppressed. On occasion they displayed considerable ingenuity in exploiting canon law to gratify their desire for a marital change. In 1621 the archbishop of Manila was plagued by numerous requests for annulments. These petitions bore a suspicious resemblance to one another. They all alleged that the interested parties had had intercourse before marriage with relatives of their wives. The archbishop accused the plaintiffs of intentionally concealing these facts, which canon law recognized as an obstacle, until the husband desired to marry someone else. The archbishop urged the king to request from the Pope a bull giving the Philippine prelates broad powers to grant absolution for this type of impediment in cases where a marriage had already been performed.[16] The monarch instructed his ambassador to the Roman curia to make such a request. Mentrida's manual, published in Manila in 1630, granted parish priests the very authority that the archbishop had requested in 1621.[17]

This episode illustrates the degree to which functional Hispanization had progressed within fifty years of the conquest. These Filipinos were sufficiently Hispanized to attempt to continue inside the framework of canon law the preconquest tradition of easy divorce.

The transition from the pagan marriage pattern to the Christian one was not always smooth. Many marriages violated some principle of canon law. There were cases of baptized natives marrying infidels according to pagan rites, or of a man marrying his widowed step-mother, or of someone else marrying a cousin within the prohibited third degree, without securing a prior dispensation.[18]

The actual sacrament of matrimony did not have to be performed inside the church itself. A priest could marry a couple in the parish residence or in the home of the bride, but the solemnities of the nuptial Mass, followed by the nuptial blessing, could be performed only inside the church, at any time of the year but during the season of Lent. Such services were, however, rare. Some contemporaries blamed the relative infrequency of nuptial Masses on the high fees charged by the clergy.[19] Although such fees were a standard custom throughout Catholic Europe, the Crown sought to delay their introduction into the Indies. It was thought that these fees might discourage the Indians from receiving the sacraments and that the Indians might be confused about the spiritual nature of the sacraments. In 1596 Philip II ordered that no sacramental fees be collected from the Filipinos.[20] These mandates went unheeded. Nor would the regulars abide by a set of tariffs, one drawn up by Bishop Salazar in the 1580's and another by Archbishop Camacho in 1698.[21] As we have already observed in the last chapter, the

religious defied episcopal authority with impunity. The Augustinians and the Franciscans, but not the Jesuits and the Dominicans,
charged substantial sacramental fees.[22] In short, most Filipino
Christians were married in the Church but not inside the churches.
Nuptial blessings were for the well-to-do.

The introduction of Catholic matrimony implied certain changes
in sexual mores. Some erotic practices, which provoked vehement
opposition among the Spaniards, were gradually suppressed.[23] In
discussing changes in sexual mores following the conquest, another
issue is pertinent. Did the Chinese, who did not settle in the islands
until after the arrival of the Spaniards, introduce sodomy to the
Filipinos? Although this allegation was made by observers whose
testimony on other matters has proved reliable, the evidence they
adduce on the question of sodomy is something less than convincing.[24]

Spanish policy was to tolerate many indigenous mores which
did not brazenly conflict with basic precepts of Spanish Christian
morality. As early as 1599, Tagalog dowry and inheritance practices as codified in Plasencia's study received recognition in the
Spanish law courts as customary law in all inter-Filipino litigations.[25] The Spaniards did not object to the pre-Hispanic tradition
of the groom providing the dowry, although this custom differed
from Spanish usage. The Spaniards did, however, view with hostility the twin customs of bride-gift and bride-price, in which the
groom rendered either labor services or a payment to his future
father-in-law. To the Spaniards it smacked of fathers selling their
daughters, perhaps against the latters' will, to the highest bidder.
Although it was the accepted practice in Spain for parents to arrange the marriage of their children, Catholic doctrine insisted that
the ultimate decision to marry must be a voluntary act of the couple
concerned.[26] Bride-service also aroused the suspicions of the
clergy. The engaged couple living under the same roof might have
opportunities for premarital sexual relations.

Plasencia's study did not mention bride-service and bride-price.
Hence these customs did not come under the protection of the

Spanish law courts. In 1628 a cedula of Philip IV ordered that no Indian in any part of the empire should make a payment or provide free labor services to his future father-in-law.[27] This legislation was not vigorously enforced in the Philippines. At the beginning of the eighteenth century Governor Zabalburu and Archbishop Camacho did in fact launch a campaign to wipe out bride-service and bride-price,[28] but just how successful they were cannot be determined until the manuscript sources for the eighteenth century are examined. For our immediate purposes the important conclusion is that many of the socioeconomic aspects of the marriage pattern in pre-Hispanic society were not materially altered during the first century of Spanish rule.

The spread and the eventual acceptance of the Christian ideal of matrimony among the Filipinos represents one of the most enduring achievements of the Spanish religious. A new standard of premarital and marital morality was set up. Like all such norms, this one was not always observed, but it was a standard destined to exercise continuing influence through the coming centuries.

The next step in the spread of Christianity was the introduction of the sacraments of penance and Holy Eucharist. Penance provided the Church with a potent weapon in the enforcement of moral and ethical standards. Nor could the introduction of this sacrament be long delayed, for all Catholics were required to confess once a year.

This sacrament could not be properly administered unless the clergy acquired a solid linguistic training. There are few references to Filipinos confessing through interpreters, as was sometimes done in Mexico. Hence a characteristic publication of the Philippine presses was the *confessionario*. These confessionaries were bilingual texts designed to aid the priests in asking the pertinent questions and in eliciting truthful answers. The first of these texts was published circa 1610 by the prolific Dominican Tagalist, Francisco de San José. By the end of the seventeenth century similar manuals circulated in several of the major languages of the archipelago.[29]

The shortage of ecclesiastical personnel was always a handicap. In the Jesuit church in Manila, for example, Filipinos had to wait from ten to fifteen days in spite of the formidable array of priests hearing confession.[30] In contrast to the concentration of people in the vicinity of Manila, the dispersal of the population in the provinces posed another set of problems. Three years might elapse before Christians had their confessions heard.[31]

The principle of confession was entirely new to the Filipinos. In their pagan cults there was nothing even remotely analogous to it. Many Filipinos first viewed the sacrament with some misgivings. They had to be persuaded that the confessor would not be angry with them if they recited all their sins.[32] Frequent rotation of regular priests, usually every three years, avoided the awkward situation of someone being compelled or refusing to confess to a priest whom he feared or with whom he had quarreled.[33] Under those circumstances a Filipino was apt to become reticent and thus endanger the validity of that particular confession. The religious scrupulously avoided imposing heavy penances, lest the people's initial distrust of the sacrament harden into opposition. Typical penances were hearing a few Masses, reciting a few Rosaries, or visiting a sick person.[34]

Once accustomed to the idea of confession, the Filipinos took to it with characteristic enthusiasm. Sharp differences of opinion, however, were expressed about whether they understood it. Ribadeneyra, the sanguine spokesman of the first generation of Franciscan missionaries, claimed that the Filipinos usually needed no prodding from their confessors. They came to confession with their consciences well examined. They recited their sins with a clarity based on a firm grasp of the doctrine. The chronicler recounted with zest cases of Filipinos not satisfied with the rigor of the penance assigned.[35] The more sophisticated Jesuit historian, Pedro Murillo Velarde, writing around 1750, was more skeptical than Ribadeneyra. He wearily complained that the inclination of the Filipinos toward quibbling and contradictions created labyrinths which confused even the most experienced confessors.[36]

In order to overcome the Filipinos' fear and embarrassment, the missionaries developed a simple question and answer technique. Brief questions were phrased, and the confessors sought to elicit truthful and succinct answers. Placing no faith in the veracity of their parishioners, and experienced in handling primitive peoples, the confessors asked the same question in a variety of ways. An example of this technique is Fernando Rey's Ilokano confessional. The manual is divided into ten sections, one for each of the Commandments, with a series of simply phrased questions for each section.

Evidently it was in the enforcement of the Sixth Commandment that the religious encountered their greatest difficulties. Intercourse with in-laws and future in-laws, incest according to canon law, seems not to have been uncommon. The Filipinos apparently could not be made to take very literally the prohibitions of the Sixth Commandment, and they sought to conceal such conduct from their confessors.[37] From a canonical point of view such prodding was necessary, for a confession in which some capital sins are deliberately concealed is not valid.[38] What all conscientious religious fought to overcome was the popular conviction that an annual absolution in the confessional gave the Filipinos license to gratify their passions and appetites during the rest of the year.[39] In enforcing standards of premarital chastity, the clergy had more success among the women than the men. The efforts of the religious were sometimes undercut by that minority in their own ranks who openly violated clerical celibacy.

The administration of penance was complemented by the introduction of the sacrament of the Eucharist. In the case of this sacrament the Mexican background must be taken into account. There was a spirited controversy in Mexico about the desirability of allowing the Indians to receive Communion. Many Spanish laymen voiced doubts as to whether the Indians were able to appreciate its spiritual meaning. Some Spanish colonists accused the Indians of being stupid, infamous sinners, and chronic alcoholics. Their understanding of the Christian doctrine was said to be insufficient. The regular clergy, on the other hand, were partisans of a course of action which avoided extremes. They did not refuse the Sacrament to all Indians, and yet the friars would not grant it indiscriminately to everyone. Candidates were carefully screened. The religious were particularly anxious that the candidates know the difference between ordinary and sacramental bread, and between the nonconsecrated and the consecrated Host. Ordinarily, a convert was not allowed to receive Communion until he had been confessing for four or five years. The selective policy of the Mexican friars received vigorous endorsement from Pope Paul III in 1537. Although the Mexican synods of 1539 and 1546 confirmed this course of action, latent opposition continued. As late as 1573 the Augustinian canonist, Pedro de Agurto, found it necessary to publish in Mexico City a treatise whose thesis was the obligation of the Church to grant Communion discriminately to qualified Indians.[40]

This same Pedro de Agurto was presented by Philip II in 1595 as the first Bishop of Cebu. He died in his see in 1608. Two years before that event his Mexican treatise was reprinted in the Philippines.[41] This may not have been a casual circumstance, for the viewpoint expressed in Agurto's work coincided with the policy that the Philippine religious followed. Communion was not refused to all converts, nor was it granted to everyone. The Dominicans defined the course of action of the other missionary orders when, at their chapter meeting held in April of 1592, they resolved to administer the Eucharist "in good time" to those Filipinos "sufficiently well indoctrinated."[42]

The religious sought to impress upon the Filipinos the meaning of the Sacrament, so that they could derive the maximum spiritual benefit from it. It was also hoped that as a result of preliminary preparation desecrations, or the Sacrament's misuse, might be avoided. Incidents recounted in the chronicles about misfortunes befalling natives who received Communion without making a worthy confession had an obvious didactic purpose.[43] Parish priests were admonished not to allow the keys of the tabernacle where the consecrated Host was kept to fall into the hands of any Filipino lest some desecration result. For the same reason the Host was never kept in the *visita* chapels, where there were no resident priests.[44]

There was striking uniformity among the orders in their methods. By the 1590's confession was open to most converts, but only a small minority received Communion, usually during the season of Lent. Only the seriously ill received the Sacrament during the rest of the year. As in Mexico, candidates were screened as to their habits and their knowledge of the catechism. During the week prior to taking Communion, those chosen heard Mass daily. Sometimes the men lived in the monastery during that week, participating in its liturgical exercises, including the midnight matins. Some religious fostered the custom that during the week prior to taking Communion husbands and wives not cohabitate. This act of abstinence, of course, was not obligatory.[45] As the seventeenth century advanced, more and more Filipinos were receiving Communion. With the falling off of missionary enthusiasm, however, the quality of preliminary instruction declined.

The introduction of the Eucharist into the Philippines did not provoke the lively controversy accompanying its previous introduction into Mexico. For that matter the same is true for the sacraments of baptism, matrimony, and penance. Sufficient precedents had already been established in Mexico so that these sacraments could be introduced into the Philippines with only a minimum of dispute.

Not many Filipinos received the sacrament of confirmation, whose administration was an episcopal prerogative. The frequently long vacancies in the suffragan sees, as well as the extensive areas covered by each diocese, made this sacrament an occasional occurrence. In the populous Laguna de Bay district adjacent to Manila no confirmations were administered for a period of twenty-five years.[46] On the islands of Samar and Leyte there were no confirmations for a span of twenty-six years.[47] The regulars were indifferent if not actively hostile to the spread of confirmation. Some bishops had used the administration of confirmation as a preliminary to enforce episcopal visitation.[48] The consequences for the Filipinos were not grave. Theologically, confirmation is a supplement to baptism. As such it is desirable but not essential for participating in the sacramental life of the Church. Much more serious was the fact that few Filipinos received either the sacraments of holy orders or extreme unction, a condition whose ultimate consequences will be examined in the next chapter.

The Christianization of the Philippines falls into three periods. The years between 1565 and 1578 were preparatory and exploratory. There was a scarcity of missionary personnel, and those available were without adequate linguistic training. The decades from 1578 until 1609, after which date the Philippines began to feel the full impact of the Dutch war, were the "golden age" of the missionary enterprise. Fired with apostolic zeal, this generation of missionaries was inspired by a seemingly boundless enthusiasm. A modest program for training a native elite was launched. Once the initial misunderstandings and the economic dislocations provoked by the conquest receded, the Filipinos in the main responded enthusiastically to the appeal of the new religion. The chronicles of the Franciscan, Marcelo de Ribadeneyra (1601), and the Jesuit, Pedro Chirino (1604), eloquently reflect the optimism animating this first generation of missionaries.

Juan de Medina's Augustinian chronicle provides a foil to the accounts of Ribadeneyra and Chirino. Serving in the Philippines from 1610 to 1635, Medina had what we might call a "second generation complex." He suffered from an acute disappointment born of his conviction that the sanguine if somewhat unrealistic hopes of the preceding generation were not materializing. Among the Augustinians the lowering of morale took place as early as the 1590's. In the other orders the falling off of enthusiasm never was as pronounced as it was with the Augustinians, but there was a decline in the seventeenth century.

The general pattern of missionary activity in the islands was similar to what had previously occurred in Mexico. The zeal of the first generation of missionaries gave way to a spirit of apathy, routine, and discouragement. The net result was the same in both regions, but the causes were dissimilar. The decline of missionary morale in Mexico was largely the result of the losing battle the regular clergy were waging with the bishops and the secular clergy.[49] In the Philippines, the falling off of missionary enthusiasm set in as the regular clergy became increasingly aware of the limits of their resources and the magnitude of their task. The crushing burdens of the Dutch war weakened Spanish resolve to push forward the ambitious program of cultural reorganization originally contemplated.

As the seventeenth century wore on, the inadequacies of the missionary effort became increasingly apparent. Three sacraments—confirmation, extreme unction, and holy orders—were of slight importance in the spiritual life of the Filipinos. In the case of penance and the Eucharist only the minimum requirements established by the Church were met. The same situation, we observed, existed for instruction in the catechism. Yet the Filipinos were Christianized in the face of the severe handicaps of a shortage of priests and a dispersed population speaking a bewildering variety of languages.

Chapter VI

The "Philippinization" of Spanish Catholicism

Given the disadvantages under which the Spanish clergy had to operate, their efforts would have proved abortive if the Filipinos had not voluntarily responded to some features of Christianity. As it happened, the Filipinos endowed certain aspects of the new religion with a ceremonial and emotional content, a special Filipino flavor which made Catholicism in the archipelago in some respects a unique expression of that universal religion. In this process of "Philippinizing" Catholicism the major role belonged to the Filipinos. They showed themselves remarkably selective in stressing and de-emphasizing certain features of Spanish Catholicism.

The Societal and Ritualistic Character of Philippine Christianity

Before the conquest, sacred and profane were often indistinguishable. The pagan religion permeated all phases of life. One of the aims of the Spanish religious was to create a Catholic community consciousness in which the teachings and the spirit of the Church would penetrate into the daily lives of the converts. The religious fostered a series of pious customs to provide daily reminders to their parishioners. The women and the children, for example, were gathered every day at the foot of the large wooden cross erected in the main plaza of each village to chant the Rosary, and in many parishes the children walked through the streets at sunset chanting the Rosary. In other parishes one of the altar boys rang a bell as he walked through the street at sunset, to remind the faithful to say one Our Father and one Hail Mary for the souls in Purgatory.[1] But these measures proved effective only in the *cabecera* villages, where there was a constant community. The majority of the Filipinos lived at some distance from the parish church.

The fiesta system and the founding of sodalities, on the other hand, reached out to embrace the whole scattered population of the parish. Although the majority of Filipinos preferred to live near their rice fields, they could be lured periodically into the *cabecera* village. The enticement was the fiesta. There were three fiestas of consequence to the Filipinos, namely, Holy Week, Corpus Christi, and the feast in honor of the patron saint of the locality. The parishioners flocked to the *cabecera* villages for these occasions. Not only did the fiestas provide a splendid opportunity to indoctrinate the Filipinos by the performance of religious rituals, but they also afforded the participants a welcome holiday from the drudgery of toil. The religious processions, dances, music, and theatrical presentations of the fiestas gave the Filipinos a needed outlet for their natural gregariousness. Sacred and profane blended together.[2]

The periodic visits which the provincial superior was obligated to make to parishes administered by his order were usually the occasion of another elaborate celebration. The visiting superior and his retinue made an *entrée joyeuse* into the *cabecera* village.[3] The European origins of this ceremony, the liturgical prototype for which was Christ's entry into Jerusalem on Palm Sunday, go back to the Middle Ages.[4] It is highly doubtful that the Filipinos were aware of the ceremony's elaborate liturgical symbolism, but they evidently relished the pageantry involved.

The founding of confraternities or sodalities of laymen and laywomen also contributed to the formation of a Christian community consciousness. Here is another example of a medieval Spanish institution which served different ends overseas. In the late Middle Ages confraternities (*cofradias* in Spanish) were voluntary associations whose religious function was the practice of piety and the performance of works of charity. Under the patronage of a particular saint or the Virgin these associations also provided a wide range of mutual aid benefits. Requiem Masses were sponsored for the deceased, their funerals paid for, and their widows and orphans assisted.

Confraternities were founded in many Indian parishes in America whence they were introduced into the Philippines.[5] In the islands the mutual aid benefits, a prominent feature of the institution in Spain, were de-emphasized. The Jesuits skillfully used their sodalities as instruments to consolidate Christianization. The members performed two acts of charity. The first was to visit the sick and the dying to urge them to receive the sacraments and to persuade the infidels to request baptism. The purpose of these visits was to discourage the ill from appealing to clandestine pagan priests for consolation. The other act of charity was for members to attend funerals. The presence of sodality members, it was hoped, might discourage ritual drinking, a custom which the clergy was anxious to suppress.[6]

The Filipinos did not respond to all forms of social indoctrination. The attempt of the Franciscans and the Jesuits to introduce processions of flagellants during the Holy Week ceremonies enjoyed, because of its novelty, some initial success. But since the principle of corporeal mortification was alien to their previous religious traditions, the Filipinos only occasionally showed any sustained enthusiasm for that typical expression of Spanish asceticism.[7] What the Filipinos did accept with gusto were the more sensual and graphic aspects of traditional Spanish observances during Holy Week. Candlelit processions of penitents dressed in hood and gown, large floats depicting scenes from the Passion, the thick

aroma of incense, and noisy music were some of the colorful ex-
ternals of Spanish Catholicism which flourished in a Philippine
setting.

Another act of penitence to which the Franciscans sought to
persuade the Filipinos was to deprive themselves periodically of
their daily bath. Ribadeneyra, the first Franciscan chronicler,
quoted with approval the pious legend that the Apostle, St. James
the Younger, never bathed during his lifetime, but he ruefully admitted that the Filipinos all too infrequently showed signs of
emulating that Apostle's example. No amount of ecclesiastical
eloquence could induce the Filipinos to give up their daily bath
at sunset, which they took for pleasure as well as for bodily
hygiene. In spite of their prejudice against bathing, the clergy had
the good sense not to interfere with this Philippine custom.[8]

Accustomed to the water since infancy, the Filipinos did, however, take enthusiastically to another aspect of Catholicism, that
is, the use of holy water. Their faith in its efficacy was almost
boundless, and their demand for it was insatiable.[9]

It is apparent that one of Catholicism's strongest appeals was
its splendid ritual and its colorful pageantry. In this respect the
Filipino attitude was not substantially different from most other
indigenous peoples of the Spanish empire. But there are special
features to the Filipino response. Singing played a prominent role
in the pre-Hispanic culture, hence the Filipinos proved eager and
talented pupils of liturgical music. They soon acquired proficiency
in singing Gregorian chants. They learned to play European instruments like the flute, the violin, and the flageolet with remarkable skill.[10] The Filipino love of pageantry expressed itself in a
variety of ways, one of which was the popular custom of shooting
off firecrackers as the Host was elevated at Mass.[11]

The pomp and pageantry of the Church's ritual contrast with
the simple edifices in which these ceremonies were ordinarily performed. Only in Manila and its environs were there many elaborate stone churches constructed in the baroque style. In the provinces the majority of the *cabecera* churches and virtually all the

visita chapels were plain, wooden structures built according to the principles of the folk architecture of the Filipinos rather than the monumental architecture of the Spaniards.[12] As a protection against the hot and humid climate these churches were built elevated on thick timbers. The walls were made of bamboo, and nipa palm leaves provided the material for the roofing. The unpretentiousness of these churches apparently did not dampen the enthusiasm of the Filipinos for the colorful rituals of the Church.

The acceptance on the part of the Filipinos of the Catholic ritual pattern had much to do with the eventual suppression of pre-Hispanic ritual drinking. Without being outright hypocrites the Spanish clergy could not oppose moderate drinking as such. Excessive indulgence they could attack as a threat to public morality. What aroused their hostility was that drinking was identified exclusively with the pagan religious observances of betrothals, weddings, and funerals. The missionaries took vigorous measures to wipe out this custom. One method was to denounce offenders from the pulpit. The culprits were ostracized for a certain period of time.[13] Often less drastic measures sufficed. In order to disentangle betrothals from ritual drinking, the religious fostered the custom that the *fiscal* conduct the ceremony in the presence of the two families, without benefit of alcoholic stimulation.[14] The sodalities contributed to the undermining of ritual drinking at the celebration of funeral rites, as we recently observed. Such a tradition could not be suddenly abolished by ecclesiastical fiat, but gradual progress was registered. Ritual drinking survived longest in the less Hispanized regions of the archipelago such as the Bisayas and Cagayan, but even there the custom was on the decline during the second half of the seventeenth century.[15] But the remarkable fact is that ritual drinking was eventually eliminated among the Christianized peoples of the islands. Ceremonial drinking disappeared after the suppression of the pagan rituals with which, in the minds of the Filipinos, it had come to be identified. The custom withered away as the pagan ritual complex was overwhelmed by the elaborate ceremonies of Spanish Christianity, in which alcoholic stimulation had no necessary function. Thus the acceptance of the Catholic ritual pattern had much to do with making the Filipinos the sober people they remain to this day.

Since Philippine society before the conquest was kinship-oriented, the Catholic custom of ritual coparenthood provided an opportunity which the Filipinos eagerly grasped, namely, to bring kinship relations into the circle of Christianity. According to the Catholic ritual, each person at baptism is required to have two sponsors, a godfather (a *compadre* or *padrino*) and a godmother (*madrina*). Godparents were also required for confirmation, on the assumption that confirmation was a completion of baptism. At weddings, godparents were optional. The notion of sponsorship does not have a Biblical but rather a customary basis, according to canon law. Baptism was traditionally regarded as a spiritual re-birth at which ceremony spiritual, as opposed to natural, parents were considered necessary. Thus a spiritual and mystical relation-ship was formed between the godparents and the godchild. No marriage, for example, between them was possible.

Some interesting innovations resulted when ritual coparent-hood (*compadrazgo*) spread to America and to the Philippines. In contrast to Spain, the tendency overseas was to expand the number of people involved. The "blanketing in" of relatives of the partici-pants was common. The relationship between godparents and parents rather than between godparents and godchildren was stressed, thereby creating a functional relationship between age equals rather than an unbalanced relationship between two genera-tions. In the colonies there were sometimes as many as twenty occasions when godparents were chosen, in contrast to the two obligatory occasions fixed by the Council of Trent. Coparenthood was often extended to include such mundane events as serious ill-ness, the first shave of a youth, or the building of a new house. The trend was to chose godparents from a superior social stratum, for the participants in the relationship were under some moral obliga-tion to aid each other. Ritual coparenthood promoted social sta-bility, especially in regard to interclass and interracial relations.[16]

Compadrazgo rapidly spread in the Philippines. Conquistadores and early encomenderos frequently served as godfathers to native chieftains and their relatives. Magellan was Humabon's sponsor.[17] Legazpi was Doña Isabel's godfather. He also served in the same capacity at the baptism of Tupas, and the *Adelantado*'s grandson was the godfather of Tupas' son.[18] During the first generation of missionary activity, the *compadrazgo* served a symbolic purpose, a visible act of reconciliation between the conquerors and the conquered.

The actual spread of *compadrazgo* is exceedingly difficult to trace. The available sources contain very little information on the subject. A tantalizing indication of the rapid spread and the social significance of ritual coparenthood can be found in an ordinance of the Audiencia (May 17, 1599) prohibiting Chinese converts from serving as godparents. The edict accused the Chinese of "having a great number of godchildren, both Christian and infidel, in order to have them ready for any emergency that may arise, and to employ them as false witnesses—to which they lend themselves with great facility, and at little cost—and for other evil purposes and intents, exchanging with them favors and assistance in their affairs. . . ."[19] If more information of this sort were readily available, it would be possible to reconstruct the historical process by which ritual coparenthood blended into or destroyed preconquest kinship relations or created new kinship ties. Since this is not possible with the sources available, *compadrazgo* must be studied in a contemporary setting, with the tools available to the social anthropologist.

Syncretic Elements in Philippine Christianity

The Filipinos' lack of a solid grasp of Catholic doctrine threatened to cause native Christianity to degenerate into outward ritual formalism. The line between veneration of the saints and idolatry was often crossed, and belief in miracles sometimes provoked a relapse into magic and superstition.

There emerged no one single cult of mass appeal comparable to the celebrated apparition of the Indian Virgin of Guadalupe in Mexico. Although there was no Philippine Virgin of Guadalupe, the Filipinos' belief in miracles was boundless and virtually uncontrollable. Few of these "miracles" received any official recognition from the Church, but such ecclesiastical discouragement did little to dampen the simple faith of the Filipinos in the ever-present powers of the supernatural. And to this day in the rural Philippines an atmosphere of the miraculous and the supernatural permeates popular Catholicism.

The suppression of outward pagan rituals did not entail the abolition of a whole accretion of superstitious customs of pre-Hispanic origin. Rather these folk customs were gradually if only superficially Christianized. Friar Tómas Ortiz's *Práctica del ministerio*, published in Manila in 1731, is an invaluable source for observing the development of this "Christianizing" process. Father Ortiz commented:

. . . the Indians [the Filipinos] very generally believe that the souls of the dead return to their houses the third day after their death in order to visit the people in it, or to be present at the banquet, and consequently, to be present at the ceremony of the *tibao*. They conceal and hide that by saying that they are assembling in the house of the deceased in order to recite the Rosary for him. If they are told to do their praying in the church, they refuse to comply because that is not what they wish to do . . . . They light candles in order to wait for the soul of the deceased. They spread a mat on which they scatter ashes, so that the tracks or footsteps of the souls may be impressed thereupon; and by that means they are able to ascertain whether the soul came or not. They also set a dish of water at the door, so that when the soul enters it may wash its feet there.[20]

One method for apprehending a thief turns out to be a classic example of the coexistence of pagan and Christian elements in which sacred and profane are interwoven. "It is reduced to placing in a *bilao*, sieve or screen some scissors fastened at the point in the shape of the cross of St. Andrew, and in them they hang their rosary. Then they repeat the name of each one of those who are present and who are assembled for this. If, for example, when the name Pedro is mentioned, the *bilao* shakes, they say that Pedro is the thief."[21]

The densely populated spirit world of pre-Hispanic Philippine religion was not swept away by the advent of Christianity. Some Filipino Catholics continued to ask permission from the spirits before doing certain things. The *nonos* had to be propitiated on occasions, such as before taking fruit from a tree or before crossing a river. Added Father Ortiz: "When they are obliged to cut any tree, or not to observe the things or ceremonies which they imagine not to be pleasing to the genii or the *nonos*, they ask pardon of them and excuse themselves to those beings by saying among many other things that the Father [the parish priest] commanded them to do it, and that they are not willingly lacking in respect to the genii, or that they do not willingly oppose their will, etc."[22] Thus did some Filipinos seek to reconcile their pagan superstitions with their Christian beliefs.

Father Ortiz's observations point up the syncretic element in Philippine Christianity during the early Spanish period. It would, however, be rash to postulate a "mixed religion" hypothesis by claiming that the Filipinos worshipped idols behind altars, adopting from Christianity only those elements which harmonized with the preconquest religion. Those preconquest rituals and beliefs which survived the conquest eventually lost their pagan identity and blended into popular or folk Catholicism. With the passing of time this process acquired increasing intensity. In the seventeenth century syncretic elements are often apparent, but in the nineteenth century they are much less so.

Toward the Spanish clergy the Filipinos were capable of showing on occasion a remarkable solidarity, even to the extent of burying, temporarily, personal animosities among themselves. An informal conspiracy of silence operated at times to keep the religious ignorant of the existence of some scandals or the continuance of clandestine pagan rituals. A Filipino who passed on such information to the priest was called a *mabibig*, a Tagalog word meaning informer or spy.²³ If his identity became known, ostracism by his fellow countrymen was apt to be his lot.

Various means of breaking through the conspiracy of silence were devised. One method was for the *fiscales* to keep the religious informed. But the *fiscales* could also be parties to the silent conspiracy. The clergy initially encouraged the writing of anonymous letters. This procedure proved not very helpful; charges made under the cover of anonymity often turned out to be false.²⁴

The conspiracy of silence began to lose its effectiveness gradually, as the daily lives and customs of the Filipinos became somewhat more Christianized. The silent conspiracy continued longest in that sphere where Spanish Christianity could offer no satisfactory substitute for traditional pagan observances. Preconquest religion, for example, stressed the causes and cures of illness. Catholicism offered little specific help in this regard. There was no Catholic ritual for curing illness, other than the appeal to prayer. The Church could only provide sacramental consolations to the ill and the dying. But the majority of Filipinos died without receiving the sacraments of penance, Holy Eucharist, and extreme unction. The absence of the Church when death loomed was a salient characteristic of Philippine Christianity. Its causes and its consequences merit some attention.

The Last Rites

Of all the sacraments that of extreme unction caused the greatest amount of controversy. Basic to an understanding as to how this controversy developed must be an awareness of the fact there were usually less than four hundred priests administering to about 600,000 Filipinos. Furthermore, the majority of the natives did not live in compact villages but in small scattered units near their rice fields. The shortage of clergy and the dispersal of the population were the two basic arguments that the regular clergy invoked to justify their refusal to administer the last sacraments in the dwellings of the Filipinos. They argued that a priest would not be justified in spending, for example, three days traveling to and from a sick person's home located in an inaccessible part of the parish, thereby depriving the remainder of his parishioners of his ministrations. In the early 1680's, Archbishop Pardo vigorously sought to enforce compliance with the canon of the Mexican Council of 1585 which ordained that the last rites be administered in the homes of the dying. That prelate's efforts, however, proved to be fruitless.

In their correspondence with Archbishop Pardo, the provincial superiors contended that they had trained the chieftains and the *fiscales* to bring the sick in hammocks to the *cabecera* church before illness had progressed too far. The provincial superiors concluded that few Filipinos died without the sacraments unless death occurred suddenly, in which case a priest could scarcely be expected to be present.[25] Independent evidence does not corroborate this claim. Not laboring under any such compulsion to rationalize as were the provincial superiors in the controversy with Archbishop Pardo, Alcina candidly admitted to his Jesuit superiors in Rome that seven out of every ten Filipinos died without the sacraments.[26]

doned their parishioners on their deathbeds. The vacuum created by the scarcity of priests and the dispersal of the population was eventually, but only partially, filled by the growth of a custom peculiar to the Philippines. Specially trained natives visited the seriously sick and, reciting the Rosary and performing other pious devotions, did bring the ill some spiritual consolation to prepare them for possible death. These visitors were called *magpapahesus*, which in Tagalog means "one who makes another call on Jesus." The genesis of this custom goes back to the seventeenth century, but it was not prevalent then. The religious superiors in their correspondence with Archbishop Pardo did not mention it. It is inconceivable that they would have neglected to do so if this practice had then been customary. Such a makeshift substitute for the last rites certainly would have eased the task of justifying their refusal to administer the last sacraments in the homes.

and from a sick person's home located in an inaccessible part of the parish, thereby depriving the remainder of his parishioners of his ministrations. In the early 1680's, Archbishop Pardo vigorously sought to enforce compliance with the canon of the Mexican Council of 1585 which ordained that the last rites be administered in the homes of the dying. That prelate's efforts, however, proved to be fruitless.

In their correspondence with Archbishop Pardo, the provincial superiors contended that they had trained the chieftains and the *fiscales* to bring the sick in hammocks to the *cabecera* church before illness had progressed too far. The provincial superiors concluded that few Filipinos died without the sacraments unless death occurred suddenly, in which case a priest could scarcely be expected to be present.[25] Independent evidence does not corroborate this claim. Not laboring under any such compulsion to rationalize as were the provincial superiors in the controversy with Archbishop Pardo, Alcina candidly admitted to his Jesuit superiors in Rome that seven out of every ten Filipinos died without the sacraments.[26]

The religious were sensitive to the charge that they had abandoned their parishioners on their deathbeds. The vacuum created by the scarcity of priests and the dispersal of the population was eventually, but only partially, filled by the growth of a custom peculiar to the Philippines. Specially trained natives visited the seriously sick and, reciting the Rosary and performing other pious devotions, did bring the ill some spiritual consolation to prepare them for possible death. These visitors were called *magpapahesus*, which in Tagalog means "one who makes another call on Jesus." The genesis of this custom goes back to the seventeenth century, but it was not prevalent then. The religious superiors in their correspondence with Archbishop Pardo did not mention it. It is inconceivable that they would have neglected to do so if this practice had then been customary. Such a makeshift substitute for the last rites certainly would have eased the task of justifying their refusal to administer the last sacraments in the homes.

Correction sheet

To replace page 82 of the second printing of *The Hispanization of the Philippines: Spanish Aims and Filipino Responses 1565–1700* by John Leddy Phelan (The University of Wisconsin Press, 1967).

The *magpapahesus* evidently had a Jesuit origin. One of the duties of the Jesuit sodality members was to visit the seriously ill. This obligation was originally envisaged as a means of destroying the influence of the pagan priests rather than as an imperfect substitute for the last rites.[27] Yet this substitute is precisely what it became in the eighteenth century and afterward, when the religious, sensitive about the accusations made in the Pardo period, felt compelled to do something toward consoling the sick and the dying.

The theological consequences of this neglect of the last rites may have been grave for many Filipinos. According to Catholic doctrine, a person dying in a state of mortal sin is destined for eternal damnation. In view of the fact that Filipinos ordinarily confessed only once a year, it is reasonable to suppose that some of the seriously ill were not in a state of grace. The most certain and direct means of winning grace is through the sacrament of penance. Because of the situation described above, this easier route was closed to most Filipinos. While it is true that even without the benefit of penance a believer can acquire grace by making what the theologians call an act of perfect contrition—an act of sorrow for sin based on the love of God—still, this act is more difficult of accomplishment for most people than is the act of imperfect contrition. The latter is an act of sorrow for sin motivated by fear of divine chastisement.[28] Considering the inadequacy of the average Filipino's doctrinal knowledge, it is certainly permissible to doubt whether many of them were capable of grasping the theological distinction between an imperfect and a perfect act of contrition. But here is where the task of the historian ends and that of the theologian begins. What can be said with certainty is that without the sacraments a believer's chances for salvation are made considerably more difficult but by no means impossible.

The more mundane consequences for the majority of Filipinos were as lamentable as were some of the theological implications. Spanish Christianity provided for the living a splendid liturgy and a colorful ritual which soon captured the imagination of most

Filipinos. The dying and their relatives, on the other hand, were deprived of the ceremonial consolations of their faith. Furthermore, the dead were usually buried without benefit of sacerdotal benediction. The dispersal of the population and the exorbitant fees charged by many priests made this ecclesiastical ceremony a privilege of the relatively wealthy. Burial fees often ranged from fifty pesos to five hundred pesos, varying according to the estimated wealth of the deceased.[29]

The Question of a Filipino Clergy

Many of the characteristics of Philippine Christianity—outward ritual formalism rather than solid doctrinal knowledge, the tendency toward idolatry, superstition, and magic, the conspiracy of silence, and the infrequency of the sacraments, especially the last rites—are largely explainable in terms of two factors. There were not enough Spanish priests to administer the sacraments and the population was highly dispersed. These conditions enabled the Filipinos to be selective in their response to Christianity and to endow the new religion with a unique emotional and ceremonial content. From the viewpoint of the Spanish clergy, the "Philippinization" of Catholicism departed too often from the norms laid down by the Church. There was only one feasible means of checking this trend, namely to train carefully some Filipinos for the priesthood. Six or eight hundred well-trained Filipino clergymen obviously could have rendered invaluable assistance in consolidating the Church's hold over the people.

In principle, the Church recognized that one of its major responsibilities in a recently converted land was to train a native clergy which in time would be able to assume the administration and propagation of the Faith among their own people. And the Crown, from 1677 onward, urged that steps be prudently taken to train a Filipino clergy. But the Spanish regular clergy adamantly refused to grant ordination to any appreciable number of Filipinos.[30] This hostile attitude of the Spanish regulars rested on a selfish desire to preserve their privileges as well as upon genuine scruples of conscience. A numerous Filipino clergy obviously would have undermined the dominant position of the Spanish regulars. According to the administration of the *Patronato*, title to the parishes was vested in the name of the various orders. The regulars could only be ousted from their benefices by the determined action of the civil authorities. Such a drastic step no governor of the Philippines would undertake, for everyone was aware that the religious were a potent factor in maintaining Spanish hegemony in the provinces. Furthermore, there were no available replacements for the regulars.

The majority of the Spanish regular clergy genuinely believed that the Filipinos were congenitally unfit for the full responsibilities of the sacerdotal state. Friar Gaspar de San Agustín voiced the sentiments of many of his brethren when he wrote:

Rather, their [the Filipinos'] pride will be aggravated with their elevation to so sublime a state [the priesthood]; their avarice with the increased opportunity of preying on others, their sloth with their no longer having to work for a living; their vanity with the adulation that they must needs seek, desiring to be served by those whom in another state of life they would have to respect and obey . . . . For the *indio* [a native-born Filipino] who seeks holy orders does so not because he has a call to a more perfect state of life, but because of the great and almost infinite advantages which accrue to him along with the new state of life he chooses. How much better to be a Reverend Father than to be a yeoman or a sexton! What a difference between paying tribute and being paid a stipend! Between being drafted to cut timber [for the shipyards] and being waited on hand and foot! Between rowing a galley and riding in one! All of which does not apply to a Spaniard, who by becoming a cleric deprives himself of the opportunity of becoming a mayor, a captain or a general, together with many of the comforts of his native land, where his estate has more to offer than the whole nation of *indios*. Imagine the airs with which such a one will extend his hand to be kissed! What an incubus upon the people shall his father be, and his mother, his sisters, his female cousins, when they shall have become great ladies overnight, while their betters are still pounding the rice for their supper! For if the *indio* is insolent and insufferable with little or no excuse, what will he be when elevated to so high a station? . . . What reverence will the *indios* themselves have for such a priest, when they see he is of their color and race? Especially when they realize that they are the equals or betters, perhaps of one who managed to get himself ordained, when his proper station in life should have been that of a convict or a slave.[31]

An enlightened Spanish Jesuit, Juan Delgado, answered these declamations with wit and skill. Delgado's apologia for the Filipinos is permeated with the atmosphere of the Age of Reason. Like his contemporary, Montesquieu, Delgado stressed that the character of men is molded in large measure by their environment. Men do not inherit vices and errors but acquire them from experience. Hence such defects are susceptible to rational correction. After urbanely demolishing Gaspar de San Agustín's dismal characterology, Delgado concluded that whatever vices and defects the Filipinos might possess had an environmental rather than a congenital origin. Give some Filipinos a sound and well-supervised education and a conscientious and well-trained native clergy would emerge, according to him.[32]

Delgado's reasoned defense of the Filipinos was not shared by the majority of the Spanish religious. In the eighteenth century pressure from the Crown and the growth of the population compelled the regulars to use some native priests. Filipinos were not admitted into the regular orders, but some received training as secular priests in seminaries operated by the regulars. The Filipino priesthood, who numbered 142 in 1750, were trained to fill only subordinate positions as secular coadjutors to the religious.[33] These Filipino clergymen did a great deal of the laborious work of the parish, but they were denied the emoluments and the prestige of heading a parish. The regulars, believing the Filipinos were fit only for subordinate positions, gave them only a minimum of training.

The growth of a native clergy sustained a severe reverse during the administration of Archbishop Basilio Sancho de Santa Justa y Rufina, who arrived in Manila in 1767. In his attempt to enforce episcopal visitation, the archbishop ousted many of the religious orders from their parishes. He replaced them with Filipino priests. He also had to fill the parishes of the Jesuits, left vacant by the expulsion of the Society from the Spanish dominions in 1767. Poorly trained and half-educated, the Filipino clergymen rendered a deplorable account of themselves. Manila wits quipped "that there were no oarsmen to be found for the coastal vessels, because the archbishop had ordained them all."[34] The most lurid fears of Gaspar de San Agustín seemed to come to pass when these semi-illiterate priests were suddenly put into positions of authority which their lack of sound training did not qualify them to fill. The result of the fiasco was a restoration of the old order. The Spanish religious returned to their parishes, with Filipino priests merely serving as assistants.

In the eighteenth century the Spanish clergy rationalized that the Filipinos were temperamentally unfit for the full responsibilities of the priesthood. The justification for the perpetuation of the system in the nineteenth century was a political consideration. In the face of rising Filipino nationalism aiming at independence, Filipino priests were regarded as potentially if not actively disloyal. The task which the Spanish clergy should have undertaken was not begun until after 1898. Under the American regime, church and state were separated. This change paved the way for undertaking that arduous task of training a competent Filipino clergy, an enterprise supervised by the Catholic hierarchy of the United States.

The Spanish missionaries were not unmindful of the universal character of their own religion, a universality based on the premise that all men are created equal in the image of God, endowed with a common origin and with a common end. It was in the service of this ideal that the religious went to the Philippines in the first place. Nor did the Spanish clergy believe that God spoke only in Spanish. They preached the gospel in many Philippine languages. But Catholic equalitarianism and universalism were essentially other-worldly. All men were created equal in the sight of God but certainly not in the sight of their fellow men. This-worldly inequalities in wealth, status, and intelligence were justified as a necessary consequence of man's imperfect and sinful nature. In the Middle Ages the concept of social inequalities was applied to individuals but not to whole races as such. So it was with Thomas Aquinas, for example. Dante, both one of the last exponents of medieval universalism and one of the first spokesmen of modern statism and imperialism, extended the concept of social inequalities from individuals to races and nations by setting up a hierarchy of races, with Rome at the top of the pyramid. The Spanish humanist, Sepúlveda, molded this Dantesque argument into a justification for Spanish imperialism overseas—the Spanish race was congenitally superior and the Indians congenitally inferior.[35] This idea became a characteristic feature of the colonial mentality. Few Spanish religious in the Philippines could discard this colonialist notion that subject peoples were congenitally inferior. In deliberately stunting the growth of a Filipino clergy, they allowed their Spanish ethnocentrism to override the universal spirit of their creed.

The consequences for the character of Philippine Christianity were momentous. A well-trained Filipino clergy could have done a great deal to root out superstitions, to promote a firmer grasp of the doctrine, and to administer the sacraments with much greater frequency. As it was, there were virtually two religions. One was the Catholicism of the Spanish clergy and the Spanish colonists, and the other was the folk Catholicism of the Filipinos, a cleavage which was sharply delineated along racial and linguistic lines. A numerous Filipino clergy certainly could have done something to bridge the gap between these two expressions of Christianity. The Spanish clergy paid a heavy price for opposing the growth of a Filipino clergy. A trend toward "Philippinization" set in over which the Spanish clergy had little or no control.

If "Philippinization" was unfortunate from a Spanish and Catholic viewpoint, it had much to recommend it in a strictly Filipino context. It meant that the Filipinos absorbed as much Catholicism as they could easily digest under prevailing conditions but not as much as the Spaniards would have wanted them to do. That limited portion of Catholicism which the Filipinos did digest became an integral part of their way of life, and they found in the Church a new sense of human dignity. Catholicism forged powerful bonds of social unity, thereby creating a much needed cushion against the severe economic stresses and strains whose exact character will be discussed in subsequent chapters.

LAND,
POLITICS,
AND
SOCIETY

Chapter VII

Exploitation
of Labor

In the Philippines, Christianization exerted an unusual influence over the political and economic developments of the colony. The Spanish were not unique among colonialists in their desire to exploit their conquered territories and peoples. But one should not overlook the fact that with the Spanish this desire was accompanied by a strong, if occasionally truculent, religious idealism. They genuinely believed that in bringing Christianity to the natives of the New World and the Philippines they were performing the ultimate service possible for one people to render another. The fact that the Spanish clergy on many occasions exploited their parishioners for materialistic ends, as has already been abundantly demonstrated, does not alter the ideal. And this religious idealism paid practical dividends. Christianization acted as a powerful instrument of societal control over the conquered people. While this spiritual ideal operated in all of the Spanish colonies, in the Philippines it was exaggerated because of the relative poorness of the archipelago's economy.

The maintenance of the Spanish regime in the Philippines was, in fact, a fiscal nightmare. The colony annually produced a substantial deficit, which was in turn met by the treasury of the much

richer viceroyalty of Mexico. Although colonization had originally
been inspired in part by grandiose commercial ambitions of exploiting the riches of the Orient, the hostility of the Dutch, the
Japanese, and the Chinese eventually made a mockery of those
dreams. Nonetheless, Spain did remain in the financially insolvent
colony, a fact which is largely attributable to pressure exerted by
the Church and which indicates the importance of altruistic motives in the actions of the Spanish government.

But imperialism, whatever the motive, is expensive, and it is
inevitable that the price will fall upon the conquered themselves.
Two irrevocable commitments of the Spanish colonial policy were
first, that the natives, as "new Christians," merited some effective
guarantees of their property rights and of the liberty of their persons, and second, that colonizing, based upon the exploitation of
native labor, had to be made profitable for the Spanish colonists.
The Crown seldom abandoned its restless attempt to reconcile these
two aims. The purpose of this chapter and the next is to examine
the nature of these Spanish economic and political experiments in
the archipelago and to assess their immediate and more permanent
consequences on the development of Filipino society.

The Spanish resorted to a wide variety of alternatives. Refusing to sanction the outright enslavement of the indigenous
population, the Crown nevertheless did insist that the natives be
made to work for the Spaniards. During the early years of the
conquest the Spanish colonists enslaved some Filipinos, invoking
a variety of legalistic pretexts. Bishop Salazar's Tondo Council
(1581), legislation of Philip II, and a brief of Pope Gregory XIV
(1591) provided for the immediate emancipation of all Filipinos
enslaved by the Spaniards and for rigorous penalties against further
enslavements. Henceforth Filipinos who accepted Spanish authority were effectively protected against enslavement. Those infidels who were actively hostile to the Spaniards (namely the
Moros and the Negritos) were subject to enslavement, but they
were too few in number to provide any appreciable source of cheap
labor.[1]

The Encomienda

The first workable compromise to emerge was the encomienda-tribute system. Originating in the Antilles, it spread to Mexico and to Peru and finally to the Philippines. This yearly tribute collected from the Indians in labor services, goods, or specie was justified on juridical grounds as a concrete recognition of Castilian sovereignty and an acknowledgment of the temporal and spiritual services rendered by the Spanish administration. Its economic justification was the need of the Spanish colonists to gain access to a supply of cheap labor. Encomenderos were supposed to protect their wards and to prepare them for baptism. All adult males between the ages of eighteen and sixty paid the tribute. Native chieftains and their eldest sons were exempt.

The *Adelantado* Legazpi soon apportioned the whole Filipino population into encomiendas. A third of the population was reserved for the Crown encomiendas. The alleged abuses of the early encomienda in the Philippines were the same catalogue of complaints that previously had come out of Mexico. Tributes far exceeded the official tariff, set at one peso (ten reales) in 1589. The tribute rolls were seldom kept up to date, with the result that sons often had to pay the tax on a dead father. The encomenderos were collecting their tribute with blood and fire methods without providing their wards with any of the protective services established by law. The agents of the encomenderos were harsh and brutal. Native chieftains, who frequently acted as tribute collectors, were a scourge. Many encomenderos compelled their wards to pay tribute in a scarce commodity, which goods the encomendero then resold at a handsome profit.[2]

What made the encomienda especially lucrative was that encomenderos sometimes collected their tribute in the form of labor services. During the 1570's and the 1580's the regular clergy articulately exposed the prevalence of these flagrant violations of the law. The virulence of the conflict between the churchmen and the encomenderos must be understood as a consequence of the severe economic crisis through which the new colony was strug-

gling to stability. The consolidation of the Sino-Philippine trade, in
which Mexican silver was exchanged for Chinese silks, and the
gradual expansion of rice production did much to alleviate pressure
on the Filipinos. This lucrative commerce with the Chinese merchants kept most of the Spaniards in the Manila area. These city-
loving people lacked any pressing incentive to settle in the provinces and to carve out for themselves large landed estates operated
by servile labor.

The principal abuse of the encomienda was remedied in 1595,
when the Audiencia in Manila drew up a computation of payments
(a *tasación*). Tribute henceforth was paid both in specie and in
kind but with products which were ordinarily plentiful in each
province. A junta convoked by Governor Acuña revised the
tasación in 1604. In the provinces, encomenderos collected four
reales in kind, one fowl, and the remaining six reales were payable
in specie.[3] Evident is the influence of the clergy, who favored a
monetary tribute because such an arrangement restricted the
opportunities for extralegal exactions by the encomenderos.

The Acuña formula produced a result similar to what occurred
in Mexico after the enforcement of the New Laws during the
1550's and 1560's. The encomienda was "tamed," to use Lesley B.
Simpson's phrase.[4] It soon became a relatively light burden on the
Filipinos, an annual head tax. The private encomienda could have
been easily liquidated, but this step was not taken immediately,
for its continuance provided the Crown with a cheap means of
pensioning military personnel. There never was a dearth of pen-
sion-seeking soldiers in the islands. The Philippine encomenderos
as well as their colleagues on the mainland repeatedly requested
that succession be made perpetually hereditary. The Crown
steadily rejected the request. Originally encomiendas in the
islands could be inherited by two successive heirs, and after 1636
by three, before they reverted to the Crown for redistribution.[5]
These rules of succession were usually violated in the Philippines
by a variety of subterfuges.[6]

Since the private encomienda was ceasing to provide a sufficient source of pensions for the military, the Crown set about to liquidate it, gradually and painlessly. The following statistics are revealing:

Private Encomiendas		Crown Encomiendas	
1608	94,310		$32,395\frac{1}{2}$
1621	97,422		33,516
1655	61,308		$46,968\frac{1}{2}$
1686	35,000		86,000
1742	$18,041\frac{1}{4}$		165,773
1766	$18,196\frac{1}{4}$		160,775[7]

The exact date of the abolition of the private encomienda is not certain, but its decline began between 1621 and 1655. The death knell was sounded in the cedula of September 17, 1721, which provided that as encomiendas fell vacant they were to revert to the Crown and were not to be reassigned to private persons or to charitable corporations.[8] The cedula was not always observed, for as late as 1789 the governor granted an encomienda to the hospital of San Juan de Dios in Manila for a period of four years.[9] Although the private encomienda withered away during the eighteenth century, the tribute tax now collected by the Crown lasted as long as the Spanish regime. In 1874 the tribute was fourteen reales, only four reales above the tariff established in 1589.[10]

In both Mexico and the Philippines the Crown sought to fill the vacuum created by the liquidation of the private encomienda with free, paid labor. In the islands this development occurred only in metropolitan Manila, whose suburbs contained some 20,000 Filipinos. They were paid wage earners who performed domestic and manual labor for the Spanish residents of the walled city and the Chinese residents of the Parian. Unlike the Indians in Mexico City, the Filipinos did not produce a numerous class of craftsmen. The skilled trades soon came to be a monopoly of the Chinese. Filipinos in the Manila area did engage in petty retail operations, but the more lucrative aspects of this trade were controlled by the Chinese.

The Manila suburbs also had to provide gratis domestic service for the convents of the five religious orders. Each order maintained in the capital a large conventual establishment which served as an administrative headquarters, an infirmary, and a receiving station for arrivals and departures on the Manila Galleon. At its triennial chapter meetings, the Augustinian convent, for example, was temporarily staffed with 300 domestics.[11] Each of the convents had the exclusive use of the labor services of one of the suburban villages.

Although these domestics received no salaries, their obligations to the convent were not onerous. For one thing, they only had to work periodically. Furthermore, all these villages enjoyed the highly desirable privilege of being exempt from draft labor service. Most of the time they were able to offer their labor services for hire in a free market. They produced very little of the food they consumed, except by the raising of some fowl. An indication of their status as wage earners is the fact that metropolitan Filipinos paid their tribute in the form of nine reales in specie and one fowl. This concentrated population was attacked on occasion for being unproductive and parasitical. Commented one zealous bureaucrat: "These settlements have become dens of thieves and vagabonds, and of hucksters and retailers who buy provisions at wholesale for their retail trade, and hence their cost; and they commit many offenses against God."[12] He suggested that the metropolitan villages be disbanded and their inhabitants be sent back to the rice paddies in the provinces. The Filipinos of Manila in reality were no more parasitical than the metropolis itself, which never carried its own weight economically, living off the resources of the provinces. The Filipinos of Manila were an outstanding example of functional Hispanization in the economic sphere. They were urbanized wage earners.

In the provinces no such functional Hispanization occurred. There no numerous class of wage earners emerged. The Filipinos continued to engage in agriculture as in pre-Hispanic times under a complex system of debt peonage and sharecropping.

The *Polo* and the *Vandala*

The relative economic equilibrium attained after the mid–1580's was shattered by the impact of the Hispano-Dutch war, which produced a severe strain on the Philippine economy between 1609 and 1648. The defense of the Philippines could not have succeeded if the government in Manila had not ruthlessly exploited the material and human resources of the islands. Since the conflict was essentially a naval war, the harshest burdens placed on Filipino labor were as woodcutters, shipbuilders, crewmen, and munitions makers.[13] Draft labor was recruited through a system known as the *polo*. Although draft labor existed in the Philippines in some form as early as 1580, its character changed radically after the coming of the Dutch war. The Philippine *polo* was modeled after the Mexican *repartimiento*.[14] All men in the community with the exception of chieftains and their eldest sons were obligated to serve periodically in the labor pool, but richer Filipinos could purchase exemption by buying a substitute for six or seven pesos.[15] *Polo* laborers seldom received even their token wages. The treasury soon fell into arrears. What kept *polo* workers alive was a monthly stipend of four pesos worth of rice provided by the village treasuries. The villages in turn levied a small annual assessment on their inhabitants for this purpose.[16]

The government did attempt to set up some safeguards to protect the interests of *polo* labor. Filipinos could not be drafted for private enterprises or for public works of a nonmilitary sort. Draft labor was not to be used when voluntary Chinese labor was available. Nor were Filipinos to be transported long distances or to different climates. Shipbuilding schedules were to be arranged so that labor drafts would not be necessary during the planting and the harvesting seasons. These humanitarian intentions of the Crown proved a dead letter in the face of the relentless exigencies created by war conditions. Working conditions for *polo* labor were usually appalling.

Perhaps more oppressive than the *polo* was the *vandala*. Meaning "purchase" in Tagalog, the *vandala* was the compulsory sale of

products to the government.[17] Manila assigned an annual quota
to each province, and the *alcaldes mayores* distributed this quota
among the villages in their provinces.[18] In the poblaciónes and
barrios the chieftains were held responsible for collecting the
quotas. Since the hard-pressed treasury was in no position to pay,
only periodically making token payments and generously distributing promissory notes, the *vandala* became in reality an extralegal
form of taxation—and a burdensome one at that. Between 1610 and
1616 the treasury owed the Filipinos some 300,000 pesos.[19] By
1619 the sum had climbed to 1,000,000 pesos.[20] These sums include
both labor services and enforced sale of goods. Although it is not
possible to break down the figures between the *polo* and the *vandala*,
the latter bulked much larger than the former in view of the nominal wages paid to *polo* workers.

   Of all the provinces, Pampanga suffered the most acutely from
the *vandala* and the *polo*. Adjacent to Manila, the products of its
fertile rice fields and its excellent timber were in constant demand.
Between 1610 and 1616 the treasury had accumulated a debt of
some 70,000 pesos to the Pampangans. That figure had risen to
200,000 pesos by 1660, when the province was inflamed by revolt.[21]
The Tagalog provinces also suffered acutely from the demands of
the war effort. The resources of the Bisayan islands were not as
densely exploited as were those of central Luzon. Yet the Bisayan
area also sustained severe and continuous damage from the depredations of the Moros, as we shall see in Chapter X.

   The demographic consequences issuing from the economic crisis
provoked by the Hispano-Dutch conflict were not insignificant, as
the following statistics of the total population under Spanish control indicate:

1606	580,820
1621	610,918
1655	505,250
1686	600,000 (rough estimate)
1766	720,000[22]

These figures come from the tribute rolls. In order to arrive at the total population, approximately one sixth must be added to the tribute statistics to cover the numerous statutory exemptions (*cabezas de barangay*, their eldest sons, elected officeholders, cantors, *fiscales*, etc.). One should use these tribute statistics with caution, but they do indicate a trend. Between 1621 and 1655 the Filipino population under Spanish control declined noticeably but not disastrously. An approximate loss of 35,222 male workers occurred out of a total population decline of some 105,688 persons. That the *polo* and the *vandala* took a heavy toll in lives is apparent. Filipinos, however, did have the alternative of fleeing to the pagan country in the mountains. Although the actual number of such fugitives cannot be determined, this practice was evidently not uncommon.[23] Such occurrences may partially, but not completely, account for the decline in the tribute rolls.

That the royal treasury had only a fraction of the funds it required to meet the mounting expenses of the war was due in part to the precipitous decline in the volume of the Manila-Acapulco trade. The prosperity of the Spanish colonists and the solvency of the treasury depended upon the safe arrival of the galleons in Manila and in Acapulco. A chain of calamities drove the treasury to the brink of bankruptcy. In 1636 no ships were dispatched from Manila to Mexico. The galleon, *Concepción*, en route to Manila was lost in the Ladrones in 1638. The Dutch in 1640 intercepted a large part of the Chinese junk fleet headed for Manila. Bad weather compelled one of the outgoing galleons to return to Manila in 1643. In 1645 the loss of the incoming galleon off the coast of Cagayan only compounded the tragedy of the disastrous earthquake of San Andrés, which reduced the proud and magnificent city of Manila to a pile of ashes and rubble. No ships came from Mexico in 1647, 1648, and 1652; and in 1654, 1655, and 1657 four galleons were lost.

The Dutch war was primarily responsible for the severe strains put on the Filipino population, and the string of calamities interfering with the galleon trade only aggravated an already desperate situation. After the treaty of Münster, which ended the Dutch

threat, and a run of better luck in the galleon trade, a gradual relaxation of the pressure on the natives resulted during the second
half of the seventeenth century. An official recognition of this improvement occurred in 1657, when the annual assessment paid by
all Filipinos to their village treasuries to provide rice for *polo*
workers was abolished.[24] Throughout this period there remained,
of course, the ever-present problem of Moro depredations. Nonetheless, the upward movement in the population curve after the
1650's substantiates the fact of gradual amelioration.

Ecclesiastical Exploitation

As champions of native rights, the regular clergy were acutely
aware of the crushing impact of the *polo* and the *vandala* on the
Filipinos. Yet they seldom recommended the system's abolition.
They concentrated on mitigating some of its worst abuses, and
this was done in temperate language. Such an attitude on the part
of the religious in the Philippines contrasts sharply with that of
their brethren in Mexico. The latter flayed the Mexican *repartimiento* in caustic language reminiscent of Las Casas' earlier denunci-
ations of the encomienda.[25] The religious in the archipelago realistically if unhappily recognized that the preservation of the Philippines as a bastion of Catholicism against the threat of conquest
from the Protestant Dutch entailed some substantial degree of exploitation of native labor. The very future of the missionary enterprise itself was linked to the success of the defense effort against
the Dutch.[26] In Mexico, on the other hand, there was no external
threat of conquest by a Protestant power. Furthermore, the Mexican economic crisis was of a more severe character than its Philippine counterpart, as we shall see in the next chapter. Hence the
mendicant orders in Mexico could not view the missionary enterprise and the exploitation of native labor as interdependent.

Although the clergy in the Philippines sought to place some
restraints on the civil power's exploitation of native labor, the
Church's record in this regard was not always blameless. Some
Augustinians, for example, showed an acquisitive instinct far at

variance with their monastic vow of poverty. They either cajoled
their parishioners into selling products for a fraction of their true
value, or they exercised undue pressure in extracting alms. Considerable quantities of rice, wax, and cloth were resold by the friars
in a private and not a corporate capacity in the Manila market and
abroad at substantial profits. The most notorious of these "clerical
merchants," Friar Lorenzo de León, whose career was chronicled
in Chapter III, was deposed as provincial superior by the Augustinians in 1607. While these practices cannot be glossed aside,
neither should they be exaggerated. Only a minority of the clergy
engaged in this type of flagrant exploitation. Actually the civil
authorities in the provinces, the *alcaldes mayores* and their deputies,
indulged in retail operations with the illegally acquired products of
the natives on a much larger scale than did the clergy.[27]

The fact remains that most of the material burden for supporting the religious establishment in the islands fell on the Filipinos,
the Crown assuming only the expense of the costly operation of
transporting the clergy from Spain to the Philippines. Two reales
of the tribute went to defray the stipend of 100 pesos and 100
bushels of rice paid to parish priests for every 500 families under
their care.[28] Every community was required to furnish rowers and
porters gratis to the clergy. Manual labor for the construction of
ecclesiastical buildings had to be provided without payment.[29]
Only the Dominicans and the Jesuits did not charge fees for the administration of the sacraments. The other orders collected fees
which were considered excessive by the civil and the episcopal
authorities. Periodic attempts of the latter to regulate the use of
native services were not very effective. Customs such as the clergy
requiring their parishioners to furnish rice, fish, and domestic
service gratis were among the practices which came under attack.[30]

As a consequence of the prolonged war emergency, the *vandala*
and the *polo* exacted a crushing toll from the Filipinos in goods, labor, and lives. The demands of the Church, some legitimate and
others extralegal, as well as the impositions of the *alcaldes mayores*,
added to the already heavy load. That the Filipinos managed to

survive this "time of troubles" can be explained principally by the evolutionary character of the economic and ecological changes which transformed Philippine agriculture during the course of the seventeenth century.

Ecological and Economic
Consequences of the Conquest

A number of factors explain how the Filipinos managed to survive
those decades of strain and stress of the Hispano-Dutch war.
Underlying all these factors, however, is the comparative mildness
and the gradualness of the ecological and demographic changes
issuing from the conquest. In this fundamental respect the postconquest situation in the Philippines differs markedly from that in
sixteenth-century Mexico. The initial Spanish impact on the
Philippines was unquestionably less painful than on Mexico. The
conquest of the islands was relatively pacific. Few belligerents
were killed in military and postmilitary operations, a fact which
contrasts with the massive loss of life in the conquest of Mexico.
In addition, the Spaniards were never attracted to the Philippines
in such numbers as they were to Mexico. There was of course the
obstacle of distance, but there was also the absence of mining and
hence of the prospect of quick and spectacular wealth.

No mining industry developed in the islands. The mining of
precious metals on a massive scale would have caused an intensive
economic revolution, as it did in Mexico. There were precious
metals in the Philippines, but they were not discovered and

systematically exploited until the twentieth century. Had these mines been developed in the sixteenth or in the seventeenth centuries, Spanish colonization might have assumed a fundamentally different character. As it happened, the small Spanish colony largely consisted of merchants, civil bureaucrats, soldiers, and the clergy, for these activities corresponded to the only vested interests of Spain in the islands. Metallic wealth, on the other hand, would have attracted thousands of Spanish colonists. Vast numbers of Filipinos would have been conscripted to operate the mines, which in Mexico was one of the most grueling forms of exploitation the Indians had to endure. Thus the absence of mining in the Philippines intensified the evolutionary character of the transition from the preconquest to the Hispanic periods.

An increased Spanish population in the islands as the result of a mining industry might also have caused miscegenation on a large scale, and the Philippines might have become a mestizo nation, as did Mexico. *Mestizaje* was ordinarily confined to the Manila area, for few Spaniards except the clergy and a handful of bureaucrats settled in the provinces. Even in the capital Filipino women were more often the mistresses than the wives of Spaniards. In those days mestizo and illegitimate were synonymous terms.[1] In addition to informal unions between Spaniards and Filipinos, there were also various mixtures resulting from miscegenation with the Chinese community in the capital.

Spaniards preferred to marry their own kind, for marriage with a non-Spaniard seldom offered economic or social advantages. For this reason the establishment of the first convent in Manila in 1621, the Franciscan Poor Clares, caused a wave of panic and indignation to sweep through the ranks of Manila's eligible Spanish bachelors. Within a few years twenty-two young ladies from Manila's aristocracy, one-half of the eligible maidens of the capital, had taken the veil. Not with equanimity did the bachelors of the capital observe these dowries flowing into the empty coffers of the convent. Protesting loudly and vigorously, they pleaded with the Council of the Indies to close the convent. Their not impertinent argument was that these girls might best serve the cause of God and king in that exposed outpost of Christianity as the mothers of future Spanish citizens.[2]

In addition to the paucity of Spanish colonists and their concentration in Manila, some demographic factors help to explain the slow growth of a mestizo class. The effects of the Spanish conquest of the Philippines, demographically speaking, were also mild in comparison to those in Mexico. In the latter country there was a sharp and steady decline of the Indian population from approximately 11,000,000 in 1519 to 4,409,180 in 1565, and by the end of the sixteenth century to about 2,500,000.[3] The vacuum created by the disappearance of the Indians was rapidly filled by a fast-growing mestizo population.

One of the main causes of the Mexican Indian decline was the spread of contagious diseases—smallpox, influenza and measles—against which the Indians had no immunity. The Filipinos escaped this simple but devastating cause of depletion through the fact that they had acquired some immunity to such diseases as the result of their frequent contacts, before 1565, with the neighboring peoples of southeastern Asia. Furthermore, Philippine geography did much to limit the advance of contagious epidemics. Diseases were not apt to spread as rapidly from island to island as they might overland, and the mountainous terrain of the islands, together with the dispersal of the population, created additional barriers against the spread of disease. As was suggested in the last chapter, the basic cause for the decline in the Philippine population in the early part of the seventeenth century—and it never became a demographic disaster—was the dislocation produced by the Dutch war.

In Mexico, the severe demographic revolution provoked an ecological revolution. The preconquest system of sedentary agriculture based on the cultivation of maize was seriously disrupted by the rapid spread of a pastoral economy. Since nature abhors a vacuum, the lands vacated by the declining Indian population were filled by countless herds of cattle, sheep, and goats.[4] Although the demographic-ecological revolution created demoralizing social consequences on the surviving Indian population, not all the long-term results were harmful to the Indians. The massive production of beef created for them a new form of food more nourishing in proteins than the preconquest staple of corn. The non-Indian population of Spaniards and mestizos, increasing both relatively and absolutely, were determined to maintain their customary standard of living. Pressure on the rapidly diminishing Indians became almost intolerable. The Spaniards first resorted to draft labor under the form of the *repartimiento*. The long-range solution was the growth of latifundia based on Indian debt peonage.[5]

Evolutionary Character of Ecological Changes

In the Philippines, on the other hand, the postconquest changes were evolutionary rather than revolutionary, most significantly as a result of demographic stability. During the seventeenth century the Filipino population under effective Spanish control varied between 500,000 and 600,000 people. In addition there may have been as many as one million Filipinos who were not Spanish subjects. The islands, in reality, were underpopulated in terms of what the land was capable of producing. What was required to stimulate production was that kind of external pressure that the war demands of the Spanish regime created. Although the initial process of expanding production imposed severe hardships on the Filipinos, long-term benefits may have resulted. As we have seen, once the strain of war conditions was removed, increased productivity facilitated the growth of a larger population, which increased steadily after 1650.

The Spaniards invariably accused the Filipinos of indolence. A frequent complaint was that they would not voluntarily grow a surplus.[6] Such an argument was, in part, a Spanish rationalization for coercion. Actually compulsion in the form of the *polo* and the *vandala* became necessary not because the Filipinos lacked industry but because the Spaniards would not adequately reward them for the toils of their labor. Although the preconquest Filipinos never were surplus farmers, they might easily have been induced to become so if the Spaniards had paid them fair prices for their products. Since the Spaniards would not do so, they had to force the Filipinos to grow a surplus. The *vandala* was an ill-camouflaged form of confiscatory taxation. That it produced results may be partly attributed to the bureaucratic system of enforcement extending down to the village level. Every *cabeza de barangay*, for example, had his annual quota. There were yearly allotments for rice, fowl, coconut palms, and abacá plants. When these quotas were not met, fines were imposed on both native chieftains and Spanish officials.[7] Every community had its inspector of palm trees and its inspector of the rice fields, both of whom enjoyed statutory exemption from the *polo* and the tribute.[8] Chosen from the Filipino upper class, the responsibility of these officials was twofold. They had to enforce the regulations of the central government in regard to food production. An equally pressing obligation was to organize protection against the various plagues of locusts which periodically threatened to destroy the crops. Although it would be rash indeed to assume that the coercive regulations of the central authorities were always enforced, it would be equally unwise to take for granted their total ineffectiveness. Production did expand in the face of a decline in the total labor force.

All contemporary accounts credit the Chinese with being more highly skilled farmers than the Filipinos. Although the majority of Chinese preferred to engage in commerce and in the skilled crafts, an appreciable number did enter agriculture. Those who did, accomplished much to raise productive efficiency. The Jesuits, who were outstandingly successful in their agrarian enterprises, employed Chinese laborers on some of their estates.[9]

The most important agricultural region of the Philippines was, and for that matter still is, the "rice basket" central plain of Luzon, which consists of the present provinces of Bulacan, Pampanga, and Nueva Ecija. The productivity of this area contrasts sharply with that of the rest of the islands, much as the cultural and political importance of Greater Manila vis-à-vis the archipelago as a whole stands out in clear relief. Of all the provinces of the "rice basket"

Pampanga was the most fertile. Situated in a valley where the delta of the Rio Grande was inundated during the rainy season, Pampanga produced two annual crops of wet rice. Of the peripheral provinces on the island of Luzon only Ilokos sent an appreciable supply of rice to Manila, usually during the months of February and March, when the winds were favorable for the sea voyage. The provinces of Cagayan and the Camarines at that time produced no food surplus.

In the Bisayan islands Panay, with its dense population, produced a rice crop second only to that of central Luzon. Panay's surplus was apt to move southward rather than northward. That island served as the base of operations for supplying the fleets and garrisons for Mindanao and the Moluccas farther to the south. Cebu with its mountainous terrain was plentifully supplied with game, but it had to import rice from the neighboring islands of Leyte, Samar, and Bohol.[10]

Fish had always figured prominently in the diet of the Filipinos. In the Spanish period the production of root crops, of which the sweet potato became the most important species, greatly expanded. Both the Filipinos and the Spaniards came to rely on it increasingly. In fact, during those periodic rice shortages, especially before the harvesting of the new crop, it was the availability of root crops which prevented mass starvation.[11]

Although the Spanish regime sponsored a significant transformation of Philippine agriculture, the basic pattern of preconquest food production, based on the cultivation of rice and root crops, fishing, and the raising of fowl and swine, was not overthrown. The agricultural innovations of the Spaniards were more of a quantitative than of a qualitative nature. The exigencies of the Dutch war required a rapid expansion of customary items. Those qualitative changes sponsored by the Spaniards supplemented rather than conflicted with preconquest patterns.

Notable changes occurred as the result of the introduction of new crops and weeds, many of which were first brought to the Philippines from Mexico on the Manila Galleon. Flora from Brazil also entered Papuasia at the same time by means of vessels coming from Brazil around Cape Horn to Guam. In 1912, E. D. Merrill made a study of the flora of a compact area of some forty square miles near Manila. Of the 1,000 known species of weeds, he identified 175 as having a Mexican or a Brazilian origin.[12]

Wheat was not cultivated in the Philippines prior to 1700.[13] Of cultivated plants the most significant novelty introduced by the Spaniards was Mexican corn, maize. It did not replace rice as the staple crop. On the contrary, all the available evidence suggests that maize production was not very large. The Filipinos did not like its taste, and they ate it only under duress. What is more to the point is that the preparation of maize for cooking required considerably more time than did the preparation of rice. Furthermore, the habit of some government officials to confiscate maize in the king's name scarcely encouraged the Filipinos to cultivate that crop extensively. Rice continued to be the staple of the diet not only of the Filipinos, but also of the heretofore grain-fed Spaniards. But maize production, small though it was, nonetheless contributed something to relieve the pressure of food shortages by creating a new form of nourishment.[14]

A revealing example of the mild character of the ecological changes in the islands is the story of cattle raising. There were no beef cattle in the Philippines before the Spaniards came. Cattle were first brought to the islands from Mexico on the Manila Galleon, but the Spaniards soon learned that the smaller variety of cattle from northern China and Japan acclimatized more easily than did the Mexican imports.[15] But the introduction of cattle was only a limited success. By 1606, some twenty years after the first shipments of cattle, there were only twenty-four ranches in the archdiocese of Manila. Each of these ranches contained herds of at least one thousand head of cattle, and some of them had as many as four thousand head. Cattle production was of limited scope, as suggested by the fact that in the fiscal year of 1632/33 the income from ecclesiastical tithes collected from cattle ranches in the archdiocese amounted to the paltry sum of 300 pesos.[16]

Cattle production supplied a limited market based on the traditional eating habits of the beef-consuming Spaniards. In the provinces the Filipinos seldom ate beef. What meat they did consume was apt to be pork and water buffalo, which were plentiful in the islands even before the conquest. Actually the Filipinos secured their proteins not from meat but from fish, which was usually varied and abundant. The fact that confessors often assigned as penance the task of bringing some meat to an invalid suggests that meat of any sort was a delicacy for most Filipinos.[17]

The Philippines never were and never could be a cattle country on the scale of Mexico, where the cattle industry grew rapidly. Only in the province of Batangas and in some other isolated areas was there the kind of succulent fodder upon which cattle could thrive. The coarse grass covering most of the unwooded land in the archipelago always has been a deterrent to extensive cattle raising. Intestinal diseases, such as hoof and mouth disease, liver flukes, and the generally hot and humid climate are other obstacles.

In addition to raising cattle the Spaniards made other experiments in animal husbandry, some of which were successful and others less so. The Manila Galleon brought several varieties of Mexican animals to the Philippines, but Spanish beasts of burden (donkeys and oxen), which had multiplied in Mexico, did not thrive in the Philippine climate. The water buffalo continued to be the beast of burden, as it had been before the conquest. Sheep and goats were relatively unimportant. Sheep could not be raised in the Philippines in spite of repeated attempts to do so. Goats and kids imported from Mexico acclimatized with difficulty. By 1650 there were only a few herds of goats and kids.

As in the case with cattle, the Spaniards found out that the Chinese and Japanese horses acclimatized more readily than did the Mexican variety.[18] There were no horses in the islands before the conquest, but their introduction did not produce a revolution in transportation.[19] The Philippine topography and climate, combined with the abundant and cheap supply of labor, assured that the rivers and coasts remain the principal highways during the Spanish regime. In the rainy seasons the trails were virtually unpassable for horses and mules, and furthermore these animals did not always thrive in that hot and humid climate. Overland transportation for the affluent was by hammocks or litters carried by native porters; the ordinary folk just walked. Because of these conditions, legislation issued in Manila designed to relieve the Filipinos of the harsh burdens of serving as porters and rowers, by requiring every community to maintain a supply of horses and mules, was seldom enforced and came to naught.[20] Not until the twentieth century have the Philippines undergone a revolution in transportation, one initiated by automobiles and highways.

The pastoral economy introduced by the Spaniards did not produce violent ecological dislocations. The Filipinos suffered from no widespread distress, for the encroachment of unfenced cattle on the landscape did not drive large numbers from their rice paddies.[21] A painful adjustment, such as occurred in Mexico, would have been required to superimpose a pastoral economy on top of the traditional agricultural economy of the islands. This adjustment proved unnecessary largely because of the fact that most of the unwooded land of the archipelago was unsuited to grazing. Thus the ecological changes introduced by the Spaniards supplemented, but they did not disrupt the preconquest agricultural economy.

Native Servitude and Labor

The same pattern of continuity also prevailed in the systems of labor. Pre-Hispanic forms were modified gradually, but not radically altered, during the early Spanish period, despite the fact that both the Spanish clergy and the civil authorities were militantly hostile to the Philippine variety of debt peonage and sharecropping. The continuance of this system was in fact the major obstacle to the growth of free, paid labor in agriculture.

Spanish failure in this regard was as complete in the Philippines as it was in Mexico. The precipitous decline of the Indian population was at the root of Spanish failure in Mexico. The sustained war emergency in the islands crippled the innovating powers of the government. The immediate demands of the defense effort took precedence over more long-range reform projects, and the net result was to strengthen preconquest patterns based on debt peonage and sharecropping.

Applying a moralistic criterion, the Spanish clergy assailed the pre-Hispanic system of labor as wanting in what they considered to be elementary forms of justice and charity. War captives were cast into dependent status not in "just wars" but in raiding expeditions that seemed to the Spaniards like sheer brigandage. The churchmen attacked the usurious character of debt peonage. As the heirs of the medieval Aristotelian doctrine against charging interest, they regarded the Philippine form of usury, which was the primary cause of debt peonage, as unmitigated avarice and morally reprehensible.[22]

Profiting from its experience in Mexico, the Spanish government vigorously opposed in the islands the extension of any form of involuntary servitude, be it operated by the Spaniards or by the Filipinos. Consequently the colonists in the archipelago were not allowed to acquire Filipino dependents. The government's highly plausible supposition was that under the administration of the colonists such a labor system would quickly degenerate into overt slavery, which it never had been among the Filipinos.[23] Between 1565 and 1586 the Spanish missionaries made vigorous attempts to abolish native servitude, but everywhere they met tenacious resistance. This institution provided native chieftains with their principal source of wealth, and it was intimately bound up with kinship ties. Its abrupt abolition, in conjunction with other changes introduced as a result of the conquest, threatened to undermine the whole fabric of native society. The clergy actually found that their making emancipation of dependents a precondition for baptism was beginning to paralyze the missionary enterprise itself. By 1586 Bishop Salazar confessed to Philip II failure on the question of native servitude.[24] The ecclesiastical-inspired attempt in favor of immediate abolition was followed by a period of experimentation (1586–99). During this stage, legislation issued in Spain sought to determine how rapidly the institution could be liquidated without undermining the economic foundations of native society.[25] During the third period (1599–1679) the Audiencia, the highest tribunal of justice in the islands, conducted an operation to restrict the scope of the system gradually and thus to pave the way for its eventual extinction.[26]

The Audiencia's policy, however, encountered difficulties as a result of the severe economic strains produced by the Hispano-Dutch war. As we have seen, the war created an urgent need for manpower and supplies, and the requisitioning of these had to be delegated, on the local level, to the native chieftains. Hence the *cabezas de barangay* acquired new and lucrative sources of enrichment, and the tendencies toward debt peonage increased. The chieftains frequently confiscated the token wages paid to *polo* laborers.[27] Furthermore, in order to purchase a substitute for the *polo* some destitute Filipinos were willing to borrow money. That meant that they sold themselves into dependent status. Those who could not meet the burdensome *vandala* quotas had little alternative but to become debtors to their local *cabeza*.[28]

With the gradual improvement in the Philippine economy following the end of the Dutch war, however, the Audiencia's restrictive policy began to yield results. Between 1679 and 1692 the whole dependent system was ostensibly legislated out of existence. As of 1692 no dependent could be transferred from one superior to another, either through inheritance or through purchase. Those of dependent status as of 1692 remained under the control of their superiors until either one of them died. All children born after 1692 were free.[29] But all forms of pre-Hispanic debt peonage and sharecropping did not disappear within a generation after the settlement of 1692. The *guiguilar-ayuey* group, whose labor services were primarily monopolized by their superiors, disappeared.[30] The sharecropper group, the *mamamahay-tumaranpuh*, on the other hand, were abolished in law but not in fact. Sharecropping founded on debt peonage continued as the prevailing labor system.

During the eighteenth century it became the custom for the owner of a piece of land to enter into a partnership with a landless native. The latter cultivated the land of the former, and the two shared the harvest. Usually this system involved a loan from the owner to the tenant at a usurious rate of interest. Toward the end of the eighteenth century sporadic attempts were made to regulate this arrangement, which was sometimes called the *casamajan*, a Tagalog word meaning partnership. Ordinances restricting to the old and the infirm the right to rent their lands and forbidding usurious interest on loans were difficult to enforce. The well-to-do among the Filipinos preferred to rent their lands under the *casamajan* system rather than to cultivate their own fields.[31]

An arrangement similar to the *casamajan* prevailed on estates owned by ecclesiastical corporations. The tenant farmer paid a nominal rent for his dwelling, and he shared the harvest with the ecclesiastical owners of the land.[32] Chinese farmers were also sharecroppers.[33]

From this discussion it will be seen that there has been a remarkable historical continuity in Philippine agricultural organization. Wealthy Filipinos have exploited their holdings by means of tenant farming and debt peonage from preconquest times to the present. The pre-Hispanic *mamamahay*, his seventeenth-century successor, the *casamajan* farmer in the eighteenth century, and the modern tenant farmer all have cultivated the land under various systems of sharecropping and debt peonage that differ among themselves only in detail but not in substance.

Land Tenure

The Spaniards introduced greater changes in the sphere of land tenure than in either agriculture or the labor system. An ancient myth, which has served only to obscure the true origins of land tenure, is that Philippine latifundia grew out of the encomienda.[34] For one thing, large-scale latifundia did not become significant in the Philippines until the nineteenth century and not before. Even in Mexico, where large estates owned by the Spaniards developed as early as the sixteenth century, the connections between the encomienda and land tenure have proved much more tenuous than was commonly supposed.[35] In the Philippines the relationship seems to be virtually nil. Legally speaking, of course, the encomienda never was a land grant, but merely the right to collect tribute from a certain number of natives. The government did make efforts to keep the encomenderos near their wards as a means of consolidating Spanish political control in the provinces.[36] If these regulations had been observed, the encomenderos undoubtedly would have acquired the ownership of land near their tributaries. But events did not follow this course. Once the initial pacification had been consummated, Filipinos seldom saw their encomenderos. The *cabezas de barangay* collected the tribute and forwarded it to the encomenderos living in the capital. After the middle of the seventeenth century the decline of the private encomienda rapidly set in. Hence all the available evidence suggests that the encomienda as such had nothing to do with the origins of land tenure.

The Spaniards introduced one significant innovation in land tenure. It was the notion of land ownership as opposed to land use, the concept that individuals and not merely groups could own land, that land itself was a source of wealth. In preconquest times landowning was communal in character, with the actual title to the lands vested in the communal barangay. Wealth was determined by how many dependents a chieftain could muster to cultivate the communally owned lands. Although Spanish law recognized communal ownership, there was a tendency for chieftains in the early Spanish period to assume the formal ownership of that portion of the barangay land which their dependents ordinarily cultivated. During the seventeenth century the trend increased, more and more Filipino chieftains acquiring the actual title to the land that their dependents cultivated. This gradual adoption on the part of the Filipinos of the European principle of individual ownership of land is clearly one enduring consequence of economic Hispanization.

How extensive this development was awaits further archival research, but a well-documented example of its beginnings is the Jesuit acquisition of the lands of Quiapo, then a suburban village of Manila. The Jesuits purchased these lands from some local chieftains. By Spanish standards this seemed an equitable arrangement, but according to preconquest usages the ownership of the land belonged to the barangay, and therefore it was not the chieftains' to alienate. Protests of the villagers of Quiapo, vigorously seconded by Archbishop Benavides, were brought to the attention of the Audiencia, and an interminable litigation ensued. But it failed to expel the Jesuits from Quiapo.[37]

There were two types of land tenure, that of preconquest and that of postconquest origin. Under Spanish law preconquest usufruct of land became titles held in fee simple. Their owners could alienate such property.[38] All lands not owned either communally or individually at the time of the conquest belonged to the royal domain, the *realengas*. Some of this land was assigned by the Crown's representatives to those Filipinos who settled in or adjacent to the multitude of newly founded communities. These lands were held not in fee simple but in fee tail. Although such real estate could be transmitted to legitimate heirs, it could not be sold without the consent of the *fiscal* of the Audiencia. Title ostensibly reverted to the Crown after failure to cultivate this land for a period of two years.[39] How vigorously these laws were enforced is uncertain. For that matter many basic questions about the origins of land tenure cannot be clarified until the Spanish archival sources are more extensively examined.

It is evident that the bulk of all cultivated lands remained in the possession of the Filipinos. Ecclesiastical estates were the largest single item of Spanish-owned latifundia, yet the Church's holdings represented only a small fraction of the total land under cultivation. As of 1768 the religious orders owned only twenty estates in the Tagalog country.[40]

Evolution of Philippine Society

Both the success and the failure of the Spanish efforts to introduce changes in Philippine systems of labor and land tenure left enduring consequences on the development of Philippine society. Here again the contrasts with Mexico are illuminating. Much though official Spanish policy desired the growth of free labor in agriculture, its attainment might have been highly inconvenient. Free labor in practice would have meant very small holdings of a subsistence variety. In such a situation there might not have been that agricultural surplus whose continuous flow provided the necessary economic underpinning of the colonial regime. The choice confronting the Spanish authorities was actually not one between free labor and debt peonage-sharecropping but rather between two forms of the latter—direct or indirect exploitation of the indigenous population. The former alternative, including Spanish-owned latifundia and Indian debt peonage, was what emerged in Mexico. The latter solution, involving smaller landholdings owned by a native upper class who were made responsible for delivering to the Spanish authorities labor and commodities, developed in the Philippines. Exploitation was of a direct variety in Mexico; in the Philippines it was indirect. The larger numbers of Spaniards in Mexico, the growth of large cities providing a market and hence an inducement for the rise of large estates, and the severe character of ecological and demographic changes account for this contrast.

The seventeenth-century crises in both Mexico and in the Philippines had much to do with shaping the character of society in both countries. Latifundia and Indian debt peonage were outgrowths of New Spain's "Century of Depression.[41] Subsequent events in the nineteenth century, such as technological changes and the abolition of ecclesiastical latifundia, served only to expand this system, whose origins go back to the seventeenth century. In the Philippines debt peonage and sharecropping, whose roots are pre-Hispanic but whose dominance was solidified during the Hispano-Dutch war, continue to this day to exercise a deep influence over that agrarian society.

Paradoxical though it may sound, the absence of Spanish latifundia in the Philippines was not an unmixed blessing. Although the leadership of the native chieftains, i.e. *principales*, may have facilitated the task of social adjustment, the Filipinos paid a price in the form of exploitation exercised by their own chieftains. Spanish latifundia would have diminished this abuse. Furthermore, Spanish landlords, if only for reasons of self-interest, would have protected their peons against excessive ecclesiastical exploitation.[42] The absence of Spanish landlords left the Filipinos virtually defenseless against the exactions of the clergy, for the native magistrates lacked the effective power to oppose the Church's demands.

In Mexico, on the other hand, latifundia of two varieties came to prevail. In the south, with its dense Indian population, Spanish landowning tended to be of smaller units than the extensive estates carved out of the northern country of the Chichimecas, where the Indian population was relatively sparse.[43] Although much of the communal property of the Indians survived intact, Spanish latifundia became increasingly predominant. The large-scale intrusion of Spaniards and mestizos into Indian Mexico weakened but did not destroy the leadership role of the native magistracy. Local administration continued to be in the hands of the caciques, but their capacity to provide creative leadership was enfeebled.[44] The role of the caciques as the intermediaries between the two races was gradually reduced in scope, since debt peons were under the direct control of the manager of the hacienda. Deprived of many sources of graft and exploitation, the wealth of the cacique class diminished. Although the Indian masses received some protection against the dual exploitation of their own chieftains and of the clergy, their lot as debt peons was scarcely enviable.

In the Philippines the class structure in native society remained more cohesive than in Mexico, for it was solidified by the performance of two kinds of services rendered by the *principales* to the colonial government. The native magistracy acted as intermediaries between the material demands of the Spanish regime and the productive capacities of the masses. Secondly, the *principales* were the local, political administrators. Heretofore attention has been concentrated on the economic role of the *principales*. What now must be explored is their complementary political role.

Political
Hispanization

Spanish legislation regarded the indigenous population of the empire as legal minors whose rights and obligations merited paternalistic protection from the Crown and its agents. For administrative purposes the natives were treated as a separate commonwealth, *la republica de los Indios*, with its own code of laws and its own set of magistrates. The segregation of the Indians from the Spanish and mestizo communities gave the Indian commonwealth a kind of ethnic-territorial reality. Among the natives there was a substantial amount of self-government. Spanish officialdom determined policy directives, but on the local level natives administered. Wherever the Spaniards colonized, they did not destroy the indigenous upper class. Rather they sought to transform such a group into a native nobility from whose ranks local magistrates could be recruited. The system of local self-government which the Spaniards introduced into the Philippines was largely of Mexican origin, with significant regional modifications. One of the most remarkable features of the whole Hispanization program was the degree to which the Filipinos acculturated to Spanish political usages. Their response was on the whole enthusiastic, rapid, and in many cases penetrating.

The Barangay

The Spanish administration transformed the barangay into the smallest unit of local government. In pre-Hispanic times these kinship units, which were the only political entities, varied from thirty to one hundred families. In the interests of administrative efficiency the Spaniards sought to standardize the size of the barangay at a figure between forty-five and fifty families. Of the 6,000 barangays existing in 1768 the average size probably came closer to thirty families.[1] The actual number of people in a barangay was apt to vary considerably. The head of the barangay was originally called a *datu*, but this title was soon Hispanized to *cabeza de barangay*, best translated into English as headman.

As early as 1573 the Augustinian prelates urged Philip II to preserve this group as a privileged class. In 1594 Philip II granted two concessions to the headmen of the Philippines, privileges previously granted to the Indian caciques in America. Both the headmen and their eldest sons were exempt from the paying of the annual tribute as well as from participating in compulsory labor projects. They also enjoyed certain honorific tokens of prestige. They enjoyed honors similar to hidalgos of Castile, including the privilege of using the Spanish "don."[2]

The primary duty of the *cabezas* was to collect the tribute tax from the members of their barangay. In addition, as we noted in the previous chapter, their responsibilities in connection with the *polo* and *vandala* provided them with inviting opportunities for extralegal enrichment and tended to increase their power. No government regulations were successful in rooting out these abuses.[3]

Two notable features of the postconquest barangay were its stability and horizontal mobility. Leadership was hereditary, with succession passing from father to eldest son. In default of heirs, machinery existed for the selection of a new *cabeza*. Every Filipino subject of the Crown had to belong to a barangay. He could change his barangay when he moved from one locality to another. A baptized person, however, could not move from one locality with religious instruction to another settlement lacking it, nor could he change barangays within the same community. The post-Hispanic barangay provided for a greater degree of horizontal mobility than did the preconquest institution. Before 1565 the cost of moving from one barangay to another was prohibitive. Not only did such a person have to pay a large fee, but he also had to offer an elaborate fiesta in honor of his former barangay.[4]

During the reign of Charles III (1759–88) enlightened despotism was in vogue among the ruling circles in Spain. One of the political aims of this movement was to create a more rational, efficient, and uniform system of imperial administration. The monarch's energetic bureaucrats were also motivated by the practical incentive to increase the royal revenues, since the expenses for imperial defense were steadily mounting. This fiscal consideration prompted an abortive attempt to abolish the barangay itself. A proposal was made to replace the headmen, in their position as tribute collectors, with the elected magistrates of the villages, the *gobernadorcillos*. To encourage efficient tax collecting the *gobernadorcillos* were to receive one-half per cent of the tribute collected. The *cabezas* were to be deprived of their cherished privilege of tribute exemption. Thus it was hoped to add 11,250 pesos to the royal revenue.[5]

These changes proposed by Governor Raón were never enforced. In 1786 the barangay was modified and given the form it retained until the end of the Spanish regime.[6] This legislation was a less drastic reform than one contemplated by Governor Raón. The *cabezas* retained their basic function as tribute collectors. The regulations abolished hereditary succession in favor of the election of *cabezas* for a minimum term of three years by the leading members of the community. During his term of office the elective headman enjoyed all the privileges that the formerly hereditary *cabezas* once enjoyed, i.e., exemption from the tribute and forced labor services. If he served for a period of more than ten years, he retained these privileges for life.

Village Government

The barangay was the smallest administrative unit. But there were also other units of local government, the most important being the *pueblo de Indios*. The latter was the forerunner of the modern *municipio* or township. A *pueblo de Indios* in the seventeenth century consisted of a principal settlement, the *cabecera*, where the main parish church was located. Attached to the pueblo was a whole series of outlying clusters of population, the *visitas* or barrios, serviced by an itinerant priest from the *cabecera*, in addition to various sitios (less than ten families). Every pueblo, which was an extensive territorial unit, was a collection of barangays. There might be more than one barangay in the *cabecera* if the population warranted it, but in the *visitas*-barrios there was generally only one barangay. Various sitios would have to be combined to form one barangay. The evolution of Philippine settlement patterns and administrative terminology may be clarified by the following chart.[7]

	PRE-CONQUEST	EARLY SPANISH	LATE SPANISH	CONTEMPORARY ENGLISH
1)	(no term)	Rancheria	Sitio	Sitio (hamlet)
2)	Barangay	*Visita*	Barrio	Barrio (village)
		Barangay	Barangay	
3)		*Cabecera*	Población	Población (town)
4)		Pueblo	*Municipio*	Municipality (township)
5)		*Cuidad*	Cuidad	City
6)		*Alcaldia mayor*	*Provincia*	Province
		Corregimiento		

The chief magistrate of the pueblo was called the *gobernadorcillo*, meaning petty governor in Spanish. In the early seventeenth century all adult males nominated three candidates for the post, and a representative of the Crown selected one nominee who served for a term of one year.[8] This system proved unworkable, causing many disputed elections. The Filipinos evidently took their local politics seriously. Some politicans vigorously pushed their candidacy for the office of *gobernadorcillo* to the point of holding "political rallies."

Support was wooed by organized fiestas in which entertainment and rice wine were supplied by aspirants to office. These "rallies" were never held in the *cabecera* villages themselves lest the clergy interfere.[9] These facts do suggest that the Filipinos were rapidly responding to some Hispanic political practices, although in a manner that did not always meet with the approval of Spanish bureaucrats.

Governor Corcuera and Governor Cruzat in 1642 and 1696 drastically restricted the franchise. The democratic arrangement in which all married males voted was replaced by a more oligarchical franchise. In the presence of the retiring *gobernadorcillo* and the parish priest the twelve senior *cabezas de barangay* nominated three candidates at an annual election held between January 1 and February 28. The governor in Manila selected one of the three nominees for all communities adjacent to the capital. The *alcaldes mayores* chose one of the nominees in the outlying provinces.[10] Although Spanish officialdom retained the final voice in choosing the *gobernadorcillos*, Filipino leadership played a substantial role in this process of selection.

Alcaldes mayores were under standing orders not to interfere with the nomination of candidates except under rigorously prescribed conditions.[11] That Spanish bureaucrats sometimes did is evident, but it is doubtful if such interventions became wholesale practice. As a deterrent to maladministration and corruption, *gobernadorcillos* were required to submit to a judicial and public review of their conduct in office.[12] This review, known as the *residencia*, was a system initiated in the Indies, where all magistrates were required to undergo it. Its effectiveness is a moot question.[13] In the small Philippine communities the *residencia* was probably even less effective than in the larger administrative units staffed by professional Spanish bureaucrats. Petty peculations on the part of local magistrates usually went unpunished if these officials had an understanding with the *alcalde* of the province.

The Filipino upper class, the *principales*, largely consisted of two groups, namely, the hereditary *cabezas* and a whole series of elected officials. Officeholders other than the *gobernadorcillo* included his deputy, a constable, an inspector of palm trees, an inspector of rice fields, and a notary. Filipinos in the service of the Church also belonged to the upper class, in particular, the *fiscales* (the sacristans) and the cantors of the choir. All these magistrates enjoyed the statutory privileges of the *cabezas*. In practice there was much overlapping in the political functions of this class. *Cabezas* were apt to be the magistrates, and the *fiscales* ordinarily were ex-*gobernadorcillos*. The principle of rotation in office was observed. *Gobernadorcillos* could not succeed themselves, but they could be reelected to office after undergoing the *residencia*.[14] The possession of wealth and the participation in the local administration tended to coincide but perhaps not in all cases.

The political authority of the local magistracy was not negligible, although it was limited. The magistrates had to conform, outwardly at least, to orders from Spanish officialdom. Although policy decisions were not theirs to make, the enforcement of the law in the villages and in the countryside was in their hands. Procrastination and evasion on their part made the local magistrates not insignificant participants in the administrative chain of command. Nor could they directly oppose the expressed wishes of the priest, who was a "petty viceroy" of the Spanish king in his parish. The clergy could often be appeased by outward observance rather than inner acceptance. Within these limitations the Filipino magistrates exercised considerable power and prestige over their fellow countrymen, and a whole class of Filipinos acquired substantial political experience on the local level.

The growth of the *principalía* class in the early Spanish period has left a deep imprint on the subsequent political development of the islands. Although the Philippines did not achieve self-government on the national scale until very recently, the Filipinos had had extensive political experience on the level of local government since the late sixteenth century. New political practices introduced by the Spaniards, such as the principles of hereditary succession, representation, election to office, and rotation in office, were meticulously observed. This system of local administration was oligarchical rather than democratic. Political office was monopolized by a small group of "bosses" in each community. Venality, widespread but petty, flourished. In the Hispanic world this system has come to be known as "caciquism."

Its legacy has proved a major obstacle to the growth of sound democratic institutions in the modern Philippines. At times it looks as if the cacique tradition had been transferred from the village level, where it was confined in Spanish times, to the national level, where it now seems to be flourishing. Some contemporary politicians have acted like *gobernadorcillos* indulging in graft and favoritism. In Spanish times graft for the individual magistrate was petty, for an officeholder's authority seldom extended beyond one small village. Now the sphere of peculation has reached out to include the whole nation. It would be unjust not to recognize the solid progress that the Filipino people have made in recent years toward creating stable democratic institutions, an achievement which has been buttressed by the spread of popular education and economic growth. But candor requires that the obstacles toward the consolidation and expansion of democracy ought not to be glossed aside. One of the major barriers is just this legacy of caciquism.

In order to enable the *pueblos de Indios* to carry out their corporate responsibilities, legislation provided that every community establish a treasury called a *caja de comunidad*. A certain amount of land from the royal domain was assigned to every new pueblo in its corporate capacity. Every Filipino deposited one half bushel of rice in the village treasury at the time he paid his tribute. These funds were supposed to provide an agricultural surplus with which to relieve distress in times of famine, to make loans payable at harvest time, to pay the nominal salaries of local officials and to finance public instruction. The supervision of the *cajas* was entrusted to the officers of the royal treasury, the *oficiales reales*, who formed an autonomous branch of the imperial bureaucracy. The judicial protection of these funds was the responsibility of the Audiencia.[15]

Bishop Salazar was one of the first to suggest that the Mexican system of communal treasuries be extended to the Philippines.[16] This institution, however, did not prosper. The Audiencia estimated in 1609 that the total value of all the *cajas* in the islands did not exceed 10,000 bushels of rice.[17] No substantial surpluses could be accumulated. The *alcaldes mayores* repeatedly borrowed from these funds without troubling to repay the loans. The stewards of the *cajas* were unable to resist the combined pressure of the religious and the *gobernadorcillos*, both of whom were anxious to spend lavishly for religious fiestas. This practice, forbidden by royal edict, was widespread. Until 1657 the village treasuries also paid a monthly stipend to *polo* laborers from a separate fund accumulated from a special assessment.

The treasury officials in Manila evidently exercised little effective control over the administration of these communal funds. The *cajas* served to finance village fiestas, to pay the nominal salaries of local officeholders, and to provide sources of graft for Spanish and native officialdom.[18] The principal purposes for which the *cajas* were set up—the accumulation of surpluses for emergencies and the financing of a system of primary education—never were fulfilled. Reform legislation issued in 1642, 1696, and 1768 did little to alter the situation.[19]

The archipelago was divided into twelve provinces called *alcaldías mayores*. Some of the more extensive provinces were subdivided into *corregimientos*. There were eight of these subdivisions. The modern provinces of the Philippines grew out of these seventeenth-century *alcaldías* and *corregimientos*, just as the *cabeceras* and *visitas* are the genesis of the contemporary *población* and barrio.

The *alcalde mayor* or the *corregidor* was the principal executive, judicial, and military officer in his district, responsible directly to the authorities in Manila, the governor and the Audiencia. The alcaldes were scarcely able to provide for themselves, let alone for their families, on their modest salary of 300 pesos annually. The irresistible temptation was to indulge in a wide variety of peculations, mostly at the expense of the natives. Although these officers were required to submit to the *residencia*, this device evidently did little to diminish these abuses.[20]

The alcaldes and their deputies, the subdelegates, were the intermediaries between the central authorities in Manila and the *gobernadorcillos* in the villages. Occupying a middle position in the administrative chain of command, their primary responsibility was to enforce locally policy directives issued in Madrid and in Manila, not to formulate policy.

The Administration of Justice

The Spanish regime provided the Filipinos with an elaborate machinery to enable them to seek redress of their grievances through the courts. A standard practice of the colonial administration throughout the Indies was to recognize the applicability of the customary law of the natives in those cases where it did not violate basic precepts of Spanish-Christian morality. In civil suits among the Filipinos, customary law applied in litigations dealing with pre-Hispanic dependent status, inheritances, and dowries. In 1599 the Audiencia defined as customary law for the whole archipelago Tagalog usages as codified by Friar Juan de Plasencia. In all criminal suits and civil cases not covered by customary law Roman jurisprudence applied.[21]

The transition from pagan to Spanish legal procedures was made as smooth as possible. Disputes antedating the conquest were settled on the basis of oral testimony. The Spanish monarchs issued repeated orders that native suits be adjudicated summarily and hence with the least possible expense to the Filipinos. As chief magistrates in the pueblos, the *gobernadorcillos* tried civil cases involving small sums. The alcaldes or their deputies heard appeals on these verdicts. In civil suits involving large sums, all criminal cases, and litigations in which the royal treasury was a party the alcaldes acted as the court of the first instance, with the Audiencia hearing appeals.[22] The Council of the Indies in Spain was the highest court of appeal for the colonies, but cases among the Filipinos were seldom referred to the Council.

Some restrictions had to be placed on the jurisdiction of the Audiencia in cases involving Filipinos. The government sought to discourage the Filipinos from spending their meager resources in needless litigations which, under the slow-moving Spanish legal machinery, were often interminable. Most observers felt that the Filipinos, like the Indians of Mexico and Peru, were all too prone to spend their time and their money in litigations merely for the sake of being embroiled in a legal controversy. As an appellate court the Audiencia reserved the right to refuse to hear cases at its discretion.[23]

Although the Crown sought to place some curbs on the litigiousness of the Filipinos, strenuous efforts were made to assist the Filipinos in their quest for justice before the Audiencia. The *fiscal* of the Audiencia, the Crown attorney, also held the post of protector of the natives and the Chinese. As such he defended them without fee. He was assisted by a solicitor and a staff of interpreters who performed their services gratis.

The regular clergy often questioned the desirability of applying Spanish judicial procedures to cases among the Filipinos. Most Spaniards, laymen and ecclesiastics alike, expressed nothing but contempt for the veracity of a Filipino's testimony. They shared the conviction, whether rightly or wrongly, that the capacity of the Filipinos for committing perjury was virtually limitless. What some religious criticized was the policy of the Audiencia of reaching decisions on the principle of *juxta allegata et probata*, without inquiring into the credibility of the witnesses. According to the religious, the Filipinos often exploited Spanish judicial processes to obtain vengeance in their feuds. Instead of murdering or assaulting his enemies, an accuser brought suit and presented false testimony, which usually produced the desired result. The accused languished in prison. The regulars claimed that the paternalistic system prevailing in the villages produced fewer miscarriages of justice.[24] Suits were settled on the basis of oral testimony, and the veracity of testimony could be checked against other local sources.

That the Filipinos sometimes exploited Roman law procedures to their ends is undoubtedly true. They used canon law for this purpose on occasion, as we observed in Chapter V. It should be realized, nevertheless, that the religious were not solely motivated by a disinterested consideration in their criticism of the introduction of Roman law usages among the Filipinos. They felt that the spread of Roman jurisprudence would tend to bring the Filipinos under the increasing jurisdiction of the civil authorities and thereby might lessen the influence and the power of the clergy.[25]

The Nonlinguistic Character of Hispanization

The native commonwealth in the Philippines was no mere legal or administrative fiction. It had more of a territorial and socioethnic reality in the islands than it ever possessed in Mexico. The vast majority of Filipinos in the provinces seldom saw any Spaniard except the local priest, who usually spoke the local language. The isolation of the Filipinos from Spanish-speaking people provides the basic explanation for the strange fact that after more than three hundred years of Spanish rule less than 10 per cent of the population spoke Spanish.[26]

As we already know, the Crown originally encouraged the clergy to preach the Faith in the native languages in order to facilitate the transition from paganism to Christianity. In the seventeenth century, however, royal policy became one of encouraging the Indians to become bilingual, and in the eighteenth century frantic efforts were made to compel the natives to adopt Spanish. Motivating this gradual shift toward "linguistic imperialism" was an ethnocentric prejudice of the Spaniards that the native tongues were not sufficiently well developed to transmit the mysteries of the Catholic creed. There was also a genuine fear among the civil authorities that idolatries and superstitions would persist until the natives abandoned the languages of their pagan past.[27]

Every community was required to set up a primary school with Spanish as the obligatory language of instruction. The monthly salary of one peso paid to school teachers obviously did not provide any economic incentive for Filipinos to enter that perennially underpaid profession.[28] Spanish-speaking school teachers were at a premium, and students were scarcer still. Parents showed no enthusiasm for sending their children to school, since their labor services could be usefully employed in the rice fields or in domestic chores. Philippine geographical particularism also imposed considerable hardships on students, most of whom had to travel long distances daily to attend classes.[29] Hence few of these civil-operated primary schools, designed to take the place of the monastic-run schools which had long since decayed, actually functioned. Punitive measures in the eighteenth century produced no appreciable change. A royal cedula that no Filipino who did not read, write, and speak Spanish could be elected to public office was unenforceable. The Crown had to retreat behind the face-saving formula that Spanish-speaking Filipinos be "preferred" for public office. Since few Filipinos spoke Spanish, the phrase was meaningless.[30]

Bureaucrats during the time of Charles III (1759–88) were apt to accuse the regular clergy of deliberately conspiring to keep the Filipinos in linguistic isolation on the supposition that non-Spanish-speaking Filipinos would be more amenable to ecclesiastical control.[31] The regulars may have been indifferent if not hostile to the spread of Castilian, but they could not have prevented the Filipinos from learning that language if certain conditions had been present.

What the Filipinos lacked was a social and economic incentive to learn Spanish, the kind of incentive with which the American regime provided them to learn English. The Americans quickly recognized the practical necessity of throwing open most of the jobs in the civil service to qualified Filipinos. English was made the *sine qua non* for obtaining these positions. The creation of an educational system from the primary grades through the university level, with English as the obligatory language of instruction, spread the new *lingua franca* within a generation. Given the isolation of the Filipinos from most social contracts with the Spaniards, the slow growth of a Spanish-speaking mestizo class, and the total absence of any socioeconomic incentive, fluency in Spanish was confined ordinarily to Filipinos living in Greater

Manila. But even there Tagalog remained the "language of the hearth."

The failure of Spanish to spread among the Filipinos did not prevent a substantial measure of political Hispanization. The explanation of this anomaly lies in the character of the political and judicial forms which the Spaniards introduced. This system was a mosaic of preconquest and Hispanic features, with the latter elements tending to predominate. The post-Hispanic barangay, for example, was profoundly Hispanized without losing continuity with its preconquest antecedent. Out of the system of local self-government, in which the principles of hereditary succession, representation, election and rotation in office were meticulously observed, grew modern political caciquism. In the administration of justice pre-Hispanic usages and Roman jurisprudence originally coexisted, but they eventually blended together. Terminological Hispanization was in time followed by a substantial degree of functional Hispanization.

The enthusiasm with which the Filipinos adapted themselves to Spanish political forms attests to their capacity for creative social adjustment. Their response to political Hispanization was in many respects as positive and as penetrating as their acceptance of certain features of Christianity. The institutions of local self-government established in the islands were substantially similar to those the Spaniards had previously fashioned for Indian Mexico.[32] The long-term results in both regions, however, were somewhat dissimilar. As we observed in the last chapter, the Philippine magistrates remained relatively affluent, largely as a result of their role in organizing the material and human resources of the native population for the benefit of the colonial government. Continued prosperity in addition to the isolation of the Filipinos from the Spanish-mestizo community strengthened the political and societal leadership of the *principales*. These conditions enabled them to play a creative role as intermediaries between the two cultures.

The loss of wealth among the Mexican cacique class caused by the spread of Spanish latifundia and debt peonage weakened the societal role of the caciques as cultural intermediaries. Hispanization often took a more direct form, with Indian debt peons coming into close contact with some Spaniards but more especially with mestizos. In some respects the Mexican Indians may have been more completely Hispanized than the Filipinos. The intrusion of mestizos into the Indian countryside, for example, was an effective agent in spreading the Castilian language among the Indians. But this more direct form of Hispanization could produce confusion and demoralization. As is well known, the Indian consumption of pulque increased alarmingly all during the colonial period. Spanish pulque producers may have encouraged this trend in order to expand the market for their product. But the Indians' alcoholism can also be interpreted as a symptom of a state of demoralization caused by the cultural cross currents in which they lived.

In the Philippines, on the other hand, alcoholic consumption declined precipitantly during the seventeenth century. This result occurred in spite of the preconquest tradition of ritual drinking associated with the performance of certain religious observances. As was pointed out in Chapter VI, ceremonial drinking disappeared after the pagan ritual complex was overwhelmed by the elaborate ritual of Spanish Catholicism, in which alcoholic stimulation had no necessary function. The fact that alcoholic consumption during the seventeenth century declined to virtually nothing is indicative of a relative lack of demoralization.

While it is a valid generalization to describe Hispanization in the Philippines as indirect rather than direct, some reservations are in order. Outstanding among them is the case of metropolitan Manila. The large Filipino population in the capital was thrown into frequent contact with the Spanish community. They became urbanized wage earners who spoke at least a smattering of Spanish and hence were more Hispanized than their cousins in the provinces. Although a small class of mestizos emerged, miscegenation between the Filipinos and the Chinese was much more frequent than between the Filipinos and the Spaniards. The simple fact is that there were far more Chinese in Manila than there were Spaniards. Both the Chinese and the Filipinos were in an inferior social category to the Spaniards. The Chinese seemed to adapt themselves more easily to the Filipinos' way of life than did the Spaniards, who ordinarily insisted on the prevalence of Spanish cultural standards. Sino-Filipino miscegenation evidently produced far fewer psychological and cultural tensions than issued from unions between Spaniards and Filipinos.

In conclusion, it seems apparent that the cultural changes introduced by the Spanish regime were of a more orderly, a more selective, and a less demoralizing character in the Philippines than in Mexico. In the making of this result three factors seem decisive. The physical survival of the Filipino population was never threatened by any of the changes accompanying the conquest. The Filipinos in the provinces were isolated from most contacts with the Spanish and mestizo population except those provided by the clergy. Thirdly, continued prosperity enabled the *principales* to act in a creative and selective fashion as the intermediaries between the two cultures. A convincing demonstration of the inward cohesiveness of native Philippine society can be found in an examination of some of the disruptive pressures aimed at overthrowing this regime.

Chapter x

Patterns
of Resistance

The military phase of Spain's conquest of the Philippines must be thought of as a continuum, a movement which began in 1565 and one which was reaching its completion in 1898. The conquest falls into three principal periods. Within a decade after 1565 Spanish control was firmly established over the maritime provinces of the northern and central portions of the archipelago. During the first half of the seventeenth century the offensive was resumed against the two major groups who had rejected Spanish hegemony—the Moros of Mindanao and the inhabitants of the mountain province of northwestern Luzon. Spanish efforts in this period yielded few lasting results. It was not until the second half of the nineteenth century that the conquest entered its third and final stage. By 1898 the backbone of resistance in both regions was broken on the eve of the overthrow of the Spanish colonial regime by the combined efforts of a Filipino nationalist revolt and the more decisive intervention of the United States.

Thus two configurations of resistance emerged during the seventeenth century. One was the outright rejection of Spanish domination by some groups. The other was an occasional desire of the Christianized Filipinos of the maritime province to overthrow Spanish hegemony.

Mindanao and the Mountain Province

The first contacts between Spaniards and Moros were sanguinary. The conflict was another clash between the Cross and the Crescent, for the inhabitants of the southern Philippines had been converted to the religion of Islam during the century prior to the Spanish conquest. Thus the Spaniards in their westward expansion to America and to the Orient had half-encircled the globe only to encounter in Mindanao the farthermost eastern advance of their ancient enemies, the Muslims. Spanish intervention in 1565 occurred just in time to halt the advance of Islam toward the central and northern portions of the archipelago. If the principal Spanish base of operations had remained in the Bisayas and had not been removed to Manila, Mindanao might have been conquered in the sixteenth century. However, early Spanish attempts at conquest and colonization, notably the expedition of Estebán Rodríquez de Figueroa (1596), failed.

The Moros vigorously retaliated against Spanish attacks. From their bases in Jolo and Lake Lanao the Moros conducted a series of devastating raids on the Christian communities in the Bisayas. These maritime and riparian settlements were an exposed and inviting prey for hit-and-run raids. Spanish efforts to defend the Bisayas from their bases at Iloilo and Cebu proved inadequate to stem the tide of Moro aggression. Jesuit missions on Leyte, Samar, Cebu, and Bohol sustained heavy damage.[1] This fact explains why the Jesuits vigorously demanded punitive measures to curb the depredations of the Moros. The enslavement of Moro raiders was authorized as early as 1570, but the Spaniards failed to capture many. As of 1606, for example, there were only fifty Mindanao captives serving as galley slaves in the Spanish fleet, whose total crew consisted of some seven hundred galley slaves.[2]

The primary objective of Spanish penetration into Mindanao in the seventeenth century was defensive in character. The founding of a perimeter of coastal presidios had two strategic purposes. One was to protect the settlements in the Bisayas. The other was to neutralize Mindanao and Jolo in the Hispano-Dutch war, for the Moros frequently coöperated with the Dutch against the Spaniards. Acting on the appeals of the Jesuit missionaries, Governor Cerezo de Salamanca dispatched an expedition in 1635 to establish the fortress of Zamboanga in southeastern Mindanao.[3] This site was strategic because leadership among the Moros had passed from the Magindanaus to the Sulus, whose headquarters were on the island of Jolo, from which they dominated the whole Sulu archipelago. In order to combat the Sulu menace, the Spaniards chose Zamboanga as their principal offensive and defensive base in that region.

An able general, Governor Hurtado de Corcuera, conducted in 1637 and 1638 a twofold offensive in which he set out to destroy the two principal centers of Moro power. At the battle of Lamitan he defeated the Moro chieftain, Kudarat, and was thus enabled to demolish the Moro citadel near Lake Lanao. Turning southward the next year he led an expedition of some 1,000 Filipinos and 600 Spaniards against the sultan of Jolo, capturing the city of Jolo after a fierce battle. Although Corcuera's campaigns momentarily relieved the pressure from Moro raids, his victories, celebrated in the Jesuit chronicle of Francisco Combés, turned out to be more spectacular than solid. They were not consolidated by territorial occupation of large areas.

It is possible, in fact, that Corcuera's expeditions against the Moros on Mindanao had a more significant effect on the status of Formosa than they did on the Moro problem. Under the influence of his Jesuit advisers, Corcuera apparently neglected the Spanish garrison on the island of Formosa, Spain's most northerly advance, in favor of concentrating on the Moro menace to the south. Corcuera's indifference may have contributed something to Spain's losing her toehold on southern Formosa a few years later to the Dutch, who were entrenched in northern Formosa. Also involved in the loss of the island was the rivalry between the Dominicans and the Jesuits. The Dominicans had set up a chain of missions in southern Formosa, which they regarded as a stepping stone to China. The Spanish Jesuits in the Philippines looked with disfavor on such a prospect. They feared Dominican encroachment on the modest but already flourishing Jesuit mission in the Celestial Empire.[4] However, in addition to these suspicions the Jesuits had the very real reason of the attacks their missions in the central Philippines had suffered from the Moros for advising concentration of military efforts in the south.

Corcuera's neglect of Formosa was a defensible decision. Given his limited resources, he had to concentrate on the most critical fronts, and the pressure of the Dutch in other areas and the depredations of the Moros required immediate attention. Formosa thus fell away from the orbit of the Philippines, to which it could conceivably have belonged because of the ethnic character of its indigenous population and because of geopolitical considerations. It is doubtful, however, whether the Chinese government would have tolerated Spanish control over Formosa for any length of time.

The tie-up between Formosa and Mindanao was to assert itself again in that critical year of 1662. No sooner had the Chinese condottiere, Koxinga, ousted the Dutch from Formosa in 1661 than he indicated aggressive designs on Manila. With Koxinga's sudden death the threat to the Spanish colony evaporated, but before the situation clarified Manila ordered the withdrawal of Spanish garrisons on the periphery, notably Zamboanga in Mindanao and the presidios in the Moluccas. The Dutch had long since won the "war of the spices," and the garrisons in the Moluccas were strategically obsolete and costly.[5] The decision to abandon Zamboanga, on the other hand, was the product of momentary panic rather than cool strategic thinking. In the eighteenth century the Spanish presidio was re-established there.

Accompanying Spanish soldiers to Mindanao were the Jesuits and the Augustinian Recollects. The first Jesuit mission, which was founded in 1596 and abandoned in 1600, was located at the mouth of the Butuan River. Re-established in 1611, the Jesuits handed it over to the Recollects in 1622. The two principal Jesuit missions were at Zamboanga and at Dapitan-Iligan. There were usually not more than eleven priests in both areas, administering to about 28,000 people. The Recollect missions were located along the coast adjacent to the mouth of the Butuan River and along the northeastern coast of the Surigao peninsula. The Recollects administered to about 20,000 people.[6]

Spanish failure in the mountain province of northwestern Luzon was as complete as it was in Mindanao but for different reasons. The mountainous terrain of that interior province made it inaccessible. The area quickly aroused the curiosity of the Spaniards as a potential source of gold and as the home of the headhunting bands who occasionally raided coastal communities. Once the lowland provinces of Pangasinan, Ilokos, and Cagayan had been subdued, the Spaniards turned their attention to the mountain region, whose inhabitants they called *Ygolotes*. In the face of the uncompromising hostility of the mountaineers and the reluctance of Manila to underwrite the expenses of a prolonged and costly territorial occupation, various military expeditions in 1591, 1608, 1635, and 1663 proved fruitless.[7] Missionaries who ventured into the area without military escort often met a martyr's death at the hands of the headhunters. In the seventeenth century the Spaniards had neither the military nor the ecclesiastical personnel to conquer the area. Occasional uprisings by the maritime peoples, the endless depredations of the Moros, and the Hispano-Dutch campaigns sufficiently taxed the limited resources of Manila without the Spanish attempting the costly operation of subduing the determined resistance of the mountain peoples.

During the administration of Governor Manuel de León (1669–77) the Spaniards undertook to stabilize the frontier. The job of creating a buffer zone between the Christianized lowlands and the mountain country was assigned to the military in cooperation with the religious. The *misiones vivas*, or active missions, were organized in outlying areas. The natives paid no tribute, and many of them were not baptized. Each mission enjoyed the protection of a few soldiers. As of 1742 there were some twenty-eight religious stationed in these missionary outposts along the rim of the mountain country. Thirteen of these friars were in the province of Cagayan.

In the slow advance from the Cagayan valley the Dominicans took the lead. In the northeastern direction they reached the Isneg-Negrito country on the Abulog river, and by 1632 they had penetrated inland as far as the Isinai country in the southeastern part of the province. Eventually they opened a land route from the Cagayan valley to Manila.

The inhabitants of the mountain province had been expelled from the lowlands by the Malay invaders who were in possession of the maritime provinces when the Spaniards arrived. Hence there had been a long tradition of hostility between the people of the mountain province and those of the lowlands. This animosity was intensified in the seventeenth century, when the maritime peoples were converted to Spanish Christianity and the mountain province remained pagan. In spite of this traditional hostility, trade of a limited sort took place between the two regions, for each area had products the other needed. The semi-Christian buffer zone, the region of the *misiones vivas*, provided a convenient neutral ground where hogs, salt, iron, and cloth from the lowlands could be exchanged for gold, wax, and cacao from the mountain country.

The existence of this trade would suggest that the relations between these two diverse regions were not consistently hostile. Raiding expeditions organized by Christianized Filipinos against the mountain pagans sometimes degenerated into elaborate farces. The Christian raiders, who received a daily ration of rice from the royal treasury, sometimes forewarned their pagan neighbors of the impending attack.[8] Another significant example of coöperation between Christian and pagan Filipinos was that many of the former who fled to the mountains to escape the crushing burdens of the *polo* and the *vandala* were hospitably received by the pagans. Although there were deep historical roots antedating the conquest which help to explain the hostility between the people of the mountains and those of the lowlands, both groups on occasion were capable of coöperating against the Spaniards.

The mountain peoples of the other Christianized islands were equally unresponsive to Spanish efforts to subjugate them. They were the fierce and warlike Negritos, who were probably the original inhabitants of the islands. The mountainous terrain and the Negritos' passionate determination to preserve their independence proved effective shields against Spanish penetration.

The successful resistance of the Moros, the mountain province, and the Negritos cannot be explained solely in terms of a rigid analysis of the weakness and strength of the Spaniards. Numerical inferiority begs the question, for all the great Spanish conquests were achieved by a mere handful of conquistadores facing vast hordes of natives. The effectiveness of the tactical advantages of the Spaniards such as the horse and gunpowder was diminished by mountain barriers as well as the hot and humid climate in both regions. It is true that during their greatest concentration of military power in the first half of the seventeenth century the Spaniards were involved in a desperate struggle with the Dutch. Therefore they were able to concentrate only a fraction of their strength against their domestic Filipino enemies. Significant though these factors may be, these explanations border on the superficial.

In order to understand the successful resistance of these peoples it is necessary to explore their cultural development. Something in their way of life made resistance both meaningful and possible. After a few military encounters the peoples of the maritime provinces submitted to the rule of the conquerors. The Moros, the inhabitants of the mountain province, and the Negritos chose the alternative path of resistance. Why?

In the case of the Moros the factor of transculturation seems decisive. The creed of Islam gave them a religious belief, one which had amply demonstrated over the centuries its dynamic capacity to resist and even, in several cases, to overwhelm Christianity. Since Spanish nationalism had been born in the *reconquista* crusade against the Moors, the conflict between the Spaniards and the Moros in Mindanao became another clash between the Cross and the Crescent. Such a war seemed just and understandable to both belligerents. Islam's sway over the southern Philippines gave the Moros a political means of organizing successful resistance, for Muslim cultural influence introduced the suprakinship unit of the state. The new institutions of the *rajah* and the sultanates were superimposed on the pre-Muslim kinships units, which lost none of their vitality. Political-military authority was centralized sufficiently to organize effective resistance, but it never arrived at the point where the Spaniards could defeat and usurp it. What made the Moros unconquerable was the sound balance in their political-military organization between pre-Muslim decentralization and Muslim-sponsored centralization. Given their acceptance of certain features of Muslim culture, resistance became meaningful to the Moros. Hence resistance became possible by exploiting Spanish weakness in such a manner as to confine Spanish control to a few coastal presidios and even to carry the war into the territory of the enemy by means of devastating hit-and-run raids.

If transculturation illuminates the character of resistance in Mindanao, it provides no clues for understanding the successful resistance of the mountain province and the Negritos. Nor does the available evidence suggest that these peoples adopted certain features of Spanish culture in order to protect themselves against conquest. No trend away from the decentralized kinship units toward political-military centralization occurred. Spanish involvements with the Dutch or the fact that the mineral and manpower resources of the region provided no compelling inducement to the Spaniards are superficial explanations for Spanish failure to subdue the mountain province. The lack of success of the Spaniards had a preconquest origin. Built into the culture of the mountain province was the pattern of resisting encroachments from the lowlands. The Spanish conquest of the maritime peoples and the latter's subsequent adoption of Christianity merely fortified the traditional determination of the mountain province to resist conquest from the lowlands. Abandoning the idea of conquest, the Spaniards were forced to settle for a stable frontier which would afford protection to the maritime provinces. And the mountain peoples in turn wanted to be left alone. Military clashes occurred along the frontier from time to time, but the aims of both belligerents were essentially defensive in character.[9]

It was not until the second half of the nineteenth century that Spanish authority began to spread into these centers of resistance which for two centuries had tenaciously repulsed every effort at penetration. Ironically this development occurred during the very decades when Spain's ancient grip over the maritime provinces was being undermined by the spread of revolutionary and nationalist sentiment aiming at independence. Superior instruments of technology such as the steamboat, which opened up the interior river system of Mindanao, increased military strength, and the vigorous determination of the Spanish authorities, who then had the means of undertaking effective territorial occupations of pacified areas, partially account for the success of this last phase of the conquest. Equally decisive was the radical change which was taking place in Spanish methods. The Spanish were beginning to distinguish between the adoption of Catholicism and the acceptance of political control. Manila was willing to tolerate non-Christian beliefs in order to win the political allegiance of the newly conquered.[10]

Costly and inconvenient though the depredations of the Moros and the mountain peoples may have been in the seventeenth century, this very hostility strengthened the Spanish hold on the maritime provinces. The protective power of Spain was the only shield those Provinces had against the raids of their hostile neighbors, a condition which helps to explain their sustained loyalty to the Spanish regime.

Revolts

The hard core of Spanish power was an area that included the central plain of Luzon (the Tagalog country), Pampanga, Pangasinan, Ilokos to the north, and the Bikol-speaking country of the

Camarines to the south. Spanish control over these regions was rapidly consummated during the 1570's. Uprisings such as the Pampanga revolt of 1585 and the Tondo conspiracy of 1587–88 were but the final stage of the conquest. No single item illustrates more concisely the firm grip of the Spanish regime over this area than the fact that between 1588 and 1762 there were only two periods of acute tension. They occurred in 1660–61 and 1745–46. Herein lies the principal explanation of why the Spaniards in the face of countless severe losses were always able to repulse their external enemies—the Dutch and the Moros. Nor were the Spanish authorities unaware of this fact. Acting on the suggestion of the procurator of the Philippine colony at the Spanish court, Philip IV in 1636 and 1642 instructed the *alcaldes mayores* to express his formal appreciation to the inhabitants of the Tagalog, Pampangan, and Bikol provinces for their fidelity.[11]

Manila itself, the very citadel of Spanish power, might have been a source of weakness in that it contained a concentrated population of some 20,000 Filipinos and some 15,000 Chinese. In response to famine conditions the same sort of floating population had twice looted Mexico City in the seventeenth century. In Manila, however, the crowds did not act in this fashion. The capital was adjacent to the "rice basket" of central Luzon. Food distribution never broke down as abruptly as it sometimes did in Mexico City, for, as we have seen, the ecological and economic changes introduced by the conquest were far less severe in the islands than in Mexico. Unlike Mexico City, where the Spanish town was exposed to the attacks of rioters, Manila was a walled and fortified town. Most of the Filipino community lived in the suburban villages encircling the walled city. The Chinese were settled in the Parian in wooden buildings within firing range of the guns of the fortress.

The resentments of the Filipinos in the face of economic hardships and dislocations had a visible scapegoat in the Chinese merchants who controlled the retail trade. The Filipinos enthusiastically coöperated with the Spaniards in periodic massacres of the Chinese community, the most notable of which occurred in 1603, 1639, 1662, and 1782. It is evident that Sino-Filipino hostility acted as a safety valve to unleash the pent-up resentments of the Filipinos. But it cannot be said that the Spanish administration cold-bloodedly fostered this racial-economic conflict in order to guarantee their hold over Manila. The Spaniards themselves were as genuinely afraid of the large Chinese colony in their midst as they were dependent upon it for a wide variety of economic services. Rather, the hatred of both the Spaniards and the Filipinos toward the Chinese created a situation favorable to the maintenance of Spanish control.

Hence Manila was a secure bastion from which the Spaniards continued to perpetuate their grip over the neighboring maritime provinces of Luzon. When revolt did sweep through the provinces of Pampanga, Pangasinan, and Ilokos in 1660, it did not represent a serious threat. The Pampangans were protesting against the crushing burdens placed on their material and human resources as a consequence of the Dutch war and its aftermath. Quick military action on the part of Governor Manrique de Lara saved Manila from the threat of invasion by the rebels. The governor negotiated with the leaders of the rebellion until his forces were sufficiently concentrated to undertake military operations. A small punitive expedition, a general amnesty for all rebels, the payment of 14,000 pesos as an initial installment on the *polo-vandala* debt of some 200,000 pesos, and a solemn promise to reduce the scope of woodcutting brought about a rapid cessation of the revolt.[12] Pampanga's fidelity to the Spanish regime up to 1660 was a partial outgrowth of the raids of the fierce Sambals who periodically terrorized that fertile valley. The Sambal threat made Pampanga as dependent on Manila as was the capital on the rice, the timber, the labor, and the soldiers of Pampanga.[13]

In Pangasinan and Ilokos the uprising of 1660–61 took on a more decided anti-Spanish character, with nativistic overtones. Malong in Pangasinan and Almazan in Ilokos proclaimed themselves kings of their respective peoples. Religious were killed, churches looted and their ornaments desecrated. Yet these provinces were rapidly pacified. Another general uprising in the Ilokano country did not occur until the period of the British invasion (1762–63).[14]

A revolt in the Tagalog provinces did not take place until the agrarian disturbances of 1745–46. In various localities the Filipinos took up arms to protest the alleged usurpation of their lands by some religious orders. The Jesuits, the Dominicans, the Augustinians, and the Augustinian Recollects among them operated some twenty large cattle ranches in the provinces of Bulacan and Batangas. Ten of these estates belonged to the Jesuits.[15]

The relative absence of revolts in the lowland provinces of Luzon is all the more remarkable in that these areas were the most densely exploited in the islands. From these provinces came in large quantities the agricultural products, the wood for shipbuilding, the labor services, and the soldiers that the Spanish administration required.

Spanish control over the Bisayas was never as penetrating as their domination of the maritime provinces of Luzon. Yet in a period of two centuries, between 1565 and the British invasion of 1762, only three major uprisings occurred in the whole Bisayan area. The Bisayans perhaps had as much need of the Spaniards as the Spaniards did of the Bisayans. The frequent raids of the Moros from Mindanao and Jolo terrorized the Bisayan settlements year after year. Spanish power was their only shield. When revolts did break out, they were apt to have a more pronounced nativistic content that the uprisings on Luzon. This trend was an outgrowth of the fact that the ecclesiastical establishment in the central Philippines was even more understaffed than were the parishes of Luzon.

In 1621 revolt swept through the island of Bohol, administered by the Jesuits. Led by a Filipino pagan priest, Tamblot, the rebels repudiated Christianity and aspired to return to the religion of their pagan ancestors. About 2,000 Boholanos joined the movement, but an expedition of fifty Spaniards and more than 1,000 Cebuans easily crushed the uprising, in January of 1622.[16]

The insurrection spread to the neighboring island of Leyte. Its leader was an aged chieftain, Bankaw, whose hospitable welcome of Legazpi was said to have evoked a formal acknowledgment from Philip II. A convert to Christianity and a loyal subject of Spain for many decades, he apostatized in his old age. Overthrow of Spanish control and the restoration of paganism were the twin objectives of the movement. Although the uprising plunged most of Leyte into chaos for a few months, a punitive expedition composed of a small detachment of Spanish soldiers and a much larger force of Cebuans quickly restored order.[17]

The year 1649, when the Hispano-Dutch war was drawing to its close, was another period of rebellious unrest in the Bisayas. The rebellion was precipitated by the order of Governor Diego Fajardo that a large detachment of Bisayan workers be sent to the shipyards in Cavite to relieve the hard-pressed Tagalogs. The religious in the Bisayas foresaw trouble and pleaded with the governor to revoke the order. The Bisayans were not accustomed to working in the shipyards, and the clergy stressed the hardships involved in Bisayans abandoning their homes and fields for distant Luzon. The fears of the religious were not groundless. When the governor's order was applied in Palapag on Samar, the standard of revolt was raised. The first act of the rebels was to liquidate an unpopular parish priest. The movement won initial successes as a consequence of the capable leadership of Juan Ponce Sumoroy. Before the insurrection was quelled the next year, it had spread to other islands. Its hard core, however, remained in Samar. The capture of the mountain citadel of Sumoroy brought hostilities to an end.[18]

An unusual revolt was one that broke out in Bohol in 1744. Under the leadership of Dagohoy, 3,000 of his followers fled to the mountains, where they repulsed all Hispano-Filipino expeditions sent against them. In fact, the rebellion did not end until 1829, some eighty-five years after its inception. Governor Ricafort pardoned the descendants of the rebels and permitted them to resettle in new villages in the lowlands. By 1829 Dagohoy's original 3,000 followers had multiplied to about 20,000 people.[19]

None of the five major uprisings which occurred prior to 1762 posed even a remote threat to Spanish hegemony over the lowlands. Each revolt was subdued by a handful of Spanish soldiers assisted by Filipino recruits, i.e., natives from a different province or island. In the absence of any clear-cut Philippine national consciousness, which did not begin to emerge until the nineteenth century, the Spaniards were able to play one ethnic group against the other.

The regular clergy played a key role. Some religious did lose their lives in the various uprisings. For this reason the clergy as a group were tireless in their efforts to pacify a recently revolted area. Their intervention usually secured a general amnesty, with the death penalty confined to a few leaders. The fact that more revolts did not break out may be traced to the appeal and authority the religious exercised over their parishioners. One bishop of Cagayan perhaps understated his case when he wrote Philip III that one religious was worth one hundred Spanish soldiers.[20]

The native constabulary was another reliable source of strength to the Spanish administration. A separate army modeled along the lines of the Spanish military organization was set up. Its officers were Filipinos, some of whom bore the high-sounding military rank of captain and master of the camp. Taught in the methods of European military science, they fought with distinction in every campaign along with Spanish troops. They were equally reliable against the regime's domestic foes and against its foreign enemies. Ordinarily a military expedition would consist of a small Spanish detachment and a much larger Filipino force. Pampanga furnished the bulk of these levies. The Spaniards usually expressed high regard for the courage and stamina of the Pampangan troops. Occasionally some uneasiness was voiced about putting arms into the hands of any native group. These fears, however, proved groundless.[21]

Along with the Church and the Filipino constabulary, the system of local administration was another factor in the maintenance of Spanish authority in the provinces. As we observed in the last chapter, the *principales* were modest beneficiaries of the colonial status quo. The preservation of the system was to their advantage. The Filipino magistracy had to maneuver between the triple pressures exercised by the Spanish administration, their desire for self-enrichment at the expense of their followers, and the discontents of their fellow countrymen. Only under conditions of acute stress did they desert the Spanish cause to lead their followers into armed rebellion. Every insurrection that did take place resulted from a case of such stress, and the *principales* provided the leadership for the revolt. Thus the class structure as well as the ethnic divisions among the Filipinos provides a *divide et impera* explanation of the long-enduring Spanish hold on the maritime provinces.

If the Filipino magistrates had to adjust to pressures exerted by the Spanish administration, they also could not be indifferent to the welfare of their followers. Only occasionally were they driven to the desperate extremity of open rebellion, in most situations preferring to use peaceful means to protect their subordinates. The kinship character of Philippine society, which retained much of its cohesiveness in the seventeenth century as a result of the survival of the barangays, made these magistrates patriarchical and paternalistic leaders of their communities. In dealing with the Spanish authorities, evasion and procrastination were effective tactics, given the decentralized character of population patterns. The *principales* seldom put pressure on the Spanish administration by means of memorials and petitions to the Audiencia in Manila and the Council of the Indies in Spain demanding reform. This alternative was closed to them, for as a class they had little formal education of the Spanish variety. They were not illiterate, but few spoke or wrote Spanish. There were no specially created schools where the sons of the chieftains could acquire a Spanish education.

In Peru, on the other hand, special schools operated by the Jesuits enabled some sons of caciques to acquire an excellent formal education by the standards of the time and place. In the eighteenth century several caciques conducted a sustained program of political agitation, designed to improve the lot of the Indian masses, inside the framework of the Spanish bureaucracy. Periodically petitioning the Crown for reforms, this Inca nationalist movement culminated in a series of extensive rebellions whose well-organized character posed a serious problem to the Spanish authorities.[22] No comparable political activity was undertaken by the Filipino *principales*, lacking as they did the educational opportunities available to the Peruvian caciques. Yet it is apparent that the *principales* provided the Filipino masses with some modest protection against the worst excesses of colonial exploitation at the same time that they oppressed their subordinates for their own personal gain and for the benefit of the Spanish regime.

Understandably enough, the leaders of these early revolts have been enshrined in the pantheon of modern Philippine nationalism as heroic precursors of independence.[23] It should be realized, however, that none of these leaders was guided by an outlook that could be called even remotely Pan-Philippine. These revolts were local uprisings executed as protests against local grievances. It took two hundred and fifty years of the *pax hispanica* before a Philippine national consciousness could become articulate. The Spanish contribution toward the formation of the modern Philippine nation was substantial. The *pax hispanica* created conditions of law and order throughout the maritime provinces of Luzon and the Bisayas, Spanish forms of political organization spread, and Catholicism gave the Filipinos a new kind of spiritual and cultural unity. Nonetheless, if the Spanish contribution should not be overlooked, neither should the role of the Filipinos be underestimated. Their capacity for creative social adjustment to new cultural stimuli has been amply demonstrated. They selectively adapted rather than arbitrarily adopted Spanish forms to old patterns. If the Filipinos revere the leaders of the early revolts as the precursors of the modern nation, they should not disparage the laborious if undramatic efforts of those Filipinos in the seventeenth century who were confronted with the difficult task of synthesizing Hispanic and indigenous elements into a somewhat harmonious whole. The modern Philippine nation owes as much to the latter group as it does to the former.

In Retrospect

Nietzsche was once supposed to have exclaimed, "Those Spaniards! those Spaniards! Those are men who wanted to be too much."[1] Spanish colonization in the Philippines is certainly a case in point. Isolated from Mexico and Spain by the breadth of the Pacific and the Atlantic, the small Spanish colony attempted to do too much. As is now rather clear, the Spanish regime's ambitious program of cultural integration was only partially implemented in the Philippines.

Immediately apparent is the deep gulf separating legislation formulated in Spain and its lack of enforcement in the islands. Philippine colonization was modeled on Mexican precedents. Conditions in the archipelago, however, did not always respond to this Mexican-inspired legislation.[2] A Hegelian formula may clarify matters somewhat. The thesis is royal legislation dispatched to the Philippines based largely on Mexican models. The antithesis is local conditions in the islands often at variance with the government's instructions. This gap was created by the Council of the Indies' unawareness of the actual state of affairs in the distant archipelago and by the instinctive impulse of the bureaucrats in

Spain to standardize practices throughout the empire. The synthesis was what actually happened in the Philippines. That may not always have been satisfactory, but it was usually a workable compromise between what the central authorities intended and what local conditions would permit.

Bureaucrats in Spain had a habit of treating the Philippine colony as if it were another province of Mexico. Administratively the islands did form an autonomous branch of the viceroyalty of New Spain, but local conditions often stubbornly resisted Mexican-oriented legislation. This proposition is true in many cases but not in all. There are two sides to the coin. Spanish activity in Mexico provided some experience that was profitably applied in the colonization of the Philippines. The relatively peaceful character of the military conquest itself is an outstanding case in point. In the organization of labor Mexican precedents proved helpful. Some of the worst excesses of the encomienda and the *repartimiento* were avoided when these institutions were transplanted to the Philippines. The Mexican experience also provided the clergy with a galaxy of pertinent models. The sacraments were introduced into the islands with a minimum of controversy largely because the lessons learned in Mexico were profitably applied. Political Hispanization among the Mexican Indians was equally useful to the Spanish authorities in setting up local self-government in the archipelago. It is apparent that previous experience in Mexico was both a help and a hindrance in the Philippines. It became an obstacle when special regional conditions were ignored.

In the Philippines the gap between the law and its observance was expanded by geographical isolation. Ordinarily it took two years to exchange communications between Manila and the Spanish court. In spite of the theoretical centralization of the Spanish monarchy, colonial magistrates often acted with a substantial degree of independence. They were able to disregard the injunctions of the authorities in Spain by invoking the "I obey but do not execute" formula. Royal orders whose implementation might create injustices or conflicts did not have to be enforced until the Council of the Indies had been made aware of the special circumstances of the area involved.[3] In few regions of the empire was this formula more frequently invoked than in the Philippines. In many cases this procedure was followed with ample justification. Royal legislation was sometimes unenforceable. Hence both the civil and the ecclesiastical authorities in Manila did have considerable maneuverability in executing orders from Spain. These same conditions enabled the regular clergy in the provinces to pursue policies often in conflict with the wishes of the civil and episcopal authorities in Manila.

If Philippine isolation from the main centers of the empire gave Spanish magistrates a comfortable latitude of freedom in enforcing orders from Spain, local conditions also allowed the Filipinos to be selective in their responses to orders emanating from Manila. All the major participants in the transformation of Philippine society—the Spanish magistracy, the episcopacy, the regular clergy, and the Filipinos—each one had some freedom in which to maneuver. The paucity of large, compact villages of the type contemplated in colonial legislation, the scarcity of Spanish colonists, the slow growth of a mestizo class, the failure of the Spanish language to spread, and the shortage of religious limited the impact of Hispanic influences on the Filipinos. The range of Filipino responses varied all the way from hostility and apathy to curiosity and enthusiasm.

The Filipinos' hostility to resettlement greatly diminished its effectiveness and its extent. Settlement patterns did change in the direction of rural concentration but not as rapidly or as completely as Spanish officialdom desired. The población-barrio-sitio complex that emerged was a compromise between the preconquest pattern of geographical particularism and the Spanish ideal of compact rural concentration.

The Filipinos responded to some forms of Spanish political organization with an enthusiasm comparable to their acceptance of Catholicism. The system of local self-government established during the seventeenth century provided the Filipinos with a whole new range of political experience. Its ultimate consequences for the political structure of the modern Philippines ought not to be underestimated. The legacy of caciquism weighs heavily on the modern Philippine nation in its quest toward creating a stable democracy.

What facilitated a relatively orderly economic transition was demographic stability. Contagious diseases did not slaughter the Filipinos, who had previously acquired some immunity against these epidemics. The defenselessness of the Indians in Mexico against smallpox and measles made the economic transition there anything but orderly. In the wake of a severe demographic crisis there followed an economic and ecological revolution. The physical survival of the Filipinos was the *sine qua non* for the evolutionary character of the economic and the ecological changes introduced by the conquest.

The founding of the Spanish colony did not entail an overthrow of the preconquest economy based on fishing, the cultivation of rice and root crops, and the raising of swine and fowl. Rather, production expanded to meet new demands. This was accompanied by some significant changes that supplemented rather than destroyed the ancient pattern of economic organization. Among these changes were the influx of skilled Chinese labor and the introduction of new plants and animals. The mild character of ecological innovations spared the Filipinos the severe and painful dislocations which similar changes produced in Mexico. Although some forms of pre-Hispanic debt peonage were eventually extinguished, preconquest sharecropping continued under another name. In the sphere of land tenure the outstanding novelty was the gradual adoption of the European principle of individual ownership of land.

The Spanish administration sought to foster the growth of free, paid labor, but only in urbanized Manila did this objective meet with appreciable success. The Dutch war emasculated the reforming energies of the regime. In the absence of Spanish-owned latifundia, exploitation was of an indirect variety, and preconquest forms of labor therefore continued, with the chieftains responsible for delivering the required quotas of labor and goods to the Spanish authorities.

The economic underpinnings of the native upper class were not swept away by the conquest. On the contrary, colonial society provide the chieftains with additional means of enrichment. Their source of wealth was twofold. The pre-Hispanic system of sharecropping and debt peonage survived in a modified form in the face of vigorous Spanish efforts to abolish it. Secondly, the *principales* were both the economic and the administrative intermediaries between the material demands of the Spanish regime and the productive capacities of the masses. As such the opportunities of these chieftains for both legal and extralegal enrichment were various. The retention of both wealth and local political power enabled the *principales* to continue to play a role of moderately creative leadership as the intermediaries between the two cultures.

The absence of Spanish latifundia partially accounts for the more indirect character of Hispanization in the Philippines. Spanish landlords in the provinces and their mestizo managers would have dried up much of the modest wealth of the Filipino upper class, and the impoverishment of the *principales* would in turn have enfeebled but not eliminated their societal leadership. Acculturation to Hispanic norms would have become direct, with the natives being thrown into immediate and daily contact with Spaniards and mestizos. This is what happened in Mexico as a consequence of the intrusion of numerous Spaniards and mestizos into the Indian countryside.

That the Filipinos benefited in some significant respects from their indirect variety of Hispanization is apparent. It meant less Hispanization but better digested. The shocks of change and the stresses of adjustment were cushioned by the fact that continuity with preconquest culture was amply preserved. Under the leadership of their *principales* the Filipinos were able to absorb a modest portion of Spanish culture without suffering from an acute case of indigestion. Filipino adjustment to Hispanization was of an orderly variety, without causing the demoralization and confusion from which primitive peoples undergoing acculturation sometimes suffer.

The Mexican Indians in some respects may have been more Hispanized than the Filipinos, but their adjustment was of a more demoralizing and painful character. The prevalence of alcoholism among the Mexican Indians can be interpreted as a symptom of this demoralization. The most concrete manifestation of direct Hispanization was the rapid emergence of a numerous class of mestizos. The mentality of the mestizos was plagued by psychological insecurity, resentments, and frustrations created by their ambiguous cultural situation. Repudiating the world of their Indian mothers, the mestizos sought to identify themselves with the world of their Spanish fathers. There, however, they were not accepted as equals.[4]

Direct Hispanization made Mexico a mestizo nation. Although the process of miscegenation imposed severe psychological and cultural tensions on both the Indians and the mestizos which are visible to this day, the mestizo character of Mexico's culture offers promising and unique possibilities of development and growth. Indirect Hispanization of the Philippine variety, partially the consequence of the fact that there were not enough Spaniards in the provinces to produce a large mestizo class, created far fewer psychological tensions. This indirect form of Hispanization, moreover, did facilitate a more orderly adjustment to cultural change.

Indirect Hispanization presupposed two conditions. One was demographic stability. The other was the physical segregation of the majority of Filipinos from most Spanish and mestizo contacts. If the Filipino population had been decimated by the spread of contagious diseases or if the Philippine countryside had been overrun by Spaniards and mestizos, the type of indirect Hispanization which did occur would not have taken place. In surveying Hispanic colonization overseas, the Philippines emerges as a moderately successful experiment. The paradox is that Spanish success issued from Spanish failure. The Spaniards did not accomplish as much as they set out to do, and this result enabled the Filipinos to absorb a modest amount of Hispanic influence without breaking too abruptly or too completely with their preconquest way of life. The Filipinos were partially Hispanized with a minimum of psychological and physical damage. The same result did not occur in either Mexico or in Peru.

In the process of acculturation the *principales* played a key role. They had to find sufficient room to maneuver against the triple pressures exercised by the Spanish administration, their own ambition for self-enrichment at the expense of their followers, and the discontents of their own countrymen. Although the chieftains were the modest beneficiaries of the colonial status quo, the kinship character of the small barangays made them sensitive to conditions of acute stress. The *principales* both oppressed their subordinates and protected them from the worst excesses of Spanish exploitation. Yet the quotas of labor and material set by the *alcaldes* had to be met. When the pressure on the *principales* became unbearable, they led the masses into open rebellion. But these insurrections were not frequent.

Philippine society had its share of stresses and strains. That these tensions did not result in more frequent explosions may be ascribed in large measure to the influence of the Church. Catholicism provided the cement of social unity. The Filipinos responded enthusiastically to the multiform appeal of Spanish Catholicism. Knowledgeable in the psychology of primitive peoples, the missionaries knew how to capture the imagination of their parishioners. Alongside doctrinal or official Catholicism there also grew up a rich and varied folk Catholicism. The growth of these popular practices, beliefs, and superstitions indicates how deeply the new religion was taking root in the daily lives of the Filipinos.

From the viewpoint of the Church, the Catholicism of the Filipinos left much to be desired. The quality of indoctrination was not always adequate, nor did the converts always participate fully in the sacramental life of the Church. Outward religious formalism rather than sound doctrinal knowledge, the triple dangers of idolatry, superstition, and magic, added to the infrequency in the administration of the sacraments, were all defects which could have been partially remedied by a well-trained Filipino clergy. Motivated by an ethnocentric prejudice and by a selfish desire to preserve their privileged position, the Spanish regular clergy stunted the growth of the Filipino priesthood. By deliberately restricting the number of Filipino priests and the quality of their training, the Spanish clergy unwittingly sponsored the "Philippinization" of Spanish Catholicism in such a fashion that they virtually lost control over the direction and shape of folk Catholicism.

What the missionaries accomplished was nevertheless remarkable, in view of the severe handicaps under which they labored. There was a constant shortage of clergy administering to a numerous and dispersed population. The maintenance of high standards of ecclesiastical discipline, difficult under any circumstance, was aggravated in the Philippines by the fact that the clergy spent most of their lives isolated from social contacts with their religious culture. The regular clergy did manage to preserve their jurisdictional autonomy vis-à-vis the bishops, in contrast to what happened in Mexico and in Peru. Yet this advantage was largely vitiated by the considerable freedom of action that the Filipinos possessed in determining their responses to Christianity. The enthusiasm and the dedication of the first generation of missionaries was followed by a trend toward apathy and discouragement. Such a decline in morale, however, was almost inevitable, especially as the clergy became aware of the magnitude of the obstacles confronting them. It would be rash indeed to argue, without taking into account the handicaps under which they operated and the limitations of their own time and place, that the regular clergy could have done a more competent job than they actually did.

In that network of relations uniting Spaniard to Filipino, neither one always understood the other's aspirations and responses. Misunderstandings hardening into mutual deceptions abounded. In terms of their limited resources, the Spaniards actually attempted to do too much. Yet they accomplished a great deal. Judged by any objective standard, Spanish colonization in the Philippines was a remarkable episode in the global expansion of Europe. As an imperialist power the Spaniards did their share in exploiting the resources of their Philippine colony, but in all fairness to that colonizing power it should be realized that Spain gave the Filipinos something in return. The *pax hispanica* created conditions of law and order throughout the maritime provinces of Luzon and the Bisayas, Spanish political institutions took deep root and Catholicism forged powerful new bonds of cultural unity. Although dependent upon the products and the labor services of the conquered population, the Spanish administration made strenuous and sometimes effective efforts to place some restraints on the scope of exploitation. And finally, Spain brought the Philippines into the orbit of Western civilization, from which they have not departed since the sixteenth century. This is in contrast to China and Japan, for example, which have been subject to intensive Western influences for scarcely a century. As a direct consequence of Spanish colonization, the Filipinos are unique for being the only Oriental people profoundly and consistently influenced by Occidental culture for the last four centuries. In an Asia dominated by revolutionary and anti-Western nationalism, the consequences of this fact are a part of the world in which we live today.

Reference
Matter

Glossary of Spanish and Philippine Terms

ALCALDE MAYOR—The governor of a province.

ADELANTADO—The governor of a frontier colony, a title granted to Legazpi by Philip II.

AUDIENCIA—The highest tribunal of justice in the islands. It also served as an advisory council to the governor.

AYUEY—Preconquest version of debt peonage among the Bisayans.

BARANGAY—In preconquest times a political-social unit; the Spanish term for a village.

BARRIO—Village.

CABECERA—A town or the capital of a parish.

CABEZA DE BARANGAY—Hereditary native chieftain who, in Spanish times, headed the smallest unit of local administration.

CASAMAJAN—A system of sharecropping prevalent in the eighteenth century.

CAJA DE COMUNIDAD—Village treasury.

CORREGIDOR—The governor of a province.

DATU—The preconquest term for native chieftain.

FISCAL—(1) Crown attorney; (2) a combined truant officer and sacristan of a parish church.

GOBERNADORCILLO—Literally meaning petty governor, the elected magistrate of a township.

GUIGUILIR—Preconquest debt peonage among the Tagalogs.

MAHARLIKA—The noble class in preconquest times.

MAMAMAHAY—Preconquest version of sharecropping among the Tagalogs.

165

Moros—The inhabitants of the southern Philippines who were converted to Islam.

Municipio—The modern term for a township.

Negritos—The pagan inhabitants of the mountains.

Población—A town.

Polo—A system of compulsory draft labor.

Pueblo de Indios—Township.

Principales—Upper classes among the Filipinos, including the hereditary *cabezas de barangay*, the elected officeholders, and people of means.

Principalía—The abstract form for the class of *principales*.

Ranchería—Seventeenth-century term for hamlet.

Sitio—Late Spanish and modern term for hamlet.

Timagua—Freemen in preconquest times.

Tumaranpuh—Preconquest system of sharecropping among the Bisayans.

Vandala—A system of compulsory sale of products to the government.

Visita—An seventeenth-century ecclesiastical term for a village serviced by a nonresident priest.

Appendix

The following maps indicate the location of the *cabecera* churches of the regular clergy as of 1655. The first map is of the central (the Bisayas) and the southern Philippines (Mindanao). The second one includes the whole island of Luzon, and the third map is of central Luzon. The term, *cabecera*, refers to the capital of the parish, where the principal parish church was located and where ordinarily one or two religious were in permanent residence. Each *cabecera* had several *visita* chapels, usually located inland from the coast and serviced by an itinerant priest. The location of the *visitas* is not included on these maps.

These maps substantiate many of the conclusions contained in Chapter IV, which dealt with the geographical aspects of the Spanish missionary effort. The archipelago was partitioned among the five branches of the regular clergy along geoethnic lines. Spanish influence was deepest in the coastal areas, less intensive in the adjacent foothills and virtually non-existent in the central, mountainous areas of the islands. In the Bisayas the capital churches were often not located directly on the coast but a short distance inland. The frequent raids of the Moros were responsible for this trend, a problem which was discussed in Chapter X. These maps also suggest the relatively tighter grip the Spaniards held on central Luzon and the Camarines than they did on northern Luzon and in the Bisayas. Mindanao was just a frontier outpost with Spanish control confined to a few strategic coastal sites. And finally these maps constitute a convincing demonstration of the intimate relationship between the early Christianization of the archipelago and the historical development of settlement patterns in the islands. Virtually all of the *cabecera* churches of 1655 constitute important centers of population today, easily located on any large map of the contemporary Philippines.

A few words of explanation about the maps themselves are in order. Space made it difficult to include the parishes, which in 1655 were suburbs of Manila and which today constitute parts of Greater Manila. I include a list of these suburbs. The Jesuit parishes were San Miguel, Santa Cruz, and San Pedro Makati. The Augustinian parish suburbs were Tondo and Malate. Those of the Franciscans were located at Dilao, Tondo, Santa Ana de Sapa, and Sampaloc. The Dominican parishes in the suburbs were in the Parian and at Minondoc.

In order to indicate the geographical dispersal of the regular clergy different symbols have been chosen to indicate the parishes administered by the various orders. The following symbols have been used.

▲ Jesuit
● Augustinian
† Franciscan
✕ Dominican
■ Augustinian Recollect

The parishes of each order are numbered consecutively, with each order having a separate sequence of numbers. The tables on the following pages identify the numbers. Older, historical names and spellings were used throughout, but the modern version follows in brackets.

Name	Province
ARCHBISHOPRIC	
Residencia de Antipolo	
1 Antipolo	Rizal
2 Baras	"
3 Taytay	"
4 Caynta [Cainta]	"
Residencia of Silang	
5 Silang	Cavite
6 Indan [Indang]	"
7 Maragondon	"
8 Cavite [Cavite City]	"
Marinduque	
9 Boak [Boac]	Marinduque
10 Gasang [Gasan]	"
11 Marlanga (barrio of Torrijos)	"
12 Sta. Cruz de Napo [Sta. Cruz]	"
BISHOPRIC OF CEBU	
13 Cebu [Cebu City]	Cebu
Bohol	
14 Loboc	Bohol
15 Baclayon	"
16 Panglao	"

Name	Province
17 Inabagan [Inabanga]	Bohol
18 Malabohoc [Maribojoc]	"
Leyte	
19 Carigara	Leyte
20 Leyte	"
21 Haro [Jaro]	"
22 Barugo	"
23 Alangalan [Alangalang]	"
24 Ocmug [Ormoc]	"
25 Baybay	"
26 Cabalian	"
27 Sorgor [Sogod]	"
28 Inundayan [Hinundayan]	"
29 Liboan [Liloam]	"
30 Dagami	"
31 Malaguicay [Malaguikay] (barrio of Tanauan)	"
32 Tambuco	"
33 Dulag	"
34 Bitto [Bito]	"
35 Abuyo [Abuyog]	"
36 Palo	"
Samar	
37 Basey	Samar
38 Guiuan	"

Name	Province
39 Balanguigan [Balangiga]	Samar
40 Catbalogan	"
41 Caluigan [Calbiga]	"
42 Batan [Batang] (barrio of Hernani)	"
43 Capul	"
Samar y Ibabao	
44 Catubig	"
45 Biri	"
46 Catarman	"
47 Bobon	"
48 Buri [Beri] (barrio of Oras)	"
49 Tubig [Taft]	"
50 Sulat	"
51 Borongan	"
Panay	
52 Oton	Iloilo
53 Ylo-Ylo [Iloilo City]	"
Island of Negros	
54 Ylog [Ilog]	Negros Occ.
55 Cabancalan [Kabankalan]	"
56 Suay	"
57 Ysiu [Isio] (barrio of Cauayan)	"
Mindanao	
58 Residencia of Yligan-Dapitan	"
59 Residencia of Zamboanga	"

FRANCISCAN †

Name	Province
ARCHBISHOPRIC	
1 Polo de Catangalan [Polo]	Bulacan
2 Meycauayan	"
3 Bocaui [Bocaue]	"
4 Binangonan	Rizal
5 Morong	"
6 Tanay	"
7 Pililla	"
8 Sta. Maria Caboan [Sta. Maria]	Laguna
9 Mavitac [Mabitac]	"
10 Sinilaon	"
11 Pangil	"
12 Paete	"
13 Lumbang [Lumban]	"
14 Sta. Cruz	"
15 Pila	"
16 Nagcarlang [Nagcarlan]	"
17 Lilio	"
18 Mahayhay [Majayjay]	"
19 Lugban [Lucban]	Quezon
20 Mauvan [Mauban]	"
21 Tayavas [Tayabas]	"
22 Baler	"
23 Atimonan	"
24 Guxmaca or Silangan [Gumaca]	"
25 Los Banos	Laguna
BISHOPRIC OF NUEVA CACERES—CAMARINES	
26 Capalonga	Cams. N.

Name	Province
27 Paracali [Paracale]	Cams. N.
28 Labo	"
29 Yndan [Vinzons]	"
30 Daet-Tarisay [Daet and Talisay]	Cams. Sur
31 Libmanan	"
32 Quepayo [Quipayo] (barrio of Calabanga)	"
33 Ciudad of Caceres [Naga City]	"
34 Milaor	"
35 Minalabac	"
36 Bula (also Baao) [Bula]	"
37 Nabua	"
38 Yriga [Iriga]	"
39 Buhy [Buhi]	"
40 Libong [Libon]	Albay
41 Polangui	"
42 Ligao	"
43 Oas	"
44 Camalig	"
45 Quipia [Jovellar]	"
46 Albay (district of Legaspi City)	"
47 Cacsaua [Cagsawa] (district of Legaspi City)	"
48 Tabaco	"
49 Milinao [Malinao]	"
50 Casiguran	Sorsogon
51 Sorsogon	"
52 Bolosan [Bulusan]	"
53 Calonga [Calongay] (barrio ot Pilar)	"

DOMINICAN ×

Name	Province
Cagayan	
1 Pata (barrio of Claveria)	Cagayan
2 Abulug	"
3 Potol [Pudtol] (barrio of Luna)	Sub-prov. of Apayao
4 Cabagan	Isabella
Babuyanes islands (not included for limitations of space)	
5 Masi (barrio of Buguey)	Cagayan
6 Piat	"
7 Camalanyugan [Camalniugan]	"
8 Nasiping [Nassiping] (barrio of Gattaran)	"
9 Iguig	"
10 Tuguegarao	"
11 Buguey	"
Pangasinan	
12 Lingayen	Pangasinan
13 Binalonan	"
14 Calasiao	"
15 Binmaley	"
16 Magaldan [Mangaldan]	"
17 Bagnotan [Bacnotan]	La Union
18 Manaueg [Manaoag]	Pangasinan

AUGUSTINIAN ●

ARCHBISHOPRIC

Name	Province
1 Tambobong (barrio of San Rafael)	Bulacan
2 Bulacan	"
3 Guinguito	"
4 Vigaa [Bigaa]	"
5 Malolos	"
6 Quinqua [Plaridell]	"
7 Calumpit	"
8 Hagonoy	"
9 Paranaque	Rizal
10 Pasig	"
11 Taguig [Tagig]	"
12 Bay	Laguna
13 S. Pablo de los Montes [San Pablo City]	"
14 Lipaa [Lipa]	Batangas
15 Baguang [Bauan]	"
16 Batangas	"
17 Taal	"
18 Tanaguang [Tanauan]	"
19 Salaa [Salao] (barrio of Rosario)	"

Pampanga

20 Bacolor	Pampanga
21 Guagua	"
22 Macaveve [Macabebe]	"
23 Lubao	"
24 Mexico	"

Name	Province
25 Candava [Candaba]	Pampanga
26 Sesmoan [Sexmoan]	"
27 Betis (barrio of Guagua)	"
28 Porag [Porac]	"
29 Minalin	"
30 Apalit	"
31 Gapan	Nueva Ecija
32 Arayat	Pampanga

Ilokos

33 Agoo	La Union
34 Baguan [Bauang]	" "
35 Tagurin [Tagudin]	Ilokos Sur
36 Santa Cruz	" "
37 Candong [Candon]	" "
38 Navarca [Navarcan]	" "
39 Bantay	" "
40 Sinay [Sinait]	" "
41 Dinglas [Dingras]	Ilokos N.
42 Batac	" "
43 Ilagua [Laoag]	" "
44 Bacarra	" "

BISHOPRIC OF CEBU—BISAYAS

Name	Province
45 Panay [Roxas City]	Capiz
46 Dumalag	"
47 Mambusao	"
48 Batang [Batan]	"
49 Pasig [Passi]	Iloilo
50 Dumangas	"

Name	Province
51 Haro [Jaro]	Iloilo
52 Octon [Oton]	"
53 Tibaguan [Tigbauan]	"
54 Guimbal	"
55 Carcar	Cebu
56 S. Nicolas de Cebu [San Nicolas] (district of Cebu City)	"

AUGUSTINIAN RECOLLECTS ■

Name	Province

ARCHBISHOPRIC

Pangasinan

1 Masinloc	Sambal
2 Bolinao	Pangasinan
3 Marivels [Mariveles]	Bataan

BISHOPRIC OF CEBU

4 Romblon	Romblon
5 Calamianes islands (not included for limitations of space)	Palawan
6 Cuyo	Palawan

Mindanao

7 Tandag	Surigao
8 Butuan	Agusan
9 Cagayan [Cagayan de Oro City]	Misamisor
10 Siargao island [Dapa]	Surigao
11 Bislig	Surigao

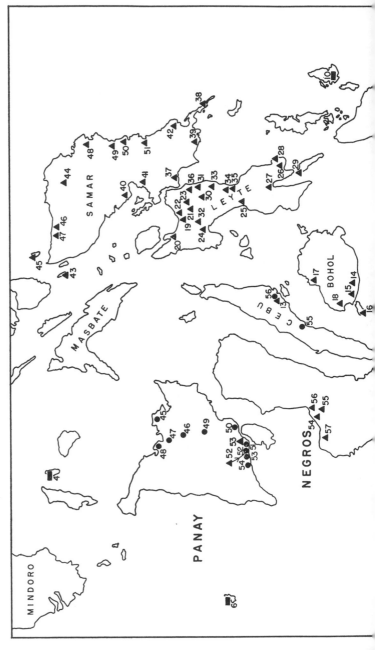

PHILIPPINES
(MAP I)

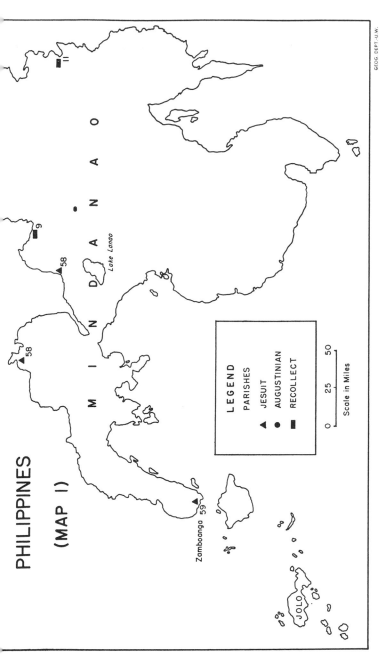

LEGEND

PARISHES

JESUIT ▲

AUGUSTINIAN ●

RECOLLECT ■

Scale in Miles

0   25   50

M I N D A N A O

Lake Lanao

Zamboanga 59

JOLO

GEOG. DEPT. U.W.

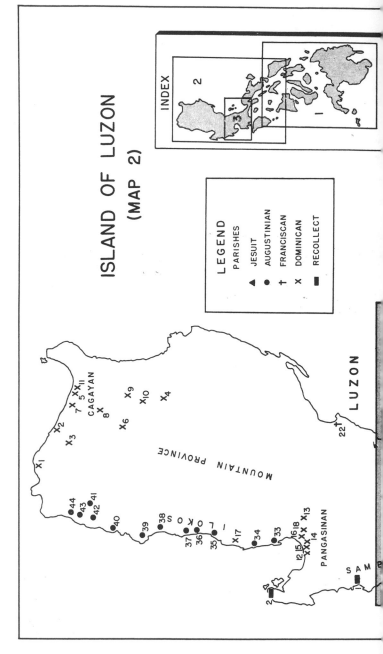

ISLAND OF LUZON
(MAP 2)

LEGEND

PARISHES

◀ JESUIT

● AUGUSTINIAN

✝ FRANCISCAN

✗ DOMINICAN

▮ RECOLLECT

INDEX

LUZON

174

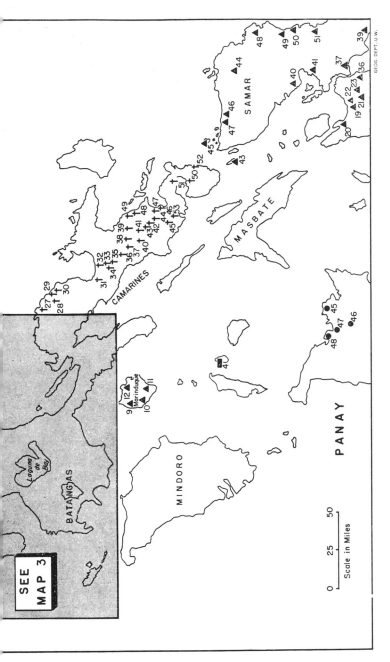

175

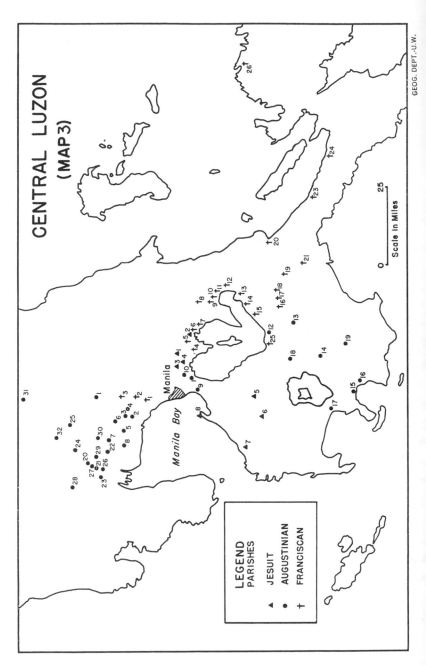

CENTRAL LUZON
(MAP 3)

GEOG. DEPT.-U.W.

Manila

Manila Bay

Scale in Miles

0   25

LEGEND
PARISHES

▲ JESUIT
● AUGUSTINIAN
† FRANCISCAN

Notes

Abbreviations used in the Notes:

AGI/AF: The *Audiencia de Filipinas* section of the *Archivo General de Indias*, Seville.

ARSI: Archivum Romanum Societatis Iesu, microfilm collection at the University of St. Louis.

BR: Emma Helen Blair and James Alexander Robertson, *The Philippine Islands, 1493–1803* (55 vols.; Cleveland: A. H. Clark, 1903–9).

In addition, works frequently referred to that are listed in the Bibliography will be cited in shortened form in the Notes.

Chapter I

1. See my *Millennial Kingdom*, pp. 5–27.
2. For a more extended treatment of this topic see my article, "Some Ideological Aspects," pp. 221–39.
3. A detailed description of the imperial bureaucracy can be found in Clarence H. Haring, *The Spanish Empire in America.*
4. Philip II to Legazpi: August 28, 1569, *BR*, XXXIV, 252.
5. See my article, "Some Ideological Aspects," pp. 221 ff. The successfully executed pacific occupation of the Philippines was followed a few years later by the promulgation in July, 1573, of the "Ordenanzas hechas para los nuevos descubrimientos, conquistas y pacificaciones," the text of which is in the *Colección de documentos inéditos relativos al descubrimiento, conquista y organización de las antiguas posesiones españolas de América y*

Oceanta (42 vols.; Madrid: 1864–84), XVI, 142 ff.

6. Andrés de Mirandaola to Philip II: Cebu, 1565, *BR*, XXXIV, 201.

7. See my article, "Some Ideological Aspects," pp. 230 ff.

8. Horacio de la Costa, S.J., "Church and State in the Philippines during the Administration of Bishop Salazar," *The Hispanic American Historical Review*," XXX (August, 1950), 314–17, 324.

9. The standard work on Sino-Spanish trade is William L. Schurz, *The Manila Galleon* (New York: E. P. Dutton, 1939). Also see the suggestive article of Pierre Chaunu, "Le galion de Manille, grandeur et décadence d'une route de la soie," *Annales, Économies-Sociétés-Civilizations*, VI (October-December, 1951), 447–62.

10. Schurz, *Manila Galleon*, pp. 63 ff. Also see his "The Chinese in the Philippines," *The Pacific Ocean in History*, H. Morse Stephens and H. E. Bolton, editors (New York: Macmillan, 1917), pp. 214–22.

11. The population of the metropolis circa 1650 was divided as follows:

The Walled City (Spanish)	7,350
Parian (Chinese)	15,000
Suburbs (Filipino)	20,124

BR, XXIV, 309; XXVII, 82; XXIX, 69, 305; XXXVI, 90–91, 203. Ventura del Arco transcripts, the Newberry Library, II, 402. Governor Vargas to Charles II: June 20, 1679, Pastells collection, St. Louis University, microfilm roll 14.

12. For a summary of the military aspect of the war see Schurz, *Manila Galleon*, pp. 342 ff.

13. W. L. Schurz, "The Philippine Situado," *Hispanic American Historical Review*, I (November, 1918), 461–64.

14. Woodrow W. Borah, *Early Colonial Trade and Navigation between Mexico and Peru* (Berkeley and Los Angeles: University of California Press, *Ibero-Americana*: 38, 1954), pp. 126–27.

15. Quoted in Schurz, *Manila Galleon*, pp. 43–44.

Chapter II

1. The overwhelming bulk of our knowledge about the character of preconquest Tagalog society comes from a study of Tagalog customs composed by a Franciscan friar, Juan de Plasencia. Written in response to the orders of Governor Santiago de Vera, it was completed in 1589. Although it was not published until 1892, the manuscript circulated in various editions from the time of its completion. This work was regarded by the Spanish law courts as the definitive statement of customary law. For the Spanish text see Francisco de Santa Inés, O.F.M., *Crónica*, II, 592–603. There is an English translation in *BR*, VII, 173–96. Friar Juan came from Plasencia in Extremadura, a scion of the noble Portocarrero family. He arrived in Manila in March of 1578 along with the first mission of the

Franciscans. Elected custodian in 1583, Plasencia was the outstanding Franciscan in the Philippines until his death in 1590. The probable author of the first printed Tagalog-Spanish catechism, he also took a leading role in resettling the population into compact villages and in fostering the spread of primary education. His study of Tagalog customs is a short account remarkable for its factual and objective description. There are few moral judgments offered. Succeeding chroniclers such as Chirino, Ribadeneyra, Colín, Santa Inés, Morga, San Antonio, and Delgado added little factual information to Plasencia's account but merely indulged in value judgments of a moralistic and ethnocentric character on the data collected by Friar Juan de Plasencia.

For preconquest society in the Bisayan area, on the other hand, there are three distinct sources. Two of them were written by early encomenderos. Diego López Povedano's account of his trip through the island of Negros (1572) and his *Antiguas Leyendas* (1578) are brief accounts rich in ethnographic and linguistic material. See *The Robertson Text and Translation of the Povedano Manuscript of 1572*, E. D. Hester, editor, transcript number 2 of the Philippine Studies Program, Department of Anthropology, University of Chicago, 1954. Also *The Ancient Legends and Stories of the Indios, Jarayas, Jiguesinas and Igneines Which Contains Their Beliefs and Diverse Superstitions*, Rebecca P. Ignacio, editor, transcript number 3 of the Philippine Studies Program, Department of Anthropology University of Chicago, 1954. Another encomendero, Miguel de Loarca, composed a more extensive description of Bisayan society in 1592. For a bilingual text see *BR*, V, 34–185.

By far the most scholarly and detailed survey of Bisayan culture is the unpublished manuscript of Francisco Ignacio Alcina (1610–74). Spending nearly forty years in the Jesuit parishes on the islands of Samar and Leyte, Alcina provided an account equally rich in ethnographic material, Filipino responses to Hispanization, and natural history. This manuscript from the library of the *Palacio de Oriente* in Madrid is now being edited for publication by my colleague in the Philippine Studies Program, Dr. Paul Lietz. This work, which I consulted in Madrid, is one of the most informative of the unpublished sources of Philippine history. Francisco Alcina (Alzina), S.J., *Historia de las islas e indios de Bisayas . . . dividida en dos: la primera natural . . . la segunda eclesiástica y sobrenatural . . . .* For biographical information see Carlos Sommervogel, S.J., *Bibliothèque de la compagnie de Jésus* (11 vols.; Brussels and Paris: Alphonse Picard and Oscar Schepens, 1890–1932), I, 260. Also see the catalogues that the Jesuit prelates in the Philippines sent periodically to Rome, *ARSI*, roll 158.

A recent publication containing significant, primary source material about the preconquest and the postconquest culture of the island of Negros is *The Robertson Translation of the Pavón Manuscripts of 1838–1839*, Fred Eggan and E. V. Hester, editors, 4 vols., transcript number 5 of the Philippine Studies Program, Department of Anthropology, University of Chicago, 1957.

2. Gregorio F. Zaide, *The Philippines Since Pre-Spanish Times* (Manila: R. B. Garcia, 1949), pp. 67–70. Eufronio Alip, *Philippine Civilization* (Manila: University of Santo Tomas Press, 1936), pp. 75–81.

3. Povedano, *Antiguas Leyendas*, in *Robertson Text*, p. 22.

4. Antonio Pigafetta, *Magellan's Voyage*, I, 152.

5. On the island of Luzon there are six major languages: Tagalog, Ilokos, Bikol (the Camarines), Pangasinan, Pampanga, and Ibanag (Cagayan). There are three major languages in the Bisayas. They are: Samar-Leyte, Hiligaynon (Panay and eastern Negros), and Cebuano.

6. Chirino, *BR*, XII, 263. One of the most useful sources of ethnohistorical material is the various accounts of early Bornean settlements on the islands of Panay and Luzon commonly referred to as the "Maragtas." See the following articles: Fred Eggan, "Bisayan Accounts of Early Bornean Settlements in the Philippines," Tom Harrisson, "Bisaya: Borneo-Philippine Impacts on Islam," and R. A. Bewsher, "Bisayan Accounts of Early Bornean Settlements in the Philippines," in the *Sarawak Museum Journal*, VII (No. 7, 1956), 22–52. Also see James A. Robertson, "The Social Structure of and Ideas of Law among Early Philippine Peoples; and a Recently Discovered Pre-Hispanic Criminal Code of the Philippine Islands," in *The Pacific Ocean in History*, H. Morse Stephens and Herbert E. Bolton, editors (New York: Macmillan, 1917), pp. 160–191.

7. *BR*, L, 216–17.

8. Morga-Retana, *Sucesos*, pp. 210–11. Antonio de Morga, a high-ranking civil bureaucrat, published his informative account in 1609.

9. *BR*, X, 303–04.

10. Alcina, *Historia*, Bk. IV, ch. 5. Before the conquest the value of a Tagalog *mamamahay* was set at six pesos and the Tagalog *guiguilir* at twelve pesos. By 1593 the price of manumission for the *mamamahay* had risen to fifteen pesos, partially the reflection of the price inflation following in the wake of the conquest. Loarca, *BR*, V, 145.

11. *BR*, XXXIV, 378.

12. Alcina, *Historia*, Bk. III, ch. 22.

13. For the Spanish interpretation of the conquest as a "liberation" see my article "Some Ideological Aspects," pp. 237–39.

Chapter III

1. For a general survey of the *Patronato* see Clarence H. Haring, *The Spanish Empire in America*, pp. 179 ff. For the primary documentation see Francisco Colín, S.J., Colín-Pastells, *Labor evangélica*, III, 671 ff. Pastells' edition of Colín, first published in 1663, contains in the notes a rich collection of primary sources dealing with Church-state relations.

2. For the Salazar period see Gaspar de San Agustín, O.S.A., *Conquistas de las islas Philipinas* . . . (Madrid: 1698), pp. 394–95. Juan Francisco de San Antonio, O.F.M., *Chrónicas*, II, 49–55. Juan de la Concepción, O.R.S.A., *Historia*, II, 47–58. For Archbishop Vásquez de

Mercado see his letter to Philip III: July 8, 1612, in *AGI/AF* 74. For the García Serrano period see Colín-Pastells, *Labor evangélica*, III, 688 ff. For Archbishop Poblete see Casimiro Díaz, O.S.A., *Conquistas*, pp. 532–34, and Colín-Pastells, *Labor evangélica*, III, 697 ff. For Archbishop Camacho see Díaz, *Conquistas*, pp. 534–36, and *BR*, XLII, 25–117.

3. Archbishop to Audiencia: June 28, 1655, Colín-Pastells, *Labor evangélica*, III, 718. In 1697 there were only sixty secular priests. *BR*, XLII, 73.

4. See the Archbishop's pastoral letter of June 14, 1772, in Juan Ferrando, O.P., and Joaquín Fonseca, O.P., *Historia de los pp. dominicos en las islas filipinas* (6 vols.; Madrid: 1870–72), V, 54–59. Father Horacio de la Costa has discussed some phases of the visitation controversy with admirable clarity in his article, "Episcopal Visitation in the Philippines in the Seventeenth Century," *Philippine Studies*, II (September, 1954), 197–216. Charles H. Cunningham's "The Question of Episcopal Visitation in the Philippines," in *The Pacific Ocean in History*, H. Morse Stephens and H. E. Bolton, editors (New York: Macmillan, 1917), 223–37, is of limited usefulness in that the author fails to control his animus against the regular clergy.

5. Memorial of Juan de Polanco, O.P., to the Council of the Indies: October 6, 1666, Colín-Pastells, *Labor evangélica*, III, 732–39. This memorial of the procurator at the Spanish court for all the regular orders in the Philippines is a masterly statement of the viewpoint of the religious, exploiting to the fullest the strong points and glossing over the weaknesses of their case. Also see the joint letter of the Philippine provincial superiors to Philip V: June 30, 1708, *AGI/AF* 302.

6. The documentation of the Camacho investigation held in 1697 and 1698 is in the *AGI/AF* 302. As a result of the abuses exposed in this inquiry, the Archbishop issued a tariff of sacramental fees, *BR*, XLII, 56–64.

7. For the testimony taken on January 23, 1593, see "Algunos excessos de los frailes," *AGI/AF* 6.

8. The documentation on the creole-peninsular rift is mountainous, as the following list demonstrates. Bishop Benavides to Philip II: July 26, 1598, *AGI/AF* 76. Alonso de Vico, O.S.A., to Bishop Benavides: June 18, 1598, Morga-Retana, *Sucesos*, pp. 436–37. Governor Tello to king: July 14, 1599, *AGI/AF* 6. Cathedral chapter to Philip III: July 10, 1599, *AGI/AF* 77. Bishop Benavides to Philip III: July 31, 1601, *AGI/AF* 76. Juan de Garrovillas, O.F.M., to Philip III: December 19, 1603, *AGI/AF* 84. Dominican prelates to Philip III: December 15, 1603, *ibid.* Bernardo de Santa Catalina, O.P., to Philip III: June 1, 1605, *AGI/AF* 74. Ditto to Philip III: June 30, 1605, *AGI/AF* 84. Pedro de Arce, O.S.A. to Philip III: May 29, 1605, *ibid.* Miguel de Cigenca, O.S.A., to Philip III: May 24, 1605, *ibid.* Colín-Pastells, *Labor evangélica*, II, 466–67. Fiscal to Philip III: July, 1606, *BR*, XIV, 167–69. Juan de Tapia, O.S.A., to Philip III: June 20, 1605, *BR*, XIII, 301–6. The only letter of León defending

his conduct in office is apparently an undated one written between 1603 and 1605 in *BR*, XIV, 31–34.

9. Cathedral chapter to Philip III: June 24, 1604, *AGI/AF* 77. Audiencia to Philip III: July 19, 1609, *AGI/AF* 20. The Augustinian chroniclers are understandably reticent about the León crisis, since it was difficult for them to defend his conduçt. Juan de Medina, O.S.A., *Historia*, p. 175. Gaspar de San Agustín, *Conquistas*, p. 522.

10. Díaz, *Conquistas*, p. 71. Juan de Medina, *Historia*, p. 209. There is a sensationalist account of the murder with all the macabre details written anonymously, probably by a Jesuit, in *BR*, XVIII, 82–89. A more sober account is that of the *fiscal* of the Audiencia to Philip III: August 20, 1615, *AGI/AF* 20. When informed of the public trial of the assassins, the authorities in Rome voiced displeasure at what they considered to be the needless public scandal with which the whole matter had been handled. Ventura del Arco transcripts, Newberry Library, I, 476.

11. The documentation of the turmoil of the 1620's is the following. Juan de Medina, *Historia*, pp. 233, 239, 254–55. Augustinian prelates to the king: July 28, 1628, *AGI/AF* 85. Governor Silva to Philip IV: July 30, 1626, *BR*, XXII, 96. The Audiencia to Philip IV: July 23, 1629, *AGI/AF* 21. Audiencia to Philip IV: August 8, 1633, *ibid.* Díaz, *Conquistas*, pp. 384–88. Augustinian prelates to Philip IV: September 9, 1637, *BR*, XXVIII, 21–25.

12. Governor Corcuera to Philip IV: June 30, 1636, *BR*, XXVI, 131–36. Franciscan Commissary-General of the Indies to Philip III: May 11, 1612, *AGI/AF* 85.

13. Alcina's report of 1660, *ARSI*, roll 165.

14. I have not seen the Gómez de Espinoza text; very few if any copies survive. For a general description of its contents see *BR* XXV, 192–93; XXXVII, 103–4; XLII, 120.

15. For a compassionate and realistic analysis of this aspect of the problem see Sinibaldo de Mas, "Informe" (1843), *BR*, XXVIII, 244.

16. Colín-Pastells, *Labor evangélica*, II, 302–3, 406 ff. Ignacio Alcina, S.J., to the general of the Society: June 24, 1660, *ARSI*, roll 165.

Chapter IV

1. For a dramatic account of the rigors and perils of the transoceanic crossing to the Philippines see Diego Aduarte, O.P., *Historia*, pp. 13–16, 22–24.

2. *Recopilación*, Bk. I, tit. xiv, law 19.

3. Ordinance of the governor: March 2, 1582, *BR*, IV, 308–9; VII, 171–72; IX, 250–51. Colín-Pastells, *Labor evangélica*, I, 436–37. *Recopilación*, Bk. I, tit. xiv, law 30.

4. The standard works on Iberian designs on China and Japan are those of Arnold Rowbothan, *Missionary and Mandarin, the Jesuits at the Court of China* (Berkeley and Los Angeles: University of California Press,

1942), and C. R. Boxer, *The Christian Century in Japan, 1549–1650* (Berkeley and Los Angeles: University of California Press, 1951).

5. For the Mexican background consult the following. Robert Ricard, *La "conquête spirituelle" du Mexique* (Paris: Institute d' ethnologie, 1933), pp. 163 ff. Lesley Byrd Simpson, "The Civil Congregation," in his *Studies in the Administration of the Indians of New Spain* (Berkeley and Los Angeles: University of California Press, *Ibero-Americana: 7*, 1934), pp. 30–129. George Kubler, *Mexican Architecture in the Sixteenth Century* (2 vols.; New Haven: Yale University Press, 1948), I, 68–103. Howard Cline, "Civil Congregations of the Indians of New Spain, 1598–1606," *Hispanic American Historical Review*, XXIX (August, 1949), 349–69.

6. For clear-cut expressions of this attitude see San Antonio, *Chrónicas*, I, 375. Pedro Chirino, S.J. *Relación*, p. 178. Marcelo de Ribadeneyra, O.F.M., *Historia*, p. 32.

7. Juan de Plasencia, O.F.M. to Philip II: June 18, 1585, *Archivo Ibero-Americano*, II (May–June, 1915), 390–91. Acts of the ecclesiastical junta of 1582 in Valentín Marin y Morales, O.P., *Ensayo de una síntesis de los trabajos realizados por las corporaciones religiosas españolas de Filipinas* (2 vols.; Manila: 1901), I, 335. Philip II to Governor Tello: May 25, 1596, *BR*, IX, 239.

8. Alonso Sandin, O.P., to Charles II [1680's], *AGI/AF* 76.

9. *BR*, XX, 231–32.

10. Vicente de Salazar, O.P., *Historia de la provincia de el Santissimo Rosario de Philipinas, China y Tvnking* (Manila: 1742), pp. 138–52.

11. Alcina's report of 1660, *ARSI*, roll 165.

12. Cedula of Philip III to the bishop of Cagayan: September 8, 1603, Pastells collection, St. Louis University, microfilm roll 33. Bishop of Cagayan to Philip III: April 12, 1605, *AGI/AF* 76. The Dominicans were somewhat more successful in Pangasinan than in Cagayan, for in the former province the population was less dispersed than in the latter. Aduarte, *Historia*, pp. 114, 153. Bishop of Cagayan to Philip IV: May 24, 1636, *AGI/AF* 80.

13. Anda's memorial of 1768, *BR*, L, 176.

14. *Ibid.*, pp. 99, 128.

15. *BR*, V, 233.

16. Early Spanish observers tended to equate barrio and barangay. Bishop Salazar, for example, urged that tributes of the natives not be collected by "barangais que son barrios en lengua castellana." Salazar to Philip II: June, 1586, Colín-Pastells, *Labor evangélica*, I, 447. Chirino wrote: "El uso de estos pueblos para su mas comodo gobierno estar partidos en barrios a la traza de parroquias que alla llaman barangais." Chirino, *Relación*, p. 33, or *BR*, XII, 211. Chirino referred to the *cabezas de barrangay* as the *cabezas de barrios*. Chirino, *Relación*, p. 187. Also see Colín-Pastells, *Labor evangélica*, I, 117–18. In sixteenth century Spain barrio was synonymous with an urban parish. In the Philippines, barrio of necessity referred to a rural cluster of population usually grouped around

a *visita* chapel. The sitio or hamlet, the smallest unit of rural organization and usually consisting of ten families or less, was ordinarily called a *ranchería* in seventeenth-century sources. I have never encountered the use of the word "sitio" in the early accounts. For the meaning of "ranchería" in the seventeenth century see *ibid.*, II, 153; Chirino, *Relación*, p. 178.

17. Dominican provincial superior to Archbishop Pardo: October 20, 1682, Colín-Pastells, *Labor evangélica*, III, 116–17. Augustinian provincial superior to Archbishop Pardo: May 8, 1686, *ibid.*, pp. 118–21. Anda memorial of 1768, *BR*, L, 155. "Ordenanzas de alcaldes (Cagayan, 1739)," ms. in possession of Professor Lesley Byrd Simpson, pp. 28–29.

18. For the historical origins of the gridiron plan and its adoption in the Spanish empire see Kubler, *Mexican Architecture*, I, 97 ff., and "Ordenanzas" of 1573 in *Colección de documentos inéditos relativos al descubrimiento, conquista y organización de las antiguas posesiones españoles* de América y Oceanía (42 vols.; Madrid: 1864–84), XVI, 142 ff.

19. *BR*, L, 255–56.

20. "Ordenanzas de alcaldes," p. 20.

21. For the cedula of April 27, 1594, see *BR*, IX, 120–21. There is a clear statement of the Crown's instinctive distrust for the principle of ethnic-territorial partition in the letter of Viceroy Enríquez to Philip II: May 20, 1576, *Cartas de Indias* (Madrid: 1877), pp. 315–22.

22. There is an extensive evaluation of the linguistic studies of the clergy in my article, "Philippine Linguistics, pp. 153–70. The most complete list of early Philippine imprints can be found in the standard work of José Toribio Medina, *La imprenta*.

23. Camacho investigation of 1697–98, *AGI/AF* 302.

Chapter V

1. A graphic description of iconoclastic activity on the part of the religious is in Francisco de Santa Inés, *Crónica*, II, 177 ff.

2. For the documentation regarding the introduction of baptism see my article, "Pre-Baptismal Instruction and the Administration of Baptism in the Philippines during the Sixteenth Century," *The Americas*, XII (July, 1955), 3–23.

3. Pedro Chirino, *Relación*, p. 233.

4. *Doctrina Christiana: The First Book Printed in the Philippines*, Manila, *1593*, Edwin Wolf, editor (Washington, D.C.: Library of Congress, 1947). Friar Juan de Plasencia (see Chapter II, note 1) is the probable author, according to Wolf's introductory essay. For background material about this *Doctrina* see my article, "Philippine Linguistics," pp. 155–56.

5. *BR*, XXIV, 268. Gerónimo de Ripalda's well-known catechism, first published in Burgos in 1591, was printed in the Philippines in only one Tagalog edition during the seventeenth century (see, J. T. Medina, *La imprenta*, II, 21). Hence it was no serious rival in popularity to the Bellarmine text.

6. In the *Doctrina* of 1593 the following key concepts were kept in Spanish: God, Trinity, Holy Ghost, Virgin Mary, Pope, grace, sin, cross, hell, church, Sunday, and the names of the sacraments. This principle of missionary policy was established in Mexico after a spirited controversy, decades before the conversion of the Filipinos. Robert Ricard, *La "conquête spirituelle" du Mexique* (Paris: Institute d' ethnologie, 1933), pp. 72–75.

7. *Archivo Ibero-Americano*, II (May–June, 1915), 393–94. Chirino, *Relación*, pp. 67–70, 97, 120, 123, 151, 184, 185, 231. Colín-Pastells, *Labor evangélica*, II, 118, 399, 409, 411. Ribadeneyra, *Historia*, p. 67.

8. For the Jesuit sources see Colín-Pastells, *Labor evangélica*, II, 127, 137; III, 135. Chirino, *Relación*, p. 242. For the Franciscans see Ribadeneyra, *Historia*, pp. 54–55. San Antonio, *Chrónicas*, II, 12–18. For the Dominicans see Adurate, *Historia*, p. 64. For the Augustinians see Juan de Medina. *Historia*, p. 75. Also see Morga-Retana, *Sucesos*, p. 206.

9. Diego de Bobadilla, S.J., "Relation of the Philippine Islands," 1640, *BR*, XXIX, 295.

10. Alcina, *Historia*, Bk. III, ch. 12.

11. There is a detailed census taken by the Jesuits of their Bisayan missions in *ARSI*, roll 158.

12. Chirino, *BR*, XII, 291–93, 295, 296, 299, 301, 317, 318; XIII, 52–54, 98–100, 134, 162, 163. Also *ibid.*, XXI, 21, 210, 221.

13. For a Latin text of the bull see Gerónimo de Mendieta, O.F.M., *Historia eclesiástica indiana* (Mexico: 1870), pp. 269–71.

14. Pablo de Jesús, O.F.M., to Pope Gregory XIII: July, 14, 1580, *BR*, XXXIV, 323–24.

15. Alonso de Mentrida, O.S.A., *Ritval*, pp. 92–98. His interpretation of Paul III's bull was derived from Alonso de Veracruz's *Speculum conjugiorum* (Mexico: 1556) written as a guide to aid the clergy unravel some of the matrimonial tangles created by the shift from pagan polygamy to Christian monogamy.

16. Archbishop García Serrano to Philip III: July 30, 1621, *BR*, XX, 86–87. Also see *Fiscal* to Philip III: July, 1606, *BR*, XIV, 158–59.

17. Mentrida, *Ritval*, pp. 88 ff. According to Rey's manual for confessors published in 1792 illicit intercourse with future in-laws continued to be not uncommon. Fernando Rey, O.S.A., *Confessonarios*, pp. 271 ff.

18. Colín-Pastells, *Labor evangélica*, II, 404–5.

19. *Ibid.*, I, 450. *BR*, VII, 317–18.

20. *BR*, IX, 225–26.

21. Camacho investigation of 1697–98, *AGI/AF* 302. For the tariff itself see *BR*, XLII, 56 ff. The Augustinians ordinarily charged two pesos for a simple marriage without the nuptial blessing. According to the episcopal tariff no fees were to be charged for this ceremony.

22. *AGI/AF* 302.

23. The most celebrated example of Philippine erotica was one first described by the famous chronicler of the Magellan expedition. Pigafetta

wrote: "The males, large and small, have their penis pierced from one side to the other near the head, with a gold or tin bolt as large as a goose quill. In both ends of the same bolt, some have what resembles a spur, with points upon the ends; others are like the head of a cart nail. I very often asked many, both young and old, to see their penis, because I could not credit it. In the middle of the bolt is a hole, through which they urinate. The bolt and the spurs always hold firm. They say that their women wish it so, and that if they did otherwise they would not have communication with them. When the men wish to have communication with their women, the latter themselves take the penis not in the regular way and commence very gently to introduce it into their vagina with the spur on top first, and then the other part. When it is inside it takes its regular position; and thus the penis always stays inside until it gets soft, for otherwise they could not pull it out. Those people make use of that device because they are of a weak nature." Pigafetta, *Magellan's Voyage*, I, 166–69. Also see Loarca, *BR*, V, 117, and Morga-Retana, *Sucesos*, p. 196.

24. Morga, Ribadeneyra, Archbishop Benavides, Archbishop Santibáñez, and Alcina, some of our most informative sources, claimed that the Chinese introduced sodomy to the Filipinos. Their principal argument was a linguistic one. They claimed that there was no word in the native languages for sodomy. The absence of a word does not necessarily prove the nonexistence of this practice, as the Spanish sources seemed to imply. Furthermore it is unprovable whether there was or was not a word for sodomy in preconquest times. The early seventeenth-century dictionaries are not now extant; and even if they were, the first vocabularies were certainly incomplete. Circa 1750 there was a Tagalog word for sodomy, *binabae*, meaning like a woman. Whether this word was of preconquest origin cannot be demonstrated. The few men who entered the pagan priesthood were effeminates and transvestites, but the Spanish sources deny that they were overt homosexuals. The linguistic argument is inconclusive, but the claim of these Spanish observers is suspect on other grounds: (1) if there was no sodomy in the Philippines before the conquest, that archipelago was one of the few regions in the world where it was unknown; (2) among the modern Filipino pagans sodomy is not unknown; (3) these Spanish observers were vituperative Sinophobes who hated the Chinese as intensely as they were dependent upon them for certain economic services. Spanish Sinophobia may be unconsciously responsible for inventing the charge that the Chinese introduced sodomy to the Filipinos. A more plausible conclusion might be that the incidence of homosexuality increased among the Filipinos as a result of the coming of the Chinese. Archbishop Santibáñez to Philip II: June 24, 1598, *AGI/AF* 74. Benavides to Philip III: July 5, 1603, and February 3, 1605, *BR*, XII, 107; XIII, 274, 278. Morga-Retana, *Sucesos*, p. 196. Ribadeneyra, *Historia*, p. 37. Alcina, *Historia*, Bk. III, ch. 21. Although placing the primary responsibility on the Chinese, Alcina does admit that a few Spaniards who

"ya no se contenta con la Venus ordinaria" were as guilty as the Chinese in introducing sexual deviations to the Filipinos.

25. Ordinance of the Audiencia: January 7, 1599, *BR*, XI, 31–32.
26. Mentrida, *Ritval*, p. 86.
27. *Recopilación*, Bk. VI, tit. i, law 6.
28. *BR*, L, 216–17.
29. For a list of these confessionals see J. T. Medina, *La imprenta*.
30. Pedro Murillo Velarde, S.J., *Historia*, pp. 5–6.
31. *Ibid.*, p. 28. Colín-Pastells, *Labor evangélica*, II, 409.
32. Aduarte, *Historia*, pp. 156–57.
33. Domingo Fernández Navarrete, O.P., *Tratados históricos*, p. 317.
34. Rey, *Confessonarios*, p. 344.
35. Ribadeneyra, *Historia*, pp. 51–52.
36. Murillo Velarde, *Historia*, p. 5.
37. Rey, *Confessonarios*, pp. 170, 208–10, 276–80, 284–87, 351–52.
38. Colín-Pastells, *Labor evangélica*, II, 409. Ribadeneyra, *Historia*, p. 51.
39. Rey, *Confessonarios*, pp. 221–24.
40. Ricard, *La "conquête spirituelle,"* pp. 148–52.
41. J. T. Medina, *La imprenta*, pp. 4–6. I consulted a photostat copy of the 1573 edition of Agurto's treatise.
42. Aduarte, *Historia*, p. 121.
43. Colín-Pastells, *Labor evangélica*, III, 113. Díaz, *Conquistas*, p. 239. Murillo Velarde, *Historia*, p. 36.
44. Mentrida, *Ritval*, pp. 48 ff.
45. Ribadeneyra, *Historia*, p. 67. Aduarte, *Historia*, pp. 74, 121, 158–59. Chirino, *Relación*, p. 140. Colín-Pastells, *Labor evangélica*, I, 361; II, 295, 343, 411.
46. *Ibid.*, III, 687–88. Bishop Salazar introduced confirmation as early as 1583. *BR*, V, 216–17.
47. Alcina's letter of 1660, *ARSI*, roll 165.
48. Colín-Pastells, *Labor evangélica*, III, 688. The infrequent references to confirmation in the chronicles of the regular orders suggests the relative lack of importance placed on this sacrament by the religious.
49. Ricard, *La "conquête spirituelle,"* pp. 285 ff. Charles Gibson, *Tlaxcala in the Sixteenth Century*, pp. 28 ff. Also see my *Millennial Kingdom*, pp. 52–55.

Chapter VI

1. Ribadeneyra, *Historia*, pp. 57, 67. Chirino, *Relación*, p. 70.
2. On June 18, 1677, Charles II dispatched a cedula to the Jesuit provincial superior (presumably to the superiors of the other orders also) ordering that each Philippine community have not more than one patron saint for whose festivities the natives were obligated to contribute. Pastells collection, St. Louis University, microfilm roll 28. This cedula apparently

meant that the Filipinos should not be required to contribute to the patronal fiesta of both the *cabecera* and the *visita*-barrio. Every male was required to make an annual contribution for this purpose at the time he made his obligatory annual confession. In 1697 this tax was fixed at three reales. *BR*, L, 218. For a description of how Holy Week was celebrated in a Jesuit parish see Chirino, *Relación*, p. 178.

3. Morga's letter to Philip II: June 8, 1598, Morga-Retana, *Sucesos*, p. 248.

4. Ernst Kantorowicz, "The 'King's Advent' and the Enigmatic Panels in the Doors of Santa Sabina," *The Art Bulletin*, XXVI (December, 1944), 207–31.

5. For general background see George M. Foster, "Cofradia and Compadrazgo in Spain and in Spanish America," *Southwestern Journal of Anthropology*, IX (Spring, 1953), 10 ff.

6. Colín-Pastells, *Labor evangélica*, II, 117. Murillo Velarde, *Historia*, p. 219. Although generally well informed, Morga showed no understanding of the effectiveness with which the religious used sodalities and fiestas as agencies of indoctrination and the enthusiastic response of the Filipinos to these techniques. Morga-Retana, *Sucesos*, p. 248.

7. The early Franciscan and Jesuit sources (Ribadeneyra and Chirino) claimed that the Filipino response was positive. This statement may be true, but the virtual absence of any references to flagellants in the later sources (San Antonio, Santa Inés, Martínez, and Colín) suggests that Filipino interest rapidly abated. Chirino, *Relación*, pp. 94, 137, 147, 176, 178, 186, 245. Ribadeneyra, *Historia*, pp. 49–50. Murillo Velarde, *Historia*, pp. 780–81.

8. Ribadeneyra, *Historia*, pp. 49–50.

9. *BR*, XXXIV, 380.

10. Ribadeneyra, *Historia*, pp. 54–55. San Antonio, *Chrónicas*, II, 12–18. Chirino, *Relación*, p. 242. Colín-Pastells, *Labor evangélica*, II, 127, 137; III, 135.

11. Acts of the First Provincial Council of Manila 1771, ms. at the Library of Congress, Manuscripts Division, Philippine Islands, Accession No. 6106–A, Box 1. Regarding the ms. see Schafer Williams, "The First Provincial Council of Manila, 1771," *Seminar*, XIII (1955–56), 33 ff. The Spaniards actually introduced a version of this theatrical custom into the Philippines. During the first Mass celebrated on Philippine soil, the guns of Magellan's ships roared a salute as the Host was elevated. Pigafetta, *Magellan's Voyage*, I, 121.

12. In the Manila area by 1620 there were only three wooden churches and twenty-seven stone churches. *BR*, XIX, 161–63. In the provinces the vast majority of *cabecera* churches and all the *visita* chapels were of wood. Alonso Sandin, O.P., to Charles II: May 20, 1685, *AGI/AF* 76. As of 1649 the Franciscans had some thirty-five *cabecera* churches in the Laguna de Bay area adjacent to Manila, eighteen of which were made of stone. The Jesuits constructed three magnificent baroque churches of stone at Silang,

Antipolo, and Taytay near Manila. Murillo Velarde, *Historia*, pp. 143–45. In the Bikol country, on the other hand, only three of the twenty-one parishes had stone churches. *BR*, XXXV, 278–87. Stone churches in the Bisayas and northern Luzon were uncommon, judging by the absence of references to such buildings. A few stone churches were built in the Bisayas during the eighteenth century.

13. See Chapter II for a discussion of ritual drinking in preconquest times. Aduarte, *Historia*, p. 65.

14. Colín-Pastells, *Labor evangélica*, II, 117.

15. Alcina, *Historia*, Bk. III, ch. 22. As late as 1739 *alcaldes* were warned to be on the alert for clandestine ritual drinking, but even in that isolated province the custom was evidently on the wane. "Ordenanzas de alcaldes (Cagagan, 1739)," ms. in possession of Professor Lesley Byrd Simpson, p. 6.

16. For the necessary background see Sidney W. Mintz and Eric R. Wolf, "An Analysis of Ritual Co-Parenthood (Compadrazgo)," *Southwestern Journal of Anthropology*, VI (Winter, 1950), 341–68. George Foster, "Cofradia and Compadrazgo," *ibid.*, IX (Spring, 1953), 1–28.

17. Pigafetta, *Magellan's Voyage* I, 153–55.

18. Juan de Grijalva, O.S.A., *Crónica de la orden de n. p. s. Augustín en las provincias de la Nueva España en quatro edades desde el año de 1533 hasta el de 1592* (Mexico: 1624), p. 125.

19. *BR*, XI, 75–76.

20. *BR*, XLIII, 105–6.

21. *Ibid.*, p. 109.

22. *Ibid.*, p. 105.

23. Letter of Gaspar de San Agustín published in Juan Delgado, S.J., *Historia sacro-profana*, p. 284.

24. *Ibid.*, pp. 314–15.

25. For the correspondence of the Dominican, Augustinian, and Jesuit superiors with the archbishop see Colín-Pastells, *Labor evangélica*, III, 115 ff. For the letters of the Franciscan and Recollect superiors see Pastells collection, St. Louis University, microfilm roll 14.

26. Alcina to General of Society, 1660, *ARSI*, roll 165.

27. Colín-Pastells, *Labor evangélica*, II, 117. Murillo Velarde, *Historia*, p. 28. Both Archbishop Camacho in 1697 and Simón de Anda in his memorial of April 12, 1768, criticized the religious for their refusal to administer the last sacraments in the homes of the sick. *BR*, XLIII, 55, and L, 175–76.

28. Hieronymus Noldin, S.J., *De sacramentis* (3 vols.; Rome: 1927), III, 253–55. Henry Davis, S.J., *Moral and Pastoral Theology* (4 vols.; London: Sheed and Ward, 1945), III, 335–57.

29. Camacho investigation of 1697–98, *AGI/AF* 302.

30. Cedula of August 22, 1677, Pastells collection, St. Louis University, microfilm roll 8. Archbishop Pardo opposed the growth of a Filipino clergy, alleging "their evil customs, their vices and their precon-

ceived ideas which made it necessary to treat them as children even when they were forty, fifty or sixty years old" *BR*, XLV, 182–83.

31. The translation is from Horacio de la Costa, S.J., "The Development of the Native Clergy in the Philippines," *Theological Studies*, VIII (July, 1947), 235–36. This discussion is lucidly presented and meticulously documented.

32. For San Agustín's letter and Delgado's reply see Delgado, *Historia sacro-profana*, pp. 273 ff. Delgado's "environmentalist" explanation of the character of the Filipinos is similar to the defense of the Mexican Indians formulated by Clavigero (1731–87). Francisco Javier Clavigero, S.J., *Historia antigua de Mexico* (4 vols.; Mexico: 1945), IV, 259. Both Jesuit historians were evidently under the spell of Enlightenment environmentalism, whose most articulate spokesman was Montesquieu.

33. A. Brou, S.J., "Notes sur les origines du clergé philippin," *Revue de l'histoire missionaire*, IV (1927), 546–47.

34. De la Costa, in *Theological Studies*, VIII, 242. For the archbishop's melodramatic confession of failure see his pastoral letter of June 14, 1772, in Ferrando and Fonseca, *Historia de los pp. dominicos en las islas filipinas* (6 vols.; Madrid: 1870–72), V, 54–59.

35. For some remarks on the Spanish and late medieval origins of this colonialist mentality see my *Millennial Kingdom*, pp. 61–63.

Chapter VII

1. In 1605 there were only 24 Mindanao galley slaves out of a total of 570 galley slaves. Audiencia to Philip III: June 30, 1605, *AGI/AF* 19. *BR*, VIII, 70–72; XXXIV, 325–31.

2. For the documentation of the early encomienda see my article, "Some Ideological Aspects," pp. 230 ff.

3. Audiencia to Philip II: June 15, 1595, *AGI/AF* 18. Governor Tavora to Philip IV: August 4, 1628, *BR*, XXII, 261–62. Morga-Retana, *Sucesos*, pp. 208–9.

4. Lesley Byrd Simpson, *The Encomienda in New Spain* (Berkeley and Los Angeles: University of California Press, 1950), pp. 145 ff.

5. Cedula of February 1, 1636, *BR*, XXV, 145–47; XIX, 273–74.

6. Dasmariñas to Philip II: June 20, 1593, *BR*, IX, 65–66. Philip III to Governor Tello: August 16, 1599, *BR*, XI, 130. *Fiscal* to king: July 21, 1599, *AGI/AF* 18. Philip III to Governor Acuña: Zamora, February 16, 1602, *BR*, XI, 272. *Fiscal* to Philip III: July, 1606, *BR*, XIV, 153.

7. The 1608 figure comes from a treasury report of August 18, 1608, *BR*, XIV, 247–48. The 1621 is Ríos Coronel's, *BR*, XIX, 285–87. The 1655 figure is another treasury report of July, 1655, Colín-Pastells, *Labor evangélica*, III, 730. The 1686 figure is from a letter of the Augustinian provincial superior to Archbishop Pardo: May 8, 1686, *ibid.*, III, 119. The 1742 figure comes from Pablo Francisco Rodríquez de Berdozido, "The Ecclesiastical Estate of the Aforesaid Philippine Islands," *BR*, XLVII, 140–42. For the 1765 figure see Viana to Charles III: July 10, 1766, *BR*, L, 78.

8. "Cédulas reales dirigidas a estas islas filipinas," ms., 2 vols., Newberry Library, II, 58–63.

9. Charles Henry Cunningham, *The Audiencia in the Spanish Colonies as Illustrated by the Audiencia of Manila (1583–1800)* (Berkeley: University of California Press, 1919), p. 110.

10. Rafael Moreno y Díez, *Manual del cabeza de barangay* (Manila: 1874), p. 35.

11. Agustín María de Castro, O.S.A., "Historia del insigne convento de San Pablo de Manila," *Missionalia hispanica*, VIII (1951), 91. It cost 12,000 pesos annually to meet the running expenses of this convent.

12. *BR*, XVIII, 311–13. In 1606 the Audiencia brought suit against the orders to compel them to restrict these settlements to the number of thirty servants per convent. The decision proved unenforceable. *Fiscal* to Philip III: July, 1606, *BR*, XIV, 169–70. Another attempt was made by the Audiencia, but again in vain. Audiencia to Philip III, July 19, 1609, *AGI/AF* 20.

13. The most informative account of Philippine shipbuilding is that of Sebastián de Pineda, *BR*, XVIII, 169–88.

14. For draft labor prior to 1609 see Morga-Retana, *Sucesos*, p. 211. For the post–1609 *polo* see cedula of Philip III: May 26, 1609, *BR*, XVII, 79–81. *Recopilación*, Bk. VI, tit. xii, law 40.

15. *BR*, XIX, 71–72.

16. The salary paid by the treasury to *polistas* was one peso monthly. Jesuit provincial superior to *fiscal*: August 21, 1616, *AGI/AF* 20. Governor Fajardo to Philip III: August 10, 1618, *BR*, XVIII, 130–31. Hernando de los Rios Coronel to king: 1619–20, *ibid*., 297–98, 316.

17. *BR*, L, 221.

18. *Ibid*., pp. 204–5. Fernández Navarrete, *Tratados históricos*, p. 304.

19. Provincial superiors to *fiscal*: 1616, *AGI/AF* 20.

20. Ríos Coronel, *BR*, XVIII, 309.

21. Augustinian provincial superior to *fiscal*: 1616, *AGI/AF* 20. Murillo Velarde, *Historia*, pp. 254–56. Circa 1650 Pampanga's annual rice quota was 40,000 bushels of rice payable in two installments. Fernández Navarrete, *Tratados históricos*, pp. 304–5.

22. The sources for these statistics were cited in note 7. The mid-century decline can be further demonstrated by statistics relative to the population of the Jesuit parishes in the Bisayan islands (Samar, Leyte, Bohol, and Cebu), who suffered as much from the depredations of the Moros as they did from the consequences of the Dutch War.

> 1622.................74,600 total population
> 1659.................52,269 total population
> 1679.................70,961 total population

The 1622 figure comes from Archbishop García Serrano's report. *BR*, XX, 230. For the 1659 and 1679 figures see the Jesuit census reports, *ARSI*, roll 158.

23. Provincial superiors to *fiscal:* 1616, *AGI/AF* 20. Fernández Navarrete, *Tratados históricos*, p. 304, 318.

24. *BR, L,* 210.

25. See my *Millennial Kingdom*, pp. 93–98.

26. This attitude of the Philippine clergy is clearly reflected in the correspondence of the provincial superiors with the *fiscal*, *AGI/AF* 20. For a characteristic example of the kind of moderate pressure exercised by the clergy to restrain the abuses of the *polo* see Philip IV's letter to the Audiencia: December, 17, 1639, *BR*, XXIX, 192–93.

27. Diego de Carate to Philip II: June 10, 1581 and Juan Pacheco Maldonado to Philip II: June 6, 1582, *AGI/AF* 34. Morga-Retana, *Sucesos*, p. 258. "Ordenanzas de alcaldes (Cagayan, 1739)," ms. in possession of Professor Lesley Byrd Simpson, p. 7.

28. *BR*, IX, 106–7. Rodríquez de Berdozido, *BR*, XLVII, 146.

29. Cedula of May 13, 1579, Colín-Pastells, *Labor evangélica*, III, 681–82.

30. "Ordenanzas de alcaldes," pp. 23–24. Memorial of Governor Dasmariñas, 1593, *AGI/AF* 6. Morga-Retana, *Sucesos*, p. 247. Rios Coronel, *BR*, XVIII, 317. Camacho investigation of 1697, *AGI/AF* 302. Cedula of March 17, 1608, *Recopilación*, Bk. VI, tit. xii, law 41, and cedula of June 18, 1594, *ibid.*, Bk. I, tit. xiv, law 81. Cedula of May 29, 1620, *BR*, XIX, 40–41; *BR, L,* 205–6, 218, 238.

Chapter VIII

1. Only occasionally do we hear of a Spaniard petitioning the king to legitimize his mestizo children, i.e., to enable them to inherit their father's property. For one such request see the petition of Pedro Sarmiento: October 14, 1581, *AGI/AF* 34.

2. The founder of the first convent of nuns of Manila was the celebrated Gerónima de Assumpción, a lady of indomitable strength of character as well as outstanding spiritual qualities, whose candidacy for sainthood was ardently championed at the Papal court by Philip IV of Spain. Sister Gerónima needed all her will power to surmount the series of noisy controversies accompanying the founding of her convent in Manila. For a hagiographical account of her life see Ginés Quesada, O.F.M., *Exemplo de todas las virtudes y vida milagrosa de la venerable madre Gerónima de la Assumpción* (Madrid: 1717). For another Franciscan account see Domingo Martínez, *Compendio histórico de la apostólica provincia de San Gregorio de Philipinas de religiosos menores descalzos de n. p. San Francisco* (Madrid: 1756), pp. 169–74. The most level-headed discussion is that of Juan de la Concepción, *Historia*, V, 9–17.

3. Sherburne F. Cook and Lesley Byrd Simpson, *The Population of Central Mexico in the Sixteenth Century* (Berkeley and Los Angeles: University of California Press, *Ibero-Americana*: 31, 1948), pp. 1–48.

4. Lesley Byrd Simpson, *The Exploitation of Land in Central Mexico in*

the Sixteenth Century (Berkeley and Los Angeles: University of California Press, *Ibero-Americana:* 36, 1952).

5. Woodrow W. Borah, *New Spain's Century of Depression* (Berkeley and Los Angeles: University of California Press, *Ibero-Americana:* 35, 1951).

6. Governor Tavora to Philip IV: August 4, 1628, *BR*, XXII, 261–62. Hernando de los Ríos Coronel, *BR*, XVIII, 317.

7. *BR*, XVIII, 317; L, 199, 211.

8. *Ibid.*, p. 108.

9. Cathedral chapter to Philip III: July 4, 1603, *AGI/AF* 77. Archbishop Benavides to Philip III: July 5, 1603, *BR*, XII, 109. Tavora to Philip IV: August 1, 1629, *BR*, XXIII, 36–38.

10. *BR*, XVIII, 93 ff. Fernández Navarrete, *Tratados históricos*, p. 322.

11. *BR*, XXIX, 298; XXXII, 93; XXXIX, 98; XXXVIII, 24–25, 28, 34. Santa Inés, *Crónica*, I, 78–79. Morga-Retana, *Sucesos*, p. 174. Alcina to General of the Society, 1660, *ARSI*, roll 165.

12. Elmer Drew Merrill, *The Botany of Cook's Voyages* (*Chronica Botanica series*, XIV, numbers 5 and 6, Waltham, Mass.: 1954), p. 237.

13. *BR*, XVIII, 179. Before wheat was grown in the islands, flour for the Host was imported from Mexico. Communion wine also was imported, shipped from Spain via Mexico and the Acapulco galleon. *Ibid.*

14. Reliable statistics about maize production must await a careful examination of the ecclesiastical tithes, the records of which are in *AGI*. Occasional references in the printed sources indicate that maize production was not large. As of 1650 a bushel of maize was worth about ninety pesos, exorbitantly expensive in contrast to the value of rice whose price fluctuated between one and four pesos per bushel. Fernández Navarrete, *Tratados históricos*, p. 322. *BR*, XXIII, 36. Alcina, *Historia*, Bk. III, ch. 6.

15. Morga-Retana, *Sucesos*, pp. 178 ff.

16. *BR*, XIV, 156–57. Colín-Pastells, *Labor evangélica*, III, 125–26. *BR*, XXV, 81. Beef production was somewhat higher than these figures would indicate, for not included in the tithes was cattle production of the ecclesiastical estates. In the province of Batangas the religious owned twenty large cattle ranches. *BR*, L, 154.

17. Fernando Rey, *Confessonarios*, pp. 343–44. Alcina reports that Jesuit priests in the Bisayas ate pork or chicken at midday and fish in the evening. Apparently they rarely ate beef. Alcina's letter of 1660, *ARSI*, roll 165.

18. *Ibid.* Fernández Navarrete, *Tratados históricos*, p. 322. He also reports that the Spaniards crossed buffaloes with cows, "and the result has been a third and very strange appearing species." *Ibid.*

19. Morga-Retana, *Sucesos*, pp. 178 ff.

20. "Ordenanzas de alcaldes (Cagayan, 1739)," ms. in possession of Professor Lesley Byrd Simpson, pp. 1–3, 37–38. *Recopilación*, Bk. VI, tit. x, law 17. *BR*, L, 198.

21. That cattle did ravage the fields in those few areas where beef production was profitable is attested by the ordinance of the Audiencia issued in 1606 authorizing the killing of cattle trespassing on adjacent rice fields owned by the natives. *BR*, XIV, 156–57. One cause for the distress culminating in the agarian insurrection of 1745–46 in the province of Batangas was the encroachment of cattle from the ecclesiastical-owned ranches on the fields of the Filipinos. *BR*, XLVIII, 27–36.

22. The Augustinian memorial of 1573, *BR*, XXXIV, 280–81. Ribadeneyra, *Historia*, p. 70. Santa Inés, *Crónica*, I, 60–62. Chirino, *Relación*, pp. 148–49. Delgado, *Historia sacro-profana*, pp. 349–52. The moralistic tone of these accounts contrasts with the dispassionate description found in the writings of Plasencia, Loarca, and Alcina. See Chapter II, note 1.

23. *BR*, VIII, 70–72; XXXIV, 325–31.

24. Salazar to Philip II: June, 1586, Colín-Pastells, *Labor evangélica*, I, 449.

25. *Ibid.*, p. 435. Alcina, *Historia*, Bk. IV, ch. v.

26. Plasencia's text was adopted by the Audiencia as customary law in all cases concerning dependent status. *BR*, XI, 31–32. Filipinos who petitioned the Audiencia for manunission often met with a favorable decision. See two letters of the *fiscales* to the king: July 10, 1610, *AGI/AF* 20, and one of November 24, 1630, *ibid.*, 21. Other regulatory acts of the Audiencia were decrees that a dependent could have only one superior and that a dependent who had been sold could not be transported beyond a distance of five leagues from the place of his habitual residence. *Fiscal* to Philip III: July 10, 1610, *ibid.*, 20. *BR*, X, 303–4.

27. Ríos Coronel, *BR*, XVIII, 297–98, 316. Unsigned letter [1598], *BR*, X, 117.

28. *BR*, XIX, 72. Provincial superior to *fiscal*: 1616, *AGI/AF* 20.

29. Cedula: June 12, 1679, *Recopilación*, Bk. VI, tit. ii, law 16. "Testimonios de los autos seguidos en Manila entre el real fiscal y el cabildo eclesiástico . . . y principales y cabezas de barangay en Pampanga sobre la libertad de Indios esclavos (1683–1684)," Pastells collection, St. Louis University, microfilm roll 32. *BR*, L, 199.

30. Delgado, *Historia sacro-profana*, p. 358.

31. *BR*, LII, 294–98.

32. *BR*, XLVIII, 142–43.

33. *BR*, XXIII, 36–38.

34. The myth that encomiendas were land grants still crops up in places where it should not. See J. E. Spencer, *Land and People in the Philippines, Geographical Problems in a Rural Economy* (Berkeley and Los Angeles: University of California Press, 1954) p. 113.

35. François Chevalier, *La formation des grands domaines au Mexique* (Paris: Institute d' ethnologie, 1952), pp. 150 ff.

36. Colín-Pastells, *Labor evangélica*, I, 424–25. *BR*, VII, 156–57.

37. Archbishop Benavides to Philip III: July 6, 1603, *BR*, XII, 117–21. Petition of Miguel Banal to Philip III: July 25, 1609, *BR*, XIV, 327–29. Philip III to Governor Silva: December 7, 1610, *BR*, XVII, 151–52. Audiencia to Philip III: July 20, 1612, *AGI/AF* 20.

38. Ordinance of Governor José Basco: March 20, 1784, *BR*, LII, 295–98.

39. "Ordenanzas de alcaldes," pp. 14–15.

40. Anda, *BR*, L, 154.

41. Simpson, *Exploitation of Land*. Borah, *New Spain's Century of Depression*.

42. *Ibid.*, p. 42.

43. Chevalier, *La formation*, pp. 403–9.

44. For the economic decline of the Mexican caciques see *ibid.*, pp. 280–85. For the decline of the caciques as creative cultural intermediaries see Charles Gibson, *Tlaxcala in the Sixteenth Century*, pp. 79 ff. For a comparison of Spanish intentions and results in the socioeconomic sphere in Mexico and in the Philippines see my article in the January, 1959, issue of the new journal, *Comparative Studies in Society and in History*, "Free versus Compulsory Labor: Mexico and the Philippines, 1540 to 1648."

Chapter IX

1. Viana to Charles III: July 10, 1766, *BR*, L, 98.

2. *BR*, XXXIV, 283. Ordinances of Governor Corcuera (1642), Cruzat (1696), and Raón (1768), *BR*, L, 203, 254–55. Hereafter cited as Ordinances. These ordinances are a richly varied source illustrating how the Filipinos were responding to many phases of Hispanization. The version in Blair and Robertson is an abridgment and an unsatisfactory one at that. I am presently editing for publication an unabridged Spanish version of these ordinances from a manuscript which Professor Lesley B. Simpson kindly put at my disposal. Morga-Retana, *Sucesos*, pp. 207–8. Cedula of June 11, 1594, *Recopilación*, Bk. VI, tit. vii, law 16.

3. "Ordenanzas de alcaldes (Cagayan, 1739)," ms. in possession of Professor Lesley Byrd Simpson, p. 22. *BR*, X, 117; XVII, 79–81; XVIII, 316; Ordinances, L, 204–5.

4. *Ibid.*, p. 194. Plasencia, *BR*, VII, 178–79. Morga-Retana, *Sucesos*, p. 210.

5. The *fiscal*, Viana, proposed this reform to Charles III in his letter of July 10, 1766. *BR*, L, 98. Governor Raón drew up the ordinance two years later, but these ordinances were not enforced until the early nineteenth century. *Ibid.*, p. 256.

6. José Montero y Vidal, *Historia general de Filipinas desde el descubrimiento de dichas islas hasta nuestros dias* (3 vols.; Madrid: 1887–95), II, 320. Moreno y Diez, *Manual de cabezas de barangay* (Manila: 1874).

7. See Chapter IV, note 16.

8. Morga-Retana, *Sucesos*, pp. 207–8.
9. "Ordenanzas de alcaldes," p. 6.
10. *BR*, Ordinances, L, 208–9.
11. "Ordenanzas de alcaldes," p. 39.
12. *Ibid.*, pp. 4–5.
13. For an over-all evaluation of the *residencia* see Clarence H. Haring, *The Spanish Empire in America*, pp. 149–53.
14. "Ordenanzas de alcaldes," p. 39. *Cabezas de barangay* in the eighteenth century could be elected to the post of *gobernadorcillo* without ceasing to act in the former capacity. *BR*, L, 255.
15. For royal legislation dealing with the *cajas* see *Recopilación*, Bk. VI, tit. iv.
16. Colín-Pastells, *Labor evangélica*, I, 449–50.
17. Audiencia to Philip III: July 19, 1609, and July 12, 1610, *AGI/AF* 20.
18. Rios Coronel discussed the abuses in the administration of the *cajas*. *BR*, XVIII, 314–15.
19. *BR*, Ordinances, L, 195, 235–36, 244 ff.
20. See Chapter VII, note 27.
21. *BR*, XI, 31–32; XVI, 321–26. Morga-Retana, *Sucesos*, p. 208. Francisco de Santa Inés, *Crónica*, I, 456.
22. *BR*, VII, 158; IX, 239–40; XI, 49–51; Ordinances, L, 196. Morga-Retana, *Sucesos*, p. 208.
23. Ríos Coronel, *BR*, XVIII, 318, and XI, 49–51. Cunningham, *The Audiencia in the Spanish Colonies as Illustrated by the Audiencia of Manila, 1583–1800* (Berkeley: University of California Press, 1919), pp. 98–104.
24. *BR*, XVII, 95–96; XX, 86; LI, 202. Rey, *Confessonarios*, pp. 170, 208–9, 221.
25. For an example of an extremist statement of this feeling widely held by the Spanish regular clergy see my *Millennial Kingdom*, pp. 85 ff.
26. *Census of the Philippine Islands*, 1903 (3 vols.; Washington, D.C.: U. S. Government Printing Office, 1905), III, 583, 594, 595, 689. Dean Worcester, *The Philippines Past and Present* (New York: Macmillan, 1930), p. 671.
27. Juan de Solórzano Pereira, *Política indiana* (5 vols.; Madrid and Buenos Aires: Compañía Ibero-Americana de Publicaciones 1930), I, 395–404. First edition is 1648.
28. Philip II to Governor Tello: May 25, 1596, *BR*, IX, 255–56. Audiencia to Philip III: July 3, 1606, *AGI/AF* 19.
29. José Duque, O.S.A., tò Charles II: March 21, 1689, *AGI/AF* 25.
30. "Ordenanzas de alcaldes," pp. 5–6. Degree of Governor Anda: November 9, 1764, "Ordenanzas para corregidores y alcaldes mayores" (Manila: 1764), p. 113 ff. See note 2 of this chapter for an explanation of this ms.
31. *BR*, XXVIII, 210–13; L, 119–24, 169–72. Also see my article "Philippine Linguistics," pp. 165 ff.

32. For Tlaxcalan responses to political Hispanization see Gibson, *Tlaxcala in the Sixteenth Century*, pp. 89 ff.

Chapter X

1. Colín-Pastells, *Labor evangélica*, I, 213; II, 506–7. Murillo Velarde, *Historia*, pp. 33, 44, 48, 77.

2. Audiencia to Philip III: June 30, 1605, *AGI/AF* 19.

3. Francisco Combés, S.J., *Historia de las islas de Mindanao y Ioló* (Madrid: 1667), pp. 197 ff. Murillo Velarde, *Historia*, p. 77.

4. Concepción, *Historia*, VI, 89–113. Also see the account of Juan de los Angeles, O.P.: March, 1643, *BR*, XXXV, 128–62. Corcuera's administration was also notable for a series of severe jurisdictional conflicts with the mendicant orders. The Jesuits usually sided with the governor against the mendicants in these disputes, for both Corcuera and the Society shared a common objective in waging war against the Moros.

5. Concepción, *Historia*, VII, 69 ff. The standard secondary work on Mindanao in the seventeenth century is José Montero y Vidal, *Historia de la piratería malayo-mahometana en Mindanao, Joló y Borneo* (Madrid: 1888), pp. 243 ff. Uprisings in Pampanga and Pangasinan, close to the center of Spanish power, were also factors precipitating the withdrawal from Zamboanga. The Sangley revolt occurred after the Zamboanga decision had been taken.

6. According to the Jesuit report published in *ibid.*, pp. 250–52, the Society administered to 4,251 families in the *residencia* of Zamboanga and 2,750 families in the *residencia* of Iligan-Dapitan for a total figure of about 28,001 people. For the Recollect figures see Luís de Jesús, *Historia general de los religiosos descalzos del orden de los ermitaños del gran padre San Avgvstín de la congregación de España y de las Indias* (Madrid: 1681), pp. 40–44.

7. The most concise collection of sources is Lorenzo Pérez, O.F.M., "Los aetas e Ilongotes de Filipinas," *Archivo Ibero-Americano*, XIV (November–December, 1927), pp. 289–346. For a brief but authoritative account see Felix and Marie Keesing, *Taming the Philippine Headhunters* (Palo Alto: Stanford University Press, 1934), pp. 62–65.

8. *BR*, L, 212–13, 248–49. Also see Chapter IV, note 17.

9. The resistance of the mountain province to Spanish penetration contrasts in some respects with the effective opposition the Spaniards met from the Araucanian Indians in central Chile. In response to the sustained pressure exerted by the Spanish colonists, who were anxious to secure an abundant supply of cheap labor, Araucanian culture underwent some intensive changes. Spanish pressure produced a counter-pressure among the Araucanians. These transformations facilitated the task of the Araucanians to preserve their independence for two hundred years. Some features of Spanish culture were adopted in order to strengthen resistance patterns. Outstanding among these changes was the emergence of a modified form of political-military centralization. In the case of the mountain province no comparable cultural changes occurred, since Spanish military, political,

economic, and religious pressure on the area was never as sustained or as intense as Spanish pressure against the Araucanians. For an evocative analysis of how Araucanian culture changed see Robert Charles Padden, "Culture Change and Military Resistance in Araucanian Chile, 1550–1730," *Southwestern Journal of Anthropology*, XIII (Spring, 1957), 103–21.

10. My colleague in the Philippine Studies Program, Paul Lietz, is presently engaged in studying for the Mindanao area various aspects of this radical change in Spanish methods of penetration.

11. *BR*, XXV, 148–49; XXXV, 125–26.

12. The sources for the Pampangan revolt are the following. Díaz, *Conquistas*, pp. 568–90. Murillo Velarde, *Historia*, pp. 254–56. Baltasar de Santa Cruz, O.P., *Historia de la provincia de santo rosario de Filipinas, Iapón y China* (Zaragoza: 1693), pp. 331–34. Concepción, *Historia*, VII, 9–35.

13. See Chapter IV, note 10.

14. Santa Cruz, *Historia*, pp. 337–40. Murillo Velarde, *Historia*, pp. 254–57. Díaz, *Conquistas*, pp. 604–6. *BR*, XXXVIII, 161–81, 181–215.

15. Concepción, *Historia*, XI, 280; *BR*, XLVIII, 27–36.

16. Murillo Velarde, *Historia*, pp. 17–18. Concepción, *Historia*, V, 20–23. Juan de Medina, Historia, pp. 226–28. Díaz, *Conquistas*, pp. 132–36.

17. The same sources as in note 16.

18. Concepción, *Historia*, VI, 247–81. Díaz, *Conquistas*, pp. 517–23.

19. Concepción, *Historia*, XII, 40–43.

20. Bishop of Cagayan to Philip III: April 12, 1605, *AGI/AF* 76.

21. *BR*, XVIII, 318.

22. John Howland Rowe, "The Incas Under Spanish Colonial Institutions," *Hispanic American Historical Review*, XXXVII (May, 1957), 155–99.

23. Gregorio F. Zaide, *The Philippines Since Pre-Spanish Times* (Manila: R. B. García, 1949), pp. 440 ff., and his *Dagohoy, Champion of Philippine Freedom* (Manila: Enríquez, Aldaya, 1941).

Chapter XI

1. José Ortega y Gasset's essay "Meditation in the Escorial" in Ortega's *Invertebrate Spain*, Mildred Adams, translator (New York: W. W. Norton, 1937), p. 208.

2. As early as 1586 Bishop Salazar, who had spent many years in Mexico, warned that Mexican-inspired legislation often conflicted with Philippine conditions. Colín-Pastells, *Labor evangélica*, I, 449.

3. Clarence H. Haring, *The Spanish Empire in America*, p. 123. Underlying the "I obey but do not execute" formula is the principle of Justinian that the prince would not willfully commit an injustice. *Recopilación*, Bk. II, tit. i, law 24.

4. For some recent characterological studies of the mestizo upon which my remarks are based see Gordon W. Hewes, "Mexicans in Search of the Mexican," *The American Journal of Economics and Sociology*," XIII (January, 1954) 209–23 and my article "México y lo Mexicano," *Hispanic American Historical Review*, XXXVI (August, 1956), 309–18.

Bibliographical Essay and List of Sources

Printed Sources

Our single most voluminous kind of sources are the chronicles published periodically by the various religious orders. They also contain considerable material on missionary activity in China and Japan, since the Philippines were the Spanish missionary headquarters for all the Orient.

Juan de Grijalva's chronicle of the Augustinian province of New Spain (Mexico, 1624) is particularly useful for the early contacts between the Augustinians and the Filipinos. Gaspar de San Agustín's account (Madrid, 1698) is a richly detailed, chronological description covering events up to 1616. Casimiro Díaz's continuation of San Agustín reached the year 1694. Abundantly informative, it is also a prolific source for information on the native uprisings in the lowland provinces.

One of the principal characteristics of Juan de Medina's Augustinian chronicle is its tone of disillusion. Serving in the Philippines from 1610 to 1635, he became discouraged and was granted permission to return to Spain. He died on board a galleon en route to Acapulco. Medina suffered from a "second-generation complex." The sanguine if unrealistic hopes of the first generation were not materializing.

Marcelo de Ribadeneyra's Franciscan history (Barcelona, 1601) is a foil to Medina's. Ribadeneyra was an eloquent spokesman of the first generation of missionaries, who were inspired by a seemingly boundless optimism about the total success of the missionary enterprise. Ribadeneyra's chronicle is invaluable for its account of Franciscan methods of indoctrination. Actually both the optimism of Ribadeneyra and the pessimism of Medina were exaggerated manifestations. Subsequent chroniclers would take a more realistic view of missionary possibilities and accomplishments.

Francisco de Santa Inés, whose work covers the period to 1600, does not add an unusual amount of new material about Franciscan activity. Juan Francisco de San Antonio's three volumes, which bear a Manila imprint of 1738–44, are more informative. Based largely on Ribadeneyra's published account and Juan de la Llave's unpublished manuscript, San Antonio's work has much detailed material dealing with resettlement and indoctrination methods. Like Santa Inés, San Antonio did not describe the seventeenth century. The Franciscan emphasis on the sixteenth century to the exclusion of the seventeenth century can only be explained in terms of events in Japan. The martyrdom of St. Pedro Bautista in 1597 was the spectacular event that absorbed a good deal of the attention of the Franciscan chroniclers. Domingo Martínez's compendium (1756) attempted to fill this wide vacuum in Franciscan historiography by covering the whole seventeenth century. Its general superficiality and its lack of detail make it, however, one of the least interesting of the Franciscan sources.

Two extra-Philippine accounts throw considerable light on Franciscan activity in the islands. They are Marcos de Alcalá's chronicle of the Discalced province of St. Joseph in Spain and Baltasar de Medina's history of the Discalced province in Mexico. The former is useful for the Spanish background of the Philippine Franciscans. The latter also contains pertinent information, for the Discalced province in Mexico was founded and maintained as a midway station linking the Discalced provinces in Spain with the Philippine province. The vast majority of Franciscans established in Mexico belonged to the Observant branch of the Order.

Four chronicles depict the exploits of the Dominicans in the Philippines. The first chronicle was written by Friar Diego Aduarte, Bishop of Cagayan (1632–36). Published in 1640 and again in 1693, Aduarte's chronicle contains a wealth of detail about initial Dominican contacts with the recalcitrant natives of the Cagayan valley. This work is also notable for its realistic tenor, avoiding the extremes of both optimism and pessimism. Baltasar de Santa Cruz published a second volume on events from 1637 to 1688. Santa Cruz's volume is more hagiographical than Aduarte's and hence less interesting for historical purposes. Vicente de Salazar's continuation covering the period from 1669 to 1700 (Manila, 1742) is invaluable for Dominican activity among the then hostile Sambals. Domingo Collantes published a volume in 1783 covering events from 1700 to 1765.

The importance of the work of the Jesuits is reflected in the literature they published. The first account is Pedro Chirino's (Rome, 1604). Based on the Annual Letters that the Jesuit authorities dispatched to their superiors in Rome, many of which were then published, Chirino's account is a rich and varied source for all aspects of missionary activity. Published three years after Ribadeneyra's, Chirino's relation is similar in tone. Both authors were first-generation missionaries. Each one was eloquently and

Bibliographical Essay

201

exuberantly optimistic, although Chirino may have been somewhat more restrained in tone than Ribadeneyra.

Francisco Colín's history (Madrid, 1663) carries the story down to 1616. What Colín did was to fill in and to expand with a prolific assortment of detail Chirino's outline. It is indeed a fine job of historical synthesis. Diego de Oña in 1706 wrote a continuation of Colín covering the period from 1611 to 1665. This innocuous chronicle fell so far short of the high standards of Jesuit historiography that the authorities had the good sense not to publish it. Of only marginal historical value, it may be consulted in manuscript form on microfilm at St. Louis University (*ARSI*, roll 167).

Pedro Murillo Velarde's account (Manila, 1749), which according to J. T. Medina is the finest example of printing done in the islands, surveys Jesuit activity from 1613 to 1749. Although it is an informative source, this work is inferior in quality to the earlier accounts of Chirino and Colín. It lacks the structural organization and the historical sense of the later books. For a Jesuit account it contains a large dose of hagiography. Juan Delgado's work, finished in 1754 but not published until 1892, is a foil to Murillo Velarde's. It is not a chronicle as such. Encyclopedic in scope, it offers a harmonious synthesis of such diverse topics as preconquest culture, missionary methods, the psychology of the Filipinos, botany, and zoology. Enlightened and urbane, Delgado belonged to that pre-expulsion generation of Jesuits who were imbued with some aspects of the spirit of the Enlightenment. Francisco Combés' history of Mindanao (Madrid, 1667) is another significant Jesuit account chronicling some dramatic chapters in that clash between the Cross and the Crescent in the southern Philippines.

For the early missions of the Augustinian Recollects the principal source is Andrés de San Nicolás' history of the Recollects (Madrid, 1664). San Nicolás chronicles the exploits of the Recollects in Spain as well as overseas for the period to 1620. The Philippine information is detailed and abundant. Luís de Jesús' continuation of the chronicle covering the decades between 1620 and 1650 is inferior in interest, since the stress is often hagiographical.

One of the classics of Philippine missionary historiography is Juan de la Concepción's fourteen volumes (Manila, 1788–92). Concepción surveyed events in the archipelago from the time of Magellan to 1759. No mere parochial account of the accomplishments of his own Recollect Order, this work synthesizes on the basis of abundant documentation and with a sophisticated historical criterion the major ecclesiastical and political events spanning a period of over two centuries. These volumes remain perhaps the outstanding example of synthetic historiography produced in the islands.

No discussion of early Philippine historiography would be complete without a reference to Antonio de Morga's account (Mexico, 1609). A conscientious and vigorous representative of the Spanish bureaucracy, he spent seven years in the islands (1595–1602), first as the principal judicial officer and later as a member of the Audiencia. His account is an invaluable source for such topics as Hispano-Dutch hostility, native self-government, the indigenous labor system, and Spanish exploitation of labor. On some controversial issues touching the clergy (episcopal visitation and clerical exploitation of labor) Morga's published account borders on the innocuous. In his private correspondence with his superiors, however, Morga made trenchant critiques of what he regarded as missionary abuses (for an example see Retana's edition of Morga, pp. 247–62).

The contrast between Morga's then unpublished correspondence and his published account of 1609 brings to light one essential characteristic of all these chronicles. They are "official" histories. Factual material was often omitted which was considered excessively controversial or which might discredit the character and the purposes of Spanish colonization. In studying the disciplinary crisis among the Augustinians, for example, information in the Augustinian chronicles turns out to be sparse and reticent. Neither do the missionary chronicles furnish much assistance in investigating ecclesiastical demands placed on native labor or the charging of sacramental fees by the regular clergy.

No objective and comprehensive picture of Philippine developments can be obtained from an exclusive reliance on the missionary chronicles. The latter must be supplemented by an examination of the voluminous correspondence between the lay and ecclesiastical figures in the islands with the authorities in Spain. A representative selection of this correspondence can be found in that monumental collection of sources compiled and edited by Emma Helen Blair and James Alexander Robertson. This collection spans the entire Spanish period from Magellan's discovery to the end of the Spanish regime. Alongside substantial selections from the ecclesiastical chronicles, there is a prolific assortment of documents from the Spanish archives. The defect of this pioneer and laborious work is not the publishing of the documents in English translation, although most scholars would feel more at ease in the original language. It is rather that the translations are usually awkward and often downright ambiguous. Nevertheless, as a collection of sources it is incomparable, especially for the sixteenth and seventeenth centuries. Forty-two of the fifty-two volumes deal with the period prior to 1700.

Some of the gaps in the Blair and Robertson series are filled by another outstanding collection of sources published by Pablo Pastells, S.J., in his edition of Colín's *Labor evangélica*. The Pastells selection is notably strong for the Sánchez mission to Spain (1586) and for its varied selection from the informative Jesuit Annual Letters. The Pastells text is still the single richest source on the question of episcopal visitation.

Perhaps the finest single collection of printed materials on the Spanish period in the Philippines is in the Edward E. Ayer collection at the Newberry Library in Chicago (see my article, "The Philippine Collection in the Newberry Library," *The Newberry Library Bulletin*, III [March, 1955], 229–36). The Newberry also has an extensive collection of Philippine linguistic items (Doris Varner Welsh, *Checklist of Philippine Lin-*

guistics in the Newberry Library [Chicago: The Newberry Library, 1950]).

The Library of Congress has an incomparable collection of twentieth century items. In addition, its holdings for the Spanish period are varied and extensive.

Manuscript Sources

Although the printed sources for the early Spanish period are abundant and accessible, they must be supplemented by manuscript sources. The Newberry has a small but choice collection of Philippine manuscripts, a calendar of which was recently published (*Calendar of Philippine Documents in the Ayer Collection of the Newberry Library*, Paul Lietz, ed. [Chicago: The Newberry Library, 1956]). For the purposes of this study, however, this manuscript collection was of real but limited value. Virtually all the significant items for the early Spanish period have been published in the Blair and Robertson series. Since the Blair and Robertson texts were sometimes ambiguous in meaning or were abridgements, it was indeed useful to be able to consult the original Spanish text. Equally convenient was the possibility of consulting the Blair and Robertson transcripts from the Spanish archives in sixteen volumes and the Ventura del Arco transcripts from the *Real Academia de Historia* in five volumes, most of whose contents appeared in some form in Blair and Robertson.

The most outstanding manuscript-on-microfilm collection containing substantial information on the early history of the Philippines located in the United States is the Knights of Columbus Foundation for the Preservation of Historic Documents at the Vatican Library at St. Louis University. In the *Jesuitica* section of this collection the most interesting Philippine items are to be found in the *Archivum Romanum Societatis Iesu*, that is, documents microfilmed from the Jesuit archives in Rome. There is, for example, a rather complete series of the Annual Letters from the Philippine province during the seventeenth century. Many of these have never been published, and several of the published texts are today scarce. Of even greater interest to the historian is the series of letters addressed by the Jesuit provincial superiors in Manila to the general of the Society in Rome. In this correspondence the provincial superiors are apt to be much more candid than in the published Annual Letters, which in the nature of things were carefully edited for public consumption. Of real value also is a large assortment of letters addressed by the rectors of the local *residencias* to the provincial superior in Manila. These letters provided the raw material from which the Annual Letters for the whole province were constructed as well as furnishing the primary material upon which the Manila authorities could make their confidential reports to Rome.

Another important section at St. Louis University is a microfilm copy of the transcripts made by Father Pablo Pastells of documents from the *Archivo General de Indias*. Only a small portion of this material concerns the Philippines as such. Of this fraction the bulk has already been published by Father Pastells in his edition of Colín's *Labor evangélica*. Nevertheless, there are a few choice, unpublished, seventeenth-century items. In another section of *Jesuitica* microfilm there are a few interesting Philippine items in the *Fondo Gesuitico al Gesu di Roma*.

The microfilm holdings at St. Louis University, as the preceding outline suggests, are of solid value for Philippine studies for the period from 1581 to 1767, when the Society was expelled from the Spanish dominions.

In both Mexico and in the Philippines there are considerable archival resources of interest. According to Herbert Bolton's *Guide to the Materials for the History of the United States in the Principal Archives of Mexico* (Washington, 1913), Philippine sources in the *Archivo General de la Nacion* are plentiful for the eighteenth century, with relatively few documents relating to the period before 1700. In the Philippines, archives sustained severe and extensive damage during the last war. Their present state is revealed in an article by Edgar B. Wickberg, "Spanish Records in the Philippine National Archives," *Hispanic American Historical Review*, XXXV (February, 1955). Poorly housed and inadequately catalogued if at all, these records are apparently abundant for the eighteenth and nineteenth centuries and scant for the period before 1700. I sincerely regret not having had the opportunity to examine these archival resources in both Mexico City and in Manila.

Such an examination might have been desirable, but it was not indispensable for the completion of this study. For the Habsburg era the richest depositories of archival records are not in the Philippines or in Mexico but in Spain. Although Philippine officials often disregarded or evaded the directives of the Council of the Indies, they found it expedient to send detailed reports to Spain justifying their course of action or inaction. These voluminous records were originally deposited in the Spanish national archives at Simancas founded by the Emperor Charles V. In the eighteenth century the *Archivo General de Indias* was established in Seville by Charles III. Today this archive is the single richest depository of manuscripts relating to the history of Spain's overseas possessions.

A three-months visit to Seville during the fall of 1954 enabled me to examine some of these Philippine records. Of the approximately one thousand *legajos* of manuscripts, more than one-half belong to the period between 1700 and 1840. The records for the two earlier centuries are, nevertheless, abundant. The great collections of primary sources edited and published by Blair and Robertson and Father Pastells are in the main selections from the *Archivo General de Indias*. It would be no exaggeration to say that these editors wisely picked out some of the choicest items. Yet these published collections are selections, and they must be supplemented by further archival consultation.

For the completion of this study I examined those *legajos* which contained the correspondence of the ecclesiastical authorities with the Council of the Indies, in particular, the correspondence of the superiors of religious orders, the archbishops of Manila, the bishops of the suffragan sees and the cathedral chapter of the archdiocese of Manila. Among the secular sources consulted were the correspondence of the governors of the colony, the members of the Audiencia, and private Spanish citizens. All these *legajos* were in the *Audiencia de Filipinas* section, and those of greatest interest proved to be the following: 6, 7, 8, 18, 19, 20, 21, 34, 35, 36, 37, 38, 39, 40, 41, 42, 43, 44, 74, 75, 76, 77, 78, 79, 80, 84, 85, 302. Archival material was of outstanding interest for the following topics: missionary logistics, pre-Hispanic dependent status, the encomienda, local self-government, the disciplinary crisis in the Augustinian order, the question of ecclesiastical visitation, the Patronato, the Church's demands on native labor, and sacramental fees.

The Philippine bundles for the eighteenth century in the *Archivo* have scarcely been exploited. In fact, few of these *legajos* have been opened by investigators. Only eight volumes in the Blair and Robertson series deal with the eighteenth century. Few items in these eight volumes are Seville documents. Actually the choice eighteenth-century selections in Blair and Robertson came from the manuscript collection purchased by Edward E. Ayer from the *Compañía de Tabacos* or from the Ventura del Arco transcripts, both of which are in the Newberry. Until these voluminous eighteenth-century sources in the *Archivo* are examined, it will be virtually impossible to make any durable conclusions about that period.

There are excellent Philippine manuscript materials in Madrid. An outstanding collection can be found in the Jesuit papers located in the *Real Academia de Historia*. The Ventura del Arco transcripts in the Newberry are copies of documents from this collection. The Blair and Robertson transcripts in the Newberry also contain some further material from the *Academia*. It would seem that many of the most interesting Philippine documents in the *Academia* have already been published. The National Library and the *Archivo Histórico Nacional* also have a few Philippine holdings.

Actually the most important Philippine collection in Madrid is not yet accessible to research. The manuscripts of the *Museo y Biblioteca del Ultramar* are stored in a Madrid basement waiting for adequate housing and cataloguing. This collection is the archive of the former ministry of *Ultramar*, which in the nineteenth century had jurisdiction over Spain's remaining colonies. Although this archive is probably the most comprehensive in existence for the nineteenth century, many casual references suggest that it also contains valuable holdings on the earlier centuries.*

A most significant manuscript relating to the Philippines is the one located in the library of the *Palacio de Oriente* in Madrid. It is the survey of Bisayan society written by Francisco Ignacio Alcina, S.J., who died in 1674. An evaluation of its contents can be found in note 1, Chapter II.

Outside Madrid there are two collections of outstanding Philippine interest. One is the library of the *Colegio de Filipinas* in Valladolid. Founded

---

* Note to second printing: This collection has recently been placed in the *Archivo Histórico Nacional*, where it is available for scholarly research.

in 1732 by the Augustinian Order as a seminary for training missionaries for the Philippines, its collection of books and manuscripts is particularly strong for the eighteenth century. The archive in Pastrana has a multitude of documents relating to Franciscan activity in the archipelago. Some of these holdings have been edited in various issues of the *Archivo Ibero-Americano*, an historical journal published by the Franciscan Order in Madrid. I regret that I was unable to visit either Pastrana or Valladolid.

List of Sources

This list of printed sources is selective rather than exhaustive. Certain items have been intentionally excluded. There is no need to include all the standard bibliographical works of reference. Works which have been cited only a few times are omitted. Particular items in the Blair and Robertson series and the Pastells edition of Colín have not been listed individually.

Acosta, José de, S.J. *De promvlgatione evangelii apud barbaros.* Salamanca: 1589.

Aduarte, Diego, O.P. *Historia de la provincia del sancto rosario de la orden de predicadores de Filipinas, Iapón y China.* Zaragoza: 1693.

Agurto, Pedro de, O.S.A. *Tractado de qve se deven administrar los sacramentos de la sancta eucharistia y extrema vnction a los Indios de esta Neuva España.* Mexico: 1573.

Alcalá, Marcos de, O.F.M. *Chrónica de la santa provincia de San Joseph de religiosos descalzos.* Madrid: 1738.

Alcina (Alzina), Francisco Ignacio, S.J. *Historia de las islas e indios de Bisayas . . . dividida en dos: la primera natural . . . la segunda eclesiástical y sobrenatural . . . .* Manuscript, library of the Palacio de Oriente, Madrid.

Astrain, Antonio, S.J. *Historia de la compañía da Jesús en la asistencia de España.* 7 vols. Madrid: Razón y Fe, 1912–25.

Blair, Emma Helen, and Robertson, James Alexander. *The Philippine Islands, 1493–1803.* 55 vols. Cleveland: A. H. Clark, 1903–9.

Borah, Woodrow W. *Early Trade and Navigation Between Mexico and Peru.* Berkeley and Los Angeles: University of California Press, *Ibero-Americana:* 38, 1954.

———. *New Spain's Century of Depression.* Berkeley and Los Angeles: University of California Press, *Ibero-Americana:* 35, 1951.

Boxer, C. R. *The Christian Century in Japan, 1549–1650.* Berkeley and Los Angeles: University of California Press, 1951.

Cano, Gaspar, O.S.A. *Catálogo de los religiosos de n.p.s. Agustín de la provincia del smo. nombre de Jesús de Filipinas.* Manila: 1864.

Chevalier, François. *La formation des grands domaines au Mexique. Terre et société aux XVIe–XVIIe siecles.* Paris: Institut d' ethnologie, 1952.

Chirino, Pedro, S.J. *Relación de las islas filipinas.* Manila: 1890. (First edition, Rome, 1604.)

Cline, Howard F. "Problems of Mexican Ethno-History; The Ancient Chinantla," *Hispanic American Historical Review*, XXXVII (August, 1957), 273–95.

Colección de documentos inéditos relativos al descubrimiento, conquista y organización de las antiguas posesiones españolas de América y Oceanía. 42 vols., Madrid, 1864–84.

Colín, Francisco, S.J. *Labor evangélica*, ed. Pablo Pastells, S.J. 3 vols. Barcelona: Henrich, 1900–1902.

Combés, Francisco, S.J. *Historia de las islas de Mindanao y Ioló*. Madrid: 1667.

Concepción, Juan de la, O.R.S.A. *Historia general de Philipinas*. 14 vols. Manila: 1788–92.

Cook, Sherburne F., and Simpson, Lesley Byrd. *The Population of Central Mexico in the Sixteenth Century*. Berkeley and Los Angeles: University of California Press, *Ibero-Americana:* 31, 1948.

Costa, Horacio de la. "Church and State in the Philippines during the Administration of Bishop Salazar," *Hispanic American Historical Review*, XXX (August, 1950), 314–36.

———. "The Development of a Native Clergy in the Philippines," *Theological Studies*, VIII (July, 1947), 219–50.

———. "Episcopal Jurisdiction in the Philippines in the 17th century," *Philippine Studies*, II (September, 1954), 197–217.

Cunningham, Charles Henry. *The Audiencia in the Spanish Colonies as Illustrated by the Audiencia of Manila (1583–1800)*. Berkeley: University of California Press, 1919.

Delgado, Juan, S.J. *Historia general, sacro-profana, política y natural de las islas del poniente llamadas Filipinas*. Manila: 1892.

Díaz, Casimiro, O.S.A. *Conquistas de las islas filipinas*. Manila: 1890.

The Doctrina Christiana: The First Book Printed in the Philippines, Manila, 1593. A Facsimile of the Copy in the Lessing J. Rosenwald Collection, The Library of Congress, Washington, D.C. With an introductory essay by Edwin Wolf. Washington, D.C.: Library of Congress, 1947.

Fernández Navarrete, Domingo, O.P. *Tratados históricos, políticos, ethicos y religiosos de la monarchía de China*. Madrid: 1676.

Foster, George M. "Cofradia and Compadrazgo in Spain and in Spanish America," *Southwestern Journal of Anthropology*, IX (Spring, 1953), 10 ff.

Gayo Aragón, Jesús, O.P. *Ideas juridico-teológicas de los religiosos de Filipinas en el siglo xvi sobre la conquista de las islas*. Manila: University of Santo Tomas Press, 1950.

Gibson, Charles. *Tlaxcala in the Sixteenth Century*. New Haven: Yale University Press, 1952.

Gómez Platero, Eusebio. O.F.M. *Catálogo biográfico de los religiosos franciscanos de la provincia de San Gregorio magno de Filipinas*. Manila: 1890.

Grau y Monfalcón, Juan. *Memorial informatorio*. Madrid: 1637.

————. *Justificación de la conservación y comercio de las islas filipinas.* Mexico: 1640.

Grijalva, Juan de, O.S.A. *Crónica de la orden de n.p.s. Augustín en las provincias de la Nueva España en quatro edades desde el año de 1533 hasta el de 1592.* Mexico: 1624.

Hanke, Lewis. *The Spanish Struggle for Justice in the Conquest of America.* Philadelphia: University of Pennsylvania Press, 1949.

————, and Millares Carlo, Augustín, editors. *Cuerpo de documentos del siglo xvi sobre los derechos de España en las Indias y las Filipinas.* Mexico City: Fondo de Cultura Económica, 1943.

Haring, Clarence H. *The Spanish Empire in America.* New York: Oxford University Press, 1947.

Hernáez, Francisco Javier. *Colección de bulas, breves y otros documentos relativos a la iglesia de América y Filipinas.* 2 vols. Brussels: 1879.

Jesús, Luís de, O.R.S.A. *Historia general de los religiosos descalzos del orden de los ermitaños del gran padre San Avgvstín de la congregación de España y de las Indias.* Madrid: 1681.

Keesing, Felix, and Keesing, Marie. *Taming the Philippine Headhunters.* Palo Alto: Stanford University Press, 1934.

Kroeber, A. L. *Peoples of the Philippines.* New York: American Museum of Natural History, 1928.

Kubler, George. *Mexican Architecture in the Sixteenth Century.* 2 vols. New Haven: Yale University Press, 1948.

Marín y Morales, Valentín, O.P. *Ensayo de una síntesis de los trabajos realizados por las corporaciones religiosas españolas de Filipinas.* 2 vols. Manila: 1901.

Martínez, Domingo, O.F.M. *Compendio histórico de la apostólica provincia de San Gregorio de Philipinas de religiosos menores descalzos de n. p. San Francisco.* Madrid: 1756.

Medina, Baltasar de, O.F.M. *Chrónica de la santa provincia de San Diego de México de religiosos descalzos de n.p. S. Francisco en la Nueva España.* Mexico: 1682.

Medina, José Toribio. *La imprenta en Manila desde sus orígenes hasta 1810.* 2 vols. Santiago de Chile: 1896 and 1904.

Medina, Juan de, O.S.A. *Historia de los sucesos de la orden de n. gran p. S. Agustín de estas islas filipinas.* Manila: 1893.

Mentrida, Alonso, O.S.A. *Ritval para administrar los santos sacramentos sacado casi todo del ritual romano y lo demás del ritual indico.* Manila: 1669.

Merrill, Elmer Drew, *The Botany of Cook's Voyages.* (Chronica Botanica series, XIV, numbers 5 and 6.) Waltham, Massachusetts: 1954.

Moreno y Díez, Rafael. *Manual del cabeza de barangay.* Manila: 1874.

Morga, Antonio de. *Sucesos de las islas Filipinas,* ed.W. E. Retana. Madrid: Victoriano Suárez, 1909.

Murillo Velarde, Pedro, S.J. *Historia de la provincia de Philippinas de la compañía de Jesús.* Manila: 1749.

Ocio y Viana, Hilario, O.P. *Compendio de la reseña biográfica de los religiosos de la provincia del santísimo rosario de Filipinas.* Manila: 1895.

Ortiz, Tomás, O.S.A. *Practica del ministerio.* Manila: 1731.

Padden, Robert Charles. "Culture Change and Military Resistance in Araucanian Chile, 1550–1730," *Southwestern Journal of Anthropology,* XIII (Spring, 1957), 103–21.

Pérez, Elviro, O.S.A. *Catálogo bio-bibliográfico de los religiosos agustinos de la provincia del santísimo nombre de Jesús de las islas filipinas.* Manila: College of Santo Tomas Press, 1901.

Phelan, John Leddy. "Free versus Compulsory Labor: Mexico and the Philippines, 1540 to 1648," *Comparative Studies in Society and History,* I (January, 1959).

———. *The Millennial Kingdom of the Franciscans in the New World: A Study of the Writings of Gerónimo de Mendieta (1525–1604).* Berkeley and Los Angeles: University of California Press, Publications in History, No. 52, 1956.

———. "The Philippine Collection in the Newberry Library," *The Newberry Library Bulletin,* III (March, 1955), 229–36. Spanish translation in *Coleccionismo,* XLII (October, 1955).

———. "Philippine Linguistics and Spanish Missionaries, 1565–1700," *Mid-America,* XXXVII (July, 1955), 153–70.

———. "Pre-Baptismal Instruction and the Administration of Baptism in the Philippines during the Sixteenth Century," *The Americas,* XII (July, 1955), 3–23.

———. "Some Ideological Aspects of the Conquest of the Philippines," *The Americas* XIII (January, 1957), 221–39.

Pigafetta, Antonio. *Magellan's Voyage Around the World,* ed. James Alexander Robertson. 3 vols. Cleveland: Arthur H. Clark, 1906.

Recopilación de leyes de los reynos de las Indias. 4 vols. Madrid: 1681.

Rey, Fernando, O.S.A. *Confessonarios.* Manila: 1792.

Ribadeneyra, Marcelo de, O.F.M. *Historia de las islas del archipielago y reynos de la gran China, Tartaria, Cuchinchina, Malaca, Sian, Camboxa, y Iappón, y de lo sucedido en ellos a los religiosos descalzos de la orden del seraphico padre San Francisco de la prouincia de San Gregorio de las Philippinas.* Barcelona: 1601.

Ricard, Robert. *La "conquête spirituelle" du Mexique.* Paris: Institut d' Ethnologie, 1933.

Rowe, John Howland. "The Incas Under Spanish Colonial Institutions," *Hispanic American Historical Review,* XXXVII (May, 1957), 155–99.

Sábada del Carmen, Francisco, O.R.S.A. *Catálogo de los religiosos agustinos recoletos de la provincia de San Nicolás de Tolentino de Filipinas.* Madrid: Asilo de Huérfanos del Sagrado Corazón de Jesús, 1906.

Salazar, Vincente de, O.P. *Historia de la provincia de el Santissimo Rosario de Philipinas,* China y Tvnking. Manila: 1742.

San Agustín, Gaspar de, O.S.A. *Conquistas de las islas Philipinas: la temporal por las armas del señor don Phelipe segundo el prudente y la espiritval por los religiosos del orden de nuestro padre San Agustín.* Madrid: 1698.

San Antonio, Juan Francisco de, O.F.M. *Chrónicas de la apostólica provincia de S. Gregorio de religiosos descalzos de n. s. p. San Francisco en las islas Philipinas, China, Japón* . . . . 3 vols. Manila: 1738–44.

San Nicolás, Andrés de, O.R.S.A. *Historia general de los religiosos descalzos del orden de los ermitaños del gran padre San Avgustín de la congregación de España y de las Indias,* Madrid: 1664.

Santa Cruz, Baltasar de, O.P. *Historia de la provincia del santo rosario de Filipinas, Iapón y China, de la sagrado orden de predicadores.* Zaragoza: 1693.

Santa Inés, Francisco de, O.F.M. *Crónica de la provincia de San Gregorio Magno de religiosos descalzos de n.s.p. San Francisco en las islas Filipinas, China, Japón, etc.* . . . 2 vols. Manila: 1892.

Schurz, William L. *The Manila Galleon.* New York: E. P. Dutton, 1939.

Scott, James Brown. *The Spanish Origin of International Law: Francisco de Vitoria and His Law of Nations.* Oxford: Clarendon Press, 1934.

Simpson, Lesley Byrd. *The Encomienda in New Spain.* Berkeley and Los Angeles: University of California Press, 1950.

———. *Exploitation of Land in Central Mexico in the Sixteenth Century.* Berkeley and Los Angeles: University of California Press, *Ibero-Americana:* 36, 1952.

Solórzano y Pereira, Juan de. *Política indiana.* 2 vols. Madrid: 1648.

Sommervogel, Carlos, S.J. *Bibliothèque de la campagnie de Jésus.* 11 vols. Brussels and Paris: Alphonse Picard and Oscar Schepens, 1890–1932.

Spencer, J. E. *Land and People in the Philippines, Geographical Problems in a Rural Economy.* Berkeley and Los Angeles: University of California Press, 1954.

Torres Lanzas, Pedro. *Catálogo de los documentos relativos a las islas Filipinas existentes en el archivo de Indias de Sevilla.* 8 vols. Barcelona: 1925–34.

Zaide, Gregorio F. *The Philippines Since Pre-Spanish Times.* Manila: R. B. Garcia, 1949.

Index

COLLOQUY ON
NEW TESTAMENT STUDIES

COLLOQUY ON NEW TESTAMENT STUDIES
A Time for Reappraisal and Fresh Approaches

Edited with an Introduction by
BRUCE CORLEY

MERCER UNIVERSITY PRESS
MACON, GEORGIA 31207

ISBN 0-86554-082-9

All books published by Mercer University Press are produced

on acid-free paper that exceeds the minimum standards set by the

National Historical Publications and Records Commission

Library of Congress Cataloging in Publication Data
Colloquy on New Testament Studies (1980 : Southwestern
    Baptist Theological Seminary)
    Colloquy on New Testament Studies.
    "Proceedings of the Colloquy . . . sponsored by and
held at Southwestern Baptist Theological Seminary,
Fort Worth, Texas, 5-6 November 1980"—Pref.
    Includes bibliographical references.
    1. Bible. N.T.—Criticism, interpretation, etc.—
Congresses. I. Corley, Bruce C., 1943—
II. Southwestern Baptist Theological Seminary.
III. Title.
BS2361.2.C64   1980   225.6   83-8192
ISBN 0-86554-082-9

TABLE OF CONTENTS

PREFACE

THIS VOLUME IS BASED on the proceedings of the Colloquy on New Testament Studies, "A Time for Reappraisal and Fresh Approaches," sponsored by and held at Southwestern Baptist Theological Seminary, Fort Worth, Texas, 5-6 November 1980. The Colloquy was made possible by funds allocated by Southwestern Seminary. The opinions, findings, conclusions, and so forth expressed in the Colloquy and in this volume do not necessarily represent the view of Southwestern Seminary. The following outline describes the program and indicates the scope of participation in the Colloquy.

Keynote Address

E. P. Sanders (McMaster University)

Seminar on the Synoptic Problem

Moderator: William R. Farmer (Southern Methodist University)

(First Session)
Principal: Helmut Koester (Harvard University)
Respondent: David Peabody (Southern Methodist University)

(Second Session)
Principal: David L. Dungan (University of Tennessee)

Respondents: John H. Elliott (University of San Francisco)
Bruce Corley (Southwestern Baptist Theological Seminary)

Seminar on Gospel Genre

Moderator: Charles H. Talbert (Wake Forest University)
Principal: John C. Meagher (University of Toronto)

Seminar on Pauline Chronology

Moderator: John C. Hurd, Jr. (University of Toronto)
Principals: Robert Jewett (Garrett-Evangelical Theological Seminary)
Gerd Luedemann (Vanderbilt University)

Participants

Harry Attridge (Southern Methodist University)
William Baird (Texas Christian University)
David L. Barr (Wright State University)
E. Earle Ellis (New Brunswick Theological Seminary)
H. J. Flanders (Baylor University)
Victor P. Furnish (Southern Methodist University)
W. Ward Gasque (New College, Berkeley)
Robert A. Guelich (Northern Baptist Theological Seminary)
Robert H. Gundry (Westmont College)
John J. Gunther (Alfred, Maine)
Charles W. Hedrick (Southwest Missouri State University)
Edward C. Hobbs (Church Divinity School of the Pacific)
Edwin D. Johnston (Mercer University)
Jack D. Kingsbury (Union Theological Seminary, Virginia)
William L. Lane (Western Kentucky University)
Richard N. Longenecker (University of Toronto)
Thomas R. W. Longstaff (Colby College)
Jack W. MacGorman (Southwestern Baptist Theological Seminary)
Allan J. McNicol (University of Texas at Austin)
Abraham J. Malherbe (Yale University)
Ralph P. Martin (Fuller Theological Seminary)
Bruce M. Metzger (Princeton Theological Seminary)

J. Ramsay Michaels (Gordon-Conwell Theological Seminary)
Keith F. Nickle (Columbia Theological Seminary)
Bernard Orchard (Ealing Abbey, London)
Grant Osburne (Trinity Evangelical Divinity School)
Norman R. Petersen (Williams College)
Vernon K. Robbins (University of Illinois)
Philip Shuler (McMurry College)
Thomas C. Urrey (Southwestern Baptist Theological Seminary)
Jerry Vardaman (Mississippi State University)
William O. Walker, Jr. (Trinity University)
Stephen G. Wilson (Carleton University)

Registered Observers

James Bartley
Robert J. Beck
C. W. Brister
James Brooks
Stephen C. Coilson
Lorin Cranford
Russell H. Dilday, Jr.
Bert Dominy
John R. Donahue
Dennis Duling
Lloyd Elder
William R. Estep, Jr.
Ian Fair
Everett Ferguson
J. David Fite
James Leo Garrett, Jr.
Roger Greene
Guy Greenfield
James Hester
Harry Hunt
Dan G. Kent
W. David Kirkpatrick
George Knight
Nobuo Kobayashi
Tommy Lea
Lynn Losie

Lane P. McGaughy
John McRay
Richard R. Melick
Watson E. Mills
Richard Mobley
Guy Moore
Enrique Nardoni
John P. Newport
Thomas H. Olbricht
Jeanette B. Peer
Robert Phillips
Terence Prendergast
Charles J. Reedy
J. J. M. Roberts
Edd Rowell
William Rustenhaven
W. Thomas Sawyer
David Scholer
Robert B. Sloan
Klyne Snodgrass
M. Jack Suggs
J. D. Thomas
Robert J. Thompson
William B. Tolar
Harold L. Twist
Jack Weir

ACKNOWLEDGMENTS

THE COLLOQUY ON New Testament Studies and this volume based on its proceedings were made possible by the joint efforts of a host of people. These are the individuals whose support makes academe possible, and although mere mention of a name does less than justice, they will now be credited.

Southwestern Baptist Theological Seminary sponsored, supplied generous funds, and provided facilities for the Colloquy. President Russell H. Dilday, Jr., who both encouraged and participated in the conference, and his administrative officers undergirded the project from its inception. They include: John P. Newport, vice-president for academic affairs and provost; Lloyd Elder, executive vice-president; John Earl Seelig, vice-president for public affairs; Wayne Evans, vice-president for business affairs; and Lawrence Klempnauer, vice-president for student affairs. The late Dean of the School of Theology, Huber L. Drumwright, Jr., gave early direction and that impetus did not slack with William B. Tolar, his successor. Special mention is due Philip Poole in public relations, and Trozy Barker and Neta Stewart for arrangements. Also Keith C. Wills, director of libraries, and Robert Phillips, assistant librarian, were very helpful in securing books, materials, and equipment.

The logistics of travel, schedule, and program arrangements required a small army of supporters; this invaluable and considerate work was directed by three graduate assistants: David Evans, Randall Parks, and Gene Wilkes. Manuscript preparation, aided by Bob Trimble in audio-visuals, was carefully done by Cathy Wyatt. The major contribution of my secretary, Mary McLerren, during the Colloquy and in preparation of this volume deserves the highest recognition (as every boss who has a good secretary knows).

The program committee appointed from the School of Theology included Thomas C. Urrey, William R. Estep, Jr., James Leo Garrett, Jr., and myself. The work of liaison was carried out by William R. Farmer, Perkins School of Theology, Southern Methodist University. Profound gratitude is expressed to him for unstinted effort in arranging the Colloquy program. Finally, from the initial planning to the publication of this volume, the cooperation and encouragement of Watson E. Mills, Mercer University Press, has been greatly appreciated.

Bruce Corley
1983

ABBREVIATIONS

AnBib	Analecta biblica
ATR	*Anglican Theological Review*
BBB	Bonner biblische Beiträge
Bib	*Biblica*
BZ	*Biblische Zeitschrift*
BZNW	Beihefte zur *Zeitschrift für die neutestamentliche Wissenschaft*
CBQ	*Catholic Biblical Quarterly*
CJT	*Canadian Journal of Theology*
ConNT	*Coniectanea neotestamentica*
CurTM	*Currents in Theology and Mission*
EKKNT	Evangelisch-katholischer Kommentar zum Neuen Testament
ET	English translation
EtHPR	Etudes d'historie et de philosophie religieuses
ETL	*Ephemerides theologicae lovanienses*
ExpTim	*Expository Times*
FRLANT	Forschungen zur Religion und Literatur des Alten und Neuen Testaments

HNT	Handbuch zum Neuen Testament
HNTC	Harper's New Testament Commentaries
HTKNT	Herders theologischer Kommentar zum NeuenTestament
HTR	*Harvard Theological Review*
JAAR	*Journal of the American Academy of Religion*
JBL	*Journal of Biblical Literature*
JES	*Journal of Ecumenical Studies*
JSNT	*Journal for the Study of the New Testament*
JSOT	*Journal for the Study of the Old Testament*
JTS	*Journal of Theological Studies*
KEK	Kritisch-exegetischer Kommentar über das Neue Testament
KlT	Kleine Texte
NedTTs	*Nederlands theologisch tijdschrift*
NovT	*Novum Testamentum*
NovTSup	Supplements to *Novum Testamentum*
NRT	*La nouvelle revue théologique*
NTS	*New Testament Studies*
PSTJ	*Perkins School of Theology Journal*
RelSRev	*Religious Studies Review*
RevExp	*Review and Expositor*
RGG	*Religion in Geschichte und Gegenwart*
RSR	*Recherches de science religieuse*
SBLASP	Society of Biblical Literature Abstracts and Seminar Papers
SBLDS	Society of Biblical Literature Dissertation Series
SLJT	*St. Luke's Journal of Theology*
SJT	*Scottish Journal of Theology*
SNTSMS	Society for New Testament Studies Monograph Series
ST	*Studia Theologica*
TDNT	*Theological Dictionary of the New Testament* (eds. G. Kittel and G. Friedrich)
TP	*Theologie und Philosophie*
TU	Texte und Untersuchungen
TUMSR	Trinity University Monograph Series in Religion
TZ	*Theologische Zeitschrift*
ZNW	*Zeitschrift für die neutestamentliche Wissenschaft*
ZThK	*Zeitschrift für Theologie und Kirche*

INTRODUCTION

Bruce Corley

T̲HIS VOLUME IS BASED on the proceedings of the Colloquy on New Testament Studies held at Southwestern Baptist Theological Seminary, 5-6 November 1980. Immediately prior to the centennial meeting of the Society of Biblical Literature, some two hundred New Testament scholars and students gathered in Fort Worth to hear and discuss papers prepared for the occasion. In several ways the Colloquy was a unique event.

Background of the Colloquy

Colloquies, festivals, and the like are now familiar scholarly happenings in the New Testament guild; for example, one can trace a notable succession of conferences on the Synoptic Gospels at Pittsburgh (1970), Münster (1976), San Antonio (1977), and Cambridge (1979).[1] Where then does this colloquy fit into the scheme of things?

---

[1]The proceedings published to date are *Jesus and Man's Hope,* ed. D. G. Buttrick, D. G. Miller, and D. Y. Hadidian, 2 vols. (Pittsburgh: Pittsburgh Theological Seminary, 1970-1971); *J. J. Griesbach: Synoptic and Text-Critical Studies 1776-1976,* ed. B. Orchard and T. R. W. Longstaff, SNTSMS 34 (Cambridge: Cambridge University, 1978); *The Relationships among the Gospels: An Interdisciplinary Dialogue,* ed. W. O. Walker, Jr., TUMSR 5 (San Antonio: Trinity University, 1978). A paper from the Cambridge Griesbach Conference, held at Pembroke College, 13-17 August 1979, that

The plain answer is that it came about not through long-term planning but by a timely convergence of ongoing dialogue, programs, and collegiality in the Southwest region.

A lively forum for scholarly enterprise has existed in the Southwest for fifteen years, namely, the Southwest Seminar on the Development of Early Catholic Christianity, an ecumenical study group founded by Albert C. Outler and William R. Farmer that now includes ten schools.[2] Along with the impetus provided by the success of the Colloquy on the Relationships among the Gospels at nearby San Antonio,[3] this setting produced the initial contacts which led to plans for a colloquy at Southwestern. After preliminary correspondence in the spring 1980, Southwestern Seminary appointed a program committee and agreed to host a conference in the fall.

There ensued a series of meetings, letters, and invitations through which papers were negotiated in three areas: the Synoptic problem, genre of the Gospels, and Pauline chronology. For each of the areas a seminar moderator (and editor) was enlisted, William R. Farmer, Charles H. Talbert, and John C. Hurd, Jr., respectively, and they in turn arranged for major papers from Helmut Koester, John C. Meagher, Robert Jewett, and Gerd Luedemann. At a later stage a major paper by David L. Dungan was offered, and major responses were prepared by David Peabody and John H. Elliott. With the program in hand, invitations were mailed to selected seminar participants, representing the full spectrum of scholarship on the topics, who were joined by a large number of observers at the Colloquy.

Since the introduction and notes for each seminar give relevant details, there is no need to discuss the papers at this point; however, a word should be said about the dialogue transcripts. The report of each seminar is accompanied by a transcript[4] of the dialogue that occurred

---

by David L. Dungan, appears in the present volume; others are scheduled for subsequent publication.

[2]The seminar brings together New Testament scholars and church historians at their point of intersection, the second century. These ecumenical and interdisciplinary discussions have led to the founding of a journal, *The Second Century: A Journal of Early Christian Studies* (vol. 1, 1981).

[3]See William O. Walker, Jr., "Introduction," *The Relationships among the Gospels,* 1-15.

[4]The transcripts were made from audio tapes of each session. The tapes have been

A TIME FOR REAPPRAISAL AND FRESH APPROACHES

between major contributors and participants in the Colloquy. This material has been edited in order to give it some shape and clarity, but it retains for the most part the anacolutha, extemporaneity, and imprecision characteristic of scholarly give-and-take. Names of the participants can be identified in full from the description in the preface. The editorial decision to publish the transcripts was based on two factors: (1) the dialogues reveal the heart of the Colloquy—a viva voce on the written page; and (2) better than any later commentary, the dialogues indicate the reception given the papers.

A Tribute to John Knox

A happy circumstance of the Colloquy was its focus on the life and work of Professor John Knox. Many of the contributors and participants were students and are friends of Knox, and the Colloquy, coming as it did near the occasion of his eightieth birthday, also gave those of us in other church and academic traditions an opportunity to pay him honor. Early in the planning, E. P. Sanders was asked to deliver the keynote address with special reference to Knox's contributions and influence in the growth of North American scholarship. The highlight of the Colloquy was an evening dinner attended by one hundred fifty guests during which greetings were exchanged with Knox who delivered a warm response via telephone to the assembled Colloquy. The *tabula gratulatoria* that was signed and presented to the honoree has the following tribute:

In Grateful Appreciation to
JOHN KNOX
For Contributions to Biblical Scholarship
and for the Enrichment of Life and Faith
in Various Church Traditions
Our Warmest Regards and Prayers for You and Yours
on the Occasion of Your Eightieth Birthday

Although this volume is not a festschrift in the strict sense,[5] it does

---

retained by the editor, and copies are filed in the audio-visual library at Southwestern Seminary.

[5]Such a work is admirably done in *Christian History and Interpretation: Studies Presented to John Knox,* ed. W. R. Farmer, C. F. D. Moule, and R. R. Niebuhr (Cambridge: Cambridge University, 1967).

feature the writings of Knox—in particular, the issues raised for Pauline chronology in his *Chapters in a Life of Paul.* Professor Knox has kindly consented to enter the discussion once again by penning the concluding essay in the volume.

Reflections on the Theme

The theme chosen for the Colloquy was "A Time for Reappraisal and Fresh Approaches," an ambitious title that requires some explanation.[6] It represents the opinion that many questions of New Testament scholarship linger between eras; older syntheses have broken down and have ceased to be productive for a younger generation of scholars. New paradigms of research have opened in several areas. The topics selected for the seminars were broached with the intention to reappraise established opinions and explore fresh approaches. The relative success or failure of the endeavor in three specific areas can be assessed by reading the essays. Here it is appropriate to explore the more general question raised by the theme: Have the times changed?

If one is to pronounce a healthy verdict on the current state of New Testament studies, it must be entered with the caveat that disarray, revision, and fundamental dissent are signs of vitality (witness the survey in Sanders's address). Apart from new questionings of the "assured results" of critical orthodoxy, there is a basic ferment not soon to subside concerning the role of the historical-critical method. In his inaugural lecture at King's College, Graham Stanton gave this item urgent priority: "For I take one of the most important tasks facing biblical and theological scholarship today to be to clarify the role of the historical-critical method."[7] The past decade has seen a growing chorus of such voices ranging from fundamentalist alarm to professional disaffection.[8] A striking and crusading example is Walter Wink whose

---

[6]The summer 1980 issue of the *Perkins School of Theology Journal* (vol. 33) carries the same theme, and its contents relate to the interests of the Colloquy.

[7]Graham N. Stanton, "Interpreting the New Testament Today," inaugural lecture at King's College, London (14 November 1978) 4.

[8]In Germany, Gerhard Bergmann, *Alarm um die Bibel: Warum die Bibelkritik der modernen Theologie falsch ist,* 5th ed. (Wuppertal: Schriftenmission, 1974); and Gerhard Maier, *Das Ende der historischen-kritischen Methode,* 3rd ed. (Wuppertal: Rolf Brockhaus, 1975; ET, St. Louis: Concordia, 1977); see the response by Peter

disaffection is not open to doubt: the "historical-critical method has reduced the Bible to a dead letter. Our obeisance to technique has left the Bible sterile and ourselves empty."[9] Wink's charge of bankruptcy has ruffled the feathers of fellow scholars, but the complaint he offers is to be taken seriously. Similar concerns have been echoed by a considerable number of scholars within the guild. They insist that the limitations of the historical-critical method must be recognized and that the study of the New Testament is a "service which it is our vocation to perform for the faith-community rather than merely for our scholarly peers."[10] One-sided orientation to the past, analytical techniques that distance and objectify the text, and specialist isolation from the concerns of theology are features of method that must be revised.

What all this means for the future of critical research is difficult to say, but it does highlight a shift of direction and new possibilities of dialogue. A most valuable byproduct of the Colloquy was to engage scholars of radically different persuasions, conservative and liberal, confessional and secular, in discussion of common topics. That reappraisal is happening could have no better evidence than the gathering of mainstream critics at a conservative Baptist institution!

Stuhlmacher in the works cited below. In this country, Harold Lindsell, *The Bible in the Balance: A Further Look at the Battle for the Bible* (Grand Rapids: Zondervan, 1979).

[9]Walter Wink, *The Bible in Human Transformation: Toward a New Paradigm for Biblical Study* (Philadelphia: Fortress, 1973) 4.

[10]Reginald H. Fuller, "What Is Happening in New Testament Studies?" *SLJT* 23 (1980): 97. The analyses by Fuller (90-100) and Stanton ("Interpreting the New Testament Today," 6-17) are much the same. Add the contributions on proper method by Paul Ricoeur, "Du conflit à la convergence des méthodes en exégèse biblique," *Exégèse et herméneutique,* ed. X. Leon-Dufour (Paris: Seuil, 1971); idem, *Interpretation Theory: Discourse and the Surplus of Meaning* (Fort Worth: Texas Christian University, 1976); Ferdinand Hahn, "Probleme historischer Kritik," *ZNW* 63 (1972): 1-17; idem, "Exgese, Theologie und Kirche," *ZThK* 74 (1977): 25-37; Peter Stuhlmacher, *Historical Criticism and Theological Interpretation of Scripture,* trans. R. A. Harrisville (Philadelphia: Fortress, 1977); Martin Hengel, *Acts and the History of Earliest Christianity,* trans. John Bowden (Philadelphia: Fortress, 1979); James D. Smart, *The Past, Present, and Future of Biblical Theology* (Philadelphia: Westminster, 1979); Nicolas Lash, "What Might Martyrdom Mean?" *Suffering and Matyrdom* in the New Testament, ed. W. Horbury and B. McNeil (Cambridge: Cambridge University, 1981); and for a similar analysis but with a proposal of abandonment, Dennis E. Nineham, *The Use and Abuse of the Bible: A Study of the Bible in an Age of Rapid Cultural Change* (New York: Macmillan, 1976).

The Way Ahead

It will surely be asked from all sides why a conservative, denominational seminary like Southwestern would sponsor a colloquy given entirely to critical questions raised in the main by liberal scholars. The anwer is twofold. First, a commitment to academic excellence hears contrary opinion and assumes that truth has nothing to fear from proper critical inquiry. T. W. Manson once wrote of an important and controversial work: "We learn not least when we are forced to articulate why we disagree."[11] Only naiveté pronounces historical-critical study dead and gone; the history of the investigation of the New Testament teaches us that faulty ideas are never silenced, they are replaced by better ones. Rather than stand in the distance and rail against the excesses of criticism, it is the better part of academic responsibility, not to say Christian stewardship, to do constructive shaping of the discipline. The mood in the guild can be described as an open invitation to involvement.

> To be sure, the current call for a reexamination of method explicitly includes the reconsideration of basic presuppositions (e.g., the general conception of history, judgments of what in principle is possible, etc.). Indeed, the breadth and open-endedness of this "newest questioning" are among its most promising and inviting traits.[12]

If Ben Meyer is right (and much indicates that he is) in his observation of an openness to correction, then one would be foolish to wrap himself in the robes of indignation and walk away.

Second, productive, enduring scholarship is done in community. At one level this means the doing of New Testament study in the context of the church; at another, the bridging of differences among critical camps within the guild itself. The emergence of new coalitions that transgress party lines is a heartening development. On issues such as the Synoptic problem adherents to a particular hypothesis can no longer be predictably labeled with a certain theological outlook. In the making of new acquaintances across academic gulfs, the Colloquy furnished a definite sense of collegiality—a belonging that extends discussion, admits differences, and marks a fruitful way ahead. It is

---

[11]T. W. Manson, review of *The Theology of the New Testament*, by Rudolf Bultmann, in the *Manchester Guardian* (19 March 1956): 5.

[12]Ben F. Meyer, *The Aims of Jesus* (London: SCM, 1979) 54.

imperative that the possibility of convergence be probed in further dialogue, even if eventually the sides agree to differ.[13]

Few approaches are radically new, and reappraisal may simply confirm a previously held tenet. The experience of the Colloquy suggests very little in the way of revolutionary findings, rather a friendly shift toward openness and cooperation in research. And, after all, are we not in a better position to meet the horizon of the text if we can bridge the horizons of interpreters?[14] This volume is offered in the spirit of collegiality that was the hallmark of the Colloquy.

---

[13]The proposal made by Fuller ("What Is Happening in New Testament Studies?" 100) to pursue dialogue with conservative evangelicals gets a hearty second from one.

[14]Positive directions out of the malaise are detailed in the major studies of the hermeneutical crisis by Peter Stuhlmacher, *Vom Verstehen des Neuen Testaments: Eine Hermeneutik,* Grundisse zum Neuen Testament, vol. 6 (Göttingen: Vandenhoeck & Ruprecht, 1979); and Anthony C. Thiselton, *The Two Horizons: New Testament Hermeneutics and Philosophical Description with Special Reference to Heidegger, Bultmann, Gadamer, and Wittgenstein* (Grand Rapids: Eerdmans, 1980).

New Testament Studies Today

E. P. Sanders

I HAVE BEEN ASKED TO "discuss the present state of New Testament studies with primary focus on North American scholarship in the context of international studies"—and to do so in very short compass.[1] It is a challenging task, but a potentially rewarding one, since it

---

[1]This paper orginated as a thirty minute talk at the Colloquy on New Testament Studies, and the format and style have not been appreciably changed. A full review of New Testament studies would quickly become a large book, and the editor and I have agreed that the present purpose would be better served by preserving the original selectivity than by an expansion which would still leave many areas out of account. There are available several accounts of New Testament scholarship, of which I shall mention three which usefully serve different purposes: W. G. Kümmel, *The New Testament: The History of the Investigation of Its Problems*, ET, S. McLean Gilmour and Howard C. Kee (Nashville/London, 1972)—on which see W. R. Farmer, *PSTJ* 34 (1980): 41-48; Patrick Henry, *New Directions in New Testament Study* (Philadelphia/London, 1979); Klaus Haacker, *Neutestamentliche Wissenschaft: Eine Einführung in Fragestellungen und Methoden* (Wuppertal, 1981). The following footnotes will pay special attention to surveys of different aspects of New Testament studies.

The present essay does not refer at all to the Gospel of John although Johannine scholarship is vast and the questions intriguing. There are two good recent reviews of Johannine research: Robert Kysar, *The Fourth Evangelist and His Gospel: An Examination of Contemporary Scholarship* (Minneapolis, 1975); and Stephen Smalley, *John—Evangelist and Interpreter* (Exeter, 1978).

imposes selectivity rather than encouraging cataloguing.[2] I want to focus on a few aspects and then mention briefly one or two promising developments.

Jesus, as one would expect, is the most discussed figure in New Testament scholarship, and it is of utmost importance to see how New Testament scholars currently understand Jesus and what the future might hold. We get a lot of help, I think, from the man whose life and work are being honored in this volume—John Knox. Some of the principal points of Knox's writings on Jesus and Christology may be briefly recalled. The following sentence is perhaps one of the most famous which he ever wrote: "If we could not trust any of the sayings or any of the deeds, we could still trust the impression of the sayer and the doer, which the Gospels convey."[3] Knox was not actually as skeptical about historical knowledge as that sentence might indicate. He thought that several things could be known about Jesus, that literary study could uncover a modicum of facts about him,[4] and, further, that future research into first century Judaism could flesh out a reasonable picture of the historical figure.[5] His point, however, was that no amount of historical knowledge of the ordinary kind could convey the reality of the man, a reality conveyed by the impression which he made not only on the immediate disciples but on the subsequent church.[6]

Knox's interest was precisely in that impression, which he regarded as the revelatory power of Jesus in the life of the church:

> Must we not all acknowledge that the God who makes himself known to us, in whatever area of our experience, is the God whom we are able to recognize there only because we have seen him first in Christ? . . . Whether we affirm or deny, the meaning of "God" is the meaning

---

[2]The Society of Biblical Literature is currently engaged in preparing a series of volumes on North American contributions to biblical and related areas of research. I have seen drafts of some of the chapters, and the volumes promise to be very useful.

[3]John Knox, *Jesus: Lord and Christ* (New York, 1958), p. 115.

[4]Knox's book *The Death of Christ* (London, 1958)—see esp. pp. 37-41; 118-20—is a good example of his interest in assessing the historical reliability of the gospel material. It also reflects clearly his view that the burden of proof rests on those who assert the reliability of any given passage (see fn. 12 below) and, further, the limited value which he attaches to mere facts.

[5]Knox, *Jesus: Lord and Christ*, pp. 6-7.

[6]Ibid., p. 3.

which Christ has given to the name. But this testimony of our own experience to the uniquely creative character of this ancient event is confirmed by our observation of the life of the church.[7]

There are several points to be made about Knox's position, but I wish to raise only two.

1. Whether directly because of his influence or not, studies of Jesus are moving more and more away from being summaries of the few indisputable words and deeds which can be attributed to him.[8] This kind of literalist historicism is, I hope, fading more and more. The notion that faith can rest on a few *ipssisima verba*, or that historical information is adequately conveyed by summarizing a small selection of words and deeds, is regrettable, whether one writes, as Knox did, "for theology and church" or takes a more secular approach. We now see studies emerging, and more are in the works, which focus on Jesus' intention[9]—and it may be reasonably argued that one is dealing with true history when one can begin to grapple with human intentionality. Human intention must always be inferred, but that does not mean that solid inferences are impossible. One must look not only at words and deeds and the kind of knowledge about social, political and religious environment to which Knox alluded; but, as he also insisted, at results.

Let me take one concrete item. One of the most important facts about Jesus, though it does not often appear in books about his "teaching," is that he left behind a group of disciples which was persecuted by at least some in Judaism. I think that this simple fact, when viewed against the social and political climate of first-century Palestine, tells us rather a lot about Jesus, although I do not know of a single "authentic" saying of Jesus which would account for it. If this

---

[7]Ibid., p. 198.

[8]The tendency to describe Jesus by summarizing the most reliable passages has been so widespread that it hardly needs documentation. The most thoroughgoing effort was that of P. W. Schmiedel, "Gospels," *Encyclopaedia Biblica*, vol. 2 (London, 1901), cols. 1765-1896. He could find only five "absolutely credible passages."

[9]Among recent works which reflect confidence in scholarly ability to penetrate what Jesus intended to accomplish, one may cite C. H. Dodd, *The Founder of Christianity* (London, 1971); J. Jeremias, *New Testament Theology I: The Proclamation of Jesus*, ET (London, 1971); E. Schweizer, *Jesus*, ET (London, 1971); B. F. Meyer, *The Aims of Jesus* (London, 1979). See further G. Aulén, *Jesus in Contemporary Historical Research*, ET (London, 1976), pp. viii, 3; H. Schürmann, "Zur aktuellen Situation der Leben-Jesu-Forschung," *Geist und Leben* 46 (1973): 300-10.

fact does tell us about Jesus, it does so because we infer causes from results. That sort of inference is delicate, but not impossible. If Jesus left behind a group of disciples which was identifiable and subject to persecution, one may infer that he himself may have had something in mind besides preaching repentance and the reign of God—topics which, if persisted in by his followers—even if they added that he was Messiah—would not bring down persecution.

I realize that the kind of inference which I am discussing is not the same as that intended by Knox, but the view of how to begin to approach the significance of a historical figure seems to me to be closely analogous.

It is noteworthy that we know about the persecution of the Christian movement more certainly from the letters of Paul than from the Synoptics,[10] and this leads me to ask about the role of studying the Synoptics in learning about Jesus, and consequently about the state of synoptic research. This constitutes a rather lengthy digression in our discussion of Knox's position on Jesus.

As I understand it, Knox's position on the literary study of the Synoptics is that such research is important but that it matters less for understanding Jesus and his "character" than New Testament scholarship has been wont to assume. Whether he would say precisely that or not, I wonder if it might not be the case. Let me first, however, survey the present state of literary studies of the gospels. By "literary studies" I have in mind at this point the classical ones: tests for authenticity, source criticism, form criticism, and redaction criticism. (Other, more recent developments will be at least touched on below.)

In general, when one looks at the state of the classical literary disciplines, one sees either uncertainty or inattention. Several British scholars in particular have recently paid close attention to the question of tests for authenticity, and I think that methodologically the field has been refined.[11] The studies which I have in mind are not a return to the

---

[10]See, for example, Gal 1:13, 23; 5:11; 6:12; 1 Cor 15:9; Phil 3:6; Matt 10:23.

[11]See especially M. D. Hooker, "Christology and Methodology," *NTS* 17 (1970-1971): 480-87; "On Using the Wrong Tool," *Theology* 75 (1972): 570-81; R. S. Barbour, *Traditio-Historical Criticism of the Gospels* (London, 1972); D. G. A. Calvert, "An Examination of the Criteria for Distinguishing the Authentic Words of Jesus," *NTS* 18 (1971-1972): 209-19; David L. Mealand, "The Dissimilarity Test," *SJT* 31 (1978): 41-50.

minute calculation of possible Aramaisms in the hope that thereby the truth about Jesus will be revealed. We see, rather, a concern for determining the kind of consideration which should go into deciding questions of authenticity: which considerations count more than others. Perhaps most telling is Professor Morna Hooker's statement that the burden of proof should be considered equally balanced. One should be able to give an adequate account of any given pericope and show reason for attributing it either to Jesus or the church.[12] This assumes that such an account has not been given, and is thus virtually a call for re-doing form criticism.

The recent work on criteria for authenticity, then, while helpful methodologically, has as one of its immediate results increased uncertainty. The old assumptions about authenticity are being questioned. I agree with the questioning, and at times have joined in it. Naturally one hopes that sooner or later we shall have better criteria than we used to. But meanwhile we "know" less than we did when we could assume that Aramaisms, poetic structure, and purity of form established the authentic sayings of Jesus.

Source criticism, so intimately connected with the early "lives of Jesus," is in well-known disarray.[13] The classical two-document hypothesis, though defended by such a learned advocate as Neirynck,[14] has been found wanting by most scholars who have studied the problem afresh since Streeter's synthesis. Their names are legion. I have in mind in particular Parker,[15] Farrer,[16] Farmer,[17] Goulder,[18] Dungan,[19]

---

[12]Hooker, "Christology and Methodology," pp. 484-87. Cf. Knox, *The Death of Christ*, pp. 37-42. Knox is of the view that the burden of proof rests on those who assert the historical reliability of any given passage in the gospels.

[13]See recently Fritzleo Lentzen-Deis, S.J., "Entwicklungen in der synoptischen Frage?" *TP* 55 (1980): 559-70 (p. 570: "Die Zweiquellentheorie ist nun aber ganz sicher kein 'Dogma'. . . ."); M.-E. Boismard, "The Two-Source Theory at an Impasse," *NTS* 26 (1979): 1-17 (the Griesbach hypothesis explains features not accounted for by the two-source theory, but the reverse is also true. There is a need to combine the two theories by considering intermediate stages of redaction as well as the final); see further fns. 16 and 20 below.

[14]See for example F. Neirynck, *Duality in Mark: Contributions to the Study of the Markan Redaction* (Louvain, 1972).

[15]Pierson Parker, *The Gospel Before Mark* (1953).

[16]Austin M. Farrer, "On Dispensing with Q," *Studies in the Gospels: Essays in Memory of R. H. Lightfoot* (Oxford, 1955); cf. now Edward Hobbs, "A Quarter-

and Boismard.[20] The problem, of course, is that it is difficult to find agreement among this formidable array of dissenters. One may distinguish broad schools. The French school generally tends to solve problems by multiplying sources. Austin Farrer proposed doing away with one, Q; and his former student, Michael Goulder, would take this tendency further. He thinks that Matthew can be explained without appeal to any source other than Mark, and Luke explained without appeal to any source other than Mark and Matthew. W. R. Farmer is the leading proponent of the revived Griesbach hypothesis, that Mark used Matthew and that Luke used Matthew and Mark. Farmer is open to the possibility that the evangelists may have used sources, such as collections of parables.[21]

I am tempted to leave the discussion there, but since one of the interests of the colloquy from which this volume originates was the synoptic problem, I suppose that I should tell you where I stand: squarely on the fence. The one thing that my own studies have convinced me of is that there was no Q. I am not convinced that there were no sources, just that there was no Q as traditionally defined.[22] The principal arguments for it are not true and the defenses of it are circular, arbitrary, and consequently unconvincing. Thus, for example, the first argument for the existence of Q—that Matthew and Luke do not agree against Mark in any significant way in wording, or at all in order—is not true. The attempt to protect the hypothesis by saying that the most substantial agreements against Mark occur when there is a

---

Century without 'Q'," *PSTJ* 33 (1980): 10-19. Note p. 19: "There is no serenity in the field of the sources of the Gospels, there are no longer 'assured results of scholarship'."

[17]W. R. Farmer, *The Synoptic Problem* (New York, 1964); "The Synoptic Problem: The Inadequacies of the Generally Accepted Solution," *PSTJ* 33 (1980): 20-27.

[18]M. D. Goulder, *Midrash and Lection in Matthew* (London, 1974); "On Putting Q to the Test," *NTS* 24 (1978): 175-234; "Mark XVI.1-8 and Parallels," ibid., 235-40.

[19]David L. Dungan, "Mark—The Abridgement of Matthew and Luke," *Jesus and Man's Hope* I (Pittsburgh, 1970), pp. 51-97.

[20]P. Benoit and M.-E. Boismard, *Synopse des quatre évangiles en français avec parallèles des apocryphes et des pères*, 2 vols. (Paris, 1972); cf. fn. 13, above.

[21]See, for example, Farmer, "Notes on a Literary and Form-Critical Analysis of Some of the Synoptic Material Peculiar to Luke," *NTS* 8 (1962): 301-16.

[22]E. P. Sanders, "The Argument from Order and the Relationship between Matthew and Luke," *NTS* 15 (1969): 249-61; "The Overlaps of Mark and Q and the Synoptic Problem," *NTS* 19 (1973): 453-65.

Mark-Q overlap cannot stand close scrutiny. That line of defense is obviously circular, but, more telling, it is arbitrary. Internal analysis of the passages (for example the parable of the mustard seed, Mark 4.30-32 *et parr.*) does not reveal two different channels of transmission. One cannot avoid the suspicion that the parable is attributed to both Mark and Q in order to eliminate a substantial agreement between Matthew and Luke against Mark in both wording and order.[23]

With regard to other points I think that there are things to be said on various sides of the fence. (I here must envisage a multisided fence.) I think that Farmer (supported by Dungan and Longstaff) has the best of it with regard to the argument from order.[24] I am intrigued by how well Goulder can explain some of the pericopes in Matthew as expansions of Septuagintal motifs,[25] and I am sure that his line of investigation deserves further attention. I think that Boismard errs in positing a source for—it sometimes seems—almost every variation among the gospels, but many of his explanations of pericopes seem to me compelling.[26] His work, by the way, touches not only the source question, but also form criticism, and his explanations of individual pericopes often seem to me better than Bultmann's.

This leaves us in a state of uncertainty, and that really is not very surprising. It is generally easier to find flaws in one hypothesis than to make another one absolutely convincing to everybody. At any rate, I think that the synoptic problem must be regarded as open, and one may be confident that an open problem will continue to attract attention.

---

[23]It is instructive for understanding the present state of New Testament scholarship with regard to the synoptic problem that Professor Koester in this volume indicates that, in his view, the existence of Q is the surest result of research on the source question. [Editor's note: The reference is to the preliminary draft presented at the Colloquy; the published essay is more cautious with regard to Q.]

[24]B. C. Butler first put his finger on this weakness in the arguments for the two-source hypothesis: *The Originality of St. Matthew* (Cambridge, 1951), pp. 62-71; cf. Farmer, *The Synoptic Problem*, pp. 50, 289-93; Dungan (fn. 19, above); Thomas R. W. Longstaff, *Evidence of Conflation in Mark? A Study in the Synoptic Problem*, SBLDS 28 (Missoula, 1977); cf. my own essay above, fn. 22. For a sturdy defense of the traditional view, see F. Neirynck, "The Argument from Order and St. Luke's Transpositions," *ETL* 49 (1973): 784-815.

[25]I give some instances in my review of Goulder's *Midrash and Lection* in *JBL* 96 (1977): 453-55.

[26]For examples I cite again my own review in *JBL* 94 (1975): 128-32.

It will already have become clear that form criticism is in need of serious reexamination. This follows not only from the fact that such scholars as Hooker and Boismard are dissatisfied with Bultmann's assumptions and his disposition of pericopes, nor simply from the fact that, over the years, scholars working within a basically Bultmannian position have modified his work.[27] Uncertainty with regard to the synoptic problem requires the reassessment of classical form criticism, which rested on the two-source hypothesis. Further, as I have argued elsewhere, the judgments with regard to laws governing change in traditions upon which the form critics relied were not securely based.[28] I regard form criticism as a very important tool of synoptic research, but we need to learn to do form criticism in a state of uncertainty about the sequence of the gospels and without relying on such assumptions as that traditions became progressively more detailed or progressively less Aramaic.

The results of redaction criticism, which has traditionally rested on the two-source hypothesis and form criticism, are, then, by definition insecure. Thus you will understand why I suggested several years ago that synoptic criticism needs to be redone from top to bottom.[29]

Central to all the literary problems of the gospels is the question of how they were composed. The theory of "pearls on a string" is, as far as I know, no longer held, having been already discarded by redaction criticism. But, still, what were the limits of compositional activity? Do the pericopes in Matthew tell us more about the history of Matthew's church or more about an inventive author? To illustrate the problem I shall name two people who stand at opposite extremes: Boismard and Goulder. Boismard, we have seen, tends to posit sources to account for variations from gospel to gospel. Goulder is confident that variations can be accounted for by appealing to the compositional techniques of the later evangelists.[30] I do not know whether or not this problem can

---

[27]The most recent *Ergänzungsheft* to Bultmann's *Geschichte der synoptischen Tradition* (ed. Gerd Theissen and Philipp Vielhauer, 4th ed. [Göttingen, 1971]) readily shows how many modifications of detail have been proposed.

[28]E. P. Sanders, *The Tendencies of the Synoptic Tradition* (Cambridge, 1969).

[29]E. P. Sanders, "The Synoptic Problem: After Ten Years," *PSTJ* 28 (1975): 71.

[30]Most scholars, following the two-source theory, have viewed the evangelists as being responsible for minor changes but have posited sources to account for major differences among the gospels.

be solved, but it may be that progress can be made and that thus there is a potential "new" field of synoptic research: the limits of compositional activity, granted some use of sources.[31]

The question which interests me more, however, is what all this has to do with Jesus. It seems to me that the insights which we have seen can be gained from Knox's writings about Jesus relativize some of the literary problems of the gospels. I say "relativize," not "eliminate," with intent. My first paper as a graduate student was on Aramaisms, and I spent a few years working on source and form criticism. I find such studies of interest, and many doubtless shall continue to do so. But the burning interest in these topics declines when it is realized that they are not going to reveal the truth about Jesus. They have an important role, for they may *eliminate* some things as being information about Jesus, but they teach us less of a positive character. Source and form criticism do, of course, have the capacity to tell us rather a lot about the growth of the Christian tradition, and possibly about the nature of Christianity in different locales. But I think that the day is over when people could think that piously counting Aramaisms, or diligently seeking the earliest source, or fervently doing the history of individual pericopes, would tell us what we want to know about Jesus—his character and his intent. In some ways the late Norman Perrin was the last representative of this way of studying Jesus, and he gave it up in his later works.[32]

---

[31]H. St. John Thackeray (*Josephus: The Man and the Historian* [New York, 1929], ch. 5) made an inventive effort to determine to what extent Josephus and his Greek assistants rewrote his sources. His view has not been widely accepted (see R. J. H. *Shutt, Studies in Josephus* [London, 1961]), but critics interested in how ancient writers composed can still learn from it. Another classical study is that of Henry J. Cadbury on Luke (*The Style and Literary Method of Luke* [Cambridge, MA, 1920]; *The Making of Luke-Acts* [London, repr. 1958]). The redaction critics do not seem to have contributed much to the understanding of compositional technique, since they have been mostly interested in theological *Tendenz*. (Compare the criticisms of redaction criticism in Norman Petersen, *Literary Criticism for New Testament Critics* [Missoula, 1978], pp. 17-20). Goulder (above, fn. 18) is, as far as I know, the only recent scholar to attempt a complete explanation of the compositional technique of one of the evangelists.

[32]Contrast Perrin's early work (*The Kingdom of God in the Teaching of Jesus* [London, 1963]—a book heavily influenced by his teachers, T. W. Manson and Joachim Jeremias, and reflecting their interest in defining Jesus by compiling *ipssisima verba*) with one of his last (*Jesus and the Language of the Kingdom* [Philadelphia, 1976]).

In our discussion of the understanding of Jesus and what can be learned from Knox about how to understand him, we have engaged in a long, but I think necessary digression about the present state of synoptic studies. I wish now to return to the point that one way of getting at Jesus' character and intent is by studying his impact and the results of his ministry.

2. When John Knox made that point he had the inner history of Christianity in mind. He wrote, as I said, for the church, and his interest was Christ's revelatory power in the church. We now see emerging, especially in North America, a whole generation of scholars who do not have this interest as the focal point of their work.[33] They want to understand the Jesus movement and the Christian movement against their social and political background and as part of the religious development of the West. They have, in short, a secular interest in Jesus and the rise of Christianity. But it is of interest, as I previously indicated, that secular historians who are willing to infer causes from results can profit from some of the insights developed by Knox. I shall return to the question of the significance of the study of religion as a subject in the humanities and social sciences, rather than as theology, below.

If Jesus is the most important figure in New Testament studies, Paul runs a very close second. Here I shall be very brief. It has long been the case that the study of Paul was dominated by German Protestant scholars and their followers. The heart of Pauline theology has, consequently, been interpreted in terms of justification by faith, and that has been understood as a forensic or juridical declaration of the righteousness of believers. Hans Hübner has recently noted that this traditional interpretation, which he still holds to be the correct one, has received two serious challenges from North America, one from the American scholar Krister Stendahl and one from the Canadian scholar E. P. Sanders.[34] Apart from the scholars named by Hübner, it is clear that the Lutheran interpretation of Paul does not

---

[33]Some of these are discussed below, in the section which deals with the influence of recent literary criticism and of sociology on New Testament studies.

[34]H. Hübner, "Pauli Theologiae Proprium," *NTS* 26 (1980): 445-73; here pp. 445, 477. Hübner does note that Stendahl was originally a Swedish Lutheran.

have the dominating force that it once had, as any survey of literature on Paul will make clear.[35]

One of the things at stake in the debate about Paul is the understanding of Judaism. Part of the power of insisting that "justification by faith not by works" is the heart of Pauline thought is that thereby a contrast is provided with the religion which Christianity is supposed to have superceded—Judaism. Judaism, it has been thought, was based on a legalistic counting of merits over against trangressions, and Paul's statement "justification by faith" has been seen as the counter to "justification by one's own (legalistic) works." As you know, the challenge to this view of Judaism has also come from North America.[36] The more favorable view of Judaism will, I think, prevail; debates about how to interpret Paul will doubtless continue.[37]

Let me now draw some threads together. We have earlier noted that work about Jesus is being done in what I have called a secular context as well as in theological faculties. It is noteworthy that most of the challenges to the traditional Christian evaluation of Judaism in the first century have come from people who worked or are working outside theological faculties. Within the confines of a Christian theo-

---

[35]Thus, for example, George Howard, *Paul: Crisis in Galatia* (Cambridge, 1979) ("the key to his thinking is his understanding of the universality of the gospel," p. 76); J. Christiaan Beker, *Paul the Apostle: The Triumph of God in Life and Thought* (Philadelphia, 1980) (the triumph of God is the center of Paul's thought, p. 355); Karl Hoheisel, *Das antike Judentum in christlicher Sicht* (Wiesbaden, 1978) (it is Paul's central christological conviction which excludes the law, not the view that it leads to self-righteousness—which would be countered by justification understood as imputed; see pp. 182, 195 ["it is better to forget the Lutheran *Problematik*"], 200); cf. also Leander Keck, *Paul and His Letters* (Philadelphia, 1979), pp. 35, 117.

[36]The principal challenge to the denigrating view of Judaism came from George Foot Moore, "Christian Writers on Judaism," *HTR* 14 (1921): 197-254; *Judaism in the First Centuries of the Common Era: The Age of the Tannaim*, 3 vols. (Cambridge, MA, 1927-1930). Moore's challenge was at least partly successful in the English-speaking world. I renewed the challenge and reviewed the degree to which it was not effective in *Paul and Palestinian Judaism* (London/Philadelphia, 1977), esp. pp. 33-59. In this work I also try to put the contrast between Paul and Judaism on grounds other than "faith" versus "legalism"; see pp. 550-52. See now also, from the German side, Charlotte Klein, *Theologie und Anti-Judaismus* (Munich, 1975; ET, 1978); Hoheisel, *Das antike Judentum*, fn. 35 above. On the relationships among the three more recent books, see my review of Hoheisel in *JES* 17 (1980): 504-506.

[37]Thus Hübner (fn. 34 above), p. 448: he fears that the weight of my presentation of Judaism—a presentation which he does not wish to challenge—will attach itself to the section on Paul—which in his view it is the duty of Lutheran scholarship to refute.

logical faculty it is overwhelmingly tempting to explain Christianity— which is assumed to be true—by contrasting it with Judaism, the religion out of which it grew, and contrasting it in a way that, perhaps unintentionally, denigrates Judaism. The reasoning goes something like this: Christianity came from Judaism; Christianity is true; therefore it is superior to Judaism and Judaism in the time of Jesus and Paul was an inferior religion.

When the scene shifts, when one enters a department of religious studies which deals with different religions on their own terms or a faculty of humanities which assesses human culture generally, the standard Christian theological assessment of Judaism naturally changes. Christian triumphalism has a much harder time surviving in such an environment. I frankly doubt that the challenges to the view of Judaism as a religion of legalistic works-righteousness would have been expressed with such force if Judaism and Christianity continued to be studied only within the confines of theological seminaries. It is simply not normal or expected to give substantial time and attention to the understanding of another religious tradition within the context of seminary education.

I might add as an aside that perhaps it should be. Nothing would please me more—or do more for the furtherance of Christian-Jewish understanding—than to establish chairs of Judaica in Christian seminaries and positions in Christian studies in Jewish seminaries. I speak from some personal experience. In 1980 I was privileged to serve as part-time visiting professor at Jewish Theological Seminary in New York. It was the first time most of the students had actually met someone from the Christian tradition teaching Christian literature. I believe that numerous misunderstandings and some ingrained mistrust were dispelled—not because of my personal merits, but by the fact of the appointment and the face-to-face learning situation. I found this to be the case, please note, at JTS, which is across the street from Union Theological Seminary. Being across the street is not the same as being on the scene.

The reassessment of other religions, which is facilitated in settings outside theological seminaries, can also have repercussions within them. When it is no longer easy to explain the greatness of Jesus or Paul by saying that they opposed Jewish hypocrisy, legalism and casuistry, those whose vocation it is to interpret Christian theology for

the church will have to look harder at what is really important in the Christian tradition and will come, I do not doubt, to a more profound understanding of Jesus, Paul, and Christianity generally.

The topic of studying the New Testament outside the limits of traditional theological settings leads me to the last principal theme of the evening, the new applications of other disciplines to the study of the New Testament. It would be claiming too much to say that these applications spring entirely from the fact that the New Testament is now studied in secular settings, since the field has periodically been influenced by innovations which arose from other disciplines. Nevertheless there is a certain chronological congruity between taking the study of the New Testament outside the walls of the seminary and the new approaches to which I now refer.

These are of several kinds, and I can do no more than make one or two brief observations. I earlier said that numerous scholars are now trying to grapple with Jesus' intention and are willing to do so, at least in part, by inferring causes from results. We must realize, however, that many of our colleagues who do literary criticism would deny that the study of literary documents will reveal original intention. Now much literary theory is deliberately ahistorical. The aim is often to study the language or the structure of the text in order to determine what the text "wants" to say, apart from the author's intention and the understanding of the original audience.[38]

The openness of New Testament scholarship to new modes of literary analysis is to be applauded. Further, I agree that the study of texts will often not reveal intention. In seeking to find out what can be known about Jesus, as I have already indicated, I find it helpful to pay more attention to facts—the call of the disciples, their continued

---

[38]In "The Act of Reading the Bible" (a paper read at the Eighth World Congress of Jewish Studies and to be published in the proceedings of that Congress), my colleague Alan Cooper argues that modern forms of literary analysis should be deliberately ahistorical. Norman Petersen, on the other hand, in his very helpful book *Literary Criticism for New Testament Critics*, argues that literary criticism should be a necessary preliminary to historical analysis (for example, pp. 20-21). He is of the view that entirely ahistorical forms of literary analysis represent a stage through which scholars in other disciplines have already passed, and he urges biblical scholars to avoid that stage (pp. 24-25). Petersen's rich and clear discussion of modern forms of literary analysis is reliable and obviates the need here to discuss structuralism and other current modes of literary criticism.

existence as a group and their persecution—than to a literary analysis of the sayings.[39] But while structuralism and some other modes of literary analysis may not offer direct help when one asks historical questions, we can all learn from them. They show us new ways of reading a text, and they bring home to us the limits of old ways.[40] I doubt, however, that ahistorical forms of criticism will sweep the field. New Testament scholarship seems always to come back to historical problems after excursions into other questions, and this will almost certainly continue to be the case. The observation that Christianity is a historical religion is so common as to be trite, but it is nevertheless true; and that fact will continue to fix attention on history. What one hopes, of course, is that diverse modes of study can be followed in a complementary way, without the methodological imperialism that often mars not only our field but also many others.

I should like to say a little more about another new direction in biblical studies, the application of the viewpoint of the social historian to the New Testament. Max Weber pioneered the application of sociology to the study of religion, but modern interest in this approach seems to stem from John Gager's book, *Kingdom and Community: The Social World of Early Christianity* (Englewood Cliffs, 1975). This is an avenue that is now being explored by numerous scholars.[41] To name two, Gerd Theissen has published several studies which shed

---

[39]Thus I think that it is sometimes possible to bypass certain forms of literary analysis in investigating at least some historical problems; contrast Petersen's view in the preceding note.

The principal scholar who has focused on "facts" rather than sayings in studying Jesus is Morton Smith in *Jesus the Magician* (New York, 1978). The fact which is for him foremost is that Jesus was known as a wonder-worker. I am presently completing a book based more on facts than sayings, which is scheduled to appear in 1983 as *Jesus and Judaism*.

[40]For a critique of the old form of literary-historical work on the gospels, see Petersen, *Literary Criticism for New Testament Critics*, pp. 11-20.

[41]Bengt Holmberg in 1978 called sociology "a field of scholarship seldom used by New Testament scholars" (*Paul and Power* [Lund, 1978], p. 5). "Seldom" is a relative term. Certainly work which falls into the category which Holmberg calls "the history of ideas" still predominates. But work which is indebted in some way or other to sociology has proliferated sufficiently that it has led to two review articles: Jonathan Z. Smith, "The Social Description of Early Christianity," *RSR* 1 (1975): 19-25; Robin Scroggs, "The Sociological Interpretation of the New Testament: The Present State of Research," *NTS* 26 (1980): 164-79. There is also an up-to-date bibliography in John H.

light on the social situation both of Paul[42] and of Jesus,[43] and Abraham Malherbe has published a very helpful work entitled *Social Aspects of Early Christianity*. I am personally most helped by, and consequently attracted to this general area when the study consists in asking a new set of questions, reading the material through different spectacles, rather than in developing and attempting to apply elaborate categories derived from sociology.[44]

The historian may indeed raise a question about the validity of applying a model derived from the study of *modern* society directly to the ancient world. Christianity is sometimes depicted as a protest movement joined by would-be upwardly mobile people whose progress was frustrated by various causes, such as their ancestry or their lack of social rank. They experienced alienation from Greco-Roman society and were thus willing listeners to the message of a new order. It is not, however, clear to me that frustration, alienation and the search for new ideas went hand-in-hand in the ancient world. It is precisely the historical reality that needs investigation.

As an example of the method which I find more illuminating and suggestive—asking about social history, rather than applying sociological models—I wish to cite the work of Wayne Meeks. Citing his work in the context of this volume has an additional advantage: it is really new, not having yet been published. Meeks promises us a large study of the social world of Pauline Christianity, and he has already written a paper bearing that title for the series *Aufstieg und Niedergang der römischen Welt*, although it has not yet appeared. I base my

---

Elliott, *A Home for the Homeless: A Sociological Exegesis of 1 Peter, Its Situation and Strategy* (Philadelphia, 1981).

I find very helpful Holmberg's comments on how to relate sociological inquiry to history-of-ideas research (*Paul and Power*, pp. 204-208).

[42]For example, "Soziale Integration und sakramenteles Handeln. Eine Analyse von I Kor. 11, 17-34," *NovT* 16 (1974): 179-206.

[43]Especially *The First Followers of Jesus. A Sociological Analysis of Earliest Christianity* (ET: London, 1978). The title in the U.S. is *Sociology of Early Palestinian Christianity*.

[44]Cf. Robert M. Grant, "The Social Setting of Second-Century Christianity," *Jewish and Christian Self-Definition I: The Shaping of Christianity in the Second and Third Centuries*, ed. E. P. Sanders (London/Philadelphia, 1980), pp. 19-20. Grant briefly reviews the earlier "Chicago school" and offers a short criticism of the recent tendency to apply modern sociological generalizations to early Christian literature.

remarks on the latter. Page numbers is the text refer to manuscript pages.

"Social world" in Meeks' definition means two things: "the environment of the early Christian groups" and "the world as they perceive it and give form and significance to it through their special language and other meaningful actions." Thus it is both the " 'world' which they share with other people who live in the Roman empire" and "the 'world' which they have 'constructed' " (p. 1). Meeks makes use of general social histories of the world in which Paul and his companions lived and worked, but the basic technique is to study that world through the writings of Paul. The focus is not on what is peculiar to Paul; just the contrary: it is on what is common and presupposed (pp. 68, 78-79). Meeks talks about reading Paul the way a social scientist would, to find out about his society. He speaks from the point of view sometimes of sociology in general, sometimes of ethnography, sometimes of anthropology (pp. 65, 79).

It would be out of place here to try to summarize the range of questions and answers in Meeks's work. Let me instead take three topics which usually lead to an analysis of Paul's theology or thought and show what Meeks does with them.

The theme of suffering is bound up, Meeks notes, with Paul's "most fundamental theological and christological beliefs." He then observes that *socially* the theme functions "to enhance the attitude of goup solidarity by emphasizing dangers from without" (p. 38). Paul's discussion of boasting in 1 Corinthians, which again is theologically significant, is viewed as a conflict between types of authority, "local, 'charismatic' power" on the one hand and "trans-local, unitive governance" on the other (p. 49).

The topic of the circumcision of Gentile converts to Christianity is theologically loaded in Paul, being connected with his discussion of the Jewish law, his so-called doctrine of justification by faith and, again, his Christology. Meeks's comment on the question of circumcision in Galatians is this:

> By abandoning these rules [i.e., such as circumcision], the Pauline Christians also gave up one of the most effective ways by which the Jewish community maintained its identity over against the pagan society within which it lived. That was precisely the practical issue at dispute between Paul and his opponents in Galatia. Would the abolition of the symbolic boundaries between Jew and Gentile *within* the

sect mean also lowering the boundaries between the sect and the
world? (p. 41).

I have quoted the last example at some length because I want to
comment on it. I must confess that I still want to know what the
Galatians thought, what the other missionaries thought, and what
Paul thought. Did the parties to the dispute know that what was at
stake in the question over circumcision was a lowering of the boundaries between the Christian sect and the pagan world? I agree with Meeks
that that turned out to be at stake, as I agree with his comments
elsewhere that Pauline Christianity maintained a tension between
being strongly sectarian and being permeable vis-à-vis pagan society
(p. 64). But was "lowering the boundaries" a conscious concern?

Let me immediately say that it may well have been. One of Paul's
conscious motives in doing away with circumcision may have been to
make the Christian message more easily accessible to Gentiles. Let me
further grant, by way of repetition, that the fact that Christianity did
not keep all the Torah, but rather "lowered the boundaries," was of
enormous consequence. I simply want to make sure that we keep our
questions and answers straight. When someone says, "that was the
practical issue," I want to know whether the disputants knew it or
whether it now can be seen to be so, or whether the answer lies
somewhere in between—and if so, just where. Thus I must confess to
an irremediable interest in exegesis and thought. The argument in
Galatians, after all, is conducted largely in terms of God's will as
revealed in Scripture, Paul's opponents apparently taking the view that
God required circumcision for admission to membership in his people,
Paul countering that the case of Abraham proves otherwise. How can
we be sure that "lowering the boundaries" was actually the issue which
was at stake? Was anyone consciously interested in a "practical issue"
at all?

As I said at the outset, I was asked to give attention to the role of
North American scholarship in the context of international studies. I
think it is obvious that it has a large role, and in particular that the
innovations in approach which I have mentioned, as well as many
which have gone unmentioned, find fecund soil in North America. I
shall continue to worry a little bit about the traditional weakness in
North American education, a solid grounding in languages and in
history. Let me make it clear that I am now referring to a general

situation, and certainly not to the work of scholars named thus far. My worry is that methodological innovation may make it even easier to escape the drudgery of the classical disciplines. What I have called the traditional North American weakness is exacerbated by a development which has brought New Testament studies new insights—the growth of departments of religious studies. Departments of religious studies have played a substantial role in the destruction of the study of foreign languages in North American universities. Language requirements have been dropped in most universities with which I am acquainted, and religious studies departments have all too willingly pretended that religion can be studied entirely in English. This is, to quote Jacob Neusner, "the propagation of the notion that we can understand what is alien without learning the language of the alien."[45] It is thus now possible for an undergraduate student to major in religion and to do several courses in New Testament with straight A's, and then to seek admission to graduate school, without ever learning a word of Greek— much less the several other languages that serious study requires. Here it is the seminaries which have been more responsible toward the discipline and the students.

If one were to wish for utopia, one would wish that the broad questions and the contact with other disciplines which are facilitated in a university context would be combined with the traditional strengths of seminary education. If that can be done—and it may well be possible—innovation can be built on a solid foundation of learning and escape faddishness. We shall penetrate more deeply the origins of Christianity and understand better its role in Western culture, thought and society.

---

[45]Jacob Neusner, "Stranger at Home: The Task of Religious Studies," Inaugural Lecture of the Department of Religious Studies, Arizona State University (Tempe, AR, 1979), p. 7. In this lecture, as well as in several other papers, Neusner offers valuable reflections on the role of religious studies in secular settings. See, for example, "Defining the Humanities: Clearing Away Some Debris," *Federation of Public Programs in the Humanities* (Minneapolis, 1979), pp. 15-24.

PART TWO

SEMINAR ON THE SYNOPTIC PROBLEM

INTRODUCTION

William R. Farmer, Moderator

T HE WORK OF THIS SEMINAR on the Synoptic Problem, featuring a major paper by Helmut Koester and a major response by David Peabody, taken together with the paper by David Dungan and the responses by Bruce Corley and John Elliott, constitutes a highwater mark for collegiality in Gospel studies in North America.

Prior to the seminar, Helmut Koester had worked out a theory by which he was able to give a reasonable account for all known forms of the Gospels from what he designates as the "Gospel of Mark," written ca. 70 A.D., but no longer extant, up to Marcion. The Gospel of Mark as it has been canonized in the church comes last in the series, just before Marcion. The literary evidence that led Helmut Koester to the view that the Gospel of Luke was composed before canonical Mark bears careful consideration. The original invitation to Koester was for him to present a paper setting forth the evidence. Koester's counteroffer was to present that part of his overall theory concerning the history and development of one particular gospel, namely, Mark. The acceptance of this counteroffer has entailed a postponement of a presentation of Koester's work on Luke and Mark which occasioned the original invitation.

Koester's explanation of the history and development of Mark's Gospel is clearly set forth in the opening paper. The response by

Peabody is equally clear. Both Koester and Peabody were given an opportunity to modify their contributions for publication. Koester made some changes. Peabody made none. This explains why, at a few points, Peabody is responding to statements by Koester which do not stand in the revised version of Koester's paper. Similarly the transcript of the discussion of Koester's paper presupposes the form in which that paper was originally presented.

David Dungan's paper "The Purpose and Provenance of the Gospel of Mark According to the 'Two Gospel' (Griesbach) Hypothesis" was originally prepared for the Cambridge Griesbach Conference, held at Pembroke College, Cambridge, England, August 1979. It appears here in the same form in which it was presented for discussion at Fort Worth. The response by John Elliott has been revised for publication as is indicated in the editorial notes at the beginning and close of his main contribution to the discussion.

By common agreement between Dungan and Elliott, Dungan will revise the published form of his paper for the volume which will contain the papers from the Cambridge Griesbach Conference in the light of Elliott's revised response to Dungan's paper presented for discussion in Fort Worth. In this way this important discussion will continue, and should be followed with interest.

Koester's opening comment in the discussion of his paper warrants the effort required to organize the seminar and publish its results: "It is better these days to write a paper for a conference like this than to publish something, because whatever you publish, nobody reads anyway."

It is unlikely that nobody will read what Koester has published in this volume. But it is certainly the case that if anyone does read carefully what is published on the synoptic problem in this volume, that person will be far better instructed than were he or she to read either Koester's or Dungan's papers without benefit of any of the evidence of lively debate these original contributions evoked, evidenced in the prepared responses and the transcripts of the discussions.

Scholarship is a living reality. First, the individual mind must do its work. But then, the ideas that are formed by original research and reflection are tested in the open forum of scholarly debate.

In the history of the synoptic problem, the colloquy in Fort Worth in November 1980 will stand out as a model for scholarly discussion.

Careful and imaginative work was responsibly considered. Let the reader be the judge of the value of the proceedings.

HISTORY AND DEVELOPMENT OF MARK'S GOSPEL
(From Mark to *Secret Mark* and "Canonical" Mark)*

Helmut Koester

T HIS STUDY PRESUPPOSES THE TWO-SOURCE hypothesis, namely, that Matthew and Luke used the Gospel of Mark and a second common source, the so-called synoptic sayings source ("Q"). It is not my intention to question or to defend this hypothesis. I am aware of the repeated doubts which have been raised with respect to the existence of "Q."[1] But the more recent discoveries of gospels based on collections of sayings of Jesus such as *The Gospel of Thomas, The Dialogue of the Saviour,* and *The Apocryphon of James*[2] may give new evidence for the hypothesis that a rich and diversified production of sayings literature constituted the matrix for the composition of this source of the Gospels of Matthew and Luke. However, I want to discuss the problem

---

*I am indebted to the detailed evaluation of my arguments presented by David Peabody at the conference at Southwestern Baptist Theological Seminary in Fort Worth, Texas, on 5 November 1980, and I gratefully acknowledge the valuable suggestions which I received from Prof. Morton Smith in a letter of 10 October 1980.

[1]Austin M. Farrer, "On Dispensing with 'Q'," in *Studies in the Gospels: Essays in Memory of R. H. Lightfoot,* ed. by Dennis E. Nineham (Oxford: Blackwell, 1955), pp. 55-86; Edward C. Hobbs, "A Quarter-Century without 'Q'," *PSTJ* 33 (1980): 10-19.

[2]English translation in James M. Robinson (ed.), *The Nag Hammadi Library in English* (New York: Harper & Row, 1977).

of the Gospel of Mark, once the pillar of the two-source hypothesis, now seen by some as a secondary excerpt from Matthew (and Luke).[3] Though such criticisms do not, in my opinion, invalidate the two-source hypothesis, they reveal a major weakness of the assumption of Markan priority: the text of the Gospel of Mark, as it is preserved in all ancient manuscripts, cannot have been identical with the text used by Matthew and Luke. Even Heinrich Julius Holtzmann, the classical advocate of the two-source hypothesis, assumed that Matthew and Luke used an earlier version of Mark.[4] Ur-Marcus hypotheses have been offered several times,[5] but none has found widespread acceptance.[6] To be sure, ad hoc explanations for the several agreements of Matthew with Luke against Mark can be proposed. But such a procedure does not offer an explanation for the problem of Mark as a whole which has been made more enigmatic through the recent discovery of a *Secret Gospel of Mark* (which will be further discussed below). It seems that even a new Ur-Marcus hypothesis will not illuminate the problem of Mark, nor will the assumption of Matthean priority. Rather, a solution may be sought in analogy to more recent studies of the Gospel of John which have recognized several stages of rewriting in

---

[3]Most recently Hans Herbert Stoldt, *Geschichte und Kritik der Markus-Hypothese* (Göttingen: Vandenhoeck & Ruprecht, 1977; ET: Macon, GA: Mercer University Press, 1980).

[4]Heinrich Julius Holtzmann, *Die synoptischen Evangelien: Ihr Ursprung und ihr geschichtlicher Charakter* (Leipzig, 1863). He later abandoned this Ur-Marcus hypothesis, cf. idem, *Lehrbuch der historisch-kritischen Einleitung in das Neue Testament*, 3rd ed. (Freiburg: Mohr, 1892), pp. 342-61.

[5]One of the more radical Ur-Marcus hypotheses was proposed by Emil Wendling, *Die Entstehung des Marcus-Evangeliums* (Tübingen: Mohr/Siebeck, 1908).

[6]For a brief survey and critique, cf. Werner Georg Kümmel, *Introduction to the New Testament* (Nashville: Abingdon, 1975), pp. 60-63. On the other hand, G. Bornkamm ("Evangelien, synoptische," *RGG*, 3rd ed. [1958]: 756) states that "Mark had a history even before it was utilized by Matthew and Luke," and that the Gospel of Mark used by Matthew and Luke was hardly identical in all details with the text of the second Gospel of the canon of the New Testament. A new version of the Ur-Marcus hypothesis was proposed by Etienne Trocmé, *La formation de l'Évangile selon Marc*, EtHPR 57 (Paris: Presses Universitaires, 1963); but Trocmé bases his hypothesis upon a comparison of Mk 14-16 with the Lukan passion narrative and concludes that the original Gospel of Mark is only preserved in Mk 1-13, and he does not believe that a comparison with Matthew would yield any arguments for an establishment of a more primitive version of Mark. I did not have access to M. Karnetzki, "Die letzte Redaktion des Markusevangeliums," *Zwischenstation* (München, 1963), pp. 161-74.

the text of this Gospel, thus testifying to the instability of such texts as they were used by early Christian communities.[7]

I

The external evidence for Mark's Gospel is weaker than that for the other canonical Gospels. Whereas Matthew and Luke are used and quoted repeatedly by the middle of the second century (Polycarp of Smyrna, *2 Clement*,[8] Justin Martyr,[9] Ptolemy's letter to Flora), there is no certain quotation from Mark before Irenaeus and Clement of Alexandria. Papias of Hierapolis[10] (ca. 100-150) mentions the existence of a gospel written by Mark; but the extant fragments of Papias' work do not contain any quotations from this gospel. Early gospel manuscripts, admittedly all from Egypt, do not give any attestations of Mark's most original text.[11] Papyri from the second century A.D. contain texts from the Gospels of Matthew (P 64 and 67), John (P 52, 66), and Thomas (Ox. Pap. 1). From the third century come six manuscripts with the text of John (P 5, 9, 22, 28, 39, 80), four with the text of Matthew (P 1, 53, 70, 77), and two with the text of Luke (P 4, 69). The earliest papyrus with the text of more than one single Gospel, P 75, contains Luke and John. But Mark appears for the first time in the mid-third-century in P 45 which contains the text of all four canonical Gospels.

The manuscript tradition reveals the lack of stability of the Markan text. The oldest extant manuscripts conclude with Mk 16:8 (P 45, ℵ, B); Eusebius and Jerome attest that most or all of the Greek manuscripts known to them did not contain anything after Mk 16:8. The longer ending of Mark (16:9-20), copied in most later manuscripts, though obviously secondary, is nevertheless old and must have circu-

---

[7]Raymond E. Brown, *The Community of the Beloved Disciple* (New York: Paulist Press, 1979); Ernst Haenchen, *Johannes-Evangelium* (Tübingen: Mohr/Siebeck, 1980).

[8]Cf. Helmut Koester, *Synoptische Überlieferung bei den Apostolischen Vätern*, TU 65 (Berlin: Akademie-Verlag, 1957), pp. 62-123.

[9]A. J. Bellinzoni, *The Sayings of Jesus in the Writings of Justin Martyr*, NovTSup 17 (Leiden: Brill, 1967).

[10]In Eusebius, *Hist. eccl.* 3.39.14-15.

[11]For a survey of attestations of Gospels in early papyri, cf. Helmut Koester, "Apocryphal and Canonical Gospels," *HTR* 73 (1980): 107-10.

lated as early as in the second century, because Tatian and Irenaeus knew it and it also appears in part of the older Syriac (sy^c) and Latin tradition. The secondary expansion of this longer ending in Mk 16:14, the so-called "Freer-Logion," is presented by Codex W, one of the oldest Gospel codices from the fourth (or fifth) century.

One major section of Mark's Gospel, although appearing in all extant manuscripts, has been seen as a later expansion: Mk 6:45-8:26. Matthew reproduces, with one exception (Mk 8:22-26), all parts of this section of Mark in the same context and in the same sequence (Matt 14:22-16:12). But Luke gives the impression that he did not read this section in his copy of Mark.[12] Rather, Lk 9:19 = Mk 8:27 follows directly upon Lk 9:17 = Mk 6:44. It is, of course, not impossible that Luke's copy of Mark had accidentally lost a few pages.[13] However, exactly this section of Mark contains a number of doublets to pericopes appearing elsewhere in Mark: Mk 6:45-54 (the walking on the water) is a variant of Mk 4:35-41 (the stilling of the tempest); Mk 8:1-10 (the feeding of the four thousand) is obviously a secondary elaboration of Mk 6:34-44 (the feeding of the five thousand); Mk 8:22-26 is one of two stories of a healing of a blind man in this Gospel (cf. Mk 10:46-52).[14] There are other unusual features in this section: Mk 7:32-36 and 8:22-26 are the only two miracle stories in the Synoptic Gospels in which the healing is accomplished through elaborate manipulations, a feature which is otherwise frequent in Hellenistic miracle healings whereas the Synoptic Gospels elsewhere only report healing through Jesus' word, gesture, or touching with the hand. In addition, Mk 7:34 is one of two Synoptic passages which report a magic word in Aramaic (ἐφφαθά). The other passage is Mk 5:41 (ταλιθὰ κοῦμ); Matt 9:25 and Luke 8:54 in their parallel versions of the raising of Jairus's daughter do not reproduce this magic formula (nor does Matt 15:29-31 in his

---

[12]Heinz Schürmann has tried to demonstrate that other parts of the Gospel of Luke prove that Luke knew this section of Mark and deleted it deliberately (*Traditionsgeschichtliche Untersuchungen zu den synoptischen Evangelien* [Düsseldorf: Patmos, 1968], p. 114, fn. 9).

[13]Most recently this was argued again by Ernst Haenchen, *Der Weg Jesu* (Berlin: Töpelmann, 1966), pp. 303-304.

[14]Haenchen (*Weg Jesu*, p. 283) shows that Mk 6:33-7:37 and 8:1-26 are two parallel compositions. This would indeed comprise the whole Markan section which is missing in Luke, except for Mk 6:33-44 (the feeding of the five thousand).

parallel to Mk 7:34). Also in its general vocabulary, Mk 6:45-8:26 contains some peculiar features. For example, the term συνίημι ("to understand") occurs four times in this section (Mk 6:52; 7:14; 8:17; 8:21) but elsewhere in Mark only once (4:12) in an allusion to Isa 6:9-10. The synonymous term νοεῖν is found twice here (Mk 7:18; 8:17), elsewhere only in Mk 13:14, the adjective ἀσύνετος ("without insight") only in Mk 7:18. It is important to note that in all these instances we are dealing with passages which are clearly redactorial. One other peculiarlity should be mentioned: The section begins and ends with the mention of Bethsaida (Mk 6:45; 8:22), a place which does not occur anywhere else in Mark.

It would be premature to draw any conclusions with respect to the more original text of Mark. But one can say with confidence that at an early date (no later than the middle of the second century) there was a version of Mark with a secondary ending containing a story of Jesus' appearance before the disciples after his resurrection, another version which ended with Mk 16:8. It seems equally probable that by the time Matthew and Luke wrote their Gospels, there was one version of Mark which included Mk 6:45-8:26 and another which did not, and it is not unreasonable to state that the former exhibits some features which are normally considered as secondary.[15]

II

There are a number of sentences or small pericopes in Mark which have no parallels in Matthew and Luke. I will discuss some of these which seem significant.

It is commonly assumed that in the apophthegma Mk 2:23-28, the original saying was: "The sabbath was made for people, and not people for the sabbath" (Mk 2:27). The second saying, "Thus the Son of Man is lord over the sabbath" (Mk 2:28) would be a secondary addition, whether or not it was once an independent saying.[16] However,

---

[15]It is not suprising to find in this section redactional features which are typically "Markan," e.g., εὐθύς; καὶ ἔλεγεν αὐτοῖς, πάλιν. Also the additions of *Secret Mark* to Mark are typical for Markan redaction. Note that stylistic and redactorial features typical of John's Gospel are insufficient arguments for the distinction between earlier draft, revision, and redaction in that Gospel.

[16]Rudolf Bultmann, *History of the Synoptic Tradition* (New York: Harper, 1963), pp. 16-17; Haenchen, *Weg Jesu*, p. 121.

Matthew and Luke reproduce only this second saying (Matt 12:8; Lk 6:5). It seems that one should reverse the traditional opinion: Mk 2:28, "The son of man (= every human being) is master over the sabbath," was the original nucleus of this apophthegma; Mk 2:27 was added at a later time: Matthew and Luke did not read it in their copy of Mark.[17]

The parable of the seed growing secretly (Mk 4:26-29) is missing in both Matthew and Luke.[18] It has been assumed that Matthew replaced it by the parable of the tares (Matt 13:24-30). But Matthew expanded Mark's parable chapter anyway (cf. Matt 13:33, 44-46, 47-50, 51-52), and parables about the sowing and harvesting were readily available.[19] Since also Luke does not reproduce Mk 4:26-29, it is better to assume that it is a later addition to the Markan text. The *Gospel of Thomas* (21) demonstrates that this parable was in circulation in independent collections of sayings and parables of Jesus.

In Mark, the pericope about the great commandment (Mk 12:28-31 = Matt 22:34-40 = Lk 10:25-28) has an appendix, Mk 12:32-34, of which there is no trace in the other two Synoptic Gospels. In a brilliant analysis, Günther Bornkamm[20] has demonstrated that this appendix about the scribe "who is not far from the kingdom of God" is an addition to Mark's Gospel which was written from the perspective of Hellenistic propaganda and employs a terminology which is distinctly different from the vocabulary of the Second Gospel. The scribe acknowledges that Jesus "in truth" (ἐπ' ἀληθείας) puts first the confession of Hellenistic Jewish propaganda that "God is One" (cf. *Hermas Mand.* 1.1); perhaps also Mk 12:29, the quote of the "Hear Israel" (Deut 6:4), which is missing in Matt 22:37 and Lk 10:26-27, is a latter insertion into the Markan text. In the repetition of the command to

---

[17]It is usually argued that the saying "The sabbath was made for people, and not people for the sabbath," was too bold for the later understanding of the church and thus deleted by Matthew and Luke. However, the criticism of the sabbath as, e.g., expressed in Col 2:16; Ign. *Magn.* 9.1; *Barn.* 15 could suggest the opposite conclusion.

[18]Philipp Vielhauer (*Geschichte der urchristlichen Literatur* [Berlin: De Gruyter, 1975], pp. 273-75) considers this Markan parable the most important, if not the only, support for an Ur-Marcus hypothesis.

[19]Cf. the new Jesus-parables in the *Apocryphon of James* (CG 1.2) 7, 22-35; 8, 16-27; 12, 20-30.

[20]"Das Doppelgebot der Liebe," in *Neutestamentliche Studien für Rudolf Bultmann*, BZNW 21 (Berlin: Töpelmann, 1954), pp. 85-93.

love God (Mk 12:33=Deut 6:5), "out of your whole understanding" (ἐξ ὅλης τῆς συνέσεως) is added[21] and the love of one's neighbor is contrasted with "burnt offerings and sacrifices" —a typical common-place of the propaganda of Jews and Christians in the Hellenistic world. Jesus admits that the scribe has answered "with understanding" (νουνεχῶς Mk 12:34; this term occurs nowhere else in the NT).

III

What has been observed so far points to a remarkable instability of the text of this gospel. In several instances, redactors have expanded its text. Another, and indeed remarkable, redactorial expansion is the story of the raising of a youth which Clement of Alexandria found after Mk 10:34 in the *Secret Gospel of Mark*.[22] The story closely parallels that of the raising of Lazarus (John 11). However, it is an older version of the same miracle story: The language is Markan,[23] with no traces of Johannine vocabulary; personal names (Lazarus, Mary, Martha) are missing; there is no delay motif as in Jn 11:3-6; no discourse of Jesus interrupts the narrative.

Peculiar is the continuation of the account in the *Secret Gospel*: the youth who was raised invites Jesus into his house, and after six days he comes to Jesus, "wearing a linen cloth over his naked body. And he remained with him that night, for Jesus taught him the mystery of the kingdom of God." Morton Smith has argued that this is the report of a mystery initiation, most likely baptism.[24]

Clement of Alexandria reports a second and similar addition to Mark's text in the *Secret Gospel* after Mk 10:46a ("And they came into

---

[21]Cf. above, the frequent appearance of the verb συνίημι in the section Mk 6:45-8:26.

[22]Morton Smith, *Clement of Alexandria and a Secret Gospel of Mark* (Cambridge, MA: Harvard University Press, 1973); text and translation pp. 445-51. My quotations are indebted to this edition.

[23]Smith (*Clement*, pp. 97-122) has given a detailed analysis of the stylistic features of the text of *Secret Mark* and compared its vocabulary to that of the four canonical Gospels (pp. 122-44). He comes to the conclusion that its style and vocabulary, insofar as it is not made up of words used by all evangelists, is predominantly Markan, contains mostly Markan grammatical peculiarities, and is connected with "Mk by 6 major parallels, of which 4 are peculiar to Mk" (p. 144; cf. the summary of conclusions on pp. 144-66).

[24]Smith, *Clement*, pp. 195-278.

Jericho"): "And the sister of the youth whom Jesus loved and his mother and Salome were there, and Jesus did not receive them." In the text of canonical Mark, 10:46 is odd, since upon "And they came into Jericho" follows immediately "and when he came out of Jericho." Nothing is said about the stay in Jericho.[25] Matt 20:29 brings only the latter remark; Lk 18:35 says: "When he was approaching Jericho." Thus, it is possible that neither of them read the first remark of Mk 10:46a in their text of Mark,[26] in other words, "And they came into Jericho" is the remnant of a report of an encounter in Jericho, that is, the meeting with the youth and his mother Salome preserved in the *Secret Gospel of Mark*.[27] Neither Matthew nor Luke read this report in their copy of Mark. If Mark was expanded at this point, probably also the name of the blind man, Bartimaeus son of Timaeus, must be assigned to the same redactor.

There was yet another version of the *Secret Gospel of Mark* which, according to Clement of Alexandria, was used by the gnostic sect of the Carpocratians. Clement reveals that it had some similarity with the *Secret Mark* used in the church of Alexandria; yet he gives but one example of the contamination found in their text ("naked man with naked man"). It is evident, however, that both the *Secret Gospel* of the Alexandrian church and that of the Carpocratians were editions of the second Gospel of the New Testament.

IV

It has been observed repeatedly that the text of the canonical Gospel of Mark contains numerous phrases and terms which differ from both Matthew and Luke, even in sections in which they are obviously dependent upon Mark. In the following I will discuss some selected instances of these Markan peculiarities.

---

[25]Mk 11:11-12 (". . . when it was late, he went to Bethany with the Twelve. And on the next morning, when they went forth from Bethany. . . .") is not analogous, because it implies that Jesus spent the night in Bethany.

[26]Luke's redactorial framework seems to be independent of Mark anyway, since he wants to locate two encounters here, the healing of the blind man "when he was approaching Jericho" (Lk 18:35), and the Zacchaeus episode "when he entered and went through Jericho" (Lk 19:10). To explain Mk 10:46 as a combination of Matt 20:29 and Lk 18:35 would suggest that the author of Mark was incredibly clumsy in the use of his sources.

[27]Smith, *Clement*, pp. 193-94.

1. Εὐαγγέλιον. The relationship between Matthew and Mark in the use of the term εὐαγγέλιον is very peculiar.[28] Only twice is εὐαγγέλιον used in the same passage in Matthew and Mark: Mk 13:10 δεῖ κηρυχθῆναι τὸ εὐαγγέλιον = Matt 24:14 κηρυχθήσεται τοῦτο τὸ εὐαγγέλιον τῆς βασιλείας. Mk 13:10 is very awkwardly placed between the persecution logia 13:9 and 13:11-12, whereas Matt 24:14, the announcement of the preaching of the gospel in the whole world, quite naturally concludes the sayings about the tribulations of the last days. Is Mk 13:10 a secondary intrusion from the text of Matthew?[29] Mk 14:9 = Matt 26:13, the second common occurrence, was either a secondary expansion of the story of the anointing in Bethany which Mark found in his source, or it was added by Mark in order to establish a relationship to the passion narrative.

Matthew has added the phrase καὶ κηρύσσων τὸ εὐαγγέλιον τῆς βασιλείας to a Markan summary statement (Mk 1:39; 6:6) in two instances (Matt 4:23; 9:35). On the other hand, none of the other occurrences of εὐαγγέλιον in the canonical text of Mark are paralleled in Matthew. Since Matthew begins his gospel with the birth narratives of Jesus, one would, of course, not expect Mk 1:1 (ἀρχὴ τοῦ εὐαγγελίου) to appear in Matthew. But in four other Markan passages Matthew might have picked up the term had he read it in his copy of Mark:

Mark		Matthew	
1:15a	κηρύσσων τὸ εὐαγγέλιον τοῦ θεοῦ	4:17a	ἤρξατο κηρύσσειν
1:15b	καὶ πιστεύετε ἐν τῷ εὐαγγελίῳ	4:17b	_____
8:35	ἕνεκεν ἐμοῦ καὶ τοῦ εὐαγγελίου	16:25	ἕνεκεν ἐμοῦ
10:29	ἕνεκεν ἐμοῦ καί ἕνεκεν τοῦ εὐαγγελίου	19:29	ἕνεκεν τοῦ ἐμοῦ ὀνόματος

---

[28]As is well known, the noun εὐαγγέλιον never occurs in Luke's Gospel. This makes it very difficult to determine whether the term occurred in Mark's most original text.

[29]In Matthew's reproduction of the persecution logia of Mk 13:9-12 in Matt 10:17-21 there is no trace of Mk 13:10.

In the latter two instances the Markan phrase is clearly a secondary expansion of an older saying. Matthew seems to indicate that this expansion was introduced only at a later stage of the development of Mark's text.[30] It may be true that all occurrences of εὐαγγέλιον in Mark belong to the same category of theological understanding of this term.[31] But also Mk 16:15 reflects the same usage, though it certainly does not stem from the hand of the same author!

2. διδάσκειν, *διδαχή.* Matthew's and Luke's parallels show that they have read the terms διδάσκειν and διδαχή in the following Markan passages: Mk 1:21, 22; 6:2, 6; (7:7); 11:18; 12:14; 14:49. But there are occurrences of these terms in Mark where the other two Synoptic Gospels do not reflect such usage in their corresponding passages.

Mk 1:27. The witnesses react to the driving out of an unclean spirit (1:23-26) by saying διδαχὴ καινὴ κατ' ἐξουσίαν. The astonishment about Jesus' "teaching with authority" had already found adequate expression at the beginning of this pericope in Mk 1:22 = Matt 7:28-29; Lk 4:22). Moreover, διδαχὴ καινή appears only once more in the New Testament: Acts 17:19 as a request for Paul's teaching (to which Paul responds with the "Areopagus Speech"): τίς ἡ καινὴ αὕτη ἡ ὑπὸ σοῦ λαλουμένη διδαχή; as the listeners attest afterwards, the content of the new teaching is "the resurrection from the dead" (Acts 19:32). Elsewhere in early Christian literature, διδαχὴ καινή is attested only in the Gospel fragment P. Oxy. 1224, 2 v. col. I: π[ο]ίαν σέ [φασιν διδα] χὴν καιν [ὴν διδάσκειν ἢ τί β] ά [πτισμ] α καινὸν [κηρύσσειν; . . .].[32] If the reconstruction is correct, the question asked by Jesus' opponents proves that "new teaching" and "new baptism" are closely related to each other.

Mk 2:13 is a redactional remark about Jesus' teaching "by the sea." It is entirely gratuitous between the story of the healing of the paralytic

---

[30]Lk 9:24 agrees with Matt 16:25 in his reproduction of Mk. 8:35. Lk 18:29 (= Mk 10:29) has ἕνεκεν τῆς βασιλείας τοῦ θεοῦ.

[31]On the usage and understanding of this term in Mark cf. Willi Marxsen, *Der Evangelist Markus,* FRLANT 67 (Göttingen: Vandenhoeck & Ruprecht, 1956), pp. 83-92; Manfred Karnetzki ("Die galiläische Redaktion in Markusevangelium," *ZNW* 52 [1961]: 265) assigns Mk 1:1; 1:14-15; 8:35 and 10:29 to the last redactor of Mark.

[32]Erich Klostermann, *Apocrypha II: Evangelien,* KlT 8, 3rd ed. (Berlin: De Gruyter, 1929), p. 26.

(Mk 2:1-12) and the account of the call of Levi (Mk 2:14). Both pericopes appear in Matthew and Luke; but there is no parallel to Mk 2:13.

Mk 4:1-2 again introduces Jesus as "teaching by the sea" (ἤρξατο διδάσκειν παρὰ τὴν θάλασσαν, Matt 13:1: ἐκάθητο, Lk 8:4 eliminates the sea altogether), emphasizes that Jesus "taught" (ἐδίδασκεν, Matt ἐλάλησεν, Lk εἶπεν) in parables, and adds the phrase καὶ ἔλεγεν αὐτοῖς ἐν τῇ διδαχῇ αὐτοῦ (no parallel in Matt and Lk).[33] A later redactor obviously had an interest in emphasizing that parables are "teaching" in a special sense. (On the relationship of parable teaching and "mystery" see below.)

While the Twelve are sent out in Mk 6:7 with "power over the unclean spirits," they return in Mk 6:30 announcing "all they had done and what they had taught" (. . . καὶ ὅσα ἐδίδαξαν); a corresponding reference is missing in Matthew and Luke (Lk 9:10 only has ὅσα ἐποίησαν). In the following introduction to the story of the feeding of the five thousand, *Mk 6:34b* says: καὶ ἤρξατο διδάσκειν αὐτοὺς πολλά. Matt 14:14 only reports that Jesus healed the sick; Lk 9:11 contains a similar remark and refers to Jesus "speaking (ἐλάλει) about the kingdom of God." The agreement between Matthew and Luke against Mark confirms that Mark's original text is not preserved. Why did a later redactor replace the remark about Jesus' healing with a reference to his teaching without any indication of the specific content? And why does such a remark about instruction precede the account of the feeding of the five thousand? Possibly this account was understood as a report of a sacramental meal and the redactor therefore inserted a remark about the proper instruction of the participants.

Mk 8:31 and 9:31 introduce the first and second prediction of the passion by (ἤρξατο) διδάσκειν and ἐδίδασκεν respectively (Matthew and Luke use δεικνύειν, εἰπεῖν). This characterizes these predictions in a special way. What is meant becomes clear when one considers two other redactorial changes. Matthew and Luke agree in their formulation καὶ τῇ τρίτῃ ἡμέρᾳ ἐγερθῆναι (Matt 16:21 = Lk 9:22). Thus, this seems to have been the Markan text they read. However, in the preserved text of Mk 8:31 one reads καὶ μετὰ τρεῖς ἡμέρας ἀναστῆναι.

---

[33]The phrase καὶ ἐν τῇ διδαχῇ αὐτοῦ ἔλεγεν also occurs in Mk 12:38. Matt 23:1 and Lk 20:45 use different formulations.

In the second and third prediction of the passion, Mark has καὶ μετά τρεῖς ἡμέρας ἀναστήσεται (Mk 9:31; 10:34) while Matt 17:23 and 20:19 have ἐγερθήσεται (Lk 9:44 has no parallel to Mk 9:31b, but Lk 18:34 corresponds with ἀναστήσεται to Mk 10:34, although it agrees with Matt 20:19 in the formulation τῇ τρίτῃ ἡμέρᾳ). At least in Mk 8:31 and 9:31 the change to ἀναστῆναι and ἀναστήσεται seems to be as deliberate as the characterization of these predictions as "teaching." It is hardly possible that "after three days" was the original reading of these predictions in Mark, because Mk 15:42 and 16:1 clearly state the resurrection "on the third day."[34] One finds the same redactorial hand in Mk 8:32a: καὶ παρρησίᾳ τὸν λόγον ἐλάλει, which does not occur in the corresponding passages of Matthew and Luke.[35] Mk 8:32a is indeed the only passage of the Synoptic Gospels which uses the term παρρησία. But one must compare Jn 16:29 (ἴδε νῦν ἐν παρρησίᾳ λαλεῖς καὶ παροιμίαν οὐδεμίαν λέγεις) and Jn 18:20 where the speaking in παρρησία is contrasted with the speaking ἐν κρυπτῷ.

Four further references to Jesus' teaching which occur only in Mark are explicitly related to the presence of the crowd: Mk 10:1; 11:17; 12:35, 37-38. In the first of these passages, Matthew's parallel passage (19:2) speaks about Jesus' healing activity: a Lukan parallel to Mk 10:1-12 is missing. In two other passages Matthean and Lukan parallels use λέγειν and εἰπεῖν instead of Mark's διδάσκειν. The reference to Jesus' διδαχή in Mk 12:38 has no parallels in Matt 23:1 and Lk 20:45.

The verb διδάσκειν is also used in the *Secret Gospel of Mark* III, 10: ἐδίδασκε γὰρ αὐτὸν ὁ᾽Ιησοῦς τὸ μυστήριον τῆς βασιλείας τοῦ θεοῦ. Morton Smith, who favors a baptismal interpretation of the nocturnal meeting of Jesus with the youth, had originally suggested that

---

[34]Smith (*Clement*, pp. 163-64) points out that "after three days" actually means "on the fourth day" and that there is an interesting parallel in Jn 11:17 and 39, i.e., in the Johannine parallel to the story of the raising of the young man in *Secret Mark*: Lazarus was raised on the fourth day in the tomb.

[35]The phrase ἐλάλει αὐτοῖς τὸν λόγον also appears in Mk 2:2 and 4:33; as in Mk 8:32, Matthew and Luke do not indicate that they read this phrase in their text. Both may have tried to avoid the absolute use of the term λόγος. But this could have been accomplished by the addition of a genitive, cf. Mk 4:14 τὸν λόγον, Matt 13:19 τὸν λόγον τῆς βασιλείας, Lk 8:11 ὁ λόγος τοῦ θεοῦ.

ἐδίδασκε is a corruption of ἔδωκεν,[36] a word which is also used in Mk 4:11 in connection with μυστήριον. He also assumes that, when baptism "declined in prestige," "there was a corresponding growth of secret teachings," a "development reflected by Matthean and Lukan emendations of canonical Mark."[37] In order to consider this problem, another Markan peculiarity must be discussed, that is, the use of the term "mystery."ⱽ

3. **μυστήριον.** According to the best textual witnesses, *Mk 4:11* reads: ὑμῖν τὸ μυστήριον δέδοται τῆς βασιλείας τοῦ θεοῦ. However, Mt 13:11 and Lk 8:10 agree in inserting γνῶναι and reading the plural μυστήρια: ὑμῖν δέδοται γνῶναι τὰ μυστήρια τῆς βασιλείας τῶν οὐρανῶν (Matt; τοῦ θεοῦ Lk). If Matthew and Luke drew their parable chapters (Matthew 13; Luke 8) from Mark 4, it is highly unlikely that both would make the same changes independently. Moreover, Matthew 13 and Luke 8 are otherwise clearly dependent upon Mark 4, and they frequently exhibit secondary alterations of the Markan text. The agreement of Lk 8:10 and Matt 13:11 cannot be explained by the assumption of Lukan dependence upon Matthew.

Joachim Jeremias has demonstrated that Mk 4:11-12 is an older saying of Jesus which was originally independent.[38] He points to the antithetical parallelism of ὑμῖν δέδοται τὸ μυστήριον and τοῖς ἔξω ἐν παραβολαῖς τὰ πάντα γίνεται. Therefore, παραβολή must be understood as "riddle," "mysterious saying." This is persuasive.[39] However, Jeremias fails to explain why Mk 4:11 uses the singular μυστήριον as antithesis to the plural ἐν παραβολαῖς, and δέδοται without γνῶναι remains awkward, if the saying speaks of the disciples' ability to understand the mysterious meaning of parables; cf. Mk 4:34: τοῖς μαθηταῖς ἐπέλυεν πάντα. All these problems are solved if one assumes that ὑμῖν δέδοται γνῶναι τὰ μυστήρια of Matt 13:11 and Lk 8:10 was also the original text of Mk 4:11.

---

[36]Smith, *Clement*, 183. But he has now withdrawn this suggestion, cf. Morton Smith, *Jesus the Magician* (New York: Harper & Row, 1978), p. 207, fn. on Mk 4:11 ff.

[37]Smith, *Clement*, pp. 183-84.

[38]Joachim Jeremias, *The Parables of Jesus*, 2nd ed. (New York: Scribner's, 1972), pp. 13-18.

[39]If Mk 4:11a and 11b are thus two antithetical parts of one saying, Matthew's insertion of another saying (Matt 13:12 = Mk 4:25) after Mk 4:11a = Matt 13:11 is clear evidence of a secondary redaction.

This hypothesis can be defended through reference to the *Gospel of Thomas* 62: "It is to those who are worthy of my mysteries that I tell my mysteries." This saying, cited as an independent unit, introduces a series of parables (*Gos. Thom.* 63, 64, 65) and uses the plural "mysteries." It is the only occurrence of the term in the *Gospel of Thomas*, as Mk 4:11 (and parallels) is the only occurrence of this term in the Synoptic Gospels. The close relationship of the saying about the "mysteries," that is, the secret words of Jesus, to the transmission of the parables is obvious in both instances. It is a very old usage. That can be demonstrated in a comparison with Paul's use of the term; it occurs either in the plural (κἂν . . . εἰδῶ τὰ μυστήρια πάντα 1 Cor 13:2; cf. 1 Cor 4:1; 14:2) or refers, in the singular, to an individual saying (for example, Rom 11:25; 1 Cor 15:51).

Jeremias assumes that the saying of Mk 4:11 was originally unrelated to the parables, but rather referred to the whole preaching of Jesus, that is, the "gospel." That is wholly untenable. On the contrary, the use of the singular μυστήριον, especially as a synonym to εὐαγγέλιον, belongs to a later period. Such understanding is most clearly documented in the deutero-Pauline Epistle to the Ephesians. The sentence ἐν παρρησίᾳ γνωρίσαι τὸ μυστήριον τοῦ εὐαγγελίου (Eph 6:19) summarizes the theological position of the Markan redactor who changed the older saying of Mk 4:11 into the present text. He knows only *one* mystery. From Eph 6:19 (cf. 3:1-7) it is clear that "mystery" and "gospel" are either identical or closely related. The redactor of Mk 4:11 is most likely the same person who also introduced into the Gospel of Mark the term "gospel" as designation of Jesus' whole message or story.

What is the relationship of this redaction of Mk 4:11 to ἐδίδασκε αὐτόν . . . τὸ μυστήριον τῆς βασιλείας in the *Secret Gospel*? Morton Smith shows that baptism was widely understood as the mystery of the kingdom of God.[40] The close relationship between "mystery" and "gospel" and "baptism" is indeed obvious in Ephesians: γνωρίσας τὸ μυστήριον, ἀκούσαντες . . . τὸ εὐαγγέλιον, and πιστεύσαντες ἐσφραγίσθητε are described as steps of initiation in Eph 1:9-13. This seems to be the "mystery of the kingdom" for the disciples" in Mk 4:11 as well as the "mystery of the kingdom" into which the youth is

---

[40]Smith, *Clement*, pp. 195ff. and passim.

initiated in the *Secret Gospel* III 10. We have observed several instances in Mark where the redactor has introduced διδάσκειν as designating special instruction related to the message of the resurrection as well as to instruction in preparation for the receiving of the "sacrament."[41]

4. βάπτισμα. The *Secret Gospel* does not expressly use this term. But in Mk 10:38b/39b, Jesus speaks of the disciples' "baptism in the same baptism in which I am baptized" (τὸ βάπτισμα ὃ ἐγὼ βαπτίζομαι βαπτισθῆναι). The sentence is parallel to "drinking the chalice which I drink" (πιεῖν τὸ ποτήριον ὃ ἐγὼ πίνω 10:38a/39a). This is generally taken as a reference to martyrdom, understood as an analogy to the death Jesus has to suffer.[42] However, the reference to the "chalice" would have sufficed. Indeed, Matt 20:22-23, in his reproduction of Mk 10:38-39, speaks of the chalice only and makes no reference to baptism. Although baptism was understood very early as participating symbolically in the death and resurrection of Jesus (Rom 6:1ff.), the interpretation of martyrdom as baptism appears only in later Christian literature.[43] It is much better to recognize the two sentences in Mk 10:38/39 referring to baptism as an interpolation which reinterprets the whole passage: it is no longer a reference to Jesus' death and martyrdom, but a "homiletic reference" to the Christian sacraments, eucharist and baptism, as Morton Smith[44] correctly notes. It must be remembered also that this Markan passage (Mk 10:35ff.) follows immediately upon the story of the raising of the youth and his initiation into the mystery of the kingdom (= baptism) which *Secret Mark* reported between Mk 10:34 and 10:35.

V

The last observation leads directly to the question of the more intimate ties of the *Secret Gospel of Mark* and its resurrection/initia-

---

[41]I agree with Morton Smith (*Clement*, p. 180) that "μυστήριον to mean 'secret' " can at the same time mean "secret process." This, however, is in agreement with deutero-Pauline and later Christian usage, but is not reflected in the genuine Pauline letters.

[42]For example, Haenchen, *Weg Jesu*, pp. 363-64. The parallels cited for this interpretation demonstrate that the drinking of the chalice is a much more widespread metaphor for suffering death; cf. Haenchen, p. 364, fn. 2.

[43]Cf. Hans von Campenhausen, *Die Idee des Martyriums in der alten Kirche*, 2nd ed. (Göttingen: Vandenhoeck & Ruprecht, 1953), pp. 60-61.

[44]Smith, *Clement*, pp. 186-87.

tion account to the redaction of the Gospel of Mark. Apparently, the redactor has not only introduced certain terms and concepts into Mark's Gospel as a whole, but has also established explicit links of the story of the *Secret Gospel* with the Markan narrative.

1. The Epileptic Child.[45] The exorcism of the epileptic child appears in all three Synoptic Gospels after the transfiguration story: Matt 17:14-21 = Mk 9:14-29 = Lk 9:38-43a. Mark's story is more than twice as long as the reproductions in Matthew and Luke. Matthew regularly abbreviates Mark's miracle stories. But in this case, Luke reproduces the same parts of Mk 9:14-29 which Matthew used in his abbreviated version. Mk 9:14b-16, 21, 22b-24, parts of 25-27 and 28 do not appear in either Matthew or Luke. Thus, the version now recorded in Mark seems to be the result of secondary expansion of a shorter account which Matthew and Luke read in their copies of Mark.

In Mk 9:14-16 several features are clearly secondary. No explanation has been found yet for the "scribes" whom Jesus, coming down from the mountain of the transfiguration, finds debating with his disciples (v. 14). Noteworthy is the description of the reaction of the crowd to Jesus' arrival: ἰδόντες αὐτὸν ἐξεθαμβήθησαν, καὶ προστρέχοντες ἠσπάζοντο αὐτόν. The verb ἐκθαμβεῖσθαι is used in the New Testament only by Mark; in addition to Mk 9:15, it appears in the Gethsemane pericope (Mk 14:33) and in the story of the finding of the empty tomb where it describes the reaction of the women to the νεανίσκος, dressed in a white robe (Mk 16:5; cf. 16:6). Mark also uses the simplex θαμβεῖσθαι several times: in the description of the reaction of the people to the exorcism in the synagogue (1:27), in the appendix to the story of the rich man (10:24), and in the introduction to the third prediction of the passion (10:32; on these two passages see below). Luke seems to have read this word in Mk 1:27, since he says in his parallel passage (Lk 4:36): καὶ ἐγένετο θάμβος ἐπὶ πάντας. The term appears once more in Luke when he describes Peter's reaction to the miraculous draught of fishes (Lk 5:9). Otherwise, there are no parallels in Matthew and Luke to Mark's use of these terms. Both θαμβεῖσθαι and the intensive form ἐκθαμβεῖσθαι describe the amazement which

---

[45] This miracle story has caused much bewilderment among scholars and has led to numerous attempts to explain its composition and redaction. For a detailed discussion cf. Ludger Schenke, *Die Wundererzählungen des Markusevangeliums*, Stuttgarter Biblische Beiträge (Stuttgart: Katholisches Bibelwerk, 1974), pp. 314-49.

befalls people in view of an extraordinary event, especially appearances of a god or some supernatural phenomenon. In the Hellenistic period, it was used frequently in the context of magic,[46] so that Plutarch could describe θάμβος as a typical result of superstition.[47]

The discussion of Jesus with the father of the epileptic boy, Mk 9:20-24, may have been part of the original story. It is, in any case, a feature that is germane to the miracle story since it stresses the severity of the disease. Matt 17:15b seems to reflect knowledge of these verses.

Deliberate alterations of a more original Markan text appear in Mk 9:25-27. Matt 17:18 and Lk 9:42b show that their common source only reported that Jesus exorcised the unclean spirit (ἐπετίμησεν κτλ.), that the child was healed (Matt ἐθεραπεύθη, Lk ἰάσατο), and perhaps a reaction of the crowd (only Lk 9:43). But the preserved text of Mark quotes the full wording of an exorcism: τὸ ἄλαλον καὶ κωφὸν πνεῦμα, ἐγὼ ἐπιτάσσω σοι, ἔξελθε ἐξ αὐτοῦ καὶ μηκέτι εἰσέλθῃς εἰς αὐτόν. This is the longest exorcistic formula fully reported in the Synoptic Gospels (Mk 1:41; 2:11; 3:5; 10:52; Lk 8:54; 13:12 and 17:14 merely report briefer commands). Surprisingly it is an exorcism for a deaf-mute person, not for an epileptic. Mk 9:17 has been changed accordingly (ἔχοντα πνεῦμα ἄλαλον), although the original description of the disease is still visible in Mk 9:18, 20, 22. The redactor, eager to demonstrate Jesus' supernatural powers, inserted a formula of exorcism which does not quite fit the occasion. Nevertheless, it is described as having been very effective. The redactor's hand is unmistakable (no parallels in Matthew and Luke): the demon departs with appropriate demonstration, the boy is left "as if dead" (ὡσεὶ νεκρός), and the bystanders say "he died" (ἀπέθανεν). Corresponding to this description is the subsequent resuscitation: Jesus takes him by the hand (κρατήσας τῆς χειρός), raises him, and he rises (ἤγειρεν αὐτόν, καὶ ἀνέστη). The vocabulary of this passage is peculiar: it is identical with death/resurrection terminology and it reappears almost verbatim in the story of the raising of the youth in the *Secret Gospel*: . . . ἀπέθανεν, . . . ἤγειρεν αὐτόν, κρατήσας τῆς χειρός (II, 24; III, 4). It also recalls the terminology in which Jesus' death and resurrection is described (cf. Mk 8:31, etc.).

---

[46]G. Bertram, "θάμβος etc.," *TDNT* 3:4-7.

[47]Bertram, ibid., p. 4.

Characteristic magical terminology appears once more in the secondary Markan redaction of the conclusion: Jesus says that "this kind cannot be exorcised unless it is done with prayer and fasting (ἐν προσευχῇ καὶ νηστείᾳ Mk 9:29).[48] Prayer is a typical practice of the magician's discipline.

2. The Third Prediction of the Passion. The second prediction of the passion (Mk 9:30-32) follows immediately upon the story of the epileptic child. In the revision of Mark preserved in the *Secret Gospel*, the third prediction of the passion (Mk 10:32-34) precedes the story of the raising of the youth, that is, in the *Secret Gospel* two "resurrection" stories are closely associated with these two predictions.

The third prediction of the passion is introduced by a description of Jesus' appearance to the disciples and followers (Mk 10:32) which is not paralleled in Matthew's and Luke's reproduction of this prediction (Matt 20:17-19; Lk 18:31-34): as Jesus goes before them "they are amazed" (ἐθαμβοῦντο) and those who follow "are taken by fear" (ἐφοβοῦντο). In the context of canonical Mark, this makes no sense. But in the context of *Secret Mark*, these words are very interesting. In the introduction to the story of the epileptic boy, which the redactor transformed into a resurrection story, he had inserted a reference to the amazement of the people at Jesus' arrival (ἐξεθαμβήθησαν, Mk 9:15). The reference to the amazement in the third prediction of the passion (ἐθαμβοῦντο) serves as introduction to a second resurrection story, the raising of the youth in the *Secret Gospel of Mark*. This suggests that the redactor of Mk 9:14-29 is identical with the redactor of the third prediction of the passion and with the person who inserted the story of the raising of the youth which is contained in *Secret Mark*.

3. The Rich Man Whom Jesus Loved. In the canonical Gospel of Mark, the third prediction of the passion (Mk 10:32-34) follows upon the so-called story of the "Rich Young Man" (Mk 10:17-31; the Lukan sequence is the same; Matt 20:1-9 inserts the parable of the laborers in the vineyard). On the whole, the Matthean and Lukan parallels show little divergence from the Markan text. But Mark has two peculiarities which do not appear in the other two Synoptic Gospels.

The first is a remark which introduces Jesus' final answer to the rich man: ὁ δὲ ᾽Ιησοῦς ἐμβλέψας αὐτῷ ἠγάπησεν αὐτόν (Mk 10:21). Such

---

[48]καὶ νηστείᾳ appears only in a part of the manuscript tradition, including P 45, the oldest manuscript with the text of Mark.

a remark appears nowhere else in the Synoptic Gospels,[49] but the *Secret Gospel of Mark* says of the youth who was raised by Jesus: ὁ δὲ νεανίσκος ἐμβλέψας αὐτῷ ἠγάπησεν αὐτόν (III, 4); and in the insertion into Mk 10:46 the *Secret Gospel* says: καὶ ἦσαν ἐκεῖ ἡ ἀδελφὴ τοῦ νεανίσκου ὃν ἠγάπα αὐτὸν ὁ' Ἰησοῦς (III, 15). This remark must have been a traditional part of the story of the raising of the youth, because its variant in John 11 repeatedly alludes to this relationship of love: "He whom you love (ὃν φιλεῖς) is sick" (Jn 11:3); "Jesus loved (ἠγάπα) Martha and her sister and Lazarus" (Jn 11:5); "the Jews said (of Jesus): behold, how did he love (ἐφίλει) him!" (Jn 11:36). To be sure, this theme is greatly elaborated in the Gospel of John. But it seems to have been part of an older form of the story as it is preserved by the *Secret Gospel of Mark*. How did such a remark get into the canonical Markan story of the rich young man? Most likely, the same redactor who inserted the story of the raising of the youth also interpolated the remark in Mk 10:21 in order to establish a connection between these two stories. But this assumption does not solve all riddles. Only Matt 19:20, 22 calls the rich man a νεανίσκος. It is exactly this term that the *Secret Gospel* uses to describe the man who was raised from the dead (III.3, 4, 6, 8). Mark does not use this term in 10:17, 31.[50] Furthermore, only Luke says of the rich man ἦν γὰρ πλούσιος σφόδρα (18:23), whereas Mk 10:22 and Matt 19:22 state: ἦν γὰρ ἔχων χρήματα πολλά. But the *"Secret Gospel"* reports of the "youth" whom Jesus raised: ἦν γὰρ πλούσιος (III.6). Whatever the answer to this problem, the remark in Mk 10:21 is best explained as a *"Secret Gospel* redaction."

A number of sayings have been attached to the story of the rich man (Mk 10:23-31), and most of these are reproduced by Matthew (19:23-30) and Luke (18:24-30). What is missing in Matthew and in Luke is the disciples' reaction to the first saying about the difficulty of wealthy people to enter the kingdom of God and the repetition of Jesus' statement (Mk 10:24): "The disciples are amazed" (ἐθαμβοῦντο!) and Jesus restates what he has said, however with a slight alteration: τέκνα, πῶς δύσκωλόν ἐστιν εἰς τὴν βασιλείαν τοῦ θεοῦ εἰσελθεῖν. The possession of wealth is no longer mentioned as an obstacle, that is,

---

[49]Cf., on the use of this term, Smith, *Clement*, pp. 119-20.

[50]Lk 7:14 calls the widow's son whom Jesus raised a νεανίσκος.

Jesus now states that it is difficult to enter the kingdom, plain and simple. Why did a redactor make this addition? Apparently it was the same redactor who also added the story about the man who had to experience death and resurrection in order to be ready for the "mystery of the kingdom of God."

4. The Youth Who Fled Naked. There is at least one more trace of the *Secret Gospel* redaction in the canonical Gospel of Mark: Mk 14:51-52. When Jesus is arrested in Gethsemane, all (the disciples) flee (14:50), but a youth (νεανίσκος) who is following Jesus "wearing a linen cloth over his naked body" (περιβεβλημένος σινδόνα ἐπὶ γυμνοῦ) is grabbed by the armed men, but lets go of his linen cloth and flees naked. The *Secret Gospel* reports that the youth whom Jesus had raised (ὁ νεανίσκος) came to Jesus after six days "wearing a linen cloth over his naked body" (περιβεβλημένος σινδόνα ἐπὶ γυμνοῦ). Exegetes have been puzzling over this incident reported in Mk 14:51-52, and have even suggested that it may be part of an old historical report.[51] But there is no trace of it in either Matthew or Luke, that is, it was missing in their copy of Mark. The scene at Gethsemane, with Jesus being "amazed" (θαμβεῖσθαι) and distressed, may have attracted the redactor to introduce the youth once more—who had been initiated into the mystery of the kingdom and now flees shamefully.

VI

The conclusion must be tentative and can be brief.

The Gospel of Mark which was written ca. 70 A.D. is no longer extant. Its text cannot be reconstructed on the basis of the manuscripts of canonical Mark, nor will Ur-Marcus hypotheses help to reconstitute the original text. But various witnesses testify to the history of the development of this gospel until it finally emerged in the form which became the basis of the manuscript tradition of this canonical writing. At least five different stages in this development can be identified:

(1a) *Proto-Mark*: In this form it was used by the author of the Gospel of Luke. This is probably the oldest stage which can be fixed with some certainty, though it is quite likely that it was preceded by one or several written sources, at least in part translated from Aramaic. Comprising many of the Markan miracle stories and the passion

---

[51]Bultmann, *History*, p. 269; Haenchen, *Weg Jesu*, pp. 502-503.

narrative, this source or these sources constitute the common *Vorlage* for both Proto-Mark and the first draft of the Gospel of John.

(1b) An expanded variant of Proto-Mark which had incorporated a new miracle catena in Mk 6:45-8:26. This expanded version was used by Matthew. It is not impossible that this copy of Mark preceded the shorter version used by Luke; in this case Luke would have used a defective copy.

(2) A thorough revision of Proto-Mark which is known as the *Gospel of Matthew*. It preserves the basic framework and outline of Mark, but establishes five major speeches of Jesus with materials drawn from Mark and especially from the synoptic sayings source as the major structural element; most of the miracle stories were assembled in a special section (Matt 8-9).

(3) In a different way Proto-Mark was revised by the author of the *Gospel of Luke*. Luke followed Mark's outline quite faithfully in the first and third part of his work (Lk 4-9 and 18-24), but made the second part, the so-called travel narrative (Lk 9:51-18:14) the primary repository for materials drawn from the synoptic sayings source and from a special source.

(4a) Whereas Matthew and Luke fundamentally altered the character of Proto-Mark and thus, in fact, created new gospels, the further development of Proto-Mark which resulted ultimately in canonical Mark was more conservative and preserved the original outline more or less intact. Also the style and language of Proto-Mark was maintained. One would, therefore, assign this development to the "Markan community." There is one stage of revision which can be more clearly identified: The *Secret Gospel of Mark*. The story of the raising of a youth from the dead and his subsequent initiation, attested by Clement of Alexandria as part of *Secret Mark*, is closely related to a number of other Markan features which were not present in the copies of Proto-Mark used by Matthew and Luke: a special understanding of Jesus' teaching in terms of resurrection and initiation, the concept of "mystery" as the sum total of Jesus' message to the disciples and probably a similar interpretation of the term εὐαγγέλιον, and the elevation of Jesus to a supernatural being endowed with magical powers and with a "new teaching."

(4b) A different edition of *Secret Mark* was used by the sect of the Carpocratians. Clement of Alexandria says that Carpocrates "pol-

luted" the *Secret Gospel*, "mixing with the spotless and holy words utterly shameless lies" (II, 8-9), such as adding to the nocturnal teaching "naked man with naked man" (III, 13) and "many other things . . . which seem to be and are falsifications" (III, 17). Morton Smith writes[52] about the relationship of these two secret gospels to each other: "The question of whether these were really Carpocratian additions, as Clement claims, or whether they were parts of the original text, is not only insoluble, but also irrelevant. Whatever they were, they made a text considerably different from Clement's secret gospel."

(5a) A large number of features which distinguish *Canonical Mark* from Proto-Mark are so closely related to the special material of *Secret Mark* quoted by Clement of Alexandria that the conclusion is unavoidable: Canonical Mark is derived from Secret Mark. The basic difference between the two seems to be that the redactor of canonical Mark eliminated the story of the raising of the youth and the reference to this story in Mk 10:46. Perhaps there are other peculiarities of Secret Mark which were eliminated, but Clement of Alexandria is not clear on the question of other differences—at least he does not feel that they are important enough to warrant a discussion. It is easy to understand why this story of the raising of the youth was not acceptable for a gospel publicly used in the church. In fact, Clement says as much.[53] As far as Clement's canonical Gospel of Mark is concerned, it was identical with the main manuscript tradition of the Markan Gospel of the New Testament as Clement's quotations from this gospel demonstrate.[54]

The redaction of Mark which produced the *Secret Gospel* must have taken place early in the 2nd century. The close similarities of this redaction and the Epistle to the Ephesians confirm this date. "Canonical Mark" would have been written some time thereafter, but before Clement of Alexandria. The Carpocratians, however, based their new edition of Mark upon the full and unabbreviated text of the *Secret*

---

[52]Letter to the author of 10 October 1980.

[53]The secret gospel is kept in the church in Alexandria "most carefully guarded, being read only to those who are being initiated into the great mysteries" (II, 2).

[54]M. Mees, *Die Zitate aus dem Neuen Testament bei Clemens von Alexandrien*, Quaderni di "Vetera Christianorum" 2 (Instituto di Letteratura Cristiana Antica: Università di Bari, 1970), pp. 55-63; the quotations are conveniently collected on pp. 59-65 of Part II.

Gospel. Clement of Alexandria believed that Mark first wrote the "canonical" (or "public") Gospel, and later produced the "secret" version of this writing. My observations, however, lead to the conclusion that "canonical" Mark was a purified version of that "secret" Gospel, because the traces of the author of *Secret Mark* are still visible in the canonical Gospel of Mark.

(5b) The additions of Mk 16:9-20 and of the so-called Freer Logion demonstrate that the history of "canonical Mark" was still continuing—and, indeed, there are typical "Markan" features in the longer ending of Mark. But the further history of the Markan text is most deeply influenced by the two major revisions of Proto-Mark, namely, by Matthew and Luke.

Seminar Dialogue
with Helmut Koester

Corley: On behalf of Southwestern Baptist Theological Seminary I would like to welcome you to the Colloquy on New Testament Studies. The morning seminar is on the synoptic problem. The moderator is William R. Farmer, from the School of Theology, at Southern Methodist University. I have agreed with him to ask David Peabody, Ph.D. candidate in the S.M.U. Graduate Program in Religious Studies, to prepare the major response to the morning's paper. David will come and Professor Farmer will moderate the session.

Farmer: I would like to begin by asking whether everyone at the table has had an opportunity to read Professor Koester's paper? Since all have read the paper I propose that we begin by asking Professor Koester to take ten or fifteen minutes to take us through his paper bringing out the main points that he wants to make. That will be followed by a similar presentation by David Peabody. Our discussion will begin with a response from Professor Koester to David Peabody's response. I think that we can get through all three of these presentations in the first hour. This will leave us a full hour for further discussion with ample opportunity for other members of the seminar to contribute. Does this procedure meet with the approval of the

seminar? Very well, we will begin, then, by asking Professor Koester to make his presentation.

Koester: I don't want to rehearse my paper since apparently it has been widely distributed. I want to say a little bit about the approach, not methodologically, but in terms of interest. As my friend Bill Farmer knows, I did not come to this paper via years of hard thinking and hard work on the question of the synoptic problem or the sequence of the Gospels. I came to it rather out of a considerable amount of work with non-canonical gospel materials and a fascination with the *Secret Gospel of Mark*.

The *Secret Gospel of Mark* has bothered me tremendously for years, because I couldn't fit it in. One reason that I couldn't fit it in was the appearance, and I think it is an appearance that is correct, that the initiation story in the *Secret Gospel of Mark* rested on an older story of a resurrection, that Jesus accomplished. It also seemed that this story of the raising of the young man is best explained as an older, more genuine version of the story of the raising of Lazarus which we have in John 11. There are no individual names which appear in the story in the *Secret Gospel of Mark*. The story is told in a rather simple, straightforward form as one would expect from a story that has circulated orally. It has no traces of the way in which the author of the Gospel of John fitted that particular story into the total framework of the Gospel of John. As we know, John 11 is at a crucial position in the Gospel of John and the author of John has done a lot to tie the story into the course of the ministry of Jesus, backwards in chapters one through ten, and forwards to the passion narrative—into which the story of the raising of Lazarus leads directly. None of these features appears in the *Secret Gospel of Mark's* version of that story. However there are a few features which appear which still tie these stories together and prove that they are one. One is the fact that in each instance a relative approaches Jesus, to be sure, *not two* sisters, *but one* sister that appears in the *Secret Gospel of Mark*. Also, then the play on the question of the love relationship between Jesus and the person who is raised, which is also prominent in John 11 where Jesus stands at the tomb and weeps and the Jews say, "How he did love him."

What would this mean for our knowledge of the development of gospel literature, in particular Mark, if indeed the *Secret Gospel of Mark* contained a story of the raising of a person which is not depend-

ent upon the Gospel of John but in every respect exhibits the features of the older forms of the tradition of miracle stories of Jesus. The question is complicated by the fact that the Gospel of John and the Gospel of Mark seem to use a number of other miracle stories that are rather closely related to each other. They are well known, not only the healing of the blind man, but also, of course, the stilling of the tempest (I don't want to go into detail here).

One very attractive solution with which I played, and in fact played with for years (and I mean years, because I first heard about the *Secret Gospel of Mark* in 1960, when Morton Smith reported about it in an SBL meeting in New York) was to assume that the *Secret Gospel of Mark* used source materials which were similar to those used by the Gospel of John, some older collection of miracle stories. In that case, the *Secret Gospel of Mark* should be an older version of the Gospel of Mark. However, that has a lot of difficulties. I just want to set aside for a moment the difficulty which arises with respect to the initiation story which follows in the *Secret Gospel of Mark*. It has a lot of difficulties because there the whole question of the sequence of the Gospels, of course, comes into play. Why then do Matthew and Luke not have the slightest reflection of this? There are other difficulties and these are seen in the fact that other features in the Gospel of Mark which tie in with the *Secret Gospel* do not seem to reflect, say, middle first-century Christianity, but rather Christianity at the turn of the century, developments as they are present in the Epistle to the Ephesians.

All right, finally challenged by Farmer, I thought I should really sit down and go into some detail. Obviously, I haven't gone into enough. Mr. Peabody will point that out to you in a moment. [Peabody had arranged to get a copy of his respone to Koester the day before.] But I was not looking for instances in the Gospel of Mark which did not occur in Matthew and Luke. I was looking for instances in the Gospel of Mark which revealed parallels to that section of the *Secret Gospel*. That is important to know in order to understand what I have tried to do. Where in Mark are there close parallels, both in terminology and in theology to what the *Secret Gospel* reflects? Lo and behold, in one case after the other, these turned out to be passages in the Gospel of Mark which have no parallels in Matthew and Luke. Or, if there were parallels to Mark in Matthew and Luke then Mark had something "peculiar." I formulate it that way (that is, that Mark had something "peculiar") because I don't want to imply anything at this point about a

solution to the synoptic problem. That is the basis for this paper. And that is also the reason why this paper does not present all instances in which Mark deviates from Matthew and Luke, but only those instances in which I find significant parallels to the *Secret Gospel* (and they are enumerated in my paper). Let me make one more point and then I'll quit. But I want to bring that point up again later in the discussion. I have become convinced that the problem, the synoptic problem, or the problem of those three Gospels, is, at the present stage of our knowledge of gospel literature, a wrong problem, because it isolates three gospels. How many gospels were probably in circulation in the last decades of the first century and at the beginning of the second century? Probably something like eleven, twelve, or even fourteen gospels is the minimum we have to work with. If we do not find a way to deal with literary relationships of the Gospels by taking account of all those gospels, we are working on an outdated model of literary criticism. I would be glad to make some more comments on this, but I say this now because my interests are primarily here; I want to challenge the scholarly world to write the literary history of the gospels in early Christianity considering all gospel materials which are available. With new discoveries, we can no longer put all of the apocryphal materials into some special boxes and suggest that they didn't exist, which scholarship has done up to the publication of Hennecke-Schneemelcher. H-S is just another method of classification which enables us to put away all that apocryphal stuff and not look at it again and return to deal just with the canonical Gospels, or just with Matthew, Mark and Luke. I don't think we are permitted to do that any longer. So let me stop here.

Farmer: Professor Koester is not only challenging other scholars to do what he has just proposed. He has himself produced a significant manuscript in which he places all known gospels in a developing sequence from Jesus to Marcion. We look forward to the day when that manuscript will be in a form suitable for public presentation. Meanwhile, we welcome very much this paper which he has prepared especially for our seminar. I am going to ask him, for the benefit of some in this room who have not had the opportunity to read the paper, to recapitulate for us his hypothesis concerning the history of the Gospel of Mark.

Koester: My hypothesis is that the gospel literature before canonization was a literature that was subject to numerous revisions and

rewritings. No matter which position you take on the sequence of the Gospels that is something we probably would agree on. I think that these revisions and rewritings were much more extensive and much more frequent than we have hitherto thought. The Gospel of Mark would be one example (let me make a footnote here—more recent research has shown that the Gospel of John must have been rewritten at least three times if not five times) of a gospel that has grown out of a number of stages of revising and rewriting. My hypothesis would be that there was an original Gospel of Mark. This Gospel of Mark was revised by Matthew and that produces Matthew; it was revised by Luke and that produces Luke; then maybe there was an in-between stage. It was revised once more by the person we can call the author of the *Secret Gospel of Mark*. We don't know enough about that *Secret Gospel of Mark* because we don't know whether Clement quotes everything from it that he knew about it. We do know, though, that the *Secret Gospel of Mark* was subsequently taken by the Gnostic sect of the Carpocratians and revised again. Clement points to individual instances where the *Secret Gospel* of the Carpocratians is different from the *Secret Gospel* that he had. And it was finally revised once more in order to produce what we now more or less have in the canon of the New Testament as the canonical Gospel of Mark. And all those who have worked with textual criticism know that even in the process of transmission after the Gospel of Mark was accepted by the canon, it was subjected to further revisions. One of these involves the well known question of the ending of Mark. That, in brief, would be my hypothesis.

Farmer: Thank you, Professor Koester. David Peabody is well known to Gospel critics from his article, "A Pre-Markan Prophetic Sayings Tradition and the Synoptic Problem," (*JBL* 97 [1978]: 391-409). First of all I will ask Mr. Peabody to pass out copies of his response, following which he will bring out the main points he has made in his response to Professor Koester's paper. [Peabody's response—to which he refers often here—appears below, following this dialogue.]

Peabody: Let me just respond in a prefatory way to the comments that Professor Koester just made. One, that he did not intend to draw attention to materials that were absent from the Gospels of Matthew and Luke, but rather intended to draw attention to materials which

had parallels to the *Secret Gospel*. This is one of the elements of his paper that I find fascinating, that the elements which relate to the *Secret Gospel of Mark* are also, even if unintentionally so, elements which are absent from the texts of Matthew and Luke. And I quite agree with him that we need a holistic approach to gospel studies and I am very much in agreement with him on the bringing of the text of the *Secret Gospel* into the mainstream discussion of Markan studies.

My response is lengthy and I would like to summarize it in two parts. The first part is simply a review of what is in my response. In the second part I delve into my response at specific points in a detailed way. I have spent the first nineteen pages or so responding to Professor Koester's presuppositions, namely the existence of Q and the priority of Mark. I do not argue with him over the question of the existence of Q. But there has appeared in the recent edition of the *Perkins Journal* an article by Edward Hobbs ("A Quarter-Century Without 'Q'," *PSTJ* 33 [1980]: 10-19) who wrote the article in honor of Austin Farrer, and he highlights again Farrer's argument that the existence of Q may indeed be doubted, that it was not improbable that Luke knew Matthew and that the minor agreements provide the strongest evidence for that doubt. These minor agreements, so called, are most conveniently found, I think now, in Franz Neirynck's work, *The Minor Agreements of Matthew and Luke Against Mark* (Leuven: Leuven University Press, 1974). Neirynck has for the first time drawn attention not only to the *positive* agreements—that is, where Matthew and Luke add something to their text of Mark on the Markan hypothesis, but also to the *negative* agreements—that is, the agreements in omission which are more relevant to our discussion today, because it is the materials which do not appear in the texts of Matthew and Luke to which Professor Koester has drawn our attention. These minor agreements argue against the existence of Q according to Farrer.

In my brief response also to the question of the priority of Mark, I suggest that this has not been demonstrated and we celebrate today the recent publication of the English edition of a book by Hans Herbert Stoldt, translated by Donald Niewyk, and published by Mercer University Press (1980). (I see some other copies on the table.) This book draws attention to the literary evidence on which we need to focus in a seminar on the synoptic problem. Minor additions, minor changes, pericopes which do not appear in the texts of Matthew and Luke but

do appear in Mark. Some of these are the materials to which Professor Koester draws our attention.

In the course of his discussion Stoldt has, I believe, demonstrated that the proof from common narrative sequence, which I take to be one of Professor Koester's reasons for continuing to believe in Markan priority, is no longer tenable. That is the first of seven arguments for Markan priority which Professor Stoldt systematically investigates as they were expounded by the classical founders of the two-document hypothesis and finds that, the proof from common narrative sequence basically supports the Griesbach hypothesis if the evidence is looked at in detail. And he finds the editorial requirements placed upon Matthew and Luke based upon the two-document hypothesis as, "scarcely believable."

Koester also argues for the priority of Mark based upon the appearance of elements of the messianic secret in the texts of Matthew and Luke. And I suggest that this argument is both unsound in its premises and in its conclusion.

Premise one is that the idea of the messianic secret was Mark's invention, and I suggest that it was not. Wrede is very explicit about that. When questioned "Was the messianic secret an invention of Mark?" he says "No, it was not. The idea is impossible." And there is evidence within the Gospels of both Matthew and Luke which indicates that the messianic secret came to them from sources apart from Mark, even on the basis of the two-document hypothesis.

The second premise is that Matthew and Luke did not share Mark's theory of the messianic secret and therefore elements of it which appear in their texts are most easily explained as their having been copied from the text of Mark. There is evidence within the Gospels—which I cite—that Matthew adds the idea from sources apart from Mark. Both Matthew and Luke heighten the idea of the messianic secret in contexts paralleled in Mark and add it to Markan contexts. If the premises are false I suggest the conclusion is also false. Wrede supports this when he says that "people who will find what I say essentially convincing will be led to doubt the priority of Mark to Matthew and Luke." Wrede continues, of course, to support Markan priority and he basically supports it on the basis of the proof from common narrative sequence which brings us full circle back to where we began with Stoldt. The proof from the common narrative sequence I believe has been dismantled by Stoldt.

While I do not agree that the application of the methodology—which Professor Koester suggests or implies to us in this argument for Markan priority—is sound, the methodology is sound. And I use that methodology explicitly in my response in two sections (II and IV).

The methodology basically presupposes that we have some clues to the solution of the synoptic problem if redactional materials which are traceable to one Gospel appear in a fragmentary form in another Gospel.

I apply this methodology [looking for a redactional phrase which is traceable to one Gospel appearing in fragmentary form in another Gospel] in section II to evidence from Markan *Sondergut*. It is evidence which I have brought forth. It is not evidence which Professor Koester has suggested. And in section IV of my paper I apply the methodology again to evidence which Professor Koester suggests that we should look at from the double and triple tradition. As Professor Farmer has said elsewhere, when the methodology was applied to some pre-Markan prophetic sayings, the preponderance of evidence supported the Griesbach hypothesis. [The reference here is to Peabody's article in the *JBL* cited above.]

In section II of my paper I begin a detailed response to the literary data and arguments which Professor Koester has put forth for his theory of two recensions of Mark, namely, that one was used by Matthew, and another more expurgated version (omitting the Mark 6:44-8:26 section) was used by Luke. And I suggest that we can once again be enlightened by putting Professor Koester and Professor Stoldt into dialogue. The evidence which Professor Koester has called to our attention is only a part of the larger body of data which Professor Stoldt isolates for us in the first chapter on "The State of the Problem" in his book, *History and Criticism of the Markan Hypothesis*.

To be specific, Professor Koester argues that Mark 6:44-8:26 should be separated from the rest of Mark and understood as a later interpolation into the text of Mark on the basis of four arguments. He suggests that Luke did not know Mark because none of this material appears in the text of Luke. In fact, there is some linguistic evidence within the section of Mark 6:44-8:26 that does appear in the text of Luke. That evidence. although fragmentary, is listed for you in section II of my response. But I am struck by the fact that not only are there agreements, these agreements also occur in the same order. As I have

reflected since I finished this paper there is some evidence of what one might call a Mark-Q overlap, because in Matthew 12 as well as in Matthew 16, these same literary bits of data occur. It would be odd, though, I would think, for us to have not only an overlap in linguistic data, but also an overlap in order in Mark and Q.

Koester's second argument is an argument from doublets. (I respond to that also in my section II.) Yes, I would agree there are a number of passages within this section which are doublets to other materials in the Gospel of Mark; but there is also a doublet internal to this section, namely, Mark 7:32-37 and Mark 8:22-26. That would seem to be inconsistent with the data which Professor Koester has brought forward to us. He also argues for a peculiar use of language. I would only suggest that the usage of συνίημι in Mark 8:17, 18 which he calls to our attention, is similar to a usage in a longer passage in Mark 4:11, 12. (the texts are quoted in full for you, in section II of my response.)

His last argument has to do with the reference to Bethsaida both at the beginning and the end of this section. I respond that there is a reference to Bethsaida in Luke 9:10 roughly in parallel to the section in question and explain how the data would make sense on the Griesbach hypothesis. I would be the first to admit, however, that this is probably one of my weakest responses to him.

But, aside from responding to his specific four arguments, I marshall other data which I believe call into serious question this theory of two recensions of Mark, one used by Matthew and one used by Luke.

The linguistic data, I believe, is laid out in full in my section II, and shows a literary relationship between two miracle stories Mark 8:22ff. and Mark 7:31ff. Neither of these stories is found in the text of Matthew or Luke, although Professor Koester might want to debate with that. I believe he thinks that there is some evidence of Mark 7:31ff. in the text of Matthew. We can go into that in detail later if necessary.

These two miracle stories relate to the ending of a third miracle story which is outside of this section, namely Mark 5:41ff., the healing of Jairus' daughter. There are a number of isolatable linguistic phenomena which occur in the same order in Mark 8:22ff. and Mark 7:31ff. There are an equally impressive number of isolatable linguistic phenomena which occur in the same order in Mark 5:41ff., parallel Mark 7:31ff. I dream a little bit about the possibility that we have here potential evidence of a conflation in the text of Mark quite apart from

what Mark may have done with the texts of Matthew and Luke. In that case the beginning of the miracle in chapter 8 and the ending of the miracle story in chapter 5 have provided the beginning and the ending of the miracle story in chapter 7. These three stories, whatever their literary history may be to one another, clearly, I believe, evidence a redactional relationship to one another that might be explained as evidence of some miracle story source which Mark has incorporated into his Gospel. But the literary characteristics which unite these three stories to one another also unite these stories to the whole fabric of the Markan Gospel. They unite the section Mark 6:44-8:26 and material outside of that section. And some of this evidence, when looked at carefully, suggests that Mark was written third. For instance, the first characteristic ὅ ἐστιν μεθερμηνευόμενον in 5:41. I list all the appearances of that formula in the Gospel of Mark. I indicate that it never appears in the texts of Matthew or Luke in a Markan parallel, whereas both Matthew and Luke can use the formula in contexts not paralleled by Mark. Presumably they would have used the formula if they had had it in their sources. I suggest that the evidence provided by the appearance of this formula within the synoptic tradition represents an unexplained agreement in omission from Mark on the parts of Matthew and Luke. The evidence suggests an anomaly for Markan priority. This is not the only bit of evidence which can be marshalled within these three miracle stories of a similar nature, and it is all laid out for you in the subsequent pages of my response to Koester's paper.

So these three miracle stories are related to one another, uniting this "interpolated" section to the rest of canonical Mark. Further they have redactional relationships to the whole fabric of the Gospel of Mark. This goes against Koester's theory of two recensions of Mark, one used by Matthew and one used by Luke. There is, in fact, further evidence which can be marshalled, that unites the whole of Mark with this section Mark 6:44-8:26. Professor Koester has isolated certain passages as "clearly redactorial" in the course of his paper. The linguistic evidence within those passages also can be found throughout the Markan Gospel. It is not limited to the section Mark 6:44-8:26.

I conclude, therefore, that it is highly unlikely that Mark went through two recensions, one used by Matthew and one used by Luke.

At the conclusion of section II of my response, I simply respond that the common omissions in the small pericopes from Mark by Matthew and Luke are equally explainable as evidence in support of

the Griesbach hypothesis, namely, that Mark comes third rather than first, and that he has supplemented and added to the texts of Matthew and Luke at points and these are some examples of those additions. He had supplementary material.

At the beginning of my section III, I suggest an alternative reconstruction of the literary history of Mark 10:46, where Mark 10:46 is understood as a result of Mark's having conflated Matthew and Luke, and I think the evidence makes very good sense on that hypothesis.

In my section IV, once again I deal with the linguistic data. This time I deal with that data which Professor Koester himself has brought to our attention. Let us look at one specific example to see how the methodology which is implicit in Koester's argument for Markan priority (his second argument for Markan priority) when applied to the linguistic data which he has isolated himself, argues for the Griesbach hypothesis. (See my section IV.)

I suggest that the term in Mark τὸ εὐαγγέλιον is uniform throughout the Gospel and that to divide the evidence based upon parallels in Matthew and Luke or the absence of parallels, is illegitimate either on Koester's reconstruction or on the basis of the Griesbach hypothesis. We should see the data whole, and if one does that one will notice that in Mark, except in two places, the linguistic phenomenon is always "τὸ εὐαγγέλιον used absolutely," much like Paul uses it, absolutely. It has a specific content for Mark. And even the variants in the text of Mark can be explained on the basis of Pauline usage. That uniformity establishes first the results of redaction criticism for the Gospel of Mark. One next must do the same for Matthew. What one notices about Matthew is that Matthew always refers to "preaching— κηρύσσειν—the gospel of the kingdom," with one exception, Matthew 26:13. One notes, on page 45, an extensive linguistic phenomenon within the text of Matthew only traceable to him, Matthew 4:23 and 9:35 (the linguistic data are laid out in front of you). And I suggest that elements of this longer linguistic agreement recur throughout the Gospel of Matthew in other contexts, and those are also listed following those two passages. The usages of Mark's "the gospel" provide no problem for advocates of the Griesbach hypothesis, and no problems for Koester's reconstruction. However, he must say that it's odd that the author of the Ur-gospel that Matthew and Luke used has the same usage as the author or the redactor of the *Secret Mark* which came later and he has to discount this data to a certain extent in order to make his

hypothesis work for him. The Griesbach hypothesis has no such problem.

When one looks at the parallel passages, one may see that τὸ εὐαγγέλιον in Mark 13:10 and in 14:9 can be well explained as evidence of a fragmentary preservation of a formula traceable to the Gospel of Matthew within the text of Mark which argues, in my view, for the priority of Matthew to the Gospel of Mark in these passages. This would constitute evidence that Mark was written after Matthew, and Koester's statement that some scholars have considered the whole verse in the case of Mark 13:10 a Matthean intrusion would be apt. Mark copied the expression from Matthew in this case. Koester says that the appearance of τὸ εὐαγγέλιον in Matthew 4:17a is odd and I suggest on the basis of the linguistic evidence laid out there that it is only odd on the theory of Markan priority. Matthew 4:17a and 17b make quite good sense redactionally speaking within the Gospel of Matthew and all one has to see is that Mark has conformed his text to his usage elsewhere, namely, providing "τὸ εὐαγγέλιον used absolutely" in that context.

There is also evidence within these materials for Luke's priority to Mark. I say that an apparent redactional feature of the Gospel of Matthew is lost in the Markan parallels. That s, the relationship of Jesus' preaching to John's proclamation. There is no direct quotation of John's preaching in Mark 1:4 or in Matthew 3:2. Rather than continuity there is in fact a distinction made between the preaching of John and that of Jesus in the Gospel of Mark. John came preaching the baptism of repentance for the forgiveness of sins. Jesus came preaching the gospel of God. Whereas one may argue that Matthew may have changed Mark's distinction into a continuity, or that Mark may have changed Matthew's continuity into a distinction, the relationship of Luke to Mark in this passage is clear. Boismard has written, "The activity of John Baptist is formulated in identical terms by Mark 1:4 and Luke 3:3, 'preaching a baptism of repentance for the forgiveness of sins.' This way of speaking is not Markan, but Lukan. The expression 'baptism of repentance' is not read elsewhere in the New Testament except Acts 13:24 and 19:4. If the formula for the forgiveness of sins belongs to primitive theology, this forgiveness of sins is not linked with repentance except in Luke 24:47, Acts 2:38, 3:19, 5:31, 8:22, and 26:18-20. The whole phrase 'preaching a baptism of repentance for the forgiveness of sins' points to Luke, not Mark as the source and the word for sins is the one that Luke uses."

The previous discussion supports Matthew's priority to Mark, this last data argues for Luke's priority to Mark as well. Therefore, all of the data is explicable on the basis of the Griesbach hypothesis. Not only is the data consistent with that hypothesis, as has been shown, some of the data argues for it.

I do the same with the other linguistic characteristics which Professor Koester has called to our attention in the following pages, διδαχη-΄/διδάσκειν, μυστήριον, and βάπτισμα. I provide in my section V data supplementary to the passages which Professor Koester has called to our attention. Two of these do not appear in the texts of Matthew and Luke. I show that these two relate to other passages within the Gospel of Mark. My section VI is my general conclusion. [At this point, Peabody read aloud the last three pages of his response to Koester, which see, below.]

Koester: I am very impressed by Mr. Peabody's detailed analysis and I think it is always an honor to write a nineteen-page paper and get a sixty-six page response to it. So, thank you very much. I have learned a lot from this paper and in order to produce the final form of my own paper for publication with footnotes and everything, I will certainly be very grateful to be able to draw on a lot of the materials to which you have brought our attention. Let me state a few points and maybe we can have time later to go into some details.

I have to say something about Wrede. The first paper I was ever asked to write in my studies of theology was on Wrede's book on the messianic secret. And I have ever since been fascinated by it. But I have to apologize for abbreviating my reference to Wrede. Whatever David Peabody has pointed out is, of course, correct. However, I was speaking about Wrede at his best and not at his worst. I think that we must today state that Wrede was wrong on a number of points.

A. Wrede was wrong in assigning the parable theory to the messianic secret. It has nothing to do with it. It is older; we now find the same secret parable theory in the *Gospel of Thomas*. It is unrelated and probably was already in existence in the context of the parable tradition whether it occurred first in Matthew, Mark, Luke, or what have you.

B. It is wrong to assign the commandments silencing the demons to the messianic secret. This is part of the exorcistic vocabulary. The demon cries out and Jesus tells them to be silent. The demon recognizes

the exorcist. That is part of the stories that have been transmitted, and
we find the same features in stories anywhere else; they are not part of
the messianic secret, specifically.

C. It is wrong to assign the contrast motif, in which it is said, "And
Jesus forbade them to speak about it, and they went out and
announced it unto all the world," to the messianic secret. Such motifs
belong to the normal arsenal of telling miracle stories.

D. And finally, I think it is wrong to explain the messianic secret as
a general and widespread theory ultimately reflecting the knowledge
that Jesus' historical life was not messianic; and that was Wrede's
primary interest, that messianic secret theory may reflect the fact that
Jesus' life was unmessianic, and he even found that reflected in the
Gospel of John. This explanation, I hope, will stay in the closet where it
belongs and not be pulled out again.

So I would not give Wrede that much credit, though I admit that
Peabody is perfectly correct to draw my attention to this matter. On
the contrary, I think messianic secret in Mark reacts to a messianic
tradition, not to an un-messianic tradition about Jesus, and particularly a messianic tradition about Jesus as reflected in the miracle
stories; and that this reaction to a messianic tradition for the author of
Mark points to the crucifixion of Jesus, as that in which Jesus' mission
is fulfilled rather than in his messianic ministry.

Whether or not Mark is dependent on Matthew and Luke, he
composed his writing according to the theological perspective of the
messianic secret. Matthew and Luke, I believe, reflect the results of
that composition in part, though they do not share Mark's theology.
That is what I thought I had learned from Wrede.

As for the synoptic sayings source, my problem is that if we do
away with Q, then we would have to reconstruct the synoptic sayings
source, because there can be no question that there were written
collections of sayings of Jesus and whoever denies that just refuses to
accept the evidence we have. If no such written collections existed, then
the whole gospel tradition, no matter which way you approach it,
becomes unintelligible.

I am very much impressed on the one hand by books like that of
Lührmann that seems to show a particular redaction of a major
collection of sayings of Jesus, which he thinks must be presupposed for
Matthew and Luke, which incidentally does not necessarily go against
the Griesbach hypothesis. But if the two-source hypothesis does not

work, one or several sayings sources are still needed to explain the development of early Christian gospel literature. And, incidentally, I think John ought to be pulled in, because we have to explain how earlier stages of the tradition of sayings and the interpretation of the tradition of sayings shaped what we later find in written gospels. Of course, there are many other problems involved here, for example, to mention one that I find important, to explain why sayings in Luke are often more original than those in Matthew, and I think there can be no question in my mind, but you will say that there may be some debate about it. But I have never doubted that the collection of sayings that appears in Luke's so-called Sermon of the Field in many ways shows that it belongs to an earlier stage of the tradition of sayings than the one that is reflected in the Gospel of Matthew. So there would be a lot that would have to be done.

Next, I would like to refer to Farmer's rule two, if you don't mind. Farmer's rule two says you have to look, to establish first the results of redaction criticism, then consider synoptic parallels; that one should first look at the results of redaction criticism in one particular writer only. I think that does not work. Because in order to establish redactional features of any particular author, one must consider synoptic parallels, in fact, all parallels, and I hope not only synoptic parallels.

I think that the so-quoted Farmer's rule two makes redaction criticism a primary method and I happen to think that redaction criticism is not a primary method, but is only an appendix of form criticism. Redaction, first of all, seems to me is the activity of fitting independent traditions into literary units. Secondly, to continue editing such compositions or materials with, at the same time, accepting more orally transmitted units into that same literary composition. At least part of the material that is incorporated in the growth of gospel literature must have been in existence, independently of literature, namely in the actual life and work of the church. Matthew did not need a written source, Q, in order to quote the Lord's prayer. And I have been singularly unconvinced by the claim that Matthew and Luke used a common literary source in order to quote the Lord's prayer. I think that is a lot of nonsense.

There is danger that gospel criticism is again becoming a literature game. And that is exactly what happens, I think, in Stoldt's book. I have not studied it in detail, I will have to go into it in more detail when I finish the final version of my paper for publication, but I am not

interested in explaining any of Stoldt's 180 plus thirty-five instances. And I am not so terribly happy with the honor ascribed to me that I have explained twenty-odd instances of Stoldt. I don't know whether I want to engage in this kind of activity, because it seems to me that we have to play back and forth between redaction and tradition, and we have to ask at the same time also how a particular tradition is reflected in one gospel and in the other, and redaction criticism is not only the search for individual instances of using the same redactional phrases, but is also a question of asking whether traditions which can be isolated and can be described in that form are indeed presented in one gospel in a comparatively early form and in another gospel in a comparatively late form.

Next, let me just say something, synoptic source theories aside. *Secret Mark* and Mark—David Peabody said somewhere that there is a simpler explanation for the redaction of the Gospel of Mark and the *Secret Gospel of Mark*, namely, that there was only one redactor. I am usually in favor of accepting the simple hypothesis instead of the complicated one; however, in the present stage of gospel research I think it is very dangerous to accept simple hypotheses. The author of *Secret Mark*, in my opinion, cannot have been the author of the oldest form of Mark's Gospel. Mark wants to order his material as a preface to the passion narrative; I think that still stands, no matter what kind of sources Mark used. The author of the *Secret Gospel* does not. Mark understands the disciples as following Jesus on his way to suffering, the author of *Secret Mark* sees them as possessing the mystery of the Kingdom, that is, the gospel of the resurrection. Mark wants to direct the disciples to an understanding of Jesus person as the coming Son of Man. The *Secret Mark* wants to direct the disciples toward an understanding of Jesus as a magician and an initiator into mysteries. That would be nice if the author of *Secret Mark* had already also written Mark 16:9ff., because that sort of clinches that. But I am not quite so daring as to claim that for *Secret Mark* though you have a lot of what the tendencies of *Secret Mark* are, in fact, in that particular ending of Mark. I think that is fascinating. But I just don't think that one can get the composition of the materials that are brought into a context of a large introduction to Jesus' passion, and combined with this very strong apocalyptic expectation which at some time might have been the primary intention of the composer of Mark, I don't think one can fit this into the intentions of the *Secret Gospel of Mark*. They seem to

be going in a very different direction and a direction that is more closely reflected in the understanding of gospel we have in the Epistle to the Ephesians. And the Epistle to the Ephesians is just as far away from Paul's kerygma as *Secret Mark* is from the original composition of the Gospel of Mark. And I say that, synoptic source theories aside.

Let me make a last comment on gospels.

Responding to some details of David Peabody's paper. I have no major interest in claiming a different Mark as the source of Luke. This was said in the preface to my paper and I will be glad to be persuaded that the Mark that Luke used contains the same materials as the Mark that Matthew used. I don't think that is a major thing. But I am interested in one other thing here that has to do with the question of redaction. Stylistic and linguistic data which appear in various sections of a writing do not have to belong to the same redactor. If we claim that, the Gospel of John is impossible to explain. We have gone through that for decades in New Testament scholarship. There is no question that you can prove that John 21 or a section like John 6:52-59 linguistically and stylistically is in complete agreement with the rest of the Gospel of John. You can prove that John 17 stylistically and linguistically is in agreement with the rest of the Gospel of John. End

Käsemann writes his perspective on the Gospel of John beginning with chapter 17, the Testament of Jesus, and comes out with an interpretation of the rest of the Gospel of John which is completely nonsensical and wrong. Why? Stylistically John 17 is the same as the rest of the Gospel, but theologically it is very different and introduces a very different perspective. I would assign John 17 to a different redactorial level. But the stylistic arguments do not work. We have to use different arguments. Stylistically a saying about the μυστήρια τῆς βασιλείας, the mysteries of the kingdom, may be almost identical terminology with another version of that saying which speaks about the singular μυστήριον of the kingdom. But theologically these two things are worlds apart. Worlds apart! To know the mysteries (plural) of the kingdom of God means to have the interpretation of transmitted sayings and parables, sayings about the future *razim*, it is the exact parallel to the use of the term mysteries, *razim* in Qumran literature. To use the singular means something very, very different. The Epistle to the Ephesians puts the singular μυστήριον and the singular εὐαγγέλιον into parallelism. Here it is one secret message or secret event which can be turned into a rite of initiation. So we have the same word,

the same vocabulary and we have to learn, I think, more and more, that you can express very different things by staying very close in vocabulary. Other linguistic data I find unimpressive. And one would have to go into a lot of details, for which there probably is no time today, but let me mention one thing. Of course, it is true that Matthew never uses the formula, "this is translated." Obviously not, because if Matthew leaves out the original Aramaic, he doesn't have to use the formula, "this is translated." I won't have to ask here what the function of an individual instance is. One more thing. I'm sorry it gets complicated but I think it is complicated. I just don't think that any gospel we have has managed to remain in isolation. We know that the Gospels, particularly Matthew and Mark and Luke, have not managed to remain in isolation with their texts when these texts were transmitted together in Gospel codexes, or in codexes of the New Testament. What we read in our edited texts, and in that respect the new edition of Aland is worse than anything that has appeared before, is a purified text. It's a purified text edited according to one very interesting principle, namely, that whatever is different in the three Gospels is to be preferred as the original reading. And since Aland has a big institute at Münster, no one is going to challenge him on this right now. Who am I to debate Aland? But, by making the text-critical decision we overlook one very important factor, namely, that very rarely were gospels in isolation very long. The text of the canonical Gospels itself, even on the basis of the text-critical evidence, has to be reconsidered. I am not sure that whenever two Gospels differ that that necessarily points to the two original readings of these Gospels. A lot of other judgments have to be taken into consideration in order to make that decision. But I don't think Gospels had any chance of staying in isolation very long in the period before our earliest manuscripts, but rather must have influenced each other. I am not embarrassed to say that there is one verse in Mark 13 which may be a Matthean intrusion. I don't think, by saying this, I have committed a sin. On the contrary, I think we have to count on much more mutual influence of gospel literature, particularly these three gospels. Now these three move together very closely, particularly in the period before the year 200. And I say particularly these three because there is a large amount of evidence that Matthew and Luke were transmitted together at a very early stage. Justin Martyr reflects his own or somebody else's gospel harmony of Matthew and Luke. Long before people even tried to write the texts of individual gospels,

debate Aland? But, by making the text-critical decision we overlook
one very important factor, namely, that very rarely were gospels in
isolation very long. The text itself of the canonical Gospels, even on the
basis of the text-critical evidence I think has to be reconsidered. I am
not sure that whenever two Gospels differ that that necessarily points
to the two original readings of these Gospels. I think a lot of other
judgments have to be taken into consideration in order to make that
decision. But I don't think Gospels had any chance of staying in
isolation very long in the period before our earliest manuscripts, but
rather must have influenced each other. I am not embarrassed to say
that there is one verse in Mark 13 which may be a Matthean intrusion. I
don't think, by saying this, I have committed a sin. On the contrary, I
think we have to count on much more mutual influence of gospel
literature, particularly these three. Now these three move together very
closely, particularly in the period before the year 200. And I say
particularly these three because there is a large amount of evidence that
Matthew and Luke were transmitted together at a very early stage.
Justin Martyr reflects his own or somebody else's gospel harmony of
Matthew and Luke. Long before people even tried to write the texts of
individual gospels, gospel harmonies were already in existence. It is, of
course, interesting that Mark and Matthew are mentioned together by
Papias, and that is in the first half of the second century. So in certain
circles of the church, and you may want to draw that circle somewhere
from Antioch via Asia Minor to Rome, these three gospels must have
been together. I don't think it's possible to separate them. John was
elsewhere, but we do know of a stage (that is in my opinion reflected in
John 21) where John is influenced by the tradition that we have in
Mark, Matthew, and Luke. But we have to draw the apocryphal
gospels into that discussion right now also. So it becomes more complex and therefore the problem of the Synoptic Gospels I don't think
can be solved as such anymore. Nor, as recent research has shown, can
the problem of John. Because the synoptic problem is also a small part
of a larger problem. In the first century and early second century, the
number of gospels in circulation must have been much larger, at least a
good dozen of which we at least have some pieces, and everybody could
and did rewrite, edit, revise, and combine, however he saw fit. That is
exactly what Papias says about the translation of the sayings that
Matthew composed and I think that is one point in Papias's statements
which probably reflects exactly the situation of his time. If Matthew

We have been treated to a very fine scholarly discussion. This represents a high water mark in the discussion of the synoptic problem, in the opinion of some of the members of this seminar. We deeply appreciate the excellent work that both of these scholars have done. We now open up the seminar for discussion. We will take first questions for Professor Koester. Let me now ask those of you who have spoken to me, to put your questions directly to Professor Koester. I call first on Dom Bernard Orchard.

Orchard: May I just say how pleased I am to be here, I think being the only Englishman here presents a very great responsibility, particularly the day after you have had your great election. The first question I would like to ask is, How can one be sure that there were any apocryphal gospels whatever, circulating in the first century? We know that they were circulating in the second century, but I don't know of any evidence anywhere that they were circulating in the first century. Secondly, I would like to say that I disagree with the whole presentation in the sense that I do not think that simple solutions can be ruled out. If you believe, of course, in the priority of Mark and Q and so on, then you are committed to complicated solutions, there's no question about it. I do not believe that simple solutions can or ought to be ruled out and that what are thought to be the work of different redactors can well be the work of the same man working and reworking his composition in the light of time and his own ideas. My question repeated: How can one be sure that the apocryphal gospels existed in the first century?

Koester: I have to answer briefly, and I don't like to make propaganda for my own publications, but the next issue of *Harvard Theological Review* (Helmut Koester, "Apocryphal and Canonical Gospels," *HTR* 73 [1980]: 105-30), which I hear should be on the desk of Scholars Press by the meeting tomorrow, will contain an article in which I have tried to show that there are at least four if not five other gospels which must have circulated that early. If one considers the external evidence, if one considers the forms of the traditions preserved in them, it seems to me likely that an early version of the Gospel of Thomas, a version of the *Unknown Gospel* that is preserved in papyrus Egerton 2, which may very well be a papyrus that is as old as our little scrap of the papyrus of the Gospel of John, the *Gospel of Peter*, one of the sources of the *Dialogue of the Savior*, perhaps also the sources of materials which are

contained in the *Apocryphon of James*, have as much claim to have circulated at an early period as the canonical Gospels have. There is no external evidence that is any worse than it is for the canonical Gospels. I know that this is something that will have to be discussed and I hope that it will be debated in the future. My interest at this point is simply to call attention to these materials because at the present situation of research what has happened is that over the last hundred years the sometimes slow, sometimes rapid publication of new materials has always been put somewhere where we can keep it without disturbing our basic theories about the canonical Gospels. And my question is simply, Is that still possible? Do we not now, with a vast amount of new materials, have reason enough to reconsider our judgments on noncanonical materials? That, of course, will require further discussion and I would be delighted if you could read my publication and maybe respond to it at some time.

Farmer: I call next on Tom Longstaff.

Longstaff: I would just like to explore, if I could, with you, Professor Koester, a little bit further one of the comments that you made, trying not to debate presuppositions or theories of the synoptic problem, but trying to explore your own understanding of Mark as you are presenting it today. You spoke at one point in your presentation this morning about a characteristic in the Gospel of Mark of the disciples following Jesus, if I heard you right, even following Jesus into martyrdom. And in view of the understanding which you are presenting to us of several redactions of Mark, can you comment at all about the motif, that we frequently find discussed in regards to Mark's Gospel, of the failure of the disciples to understand both the nature of discipleship and the nature of messiahship, and in connection with this the possibility of some element of persecution in final redaction.

Koester: Yes, I think that the sayings about discipleship which begin after the confession of Peter at Caesarea Philipi are deliberately put into that context (chapters 8-10) and, in some way, reflected once more in chapter 13, that these indeed express not necessarily the demand to the disciples to martyrdom, but the demand to the disciples to take up the cross and follow after him, which is repeated in a number of different versions. It seems to me also that exactly here the intrusion of

the gospel concept of εὐαγγέλιον is interesting, and shifts the focus of that suffering theology considerably. That, indeed, the simple saying that the disciples have to take upon themselves their cross and follow after Jesus, is the version that the author of the Gospel of Mark wanted to bring home. And because of the gospel additions or later additions that shift the focus in different directions, that the disciples then afterwards flee, and so forth, may be very well part of the same problem. And they don't come off very well as great followers, we know that, and I don't think that contradicts the invitation of Jesus to follow after him on his way to Golgotha. I think it is a very substantial part and there I would indeed follow Wrede, namely, that the confession of Caesarea Philippi and the transfiguration is the turning point which puts forward the concept of a possible understanding of Jesus as it is focused in the cross, whereas the first part of the Gospel of Mark emphasizes very strongly that not understanding Jesus is focused on what Jesus is doing in terms of miracles and in terms of distributing the bread, his messianic dealings. I do see in those two factors the unifying feature of the Gospel of Mark.

Question: Through all of the levels of redaction this remains basically unchanged?

Koester: It does and does not. We could go into more detail concerning the healing of the epileptic child, in Mark 9. That story, I have always understood—I'd be glad to be corrected—as a really spectacular story, because Jesus does miracles. The one time the disciples try to do it themselves, they fail. And that seems to me to be the intention of the story—why it was originally put there and why it was told in this way. But that redactor, whom I would identify with the *Secret Gospel* redactor, changed that story. It becomes another instance of Jesus accomplishing a resurrection, no longer emphasizing the failure of the disciples. So further redaction would shift the focus in a different direction. That holds true also if one assumes the story is taken from Matthew. Obviously that resurrection emphasis is not in Matthew, but even if the story is taken from Matthew the story could very well be taken from Matthew and could have stood there in the form of Matthew, and be revised by the *Secret Gospel* redactor. I would think that would have been the case because the author of Mark with the one miracle story that is told after the confession, the only miracle story

that is told after the confession which has the disciples trying to act, comes out as a failure. And that could have been written by Paul.

Farmer: David Dungan.

Dungan: Granted that the past two hundred years of textual investigation has made us very conscious of the fluid condition of gospel production and redaction in the first and second centuries, my question is, If there were so many versions and revisions in the second generation, why doesn't, for example, the church father Irenaeus say more about them? He certainly was privy to authentic oral tradition, going back through Polycarp to the apostle John. Now Irenaeus focuses on four main gospels by name, Matthew, Mark, Luke, and John, and he focuses on writings in use by the Valentinians. Why doesn't he mention all the other gospels you say there were?

Koester: Farmer just said I should be brief. That's a big question. It is a good question, David. I am skeptical with respect to Irenaeus's claim to have been privy to a lot of oral tradition. He may have been only three-and-a-half years old when he saw Polycarp or sat at his feet. Irenaeus clearly, though, reflects a tradition that is close to Polycarp; Polycarp has apparently used Matthew and Luke, and he reflects a tradition that is very close to the western Asia Minor region. Papias of Hierapolis is not far away and he knew Mark. So those three we have together and at sometime during the second century the Johannine tradition must have been built up very strongly in Ephesus; not yet either known to Polycarp or welcomed by Polycarp, because Polycarp is strangely silent about the Johannine tradition. That Irenaeus does this seems to be one step forward in uniting different traditions of gospels together and, in fact, very contradictory traditions of gospels. If one goes through the whole picture of localizing early gospel traditions, probably the picture will emerge that gospels were local gospels in the beginning. But before the year 100, local gospels become more, namely, local gospels cross the paths of other local gospels, and one day I would like to write the history of the gospels in the first two centuries as a history of church political developments. And one may be able to read the church policies in the history of the gospels. These are often conscious decisions of acceptance and rejection and revision

as one might see in John 21 as the conscious revision of John that wants to bring the tradition under the name of Peter together with the tradition under the name of John, or the beloved disciple or whoever. A momentous thing has happened here in the uniting of different branches of the development of early Christianity of an earlier time. So I would look for a solution, for an answer to your question in this direction. That might be enough at this point.

Farmer: William Walker.

Walker: If we assume that there were noncanonical written materials in the first century, certainly in the second century, but if we also acknowledge that these materials are generally fragmentary, in some cases known only by attestation, in some cases purely hypothetical, how can we actually use such materials in attempting to reconstruct the history of the gospel tradition and in particular, how can you speak as you do of the tendencies of the *Secret Gospel of Mark* when we have so little of the actual content of that gospel and know so little about it?

Koester: I don't know what happened to the *Gospel of Peter* between, say, the first or second century when it was originally written, and the time when it was copied as an amulet in the eighth century and put into the tomb of a Christian monk. That makes it very difficult because, for one thing, the canonical Gospels were fairly well treated after the third century. The apocryphal gospels weren't necessarily treated as well. And I recognize the difficulty, but that does not eliminate the task of giving these voices their due. What I would add to this is that there is even more reason for us to practice empathy because we are dealing here with documents of persecuted minorities. These documents have not been given the care that has been given to New Testament manuscripts from the third century or until the time of their scrutiny in Aland's Institute in Münster. And a lot of work has to be done; I think we have to do text-critical work on the *Gospel of Peter*. One cannot just say this must have been a gospel from the first century; one would have to sit down and say, now, what is late and what is early. We have learned to do that for the canonical Gospels, so let's get to work with the apocryphal materials, accordingly.

Farmer: Jerry Vardaman.

Vardaman: I was very much taken with the question of Professor Orchard, "How can we know that there were apocryphal gospels in the first century?" One of your gospels that you used, Egerton papyrus 2, was not dated by the editors to the first century. They dated it to the second century, about mid-second century. What kind of calisthenics do you use to get it in the first century?

Koester: I did not say in the first century; in the second century, of course. Of course, there is no evidence whatsoever for any Christian writing in the first century. We assume that Paul lived and wrote in the first century, but we have no piece of papyrus from the first century. The editors, Grenfell and Hunt, dated the papyrus Egerton 2 as reflecting a hand that was used in datable papyri up to the year 120, I believe, is the statement they make. The same judgment that is used for the dating of papyrus Egerton 2 has been used with respect to the dating of papyrus 52, which is the oldest piece of any canonical Gospel. That leaves the time for the dating for the Gospel of John open, as sometime before 120, and leaves the time for the dating of papyrus Egerton 2 open, as sometime before 120. So we have here two of the oldest pieces, unless somebody proves otherwise. I know there is some discussion about the imitation of older hands, and later copying, and so on. But that may very well put our oldest evidence for the Gospel of John into the third century as well. I think it is unjust to prove only that apocryphal manuscripts were written late and never to prove that that's the case of the canonical ones, too. We have very early evidence for one canonical gospel, interestingly enough—John, which was the canonical gospel that still not very long ago many, many scholars believed to have been written late in the second century. We have very early evidence for one apocryphal gospel. And, in fact, as one lists all external evidence for apocryphal and canonical gospels side by side, they draw even. The external attestation for apocryphal gospels is just as good as it is for canonical gospels. There's no difference, in terms of manuscripts, or in terms of quotations by others.

Farmer: William Lane.

Lane: It is obvious throughout the paper that the interpretation of the data is exceedingly important. You find, for example, a possible sacramental motif in the feeding of the five thousand and that then

feeds in with your interpretation of Mark 10:38-39 as sacramental as well. Now taking that as a basic principle, how would you respond if someone were to suggest to you that rather than Mark 14:51-52 (the account of the youth who fled naked) being another evidence of the redaction of canonical Mark by the author of the *Secret Gospel*, that it was precisely the other way around, that the author of *Secret Mark* was faced with a question posed by that pericope and provided an answer? The identity of the young man who fled naked is a young man whom Jesus has raised from the dead, and so Mark 14:51-52 actually becomes the promoter, as it were, of a new piece of tradition. A piece of tradition which was cast in Markan style as you have attested can be done very skillfully by the redactors at various stages and what we have in fact, in *Secret Mark*, is a response to that enigmatic passage in canonical Mark 14:51-52.

Koester: I think one has to discuss these alternatives. What is remarkable though is that Mark 14:51-52 of the young man who fled naked is a very difficult piece to evaluate as a tradition in its own right. It is not a story in itself. The story that the *Secret Gospel of Mark* perhaps interpolated in the context of Mark 10 is indeed a story in its own right. It can be thought of as an independent piece of tradition. It has many affinities to John. It looks like an older version of John 11. It is a piece of tradition you can isolate, whereas the piece that is found in Mark 14 cannot be isolated very easily because you have to explain what it is, in terms of form and genre—and that I find difficult. And of course, it is not only that piece alone that has affinities to the *Secret Gospel*.

Lane: I was intrigued why you did not relate the tradition concerning the young man in 14:51-52 to the νεανίσκον in 16:5, the youth in white at the tomb.

Koester: I have several pages on that which ended up in my wastepaper basket. Let me make one other remark here. If there was a lot of that in the very early version of Mark, we have to discuss more seriously also the whole question of the relationship of Jesus, quoted in Morton Smith's terms of Jesus the magician, to the whole question of rites and initiation rites; reflection of that and the number of pieces which are in the Gospel of Mark, maybe including the νεανίσκος of Mark 16.

Farmer: In closing I'd like to call on Allan McNicol.

McNicol: I'm intrigued by the work on Mark 10:32 and the use there of ἐφοβοῦντο and ἐθαμβοῦντο; and you say flatly in your paper, "In the context of canonical Mark, this makes no sense." And that's true, just following the context I agree with you that the disciples were acting strangely given the context. But isn't this another example of Mark's redactional work with regard to the secret; isn't that as good an explanation as resorting to a theory about the *Secret Mark*?

Koester: I do think that is redaction. And that would also be, of course, in part an answer to Bill Lane's question, "Has the *Secret Gospel of Mark*, the author of the *Secret Gospel of Mark*, left his traces elsewhere, not just the one story of the young man?" It has to do with that part of the composition.

In closing, if I may, I would like to read just two sentences of a letter that Morton Smith wrote to me after having read my paper. At the end he says, "you really have a lot of different gospels of Mark. And I am quite happy to be left with that suggestion. You speak about proto-Greek Mark, enlarged proto-Greek Mark, Clement's secret gospel, the Carpocratians' secret gospel, and canonical Mark. To these I should add, as you know, a proto-Aramaic Mark and probably a proto-proto-Greek Mark and a proto-Greek John. From now on synoptic source criticism will have all the classic simplicity of three-dimensional chess."

Farmer: I should say that we have written apologies from all the members of the seminar whose names were listed, but who, because the seminar has been shifted to the earlier hour, were unable to be here. In behalf of, not only the members of the seminar, but the other participants in the colloquy and the observers, Helmut, let me extend to you our deepest appreciation for your coming to Fort Worth and for the preparation of your paper, and we look forward to having it in an edited form for publication in the volume of papers that will come out in due course. I would be remiss if I did not at this time also—before we break up precisely at one minute past twelve-thirty—if I did not express our appreciation to Professors Tom Urrey and Bruce Corley for all of the work that they have done to make this day possible.

THE LATE SECONDARY REDACTION OF MARK'S GOSPEL AND THE GRIESBACH HYPOTHESIS: A RESPONSE TO HELMUT KOESTER

David Peabody

W E MAY BEGIN BY expressing our appreciation to Professor Koester for his thought-provoking paper. It certainly is in keeping with the theme of our gathering. It provides both reappraisal and a fresh approach.

Not the least of Dr. Koester's contributions is his decision to include a discussion of the relationship of the "Secret Gospel of Mark" to canonical Mark. The academy is long overdue in drawing the work of Morton Smith on *Clement of Alexandria and a Secret Gospel of Mark* into the mainstream discussion of Mark.[1]

By the topics he includes in his paper Koester reminds us of the interrelationships of frequently isolated fields of inquiry, source criticism, patristics, text criticism, redaction criticism, and gnostic studies.

Koester presupposes solutions to basic questions within these disciplines which, in an earlier period, were generally accepted. He offers an explanation for literary data from the canonical Gospel of Mark which are problematic for Markan priority. Koester suggests that "canonical Mark" must be understood as the product of a development in the

---

[1] Morton Smith, *Clement of Alexandria and a Secret Gospel of Mark* (Cambridge: Harvard University Press, 1973).

Markan text through two recensions, Ur-Marcus 1, used by Luke, and Ur-Marcus 2, used by Matthew, and, at least two, probably three, and maybe four or five, redactions. The first (and second?) redaction was provided by the redactor of Ur-Marcus whose work is characterized by the various elements of the messianic secret. A second redaction was provided by a Secret Gospel redactor who performed his work after Matthew and Luke had been completed. Since this redactional step was performed after Matthew and Luke had been completed none of this material was available for them to copy from their texts of Mark. A third redaction was provided by the final redactor who, most likely, removed some of the work of the Secret Gospel redactor. This stage of Mark is preserved in the canon. In light of Clement of Alexandria's letter to Theodore, a fourth redaction of Mark's Gospel was provided and used by the Carpocratians. This fourth redaction was an expanded version of the Secret Gospel of Mark also known to Clement.

The data Koester has marshalled are impressive, and his suggestion concerning the development of canonical Mark deserves serious consideration if the presupposition of Markan priority is to be maintained.

In the course of this response, however, this and other presuppositions accepted by Koester will be reexamined and the relevant data will be expanded and refined. In the process an alternative suggestion for understanding canonical Mark will be explored which explains the data isolated by Koester as well, if not better, than the suggestions he has made. That suggestion is that Griesbach was correct. Mark is best understood as a later gospel based upon a conflation of the text of Matthew with that of Luke. Therefore, the contribution of the final redactor, perhaps the *only* redactor, of Mark is most likely to be found in the additions he provides to the narrative and the alterations he makes in the texts of his sources, Matthew and Luke. It should not be surprising then if Mark, being later, as Wrede noted, has a character more akin to that of the second century apocryphal gospels than do his sources, Matthew and Luke.[2]

---

[2] William Wrede, *Das Messiasgeheimnis in den Evangelien: Zugleich ein Beitrag zum Verständnis des Markusevangeliums*, (Göttingen: Vandenhoeck & Ruprecht, 1963), p. 148. (ET: J. C. G. Greig, *The Messianic Secret*, [Cambridge: James Clark & Co. 1971], p. 148). Wrede says, "Schleiermacher already spoke of the Gospel's tendency to have an apocryphal character. We may leave on one side precisely what he meant by that, but this much seems certain to me: that if Mark's gospel were to come to

I. Koester's Presuppositions

The "Q" Question. Koester has claimed in his first paragraph that "the existence of Q cannot be doubted" and, in his second paragraph, that its existence is receiving "new support."

Edward C. Hobbs has recently contributed an article to the *Perkins Journal* entitled "A Quarter-Century Without Q" in which he traces the history of the doubt about the existence of "Q" from its origins in Austin M. Farrer in 1953 through various doubters both in this country and abroad for the next twenty-five years.[3]

It would be fair to say that Hobbs has been far from exhaustive in listing all of those who find the "Q" hypothesis unconvincing. As Hobbs says, "many, even if not 7,000, have not bowed the knee to Q."[4]

Hobbs reminds his readers that the "Q" hypothesis depends upon "the improbability of Luke having seen Matthew."[5]

Farrer, in whose memory and honor this essay by Hobbs was composed, demonstrated that this was not in the least improbable.[6]

In fact there was a good bit of evidence against the "Q" hypothesis. In Farrer's judgment, emphasized by Hobbs, the so-called minor agreements of Matthew and Luke remain "one of the powerful arguments against 'Q'."[7] In part Koester has responded to this argument in the course of his paper. Whereas Streeter sought to explain the *positive* agreements of Matthew and Luke against Mark, that is, their common changes or additions,[8] Koester is seeking to explain many of the *negative* agreements of Matthew and Luke against Mark, that is, their common omissions.

---

light for the first time today from some tomb, this verdict on it would not be passed only in an isolated instance and many of the features belonging to it would be recognised without the slightest difficulty, whereas at present a certain critical habit of mind refuses to look at them at all."

[3]Edward C. Hobbs, "A Quarter-Century Without 'Q'," *PSTJ* 33 (1980): 10-19.

[4]Ibid., p. 18.

[5]Ibid., p. 12.

[6]Austin M. Farrer, "On Dispensing with 'Q'," in Dennis E. Nineham (ed.), *Studies in the Gospels: Essays in Memory of R. H. Lightfoot* (Oxford: Basil Blackwell, 1955), and Hobbs, "Without 'Q'," pp. 14-16.

[7]Hobbs, "Without 'Q'," p. 14.

[8]B. H. Streeter, *The Four Gospels: A Study of Origins* (New York: MacMillan, 1925), pp. 293-331.

This is not the place to argue the "Q" question. But statements that "the existence of Q cannot be doubted" or that belief in its existence is receiving "new support" sound very different from Hobbs's conclusion about the contemporary situation. Says Hobbs, "There is no serenity in the field of the sources of the Gospels, there are no longer 'assured results of scholarship'."[9] The academy could well profit from a debate between Koester and Hobbs over the existence of "Q".

The Priority of Mark. Koester has conceded that arguments based upon the alleged "Hebrew" character of Mark or belief that "Mark reflected more directly the genuine historical ministry of Jesus" are no longer tenable. However, he is willing to defend Markan priority with two arguments.

Koester's first argument for the priority of Mark appears to be "the argument from common narrative sequence." The inconclusive nature of the argument from common narrative sequence has been demonstrated in the literature since the time of B. C. Butler.[10] Most recently, however, Hans Herbert Stoldt, in his *Geschichte und Kritik der Markus-Hypothese*, has critically reviewed the works of the classical founders of the two-document hypothesis, Christian Gottlob Wilke, C. H. Weisse, H. J. Holtzmann, Paul Wernle, and Bernhard Weiss.[11] Following his discussion of each of these founders of the two-document hypothesis Stoldt examines seven arguments which were used by these founders as proof of Markan priority. "The Proof from Common Narrative Sequence" is the first of these. Stoldt writes:

> Hence the whole argument that the Gospel of Mark has a common narrative line in Matthew and Luke—so that these two are constructed "as if of their own accord" after the Markan order—rests on a preconceived opinion and is not secured or supported by reality. The truth is that *there is neither a continuous actual nor even a merely reconstructible common narrative line.* What then is there? *There are only shifting parallels between Mark on the one hand and Matthew and Luke on the other—sometimes with one, sometimes with the other.*

[9]Hobbs, "Without 'Q'," p. 19.

[10]B. C. Butler, *The Originality of St. Matthew: A Critique of the Two-Document Hypothesis* (Cambridge: University Press, 1951).

[11]Hans Herbert Stoldt, *Geschichte und Kritik der Markus-Hypothese* (Göttingen: Vandenhoeck & Ruprecht, 1977) (ET: Donald L. Niewyk, *History and Criticism of the Marcan Hypothesis* [Macon, GA: Mercer University Press, 1980]).

Now the remarkable, distinctive, and hence decisive fact here is one that may be derived logically: With the exception of those passages where all three authors are periodically in agreement or where Mark gives his own special material (as, for example, the two miracles of healing the deaf-mute and the blind man of Bethsaida), Matthew and Luke alternate in running parallel to the Gospel of Mark; that is to say, at the same moment that the parallelism of one of these two Evangelists to Mark ceases, the parallelism of the other one to Mark begins. Mark is therefore always—well, what? The *"accompanied,"* as Wilke claimed, or is he the one *accompanying*? In the first instance the initiative thereto would lie with Matthew and Luke—in the second instance, however, with Mark. In the first case Mark would possess priority, in the second posteriority. The "accompanied" Mark would have provided the basis for Matthew and Luke; the accompanying Mark, however, would have used these two sources.

Let us suppose that Mark were indeed the accompanied, as advocates of Markan priority claim. How then could the alternating accompaniment of Matthew and Luke be explained? According to the unanimous opinion of supporters of the Markan hypothesis, both had the Gospel of Mark in front of them and used it as a model, independently and without knowledge of each other. How, then, does this rhythmical change in the "accompaniment" of Mark come about? Can it be explained at all?

It is completely inexplicable—unless through a transcendental contact. What a mysterious understanding would have had to exist between the two for Luke to have known exactly when Matthew stopped accompanying Mark; that he then should have jumped in, at that same moment and without being told, in order to assume the accompaniment in place of Matthew, until some time he stopped again, to be replaced by Matthew. This would have had to go on, back and forth, throughout the entire Gospel of Mark, from beginning to the end. What magical events could have caused this repeated exchange of roles, and in uneven sequence and length at that? What utterly enigmatic understanding would have prompted the first and third Evangelists to sense, without knowledge of each other, when the other departed from the narrative sequence of Mark, and what uncanny parapsychological contact could, from time to time, have sent out the magical impetus for them once more to take their turns accompanying Mark? The whole conception is—well, let us just say, scarcely believable.[12]

While there may yet be reasons to advocate Markan priority, "The Proof from Common Narrative Sequence" is not one of them. According to Stoldt, the evidence, when carefully examined, *actually supports the Griesbach hypothesis.*

---

[12]Stoldt, *Kritik*, pp. 131-32; ET, pp. 141-42.

Koester's second argument for the priority of Mark is his claim that "the redactorial work of Matthew and Luke presupposes many sentences and phrases which were added by Mark to older materials . . . The author of Mark's Gospel created himself all references to the messianic secret—Matthew and Luke do not share this theory, but still reveal in their texts that their common source was determined by it."

In light of the actual evidence within the Synoptic tradition, however, one may question whether Koester's claims and conclusions can be sustained. Certainly the man who brought "the messianic secret in Mark" to the forefront of Markan studies, William Wrede, did not think so.

Koester seems to imply that it was Wrede's view that "the author of Mark's gospel created himself all references to the messianic secret." Actually Wrede says:

> Is the idea of a messianic secret an invention of Mark's? The notion is quite impossible.
>
> This can be seen from Mark itself. In it, the entire life of Jesus is shot through with the various motifs of this idea. The individual conceptions occur in a multiplicity of variants. In them there is much that is unresolved. Material of this kind is not the work of an individual.
>
> This is clearly instanced when the contents are taken into consideration. How would Mark come to introduce such an idea into a tradition that knew nothing of it? There is no discernible reason for his doing so. Historically speaking, the idea cannot be fully understood just from Mark directly. We find it there ready-made, and Mark is under its sway, so that we cannot even speak of a *Tendenz*. But what is its origin? We have to do with an idea which must have dominated *fairly* large circles, even if not what one would necessarily call *large* circles.
>
> It is not thereby intended to deny Mark a share, and even an important share in presenting this.[13]

Koester says that Matthew and Luke do not share Mark's theory of the messianic secret. If this is true, then one would not expect there to be elements of the messianic secret in Matthew or Luke except in passages where they have inadvertently copied it from Mark. But such passages which contain the messianic secret and do not derive from Mark do exist in both Matthew and Luke. Wrede knew there was such evidence in the texts of Matthew and Luke and frequently called

---

[13]Wrede, *Messiasgeheimnis*, p. 145; ET, p. 145.

attention to it.[14] Wrede's knowledge of these texts presumably led him to the conclusion that the messianic secret was "an idea which must have dominated *fairly* large circles, even if not what one would necessarily call *large* circles."

Wrede identifies many elements of the messianic secret when he says:

> As to what particularly concerns the idea of the secret, Mark has expressed it most forcibly in the prohibitions, and alongside these, in a whole series of vivid ideas—whether he invented these himself or found them already in his sources. As such we have become familiar with the idea of Jesus being alone with his disciples and especially with his confidants; his secret journeying; his withdrawal from the people into isolation; and his visiting the house or sending sick people home to their houses.[15]

By "prohibitions" Wrede has in mind Jesus' charges to silence following a healing or some teaching imparted to his disciples in private. Elsewhere Wrede identifies the "contents of the secret":

> Secret is the wonder-working which is the characteristic of messiahship and would betray it.
> Secret is the whole teaching of Jesus because it is completely hidden from the crowd.
> Secret in particular is the meaning of the parables, as it is only disclosed to the disciples, and even to them not without interpretation.[16]

Matthew 9:27-31 is Matthean *Sondergut*.

> And as Jesus passed on from there, two blind men followed him crying aloud, "Have mercy on us, Son of David." When he entered the house, the blind men came to him; and Jesus said to them, "Do you believe that I am able to do this?" They said to him, "Yes, Lord." Then he touched their eyes, saying, "According to your faith be it done to you." And their eyes were opened. And Jesus sternly charged them, "See that no one knows it." But they went away and spread his fame through all that district.

In this pericope alone one finds "the idea of Jesus being alone with his disciples," "his withdrawal from the people into isolation," "his

---

[14]For example, ibid., pp. 152, 166-67; ET, pp. 153, 167.

[15]Ibid., p. 135; ET, p. 135.

[16]Ibid., p. 80; ET, p. 80.

visiting the house," and a typical prohibition, "And Jesus sternly charged them, 'See that no one knows it.'" Even Wrede must say of this pericope, "the secret is mentioned entirely in the Markan fashion."[17] But the story did not come from Mark. The story and all the elements of the messianic secret within it are Matthean *Sondergut*.

The parable of the wheat and the tares (Matt 13:24-30) and its interpretation (Matt 13:36-43) are two other passages of Matthean *Sondergut*. The introduction to Matthew's explanation of the parable of the wheat and the tares reads, "Then (Τότε) he left the crowds and went into the house. And his disciples came to him, saying, 'Explain to us the parable of the weeds of the field.'"[18]

In this pericope one finds "the idea of Jesus being alone with his disciples," "his visiting the house," "his withdrawal from the people into isolation," and the "secret in particular" as "the meaning of the parables, as it is only disclosed to the disciples, and even to them not without interpretation."

A similar request for the explanation of a parable is found in Matthean *Sondergut* at Matt 15:15-16. After Jesus discusses "what makes a person unclean" and uses the metaphorical language of "plants" and "blind guides" to describe the reaction of the Pharisees to this teaching, Peter requests, "Explain (φράσον) the parable to us."[19]

Both this passage (Matt 15:15-16) and the previous one (Matt 13:36) conform to the parable theory reflected in the passage from Isa 6 which Matthew quotes in a much fuller form than Mark, at Matt 13:14-15, compare Mark 4:12. In this regard note also Matt 12:16-21. Following the statement "And many followed him and he healed them all, and ordered them not to make him known," words similar to Mark 3:12, Matthew introduces a quotation from the book of Isaiah. The introductory formula for this quotation is typical of Matthew (ἵνα

---

[17]Ibid., p. 152; ET, p. 152.

[18]Τότε appears in the text of Matthew 90 times; in the text of Mark 6 times, all but one of which is paralleled in Matthew (Mark 13:27). It appears in Luke 15 times; 8 times it appears without parallel in Matthew or Mark.

The verb διασάφησον ("explain") is found in Matt 13:36 and 18:31 but nowhere else in the NT.

[19]The verb φράσον ("explain") is found in the variant to Matt 13:36 and Matt 15:15 but nowhere else in the NT.

πληρωθῇ τὸ ῥηθὲν διὰ᾽ Ἡσαΐου τοῦ προφήτου λέγοντος).[20] One of the phrases in the quotation from Isaiah apparently has the force of supporting Jesus' charge to silence (Matt 12:17) with a proof from prophecy, "He will not wrangle or cry aloud, nor will any one hear his voice in the street." Neither the quotation nor any part of the introductory formula is found in the text of Mark.

As a fourth example of the messianic secret in Matthew apart from a Markan parallel one may cite Matthew 20:17. In introducing the third passion prediction only Matthew says that Jesus took the twelve aside privately (κατ᾽ ἰδίαν).

The same type of heightening of the messianic secret can be found in Luke. Following the second prediction of the passion, Mark reads, "But they did not understand the saying and they were afraid to ask him." By contrast Luke says, "But they did not understand this saying *and it was concealed from them that they should not perceive it*, and they were afraid to ask him about this saying" (Mark 9:32/Luke 9:45).

To this evidence Wrede adds:

> In the third prophecy of suffering, however, Luke indeed passes over the introduction about Jesus' going on ahead to Jerusalem (Mark 10:32ff) but as if by way of substitution he refashions a remark to the same kind as the previous one (Luke 9:45), 18:34, "But *they* understood none of these things; this saying was hid from them, and they did not grasp what was said."[21]

Compare also Luke 9:18/Mark 8:27. Mark reads, "And Jesus went on with his disciples to the villages of Caesarea Phillipi and on the way he asked his diciples, 'Who do men say that I am?'" Luke introduces a different setting, "Now it happened that as he was praying alone (κατὰ μόνας) the disciples were with him and he asked them . . ."[22] Only in Luke is the instruction imparted while Jesus is alone. In Mark he is in public, "on the way."

From the evidence displayed here one must challenge Koester's premises. Neither Wrede nor the texts from the Gospels themselves will sustain the claims that (1) "the author of Mark's Gospel created himself

---

[20]Cf. Matt 1:22; 2:15; 2:17; 2:23; 4:14; 8:17; 12:17; 13:35; 21:4; 27:9, cf. 26:36.

[21]Wrede, *Messiasgeheimnis*, pp. 166-67; ET, p. 167.

[22]The construction καὶ ἐγένετο ἐν infinitive is typical of Luke—5:12; 14:1; 24:15; 24:4. For 9:18, compare particularly 11:1.

all references to the messianic secret" or that (2) "Matthew and Luke do not share Mark's theory of the messianic secret."

In answer to the question, "Is the idea of a messianic secret an invention of Mark's?" Wrede responds, "The notion is quite impossible." In fact, it is "an idea which must have dominated fairly large circles . . ." The evidence from the Gospels confirms that the messianic secret found its way into the Synoptic tradition by avenues apart from Mark.

Further, how is it possible to conclude that Matthew and Luke do not share the theory of the messianic secret when Matthew can introduce the idea into his text from source material apart from Mark (as at Matt 9:27-30 or 13:36-43 or 12:16-21) or when Matthew and Luke can introduce the theme into a Markan pericope where Mark has no element of the messianic secret (as at Matt 15:15-16, 20:17 or Luke 9:45, 18:34, or 9:18)?

Perhaps one will argue that all these passages in Matthew and Luke and others which might be cited did derive from Mark, Ur-Marcus, but have dropped out of the text known to us. If such be the response then the combination of science and art which is exegesis ceases to be science at all. The total lack of controls which such a hypothesis requires would not be recognized as science at all, and the art would be limited only by the imagination of the creative artist.

Even if these premises could be sustained could the conclusion that Matthew and Luke are secondary to the text of Mark be sustained based solely upon the evidence supplied by the appearance of the various elements of the messianic secret within the Synoptic tradition? Again William Wrede did not think so. Quite the contrary.

In his chapter on "Mark in Retrospect," Wrede says, "those who find essentially convincing the view of Mark here expounded will probably be easily led to doubt the priority of Mark in relation to Matthew and Luke."[23] Clearly Wrede thought the messianic secret in Mark was a strong sign of the secondary character of Mark to Matthew and Luke. Wrede's judgement would appear to conflict with that of Koester.

Why then did Wrede continue to accord Mark priority? He tells us in this same context:

---

[23]Wrede, *Messiasgeheimnis*, p. 148; ET, p. 148.

> Certain supports for according priority to Mark, and in particular the idea that the line of development taken by the public life of Jesus is still discernible there, have shown themselves unsound. But even if these collapse, sufficient props of better timber still remain. To be specific, I agree with Holtzmann—and I may add also with Wernle—when Holtzmann remarks that the strength of the Markan hypothesis really lies in the fact that the sequence of the narratives in Mark underlies the sequence in Matthew and Luke.[24]

In conclusion then, if Koester is looking to Wrede for support for his belief in Markan priority, he will look in vain. First, Wrede does not claim that his data suggests Markan priority. Rather he suggests that his data will lead to doubt about the priority of Mark.

Second, Wrede had confidence that "The Proof from Common Narrative Sequence" as argued by Holtzmann and Wernle was enough to counter-balance the doubt created by his data as to the priority of Mark. But Stoldt has shown that all of the arguments for Markan priority including "The Proof from Common Narrative Sequence" as presented by Holtzmann, Wernle, and others are no longer able to bear the weight of such a counter-balance.

Therefore, if Wrede's own data lead to doubt about Markan priority, and if the argument marshalled by Holtzmann and Wernle which Wrede used to counterbalance that doubt is, as Stoldt has demonstrated, no longer tenable, then what remains in Wrede to which advocates of Markan priority can appeal in support of that hypothesis? If Wrede had not been able to appeal to "The Proof from Common Narrative Sequence," his work, by his own admission, would have to be used as evidence which leads to doubt about the priority of Mark.

While one must challenge both the premises and the conclusion involved in Koester's second reason for advocating Markan priority one may affirm in principle the methodology involved in his argument. A similar method has been suggested by our moderator, W. R. Farmer. In a paper prepared for the national S. B. L. meeting in Atlanta in 1971 entitled, "Redaction Criticism and the Synoptic Problem," Farmer wrote:

> The method presupposes the sound principle of criticism widely recognized in humanistic studies.

---

[24]Ibid., pp. 148-49; ET, pp. 148-49.

Namely: What is stylistically characteristic of one writer, generally speaking, will inadvertently, at least in fragmentary form, sometimes come into the text of another providing the second writer frequently and closely copies the first.

Or to put the matter another way, when we find sentences or collocations of words which recur mainly or exclusively in the text of (one Gospel) so that they appear to be favorite or habitual expressions of the writer, we are in possession of redactional evidence which presumably could throw light on the Synoptic Problem. By itself such evidence would hardly be decisive. But if there were significantly fewer cases (or perhaps better, none at all) where the reverse could be shown to be true, then we would have one methodological possibility of making Redaction Criticism of service in solving the Synoptic Problem.[25]

Farmer's method includes three rules: (1) *"Consider the whole.* Having considered the whole, and having isolated what may be regarded as redactional in (one Gospel) it is relatively simple to check to see whether what is redactional in (one Gospel) shows up in the text of (either of the other two Gospels)."[26] (2) *"Establish first the results of redaction-criticism, then consider synoptic parallels."*[27] (3) *"When considering any particular example of redaction, give due weight to the ways in which that redactional passage can be clearly identified as from the hand of the final redactor.* This rule is important because what can be shown to have come from the hand of the final redactor (or evangelist), cannot be explained by appeal to hypothetical sources, for example, Ur-Marcus."[28]

The Seminar on the Synoptic Problem of the Society for New Testament Studies has affirmed the methodology as one valid means of solving the synoptic problem. However, that seminar recognized the great importance of rule 2, "Establish first the results of redaction-criticism, then consider synoptic parallels." To the end of "establishing first the results of redaction-criticism," this seminar has requested that comprehensive lists of the redactional characteristics of each of the

---

[25]W. R. Farmer, "Redaction Criticism and the Synoptic Problem," *SBLASP* 1 (1971): 239-50.

[26]Ibid., p. 239. The words in the three sets of parentheses are substitutions for Farmer's "Matthew," "Matthew," and "Mark or Luke," respectively. The italics are his.

[27]Ibid., p. 242. Italics are his.

[28]Ibid., p. 245. Italics are his.

Synoptic Gospels be compiled. Until all three such lists are available, one for Matthew, one for Mark, and one for Luke, any consideration of Synoptic parallels will be somewhat premature.[29] A conclusive judgment as to how the linguistic evidence weighs in balance can only be made by applying this methodology to the entire texts of all three Gospels with these comprehensive lists of the redactional characteristics of each Gospel in hand. Short of such a procedure any judgment as to the mutual relationships among the Gospels must be considered tentative and incomplete.

However, short of considering the whole texts of all three of the Synoptic Gospels one can apply the method to test cases. One may choose a single linguistic phenomenon within the Synoptic Tradition and do an exhaustive study of all of its appearances within the whole of all three Gospels. In short, one "considers the whole" of a selective sample. In fact, such a procedure will be applied to the linguistic data isolated by Koester in the course of this response.

This methodology has been applied elsewhere to some pre-Markan prophetic sayings isolated by Werner Kelber. When the methodology was applied in that case it was concluded that "the preponderence of evidence supports the Griesbach Hypothesis."[30]

II

Having responded to Koester's presuppositions and questions of method it is time now to consider the actual data from canonical Mark to which Koester has drawn our attention.

First, Koester observes that there are "sentences or small pericopes in Mark which have no parallels in Matthew and Luke." Later he observes "that the text of the canonical Gospel of Mark contains numerous phrases and terms which differ from both Matthew and Luke, even when these two later gospels are obviously dependent upon Mark."

In the history of the discussion of the synoptic problem such evidence represents part of a large "remainder of data" which is left

---

[29]This work on the Gospel of Luke has been done by Franklyn J. G. Collison, "Linguistic Usages in the Gospel of Luke" (Ph.D. dissertation, Southern Methodist University, 1977).

[30]David Peabody, "A Pre-Markan Prophetic Sayings Tradition and the Synoptic Problem," *JBL* 97 (1978): 391-409.

unexplained by the theory of the dependence of Matthew and Luke upon the texts of Mark and "Q". While it may not have been Koester's primary intent to defend Markan priority in the course of his paper this is the import of much of his argument.

But the data to which Koester draws attention are only parts of a larger whole, the entirety of which must be explained if Markan priority is to be successfully defended.

Toward the end of his chapter on "The State of the Problem," Stoldt has written:

> The problems inherent in the Markan hypothesis can be read between the lines of this general overall view. These problems define more precisely the task with which the protagonists of the Markan hypothesis saw themselves confronted in trying to prove its validity. They were obliged to answer the following questions and to furnish a solution to the problem which they embraced—a solution which had to be more convincing than the one found by Griesbach:
> (1) Where did the extensive additional substantive material shared by Matthew and Luke alone come from?
> (2) How could it be that the additional substantive material in the Gospel of Mark failed to appear in Matthew or in Luke, if Mark had been their source?
> (3) How can it be explained that in 180 cases Matthew and Luke, independently and without knowledge of each other, joined in leaving out and ignoring the identical phrases and sentences of the Gospel of Mark—if this had been their source?
> (4) How was it possible that both the first and third Evangelist without having contact with each other, and in spite of their separate style of work, nevertheless in thirty-five cases added to the text of Mark in exactly the same places and in exactly the same phrasing?
> (5) What caused both Matthew and Luke, in another thirty-five cases, independently to agree in replacing a word which according to the hypothesis, they found in the text of Mark, with the same similar sounding new word?
> (6) What caused the other two synoptic writers, independently and without personal contact, in twenty-two cases to make exactly the same small modification in an identical manner to a word they both had in common in the text of Mark?[31]

It is to Stoldt's credit to have *explicitly* formulated and systematically articulated these six questions from his own research. It is probable, however, that questions similar to these could have been collected from several authors in the literature. But Stoldt represents both the

---

[31]Stoldt, *Kritik*, pp. 25-26; ET, pp. 21-22.

6850

most recent and one of the most systematic critiques of Markan priority to appear in the literature. He is therefore the leading candidate to represent the opposition.

It is to Koester's credit *implicitly* to have suggested answers to these questions. Whether he had these or similar questions in mind as he composed his paper one cannot know. Certainly Koester makes no explicit reference to the work of Stoldt, or any other opponent of Markan priority for that matter, in the course of his discussion of this literary data.

It may be helpful, however, in a seminar addressing the synoptic problem to perceive these two, Koester and Stoldt, in dialogue. By such a perception the discussion of the synoptic problem may advance.

Henceforth, then, any statements about Koester's "answers" to Stoldt's questions should be understood as a dialogue of this respondent's making and should *not* be understood to impute to Koester any intention apart from what can be known from his own explicit statements.

Stoldt may be perceived as one of the most formidable opponents of Markan priority while Koester may be perceived as a significant defender of Markan priority. Where these two agree will represent an advancement of the discussion of the Synoptic Problem. A continuing difference of opinion may aid scholars in structuring a research agenda for the future. With this understanding we may now proceed with a discussion of the actual data highlighted by Koester.

In the course of his paper, Koester has suggested answers to parts of all of these six questions posed by Stoldt. Koester, of course, relies upon the hypothetical source "Q" as his answer to question 1. He has also explained one of the thirty-five cases mentioned by Stoldt in question 4 (Mark 4:11 and parallels). He explains one of the thirty-five cases mentioned by Stoldt in question 5 (Mark 8:31 and parallels) and he explains one of the twenty-two cases mentioned by Stoldt in question 6 (Mark 4:11 and parallels).

Koester's major responses, however, are to questions 2 and 3. He answers question 2 in two ways and question 3 in one of these same two ways.

Stoldt's Question 2: "How could it be that the additional substantive material in the Gospel of Mark failed to appear in Matthew or in Luke if Mark had been their source?" Stoldt identifies the material he has in mind when he says:

Mark also exhibits a whole series of additional textual details that go beyond Matthew and Luke, above all in three particular pericopes:
(1)   the miracle of the healing of the deaf-mute (7:32-37).
(2)   the account of the healing of the blind man from Bethsaida (8:22-26).
(3)   the parable of the growing seed (4:26-29) and further,
(4)   the brief, but in content significant note (3:21):
"And when his friends heard it, they went out to sieze him, for they said, 'He is beside himself'."
These four cases concern themselves with material in Mark for which there is no corresponding testimony in the Gospels of Matthew and Luke. The following must also be considered:
(5)   a quite surprisingly large number of passages in the second Gospel in which minor additional details extend *beyond the particular text parallels which Mark shares with Matthew and Luke*—180 in number.[32]

Koester explains these data which are peculiar to the Markan Gospel in two ways. His first explanation is that Matthew and Luke used two different recensions of Mark's Gospel, one which included Mark 6:45-8:26 used by Matthew and one which omitted Mark 6:45-8:26 used by Luke. Any omissions common to Matthew and Luke which occur between these verses in Mark are therefore explained by the fact that Luke did not have access to this material. Whereas Matthew *chose to omit* some of this material (only Mark 8:22-26 in Koester's opinion), Luke *did not choose to omit*. He had no choice. The material was not in his copy of Mark in the first place. The fact that Matthew and Luke agree in omitting material from this section of Mark is accidental.

Koester defends his thesis of two early recensions of Mark by appeal to four arguments. First, almost none of the material in this section of Mark appears in Luke; second, the section contains doublets to material in other sections of Mark; third, the section has some unusual content and vocabulary features; and fourth, the section begins and ends with a reference to Bethsaida.

While it is true that almost no material within this section of Mark appears in the text of Luke, some few linguistic ties between Matthew, Mark and Luke do appear within this section. Further, it is noteworthy that these few details appear in the same order in all three gospels.

---

[32]Ibid., p. 15; ET, p. 10.

Mt 16:1	πειράζοντες / ἐπηρώτησαν αὐτὸν σημεῖον ἐκ τοῦ οὐρανοῦ ἐπιδεῖξαι αὐτοῖς.
Mt (12:38)	λέγοντες διδάσκαλε, θέλομεν ἀπὸ σοῦ σημεῖον ἰδεῖν.
Mk 8:11	ζητοῦντες παρ᾽αὐτοῦ σημεῖον ἀπὸ τοῦ οὐρανοῦ, πειράζοντες αὐτόν.
Lk 11:16	πειράζοντες / σημεῖον ἐξ οὐρανοῦ ἐζήτουν (παρ᾽) αὐτοῦ.

Mt 16:4	γενεὰ	πονηρὰ καὶ μοιχαλὶς	σημεῖον / ἐπιζητεῖ,
Mt 12:39	γενεὰ	πονηρὰ καὶ μοιχαλὶς	σημεῖον / ἐπιζητεῖ,
Mk 8:12	τί ἡ γενεὰ αὕτη		ζητεῖ σημεῖον; ἀμὴν λέγω ὑμῖν,
Lk 11:29	ἡ γενεὰ αὕτη γενεὰ πονηρά ἐστιν·		σημεῖον / ζητεῖ,

Mt 16:4	καὶ σημεῖον οὐ δοθήσεται αὐτῇ εἰ μὴ τὸ σημεῖον Ἰωνᾶ.
Mt (12:39)	καὶ σημεῖον οὐ δοθήσεται αὐτῇ εἰ μὴ τὸ σημεῖον Ἰωνᾶ τοῦ προφήτου.
Mk 8:12	εἰ δοθήσεται τῇ γενεᾷ ταύτῃ σημεῖον.
Lk 11:29	καὶ σημεῖον οὐ δοθήσεται αὐτῇ εἰ μὴ τὸ σημεῖον Ἰωνᾶ.

Mt 16:6	ἀπὸ τῆς ζύμης	τῶν Φαρισαίων
Mk 8:15	ἀπὸ τῆς ζύμης	τῶν Φαρισαίων
Lk 12:1	ἀπὸ τῆς ζύμης, ἥτις ἐστὶν ὑπόκρισις, τῶν Φαρισαίων	

On the hypothesis that Luke had neither Matthew nor Mark as his source for this section, (1) how is one to explain these linguistic agreements? and (2) how is one to explain the fact that they appear in the same order in all three Gospels? This agreement in order is in spite of the fact that, while the details appear in the same pericope in Matthew/Mark, they are in three separate pericopes in the text of Luke.

While it is certain that there are pericopes within this section of Mark which are doublets to material elsewhere in that Gospel, there is also a doublet within this section of Mark (7:32-37 and 8:22-26). What reason can be given for a doublet within this potential interpolation in the text of Ur-Marcus?

While there is a greater concentration of uses of συνίημι in the section 6:45-8:26, just how different is the usage in 4:12 from that in 8:17-18? Both as to content and as to language these two "allusions to Isaiah" would seem to belong to the same redactional stage of the Gospel. "And he said to them, 'To you has been given the secret of the Kingdom of God, but for those outside everything is in parables; so that they may indeed see (βλέποντες βλέπωσιν) but not perceive, and may indeed hear (ἀκούοντες ἀκούωσιν) but not understand (συν-ιῶσιν) lest they should turn again and be forgiven'" (Mark 4:11-12). "Do you not yet perceive or understand (συνίετε)? Are your hearts

hardened? Having eyes do you not see (βλέπετε) and having ears do you not hear (ἀκούετε)?" (Mark 8:17-18).

As for the fact that Mark 6:45-8:26 both begins and ends with a reference to Bethsaida and that Mark never mentions the city elsewhere in his Gospel, it is noteworthy that the last geographical reference made in Luke's Gospel before this "Markan ʼomission" is to Bethsaida (Luke 9:10). Matthew and Luke agree on the use of the place name in the sayings tradition preserved at Matt 11:21/Luke 10:13 but otherwise they do not mention this city elsewhere in their Gospels either. One could argue that there must be some relationship between the appearance of a reference to Bethsaida at Luke 9:10 and Mark 6:45.

In Luke Bethsaida seems to be the location for the feeding of the 5,000, a tradition preserved in all three Gospels. Matthew simply says the feeding took place "in a desert place" (Matt 14:13; compare Luke 9:12).

If Mark wanted to conflate the texts of Matthew and Luke, he could agree with Matthew on the locale of the feeding story and place his subsequent story in Bethsaida. This makes better sense than Luke's obviously contrived urban locale for the feeding anyway. Mark could then follow Matthew until Matthew's text reached a point common with (caught up with?) Luke's. Again in order to harmonize with Luke's geography, it would be necessary for Mark to bring Jesus back to where he started when Mark departed from Luke in the first place, namely Bethsaida (Mark 8:22). This is not to say this *was* Mark's procedure, but it would explain the data on the basis of the Griesbach hypothesis.

This, Koester's first, answer to Stoldt's Question 2 has the effect of eliminating two of the most extensive agreements of Matthew and Luke against Mark in omission, namely items 1 and 2 in Stoldt's list, the miracle of the healing of the deaf mute (7:32-37) and the account of the healing of the blind man from Bethsaida (8:22-26). In addition, in Stoldt's list of "*minor additional details in Mark that extend beyond the text of Matthew and Luke, including passages where Matthew or Luke are lacking,*" items 82-95 could also be explained.

The similarity between these two most extensive agreements of Matthew and Luke against Mark in omission, the healing of the deaf mute (Mark 7:32-37) and the healing of the blind man at Bethsaida (Mark 8:22-26) has long been noticed. However, what has escaped the notice of the commentators is the similarity of Mark 7:32-37 to Mark

MARK 8:22-24a

22 Καὶ
ἔρχονται εἰς Βηθσαϊδάν.

Καὶ φέρουσιν αὐτῷ
τυφλὸν
καὶ παρακαλοῦσιν αὐτὸν ἵνα
αὐτοῦ ἅψηται.

23 Καὶ ἐπιλαβόμενος τῆς χειρὸς
τοῦ τυφλοῦ
ἐξήνεγκεν αὐτὸν

ἔξω τῆς κώμης,

καὶ πτύσας
εἰς τὰ ὄμματα αὐτοῦ,
ἐπιθεὶς τὰς χεῖρας αὐτῷ,
ἐπηρώτα αὐτόν,
Εἴ τι βλέπεις;
24 καὶ ἀναβλέψας

ἔλεγεν, . . .

MARK 7:31-36a

31 Καὶ πάλιν ἐξελθὼν ἐκ τῶν ὁρίων Τύρου
ἦλθεν διὰ Σιδῶνος εἰς τὴν θάλασσαν
τῆς Γαλιλαίας
ἀνὰ μέσον τῶν ὁρίων Δεκαπόλεως.
32 Καὶ φέρουσιν αὐτῷ
κωφὸν καὶ μογιλάλον,
καὶ παρακαλοῦσιν αὐτὸν ἵνα
ἐπιθῇ αὐτῷ τὴν χεῖρα.

33 καὶ ἀπολαβόμενος

αὐτὸν
ἀπὸ τοῦ ὄχλου
κατ' ἰδίαν
ἔβαλεν τοὺς δακτύλους αὐτοῦ
εἰς τὰ ὦτα αὐτοῦ
καὶ πτύσας

ἥψατο τῆς γλώσσης αὐτοῦ,

34 καὶ ἀναβλέψας
εἰς τὸν οὐρανὸν
ἐστέναξεν,
καὶ λέγει αὐτῷ,
Ἐφφαθά,
ὅ ἐστιν,
Διανοίχθητι.
35 καὶ ἠνοίγησαν αὐτοῦ αἱ ἀκοαί,
καὶ εὐθὺς ἐλύθη ὁ δεσμὸς
τῆς γλώσσης αὐτοῦ,
καὶ ἐλάλει ὀρθῶς

36 καὶ διεστείλατο αὐτοῖς
ἵνα μηδενὶ λέγωσιν· . . . .

MARK 5:41-43

41 καὶ κρατήσας τῆς χειρὸς
τοῦ παιδίου

λέγει αὐτῇ,
Ταλιθα κουμ,
ὅ ἐστιν μεθερμηνευόμενον
Τὸ κοράσιον, σοὶ λέγω, ἔγειρε.
42 καὶ εὐθὺς ἀνέστη τὸ κοράσιον

καὶ περιεπάτει,
ἦν γὰρ ἐτῶν δώδεκα.
καὶ ἐξέστησαν εὐθὺς ἐκστάσει
μεγάλῃ.
43 καὶ διεστείλατο αὐτοῖς πολλὰ
ἵνα μηδεὶς γνοῖ τοῦτο, ...

5:41-43 as well as 8:22-26. Note, however, that Koester relates Mark 7:34 and Mark 5:41 by the link of the magic word in Aramaic.

The evidence displayed by comparing the three accounts in a Greek synopsis would seem to indicate that the same hand is responsible for the editing (or composition *de novo*) of all three stories. Given the manner in which the linguistic agreements between Mark 7 and Mark 8 *cease* at precisely the point where the linguistic agreements between Mark 7 and Mark 5 *begin*, it would be tempting to suggest that Mark 7:32-37 has been composed by some redactor who conflated elements from Mark 8:22-23 with elements from Mark 5:41-43 in sequence and thereby created something new (Mark 7:32-37) out of two previously existing sources. This, of course, is how Mark is envisioned to have worked with Matthew and Luke on the basis of the Griesbach hypothesis.

Such a thesis would be doubly nice inasmuch as almost every word of this supposedly conflated material and the two sources which were used for the conflation are absent from the texts of both Matthew and Luke. Thereby one could demonstrate that Mark's Gospel evidences the characteristics of conflation quite apart from whatever his relationship to the other two Synoptists might have been.

Of course evidence for conflation does exist within the Markan Gospel of just this kind, namely at Mark 1:2-3 where elements of Mal 3:1, Exod 23:20, and Isa 40:3 have been conflated and the whole erroneously attributed to Isaiah. It is also possible, however, that Mark 5:41-43 and Mark 8:22-23 were formulated on the basis of Mark 7:32-37 rather than the other way around. In that case this redactor would be a disintegrator rather than a conflator. While these two views of the literary history of these three pericopes in Mark must remain in the realm of hypothesis what is at the level of scientific certainty is that the three stories are related to one another at some level of redaction rather extensively.

The linguistic agreements displayed here are sufficient to indicate that one is in touch with the hand of some redactor of the Markan Gospel and that redactional work is not limited to the section Mark 6:45-8:26. This redaction is not limited to material which, in Koester's view, was not available to Luke (Mark 6:45-8:26). Both Matthew and Luke record the story of the healing of Jairus' daughter and the story of the healing of the woman with the hemorrhage which is interpolated into it (Matt 9:18-26/Mark 5:21-43/Luke 8:40-56).

Some of the linguistic evidence which unites these three passages to one another in Mark is limited to these three passages within that Gospel.

(1) The use of an Aramaic healing word
Mark 5:41 ταλιθά κοῦμ
Mark 7:34 ἐφφαθά
(2) The use of spittle as a means of healing
Mark 7:33 καὶ πτύσας
Mark 8:23 καὶ πτύσας
(3) The introductory words καὶ φέρουσιν αὐτῷ
Mark 7:32 Καὶ φέρουσιν αὐτῷ κωφὸν καὶ μογιλάλον
Mark 8:22 Καὶ φέρουσιν αὐτῷ τυφλόν

If all the linguistic characteristics which unite these passages to one another were like these three above, one might postulate that such evidence was evidence of a miracle story source incorporated into the Gospel of Mark. But such is not the case.

Other linguistic data found within these passages link these three healing narratives to the total fabric of the Markan Gospel. In order of their appearance within these passages beginning with Mark 5 and taking up the characteristics in Markan order, the linguistic data are as follows:

(1) ὅ ἐστιν μεθερμηνευόμενον Mark 5:41
This full formula for translation also appears in the text of Mark at 15:22 and 15:34. The shorter formula which may be considered a subcategory of the larger formula used at Mark 5:41, ὅ ἐστιν, also appears in the Gospel of Mark at 3:17, 7:11, 7:34, 12:42, 15:16, and 15:42. Compare also the formula τοῦτο ἐστίν at Mark 7:2. Other examples of translation within the Gospel of Mark appear at 5:9, 9:43, 10:46, and 14:36 without any formula.

Neither the formula ὅ ἐστίν nor the fuller ὅ ἐστιν μεθερμηνευόμενον is ever found in the Gospels of Matthew or Luke where there is a Markan parallel. At Matt 27:34/ Mark 15:22 Matthew reads ὅ ἐστιν. . . λεγόμενος. At Matt 27:46/ Mark 15:34 Matthew reads τοῦτ᾽ ἐστιν. In both of these places Mark has the longer formula, ὅ ἐστιν μεθερμηνευόμενον.

While one does not find this formula in the texts of Matthew or Luke when Mark is in parallel with them both Matthew and Luke can use the formula in contexts independent of Mark. At Matt 1:23 the fuller formula appears. At Acts 4:36 the fuller formula also appears. Assuming the common authorship of Luke and Acts this evidence indicates that both Matthew and Luke had no objection to the formula and presumably would have used it if it had appeared in their source(s).

The evidence provided by the appearance of this formula within the synoptic tradition represents another unexplained agreement in omission from Mark on the parts of Matthew and Luke. The evidence is an anomaly for Markan priority.

(2) ἦν γὰρ ἐτῶν δώδεκα Mark 5:42

Glosses which begin with ἦν/ἦσαν γάρ are frequent in the text of Mark (1:16, 1:22, 2:15, 5:42, 6:31, 6:48, 10:22, 14:40, 16:4).

Five of these also appear in the parallel text of Matthew (Mark 1:16/Matt 4:18; Mark 1:22/Matt 7:29; Mark 6:48/Matt 14:24; Mark 10:22/Matt 19:23/Luke18:23; Mark 14:40/Matt 26:43). One of these appears in the parallel text of Luke (18:23).

While the construction never appears in the text of Matthew apart from a Markan parallel Luke is capable of using the construction in non-Markan contexts (8:40, 23:8) and in passages where the construction is not found in the parallel (9:14).

The usage supports Markan priority to Matthew but the data are inconclusive with regard to Mark's relationship to Luke.

(3) καὶ ἐξέστησαν. . . ἐκστάσει Mark 5:42

The use of the verb with a cognate accusative or dative is listed by Frans Neirynck as characteristic of Mark, "Duality in Mark," *ETL* 47 (1971): 396-97. Neirynck lists 27 examples.

(4) καὶ διεστείλατο αὐτοῖς . . . ἵνα μηδείς Mark 5:43

8:30	Καί	ἐπετίμησεν	αὐτοῖς	ἵνα μηδενὶ	λέγωσιν περὶ αὐτοῦ
7:36	Καί	διεστείλατο	αὐτοῖς	ἵνα μηδενὶ	λέγωσιν
5:43	Καί	διεστείλατο	αὐτοῖς πολλὰ	ἵνα μηδεὶς	γνοῖ τοῦτο
9:9	Καί . . .	διεστείλατο	αὐτοῖς	ἵνα μηδενὶ . . .	διηγήσωνται
8:15	Καί	διεστέλλετο	αὐτοῖς		λέγων
1:43	Καὶ	ἐμβριμησάμενος	αὐτῷ	μηδενὶ μηδὲν	εἴπῃς . . .
1:45	. . . ὥστε	μηκέτι	αὐτὸν	δύνασθαι	φανερῶς
3:12	Καὶ πολλὰ	ἐπετίμα	αὐτοῖς	ἵνα μὴ αὐτὸν	φανερὸν ποιήσωσιν
7:24	Καὶ . . . οὐδένα	ἤθελεν γνῶναι		καὶ οὐκ	ἠδυνάσθη λαθεῖν
9:30	καὶ οὐκ	ἤθελεν		ἵνα τις	γνοῖ

With the exception of a variant at Matt 16:20/Mark 8:30 which reads ἐπιτιμάω, the verb διαστέλλομαι is found only in the Gospel of Mark (5:43, 7:36, 8:15, 9:9), Acts 15:24, and Heb 12:20.

As the preceding chart demonstrates διαστέλλομαι is the verb which Mark chooses in "charges to silence" within his Gospel. This literary construction therefore is a major element in the messianic secret motif in Mark.

Luke has a statement in his parallel to Mark 5:43 which is similar to that in Mark but the verb παραγγέλλω appears at Luke 8:56 for this Markan verb.

Matthew has statements similar to Mark 9:9/Matt 17:9 and Mark 8:15/Matt 15:5 but once again the verb διαστέλλω is not found in either text of Matthew.

The evidence, on the hypothesis of Markan priority, represents a minor agreement of Matthew and Luke against Mark to avoid the verb διαστέλλω . As such, the evidence represents another anomaly for Markan priority.

(5) πόλλα adverbial Mark 5:43

See Mark 3:12, 5:10, 23, 38, 43, 6:20, 9:26. Note also perhaps 1:45 and 15:3 cited by Hawkins, *Horae Synopticae*, 2d ed. (Oxford: Clarendon, 1968), p. 35. See also possibly 6:34, 9:12, 12:27, 10:48.

Of the top nine candidates for this construction in Mark, which are listed first, not one instance of this usage is found in the parallel text of Matthew or Luke although parallel contexts are frequent. See Mark 3:12/Matt 12: 17; Mark 5:10/ Luke 8:32; Matt 5:23/Matt 9:18; Mark 5:38/Matt 9:23/Luke 8:52; Mark 5:43/Luke 5:56; Mark 15:3/Matt 27:12.

The evidence, on the hypothesis of Markan priority, represents a minor agreement of Matthew and Luke against Mark to avoid the use of πόλλα adverbial. As such the evidence represents another anomaly for Markan priority.

(6) καὶ παρακαλοῦσιν αὐτὸν ἵνα Mark 7:32

The use of παρακαλέω to mean "beseech" rather than "comfort" is found in a construction similar to this one at Mark 5:10, 12, 18, 23; 6:56; and 8:22. Other uses of παρακαλέω in Mark appear at 1:40 and 5:17. Frequently the beseeching involves the request that Jesus touch someone (1:40, 5:23, 7:32, 8:22, 6:56).

The construction and the verb are frequently found in the parallels in Matthew and Luke: Mark 5:17/Matt 8:34; 5:10/Matt 8:31/Luke 8:31; Mark 5:12/Luke 8:32; Mark 5:18/Luke 8:38; Mark 5:23/Luke 8:41; Mark 6:56/Matt 14:36. The verb is found also in Matt 8:5, 18:29, 32, 26:53 and Luke 3:18, 7:4, 15:28 where it is not present in Mark.

The data are inconclusive as to the mutual relationships among the Gospels.

(7) ἐπιθῆς τὰς χεῖρας Mark 7:32

"Placing (ἐπιτίθημι) hands" as a healing method is found in Mark 5:23; 6:5; 7:32; 8:23, 25 and in the longer ending of Mark [16:18].

With the exception of Mark 5:23/Matt 9:18 this expression is not found in the parallel texts of Matthew or Luke. Both Matthew (19:13-15) and Luke (4:40, 13:13) can use it independent of a Markan parallel, however.

The evidence constitutes another anomaly for Markan priority. Inasmuch as both Matthew and Luke can use the idea in contexts apart from Mark presumably they would have used the idea if it appeared in their source. With one exception (Mark 5:23/Matt 9:18), however, Matt and Luke agree to avoid the construction when it is found in the parallel in Mark. At Matt 9:18 the singular for hand is used and the participle is not found as in Mark 5:23.

(8) ἀπὸ τοῦ ὄχλου Mark 7:33

ἀπὸ τοῦ ὄχλου with the meaning "away from the crowd," i.e.,

"privately," is found only here and Mark 7:17 in the whole of the NT. Luke uses the construction at 9:38, 19:3, and 19:39 but with the meaning "from" or "out of" the crowd.

No conclusions may be drawn as to the mutual relationships among the Gospels.

(9) εὐθύς Mark 7:35

The expression is so common in Mark as to be found on almost every page of Greek text. It appears in the text of Matthew 7 times, always in a text parallel to Mark (Matt 3:16/ Mark 1:10; Matt 13:20/Mark 4:16; Matt 13:21/Mark 4:17; Matt 14:27/Mark 6:50; Matt 21:2/Mark 11:2; Matt 21:3/Mark 11:3; Matt 26:74/Mark 14:72.

The term appears once in Luke (6:49) in a context not paralleled by Mark.

The term appears three times in John, once in Acts, and nowhere else in the NT.

The evidence is consistent with a theory that Mark is prior to Matthew but inconclusive as to Mark's relation to Luke.

(10) Καὶ ἔρχονται εἰς βηθσαϊδάν Mark 8:22

The formula Καὶ + 3rd person plural of ἔρχομαι + εἰς + a place name introduces a section in Mark at 8:22, 10:46, 11:15, 11:27, 14:32.

8:22, 10:46, 11:15 have no parallels in the texts of either Matt or Luke although 10:46 and 11:15 have parallel contexts in both the other gospels. 11:27 is parallel to Matt 21:23 and 14:32 is parallel to Matt 26:32 but the construction in Matthew is quite different from that described for Mark.

The evidence is inconclusive as to the mutual relationships among the Gospels.

The foregoing evidence witnesses to a significant layer of redaction throughout the Gospel of Mark. The evidence unites Mark 7:32-37 and Mark 8:22-26 with Mark 5:41-43. Thereby the section Mark 6:45-8:26 is united with the rest of canonical Mark at a significant level of redaction. Further, the literary evidence which unites these three pericopes to one another is found throughout the Gospel of Mark. This is confirming evidence that the section Mark 6:45-8:26 is not to be separated from the rest of canonical Mark. The same redactor's hand is present throughout. This evidence argues against Koester's theory of two recensions of Ur-Marcus.

In his discussion of Mark's use of συνίημι, νοεῖν, and ἀσύνετος Koester identifies specific passages (Mark 6:52; 7:14; 8:17; 8:21; and 7:18) as "clearly redactorial." The linguistic evidence within these passages also can be used to demonstrate that the same redactor who edited Mark 6:45-8:26 also edited the remainder of the Gospel.

The same editor who is responsible for Mark 6:52 and 8:17 where lack of understanding about the loaves is attributed to "a hardness of heart" (ἡ καρδία πεπωρωμένη) probably also contributed Mark 3:5 about the hardness of heart (ἐπὶ τῇ πωρώσει τῆς καρδίας αὐτῶν) of those in attendance at Jesus' healing in the synagogue (Mark 3:1-5). Note that this part of Mark 3:5, like the same parts of Mark 6:52 and Mark 8:17, has no parallel in the Gospels of Matthew or Luke.

The same hand responsible for Mark 7:14, Καὶ προσκαλεσάμενος πάλιν τὸν ὄχλον ἔλεγεν αὐτοῖς ἀκούσατε, probably also contributed Mark 3:23, 8:1, 8:34, 10:42, 12:43, and perhaps also 15:44.

Mk 8:34	Καὶ προσκαλεσάμενος	τὸν ὄχλον σὺν τοῖς μαθηταῖς αὐτοῦ		εἶπεν	αὐτοῖς
Mk 7:14	Καὶ προσκαλεσάμενος πάλιν	τὸν ὄχλον		ἔλεγεν	αὐτοῖς
Mk 12:43	Καὶ προσκαλεσάμενος	τοὺς μαθητὰς αὐτοῦ		εἶπεν	αὐτοῖς
Mk 10:42	Καὶ προσκαλεσάμενος	αὐτοὺς	ὁ Ἰησοῦς λέγει	αὐτοῖς
Mk 8:1	προσκαλεσάμενος	τοὺς μαθητὰς		λέγει	αὐτοῖς
Mk 15:44	Καὶ προσκαλεσάμενος				
Mk 3:23	Καὶ προσκαλεσάμενος	αὐτοὺς	ἐν παραβολαῖς	ἔλεγεν	αὐτοῖς

Πάλιν in Mark 7:14 is also a typical redactional feature of the whole of Mark's Gospel (2:1; 2:13; 3:1; 3:20; 4:1; 5:21; 7:14; 7:31; 8:1; 8:13; 8:24; 10:1; 10:10; 10:24; 10:32; 11:3; 11:27; 12:4; 14:39; 14:40; 14:61; 14:69; 14:70bis, 15:4; 15:12; 15:13). Only six of these twenty-eight uses of πάλιν appear in either Matthew or Luke (Mark 10:24/Matt 19:24; Mark 12:4/Matt 21:36; Mark 14:39/Matt 26:42; Mark 14:40/Matt 26:43; Mark 14:70/Matt 26:72; Mark 15:12/Luke 23:20). Πάλιν seems to be a major clue to the structure of Mark. The word asks the reader to reflect back on an event or linguistic similarity in the text which precedes the use of πάλιν. By way of illustration, while there are a number of passages to which πάλιν may refer back when it appears at Mark 7:14 (5:21, 6:45, 6:55) one of the most attractive candidates is Mark 3:23.

Mk 3:23 καὶ προσκαλεσάμενος   αὐτοὺς ἐν παραβολαῖς ἔλεγεν αὐτοῖς
Mk 7:14 καὶ προσκαλεσάμενος πάλιν τὸν ὄχλον   ἔλεγεν αὐτοῖς

This is a good example of how πάλιν may refer back to a previous event or to previous similar language. If 7:14 refers back to 3:23, the redactor is calling attention to both, a previous event and previous language. Such similarities in events, such similarities in language, and

this retrospective use of πάλιν which calls attention to these similarities are most likely contributions of the final redactor of the Gospel who saw the Gospel of Mark as a literary whole.

The same hand who contributed καὶ ἔλεγεν αὐτοῖς in Mark 8:21 is probably also responsible for Mark 2:27, 4:2, 4:11, 4:21, 4:24, 6:4, 6:10, 7:9, 9:1, 11:17, 8:21, and 9:31. The shorter καὶ ἔλεγεν may also be from this hand (4:9, 4:26, 4:30, 4:41, 14:36).

The combination of words καὶ ἔλεγεν αὐτοῖς never occurs in the Gospel of Matthew and only once in the Gospel of Luke, in a passage parallel to Mark (Mark 2:27/Luke 6:5). At times, the phrase is not in the parallel at all (4:21, 6:10, 7:9, 9:1, 8:21) and it is frequently found where Matthew and Luke agree on the use of εἶπεν (see Mark 9:31, 6:4, 4:11, and 3:23 and their parallels).

In short, the redactional features of this section of Mark are the same redactional features which permeate the whole of canonical Mark. It is Koester's presupposition of Markan priority which leads him to suggest that Mark went through two early recensions. The linguistic data listed above which relate Mark 6:45-8:26 to the rest of Mark are only suggestive and far from exhaustive. The data presented have been limited to data which appear in passages Koester identified, as "clearly redactorial." There are other data that could be marshalled as evidence that the same redactor who has redacted Mark 6:45-8:26 has also redacted the remainder of Mark.

Were this section of Mark in the Gospel of Luke it would never occur to anyone to separate Mark 6:45-8:26 from the remainder of the Gospel. We have already presented data which may indicate that Luke did know this section of Mark/Matthew. He chose to omit it, however. Compared to Matthew and Mark it is clear that Luke does not like doublets or even the same turn of phrase in the same immediate context. If Mark 6:45-8:26 is characterized by doublets to the rest of Mark (the same is true of the parallel section of Matthew) then one would have a good explanation for why that material would have been omitted by Luke. It conforms to Luke's style to avoid doublets. It is not necessary to postulate two early recensions of Mark to explain Luke's text.

One may conclude this section by noting that the redactional evidence calls into question Koester's first way of explaining the common omissions of Matthew and Luke against Mark in the section

Mark 6:45-8:26, that is, his theory of two recensions of Ur-Marcus.

(1) There is strong literary evidence which links the miracle story tradition of Mark 7:32-37 and 8:22-26 to the miracle story tradition in Mark 5:41-43. The same redactor is most likely responsible for all three. Further, many of the linguistic characteristics which unite these three stories also permeate the whole of the Markan Gospel. This evidence unites this miracle story matrix with other non-miracle story contexts both within Mark 6:45-8:26 and outside of that section.

(2) On the basis of verses which Koester has identified as "clearly redactorial" more linguistic evidence has been marshalled which unites this section of Mark with the whole of the Gospel.

(3) The section Mark 6:45-8:26 becomes a meaningful literary unit within Mark essentially because it does not appear in the text of Luke. The arguments from special language and geographical details merely substantiate that major argument. But some evidence has been presented here which may suggest that Luke in fact did know this section of Mark/Matthew. A redactional analysis of Luke reveals that he would have a stylistic reason to omit Mark 6:45-8:26/Matt 14:22-16:12. He avoids doublets and there are many in this section of Mark/Matthew.

If Luke did know this section of Mark, then on the basis of the two-document hypothesis the agreements in omission of Matthew and Luke against Mark within this section would still need to be explained. In particular why would two writers using a common source both agree to omit material which is so clearly redactional in that source (Mark 7:32-37 and Mark 8:22-26)?

Let us proceed now with Koester's second answer to Stoldt's Question 2: "How could it be that the additional substantive material in the Gospel of Mark failed to appear in Matthew or in Luke, if Mark had been their source?"

Koester's second answer to this question is his theory of a Secret Gospel redactor of Ur-Marcus who edited and added details to Ur-Marcus after Matthew and Luke had been composed. Matthew and Luke therefore do not omit these sections which are found in canonical Mark. On Koester's reconstruction, they were not present in the copies of Mark known to Matthew and Luke. This redactional material isolated by Koester demonstrates the secondary character of canonical Mark relative to Matthew and Luke. Here Koester and advocates of the Griesbach hypothesis are in perfect agreement. All of the data

Koester attributes to the Secret Gospel redactor would be attributed to the final redactor of Mark, the Evangelist, on the basis of the Griesbach hypothesis. No earlier redactions or recensions of Mark's Gospel would be required.

Advocates of the Griesbach hypothesis have no need to argue with the data Koester has brought forth in sections IIff. of his paper, except perhaps to draw attention to further supporting examples within the text of canonical Mark and to suggest alternative reconstructions of the literary history of particular sections of Mark.

For example, there is no problem in understanding Mark 2:27 about the Sabbath being made for persons or Mark 4:26-29, the parable of the seed growing secretly, or Mark 12:32-34, the expansion of the teaching about the great commandment, as later additions to the text of Mark which were made following the composition of the Gospels of Matthew and Luke. The data support the hypothesis that Mark was composed after Matthew and Luke and supplemented them at points.

III

Koester's suggestion that the character of the text of the Secret Gospel quoted by Clement is the same as a redactional stage within canonical Mark is attractive. However, Clement of Alexandria was closer to the events than we are, and he may have known of what he spoke, namely, that the same author who was responsible for canonical Mark also wrote an expanded version for the church at Alexandria following his completion of the original at Rome.

Therefore, an alternative suggestion to that made by Koester might be made regarding the literary history of Mark 10:46 and the story which follows Mark 10:46a in the Secret Gospel of Mark. It is correct to note that "the text of canonical Mark 10:46 is odd." "And they come into Jericho. And as he was coming out from Jericho . . . . " As Koester is certainly aware, this text has been marshalled as evidence of the conflationary nature of Mark's Gospel. If Mark was written after Matthew and Luke and was making use of both, when he came to Matt 20:29/Luke 18:35 he was confronted with a problem. The healing narrative which follows in both Matthew and Luke is the same with the obvious difference that Matthew has two blind men to Luke's one. There is, however, a discrepancy between Matthew and Luke as to the

occasion for the healing. Matthew says it happened, "as they were going out from Jericho." Luke says it happened, "as he was drawing near to Jericho." Mark resolves the difficulty by adopting both references, "And they come into Jericho. And as he was going out from Jericho." That these references come from two sources may be confirmed by a small literary detail in the Markan text. Mark uses a plural subject (like Matthew) in his first sentence and a singular subject (like Luke) in his second sentence. Mark's difficulty is solved. He has harmonized the accounts of Matthew and Luke.

The resultant text of Mark, however, is odd. According to Mark 10:46 Jesus goes into Jericho and out of Jericho but nothing happens in Jericho. There is a need for some action to take place in this city. That need is supplied by the second edition of Mark, the Secret Gospel. The Secret Gospel supplied the required story and includes a character, Salome, who, apart from canonical Mark (15:41 and 16:1), is unknown to the readers of the NT.[33]

IV

In section IV of his paper Koester provides answers for some of the data isolated by Stoldt in his list of 180 "minor additional details in Mark that extend beyond the text of Matthew and Luke, including passages where either Matthew or Luke are lacking." He also begins to answer Stoldt's Question number 3: "How can it be explained that in 180 cases Matthew and Luke, independently and without knowledge of each other, joined in leaving out and ignoring the identical phrases and sentences of the Gospel of Mark—if this had been their source?"

Koester's answer to this question is the same as his second answer to question 2: A Secret Gospel redactor of Ur-Marcus edited and added details to Ur-Marcus after Matthew and Luke had been composed. Matthew and Luke therefore do not omit these sections which are found in canonical Mark. On Koester's reconstruction, they were not present in the copies of Mark known to Matthew and Luke.

But the data are more complicated here than in section II of the paper. In section II none of the data are found in parallels in Matthew

---

[33]It is interesting that the other interpolation into canonical Mark which the Secret Gospel records takes place in Bethany. At Mark 11:11-12 one finds the same sort of difficulty as one finds in Mark 10:46. Jesus goes into Bethany and comes out of Bethany but nothing happens in Bethany.

or Luke. This is not the case in section IV. Some members of the categories Koester has isolated do appear in parallels in Matthew and Luke. Therefore Koester must either distinguish the usages which appear in the parallels from the usages which do not or he must discount the data found in the parallels in some other way. If the Secret Gospel redactor did his work after Matthew and Luke were completed, it would be impossible for his hand to show up in the texts of Matthew or Luke.

The same problem, of course, confronts the advocate of the Gries-bach hypothesis. How is it that a usage traceable to the hand of Mark shows up in the parallel texts of Matthew or Luke if Mark was composed after these two Gospels had been completed? Here are some suggestions.

(1) Εὐαγγέλιον. The usage of this term in Mark is uniform. To divide the evidence in Mark on the basis of parallels in other Gospels is illegitimate either on Koester's reconstruction or on the basis of the Griesbach hypothesis. The literary evidence should be viewed as a whole.

Rule 2 of Farmer's methodology for making redaction criticism of service in solving the synoptic problem should be remembered, "Establish first the results of redaction-criticism, then consider synoptic parallels." When the evidence is viewed as a whole it can be seen that there is absolutely no difference in the Markan use of this term in the texts parallel to Matthew and Luke and the texts where no parallel is present. The redactional work that is reflected by this one term in Mark is of one cloth.

With the exceptions of Mark 1:1, "Gospel of Jesus Christ," and Mark 1:14, "Gospel of God," wherever "the gospel" is used in Mark it is used absolutely (1:15; 8:35; 10:29; 13:10; 14:9; [16:15]). This is even the usage of the longer ending of Mark (16:15). Mark's use of "gospel" is very nearly uniform. He refers to "the gospel" as does Paul on many occasions in an absolute way as if "the gospel" has some specific content (Rom 1:16; 10:16; 11:28 passim). Even the Markan variants, "Gospel of Jesus Christ" (1:1) and "Gospel of God" (1:14) are understandable as Pauline. For "Gospel of God," see Rom 1:1; 15:16; and 2 Cor 11:7. For "Gospel of Christ," see Rom 15:19; 1 Cor 9:12; 2 Cor 2:12. But "Gospel of *Jesus* Christ" is found nowhere else in the NT.

This uniform usage is most easily explained if one hand is responsible for all of the occurrences of "the gospel" within the text of Mark. In

this case Koester's theory of multiple redactions of the Markan Gospel has obscured the uniformity of the data.

On Koester's hypothesis one properly should conclude that the author of Ur-Marcus (13:10; 14:9) uses τὸ εὐαγγέλιον in exactly the same way as the Secret Gospel redactor (1:15; 8:35; 10:29). Koester chooses to ignore this fact, however, and to minimize its significance for his hypothesis. Of 13:10 he admits, "some scholars have considered the whole verse 'a Matthean intrusion'." He can only attribute 14:9 to "tradition".

In the foregoing we have "established first the results of redaction criticism" for the Gospel of Mark. We next must do the same for Matthew before we may properly "consider synoptic parallels."

What is constant about Matthew's use of "gospel" is that it is always used in a context of "preaching" (κηρύσσειν). (Matt 4:23; 9:35; 24:14; 26:13 are all the appearances of the word "gospel" in the text of Matthew.) In addition, with one exception (Matt 26:13), Matthew always refers to "preaching" τὸ εὐαγγέλιον τῆς βασιλείας. The extensive verbatim agreement between Matt 4:23 and 9:35 presumably puts us in touch with the hand of some redactor of Matthew's Gospel in which these elements are but parts.

4:23   Καὶ περιῆγεν. . .διδάσκων ἐν ταῖς συναγωγαῖς αὐτῶν
9:35   Καὶ περιῆγεν. . .διδάσκων ἐν ταῖς συναγωγαῖς αὐτῶν

καὶ κηρύσσων τὸ εὐαγγέλιον τῆς βασιλείας
καὶ κηρύσσων τὸ εὐαγγέλιον τῆς βασιλείας

καὶ θεραπεύων πᾶσαν νόσον καὶ πᾶσαν μαλακίαν
καὶ θεραπεύων πᾶσαν νόσον καὶ πᾶσαν μαλακίαν

Elements of this longer redactional formula in Matthew recur throughout that Gospel. For διδάσκων ἐν ταῖς συναγωγαῖς αὐτῶν compare also Matt 13:54, ἐδίδασκεν αὐτοὺς ἐν τῇ συναγωγῇ αὐτῶν. See also Matt 11:1, τοῦ διδάσκειν καὶ κηρύσσειν ἐν ταῖς πόλεσιν αὐτῶν. For κηρύσσων τὸ εὐαγγέλιον τῆς βασιλείας compare Matt 24:14, καὶ κηρυχθήσεται τοῦτο τὸ εὐαγγέλιον τῆς βασιλείας and Matt 26:13, κηρυχθῇ τὸ εὐαγγέλιον τοῦτο. Note that in both cases τοῦτο modifies τὸ εὐαγγέλιον and therefore may be said to be consistent with Matthean style. For θεραπεύων πᾶσαν νόσον καὶ πᾶσαν μαλακίαν compare Matt 10:1, θεραπεύειν πᾶσαν νόσον καὶ πᾶσαν μαλακίαν.

The usages of "the gospel" which are not found in the parallel texts of either Matthew or Luke (Mark 1:1, 1:15, 8:35, 10:29, [16:15]) present no problem for a theory of Markan redaction which follows the composition of Matthew and Luke. Either Koester's hypothesis of a later Secret Gospel redactor or the Griesbach hypothesis will explain the data.

The problematic passages are those with parallels in the other Gospels (Mark 1:14/Matt 4:17a, Mark 13:10/Matt 24:14, Mark 14:9/Matt 26:13).

Luke never uses the term "gospel" in the course of his first volume, but see Acts 15:7, "word of the gospel," and Acts 20:24, "gospel of the grace of God." With Luke out of the picture one has only to ask, "Has Mark abbreviated Matthew's longer 'preaching τὸ εὐαγγέλιον τῆς βασιλείας' or has Matthew elaborated Mark's shorter τὸ εὐαγγέλιον used absolutely?"

Advocates of the Griesbach hypothesis must explain τὸ εὐαγγέλιον in Mark 13:10 and 14:9 on the basis of Mark's use of Matthew. The long redactional phrase preserved in Matt 4:23 and 9:35 is never found in Mark or Luke, and elements of this longer redactional formula recur throughout Matthew's Gospel.

If the phrase κηρυχθήσεται τοῦτο τὸ εὐαγγέλιον τῆς βασιλείας at Matt 24:14 is an example of the recurrence of one element of a longer redactional formula present only in the Gospel of Matthew, then the appearance of τὸ εὐαγγέλιον at Mark 13:10/Matt 24:14 represents the fragmentary preservation within the Gospel of Mark of a formula traceable to the Gospel of Matthew. This would constitute evidence that Mark was written after Matthew. Koester's statement that "some scholars have considered the whole verse a Matthean intrusion" would be apt. Mark copied the expression from Matthew in this case.

Matt 26:13 is the exception to Matthew's usual expression. At Matt 26:13 τὸ εὐαγγέλιον τοῦτο is read instead of τὸ εὐαγγέλιον τῆς βασιλείας. The reference to "preaching" is still present in Matt 26:13 as in all other Matthean uses, and the pronoun τοῦτο found here is also present at Matt 24:14. One could argue that the pronoun is consistent with Matthew's style also. Mark 14:9/Matt 26:13 could also be explained by Mark's dependence upon Matthew. At both Matt 24:14/Mark 13:10 and at Matt 26:13/Mark 14:9, Mark would have altered the text of Matthew in a manner which is consistent with his usage elsewhere in his gospel.

On the basis of Markan priority one must imagine that Matthew has seen Mark's brief usage of τὸ εὐαγγέλιον at Mark 14:9 and added τοῦτο as he copied it. Previous to this Matthew would have added the same pronoun to his text of Mark at Matt 24:14/Mark 13:10. In addition at Matt 24:14 Matthew would have expanded Mark's formula in a further way by adding τῆς βασιλείας. Then, in contexts previous to both of these and in sections of his gospel not paralleled by Mark, Matthew would have used the expanded formula which he created from the Markan usage at Mark 13:10/Matt 24:14 as a part of a much larger redactional formula within his Gospel preserved both at Matt 4:23 and 9:35. If the less complicated hypothesis is to be preferred then the evidence in balance supports the priority of Matthew to Mark in these verses.

Only on the theory of Markan priority is Matt 4:17/Mark 1:14 "surprising." Matt 4:17a is quite in conformity with Matthean style elsewhere in his Gospel.

4:17a	Ἀπὸ τότε ἤρξατο ὁ Ἰησοῦς κηρύσσειν καὶ λέγειν	
16:21	Ἀπὸ τότε ἤρξατο ὁ Ἰησοῦς δεικνύειν	τοῖς μαθηταῖς αὐτοῦ
11:7	ἤρξατο ὁ Ἰησοῦς	λέγειν τοῖς ὄχλοις

The preaching of Jesus at Matt 4:17b reflects continuity with John's proclamation within that gospel.

4:17b	Μετανοεῖτε ἤγγικεν γὰρ ἡ βασιλεία τῶν οὐρανῶν
3:2	Μετανοεῖτε ἤγγικεν γὰρ ἡ βασιλεία τῶν οὐρανῶν

This apparent redactional feature of the Gospel of Matthew is lost in the Markan parallels. There is no direct quotation of John's preaching in Mark 1:4/Matt 3:2. In fact, a distinction is drawn between the preaching of John and that of Jesus in the Gospel of Mark. John came "preaching a baptism of repentance for the forgiveness of sins," and Jesus came "preaching the Gospel of God."

Whereas one may argue that Matthew may have changed Mark's distinction into continuity or that Mark may have changed Matthew's continuity into a distinction, the relationship of Luke to Mark in this passage is clear. Boismard has written:

> The activity of John the Baptist is formulated in identical terms by Mark 1:4 and Luke 3:3: 'preaching a baptism of repentance for the

forgiveness of sins.' This way of speaking is not Markan but Lukan: The word 'repentance' is nowhere else read in Mk, but eleven times in Luke/Acts. The expression 'baptism of repentance' is not read elsewhere in the NT except Acts 13:24 and 19:4; if the formula 'for the forgiveness of sins' belongs to primitive theology (Matt 26:28, Col 1:14, Eph 1:7) this forgiveness of sins is not linked with 'repentance' except in Luke 24:47, Acts 2:38, 3:19, 5:31, 8:22, 26:18-20.[34]

The whole phrase "preaching a baptism of repentance for the forgiveness of sins" points to Luke, not Mark as the source and the word for "sins" is the one Luke uses.

The previous discussion supports Matthew's priority to Mark. These last data argue for Luke's priority to Mark as well. Therefore, all of the data are explicable on the basis of the Griesbach hypothesis. Not only are the data *consistent with* that hypothesis. As has been shown, some of the data *argue for* it.

On the basis of the Griesbach hypothesis the same redactor who *added* τὸ εὐαγγέλιον to the tradition at Mark 1:1; 1:14; 1:15; 8:35; 10:29 also conformed his sources to this usage at Mark 13:10 and 14:9. This same redactor may also be responsible for the same usage in the longer ending of Mark (16:15). The Griesbach hypothesis has no difficulty with the fact that the usage in Mark when a parallel in Matthew or Luke is present is no different from a usage in Mark when no parallel is present. On Koester's reconstruction the agreement of the redactor of Ur-Marcus with the Secret Gospel redactor on this usage is problematic. It is better understood as the work of a single redactor.

In the course of his discussion of Mark's use of εὐαγγέλιον, Koester has responded to numbers 1, 4, 98, 122 in Stoldt's list of "minor additional details in Mark that extend beyond the text of Matthew and Luke . . ."

(2) διδάσκειν/διδαχή. As in the case of τὸ εὐαγγέλιον Mark's use of διδάσκειν/διδαχή in passages without parallel in Matthew or Luke presents no problem for the Griesbach hypothesis nor for Koester's reconstruction of a late secondary Secret Gospel redaction (Mark 1:27; 2:13; 4:1-2; 8:31; 9:31; 10:1; 6:34; 12:35, 38).

Again one may ask whether there is any real distinction between the use of these terms in Mark when a parallel is present and when there is

---

[34]P. Benoit and M.-E. Boismard, *Synopse des quatre evangiles en francais*, II (Paris, 1972), p. 26. I am indebted to Harold Riley for this reference and its translation.

not. On Koester's hypothesis one may ask, "Is the work of the redactor of Ur-Marcus any different from that of the Secret Gospel redactor?" In at least one case, the answer is "No." By quoting the Greek three times, Koester has drawn attention to the fact that Mark frequently uses the auxiliary ἄρχομαι in combination with the infinitive διδάσ-κειν in passages he attributes to the hand of the Secret Gospel redactor of Mark (4:1; 6:34b; 8:31). Ἄρχομαι plus the infinitive is particularly frequent in Mark, and the combination of καὶ ἤρξατο διδάσκειν to introduce a teaching of Jesus appears in Mark four times, the three verses noted by Koester (4:1; 6:34b; and 8:31) *and* Mark 6:2 (cf. Matt 13:54). The Matthean parallel has the simple imperfect, ἐδίδασκεν. There is therefore no distinction in the use of this term in the redaction of earlier tradition carried out by the author of Ur-Marcus and the Secret Gospel redaction.

Koester has presupposed that the appearance of these words, διδάσκειν/διδαχή, in passages parallel to Mark 1:21, 22; 6:2; 6:7; (7:7); 11:18; 12:14; and 14:49 appear there because they were copied there from Ur-Marcus by Matthew and Luke. But the evidence may suggest a different solution to the Synoptic Problem.

In the Gospel of Matthew one finds a formula repeated at Matt 7:28 and Matt 22:33:

Mt 7:28   ἐξεπλήσσοντο οἱ ὄχλοι ἐπὶ τῇ διδαχῇ αὐτοῦ
Mt 22:33   οἱ ὄχλοι ἐξεπλήσσοντο   ἐπὶ τῇ διδαχῇ αὐτοῦ

In Matthew the formula is identical in both cases with the exception of the reversal of word order of subject and verb.

In the Gospel of Mark one finds a formula repeated at Mark 1:22 and Mark 11:18:

Mk 1:22   καὶ   ἐξεπλήσσοντο ἐπὶ τῇ διδαχῇ αὐτοῦ
Mk 11:18   πᾶς γάρ ὁ ὄχλος ἐξεπλήσσετο   ἐπὶ τῇ διδαχῇ αὐτοῦ

In Mark the formulas vary a good bit more than they do in Matthew. Καί in Mark 1:22 parallels γάρ in Mark 11:18; the subject is unexpressed in Mark 1:22. The subject πᾶς ὁ ὄχλος appears in Mark 11:18; πᾶς ὁ ὄχλος appears as the subject of a sentence in Mark 2:13, 4:1 and 9:15. The verb in 1:22 is plural while the verb in Mark 11:18 is singular to agree with the expressed subject, πᾶς ὁ ὄχλος.

In the Gospel of Luke one finds a similar formula at Luke 4:32; but nowhere else in that gospel: καί ἐξεπλήσσοντο ἐπὶ τῇ διδαχῇ αὐτοῦ.

Matt 7:28 is parallel to Mark 1:22 and Luke 4:32. Matt 22:23 may or may not be parallel to Mark 11:18. Inasmuch as the formula is repeated in both the text of Mark and the text of Matthew but only occurs in the text of Luke in a passage in parallel with both Matthew and Mark, one may conclude that "the presence of this formula in the Gospels of Matthew and Mark is due to some preference on the part of those redactors, while its presence in the Gospel of Luke may readily be accounted for by copying."

Luke is secondary to either Matthew or Mark on the basis of this evidence alone. What then is the indication of the direction of literary dependence between Matthew and Mark?

An independent view of the data in the Gospels of Matthew and Mark reveals that the evidence for redactional kinship is greater in the Gospel of Matthew than it is in the Gospel of Mark. If Mark 11:18 is parallel to Matt 22:33, there is nothing in either text of Mark which appears to be redactional, ἐπὶ τῇ διδαχῇ αὐτοῦ, which could not be explained by Mark's dependence upon Matthew. The reverse is not true. The plural subject οἱ ὄχλοι and the plural verb in both texts of Matthew cannot derive from Mark. In balance then it would appear to be more likely that Mark represents a fragmentary preservation of a formula traceable in the Matthean Gospel than the reverse. The alteration of οἱ ὄχλοι to πᾶς ὁ ὄχλος at Mark 11:18/Matt 22:33 conforms to Markan style elsewhere in his Gospel (2:13; 4:1; 9:15).

If Matt 22:33 is not parallel to Mark 11:18, then the direction of literary dependence is inconclusive from this data inasmuch as both Matthew (22:33) and Mark (11:18) use the formula in contexts independent of one another as well as in parallel with one another (Mark 1:22/Matt 7:28).

The use of καὶ περιῆγεν . . . διδάσκων at Mark 6:7 is evidence of the secondary nature of Mark to Matthew in that passage. These words are clearly traceable to a formula only found in the Gospel of Matthew; see Matt 4:23 and 9:35 above. The words καὶ περιῆγεν, in fact the root verb itself, is found nowhere in the Markan Gospel outside of Mark 6:7/Matt 9:35. The presence of this formula in the Gospel of Matthew "is due to some preference on the part of Matt while its presence in the Gospel of Mark may readily be accounted for by copying."

While at the moment there appear to be no indicators of the direction of literary dependence suggested by the common usage of διδάσκειν/διδαχή in passages parallel to Mark 1:21; 6:2 (7:7); 12:14; and 14:49, such indicators as do exist in Mark 1:22; 6:7; and 11:18 point to Mark's dependence upon Matthew rather than the opposite which Koester presupposes.

On the basis of the Griesbach hypothesis, the same redactor who added διδάσκειν/διδαχή to the tradition at Mark 1:27; 2:13; 4:1-2; 8:31; 9:31; 6:34; 12:35; and 38 also adopted it from his sources at 1:21; 6:7 and 11:18. No conclusions can be drawn at this time about Mark 1:22; 6:2 (7:7); 12:14; or 14:49. The evidence of the double and triple tradition points in the same direction as the evidence from Markan *Sondergut*, namely, that Mark is a Gospel which reflects a late secondary redaction which was performed on the text of Mark after the Gospels of Matthew and Luke were completed.

The further evidence which Koester cites under his discussion of διδάσκειν/διδαχή could be expanded as follows:

Mark 1:27. No further data.

Mark 2:13. The larger literary relationship between Mark 2:13 and 4:1 should be noted:

2:13	Καὶ	4:1	Καὶ
	ἐξῆλθεν		
	πάλιν		πάλιν
			ἤρξατο διδάσκειν
	παρὰ τὴν θάλασσαν		παρὰ τὴν θάλασσαν
	καὶ		καὶ
	πᾶς ὁ ὄχλος		
	ἤρχετο		συνάγεται
	πρὸς αὐτόν,		πρὸς αὐτὸν
			ὄχλος πλεῖστος,
			ὥστε αὐτὸν εἰς πλοῖον ἐμβάντα
			καθῆσθαι ἐν τῇ θαλάσσῃ
			καὶ
			πᾶς ὁ ὄχλος
			πρὸς τὴν θάλασσαν
			ἐπὶ τῆς γῆς ἦσαν
	καὶ ἐδίδασκεν αὐτούς		καὶ ἐδίδασκεν αὐτοὺς
			ἐν παραβολαῖς

πολλά
καὶ ἔλεγεν αὐτοῖς
ἐν τῇ διδαχῇ αὐτοῦ
ἀκούετε

Like the πάλιν of Mark 7:14 discussed earlier (cf. 7:14 and 3:23) the πάλιν of Mark 2:13 refers the reader back to Mark 1:16. The πάλιν of Mark 4:1 refers the reader back to 2:13. This makes Mark 2:13 a pivotal verse which ties what follows in the Markan Gospel with what has preceded. Mark 2:13 is best explained as the work of some redactor who saw Mark's Gospel as a literary whole and provided shape for that whole by the arrangement of events. This redactor was most likely the final redactor.

Mk 1:16   Καὶ παράγων   παρὰ τὴν θάλασσαν
Mk 2:13   Καὶ ἐξῆλθεν   πάλιν   παρὰ τὴν θάλασσαν. . . . καὶ ἐδίδασκεν αὐτούς
Mk 4:1   Καὶ   πάλιν   ἤρξατο διδάσκειν   παρὰ τὴν θάλασσαν.
                                           . . . καὶ ἐδίδασκεν αὐτοὺς

The phrase πᾶς ὁ ὄχλος is also found in Mark 4:1, 9:15, and 11:18. This is one of several redactional links which join Mark 2:13 to Mark 4:1.

Mark 4:1-2. The phrase καὶ ἤρξατο διδάσκειν unites Mark 4:1 to Mark 6:2; 6:34b; and 8:31; see the discussion above. The phrase καὶ ἐδίδασκεν . . . καὶ ἔλεγεν αὐτοῖς unites Mark 4:2 to 9:31 and 11:17. This is one subcategory of a larger redactional category characterized by the words καὶ ἔλεγεν αὐτοῖς; see the discussion above. The phrase καὶ ἔλεγεν αὐτοῖς ἐν τῇ διδαχῇ αὐτοῦ + 2nd person plural imperative unites Mark 4:1 to 12:38.

Mk 4:1   καὶ ἔλεγεν αὐτοῖς ἐν τῇ διδαχῇ αὐτοῦ   ἀκούετε
Mk 12:38 Καὶ   ἐν τῇ διδαχῇ αὐτοῦ ἔλεγεν βλέπετε

One may take note of the potential relationship of these verses in Mark to Mark 8:18:

Mk 8:18   ὀφθαλμοὺς ἔχοντες οὐ βλέπετε
          καὶ ὦτα ἔχοντες οὐκ ἀκούετε

Mark 8:32a. The same hand responsible for Mark 8:32a καὶ παρρησίᾳ τὸν λόγον ἐλάλει probably also contributed Mark 2:2 and 4:33.

Mk 2:2   καὶ   ἐλάλει αὐτοῖς τὸν λόγον

Mk 4:33   Καὶ τοιαύταις παραβολαῖς   ἐλάλει αὐτοῖς τὸν λόγον

Mk 8:32a   καὶ παρρησίᾳ   τὸν λόγον ἐάλει

This redactor uses the term ὁ λόγος, like the term τὸ εὐαγγέλιον, absolutely (1:45; 2:2; 4:14; 4:16; 4:17; 4:18; 4:19; 4:20; 8:32; 9:10; 10:22; [16:20]).

Mark 10:1. The words in Mark 10:1 unite it with Mark 7:24.

Mk 7:24   ᾽Εκεῖθεν δὲ ἀναστὰς ἀπῆλθεν εἰς τὰ ὅρια Τυρου καὶ

Mk 10:1 Καὶ ἐκεῖθεν   ἀναστὰς ἔρχεται εἰς τὰ ὅρια τῆς ᾽Ιουδαίας [καὶ]

Mark 11:17. The phrase (διδάσκων) ἐν τῷ ἱερῷ unites Mark 11:15,17 with 14:49 and 12:35. Note that these words in Mark 14:49 in the scene in the Garden of Gethsemane reflect back to Mark 11:15,17 but also to Mark 12:35. There is no parallel in either Matthew or Luke to these words in Mark 12:35.

Mark 12:38. The phrase καὶ ἤκουεν αὐτοῦ ἡδέως relates Mark 12:38 to Mark 6:20. Neither passage is found in the parallels of either Matthew or Luke.

In addition to those passages discussed by Koester under the heading of διδάσκειν/διδαχή and beginning with those suggested by Koester, one needs also to consider Mark 1:16; 1:45; 2:2; 4:14, 16, 17, 18, 19, 20; 4:33; 6:2; 7:24; 8:32; 9:10; 9:15; 9:31; 10:22; 11:15, 17, 18; 12:35; 12:38; 14:49; and 16:20 as potential passages where the work of the secondary late redactor has been performed. The vast majority of this material has no parallels in the text of Matthew or Luke. 1:45; 4:33; 8:32; 9:10, 15; and 12:38 have no linguistic ties to the parallel Gospels whatsoever. Is this the work of some later redactor reworking an already existing piece of literature, or is this evidence more easily explained as the work of the redactor responsible for the shape of the Gospel in its original form?

In the course of his discussion of Mark's use of διδάσκειν/διδαχή Koester has responded to numbers 16, 36, 37, 97 of Stoldt's list of "minor additional details in Mark that extend beyond the text of Matthew and Luke . . . "

(3) μυστήριον. At this point Koester takes up a positive minor agreement of Matthew and Luke against Mark rather than a common omission from these Gospels. He discusses number 4 in another of

Stoldt's lists. This is a list of "concurrence of Matthew and Luke in diverging from Mark's word form"; Stoldt lists twenty two examples and from this list formulates his question number 6, "What caused the other two synoptic writers, independently and without personal contact, in twenty-two cases to make exactly the same small modification in an identical manner to a word they both had in common in the text with Mark?"

Koester answers that in the case of μυστήριον Matthew and Luke have preserved the original text of Ur-Marcus but the Secret Gospel redactor changed Ur-Marcus and thereby created this minor agreement of Matthew and Luke against Mark now preserved in canonical Mark. Ur-Marcus is a valuable hypothesis for an advocate of Markan priority because one can make such appeals to the text of the lost Ur-Marcus to explain those places within the triple tradition where Matthew and Luke agree against canonical Mark, as Koester does here.

Of course, with this gain for the Markan hypothesis there is also a loss with regard to the possibility of redaction criticism of Matthew and Luke. As redaction criticism is usually practiced on Matthew and Luke, great emphasis is put on the changes Matthew and Luke have made in their Markan exemplar. Once one admits that we no longer have access to the source used by Matthew and Luke, such a procedure undertaken by redaction critics is called into serious question. How can one know what Matthew and Luke have changed in their source if that source is no longer available?

Koester has claimed that "the agreement of Lk 8:10 with Matt 13:11 cannot be explained by the assumption of Lucan dependence upon Matthew." It should be remembered that *all* of the agreements within the triple tradition should be added to the minor agreements in order to grasp the total evidence available for the direct literary relationship of Matthew and Luke. This evidence from Matt 13:10 and Luke 8:10 alone looks like this:

Mt 13:11   ὑμῖν δέοται γνῶναι τὰ μυστήρια τῆς βασιλείας τῶν οὐρανῶν ἐκείνοις δέ

Lk 8:10   ὑμῖν δέοται γνῶναι τὰ μυστήρια τῆς βασιλείας τοῦ θεοῦ   τοῖς   δέ

Just why "Luke 8:10 cannot be explained by the assumption of Lukan dependence upon Matthew" is not clear at all given this high level of verbatim agreement.

In his discussion of Mark 4:11 Koester cites with approval the work of Jeremias. To be sure, Jeremias argues that Mark 4:11 is a primitive saying of Jesus, but Jeremias limits his discussion to Mark 4:11. He says nothing about the parallels in Matthew or Luke.[35] Koester argues that Matt 13:11-13 is a secondary redaction of Mark 4:11. Mark's saying is characterized by antithetical parallelism. According to Jeremias, this is one of the signs of the primitivity of Mark 4:11. According to Koester, Matthew has inserted an independent saying into the middle of an older saying found in Mark; this is a sign of Markan priority in this verse. Matthew represents a secondary expansion of the text which interrupts the original parallelism found in the primitive Markan text.

The evidence in Matthew, however, when considered independently of Mark, will not sustain this "interpolation thesis." Matt 13:11 taken by itself reflects antithetical parallelism.

Mt 13:11   ὑμῖν   δέοται γνῶναι τὰ μυστήρια
            ἐκείνοις δὲ οὐ   δέδοται

The object of the verb in the second member of the parallelism is the same as the object of the verb in the first member. It is simply left unexpressed in the second member. The verse reflects good Semitic style. To suggest that λαλῶ in Matt 13:13 is parallel to δέδοται in Matt 13:11 and that ἐν παραβολαῖς in Matthew 13:13 is parallel to γνῶναι κτλ., as Koester does, is simply to read Matthew through the eyes of Mark.

Jesus' answer in Matt 13:13 reflects the disciples' question in Matt 13:10.

Mt 13:10 διὰ τί   ἐν παραβολαῖς   λαλεῖς αὐτοῖς
Mt 13:13 διὰ τοῦτο ἐν παραβολαῖς αὐτοῖς λαλῶ

Matt 13:13 is therefore in no way the conclusion to the saying in Matt 13:11.

---

[35]Joachim Jeremias, *Die Gleichnisse Jesu*, 8th ed. (Göttingen: Vandenhoeck & Ruprecht, 1970) (ET: S. H. Hooke, *The Parables of Jesus*, 2nd ed. [New York: Scribner's, 1972], pp. 13-18).

Like Matthew, Luke frames the saying with a question and answer in similar language.

Lk 8:9   τίς   αὕτη εἴη ἡ παραβολή
Lk 8:11 ἔστιν δὲ αὕτη   ἡ παραβολή

The saying however is different.

Lk 8:10 ὑμῖν δέδοται γνῶναι τὰ μυστήρια τῆς βασιλείας τοῦ θεοῦ
Lk 8:10 τοῖς δὲ λοιποῖς   ἐν παραβολαῖς

In Luke ἐν παραβολαῖς is not parallel to τά μυστήρια either. Even in Mark ἐν παραβολαῖς is not parallel to μυστήριον; τὰ πάντα is.

Mk 4:11 ὑμῖν   τὸ μυστήριον δέδοται τῆς βασιλείας τοῦ
         ἐκείνοις δὲ τοῖς ἔξω ἐν παραβολαῖς τὰ πάντα   γίνεται

In Matthew, "to know the mysteries of the kingdom of heaven" is given to the disciples; in Luke "to know the mysteries of the kingdom of heaven" is given to the disciples. In Matthew "to know the mysteries of the kingdom of heaven" *is not given* to "those"; in Luke "to know the mysteries of the kingdom of heaven" *is given* to "the rest," only it is given in parables.

There is a conflict between Matthew and Luke. Is "knowledge of the mysteries of the kingdom of heaven/God" *given* to "those/the rest," as Luke suggests, *or not*, as Matthew suggests? Mark solves the difficulty by going his own way. The gift of "the myster*ies*" to those outside is left open. Mark's interest is in *the single mystery* used absolutely, like "the gospel" used absolutely, and "the word" used absolutely.

The plural is admitted by Koester to be an old Pauline idea; the singular, a later deutero-Pauline concept. This evidence fits a development of the tradition from the older ideas of Matthew and Luke to the later idea in Mark. There is no need to postulate an earlier version of Mark which was the same as the texts of Matthew and Luke.

(4) βάπτισμα. In his discussion of Mark's use of βάπτισμα, Koester discusses number 124 in Stoldt's list of "minor additional details in Mark that extend beyond the text of Matthew and Luke . . ." In the whole of section IV Koester responded to nine of the items in this list of Stoldt's (1, 4, 16, 98, 122, 36, 37, 97, and 124). He has also called attention to Mark 6:34b καὶ ἤρξατο διδάσκειν αὐτοὺς πολλά, which could be added to Stoldt's list.

In section II of his paper Koester responded to items 25, 3, and 146. Up to this point Koester has dealt with a total of 13 of 180 items in Stoldt's list.

V

In section V of his paper Koester discusses numbers 102, 103, 104, 105, 106, and 123 of Stoldt's list when he discusses "The Epileptic Child." Under "The Rich Man Whom Jesus Loved" Koester discussed numbers 120, 121, of Stoldt's list. In addition to the linguistic data discussed by Koester the following should be considered.

1. The Epileptic Child. The exorcism in Mark 1:23-27, paralleled in Luke 4:33-37, shows a striking linguistic and structural similarity to Mark 9:24-26 where no parallel exists in either Matthew or Luke.

Mk 1:25-27	Mk 9:24-26
	ἰδὼν δὲ ὁ ᾽Ιησοῦς
	ὅτι ἐπισυντρέχει ὄχλος,
καὶ ἐπετίμησεν αὐτῷ	ἐπετίμησεν τῷ πνεύματι τῷ ἀκαθάρτῳ
ὁ ᾽Ιησοῦς	
[λέγων]	λέγων αὐτῷ
	τὸ ἄλαλον καὶ κωφὸν πνεῦμα
	ἐγὼ ἐπιτάσσω σοι,
φιμώθητι καὶ	
ἔξελθε ἐξ αὐτοῦ	ἔξελθε ἐξ αὐτοῦ.
	καὶ μηκέτι εἰσέλθῃς εἰς αὐτόν.
	καὶ κράξας
καὶ σπαράξαν αὐτὸν	καὶ πολλὰ σπαράξας
τὸ πνεῦμα τὸ ἀκάθαρτον	
καὶ φωνῆσαν	
φωνῇ μεγάλῃ	
ἐξῆλθεν ἐξ αὐτοῦ.	ἐξῆλθεν.

The setting for the private instruction about the exorcism just performed in Mark 9:14-28 is typical of Mark. See also Mark 4:10; 5:38; 7:17; 10:10; 9:33. Refer to the chart below.

Mk 9:28	Καὶ εἰσελθόντος αὐτοῦ	εἰς οἶκον	οἱ μαθηταὶ αὐτοῦ . . . ἐπηρώτων αὐτόν . . .	καὶ εἶπεν αὐτοῖς
Mk 7:17	Καὶ ὅτε εἰσῆλθεν	εἰς οἶκον . . .	ἐπηρώτων αὐτὸν οἱ μαθηταὶ αὐτοῦ	καὶ λέγει αὐτοῖς
Mk 10:10	Καὶ	εἰς τὴν οἰκίαν	οἱ μαθηταὶ ἐπηρώτων αὐτόν.	Καὶ λέγει αὐτοῖς
Mk 9:33	Καὶ	ἐν τῇ οἰκίᾳ . . .	ἐπηρώτα αὐτούς	καὶ λέγει αὐτοῖς

Mk 5:38   Καὶ ἔρχονται   εἰς τὸν οἶκον . . .   λέγει αὐτοῖς
Mk 4:10   Καὶ ὅτε ἐγένετο κατὰ μόνας   ἠρώτων αὐτὸν οἱ περὶ αὐτὸν σὺν τοῖς δώδεκα . . .   καὶ ἔλεγεν αὐτοῖς

The actual "raising" of the epileptic in Mark 9:27 is performed in language similar to the "raising" of Peter's mother-in-law at Mark 1:31 and the "raising" of Jairus' daughter at Mark 5:41.

Mk 1:31 Καὶ προσελθὼν ἤγειρεν αὐτὴν κρατήσας τῆς χειρός   καὶ ἀφῆκεν αὐτὴν ὁ πυρετός καὶ διηκόνει . . .
Mk 9:27 Ὁ δὲ Ἰησοῦς   κρατήσας τῆς χειρός αὐτοῦ   ἤγειρεν αὐτὸν καὶ ἀνέστη
Mk 5:41 Καὶ   κρατήσας τῆς χειρός τοῦ παιδίου . . . ἔγειρε καὶ εὐθὺς ἀνέστη τὸ κοράσιον καὶ περιεπάτει

Note also the linguistic similarity between Mark 9:31; 7:24; and 5:43.

7:24   Καὶ   εἰσελθὼν εἰς οἰκίαν οὐδένα ἤθελεν   γνῶναι
9:31   Κἀκεῖθεν ἐξελθόντες. . .   οὐκ   ἤθελεν ἵνα τις   γνοῖ
5:43   Καὶ διεστείλατο αὐτοῖς πολλὰ   ἵνα μηδεὶς γνοῖ

2. The Third Prediction of the Passion. No further data.

3. The Rich Man Whom Jesus Loved. No further data.

4. The Youth Who Fled Naked. The language of this passage is similar in form to the language which describes the "young man" at the tomb in Mark 16:5. These two passages (14:51 and 16:5) preserve all the Markan usages of νεανίσκος and περιβάλλω.

14:51   Καὶ   νεανίσκος. . .περιβεβλημένος. . .καὶ. . .ὁ δὲ. . .
16:5   Καὶ. . .νεανίσκον. . .περιβεβλημένον. . .καὶ. . .ὁ δὲ. . .

VI

Koester suggests that the redaction of the Secret Gospel is identical with a significant layer of redaction within canonical Mark. On this point one may concur. The evidence for such a relationship is very strong. The linguistic ties between canonical Mark and the Secret Gospel, highlighted by Koester, are fascinating. In fact, there are further linguistic and structural ties between the two works.

The evidence is certainly strong enough to suggest common authorship of the Secret Gospel and much of the redactional material in Mark. If anything, the evidence is *too* strong. The high density of identifiable Markan redactional characteristics within the relatively brief text of the Secret Gospel preserved by Clement might be explained as the work of a conscious imitator of Markan style not unlike the author of Ephesians imitated Paul.

The question for continuing discussion is whether the redactor of the Gospel of Mark identified by Koester as the Secret Gospel redactor should be understood as the second or third redactor to have edited the Markan Gospel or whether the redactor identified by Koester is the *only* redactor of the Markan Gospel.

Koester has identified sections of Mark's Gospel which are, in his view, clearly secondary to the texts of Matthew and Luke. On this point there is no dispute between Koester and advocates of the Griesbach hypothesis. In twenty of 180 cases isolated by Stoldt (25, 3, 146, 1, 4, 98, 122, 16, 36, 37, 97, 124, 102, 103, 104, 105, 106, 123, 120, 121) Koester agrees that the evidence is best explained on a theory that canonical Mark was redacted following the composition of Matthew and Luke. Further, Koester suggests that all twenty of his examples reflect a theological integrity and clearly secondary character relative to Matthew and Luke. In fact, these twenty examples reflect a theological character similar to that of the deutero-Pauline Epistle to the Ephesians.

Koester goes beyond Stoldt in drawing attention to further examples of "minor additional details in Mark that extend beyond the text of Matt and Luke." (For example, 6:34b; 9:32; 10:34; 14:34; 16:5; 1:27; 10:24; 10:32; and 14:51-52. It is difficult to understand how Stoldt missed this last one.) These examples also demonstrate the secondary character of Mark to Matthew and Luke in Koester's opinion. Numerous other examples have been isolated in this response to Koester. The amount of material within the Gospel of Mark which (1) can be demonstrated as redactional within that Gospel and (2) has no parallel in Matthew or Luke is very impressive indeed. Three of the most impressive examples are Mark 7:32-37, Mark 5:41-43, and Mark 8:22-26.

This type of evidence appears throughout the Gospel of Mark. There is no recognizable difference, on the basis of this redactional material, between Mark 6:45-8:26 and the rest of Mark's Gospel. It is highly unlikely that Mark went through two recensions. The absence of Mark 6:44-8:26/Matt 14:22-16:12 from the text of Luke can easily be explained on the basis of a demonstrable Lukan *Tendenz* to avoid doublets.

Whereas Koester's arguments for a relationship between canonical Mark and the Secret Gospel and his arguments regarding the secon-

dary nature of Mark to Matthew and Luke in particular redactional passages are attractive, his arguments for the priority of Mark in the double and triple tradition are not convincing.

Koester's data, taken from Markan *Sondergut* and the "minor additional details in Mark that extend beyond the text of Matthew and Luke," argue for the secondary character of Mark to Matthew and Luke. The direction of literary dependence which is suggested by the linguistic evidence within the double and triple tradition, as demonstrated in section IV of this response, in balance, moves in the same direction—Mark is secondary to Matthew and Luke.

At times Koester's presupposition of Markan priority actually keeps him from viewing the data as a whole, even within Mark, as in the case of Mark's use of τὸ εὐαγγέλιον. The agreement in usage of this term between the redactor of Ur-Markus and the Secret Gospel redactor is problematic for Koester's theory of multiple redactions of Mark. Actually the linguistic data within the Gospel of Mark support the view that Mark's gospel was redacted once, after the gospels of Matthew and Luke were completed.

All of the data presented by Koester are *consistent with* the Griesbach hypothesis. Some of the data (discussed in section IV) go farther and actually *argue for* the Griesbach hypothesis.

THE PURPOSE AND PROVENANCE OF THE GOSPEL OF MARK ACCORDING TO THE "TWO-GOSPEL" (GRIESBACH) HYPOTHESIS*

David L. Dungan

RETHINKING THE RELATIONSHIPS of the Gospels to each other, and with this the specific circumstances that gave rise to each one, is not made easier by our old habits of thinking and our old ways of looking at each one. In this case, the decades-long custom of thinking of Mark as a "primitive" Gospel, or of regarding Matthew and Luke as efforts to improve Mark's Greek, Mark's "offensive theology," and so on, all conspire to hamper our efforts at viewing Mark in a new and fresh way. Even more insidious (because so little recognized) is the massive blockade across our path resulting from uncritical reliance upon gospel synopses (particularly Huck-Lietzmann and Aland) whose structure and arrangement so thoroughly presupposes the two-document hypothesis that it is virtually impossible to perceive Mark's relation-

*This paper was read in a slightly different version at the Cambridge Griesbach Colloquium, 13-18 August 1979. Research for it was made possible by a grant from the National Endowment for the Humanities (Summer Stipend). I wish to thank Prof. Maria Grossmann of the Andover-Harvard Library for her generous assistance, and also Dr. Richard Marius and Dr. Lanier Smythe for their unfailing hospitality. Finally, although illness prevented him from attending the Colloquium, I owe much of the inspiration for this paper to an earlier conversation with Dr. Hans-Herbert Stoldt, to whom it is gratefully dedicated.

ships to the other Gospels in an alternative way.[1] Working out new visions of the rise of Christianity and the manner in which these "memoirs of Christ" appeared must take place in spite of real mental blocks, therefore, and it will be a laborious and time-consuming process. What is presented here will of necessity be very elementary and can be offered only as a preliminary result.

A. The Key Feature of Mark That the "Two-Gospel Hypothesis" Explains

The task of this paper is to provide a plausible historical explanation for the very existence of the Gospel of Mark. Posed in Griesbachian terms, the issue is as follows: who in the early church, already (*ex hypothesi*) possessing the Gospel of Matthew and Luke-Acts, would use them to produce yet another account, with precisely the structure and contents of canonical Mark? Now, before we attempt to answer this complex question, let us be as conscious as possible regarding the central, objective, literary data that J. J. Griesbach first[2] noticed, which became the essential basis of his hypothesis. I refer to the "phenomenon of order" (as it has come to be called), which remains to this day the sine qua non of the "Two-Gospel Hypothesis" (as the neo-Griesbachian school now prefers to call it). Let us hear his statement of this phenomenon, as described in 1794:

> Mark compiled his whole work [that is, apart from about 24 verses...] from the works of Matthew and Luke in such a manner that (A) it can easily be shown what he took from the one and what he took from the other; (B) he retained the order preserved by Matthew in such a way that wherever he forsakes it he sticks to the path of Luke and follows the order of his narrative step by step, to such an extent that, (C) the

---

[1]See my article, "Theory of Synopsis Construction," *Biblica* (September 1980), which examines more than thirty synopses according to their structure and purpose, with special observations regarding the biased presentations of Aland and Huck-Lietzmann. See also J. B. Orchard, "Are All Gospel Synopses Biased?" *TZ* 34 (1978): 149-62; and, idem, *A Synopsis of the Four Gospels*, published jointly by Mercer University Press, Macon, GA and T. & T. Clark, Edinburgh, December 1981.

[2]Apparently there is some reason to suspect that Griesbach actually became aware of this theory while in London, where he picked up a copy of a book by Henry Owen, *Observations on the Four Gospels; Tending Chiefly to ascertain the Times of their Publication; and to Illustrate the Form and Manner of their Composition* (London, 1764). Since Owen's book is rather difficult to find these days, the present writer will be glad to make a copy of his edition for those who may like to have one.

verses and words where he passes from Matthew to Luke or returns from Luke to Matthew can not only be pointed out, but also (D) the probable reason can generally be given.[3]

And further:

When Mark has closely adhered to either Matthew or Luke for a long stretch, he often passes with a sudden leap from one to the other, but soon returns to his former guide; and this could not have been done unless he had simultaneously seen and compared the works of each.[4]

In other words, Griesbach's hypothesis came to him, according to his own explicit statement, as a result of careful empirical observation of the texts of all three Gospels simultaneously, and not—as was the custom of his day—from deductions based upon the early patristic tradition concerning the origins of the Gospels. Maybe Griesbach was specially prepared for this approach after years of careful, minute comparison of the Gospels during his text-critical research; I can't say. At any rate, it apparently dawned on him one day that the answer to the riddle of the relationships of Matthew, Mark, and Luke was that Mark had woven the accounts of Matthew and Luke into a composite narrative, paragraph by paragraph, sentence by sentence, and even word by word.[5] Where his two sources had the same story in the same order, Mark invariably copied it; in between, he drew from now one, now the other. Interestingly enough, the process Mark is envisioned as having followed bears a striking resemblance to the very method Arrian explicitly says he used in writing his *Anabasis of Alexander*:

Wherever Ptolemy the son of Lagos and Aristoboulos the son of Aristoboulos have both written the same accounts (ταὐτά) concerning Alexander the son of Philip, these I have written as being completely true (πάντη ἀληθῆ). But those accounts which are not the same, from

---

[3]J. B. Orchard and T. R. W. Longstaff, eds., *J. J. Griesbach: Synoptic and Text-Critical Studies 1776-1976*, SNTSMS 34 (Cambridge, 1978), p. 108.

[4]Ibid., p. 113.

[5]A word of caution: it is best to begin by consulting Griesbach's own chart, if one wishes to verify his description of the phenomena; see Orchard and Longstaff, *Griesbach*, the chart given on pp. 108-13. Currently popular synopses tend to obscure the evidence. For the most recent examination of Mark as a conflation of Matthew and Luke, see T. R. W. Longstaff, *Evidence of Conflation in Mark? A Study in the Synoptic Problem*, SBLDS 28 (Scholars Press, 1977), esp. appendix, "The Structure of Mark."

them I have chosen those which seemed to me more believable (πιστότερα) and more worth telling (ἀξιαφηγητότερα).[6]

(It is one of the more irritating features of current source-critical discussion to observe the way in which this argument from order is being used by adherents of the Two-Document Hypothesis to prove precisely the opposite conclusion Griesbach arrived at. However, this is possible, as B. C. Butler noticed more than three decades ago, and as Hans-Herbert Stoldt has now so brilliantly demonstrated, only because of a chain of mistaken inferences, careless and illogical reasoning, and circular argument stretching from Christian Hermann Weisse through H. J. Holtzmann in Germany and B. H. Streeter in England, to our own time. May I repeat: adherents of the priority of Mark have *never shown* how this very same argument from the phenomenon of order can legitimately prove that canonical Mark was written *first*.[7])

From a Griesbachian point of view, then, it is this objective phenomenon of order which constitutes the basic starting point for the theory: wherever Matthew and Luke had the same account in the same order, that Mark invariably took over into his narrative; in between he took from the one or the other (mixing in details from the account he was *not* following). Only rarely did he depart from both simultaneously. That is the objective phenomenon of order stated in bare outline as it underlies the "Two-Gospel Hypothesis." As such, therefore, this phenomenon must also be the primary fact to be explained historically.

But let us be more specific about it. Several puzzling aspects of this phenomenon require explanation. For example, why would anyone go to the trouble of composing another "memoir of Christ" in which he sought mainly to repeat carefully what two earlier memoirists had written, and yet, at the same time, to leave out lots of material that seems, to us at any rate, so precious and important? On the other hand,

---

[6]Flavius Arrianus, *Anabasis of Alexander*, 1 Pref. (my trans.).

[7]See the especially lucid statement of this challenge to the adherents of the two-document hypothesis by W. R. Farmer, *The Synoptic Problem* (Macmillan, 1964; Mercer University Press, 1981), p. 213. It is my considered opinion that this particular query is fatal to the classical form of the two-document hypothesis. For a fuller description of the complete lack of probative logic in all five of B. H. Streeter's main arguments for the priority of Mark, see my article, "Mark—the Abridgement of Matthew and Luke," *Jesus and Man's Hope*, 2 vols. (Pittsburgh Theological Seminary, 1970), 1:54-74.

how could the author supposedly copy his sources carefully and at the same time regularly spoil the good Greek style and constructions they both contained? Again, why would he want to leave aside so much teaching material (the Sermon on the Mount!) if he was free to copy from the one or the other at will? Why did he omit all mention of the birth narratives? Why did he select and shape his material in order to place such heavy emphasis upon Jesus' suffering and death?

These and many more questions—all arising out of the fundamental observation regarding the phenomenon of order—must be answered satisfactorily for the Two-Gospel Hypothesis to attain scholarly acceptance as a viable hypothesis regarding the composition of the Gospels. However, for the moment I wish to focus attention on the fundamental phenomenon of order itself. What could have been the *purpose* in producing such a combined account as we are now supposing Mark to have been? And secondly, since the purpose for writing Mark can hardly be understood apart from the religious situation of the actual Christians who desired to bring this Gospel into being, we are necessarily required to ask also concerning the *provenance* of Mark. Our starting point will be provided by these two clues: first, on the Griesbachian view, Mark represents a careful blending of the Jewish-Christian Gospel (= Matthew) with the Pauline-Gentile reinterpretation (= Luke). Second, the appearance of this Gospel was unanimously ascribed to the apostolic activity of Simon Peter, during his last days in Rome. With these two clues in hand, let us proceed rather cautiously by having a look at that other alleged relic of Simon Peter's Roman ministry, the so-called First Epistle of Peter, in order to see what light it may shed (if any) on the situation surrounding the composition of the Gospel According to Mark.

B. Some Characteristics of the "Christianity" of 1 Peter

Who wrote 1 Peter? According to Eusebius, there never was much doubt among the bishops in apostolic succession congregations that this short epistle was a genuine writing from the apostle Peter.[8] However, as many scholars have pointed out, if this really is a letter by the apostle Peter, why is it written in such excellent Greek? Didn't Luke say Simon Peter was an "uneducated (ἀγράμματος) and common

---

[8] *Hist. eccl.* 3.3.25.

(ἰδιώτης) man" (Acts 4:13)? Furthermore, if it is a letter from Peter, why does it sound so *Pauline* in its phraseology and in its Christology? Or again, if it is from the foremost disciple, the leader of the Twelve, then why does it sound so distressingly unoriginal, packed as it is with phrases that very much resemble clichés? And, finally, why would the apostle to the circumcision be writing a general epistle to such a peculiar destination, namely, "the exiles in the Dispersion of Pontus, Galatia, Cappadocia, Asia, and Bithynia,"—that is, the territories (at least in part) of the Pauline mission? Questions such as these have led many to reject the testimony of the early tradition, and to label 1 Peter as a blatant pseudepigraph, similar in content and purpose to the Pastoral Epistles. I do not share this viewpoint for the following reasons.

The "Pauline" flavor of the letter is more a matter of striking phrases than inner spirit. We may point to the following strikingly Pauline formulations:

> Live as a free man, yet without using your freedom as a pretext for evil (2:16).
> (Christ) himself bore our sins in his body on the tree so that we might die to sin and live to righteousness (2:24).
> Above all, hold unfailing love for one another, since love covers a multitude of sins (4:8).
> As each one has received a gift (χάρισμα), employ it for one another as good stewards of God's varied grace (χάρις) (4:10).
> Rejoice insofar as you share Christ's sufferings (4:13).
> Peace to all of you that are in Christ (ἐν Χριστῷ) (5:14).

However, surprising as some of these may be, J. H. Elliott rightly protests against a onesided reading of 1 Peter—what he calls its "Pauline bondage."[9] As F. Bovon observes, when the author of 1 Peter wrote "so that we might die to sin and live to righteousness," "n'a plus la même sens que chez Paul. *Dikaiosune à* pris, dans 1 Pi., un sens judéo-chrétien. C'est l'ordre du royaume qui doit regner dans la communauté et qui dépend de l'activité morale des fidèles (cf. 3:14)."[10] Bovon discusses several similar examples, and then gives a list of major Pauline themes which are completely lacking in 1 Peter.

---

[9]J. H. Elliott, "The Rehabilitation of an Exegetical Step-child: 1 Peter in Recent Research," *JBL* 95 (1976): 248.

[10]François Bovon, "Foi chrétienne et religion populaire dans la première épître de Pierre," *ETR* 53 (1978): 30.

The most impressive thing about 1 Peter, in fact, is that it is a masterful compilation of all sorts of themes, some of which are Pauline in origin. However, recognition of this fact brings us to our second, perplexing question: why is the letter, except for two brief, and thoroughly suspicious, self-references at the beginning and the end, so totally lacking in the characteristic fire or personal idiosyncracies we naturally expect from the impetuous prince of the apostles, the pillar of the church? The language of this epistle reveals nothing of the personality we find so vividly etched in the Gospel accounts, or Galatians 2, or Acts 10. On the contrary, C. Spicq termed 1 Peter as "le plus dense résumé de la foi chrétienne et de la conduite pratique qui en dérive . . . dans le corpus épistolaire du Nouveau Testament."[11] Other commentators have not been so positive. Martin Dibelius thought it had been compiled from so many sources that it was a mere "sociological result." Bishop Carrington lamented that 1 Peter had "nothing original to say."[12]

Reactions of this sort seem, in my view, to be the result of getting off on the wrong foot. Rather than coming at 1 Peter with preconceived ideas as to what we should find in it because of things we have read in other parts of the New Testament, it seems wiser to begin with 1 Peter itself and seek to grasp its nature and purpose upon its own terms. Rather than looking for the headstrong man revealed in the Gospels, we should be open to the possibility that the author of 1 Peter has carefully *avoided* overheated, rhetorical argumentation or novel theological formulations (such as we see in the Pauline epistles). This letter may in fact be the result of a careful attempt to be simple, comprehensive, and traditional. Before we conclude this discussion of authorship, let us briefly examine some of the different kinds of materials in 1 Peter.[13]

---

[11]C. Spicq, "La prima Petri et le témoignage évangélique de saint Pierre," *ST* 20 (1966): 37.

[12]Philip Carrington, *The Early Christian Church*, 2 vols. (1957); this reference is 1:209.

[13]For what follows, I am indebted to the excellent discussion of Bovon, "La première épître de Pierre," pp. 25-41. Two other especially rich studies along these lines are E. G. Selwyn, *The First Epistle of St. Peter*, 2nd ed. (London: Macmillan, 1955); also R. Gundry, "Verba Christi in 1 Peter," *NTS* 13 (1967): 336-50, and idem, "Further Verba on Verba Christi in First Peter," *Bib* 55 (1974): 211-32.

(a) Kerygma and Liturgy. 1 Peter contains a succinct kerygmatic summary: Jesus Christ has appeared in these last days according to the foreknowledge of God; his life was one of obedience which led to his sacrificial death for the sake of freedom for all who believe in him; he thus became the precious cornerstone of a holy nation, a chosen people, made up of those who have heard the Gospel and been reborn as living stones; these now live in love and harmony with each other and peaceableness toward all those around them. Entry into the spiritual household is by baptism and confession of faith (not merely by πίστις ἐξ ἀκοῆς as in Rom 10:17). Indeed, 1 Peter is noteworthy for its pervasive baptismal language and fragments of baptismal hymns.[14]

(b) Pauline Themes. 1 Peter faithfully expresses certain basic Pauline insights, although not in such a way as to require us to view the author as belonging to "the Pauline school." For example, "He himself bore our sins in his body on the tree that we might die to sin and live to righteousness" (2:24; cf. Rom 6:5-11). The redemption of the Christian is understood as liberation, freedom—but not freedom to commit license (2:16; cf. Rom 6:18; Gal 5:13). This liberation has been bought by Christ's blood as a ransom (1:18f.; cf. Rom 3:25; 5:9f.; Col 1:20; 1 Tim 2:6). At the same time, Christ's death is an example to us, that is, the Christian really participates in Christ's suffering and death (2:21; 4:13; cf. Phil 2:5-13; Gal 6:12-17; Rom 12:1). The life of the community is characterized internally by love (1:22; 3:8; 4:8; cf. Rom 13:8-10; 1 Cor 13) and by God's varied grace (4:10-11; cf. Rom 13:11-14; 1 Cor 12). Externally, it is marked by hospitality and peacefulness (2:12; 3:15-16; cf. Rom 12:14-21), especially by honor and obedience toward the government (2:13-17; cf. Rom 13:1-7). For all things are under the sign of judgment, which is coming swiftly (4:7-9; cf. Rom 13:11-14).[15]

---

[14]See R. Bultmann, "Bekenntnis- und Liedfragmente im ersten Petrusbrief," *ConNT* 11 (1947): 1-14, reprinted in *Exegetica, Aufsätze zur Erforschung des Neuen Testaments*, ed. E. Dinkler (Tübingen, 1967), pp. 285-97; also M.-E. Boismard, *Quatre hymnes baptismales dans la première épître de Pierre*, Lectio Divina 30 (Paris, 1961); references from Bovon, p. 29, n. 8.

[15]This is not the place to enter into discussion concerning the exhaustive lists and charts of Selwyn, who built upon the research of Bigg, Carrington, and others. Perhaps I may just draw attention to the important recent study by William Dalton, S.J. of the well-known *crux* in 1 Pet 3:18ff., which traditionally has been interpreted to refer to Christ's *descensus ad inferos*. Dalton's research led him to the conclusion that this passage actually refers to Christ's victorious ascent through the upper realms of evil

It is important to notice which Pauline doctrines are *not* to be found in 1 Peter: justification by faith alone, the futility of the law of Moses for saving righteousness before God, the sharp distinction between the circumcision and the uncircumcision in the divine economy (*Heilsgeschichte*). In view of the marked Pauline echoes which are here, it is most intriguing to speculate on the possible explanation for the absence of these cardinal tenets of his. It is not that we have left the Pauline world behind. Rather, we seem to be in a context, similar to that apparently reflected in the Epistle to the Ephesians (for example, 2:20): the setting now is *one* "brotherhood" throughout the world established on Christ and the apostles (1 Pet 2:17; 5:9).[16]

(c) **Use of the LXX.** A number of central themes from the LXX have also been beautifully woven into the texture of this epistle: "Be ye holy for I am holy" (1:16; cf. Lev 11:44f.; 19:2); "the stone rejected by the builders is become the chief cornerstone" (2:7; cf. Ps 118:22); "a kingdom of priests, a holy nation" (2:9; cf. Exod 19:6). Interestingly, the LXX quotations tend toward the ethical or sapiential sections of the Old Testament; for example, "keep your tongue from speaking evil" (3:10-12; cf. Ps 34:12-17), and, "God opposes the proud but gives grace to the humble" (5:5; cf. Prov 3:34). Again, it might be worth noticing what has been passed over (although this kind of argument can hardly be pressed very far): the kingdom of God/Messiah from David's line; Gentile idolatry; and so forth.

(d) **Popular Hellenistic Religious Ideas.** Bovon's analysis is unique in the way he has seen that a number of motifs in 1 Peter were neither particularly Christian nor Jewish (if we may so distinguish at this early a date), but were rather common Hellenistic religious ideas: wholesome communal life is based on harmony (ὁμονοῖα); one must submit to the external conditions of existence without losing one's internal freedom (ἀπαθεῖα); and so forth.[17] What is different in 1 Peter, of course, is that these goals are now to be really achieved through the "good news" of the Christians. But popular commonplaces are sprinkled throughout the letter:

---

spirits into the upper heavens, in close parallelism with Pauline cosmology; see W. Dalton, S.J., *Christ's Proclamation to the Spirits. A Study of 1 Pet 3:18-4:6*, AnBib 23 (Roma 1965), pp. 57, 194ff.

[16]Bovon, "La première épître de Pierre," p. 31.

[17]Ibid., pp. 34-37.

Establish harmony (3:8)
To be happy, do good (3:10-11)
Suffering is not futile; it proves your real strength and redounds to
    God's glory (1:6-7)
Let your life be a good example to others (2:12)
Do not return evil for evil (2:12, 14)
Rulers must be obeyed because they punish evildoers and praise
    law-abiding citizens (2:13-17)
Slaves must obey their masters (2:18f.)
Wives should be submissive, husbands considerate (3:1, 7)
God exists and is powerful and will save those who please Him (1:5);
He will soon judge the whole world (4:17)[18]

One further word about what is *not* in 1 Peter. Many commentators have been puzzled by the total absence of any explicit reference to the sayings of Jesus. All sorts of other authorities crowd in, either by allusion or by direct quotation. But the teachings of Jesus, for whatever reason, simply do not play an explicit role in this letter. On the other hand, the *person*, the *action*, that is, the example of obedience unto death, that is of paramount importance for the whole letter.

This concludes our brief survey of the traditional materials in 1 Peter. Well may we concur in Bovon's characterization of the author of 1 Peter: "un homme des références," or the view of C. Spicq, who sees 1 Peter as an "epistle of the tradition."[19] What has not been generally noticed, however, is that the tradition in question is quite strikingly a blend of Jewish-Christian and Gentile-Christian, or the Jerusalemite and the Pauline.

---

[18]Ibid., p. 27. Cf. A Bonhöffer, *Epiktet und das Neue Testament*, Religionsgesch. Versuch. u. Vorarb. 10 (Giessen, 1911), for the following similar ideas in Epictetus and 1 Peter:

Theme	Epictetus	1 Peter	Page # in Bon.
"God is our Father and will protect us"	*Diss.* 1 9.5	1:17	292
"Do good and don't worry about what others think"	*Ench.* 35	4:4	332
"Do not return evil for evil"	*Ench.* 42	3:3	333
"Fear God, not an evil emperor - but do not disrespect his office!"	*Diss.* 1 29.9-29 cf. 1 30.1-7	2:13-17	304
"Women should be meek"	*Ench.* 40	3:1-4	333

[19]Spicq, "La prima Petri," p. 37.

But it is when we return to the question of the authorship of 1 Peter that this confluence of traditions stands out most strikingly. In 5:12, the author has written: "By Silvanus, a faithful brother as I regard him, I have written briefly to you." Silvanus—one of the apostle *Paul's* trusted co-apostles (see 1 Thess 1:1; cf. Acts 15:40)—now to be the bearer of this letter from the apostle Peter to a large area of the Gentile (Pauline?) mission field.[20] This is the same Silas/Silvanus who was entrusted with the Jerusalem council decree when it was sent out to the Gentile congregations (Acts 15:22), because he was already at that time a trusted "leading man" in the eyes of the Jerusalem leadership, in fact, a "prophet" (Acts 15:32). Presumably, he could be depended upon to contribute a certain skill in bilingual situations, as well as draw upon the support of the apostle Paul among his congregations. Silvanus' years of close collaboration with the Pauline mission could well account for the "Pauline coloration" 1 Peter has, if Peter chose to use him as his secretary. Indeed, I do not find it implausible that the apostle Peter knew exactly what he was doing by sending his old friend Silas/Silvanus, a recognized colleague of the apostle Paul, to the Pauline congregations in Asia, Pontus, Bithynia, Galatia, and elsewhere, with a letter of exhortation having marked Pauline accents. As such, it could be a kind of mediation between the two divergent, and at times hostile, branches of the early church—the Gentile and the

---

[20]Following C. F. D. Moule and others, I take 1 Peter to have actually been a *letter*; see Moule, "The Nature and Purpose of 1 Peter," *NTS* 3 (1956-1957): 1-11. The relatively high number of citations or allusions in Polycarp *ad Phil.* suggests that he (and presumably other churches in Asia) actually received it; indeed, it was his "special favorite" (C. Richardson). J. Moffatt, *Introduction to the Literature of the New Testament*, 3rd ed. (Scribners, 1918), p. 336, provides the following list of citations of 1 Peter in Polycarp *ad Phil*:

1 Peter	1:8, 12	1:13, 21	3:9	2:11	3:13	4:7	2:21
Pol. *ad Phil.*	1:3	2:1	2:2	5:3	6:3	7:2	8:1-2

For a discussion of the issue whether the regions listed in the "address" presuppose a real itinerary, see C. J. Hemer, "The Address of 1 Peter," *ExpTim* 89 (1978): 239-43. Anglo-American scholarship tends to hold this letter to have been written by Peter or his immediate circle with his approval; see most recently J. H. Elliott, "The Rehabilitation of an Exegetical Step-child." For a good exposition of the point of view opposite to most of the critical positions here taken, see, for example, N. Brox, "Zur pseudepigraphischen Rahmung des ersten Petrusbriefes," *BZ* 19 (1975): 78-96; and idem, "Tendenz und Pseudepigraphie im ersten Petrusbrief," *Kairos* 20 (1978): 110-20.

Jewish—and a very skillful one at that. Of course, the beautiful exposition, the fluent Greek, the signs of rhetorical sophistication: we shall have Silvanus (at least in part) to thank for these.[21] But the fervent, pastoral spirit animating the whole letter, the brave encouragement, the complex reconciling purpose behind the diverse traditions crafted into the remarkably harmonious flow of expression—these reveal the heart and mind, I suggest, of none other than the apostle Peter himself.

C. Peter's Response to the Conflict between Jews and Gentiles within the Early Church

I wish to retract the reservations I once published[22] concerning W. R. Farmer's original suggestion as to the purpose for which the Gospel of Mark was composed. Farmer wrote:

> There is no reason to doubt that the Gospels of Matthew and Luke would have been very popular in the churches for which they were originally written. But in places like Alexandria or Rome, or any place where no one Gospel was clearly recognized as *the* Gospel to be read in church, the question of which Gospel to read on any given occasion would have been a very practical question of no little moment. Lectionaries were finally developed to guide the Church in just such

---

[21]For a judicious appraisal of the evidence concerning the possible role of Silvanus, see esp. Selwyn, *St. Peter*, pp. 9-17, and (for the earlier discussion) Moffatt, *Introduction*, pp. 331-38. I think Selwyn has unearthed a most remarkable set of parallels in phraseology, theology, and central concerns between 1 and 2 Thessalonians with 1 Peter on the one side (the two Pauline letters "co-written" by Paul and Silvanus), and Hebrews and 1 Peter on the other, which led him to this tantalizing query: "The author of Hebrews may have read 1 Peter and been haunted—as who would not be?—by its language. But is it not equally possible that among 'those from Italy' (Heb 13:24) who were beside [the author] as he wrote, there was one who had been the close associate of St. Paul in writing to Thessalonica and of St. Peter in his First Epistle?" (pp. 465-66). For the evidence, see Selwyn, pp. 442-49 (table XIV), and pp. 463ff. D. Daube has a very informative study showing that at numerous key points, where the same idea is expressed in 1 Peter and the Pauline epistles, 1 Peter will tend to use a participle as if it were an imperative (a usage Daube parallels from numerous Mishnaic texts) while the Pauline epistle has the imperative proper. Daube concludes that his study has undermined "one of the arguments against the authenticity of 1 Peter, its so-called Pauline character": see Selwyn, "Appended Note: Participle and Imperative in 1 Peter," pp. 467-88.

[22]See "Mark—the Abridgement of Matthew and Luke," 1:94. Probably no other single aspect of Farmer's restatement of the Griesbach scenario drew heavier fire than this one of the probable circumstances that would have caused a gospel like Mark to have been written if Matthew and Luke were already extant; see esp. the comments of C. L. Mitton (echoing the earlier views of B. H. Streeter) quoted on p. 93 of my essay.

matters. . . . [In this context, Mark was composed as an effort to reproduce] the great core of the undisputed tradition common to the most highly regarded of the existing Gospels, [so as to maintain] some overall semblance of impartiality vis-à-vis points of dispute between partisans of these Gospels.[23]

I am now more inclined to think that this hypothetical conjecture well describes the Gospel of Mark when it is viewed as the abridgement of Matthew and Luke, because 1 Peter, the other relic of the Petrine legacy in the New Testament, shows its author to have been precisely the type of "churchman" described in Farmer's conjecture. Let me explain more fully.

We may see the following situation developing toward the latter days of Peter's ministry. The acrimonious conflict between Paul and his Gentile, non-Torah observing Christians on one side, and the "hard-line" circumcision party in Jerusalem and elsewhere on the other, had only deepened over the years, despite efforts by both Paul and Peter, not to mention James the Lord's brother, to bridge the conflict. Jealousy, suspicion, and bitter rivalry were threatening to split asunder the bonds holding the brotherhood of Christ together. Of those responsible for the inner unity and vitality of the brotherhood, it was the apostle Peter more than anyone else who got caught in the middle of this conflict, since it was he who had advocated first (through divine guidance, Acts 10) the fundamental principle of table-fellowship that had opened the door to Gentiles as equals in the church. As a result, he was pulled in both directions: toward his old Jewish compatriots and fellow-apostles (cf. Acts 11:2f.) as well as toward the fervent new Gentile converts, among whom Paul/Saul was having such amazing success (cf. Acts 10:34-35, 47).

Suddenly the whole situation was brought to a fresh level of crisis by the appearance of an apparently officially authorized narrative about the Lord, which set down in virtually uncompromising terms the whole issue with regard to the laws of Moses: "Do not imagine that I have come to abolish the Law or the Prophets. I have come not to abolish but to complete them. I tell you solemnly, till heaven and earth disappear, not one dot, not one little stroke, shall disappear from the Law until its purpose is achieved. Therefore, the man who infringes

---

[23]W. R. Farmer, *The Synoptic Problem*, pp. 279-81.

even one of the least of these commandments, and teaches others to do the same will be considered the least in the kingdom of heaven; but the man who keeps them and teaches them will be considered great in the kingdom of heaven" (Matt 5:17-19, *Jerusalem Bible*).

There can be no doubt that Peter's name and/or authority was used to defend the appearance and many of the positions taken in the Gospel of Matthew. At any rate, it must have been an especially embarrassing event for him, and above all for Paul, and his Gentile Christians. Not long after, a second narrative appeared from the side of the Gentile church which told the whole story in a noticeably different way; Torah sayings were either removed altogether or given minor consideration; obscure Jewish concepts and apocalyptic themes were reinterpreted along vaguely moralistic, universal lines; Jesus the Christ appeared much more sharply as the savior of the common man—the outcast, the poor, the dispossessed. But most important was the work which was appended to the basic narrative about Jesus of Nazareth, namely, a brilliant flanking maneuver in the form of a continued narrative of the history of the early apostles in such a way that the early Jerusalem leadership—that is, Simon Peter— was both accorded due honor, and at the same time subtly slipped into the shadows following the appearance and meteoric career of the apostle Paul, whose account was punctuated by no less than three repetitions of the Lord Jesus' calling of Paul into his service.

Clearly, either writing, taken in isolation, posed a deadly threat to the tenuous unity of the brotherhood. At many points, indeed in some mysterious way totally, each was perfectly accurate as a portrayal of the Savior as known and worshiped by each branch of the church. Thus Peter and others had little choice but to try to endorse and to make as much use as possible of each account, in worship services, catechetical instruction and letter writing. What is now extant as "the First Epistle of Peter" (a designation that arose much later during the canonization process) is one such attempt. Thus by example as well as by instruction, Peter and others struggled to keep bridges over the widening gap separating the extreme factions on either wing. The conflict was probably not so much between Paul and James the Just as it was between the Paulinists and the Jerusalem "circumcision party." Peter must have watched this deepening antipathy with profound sadness and anguish. Had the Lord Jesus Christ died so that his followers could revile each other in his name?

The truth was, as many realized, each extreme needed the other: the Jewish rigorists were in danger of putting a Mosaic strait-jacket on the outpouring of the Holy Spirit among the Gentiles; even the Lord had not remained so aloof. The Paulinists on the other hand could and did plunge into flagrant antinomian excesses, calling them "gifts of the Spirit." Both were dead ends, as far as the full vital fellowship in Christ was concerned. Peter steadfastly avoided any indication of choosing sides—if 1 Peter is any indication of his type of Christianity.[24]

Eventually, under circumstances which are still cloudy to us, he came to work among the Christians in the imperial capital, Rome, and was there at least for a time while the apostle Paul also was there (under house arrest). Both were subsequently caught up in the wave of lynchings and arrests of Christians instigated by the demented Nero. The sudden loss to the church of its two leading missionary apostles undoubtedly sent a traumatic shock throughout the scattered communities of the Christian brotherhood. To some, Nero even loomed up as the very personification of the Evil One predicted by the Lord himself (cf. Rev 13). One reaction is preserved in the grave and beautiful dialogue between Jesus and Peter in the 21st chapter of John's Gospel:

> A third time Jesus said to Peter, "Simon son of John, do you love me?" Peter was upset that he asked him the third time, "Do you love me?" and said, "Lord, you know everything; you know I love you." Jesus said to him, "Feed my sheep. I tell you most solemnly, when you were young you put on your own belt and walked where you liked. But when you grow old you will stretch out your hands, and somebody else will put a belt around you and take you where you would rather not go." In these words he indicated the kind of death by which Peter would give glory to God. After this he said, "Follow me." (*Jerusalem Bible*)

---

[24]One of the major hindrances I have experienced in presenting views such as the one outlined in this paper is the opinion scholars have of Peter because of the vivid scene painted by the apostle Paul in the second chapter of Galatians. In this portrayal, obviously, Peter comes off distinctly second-best; a mere wishy-washy tool of whichever group could exert the most pressure upon him. Need we be reminded not to take this report at face value, as if it were a complete and accurate account of what actually transpired on that occasion in Antioch? Need we be reminded that this story is being told to Galatian Gentiles who may never have met Paul, let alone Peter, or any of the other principals of that occasion? And that Paul is hopping mad about somebody's attack on his apostolic status, who is apparently using Peter's name and example as that of a real apostle? Do we need to be reminded of what Paul can say when he gets this angry? It would be most interesting to hear *Peter's* account of what happened on this occasion.

Fateful words. This brief passage is an extraordinarily moving tribute from one of the original three disciples, the "disciple whom Jesus loved," to one of the others, "the Rock." Of course, those who were Peter's associates must have felt the loss most keenly. For instance, 1 Pet 5:13 mentions a "Mark, my son," whom the early tradition unanimously identified as John Mark, the son of Mary (Acts 12:12) the sister of Barnabas (Col 4:10). This John Mark had traveled as co-worker with Barnabas (Acts 15:39) and later was a "co-laborer" with Paul in Rome (Col 4:10; Phlm 24). His family home may have been one of the important meeting places of the Jerusalem Christians, for it was here that Simon Peter first went when he was released by the angel from Herod's imprisonment (Acts 12:12). What would John Mark, Peter's "son," have done in the period following the brutal death of his beloved "father"?

Two things should be borne in mind as we seek to answer this question. First of all, not long after the death of Peter and Paul, the hated regime of Nero abruptly came to an end when he committed suicide (June A.D. 68). A brief outburst of civil war erupted as different factions lunged for the fallen reins of power. Soon the powerful Flavian family gained the throne, and for a little more than a decade, there ensued one of the happiest periods in all of Rome's imperial history. It was a deeply needed time of healing after the terrible, strife-torn years of the Julio-Claudians. Vespasian and Titus repealed the sentences, fines, banishments, and other forms of punishment stemming from Nero's constant sense of *laesa maiestas*.[25] They cleaned up the city, built parks, the Colosseum, and strengthened the city defenses. They gave careful attention to the affairs of the provinces. Within a short time, they had completely won the devotion of the Roman people by their humble, dignified, and honest handling of the affairs of government.

This period (approx. 69 to 81, and possibly beyond) was especially favorable to the spread of Christianity in the city of Rome. There already was a flourishing, somewhat assimilated Jewish community in the southwestern suburbs of the city, as the Jewish catacombs reveal. And, apart from the rather dubious activities of the highly visible

---

[25]Dio Cassius LXV.9.1; 10.1-6; LXVI.19.1-2; cf. Suetonius, *Vespasian* XII-XV; *Titus* VII.3-VIII.5.

Jewish courtiers, Josephus, Herod-Agrippa II and his much-wed sister Bernice, there is ample evidence that "the Jewish philosophy" was still a matter of intellectual interest on the part of some Gentiles.[26] It rested on a total repudiation of Judean nationalistic pretensions, and instead viewed the glorious Hebrew heritage in universalist terms, that is, as of potentially saving benefit to all peoples.[27]

The evidence for Christian converts among the Roman nobility during this period is very scant but not non-existent.[28] For example, within the imperial family itself, Flavius Clemens, the son of Vespasian's older brother Flavius Sabinus, may have been a Christian. The first cousin of Titus and Domitian, both he and his wife, Flavia Domitilla, are generally thought to have been Christians, and her family later donated land for one of the earliest Christian cemeteries (now on the Via Ardeatina). Domitian later beheaded his cousin Flavius Clemens and banished Domitilla "for adopting Jewish customs."[29] Whether with the family of Flavius Clemens and his wife we have to do with "genuine Christian faith" (whatever that might mean in that context) or rather with "Judaizing," as Dio says (and it may

---

[26]For an especially illuminating analysis of the privileged positions of Jews as a cultural entity in the Mediterranean οἰκουμένη, see Victor Tcherikover, *Hellenistic Civilization and the Jews*, trans. S. Applebaum (Jewish Publication Society, 1961), pp. 301-32. It is a status difficult for us later Westerners to conceive, given our centuries of cultural hatred of the Jews. However, neither Philo nor 4 Maccabees nor Josephus nor the apostle Paul can be rightly understood as long as we remain unaware that—prior to Domitianus—the prevailing international *governmental* policy toward the Judean Hebrews was one of respect, honor, and admiration.

[27]One of the best statements of this "philosophy," though getting a bit outdated, is E. R. Goodenough, *By Light, Light. The Mystical Philosophy of Hellenistic Judaism* (New Haven, 1935).

[28]We know of a woman named Pomponia Graecina who was arraigned for "alien superstition" during the consulate of Nero, or around the year 57; Tacitus *Annals* XIII.32. Somewhat later, another member of the nobility, M. Acilius Glabrio, consul with Trajan in the year 91, was killed by Domitian on suspicion of treason, but the actual cause may have been leanings toward the Christian sect; see Suetonius, *Domitian* 10.2; cf. Dio Cassius LXVII.14.3.

[29]"And by the same year [95] Domitian slew along with many others Flavius Clemens the consul, although he was a cousin and had to wife Flavia Domitilla who was also a relative of the emperor's [namely, she was Domitian's sister's daughter]. The charge brought against them both was that of atheism, a charge on which many others who had drifted into Jewish ways were condemned. . . . Domitilla was banished to Pandateria." See Dio Cassius LXVII.13.

amount to the same thing), nevertheless we can see present, within an important branch of the imperial family, a love of "philosophy" and things at least semi-Christian which actually lingered on afterward as a happy memory in the minds of Christian "philosophers" of the following generations, prompting many of them to protest strenuously against the subsequent decades of suppression dealt Christianity by Hadrian and his successors. Well might Melito cry out to Marcus Aurelius:

> [Why is] the race of the pious now being persecuted in a way contrary to all precedent? . . . The philosophy current among us flourished in the first instance among barbarians; and, when it afterwards sprang up among the nations, . . . it proved to be a blessing of most happy omen . . . [Therefore, thou shouldst] protect that philosophy which has grown up with thy empire, . . . to which thy more recent ancestors paid honor, along with the other religions in the empire. . . . Nero and Domitian alone of all the emperors . . . cared to bring any impeachment against our doctrines.[30]

If we may assume, then, a great atmosphere of relief and calm in the Roman capital, following the terrifying final days of Nero and civil war, during which there appeared to be even a brief wave of sympathy for the down-trodden "Christians," to whom would the educated and influential Romans have turned who desired to know more of this curious sect? The famous Paul was dead, although a few of his trusted assistants were still in the city. Likewise the prince of apostles, Simon Peter. But here is his close associate, his trusted companion and translator, John Mark! He was the one who accompanied the old man when he spoke! Pressed for accounts of what the apostle Peter used to say,[31] what did John Mark produce?

---

[30]A fragment of an oration addressed to Marcus Aurelius Antoninus; see *Ante-Nicene Fathers*, 8:758. Cf. Eusebius, *Hist. eccl.* 3.17: "Domitian, having shown great cruelty toward many, and having unjustly put to death no small number of well-born and notable men at Rome, and having without cause exiled and confiscated the property of a great many other illustrious men, finally became a successor of Nero in his hatred and enmity toward God. He was in fact the second that stirred up a persecution against us, although his father Vespasian had undertaken nothing prejudicial against us."

[31]That John Mark composed the Gospel called after him following Peter's death, rather than while he was still alive (as later traditions envisioned the situation) has, I think, been conclusively demonstrated by E. Kalin, "Early Traditions about Mark's Gospel," *CurTM* 2 (1975): 332-41. Cf. J. J. Griesbach's strikingly similar discussion (apparently unknown to Kalin) in Orchard and Longstaff, *Griesbach*, pp. 114-18.

At this point we need to turn to our second thing to bear in mind. As with Silas/Silvanus, John Mark was another of these unusual "joint apostles" whom Peter relied on; skillful linguists who had been active in both the circumcision and the uncircumcision mission as messengers of Jesus Christ. As such, there is no reason to think that John Mark would persist in presenting, nor would these educated Romans desire to receive, only the polarized version of the Gospel currently in use in either faction of the churches. Disputes over the law of Moses, penetrating and subtle theological teachings by Paul—these would be unlikely to strike their inquiring Roman minds as being of the essence. More important, any Judean political overtones in the message, in view of the recent bloody revolt in Jerusalem, would have been distinctly out of place. No, what was important was the bedrock message of the new faith: the Savior had appeared bringing victory over death—and this word John Mark endeavored to reproduce. Using the apostle's public speeches as his guide and model,[32] John Mark drew upon them and the two other accounts Peter himself had often used, the Gospels of Matthew and Luke. In this way, he produced the kind of narrative Peter implicitly supported—one that preserved the heart of the faith, the central testimony to Jesus Christ the savior, yet one which did not take sides in the various partisan struggles between Jew and Gentile in the church.

D. The Petrine Legacy: the Gospel of Mark as a Kerygmatic Suture Binding Together the Jewish and Gentile Divergency in the Early Church

It would transcend the limits of this essay to discuss in any detail the characteristics of the Gospel of Mark that reveal its birth under these presumed conditions. However, we may briefly enumerate some of the more important features:

(a) As with the epistle of 1 Peter, the Gospel of Mark is a skillful and meticulous blending of earlier traditions (kerygmatic, liturgical, catechetical, Hellenistic didactic, LXX), representing the common ground of the brotherhood. There would have been no effort to be innovative, or risk bold new formulations.

(b) The typical Petrine kerygma (cf. Peter's speeches in Acts 2, 3, 10) provided the framework and model for the whole Gospel of Mark.

---

[32]For a well-worked-out exposition of this possibility, see W. R. Farmer, "Modern Development of Griesbach's Hypothesis," *NTS* 23 (1977): 275-95; esp. 283ff.

This could account for the omission of any material in Matthew and/or Luke dealing with Jesus' infancy and youth.[33] Furthermore, Mark carefully recast the materials he took up into a vivid *aural* presentation, that is, presenting them as a vivid oral narrative, as would befit Peter's eye-witness speaking style.

(c) Within the basic requirements described in (b), Mark used his sources (Matthew and Luke) in the following way: wherever Matthew and Luke had the same account in the same order, these he invariably took over; in between, he followed one or the other although he tended to stick to Matthew most of the time (but working in Luke's variations where appropriate).[34]

(d) The center of gravity in Mark (as compared with Matthew and Luke) consists in the power of the Lord Jesus, not his doctrine. (N.B. the same feature of 1 Peter described above.) The striking disdain for the niceties of the laws of Moses in Mark is a subject too complex to discuss here; note only the appearance of the important Petrine missionary concession regarding Gentile foods in the Markan addition to Matthew/Luke in 7:19-20. As for the heightening of narrative focus upon Jesus' supernatural powers over Satan, we may here only point to the sharp curtailment of the temptation account, and Mark's vigorous

---

[33]Ibid., pp. 283ff.

[34]One of the most effective ways to verify the compositional activity of Mark using currently available instruments is the colored diagram by Allan Barr, *A Diagram of Synoptic Relationships* (Edinburgh, 1938). Using the three columns on the left (representing vertical schematic outlines of Matthew, Mark, and Luke), notice the great preponderance of pink lines connecting similar pericopes between Matthew and Mark on the one side of Mark, and similarly the great number of pink lines connecting similar pericopes between Mark and Luke on the other side. The great thing to note is that these similar pericopes are all *in order* in Matthew on one side, and in Luke on the other. That's what the pink line means. Then observe the heavy black lines on Matthew's side of Mark, and a few heavy black lines on Luke's side. These represent pericopes in Mark which are not in the original order of one of the other two. Now, taking a ruler, hold it up to one of the places where there is a black line coming over to Mark from Matthew—look across to the other side of that pericope in Mark; behold, a *pink* line. *None* of the black lines coming to Mark from Luke; look across on that pericope to the Matthean side: behold, a *pink* line. *None* of the black lines on one side is not met by a *pink* line on the other; hence, according to Barr's chart, Mark was following one or the other at all times. Except, of course, for about 24 verses of his own material. It is worth checking out. I know of no more convincing *visual* demonstration of Griesbach's original observation. Of course, there are problems with Barr's chart; but these are in process of finding remedy.

expansions of *all* of the healing accounts that were contained in Matthew and Luke.

(e) Mark's pervasive emphasis upon Jesus' supernatural power over Satan was compensated on the one side by a new insistence upon Jesus' *secret identity* as Savior while on earth (cf. 1 Cor 2:6-8), and on the other, by Mark's long *expansion* in the apocalyptic prediction materials, which predicted Jesus' imminent return to earth with the whole angelic army to save his own, and wreak vengeance upon his enemies.[35]

(f) The climax of the whole account—long noted by gospel scholars—is of course the vivid description of Jesus' suffering and death and resurrection. This would have been all the more fitting to those in the inner circle surviving the brutal deaths of the apostles Peter and Paul, as they sought to find ways to express the meaning of their deaths in the light of the equally brutal death of the savior. However, the centrality of the theme itself was there already in Peter's consciousness (cf. 1 Pet 5:1-11).

These brief suggestions will have to suffice for the time being. At least they provide some indication how prominent features of the Gospel of Mark, when viewed in terms of the Two-Gospel (Griesbach) Hypothesis, would be explained. To be sure, there are also a number of curious features of Mark which also must be taken into account. But the main feature with which we are concerned in this essay, namely, the central fact of Mark as a careful stitching together of his two principle sources has, I think, been provided with a plausible historical setting. In fact, when viewed as the principle remnant of Peter's apostolic ministry and his legacy through Mark, it becomes profoundly significant. For it is nothing less than the permanent, unbreakable suture between Matthew and Luke, a bond of common kerygmatic affirmation uniting the Jewish heritage with the Pauline clarification.

E. Conclusion

In Luke's memoirs of the Christ, at the last supper Jesus turns and says to Peter, "Simon, behold, Satan demanded to have you that he

---

[35]The lengthy Markan addition to the end of the Synoptic apocalypse was so striking in Farmer's estimation that he thought it might contain the clue explaining the Markan composition as a whole; see *Synoptic Problem*, pp. 278ff.

might sift you like wheat, but I prayed for you that your faith may not fail; and when you have recovered, *strengthen your brethren!*" (Luke 22:31-32, *Jerusalem Bible*).

In our day, it may be the case that we have lost sight of the most important contribution of all by the apostle Peter on behalf of the brotherhood. When we think of Simon Peter we tend to recall his decisive confession at Caesarea Philippi as being of paramount importance, or perhaps his being with Jesus on the mount of transfiguration. But casting a dark shadow over these events are his sleeping at Gethsemane and his terrible thrice-repeated denial of Christ.

Nevertheless, we also recall Paul's strange words to the effect that the risen Lord "appeared first to Cephas and secondly to the Twelve" (1 Cor 15:5), which surely suggests that Simon Peter had been somehow reinstated into his original position of prominence among the Twelve. This accords with the picture we see in the early chapters of Acts, where he is clearly the indomitable spokesman for the community, the strict disciplinarian, and the one who courageously opens The Way to Gentiles. But then it seems as if Peter and his followers silently and mysteriously pass off the scene and are never mentioned again, except for a brief reference in chapter 15 concerning the Jerusalem council. What really became of Simon Peter? It is as if he and his activities pass behind a cloud. All we know of his later ministry, including the rather improbable twenty-five years at Rome, come from scattered notices here and there. He appears to have been active in a number of places outside of Palestine, until his final ministry and martyrdom at Rome. What was "the Rock" doing all this time?

It is one of the unexpected by-products of the renewed interest in the Griesbach hypothesis that Peter's later activity begins to re-emerge out of the mists of time possessed of a striking coherence and purposefulness. I refer not only to that "step-child of New Testament research," 1 Peter, but now also to the Gospel of Peter According to John Mark. In a curious way, the two are remarkably similar to each other (when Mark is viewed along Griesbachian lines). Could this be more than forced coincidence? To repeat what I conjectured above, I feel quite sure that Simon Peter must have become increasingly concerned with the conflict that had broken out between the Jerusalem circumcision party and the Paulinist Gentile congregations—a conflict which was hardly resolved by the Jerusalem council. I also think that Peter and many others could clearly see that this struggle was tearing apart the

whole fabric of Christian fellowship. But what could be done to overcome it? What higher unity could save the Brotherhood from imminent self-destruction? At this point, the peculiar characteristics of the epistle we call 1 Peter begin to make a strange kind of sense. Simple, devoid of controversial themes, written with the aid of the skilled Pauline co-worker Silvanus (whom Peter makes sure to call his "faithful brother"), he writes an encouraging and uplifting circular letter which draws as fully on the Jewish as well as the Pauline points of view—there we see revealed the essential style of Peter's later ministry, the actual way he sought to "strengthen his brethren." Although he died not long after this letter was written, Peter was responsible for another of these "blending documents," namely the Gospel written by John Mark, his "son." This was his masterstroke, however, and could well have been some time in preparation, especially if we consider that Mark would have drawn on a number of Peter's actual sermons in Rome, where he had already begun using both written Gospels simultaneously in an attempt to hang onto the shared, kerygmatic essence of Matthew and Luke.

It remained for the Christian leadership in the next century, however, to benefit most fully from Peter's far-sighted achievement. For if it had not been for the unbreakable kerygmatic suture so carefully sewn between the Gospels of Matthew and Luke, the second century orthodox leadership probably would not have had the ammunition to survive the ravages of the Marcionite heresy. As Tertullian and Irenaeus amply testify, the church of their day was almost hopelessly riddled with the Marcionite disease, almost fatally sick with it. Variations of Christianity minus its Jewish heritage were everywhere, bilious and grotesque phantasmagorias of otherworldly religious fanaticism. *What Peter actually achieved was to enable his successors to preserve the Jewish heritage for Gentile Christianity.*

When Mark began the task of putting into writing the kerygmatic unity Peter had sought during his apostolic ministry, working possibly with the direct encouragement of certain members of the Flavian household, he must have proceeded with utmost caution. Yet his accomplishment has stood the test. The Jerusalem Gospel of Matthew was locked so tightly to the Pauline Gospel of Luke that it was only by a violent act of assault, such as that carried out by Marcion of Pontus, that the Christianity of the apostle Paul could be torn free from its Jewish roots. And the very violence of Marcion's assault provoked

such a shocked counter-reaction that his policy and theology was decisively repudiated on all sides, and the congregations belonging to the orthodox, "catholic" persuasion began their own process of self-definition (= canonization) so as to prevent any future eruptions of this sort from ever happening again.

Rightly, then, did Jesus predict of Cephas, "Thou art Petros, and upon this rock will I found my church, and the gates of Hell will not prevail against it."

SEMINAR DIALOGUE WITH DAVID DUNGAN

Moderator: David, I will ask you to take us briefly through your paper and then I'll ask Bruce Corley to present his response to your paper. I'll give you the opportunity to respond briefly to Corley. Then we will ask Professor Elliott to make his response to your paper and you will have an opportunity to respond to him. After that we will open the discussion to all members of the seminar.

Dungan: Thank you, Bill. I really appreciate the efforts of Bruce Corley and Tom Urrey and the organizers to set up this special session on this paper. I am very pleased also to see the men here who have done a lot of work on 1 Peter, and I think that this will aid the discussion greatly because so much of what I am about to say turns on the understanding of 1 Peter, characteristics of 1 Peter, as they might relate to the Gospel of Mark.

Very briefly, my assignment when I wrote this paper was to explain why anyone in the early church who already had a Gospel of Matthew and a Gospel of Luke would produce something like a Mark, which is a short account that leaves out most of the teachings of Jesus that are found in the other two larger gospels. It leaves out the infancy account. Why would anyone do a thing like that? Scholars have asked us these questions for years.

My first inclination, as I set about researching an answer to this question, was to follow out a lead I developed in an article I wrote several years ago, namely, to focus on the phenomenon of order (as it appears to the Griesbach theorist). This meant that I had to look for any individual or group who would take Matthew and Luke, line them up and make a careful copy of the places where they overlap in their order of events (which is what Mark is to a great extent). But before I really got into my research, I thought I had better first take a look at the other material in the New Testament associated with the apostle Peter's name. Maybe I would find some clues. After all, the earliest tradition associates Peter with several writings in the New Testament. So I have to confess to everyone, this was the first time I carefully examined 1 Peter and the recent research associated with it. I had just sort of skipped over it in graduate school because our teachers put it down as essentially a document of clichés. They told us that the beautiful phrases never lead anywhere, that 1 Peter in no way resembled the intellectual depth of the genuine letters of Paul. As my teacher, Krister Stendahl, said one time, "Deep down 1 Peter is shallow." So, with this block in my mind, I had never read 1 Peter or studied it or anything. But when I began to examine it carefully this time, I suddenly became struck by some extraordinary similarities with what the Gospel of Mark looks like, if one assumes the Griesbach theory. This discovery completely re-oriented my research and is the reason for the direction the paper takes.

Now to summarize my paper very briefly. To begin with, I decided that I had to isolate at least one *central* feature of the Gospel of Mark that needed explanation, and then work toward that. In one sense, there are a lot of things in the Gospel of Mark that beg for explanation. But what must we be prepared to explain if we assume the Griesbach theory (or I would rather call it the two-gospel theory)? What is the most central, most essential, most important thing that one must account for historically, if one assumes that certain early Christian churches already had the Gospels of Matthew and Luke and still produced another Gospel like Mark? I decided that the main feature to focus on was this dominant formal characteristic: namely, that if you take Matthew and Luke and lay them down side by side, *at all the points where they have a similar story in the same order of events, Mark will have the same story in the same common order*. This triple

concurrence in order of pericopes is what led Griesbach to his original hypothesis.

Now Griesbach was not a professional source critic, or a form critic; he was a *text* critic. And, working as text critics do, he was quite accustomed to looking for evidence of the influence of one manuscript of the Gospel text on the text of another. So, as Griesbach was studying these textual matters, he visited London where he may have seen a book by an Englishman named Henry Owen, who had said that it was his view that Mark was composed by a skillful combination of excerpts from Matthew and Luke. Not long after, Griesbach published this theory (without any reference to Owen) as his own view. In other words, I am talking about the primary structural feature, the essential characteristic that *Griesbach* thought he saw, when he compared all three Synoptic Gospels. Therefore, I feel some justification for saying that it is this feature which needs most to be explained historically. I might add that he never attempted to do so himself. So we are in "untrod territory."

Stated more precisely, the phenomenon is this: wherever Matthew and Luke had the same account in the same order, that account the author of Mark invariably took over into his narrative. Between those points of agreement, Mark sandwiched in material taken from one or the other. Only rarely did the author of Mark depart from both Matthew and Luke simultaneously. (N.B.: For some strange reason, Markan priorists have always claimed that this very same argument establishes Mark's *priority*—an utter impossibility.)

Once I had isolated the basic feature to be explained, I then looked at the Epistle of 1 Peter, since it was the other writing in the New Testament universally associated with the apostle Peter. I looked for similar structural characteristics in 1 Peter. And the very first thing that I noticed was the fact that the scholarship on 1 Peter is unanimous in saying that it is an extraordinary *composite* document, made up of phrases and terms and ideas that reflect the whole spectrum of early Christian catechetical teaching. There are phrases that are distinctively Pauline in character. "Christ bore our sins in his body on the tree so that we might die to sin and live to righteousness." That's a beautiful Pauline phrase. "Peace to all of you who are in Christ," *en Christo*. Sprinkled throughout the letter are these Pauline bell-ringers. Then there are numerous beautiful phrases worked in from various parts of

the Greek Old Testament, the Septuagint. In short, the thing that caught my attention right away was this extensive use of compilation. I thought, Aha! Here is another "mixture" of earlier traditions associated with the name of the same apostle. Then it dawned on me that what we have here is somebody writing an *intentional* mixture of a certain kind. Maybe the fact that the material in 1 Peter doesn't sound "original" or controversial, but just expresses the great middle ground of the Church's teachings, maybe that was its intended goal. Then I suddenly realized that maybe what we have as an intentional act of the author of Mark (on the Griesbach hypothesis) was precisely the same kind of intentional act by the author of 1 Peter.

I won't go through the material that I have collected of the diverse types of tradition in 1 Peter. I will just mention them briefly, since everyone who will be discussing this paper has read this already. First Peter contains a kerygmatic summary focusing primarily on the passion, death, and resurrectional victory of Christ. The Pauline themes I've already mentioned, the use of the LXX I have already mentioned. One particularly interesting feature, that I found in an article by a French author, François Bovon, I do want to emphasize: 1 Peter contains a number of very popular ideas belonging to the wider Hellenistic world. Not typically Jewish or Christian or anything. For instance, "seek harmony." "If you want to be happy do good." "Let your life be an example to others." "Do not return evil for evil." "Slaves should obey their masters, wives should be submissive to their husbands, and considerate." "God exists and he will save those who please him and he will judge others." Bovon rightly noted that these platitudes in 1 Peter were typical of the wider Gentile culture at that time. I thought this shed a very interesting light on 1 Peter, and also on the Gospel of Mark, for it has many of the same features of popular Hellenistic piety that Bovon identified in 1 Peter.

Then I turned up another very intriguing feature of 1 Peter, namely the curious hints regarding authorship in chapter 5. You remember where the text reads: "By Silvanus, a faithful brother as I regard him, I am writing to you." Well, who is this Silvanus; the assistant of the apostle Paul? If so, what is he doing here as the secretary of the apostle Peter? Back to the drawing boards. I had to do some work on this little known Silvanus. Who was he and where did he come from? I hardly had time for more than a preliminary examination of the secondary literature, but I unearthed some fascinating information in the process.

It turned out that Silvanus was also present at the Jerusalem council, at least according to the Acts account of it, and was appointed to carry the council decree around to the churches with another brother. I concluded from this that this Silvanus had been bilingual. I could also see, assuming the Acts account had some veracity to it, that he had been somebody both sides present at the Jerusalem council could trust, that is, both pro-Pauline and Jerusalem rigorists. This suggested that he was something of a diplomat, a less controversial leader. In another place in Acts 15, he was also described as a "prophet." From all this it was obvious, taking into account Paul's heavy reliance upon him, that Silvanus was one of the major members of the second echelon leadership.

From this information, I thought it possible to hazard a guess regarding the peculiar address of 1 Peter, with its strange list of provinces in Asia. Taking into account the apparent use of a number of "Pauline themes" and the even more liberal and fluent use of Old Testament phrases, not to mention the skillful Greek style, features which pointed toward an author with considerable rhetorical skill, I decided we had a polished product which was, judging from the list of destinations of the letter (or copies of it), a kind of circular letter, an "open letter" to the churches in those areas. As such, it made sense to suppose that the bilingual Silvanus not only helped write the letter, but also was its bearer to at least some of the provinces mentioned.

Going back to the Gospel of Mark, I hypothesized the following historical scenario: the well-known tradition about the apostle Peter working in Rome for twenty years before his death has little evidence to support it, although this may change as more evidence becomes available. At the moment, only the most conservative Catholic scholars hold to this view. That Peter was in Rome for some period, few doubt, but exactly when he was in Rome and what he did there is at present impossible to say due to an almost complete absence of data. The very ancient tradition that he was martyred there is of course well known and widely accepted. That he was martyred about the same time Paul was, that is, during Nero's persecution, is much more disputed, partly because we know so little about Paul's last days also. At any rate, working from what scant indications there are, I said something like this: 1 Peter looks like a letter that the apostle Peter sent out, using Silvanus as a secretary, when he was fully prepared for his own imminent death at the hands of Nero's police. As the leader of the

despised Christian sect, he was all too obvious a target. Further, Peter and others may have been filled with apprehension that what Nero was about to do to him and other Christians in Rome would also be carried out against other Christian communities in the eastern provinces. In this sense, 1 Peter may have been only one of several circular letters Peter sent eastward, warning of the coming peril—and was the only one to have survived the vicissitudes of time. Then, sure enough, under conditions that are very hazy, both Peter and Paul were arrested and executed, perhaps within a three or four year period, Peter probably first. Obviously, his death would have devastated the whole early Christian church.

Who would have tried to hold things together during this period in Rome? We can only conjecture, but I suggest that it was another one of Peter's capable second echelon assistant apostles, namely, John Mark. Of a prominent family in Jerusalem, his mother owned the house where Christians often met in Jerusalem. That's where Acts says Peter went after he came out of prison in Jerusalem. According to Colossians, the prominent apostle Barnabas was an uncle of this John Mark. And here he is referred to in 1 Peter as "my son." In other words, John Mark was another one of those second echelon apostles who had worked with *both* Paul and Peter. He was apparently in good standing in Jerusalem Christian circles as well as in the Pauline churches.

Now what would this versatile, respected second echelon leader have done in the days immediately following Peter's death? Especially if you take into account the radical change that came over the city of Rome following the assassination of Nero, the year of the three emperors, and finally the accession of the Flavian house to the throne. We have ample evidence that Rome breathed a huge sigh of relief. For once the whole city was at peace. Vespasian and Titus were honest, capable rulers, and as such, very popular with the people. Of more interest to us, however, is the evidence that they were not antagonistic in principle toward the Jews or Christians. Of course, they punished those Jews who wanted to foment rebellion. But they didn't hound down law-abiding, peace-loving Jews. Nor did they hound down the Christians. In fact, we have faint evidence of certain high level Romans becoming interested in the Christian message at this time.

Now, if that is the situation of the church in Rome during the 70's, what kind of message would an apostle who had been close to Peter

and Paul, such as Silvanus or John Mark have proclaimed? What would the gospel have been that such a leader would have preached to Roman Christians at that time? My basic suggestion is that it would have been a message setting forth the unshakable center of the faith. Not one which emphasized either the Pauline or the Jerusalem extremes. It would have been a consolidating message. Now I argue in my paper that, during his latter years, the apostle Peter had sought to avoid both the rigid pro-Mosaic law orientation of the Jerusalem church, as well as the hyper-antinomian excesses of some of Paul's adherents. This course naturally brought him into considerable tension with both sides, as Galatians 2 amply demonstrates. As part of this policy, I suggested that Peter had and used both the Gospels of Matthew (representing the Moses rigorists) and Luke (representing the Pauline viewpoint) in his public preaching, emphasizing those aspects where both were similar. Then after Peter died, his close assistant Mark put into written form what Peter had striven to do in his preaching, namely, identify and emphasize the higher ground of faith shared by the two then still unreconciled branches in the Christian church—the Jewish Christian rigorists and the Pauline antinomians. In this manner the Gospel we call "According to Mark" was produced. I'll stop with that.

Corley: Some five years ago, I found a very surprising matter, namely, that F. C. Baur and Johannes Munck agreed that Romans 9-11 was the central portion of the letter but for quite contradictory reasons. In fact, they are unalterably opposed to one another as to the significance of that centrality. Upon reading David's paper, a curious agreement and disagreement with Baur has surfaced once again. Professor Elliott and I have conspired a bit in our responses; therefore, I will deal with the more philosophical problem of Roman provenance and the development of a research paradigm which features the contribution of Baur. I will do that in two ways. First, a point about my concurrence with David on 1 Peter and then a dissenting analysis of Baur's argument concerning the Synoptic Gospels and Petrine-Pauline problems in the New Testament.

I concur with David in his argumentation for the authenticity of 1 Peter, and I take it as a very positive by-product of the reopening of the synoptic problem. In fact, one of the most profitable fallouts of a new

research paradigm may be in significant areas outside the target itself, the Synoptic Gospels. I call your attention to the publication of Professor Ellis's paper (*NTS* 26 [1980]: 487-502) in which he deals with the problem of dating the New Testament and, if you will, some constraints on how we play with the data. I have paraphrased these, and since he is here, he can correct them if I am mistaken: (1) no unilinear or dialectical ground rules; (2) no stylistic or literary critical hammerlocks; and (3) no Aramaic trump cards because Palestine was not a Semitic island in the Greco-Roman sea. I do not find these notions preposterous, indeed, Professor Ellis's argument concerning Jude called for, in his own words, another look at 2 Peter; likewise, I think that David's assumptions about Mark have brought us to a place that we can look again at 1 Peter.

I also support the attempt to keep Peter from coming off second best in the apostolic record. I particularly enjoyed David's discussion of the clash reported in Galatians 2. I have repeated to all of my introductory classes in one form or another Dungan's plaintive query: "It would be most interesting to hear *Peter's* account of what happened on this occasion." James D. G. Dunn and F. F. Bruce are also right-headed here: "Peter was probably in fact and effect the bridgeman who did more than any other to hold together the diversity of first-century Christianity" (Dunn, *Unity and Diversity in the New Testament*, p. 385, quoted with approval and confession to a changed attitude by Bruce, *Peter, Stephen, James, and John*, p. 43).

But the suggestion of kerygmatic suture between Jewish and Gentile divergency, I think, cannot avoid a hangover problem that points back to F. C. Baur. It seems to me that we must return to where the discussion of Griesbach and Petrine-Pauline problems crumbled. Stoldt argues that the sinister figure in the rejection of the Griesbach hypothesis was D. F. Strauss. That may be so in terms of theological reaction to *Leben Jesu*, but I feel that David's paper points us to another figure—Baur—and to the issue—methodological premises for reading the New Testament holistically in terms of *Tendenz* criticism. With that in mind may I comment on the critical position of the Tübingen school which, I would argue, was steadily eroded by a growing gravitation to the priority of Mark.

Baur did not believe that the question of the sequence of the Gospels could be settled by appealing to purely literary considerations

of the phenomena of agreement and disagreement. On this basis alone, it could equally be argued that Mark was the earliest or the latest of Synoptic Gospels. What was needed in addition to comparative literary analysis was a study of theological tendencies of the gospels. The notion of three moments or epochs in the historical development was already in place in Baur's thinking by 1826 and developed in contrast to Strauss. Even after the open break with Strauss in 1846-1847, Baur carried on his program, applying it in particular to the Gospel of Mark in an 1851 monograph, *Das Markusevangelium nach seinem Ursprung und Charakter.*

Mark's tendency is "to round off the gospel stories," so says Baur, "into an harmonious, ordered, clearly arranged whole." He demonstrates this (pp. 1-110) by showing that Mark depends primarily on Matthew for order and content but with fundamental intention of freeing the document from special Jewish-Gentile conflicts. Thus, Mark effects a resolution, resolution coming at the end of Baur's second epoch of Pauline and Jewish conflict. Because Baur dates Matthew about A.D. 130, Mark can only come in the second quarter of the second century. He believed Mark to be a late, compromising Petrine-Pauline gospel, a second-century combination of Matthew and Luke. Now, my question is, how can Dungan and myself, since I have agreed with him somewhat, save ourselves from the lap of F. C. Baur? Well, we can reject his methodological premise. But, if we reject all notions of tendency, then I think we must reject Dungan's thesis because it deals with tendency of a particular kind. It is proper to reject Baur's conclusions about inexorable moments of development (and here I again appeal to Professor Ellis's article) but not his starting point.

Those who combated F. C. Baur can help us out at the point of what we do with him. B. W. Bacon wrote three important pieces that bolstered Markan priority in an attempt to dislodge Baur's view of the Gospel as a late synthesis. A relevant section occurs in his book, *Is Mark a Roman Gospel?* He writes (p. 105):

> The interpretation to which some expression has been given in the foregoing enquiry [sic] rests upon a comparison between Mark and the Pauline epistles, more especially Romans. It differs widely indeed from the famous theory of Baur, though *its starting point is the same* [my italics] the great division attested by Paul (Gal 2: 1-10) of the missionary field into a Petrine apostolate of the circumcision, and a Pauline apostolate of the Gentiles. The reconciliation in catholicity

which the Tübingen critics place in the age of Justin and Irenaeus, we
find already attempted (and to a heroic degree accomplished) by Paul.

Bacon handled so-called Petrine influences in Mark by making 1
Peter, their source, a pseudonymous Pauline tract issued from Rome;
therefore, the Papias testimony is nothing more than an apologetic
device to bring the Petrine churches under the aegis of the Pauline
gospel, which was Mark. In order to resist Baur, Bacon had aligned
himself with a group of critics beginning with Volkmar (1857) who
argued that Mark, seen by way of allegorical interpretation, was
thoroughly Pauline, thus overturning the Tübingen notion of synthesis
with Peter. In other words, by removing all traces of Petrine tradition
in Mark, Bacon scotched Baur.

Now it is at this point, that I wish to widen the discussion and thesis
of Professor Dungan. I don't think that you can put all the eggs in the
Petrine basket anymore than Bacon could put all the eggs in the
Pauline basket. A one-sided Paulinism in Mark did not prevail. We
should note the succession of monographs down to Werner (*Der
Einfluss paulinischer Theologie in Markusevangelium* [1923]) which
rejected the idea that Mark was Pauline, and as late as Kelber's volume
the same mood prevails. One could marshall several advocates for the
following consensus: if Mark is a Pauline gospel, it is a Paulinism such
as Peter would also have endorsed, meaning that Mark's production is
the redaction of a balanced or neutral Hellenistic gospel tradition (cf.
Kümmel, *Introduction*, pp. 94-95). I think, however, this consensus
rests safely only so long as the two-document hypothesis holds sway.

I would argue that Mark is the product of a historical resolution
effected early in Rome and initiated by the key apostles—Paul and
Peter, that is, accept the Roman tradition at face value. The Roman
connection of Paul, Peter, and Mark is remarkably firm in the external
evidence. It is difficult to imagine a historical nexus that can claim
more consistent testimony in the New Testament and the fathers than
this one. Two points can be made here: (1) to trace the movements of
Peter and Paul to Rome in the years of Claudius and/or Nero is no
far-fetched procedure (cf. J. A. T. Robinson, *Redating*, pp. 111-17,
140-50), and (2) the Papias testimony can be profitably interpreted as
an apology for Mark's Gospel being an apostolic witness not the least
inferior to Marcion's "improved edition" of Luke (so R. Martin, *Mark:
Evangelist and Theologian*, pp. 80-83).

I am inclined, therefore, to add 1 Peter to the pre-Marcionite Roman canon (along with Matthew, Luke-Acts, and Romans) on the assumption that it is genuinely Petrine. This seems to me crucial: it saves Mark from a one-sided Paulinism which has been rejected and also from a one-sided Petrinism which I fear will be rejected, and it takes seriously the New Testament and the patristic witnesses. I do agree with Albert Outler who proposes that Romans is Mark's "Q" in the important "sense that Paul's *soteriology* and Mark's 'memoirs' support each other" (*PSTJ* 33 [1980]:7). The historical nexus of Paul, Peter, and Mark in the Roman church has a literary counterpart in the relationship of Romans, 1 Peter, and the Gospel of Mark (this could be extended to the speeches of Acts). The upshot of the historical connection is that Mark falls heir to a Pauline-Petrine resolution in the Roman church. In literary terms this means that Mark's Gospel conflates the Pauline kerygma of Romans and the Palestinian Jesus-tradition of 1 Peter. The literary relationship of 1 Peter and Romans is widely recognized, but there is little agreement on how this circumstance came to be. I suggest that they both draw on common materials and that neither is dependent on the other. The attempts to demonstrate either Pauline or Petrine influence on Mark are multitudinous (Kümmel alone lists thirty-five names). Nevertheless, I am unaware of a post-Farmer study which probes the three-fold connection of Romans, 1 Peter, and Mark. I have done preliminary research on the motif of Israel's hardness and stumbling in unbelief in Mark 4, Romans 11, 1 Peter 2 (which is Professor Elliott's long-time study), and Acts 28. There are affinities at several levels of vocabulary, theological motifs, and structure. The most profitable avenue for me has been to take this matter from Marcion backwards, concentrating on Rome and the Roman-shaped patristic evidence, such as 1 Clement. It takes no stretch of the imagination for me to accept the proposal that at Rome there must have been gospel traditions or books like canonical Matthew and Luke but not quite the same.

Dungan: Let me respond, regarding the issue of Baur. I am very struck by the way in which you start because that was the first thing that Rengstorf said after I read this paper at Cambridge. He got very agitated and when he was out in the courtyard at Pembroke College, he grabbed me by the arm and said, "I am very interested in your paper, but *we must get behind Baur!*" Well, I didn't understand what he meant

at the time, and in a way, I still don't. What does it mean to "get behind
Baur?" I guess it means the same thing that you just said, that we have
got to find some way to not sound like Baur, even though he may have
had some truth. But what is so frightening about Baur? Maybe what's
so frightening about Baur is that he viewed the development of Christian theology *according to some other principle* (not part of the Gospel), that is, a mechanical or "abstract," conception of the way history
unfolds. In other words, he implicitly denied that Christian theology
arose out of Christian experience of God; in one sense, he denied the
sovereign freedom of the Holy Spirit. As a result, Baur's view of the
development of Christian history was in one sense "natural," like trees
growing. Somebody has view one, somebody else has the opposite
view, and then somebody else comes along and somehow "synthesizes"
the two together into a "higher unity," which itself then becomes the
basis for a new three-step development, ad infinitum. Maybe that's
what "Baur" stands for; an insidious undermining of the autonomous-
ness or theonomousness of Christian faith. But I'm still not sure. In any
case, I want to thank Bruce for bringing our attention to the danger
there. Let me just see if I can give a quick suggestion how to avoid
"Baur."

First off, I really do see two main factions or wings within the
Christian movement in the earliest period (30s, 40s, 50s), the Judaistic
Mosaic rigorists and the Pauline antinomians. Each had its apostolic
leader, slogans, and "turf." Now attempts to bridge the gulf between
these two rival branches did not arise *subsequently* (à la Baur); these
attempts arose because the unity was already there among the top
apostles: James, Peter, and Paul. In other words, efforts to hold the
church together were made because there had been unity from the
start, from the time Paul first went up to Jerusalem. He met with James
and with Peter, and as Paul says, they "added nothing" to his gospel.
They gave him and Barnabas "the right hand of fellowship." A truly
momentous meeting. Incidentally two important related issues also fit
in at this point. This unity of these three is simultaneously the *start* of
the Christian canonization process that produced *our* Bible (as distinct
from Marcion's truncated, non-Jewish version), and also is the real
meaning of that process so misleadingly labeled "Urkatholicismus"
(another legacy of Baur's). The beginning of harmonizing the divisive
issues, of searching for institutional forms that will strengthen the

nascent Christian faith—these are all part of this initial meeting between Paul, Peter and James in Jerusalem. These trends do not come afterward, as Baur argued. Rather, they are part of the whole Gospel from the very start. Well, that's my answer to Baur. I'm not sure it is the whole problem, though, so I would welcome other comments.

Let me comment briefly on the point you made regarding what Paul says about Peter at Antioch. My understanding of that situation is that Peter was the one who acted in accord with the accepted protocol, while Paul seems to represent an extreme. We make a big mistake if we take Gal 2 as a full, accurate account of what happened. On the contrary, in my view Peter represented "mainline Christianity" in that he was trying to *not* make an issue out of Jewish sensitivities regarding Gentile food. It was a kind of working consensus that admitted Gentiles into the fellowship despite the obvious fact that they regularly ate polluted foods. Paul said, "Never mind, you Jews shouldn't make an issue out of it. But if you can't handle that kind of freedom, and can't eat with those Gentiles, then don't give up your Judaism, but don't try to force those Gentiles to conform to your food laws either. Simply agree to disagree and let it go at that." It was not supposed to be that important as far as fellowship in the Gospel was concerned. Well, what happened? Peter is eating with these Gentiles when some brothers show up from Jerusalem. They are horrified and get all uptight about him, and so he stops eating with the Gentiles for their sake. Naturally this makes the Gentiles upset, but Peter is trying to work with both sides. So what does Paul do? According to Galatians 2, he humiliates Peter in front of everybody—hardly an act of Christian charity—for vacillating, and yet we can see in 1 Corinthians 8 that Peter acted precisely the way Paul advises his Corinthian brothers and sisters to act regarding foods! So Galatians 2's scenario strikes me as a bit hypocritical on Paul's part—but he undoubtedly had his reasons.

A final comment on the Gospel of Mark being "thoroughly Pauline." Dom Bernard doesn't agree with me, but I think that the Gospel of Mark tends to agree more with Matthew than with Luke; that is to say, in general Mark agrees with *the Jerusalem version* of the story of Jesus throughout most of the text of Matthew, as compared to Luke. Sometimes Mark will follow Luke's alteration of the Matthean account, but note that Mark abandoned Luke's whole middle section. Also Mark does not accept Luke's version of the Passion events,

especially from the Lord's Supper onward. So, it seems to me that if there is a kind of "tilt" to Mark, it's a curious kind of thing where Mark has the Jerusalem traditions, but he gives them a Pauline kerygmatic twist in language.

Corley: David, I don't know whether you have read Baur's book or not. That is his exact argument. I'm talking about the last statement you made concerning Matthew as the primary moving force in Mark.

Elliott: Since we are going to be talking about the date of Peter, because David talks about the date of Peter and since I don't want to repeat myself, I am going to pass out something that I presented at the Society of New Testament Studies at Toronto this summer. It's on the date of 1 Peter. We had a seminar in which we discussed various positions on the dating of New Testament documents and F. F. Bruce defended an earlier dating and I defended a later dating of 1 Peter and here are my reasons for a later dating.

[Editor's note: At this point in the discussion Elliott, at the invitation of the moderator, began to make his response to Dungan's paper. A revised version of the text from which he read is provided below. By mutual agreement between Dungan and Elliott, Dungan's response to Elliott's original response is omitted. Dungan will take Elliott's revised response into account at some appropriate time in the future. The record of the discussion takes up with the contribution of Edward Hobbs which followed Dungan's response to Elliott.]

Hobbs: May I raise what I suppose is a minor issue and yet it does have to do with the question of the extent to which 1 Peter is Pauline. I am troubled by something that you did, David, which appears very often in arguments about whether something is Pauline or Petrine. You say it is important to know which Pauline doctrines are not to be found in 1 Peter, justification by faith alone, futility of the law of Moses for saving, righteousness before God, the sharp distinction between circumcision and uncircumcision. Now, if I were to apply that criterion for deciding whether a letter bearing Paul's name or even one of the so-called seven undoubted letters were from Paul, only Romans and Galatians could pass that test. I don't know any letter by Paul that

includes all the Pauline doctrines. So since Paul himself doesn't manage to get these things in letters about the length of 1 Peter, why should the so-called Paulinism of 1 Peter be discredited simply because these don't come in. I find that a very troublesome argument.

Dungan: Fair enough.

Farmer: If we say that 1 Peter is Petrine, whether by Peter himself or by some Petrine school, does that necessarily preclude the possibility that there will be features in 1 Peter that are faithful to some mutual theological position that might have been shared by Peter and Paul?

Elliott: No, I wouldn't think that calling the document of 1 Peter Petrine would exclude any relationship with Paul. I am really concerned about the predominant mode of New Testament thought which seems to take 1 Peter, at least German thought, as a Pauline document and when it uses the word Pauline, it means *cold* from Paul. First of all, I have a difficulty imagining how that would even work in practical life. Did Peter kind of hang around with Paul and write these things down so that he could later use them or did he memorize them and so forth? Edward talks about Lutheran predispositions and presuppositions. There is one Lutheran predisposition, and I speak as a Lutheran, namely, that if Paul is going to be the measure of what is good, then I can understand why Stendahl would say, 1 Peter is a very superficial document; shallow, providing you assume that justification by faith is the depth of the Christian gospel. But what I am suggesting is that we look at this document on its own terms. First of all we do find a breadth of tradition, and it would be reasonable to assume that much of that emphasis would be similar to an emphasis of Paul, and if 1 Peter is located in Rome, if it has a Roman provenance, it would be even more reasonable to assume an association of as much of the common Christian tradition as possible. After all, this is a small little sect that we are talking about and any small little sects that I know of are very concerned about emphasizing everything that is common to us that distinguishes us from the others. So I think it would be, to use a contemporary term, extremely counter-productive for Peter to be running around pointing out how he differs from Paul. We would assume the opposite.

Gundry: Professor Dungan, it seems to me that you have not made an argument for Mark's use of Matthew and Luke; rather you have made an attempt to dispose of an objection to Mark's using Matthew and Luke by providing a hypothetical, but historically realistic occasion for Mark's using Matthew and Luke, namely, the need to bring together the Jewish and the Gentile wings of the Christian church. Three questions come to my mind with respect to your hypothesis. First of all, I am wondering whether or not you don't underestimate the Gentile thrust in Matthew—a thrust which begins with the Gentile women and genealogy of Jesus; continues with the exchanging of Jewish shepherds for Gentile magi in the nativity story; becomes most startling in the Christianizing of Pontius Pilate and his wife; and reaches a resounding climax in the Great Commission, "Go make disciples of all the nations," or as it might be translated, "all the Gentiles." So it is hard for me to think that the undoubted Jewish Christian features in Matthew make Matthew represent Jewish Christianity in opposition to the Gentile Christianity represented by Luke. That is the first question.

Dungan: Can I just take them one at a time. Let me just ask about this genealogy. I thought Matthew had the royal Davidic genealogy.

Gundry: I am not calling in question the Jewish features of that, but it seems to me that you have very strong Gentile features as well, so that it seems to me that Matthew is a more ecumenical gospel.

Dungan: I know that's what you wanted to say and I need to pay attention to that and of course it isn't to the interest of the theory to overdo it with regard to Matthew. But let me ask you once more; did you say that shepherds came to see Jesus in Matthew?

Gundry: No, the exchanging of Jewish shepherds in Luke's nativity story for Gentile magi.

Dungan: I see. I'm not sure what you mean by "exchange," but in any case, the objective literary demonstration of Mark as a conflation of Matthew and Luke has been done elsewhere, I wasn't supposed to provide that proof. I would be glad to do it, but let's have your second question.

Gundry: Well, the second question is this. It is well known that whoever copied whom in Matthew, the disciples have a good press, and comparatively speaking in Mark the disciples have a bad press. Under your hypothesis, why does Mark blackball the original disciples, that is, those who founded the Jewish Christian church. The blackballing doesn't sound to me like an attempt by Mark or Peter behind Mark to pour the oil on troubled ecclesiastical waters.

Dungan: Yes, I think that is a fair point. I don't have an easy answer for that. You could extend that problem. By comparison with Matthew, Jesus' family in Mark comes off very bad.

If you look at Mark's story regarding Jesus' relatives in Mark 3:21-25, there appears to be a most surprising critical attitude toward Jesus' family's behavior during that event. In other words, you could expand your question: in Mark as compared to Matthew, not only does Peter himself come off looking pretty bad, so do Jesus' relatives as well as the disciples. I'm at a loss for an explanation for this. You've asked a difficult question. The only thing that I could say that may be pertinent now is that if you look at the behavior of the apostles in *Apollonius of Tyana*, they too are cast in the image of doubting, faltering, cowardly followers. No doubt the purpose is to heighten the contrast between them and the glorious courage and strength of the leader. But I admit that's far from sufficient.

Gundry: A third question; this is my last. It occurs to me that a good test case for your hypothesis might be the pericope on true and false defilement because that pericope deals with a question that was at issue in the church and was debated by Jewish and Gentile believers. Now, when you compare Mark 7:19 and Matthew 15:17, you discover that under your hypothesis Mark inserts the phrase that Jesus "cleansed all foods." An insertion that hardly sounds conciliatory so far as the Jewish Christian church is concerned, does it? It hardly agrees with Peter's withdrawing from table fellowship with Gentiles in Antioch, does it?

Dungan: I've already touched on how I would regard Peter's alleged behavior at Antioch. But in response to your question, that phrase in Mark could have come straight out of Acts 10 where Peter proclaims as

a divine revelation the principle that all foods are clean. Be that as it may, I still must concede your point that the addition in Mark 7 would not have pleased the Jerusalem rigorists in the least. But the issue here I think is to see the larger framework of the needs of the Christian church *in Rome*. What would a leader of it have wanted in this combination of Matthew and Luke?

Ellis: Two comments. First on the question of mission practices in the early church. I question whether we should take Paul as sort of the headline, and that everything else must be tributary to him. Missionary activity in provinces Paul did not visit could be contemporaneous with him. We should understand the Christian mission to be much more multipronged than many have traditionally understood it. And so that seems to me to have some bearing on the kind of dating we give to 1 Peter. I agree with David in that I don't see the destruction of Jerusalem. I don't see the prophecies of the destruction of Jerusalem in the gospels as reflective of the event. It seems to me they are entirely based on Old Testament analogies of 586 and with some analogy of 722 destruction of Samaria. So I would go with you on this. I do have some questions about what seems to me to be a kind of Hegelian pattern of Luke versus Matthew, mediated by Mark. I have some problems there. But, on the matter of Matthew 15, I have studied the general questions much less than the rest of you have, but one area that has intrigued me in the gospels has been this matter of what is analogous to the midrash patterns, both the proem-homily and the *yelammedenu*. You get the *yelammedenu* pattern in Matthew 15, also in Matthew 12. One sees this pattern in the rabbis whom I assume did not grow from the Christians. This pattern is better duplicated in Matthew. In the Markan text this pattern is broken. Now, one can always argue, and several of our colleagues have argued, that Matthew has subsequently made Jesus into a Jew. I have some problems with that kind of historical sequence. So, in terms of the literary analysis of those two passages, I think that one can argue for the priority of the Matthew pattern as over against the Markan. I am, as some of the rest of you, disillusioned with the two-document hypothesis; and I am not decided on which way to go to find an alternative, but I just would follow up on Bob Gundry's comment on Matthew 15 with that.

Elliott: Could I respond to what Earle said about mission practices? Just to clarify, we are talking about 128,000 square miles of territory and it

seems to me that we have to realistically allow enough time for Christians to have extended a network in 120,000 square miles of territory in Asia Minor. And the mission activity of Paul, which covers ten years at best in this area, is restricted in all of the literature we have to Asia alone and the lateral parts of Asia; lateral part of influx into the broad area of Syria of a number of the Jewish Christians bringing this strong tradition and raising the questions once again that were supposedly resolved in the Petrine legacy. Matthew could be for a congregation that had to assimilate this very conservative element into a congregation that was already somewhat integrated in the Jewish Christian sense of the word.

Dungan: I am at the moment open to any proposals regarding the origin of the Gospel of Matthew. I used to say that the problem which needed careful explanation in Matthew was the attack on the Pharisees in chapter 23. I just could not understand how it could represent anything in Jesus' actual ministry, since so many of Jesus' positions elsewhere in Matthew were good *pharisaical* positions. And so I would ask myself, where did that vicious diatribe in chapter 23 come from? The answer I tended to give was that it came from *Matthew*, not Jesus, and that it reflected *his* situation in the period after the revolt in 66. As everyone knows, the deal struck between Yohanan ben Zakkai and Vespasian turned out to be a dreadful development from the Christian point of view. How dare these quisling Pharisees now nestled in the lap of Roman violence, portray themselves as the arbiters of the heritage of Israel? It was the messianic community founded by Jesus the Messiah-designate who saw *themselves* as the ones who were to preserve the true heritage of Israel. As such, these Jewish Christians were outraged at the Pharisee hypocrites, came the bitter invective in chapter 23. That was my scenario. But now, as I tend to think Matthew was written much earlier, I am unclear what kind of situation in an earlier time could have produced chapter 23 (for it still remains a kind of anomaly for me in Matthew). There is probably a lot that I'm missing, but at any rate, that is in answer to you.

Corley: Can we revise David's thesis a bit? Not the problems of Jewish-Gentile divergence; rather, the divergence between the Pauline kerygma of the ascended Lord and the persecution and suffering entailed in the *imitatio Christi.* How would Matthew fit into that pattern? Let's talk in terms of the two tendencies being the kerygma of

the ascended Lord (Paul-Luke) and *imitatio Christi* (1 Peter-Matthew).

Gundry: Well, I would not have any objection to seeing in Matthew a very strong emphasis on the theme of persecution and suffering of Christ. Despite Doug Hare's thesis with which I just cannot agree, it seems to me that Matthew constantly plays up the theme of persecution of Jesus' disciples so that in that respect I could happily subscribe to your suggested revision of David's thesis. What is Mark trying to do now, if you assign Matthew and Luke to those two classifications?

Corley: I am not a synoptic student at all; my work has been in Paul. But my notion would be that somewhere among Weeden and all these people people writing on Mark, you have to decide what you think Mark is about. My feeling is that there is in Mark a resolution of these two matters, namely, how the triumphal, glorious Christ is so through his passion and suffering.

Gundry: Wasn't David trying to propose a historically realistic situation or occasion for Mark's writing? What would that occasion be under your revision?

Corley: My connection is Romans, 1 Peter, and Mark in the Roman community. I agree with Elliott that the Roman situation must be the key to all this, and the purpose and provenance of Mark must be related to the Roman situation.

Guelich: I can't see where your analogy or your division fits either Matthew or Mark, and that's where I have a problem answering your question, Bruce, because I see persecution motifs in Matthew very strong, certainly relocation from the Olivet discourse into the mission discourse of Matthew 10 and 1—as you know, that is one of the main motifs behind discipleship in Mark's gospel. So, the so-called *imitatio Christi* fits in one sense both patterns, Matthew and Mark. I have a hard time thinking that Mark represents the Pauline kerygma as you have described it. I am not sure the Pauline kerygma ever simply focuses on the death-resurrection of Jesus. I think that Mark is simply doing what Paul did when he preached, and what Peter did when he

preached the *Evangelion*. So, I can't answer your question, because I don't see the categories fitting either/ or. I am not trying to debate that question but I think that you can answer that both Matthew and Mark, in their own way, fit both patterns if you extend them broadly enough.

Elliott: I would like to suggest that maybe we can stop asking the wearying question about which represents the thesis and which represents the antithesis. I think that is giving us a bum steer. I don't mean to suggest that we not look for conflict. I think Tyson is right when he suggests that conflict is one of the motivating dynamics of the early Christian community. It is one thing to imagine that there is inevitably going to be difference of opinion, conflict. It is quite another to try and find a document in the New Testament that represents wholesale, one position. Baur himself suggests Luke-Acts as the unifying document. David is suggesting that Luke-Acts represents one polarity so, therefore, I would suggest that we stop trying to find the thesis and the antithesis, but we rather ask about dependencies of a given church within a given locality, namely Rome. And it seems to me one can show through the literature associated with Rome an interest in consolidation, both liturgical consolidation and the binding together of traditions. Already in Clement, there is an interest in the united appeal to Peter and Paul whatever their differences might have been, and then an interest in the Roman community and churches abroad. Rome is the first community which presumes to tell other churches anywhere else in the world how to behave and we have been dealing with that ever since. If Mark is assigned as a book to Rome and the community of Rome is interested in the world-wide brotherhood, then what's happening might reflect an awareness and an interest in what's happening in other parts of the world. And, since there is the tendency of the Roman literature to stress the unity of the church, you've got something going for the hypothesis. That's about all that I am willing to say at this point, but I think it is worth pursuing.

Farmer: We have time for two or three more questions. Abe Malherbe.

Malherbe: Yes, I want to attach to what Jack has just said about certain documents being placed in this conflict model. I am very suspicious about this conflict model. And in that connection, David, if

one looks at the Luke-Acts side of your equation, I wonder if the mediation by Peter which you see in Mark and 1 Peter, is not in fact already to be seen in Acts. Is this not precisely what Peter does in the conference in Acts 15 when he is in Paul's corner? And it is interesting when one looks at the story in this connection that it is Peter who functions in the Cornelius incident in 10 and 11 and then who refers to it in 15. And I think it goes beyond that. I am also suspicious of the notion that whenever anybody says that you are saved by grace or faith, then it is Pauline. I think it is striking that when Peter gets up and argues for Paul in Acts 15 that you really have the kind of Pauline stuff I think is on a level not that different from the so-called Paulinism that one has in 1 Peter. It seems to me that on the Lukan side, one already has Peter as the mediating person.

Hobbs [*to Dungan*]: It seems to me that if you are going to argue that Mark is trying to represent the Petrine legacy and mediate, we come to the confession of Peter and we see the author looking at Matthew, who has Peter make this confession, has Jesus praise him and install him as pope, and then the condemnation of him as Satan, when he tries to discourage Jesus from the Passion, and tell him to get behind him; then he looks at Luke who, on the conventional Markan priority hypothesis, is very simple. Matthew and Luke in their different ways want to save Peter's hide. Matthew, by first making him pope, and Luke, by just eliminating the protest. But he looks in Luke and there is no such thing at all. Now, why is it that Mark would look at that and pick out something he only finds in Matthew that damns Peter, that he calls him Satan, because of his rejection of the Passion, no rehabilitation of him, and yet he avoids the blessing of Peter, et cetera? It seems to me that that is characteristic of so much of the bad press that the Twelve get and, above all, Peter gets. You don't have to follow Schreiber or Weeden all the way to accept the evidence that that kind of press is very bad. And you have differing kinds of rehabilitation in Matthew and Luke on the Markan priority hypothesis. Luke is very simple; he just cuts these things out, one after the other. Matthew rehabilitates Peter very beautifully by putting Peter in charge of the church. It is difficult for me to perceive on your scenario, how Mark could have behaved as he has.

Dungan: Your point is very well taken, Ed. Let me first just note that what you've pointed out about Luke is still acceptable—on the Gries-

bach hypothesis. That is, it is easy to see him going through and removing the negative features in Matthew's account. But also, Luke is not interested in preserving such a prominent place for Peter as Matt 16:17-19 gives to him. Presumably, neither was Peter, if Mark is any indication.

To answer your question in a brief, sketchy way, I think you can look at Mark's account and see the characteristic preservation of the material that *both* Matthew and Luke have (Jesus' question, Peter's answer, the command to silence, the prediction of suffering, death and resurrection) and also the inclusion of the warning to Peter following his protest that Mark saw in Matthew (but not in Luke). Of course, Mark has softened the saying just a bit, by leaving out the σκάνδαλον εἶ ἐμοῦ, hasn't he? But why didn't Mark preserve that extraordinary sweeping authorization recorded in Matt 16:17-19?

I don't have a simple answer to this. What comes to mind, however, is the incredible thing which happened to this religious movement immediately after the brutal murder of its leader—the Holy Spirit picks the surviving one of the pair of intimate disciples chiefly responsible for betraying their master to the authorities. The implications of that fact for the early Christian experience of divine grace blows my mind away. Who could possibly pick up after Jesus Christ had been so horribly killed? *Not Simon Peter*?! Now the passage in all the Gospels that seems to me to speak directly to this profoundly unexpected and significant event is the haunting prophecy Jesus gives to Peter, in Luke's unique version of their last dinner together (Lk 22:31). "Simon, Simon; Behold, Satan demanded that he might sift you like wheat. But I prayed for you that you not be deprived of your faith. And you, once you have repented and come back, *strengthen your brothers*." It was out of this experience of divine acceptance that Simon Peter rose to the point where he could see that neither Jewish (nor Gentile!) scrupulosity counted for anything—only the new person in Christ Jesus. How would he recount stories of the way he had been? Blind, confused, arrogant, and, certainly, passionately committed. But to what? No, I think that the Peter we see after the resurrection appearances is almost another man. What intrigues me is, what kind of gospel accounts was *he* responsible for . . . ? Can our Gospel According to Mark be something like his legacy? A legacy we can also see in 1 Peter and the speeches in Acts?

THE ROMAN PROVENANCE OF 1 PETER AND THE GOSPEL OF MARK: A RESPONSE TO DAVID DUNGAN

John H. Elliott

Anyone who wants to challenge dominating and often domineering assumptions of the exegetical guild has my admiration and my ear. The field of exegesis, alas, is no less prone to opiniosclerosis and the sanctification of "conventional wisdom" than any other of the would-be scientific disciplines. While research on 1 Peter has occupied my attention more than the question of gospel relationships, I can sympathize with Professor Dungan's desire to break with "old habits of thinking" and to explore alternate approaches to unresolved exegetical problems. Our understanding of 1 Peter, no less than our comprehension of Mark, has been hampered by a tendency to allow revered though untested hypotheses to predetermine the very questions we bring to the text, let alone the evidence we find useful for its interpretation. Therefore I welcome this attempt of Dungan's to widen the perspective on the issue of the relationship of the Synoptic Gospels through an attempt to situate one of these gospels within the broader stream of early Christian history and tradition; specifically, to explore the possible links between the historical situation and sociological-theological strategies of Mark and 1 Peter. As Dungan himself indicates in his introduction, there is an implied question here which transcends the more narrow issue of literary relationships among the New Testament writings; to wit: is it possible to find a fresh approach

to this literature which will provide us with "new visions of the rise of Christianity," its dilemmas and dynamics?

The issues which Dungan addresses here are quite comprehensive in scope and the hypotheses to be examined, quite numerous. Since the brunt of his proposal concerns a possible relation between the Gospel of Mark and the first letter of Peter, I shall restrict the bulk of my response to the issue of this relationship and its possible bearing on the matter of social and theological developments within the early Christian movement. Since Dungan's ultimate intention here is to test the plausibility of the Griesbach hypothesis, however, it will be necessary to make some judgment on the extent to which his comparison of Mark and 1 Peter relates to and possibly supports this hypothesis. As will become clear in the remarks which follow, I concur more with the approach which Dungan proposes than with his specific conclusions. The scenario which he suggests concerning Mark's situation and purpose of composition, in my opinion, remains open to serious question. The case, however, is not closed. Therefore, in order to move the discussion along, I shall close my response with some suggestions for a future study agenda.

Dungan's Proposal

In his essay Dungan wishes to test a specific aspect of the Griesbach hypothesis regarding the composition of the Synoptic Gospels. His interest in the purpose and provenance of Mark proceeds from his acknowledgment that any attempt to make this hypothesis plausible must provide a reasonable account of the motives as well as the methods behind Mark's redaction of the material of Matthew and Luke upon which he was presumably dependent. This account, Dungan further acknowledged, must involve a consideration of historical as well as literary factors. A chain of hypotheses leads Dungan from the Gospel of Mark to the first letter of Peter. He hypothesizes that:

> (1) canonical Mark is subsequent to, dependent upon, and "a careful blending" of the Gospels of Matthew and Luke;
> (2) the Gospel of Matthew is to be regarded as "a Jewish-Christian" work and Luke, its "Pauline-Gentile reinterpretation";
> (3) the Gospel of Mark is ascribable "to the apostolic activity of Simon Peter, during his last days in Rome"; and
> (4) 1 Peter may also be regarded as a "relic of Simon Peter's Roman ministry."

A comparison of two documents which may be taken as representative of the "Petrine legacy," he suggests, may shed some light on the situation surrounding the composition of the Gospel According to Mark. Drawing from 1 Peter some conclusions regarding a "mediatorial" role of Simon Peter and Petrine theology, he proposes that the Gospel of Mark may be seen as an analogous kind of "suture" between Jewish-Christian and Gentile-Christian divergency in the early church. A thorough evaluation of this proposal would require an examination not only of the links which Dungan has drawn between Mark and 1 Peter but also of the evidence he offers to substantiate his first two hypotheses concerning Matthew, Luke, and Mark. Since Dungan himself makes no attempt to substantiate the latter, I shall restrict my attention to a consideration of the former.

An Evaluation

On the whole it would appear that this thesis raises as many questions as it intends to solve. My general impression is that although Dungan has identified certain important "characteristics of the 'Christianity' of 1 Peter" (section B of his essay), his description of "The apostle Peter's response to the conflict between Jews and Gentiles within the early Church" (section C) is a misguided interpretation of 1 Peter along Baurian lines. What he suspects is true concerning the situation and strategy of Mark he incorrectly attributes to 1 Peter. In my opinion, if there is a similarity between the provenance and purpose of these two documents, this will have to be examined along somewhat different lines. Thus his conclusions regarding the mediating role of Mark (section D) still await demonstration.

With certain qualifications I would concur with Dungan's delineation of the content of 1 Peter (section A). The letter does employ a wide range of kerygmatic, liturgical, catechetical and parenetic traditions which derive not from a narrow "Pauline" current but rather a broad stream of Jewish-Christian Palestinian and Hellenistic-Christian diasporaic tradition. Neither this inclusive content nor its general address (1:1) to four Roman provinces in Asia Minor (including Bithynia-Pontus and Cappadocia for which there is no record of Pauline activity) warrant the assignment of this letter to a supposed "Pauline school." Nor are the themes which Dungan enumerates exclusively

"Pauline" themes.[1] The ecumenical or catholic scope of the tradition which the letter incorporates is, as Dungan surmises, an important indication of the roots of its composer(s) as well as of their interests in the solidarity and consolidation of the Christian brotherhood. In its explicit message as well as its integration of tradition, 1 Peter represents an urgent attempt at enabling its addressees to form and maintain a united front against the hostile societal forces whose discriminating and harrassing policies threaten to undermine the brotherhood's cohesion and commitment.[2]

While I agree that 1 Peter clearly incorporates a "blend" of Christian traditions from Palestine and the Diaspora,[3] I do not agree with what Dungan deduces from this fact. Here we are dealing with an important issue concerning method. Tradition analysis alone is an

---

[1]The similarities between 1 Peter and the Pauline literature are due to the use of a common body of tradition. Although the older theory that 1 Peter represents a product of later Paulinism still has its advocates, recent Petrine commentators have shown the distinctive and discernably non-Pauline features of its composition. For the former view, e.g., K. M. Fischer, *Tendenz und Absicht des Epheserbriefes* (Göttingen: Vandenhoeck und Ruprecht, 1973), p. 15, n. 3; H.-M. Schenke, "Das Weiterwirken des Paulus und die Pflege seines Erbes durch die Paulus-Schule," *NTS* 21 (1975): 505-18, esp. 515-16; H. Goldstein, *Paulinische Gemeinde im Ersten Petrusbrief*, Stuttgarter Bibelstudien 80 (Stuttgart: Katholisches Bibelwerk, 1975); P. Vielhauer, *Geschichte der urchristlichen Literatur. Einleitung in das Neue Testament, die Apokryphen und die Apostolischen Väter* (Berlin: W. de Gruyter, 1975), pp. 580-89. For the latter view see e.g., J. H. Elliott, "The Rehabilitation of an Exegetical Stepchild: 1 Peter in Recent Research," *JBL* 95 (1976): 243-54, esp. 246-48; N. Brox, "Tendenz und Pseudepigraphie im ersten Petrusbrief," *Kairos* 20 (1978): 110-20; idem, "Der erste Petrusbrief in der literarischen Tradition des Urchristentums," *Kairos* 20 (1978): 182-92; idem, *Der erste Petrusbrief*, EKKNT 21 (Köln: Benziger; Neukirchen-Vluy: Neukirchner, 1979), pp. 47-51; L. Goppelt, *Der erste Petrusbrief*, KEK 12/1; 8th ed. (Göttingen: Vandenhoeck und Ruprecht, 1978), pp. 47-56; A. Lindemann, *Paulus im ältesten Christentum: Das Bild des Apostels und die Rezeption der paulinischen Theologie in der frühchristlichen Literatur bis Marcion*, Beiträge zur Historischen Theologie 58 (Tübingen: Mohr, 1979), pp. 252-61.

[2]See J. H. Elliott, *1 Peter: Estrangement and Community*, Herald Biblical Booklets (Chicago: Franciscan Herald Press, 1979), and for a fuller development, J. H. Elliott, *A Home for the Homeless: A Sociological Exegesis of 1 Peter, Its Situation and Strategy* (Philadelphia: Fortress, 1981); see also J. H. Elliott, *1-2 Peter, Jude*, Ausburg Commentary on the New Testament (Minneapolis: Augsburg, 1982); and, most recently, my article "Salutation and Exhortation to Christian Behavior on the Basis of God's Blessings (1:1-2:10)," *RevExp* 79:2 (1982): 415-25.

[3]This formulation is more accurate than it is to speak, as Dungan does, of "Jerusalemite" and "Pauline" traditions.

insufficient indicator of a document's situation and purpose. For a determination of the latter, attention must also be paid to explicit and implicit, internal and external evidence of those factors which motivated and shaped the selection, arrangement, and accentuation of such tradition in any given document. Instead of seeking this evidence in 1 Peter and Mark, Dungan has rather resorted to a hypothetical situation which he never fully examines or demonstrates—a rift between two theological extremes in the early church. More on this below.

Finally, in regard to Dungan's sketch of "the 'Christianity' of 1 Peter," I also agree that the explicit references to "Silvanus, the faithful brother" (5:12) and "Mark, my son" (5:13), in conjunction with the ascription of the letter to "Peter, an apostle of Jesus Christ" (1:1), are important clues as to the provenance and socioreligious perspective of the letter. However, his attribution of the literary style of the letter to Silvanus, on the one hand, and its pastoral spirit to "the apostle Peter himself," on the other, and the association of the former with Gentile and the latter with Jewish influence, constitutes no more than an arbitrary assertion which defies demonstration. As I have attempted to show elsewhere on the basis of the comparative evidence from 1 Peter and Acts, especially chapter 15[4], the most that can be postulated with any degree of plausibility is that these personal names in 1 Peter suggest the existence of a Petrine group in Rome (symbolized by the term "Babylon" in 5:13), three of whose members were known to and highly respected by branches of the Christian movement in Palestine and Asia Minor as well as in Rome. In a letter stressing the unity of the worldwide brotherhood in the face of worldwide oppression (5:9), these persons represent the unity of diverse geographical areas of the church in its concerted resistance to a hostile non-Christian society (2:11-12; 4:2-5, 12-19). The tension of which 1 Peter explicitly speaks concerns not an internal rupture between Jewish and Gentile branches of the church, as Dungan suggests, but rather a conflict between the elect and holy people of God (2:4-10) and an oppressive society of non-believing "Gentiles" (2:12; 4:3). The very composition and dispatch of this personalized letter, as well as its use of diverse traditions,

---

[4]J. H. Elliott, "Peter, Silvanus and Mark in 1 Peter and Acts: Sociological-Exegetical Perspectives on a Petrine Group in Rome," *Wort in der Zeit*, Neutestamentliche Studien, K. H. Rengstorf Festschrift, ed. W. Haubeck and M. Bachman (Leiden: E. J. Brill, 1980), pp. 250-67.

exhortation to concerted resistance and reference to key figures who have traveled from Palestine through Asia Minor to Rome all attest to an urgent interest in Christian consolidation. According to 1 Peter, however, the conflict which necessitated this effort at solidarity was caused by outside opposition to the Christians and not by internal theological disparities within the Christian movement.

With these remarks I have already begun to touch on my major disagreement with Dungan's thesis; namely, his reconstruction of "the apostle Peter's response to the conflict between Jews and Gentiles within the early church" (section C of his essay). Dungan postulates that the apostle Peter himself wrote 1 Peter or at least that he was alive and was the guiding "spirit" behind its composition. Thus he assumes for the letter a date of composition prior to the apostle's death (most likely c. 65-67 C.E.). He also assumes that Peter knew and used the Gospels of Matthew and Luke which then presumably existed prior to 67 C.E. Furthermore, he claims that Peter's purpose in writing was to unite, or mediate between, two rival factions in the Christian movement (represented by Matthew and Luke) which threatened "the tenuous unity of the brotherhood." I do not think that an exegesis of 1 Peter can support any of these postulates.

First of all, a mid-sixties date for the composition of 1 Peter is most unlikely.[5] This, in itself, however, is not detrimental to Dungan's thesis

---

[5] A constellation of factors suggest that 1 Peter was written somewhere in the mid-Flavian period, ca. 73-92 A.D. Numerous echoes of Paul's letter to the Romans in 1 Peter and of Petrine material in 1 Clement establish the Roman provenance of all three and the lower and upper limits, respectively, of 1 Peter's date of composition. Within this general time-frame (ca. 58-96), further considerations favor a post-70 dating:

—The scope of the address in 1 Pet 1:1 (four provinces comprising 128,000 sq. mi., and two provinces not reached by Paul [Bithynia-Pontus and Cappadocia]) requires sufficient time for the spread of Christianity subsequent to the mission of Paul.

—The chief issue and focus of 1 Peter is no longer an internal Jewish struggle over the self-definition of the messianic people as with Paul but the identity and interaction of the Christian brotherhood vis-à-vis an alien society.

—In 1 Peter the brotherhood is in the process of distinguishing itself from, and appropriating the status of, ancient Israel (1:4, 10-12; 2:4-10); it associates the Jews with the ἔθνη as non-believers (2:12; 4:3) and as the attacking "lion" (5:8); and is known by a distinctive sectarian label, Χριστιανός (4:16). For the spread of such usage from Antioch (Acts 11:26) and Caesarea (Acts 26:28) to Asia Minor and Rome, again sufficient time must be allowed.

—The breadth and diversity of the tradition employed in 1 Peter suggests a growth and coalescence of tradition subsequent to the Pauline period.

concerning the relation of 1 Peter, Matthew, and Luke. The earlier one dates 1 Peter which supposedly was posterior to and dependent upon canonical Matthew and Luke, the earlier one then would have to date these Gospels and the more implausible the theory becomes.

There is, however, a more cogent reason for doubting that Peter and/or his associates knew, used, or "endorsed" the (then extant) Gospels of Matthew and Luke; namely, the content of the letter itself. A literary and form critical comparison of the letter and these gospels reveals no indications of direct literary dependence (of 1 Peter upon

---

—The shift from a positive (Romans 13) to a neutral stance regarding Roman government (1 Pet 2:13-17) would be accounted for by Nero's pogrom against the Christians in Rome as viewed from the distance of a decade or more.

—1 Pet 5:1, if not an overt reference to Peter's death, at least implies through its parallel with 4:13 and 5:2-5a, his similar experience of suffering as a witness and his similar status and share in glory, i.e. the experiences which authenticate the message and unite recipients and senders.

—"Babylon" (1 Pet 5:13) as a symbol for Rome (with varying implications) appears only, 1 Peter aside, in literature composed after the destruction of Jerusalem (70 A.D.): Or. Sib. 5:143, 159; 2 Bar 11:1; 67:7; 4 Ezra 3:1, 28, 31; Rev 14:8; 16:19, etc.

—In 1:1 the commencement of the address with Pontus and the sequence of provinces (Pontus-Galatia-Cappadocia . . .) may reflect not only the intended route of the letter (so Hort, Hemer) but also the alteration of these provincial boundaries undertaken by Vespasian in 72 A.D. (Parts of Pontus not belonging to Bithynia-Pontus were, along with Cappadocia and Lesser Armenia, annexed to Galatia, thereby forming "Greater Galatia.") An emissary, in proceeding from coastal N. Pontus southward would first traverse northern Galatia (expanded by Gal. Pontus) and then Cappadocia proper (rather than Pontus, then Cappadocia, then Galatia, as previously).

On the other hand, there is reason for also dating 1 Peter prior to 92 A.D.

—The situation and suffering described in 1 Peter cannot be ascribed to any universal (see 5:9) official anti-Christian imperial policy or to the limited actions of Nero and Domitian in Rome or of Pliny in (Bithynia-) Pontus. The hostility and harassment of the local populace was the result of ignorance (2:14; 3:15) and traditional native suspicion of the wrongdoing (2:12, 14; 4:15) of strangers and aliens (1:1, 17; 2:11), their exclusiveness (4:3-4), and peculiar religious loyalties (4:14, 16).

—Pliny, though writing of Pontic Christians (*Epistles* 10.96), describes a different and later situation. His reference to some Christian defections "twenty years" earlier, a development not yet encountered in 1 Peter, establishes the year 92 A.D. (112 A.D. minus 20) as the upper limit of 1 Peter's dating. This coincides, approximately, with the anti-Christian initiatives of Domitian in Rome and the situation in the province of Asia portrayed in Revelation (ca. 95). Prior to these last years of Domitian, the Flavian period was marked by a relative tranquillity which encompassed Imperial-Christian relations as well.

—Revelation, though addressed to Christians of Asia, also describes a different and later situation than that in 1 Peter. In contrast to 1 Peter, many believers have

either or both Gospels) but only a varied common use among all three writings of certain dominical logia in a fluid state of transmission.[6] Such literary affinities which result from the common use of a still flexible source of material in no wise demonstrate that 1 Peter was later than and dependent upon canonical Matthew and Luke.

Thirdly, 1 Peter gives no hint of being an *Unionsdokument* whose purpose was to reconcile two divergent theological positions represented in the Gospels of Matthew and Luke. However one might be inclined to attribute such a purpose to Mark, it fits neither the compositional strategy nor the situation of 1 Peter. The conflict described in this letter is not, as Dungan suggests, an *internal* Christian dispute between "non-Torah observing Christians" and a "hard-line circumcision party in Jerusalem." It is rather, as already indicated, a struggle between a sectarian brotherhood of locally harassed, slandered and maligned and suffering Χριστιανοί (1:6-7; 2:11-12, 18-25; 3:6, 13-17; 4:1-4, 12-19; 5:8-9, 10) on the one hand, and, on the other, a hostile, discriminatory non-Christian society composed of antagonistic Jews and pagans identified together as ἔθνη (2:12; 4:3) and symbolized as a menacing "roaring lion seeking to devour you" (5:8). The conflict, that is, is a predominantly *external* social-religious struggle involving the forces of assimilation-accommodation and the counter-forces of sectarian resistance through social separation, increased group-consciousness, and socioreligious cohesion.[7] Such resistance to outside

---

suffered martyrs' deaths (2:13; 6:9-10; 16:6; 18:24; 19:2) and the attitude toward Rome is a thoroughly negative one.

In the period thus bounded by the years 73 and 92 A.D. the Christians at Rome would not only have had time to consolidate locally following the Neronian pogrom. They would also have had opportunity to develop the vision of the worldwide brotherhood which 1 Peter reflects. In 1 Peter the concern of the Christians at Rome for the unity and solidarity of the Christian movement receives its first articulation. However, this ecumenical interest is soon echoed and celebrated in the literature which immediately follows (1 Clement; Ignatius, Romans inscr. and 3:1; cf. Hermas, Vis. 2.4.3).

[6]On the use of tradition in 1 Peter, including the dominical logia in particular, see Elliott, "Rehabilitation," pp. 247-48, and the literature cited there in notes 19-22. For more recent studies see Brox, "Tradition"; and Goppelt, *Der erste Petrusbrief*, pp. 47-56; and the various overviews of issues and literature in Charles Perrot et al., *Etudes sur la première lettre de Pierre*, Lectio Divina 104 (Paris: Editions du Cerf, 1980).

[7]For the recent concurrence on this analysis of the situation of 1 Peter see the commentaries of Brox and Goppelt; N. Brox, "Situation und Sprache der Minderheit im ersten Petrusbrief," *Kairos* 19 (1977): 1-13; and Elliott, *A Home for the Homeless*.

pressures is encouraged and reinforced in 1 Peter through appeal to the religious tradition, the persons, and the common experiences and hopes which unite the family of God with their suffering and exalted Lord. Of the situation which Dungan envisions I can find no trace.

Since 1831 when F. C. Baur first applied his famous *Unionsthese* to 1 Peter, various attempts have been made to find in 1 Peter or the apostle to whom this letter is ascribed some mediating or reconciling force between conflicting theological parties. Norbert Brox, one of the most recent commentators on 1 Peter, has submitted such attempts to rather penetrating critique.[8] On the whole, he finds that proponents of such a view tend to approach 1 Peter with a predetermined conception of Peter and the early Christian scene in mind and then attempt to force the letter into a precut mold. When the letter is examined on its own, however, the external nature of the conflict which it describes is explicitly clear: believing brotherhood versus non-believing society. To attempt to discover some *implicit* hint of any kind of Jewish-Christian versus Gentile-Christian tensions or any signal of a harmonizing or mediating *Tendenz* in 1 Peter is pointless and contrary to the principles of sound exegesis. On this score I think Dungan has seriously misread 1 Peter. It is a pastoral word of encouragement and consolation in the face of societal harassment, not a product of internal *Unionspolitik*.

If agreement is attainable on this point, then two possibilities are left regarding the relation of 1 Peter and the Gospel of Mark. If there is still some reason to suspect the possibility of a link between the letter and the Gospel in terms of a similar provenance and purpose, then Dungan's reconstruction of Mark's situation and strategy might have to be revised so as to accord more with the situation and strategy of 1 Peter. On the other hand, if the provenance and purpose of both documents are quite different, then the situation of Mark and its strategy must be established through means other than a comparison

---

[8] F. C. Baur, "Die Christuspartei in der korinthischen Gemeinde. Der Gegensatz des paulinischen und petrinischen Christentums in der ältesten Kirche," *Zeitschrift für Theologie* (1831); idem, "Über den Ursprung des Episkopats in der christlichen Kirche," *Tübinger Zeitschrift für Theologie* 3 (1838): 141-43. For English translations of excerpts of these essays see W. G. Kümmel, *The New Testament: The History of the Investigation of its Problems*, trans. S. M. Gilmour and H. C. Kee (Nashville: Abingdon, 1972), pp. 127-43. See the studies of Brox cited in notes 1 and 7 above.

with 1 Peter. Before taking the latter course and abandoning altogether the comparison which Dungan has proposed, I would favor first exploring further the former possibility.

The hypothesis that Mark is a "kerygmatic suture binding together the Jewish and Gentile divergency in the early church" cannot be made plausible through a comparison of Mark and 1 Peter. If Mark is to be regarded as later than and dependent upon canonical Matthew and Luke, this too must be demonstrated through means other than a comparison with 1 Peter. What a comparison of Mark and 1 Peter might reveal, however, are certain features of the tradition and perspective of a community of which they were both products, namely the Christian brotherhood at Rome. If, through an analysis of all the evidence pertaining to early Christianity at Rome, an inventory and profile of its typical features could be constructed, then the common as well as distinctive features of any one or more of the writings of the Roman community might be brought to clearer light.

A Suggested Agenda for Further Discussion

Despite our disagreements over the purpose of 1 Peter, Dungan and I seem to concur on three important points regarding the relation of 1 Peter and Mark. First, they appear to be roughly contemporaneous. Although Dungan would date 1 Peter in the mid-sixties, there are, as I have indicated above, more compelling reasons for assigning 1 Peter to the mid-Flavian period (ca. 73-92 C.E.). This coincides with the date which Dungan proposes for Mark. Secondly, the figure of Mark, at least to the thinking of the early church from Papias onward, was an important link between the letter of 1 Peter (5:13), its ascribed author (the apostle Peter, 1:1), and the reputed author of the second Gospel.[9]

---

[9]The historical basis and possible *Tendenzen* underlying such linkage remain, of course, open to question. Who was the Mark mentioned in 1 Peter 5:13—the John Mark from Jerusalem known from Acts, an otherwise unknown Mark? Or was the personal reference in 1 Peter simply part of the literary device of pseudonymity? Were the Mark of 1 Peter and the Mark to whom the second Gospel was ascribed one and the same person? Was it 1 Pet 5:13 which suggested to Papias the association of the apostle Peter and the author of the second Gospel or was he passing on reliable historical testimony (via the presbyter) to such an association? Do the implicit motives behind the Papias account outweigh its historical reliability?

It is interesting to note that on this point Dungan disagrees with Griesbach's own dismissal of the Papias and patristic tradition as historically unreliable and irrelevant to the actual circumstances of the composition of the Markan Gospel. For Griesbach's

Thirdly, it is likely that both the Gospel of Mark and 1 Peter originated among Christians in the city of Rome.[10]

In addition to these general points of contact, Dungan (Section D) has called attention to several similarities in the content and focus of the Markan Gospel and 1 Peter:

- a similar blending of earlier traditions representing the common ground of the brotherhood and a more conservative than innovative spirit of composition
- a common echo of the Petrine kerygma which focused on Jesus's suffering, death and resurrection
- a mutual accentuation of Jesus's power rather than his doctrine
- a similar apocalyptic interest in Jesus's imminent revelation and return
- a common stress on the bond of suffering which links the experience of the Lord with that of his disciples and martyr-witnesses.

The list could be expanded to include further similarities.

---

position see *The Dissertation of J. J. Griesbach, Doctor of Theology and Principal Professor in the University of Jena, in which he demonstrates that the entire Gospel of Mark has been extracted from the Gospels of Matthew and Luke, written in the name of the University of Jena (1789-90), now revised and furnished with many additions.* A translation by Bernard Orchard, O.S.B., from P. Gabler's edition of the works of J. J. Griesbach: *Jo. Jacobi Griesbachii Opuscula Academica*, 2:358-425 (Rome: Beda College, 1975), pp. 26-33; cf. also p. 59. For more recent divergent assessments of these problems see, among others, E. R. Kalin, "Early Traditions About Mark's Gospel," *CurTM* 2 (1975): 332-41; R. Pesch, *Das Markusevangelium*, part 1, HTKNT 2 (Freiburg-Basel-Wien: Herder, 1976), pp. 3-11, and the literature cited on p. 11; N. Brox, "Tendenz" (fn. 1 above); U. H. J. Körtner, "Markus der Mitarbeiter des Petrus," *ZNW* 71 (1980): 160-73; and Elliott, "Peter, Silvanus and Mark in 1 Peter and Acts."

[10] Although the provenance of Mark is still vigorously debated, the studies of B. W. Bacon (*Is Mark a Roman Gospel?* Harvard Theological Studies 7 [Cambridge: Harvard University Press, 1919; reprinted, New York: Kraus Reprint Co., 1969]) and S. G. F. Brandon ("The Markan Gospel: An Apologia ad Christianos Romanos," ch. 5 of *Jesus and the Zealots* [New York: Charles Scribner's Sons, 1967], pp. 221-82) have compiled the most extensive and persuasive arguments for the Gospel's Roman origin. On the Roman provenance of 1 Peter there is a more general consensus. See the commentaries of Brox, Goppelt, J. N. D. Kelly (*The Epistles of Peter and Jude* HNTC [New York: Harper and Row, 1969]) and E. Best (*1 Peter*, New Century Bible [London: Oliphants, 1971]); also Elliott, *1 Peter*, and *A Home for the Homeless.*

Both documents are products of a marginal sectarian community intent upon establishing its specific identity over against both Judaism and Greco-Roman society.[11] Both distinguish those who accept Jesus from those who reject him, the righteous elect from the sinners, those who follow the will of God from those following human ordinances and customs, insiders from outsiders.

According to both documents the relation of the Christian elect to the non-believing outsiders is one of tension and conflict. For both 1 Peter and Mark suffering is the cost of discipleship.[12] In both writings the kerygma of the Lord's suffering serves as rationale for the sufferings of his followers. In the Christology of both writings the suffering servant of God tradition with its Isaianic roots plays an important role.[13]

Further Christological traditions and images common to both include the messianic *lithos* tradition drawn from a complex of Old Testament sources,[14] the exaltation of the Lord to God's right hand,[15] and the image of the Lord as shepherd.[16]

Related ecclesial motifs and symbols common to both include the depiction of the faithful as sheep once scattered but eventually gathered,[17] as the "elect" of God[18] and as disciples who follow in the footsteps or way of their suffering yet vindicated Lord.[19] Chief among such ecclesial images is the portrayal of the believing community as the family or household of God, the brotherhood of faith. This seems to have been particularly characteristic of early Roman Christianity,

---

[11]On Mark see the instructive study of J. A. Wilde, *A Social Description of the Community Reflected in the Gospel of Mark* (Dissertation, Drew University; Ann Arbor: University Microfilms International, 1978). On 1 Peter see the works listed in fn. 7 above.

[12]On the situation of Mark see B. M. F. van Iersel, "The gospel according to St. Mark—written for a persecuted community?" *NedTTs* 34 (1980): 15-36; on 1 Peter see the works listed in fn. 7 above.

[13]Mark 10:45 / 1 Peter 2:21-25; see also Mark 9:12; 14:60-61; 15:4-5.

[14]Mark 12:1-12 / 1 Peter 2:4-10.

[15]Mark 12:36; 14:62 / 1 Peter 3:22.

[16]Mark 14:27 / 1 Peter 2:25; 5:4.

[17]Mark 14:27 / 1 Peter 2:25; 5:2.

[18]Mark 13:20, 22, 27 / 1 Peter 1:1; 2:9; 5:13.

[19]Mark 1:16-20 and passim / 1 Peter 2:21.

where natural familial ties were replaced by the bond of faith, the concept of family was universalized to include *all* who believed, and moral instruction focused upon household roles, relationships, and responsibilities.[20]

Both documents, furthermore, reflect a conservative Christian stance vis-à-vis civil government. As Mark's account of the passion seeks to exonerate the Romans in the case of Jesus' execution and highlights the confession of a Roman soldier (15:39), so in 1 Peter Christians are encouraged to regard the emperor and his governors as those charged with maintaining justice (1 Pet 2:13-14).

Finally in this by no means exhaustive list, both writings reflect and support a universal mission of the faithful, a propagation of the gospel to *all* humanity in *all* corners of the earth.[21] They are both products of a community with ecumenical rather than only local interests.

Such similarities would seem to warrant a more extensive and detailed comparison of the Gospel of Mark and 1 Peter. Since the last such analysis was the rather superficial study of Ernst Scharfe, *Die petrinische Strömung in der neutestamentlichen Literatur,* in 1893,[22] Dungan's proposal is certainly to be welcomed. It would seem to me, however, that this theory concerning a common preservation of the "Petrine legacy" offers too narrow a base for explaining the commonalities of Mark and 1 Peter. If both documents originated at Rome at approximately the same time and under similar circumstances, would it not be more appropriate to consider them as writings illustrative of the Christian movement at Rome. That which they have in common might then be seen to involve traits typical of the Roman brotherhood, its composite tradition, its experience, and its worldwide vision of the Christian mission.

To pursue this possibility, it would be advisable to make an inclusive comparison of *all* early Christian literature of the first century with

---

[20]Mark 3:21-35 and further οἶκος-οἰκίᾳ occurrences / 1 Pet 2:5; 4:17; household exhortation: Mark 9:33-37; 10:2-31 / 1 Pet 2:13-3:7; 5:1-5. For a comprehensive analysis of the οἶκος as a socioreligious model in 1 Peter and related literature see ch. 4 of my *A Home for the Homeless.*

[21]Mark 11:17; 13:10, 27; 14:9 / 1 Pet 2:12; 3:1; cf. 5:9.

[22]E. Scharfe, *Die petrinische Strömung in der neutestamentlichen Literatur: Untersuchungen über die schriftstellerische Eigentümlichkeit des ersten Petrusbriefs, des Marcusevangeliums und der petrinischen Reden der Apostelgeschichte* (Berlin: Reuther und Reichard Verlag, 1893).

a possible Roman provenance. This would include Paul's letter to the Romans, Mark, 1 Peter, and 1 Clement. At a subsequent stage of analysis later writings such as Hermas as well as more questionable documents such as the Epistle to the Hebrews and the Epistle of James could also be examined.

Such a comparison might include an investigation of the following items: (1) sources and traditions (and their various provenances) which this literature has in common; (2) similar compositional features and emphases such as those regarding Mark and 1 Peter as listed above; (3) similar socioreligious perspectives on the identity of the Christian community at Rome, the nature of its distinctiveness and its modes of symbolization, the norms and means by which social cohesion and religious conformity is regulated, structures of organization and authority; (4) similar attitudes toward civil authority; (5) similar interests of Roman Christianity in the course of the Christian movement beyond the city of Rome, especially interest in the consolidation and internal cohesion of the worldwide movement; and (6) where possible, the kind of attention accorded the apostle Peter, the significance and role attributed to him, tradition associated with him, theological and social perspectives linked to his name, and persons associated with him and possibly responsible for the preservation and transmission of a "Petrine legacy."

At first glance, such an agenda might appear to take us far beyond the immediate issue of Dungan's essay, namely a reconstruction of the historical situation of Mark and the relation of this Gospel to the Gospels of Matthew and Luke. It would, however, be consistent with the approach to this issue which Dungan has taken. It would provide us with a broader data base for the comparison which he has suggested. It would illuminate more clearly the social context of the Roman community within which and for which the Gospel of Mark was composed. Finally, through a clarification of the theological traditions, interests, and accents of the Roman community or communities, it would provide a wider basis for determining the situation and strategy of one of its writings in particular, namely the Gospel of Mark, and thus a more adequate means for assessing the plausibility of the Griesbach hypothesis in general.

Seminar on
Gospel Genre

Introduction

Charles H. Talbert, Moderator

WHEN SOUTHWESTERN BAPTIST THEOLOGICAL SEMINARY decided to sponsor the Colloquy on New Testament Studies, 5-6 November 1980, and elected to focus on gospel genre as one of the three areas of concern, the program committee looked for someone who was not already registered on the genre question but who had competence in literary, theological, and exegetical matters. Professor John C. Meagher of St. Michael's, the University of Toronto, seemed an ideal selection. Professor Meagher was assigned the topic, "The Implications for Theology of a Shift from the K. L. Schmidt Hypothesis of the Literary Uniqueness of the Gospels." In this title, theology was understood to mean both biblical theology engaged in the interpretation of the message of the gospels and systematic theology in its quest for current relevance.

Background

The selection of the topic of gospel genre was due to the fact that for more than a decade, especially in North American New Testament scholarship, it had been a matter of scholarly debate. Since the mid-1960s there had been a serious attempt to overthrow the then-reigning critical orthodoxy that went back to K. L. Schmidt's, "Die Stellung der Evangelien in der allgemeinen Literatur," in *Eucharisterion: Herman*

Gunkel zum 60. Geburtstag,[1] and that had become popularized in the synthesis of Rudolf Bultmann.[2]

The attack on the thesis of the Gospels' literary uniqueness emerged as a response to several independent developments There was first of all the shift in theological mood. The Barthian stress on the theological uniqueness of the Christian message had been replaced by one in which there was a reaffirmation of the continuities between religion and culture.[3] In the second place, there was the related openness of biblical scholars to the perspectives of nonbiblical literary criticism. One of the aspects of current thinking about interpretation in nonbiblical circles has been a renewed interest in genre criticism.[4] This concern for a critique of "reader" as rigorous as that developed for "text" and "author" has spilled over into New Testament research generally. Consequently, North American scholarship has found a new focus in the study of the epistolary genre of antiquity as it relates to the New Testament letters,[5] in the quest for a definition of apocalyptic,[6] in the reexamination of the forms of the various components of the Gospels,[7] as well as its concern for the nonuniqueness of the Gospels as wholes.[8] In the third place, there were developments within New Testament research that seemed to call for an explanation that went beyond what the Schmidt-Bultmann posture dictated: for example, the relation of

---

[1]H. Schmidt, ed. (Göttingen: Vandenhoeck und Ruprecht, 1923), pp. 50-134.

[2]"Evangelien," *RGG*, ed. H. Gunkel et al., 2nd ed. (Tübingen: J. C. B. Mohr [Paul Siebeck], 1928), 2:418-22; *History of the Synoptic Tradition*, trans. J. Marsh (New York: Harper & Row, 1963), pp. 373-74; *Theology of the New Testament*, trans. K. Grobel (New York: Scribner's, 1951), 1:86.

[3]James M. Robinson, "On the *Gattung* of Mark (and John)," *Jesus and Man's Hope* (Pittsburgh: Pittsburgh Theological Seminary, 1970), 1:104.

[4]Mary Gerhart, "Generic Studies: Their Renewed Importance in Religious and Literary Interpretation," *JAAR* 45 (1977): 309-25.

[5]William G. Doty, *Letters in Primitive Christianity* (Philadelphia: Fortress, 1973), offers an overview. The major work has been done by John White's group in the Society of Biblical Literature.

[6]John J. Collins, ed., *Apocalypse: The Morphology of a Genre*, Semeia 14 (Chico CA: Scholars Press, 1979).

[7]The Miracle Stories Group and the Pronouncement Stories Group in the Society of Biblical Literature typify this movement.

[8]In the early seventies there was a Gospel Genre Group in the Society of Biblical Literature.

the form of the apocryphal gospels to that of the canonical Gospels[9] and the alleged independence of the Fourth Gospel from Mark.[10] These independent developments became converging lines of evidence to compel the reopening of the question of the genre of the canonical Gospels in the late sixties and seventies.

During the period of challenge to Schmidt-Bultmann two different types of answers were offered as to the literary affinities of the canonical Gospels. On the one hand, the Jewish milieu was suggested as the clue to the genre of the Gospels. Possiblities included both Old Testament parallels such as the Moses traditions[11] or the Elijah-Elisha stories[12] and the theory of the Gospels as Christian midrashim following the Jewish lectionary cycle.[13] None of these options gained much of a following.

On the other hand, the Greco-Roman milieu seemed to offer unlimited possibilities. (1) Moses Hadas and Morton Smith, *Heroes and Gods* (New York: Harper & Row, 1965), suggested aretalogy as a literary analogy for the Gospels. This volume gave momentum to the movement. (2) David L. Barr, "Toward a Definition of the Gospel Genre: A Generic Analysis and Comparison of the Synoptic Gospels and the Socratic Dialogues by Means of Aristotle's Theory of Tragedy" (Ph.D. dissertation, Florida State University, 1974), worked with the Socratic dialogue. (3) Philip L. Shuler, Jr., "The Synoptic Gospels and the Problem of Genre" (Ph.D. dissertation, McMaster University, 1975), proposed encomium biographies as the appropriate literary analogy for the Gospels. (4) Jack Suggs, "Gospel, Genre," in *Interpreter's Dictionary of the Bible,* Supplementary Volume, ed. K. Crim (Nashville: Abingdon, 1976), pp. 370-72, suggests biographical

---

[9]Helmut Koester, "One Jesus and Four Primitive Gospels," *Trajectories through Early Christianity,* ed. J. M. Robinson and H. Koester (Philadelphia: Fortress, 1971), pp. 158-204.

[10]James M. Robinson, "On the *Gattung* of Mark (and John)," *Jesus and Man's Hope,* 1:104; and "The Johannine Trajectory," *Trajectories through Early Christianity,* p. 266.

[11]Dom Aelred Baker, "Form and the Gospels," *Downside Review* 88 (1970): 14-26.

[12]Raymond E. Brown, "Jesus and Elisha," *Perspective* 12 (1971): 85-104.

[13]M. D. Goulder, *Midrash and Lection in Matthew* (London: S.P.C.K., 1974); idem, *The Evangelist's Calendar: A Lectionary Explanation of the Development of Scripture* (London: S.P.C.K., 1978).

affinities. (5) Gilbert G. Bilezikian, *The Liberated Gospel: A Comparison of the Gospel of Mark and Greek Tragedy* (Grand Rapids: Baker Book House, 1977), sees some affinities with tragedy. (6) Charles H. Talbert, *What Is A Gospel?* (Philadelphia: Fortress, 1977), proposes cultic biography. (7) David R. Cartlidge and David L. Dungan, *Documents for the Study of the Gospels* (Cleveland: Collins, 1980), affirm biographical ties. (8) Vernon K. Robbins, "Mark as Genre," in *SBL 1980 Seminar Papers*, ed. Paul J. Achtemeier (Chico CA: Scholars Press, 1980), pp. 371-99, offers the suggestion of eschatological memorabilia within a tragic mode.

At the present moment, among those who are working with the problem most directly, the burden of proof seems to have shifted from those who wish to falsify the Schmidt-Bultmann hypothesis of the literary uniqueness of the Gospels to those who would deny that the canonical Gospels belong in some way to the biographical genre of Mediterranean antiquity.[14] This is not to say that all of the questions have been answered, only the basic one. It is among the biographical literature of antiquity that one finds the greatest affinities with the canonical Gospels. Exactly how the Gospels fit into the *bios* literature remains for future research to clarify. In recognition of this significant shift in scholarly opinion, Professor Meagher was asked to explore the implications for theology of the movement that had taken place in the preceeding fifteen years (though, in all fairness to him, he was not asked to agree with the shift, and in fact did not, choosing to remain noncommittal on the matter).

The Paper and the Seminar Discussion

Meagher's paper offered a description of K. L. Schmidt's position and a critique of it, as well as his answers to the two questions of relevance. Regarding the significance of the shift away from Schmidt for the study of the theology of the Gospels, Meagher hoped for little. The shift, he said, is likely to result not so much in an increased precision of knowledge about the theology of the Evangelists as in a growing sobriety about how much we can expect from redaction

---

[14]D. E. Aune, "The Problem of the Genre of the Gospels," *Gospel Perspectives: Studies of History and Tradition in the Four Gospels*, ed. R. T. France and D. Wenham (Sheffield, England: JSOT Press, 1981), has produced a confused and confusing essay that does nothing to advance research.

cr[...] [sign]ificance of the shift for systematic theol-
og[...] opens the possibility of rethinking the issue
of [...] the world which Schmidt so closely wedded
to [...]

[...]cussion rarely touched on either of these points
o[...] [...]r picked up on various details of the paper. (1)
There was an ex[...]sion of appreciation for Meagher's recognition
that genre can be either conscious or unconscious (Barr). (2) There was
a concern for clarity about the conception of genre being assumed in
the paper: classical or modern (Robbins). (3) There was a question
about an assertion made in an earlier form of the paper to the effect
that gospels ceased to be written after the earliest period of the church,
something deemed inaccurate (Dungan). (4) There was a query about
what difference it would make in genre discussions if the two-source
theory were not assumed (Farmer). (5) There was general astonishment that Meagher did not wish to concede that the Gospels were *bios*
literature.

Where the discussion did touch on Meagher's two points of relevance, it was on how genre criticism affected one's reading of the
Gospels. On the one hand, it was recognized that the value of genre
criticism is that it contributes to the readers' expectations when they
read a piece of literature (Barr, with Meagher's agreement). On the
other hand, there was an expressed concern that genre criticism remain
the servant of the interpretative process and not become its master
(Ellis). Perhaps because none of the participants was a systematic
theologian, at no time did the group explore the suggestion made by
Meagher about the relevance of the shift for the God-world question.

Conclusions

The seminar was important in several ways. (1) It reaffirmed as a
crucial task of interpretation the location of the nonuniqueness of a
gospel by which the reader can tune in to what is being offered. For
example, redaction criticism can trace a theological theme throughout
a gospel but what it cannot do is to arbitrate among the many competing themes in a gospel and assign positions of relative importance to
them. Genre criticism holds out the possibility of such a task of
arbitration.[15] (2) It eliminated some dead ends in research. For exam-

---

[15]David E. Garland, "A Review of *Matthew*, by Jack Dean Kingsbury," *RevExp* 74
(1977): 567-68, puts the problem well: "Perhaps it is an embarrassment that a method

ple, the discussion gave no encouragement to the possibility that genre criticism will help solve the synoptic problem.[16] (3) It left open for future discussion the systematic theological implication of the shift away from Schmidt's position. Does the shift demand a corresponding alteration in theological posture so that the uniqueness of the Christian message is vitiated—as many seem to fear—or is the shift at the literary level theologically neutral—as I personally think? Here is an agenda for a future meeting.

---

which purports to be especially suited for unearthing an author's purpose has produced so many purposes for Matthew. Kingsbury briefly passes over twelve proposals and then offers his own."

[16]Philip L. Shuler, "The Griesbach Hypothesis and Gospel Genre," *PSTJ* 33 (1980): 41-49, relates his view that the gospels are biographies to the Griesbach hypothesis. While this is possible, it is not necessary. Shuler rightly concludes: "The question of priority cannot be solved by the work of the genre critic" (p. 49).

uniqueness. For the conversation which we here pursue was in effect initiated by Justin's characterization of the gospels as the "memoirs" of the apostles, thus offering the earliest surviving proposal to classify the literary type to which the New Testament books of Matthew, Mark, Luke, and John belong.

By assimilating the gospels to Xenophon's Ἀπομνημονεύματα or *Memoirs* of Socrates, Justin undoubtedly meant to locate and dignify these curious Christian compositions within the literary land-scape of Roman-Hellenistic culture. If his strategy was apologetically successful, it has nevertheless fared badly in the long run. His categori-zation has been rebuffed by the more demanding standards of modern scholarship, and he has been often scolded for confusing and mislead-ing the discussion of gospel genre. The gospels are not memoirs.[2] They conspicuously lack the characteristic personal reminiscing voice that belongs to that literary type. What then are they? And in what way does it matter?

The convenient answer to the first question is simple. They are gospels. Their general resemblance to one another, and to apocryphal texts that are called by the same name, is plain. Antiquity bestowed upon this literary type the category *gospel*, and the name conveniently stuck. There is no clear evidence that any earlier works were so designated. Apparently, what we call gospels were perceived very early as special forms of literature, sui generis in character. There is nothing just like a gospel except another gospel.

Does that make the gospels unique? Yes and no. Yes, insofar as the gospels have shared characteristics that simply do not occur in any other extant literature, except in imitation of the four canonical books. But also, no, insofar as the gospels share characteristics with other literary types. If the gospels are unique, so are the *Upanishads*, the *Talmuds*, and the *Screwtape Letters*. And so, at another level of particularity, is this paper. Uniqueness may be taken for granted. What matters is to locate the relevant sorts of nonuniqueness by which we

---

[2]In a sense, of course, they are; but I do not think that we can profit from following Justin's generic lead any more than we can gain important interpretive insight on the Pharisees, Sadducees, and Essenes (and Zealots!) from the fact that Josephus referred to them as "schools of philosophy." The two cases seem to me to be exactly parallel as attempts to register Jewish realities in the nearest analogous category of Hellenistic culture: I doubt that either Justin or Josephus really read for themselves in this way.

come to tune in properly on what is being offered, so that our appropriation of the offering may be apt. It is important to me that you understand these remarks as an academic paper rather than as, say, the transcript of an extraordinarily dull nightclub act. It is also, needless to say, important to you. The gospels were put together for the purpose of being read. Read as what?

At that stage of the question it simply will not do to say that they were meant to be read as gospels. That begs the question. Luke's prologue rules out the possibility that gospels are meant to be read as direct all-stations-alert communications by the Holy Spirit. One may of course overrule Luke, and choose to read the gospels as just that. But such a choice is finally arbitrary, and merely postpones the question of genre. What are the gospel-mediated communications of the Holy Spirit to be read as? We cannot escape the problem of genre. The gospels are literarily unique. To know how to read them, we must go beyond this trivial truth to discover just what sorts of nonuniqueness guided their authors into the supposition that their readers would understand them. And that is precisely what Karl Ludwig Schmidt proposed to do, while asserting that their measure of environmental nonuniqueness made their measure of literary uniqueness both large and important.

The K. L. Schmidt Hypothesis

Schmidt's hypothesis offers to resolve the problem by situating the gospels, both in their uniqueness and their nonuniqueness, in the communal cult of Jesus Christ. For him, the uniqueness of the literary form and the principle of its intelligibility derive from a single common source, the uniqueness of the Christian religion as expressed in the materials formed and handed down in the cultic life of a community "which regarded itself as the people of God (church) of the old and new covenants,"[3] centrally preoccupied with the Christ-myth. The process

---

[3] "Der Gemeinde, die sich als das at.lich-nt.lich Volk Gottes ("Kirche") darstellte," *RGG*, vol. 3 (Tübingen, 1929), col. 114: this is of course the second edition of *RGG*, and comes from Schmidt's article on "Jesus Christus," which will be cited subsequently simply as *RGG²* with the relevant column number. The translation is the work of R. A. Wilson, and appears in *Twentieth Century Theology in the Making*, vol. 1, ed. Jaroslav Pelikan, Themes of Biblical Theology, published first by Collins and Harper & Row in 1969; but in that edition there is nearly a full page of redundancy on 95-96, which was corrected in the Harper Paperback of 1971. My citations will therefore be of the latter, signaled by *TCT*, and can be found about a page later in the 1969 edition— e.g., the present quotation falls on p. 100 of the 1971 ed., 101 of the 1969.

of gospel formation was grounded in the life of the community; "the stronger the life of the community is, the stronger will be the transmission of that which holds the community together."[4] The resulting tradition eventuated in gospels not by any creative originality on the part of authorial evangelists, but by natural necessity: "This form was clearly the only one appropriate to the material which went to make up the gospels."[5]

It is basically as simple as that. The evangelists were merely "*compilers* of traditional material,"[6] not literary personalities. The real authorship of the gospels belongs to the "Community, out of whose communal life early Christian literature, and especially the gospels, took shape."[7] The evangelists stayed out of the way in compiling the natural result: "The compilers of these pieces . . . did not on the whole make substantive changes"[8] and the gospels are accordingly "*cultic folk-books*, or perhaps *popular cult-books*."[9] The content of the gospels was brought to the brink of compilation by a transmissional tradition graced by "the fidelity to the material which characterizes all popular tradition"[10] and it is this that assures its reliability—"that the people as community became bearer and creator of the tradition makes its content reliable."[11] The resulting texts "are proper not only to

---

[4]"Je stärker das Gemeindeleben ist, desto stärker wird die Überlieferung von dem, was die Gemeinde zusammenhält" (Karl Ludwig Schmidt, "Die Stellung der Evangelien in der allgemeinen Literaturgeschichte," in the Gunkel Festschrift entitled *EYXA-PIΣTHPION: Studien zur Religion und Literatur des Alten und Neuen Testaments*, part 2 (Göttingen, 1923), p. 118; subsequent references to this seminal piece will be signaled by "Stellung." Translations mine.

[5]"Diese Form ist offenbar als die einzige dem Stoff, den es in den Evangelien darzulegen galt, kongenial gewesen" (*TCT*, 100; *RGG*[2], 114).

[6]"Die *Evangelisten* im ganzen *nicht Schriftstellerpersonlichkeiten sondern Sammler* eines anvertrauten Gutes gewesen sind" (ibid.).

[7]"Gemeinde, aus deren Gesamtleben heraus die urchristliche und vor allem die Evangelien-Literatur geformt ist" ("Stellung," 89).

[8]"Die Sammler dieser Stüke haben . . . im ganzen nicht durchgreifend geändert" ("Stellung," 91).

[9]"*Kultische Volksbücher* oder auch *volkstümliche Kultbücher*" ("Stellung," 124).

[10]"Die Gebundenheit an den Stoff, die alle Volksüberlieferung und in besonderem Masse die esoterische Jesus-Überlieferung auszeichnet, nimmt immer mehr ab" (*TCT*, 100; *RGG*[2], 114; cf. "Stellung," 131).

[11]"Dass das Volk als Gemeinde Träger und Schöpfer der Überlieferung gewesen ist, sichert dieser ihren Gehalt" ("Stellung," 124).

specific authors or redactors, but rather to the people itself, which brought forth this tradition out of itself."[12]

The gospel genre therefore derives its uniqueness from the cultic tradition, mediated by the sheer absence of any self-conscious literary character, and derives its intelligibility from its rootedness in the early Christian communal cult. It is the signet impress of primitive Christian religious life. And as its source of uniqueness determined its emergence, so it determined its deterioration. Hellenistic culture nibbled at successive gospels, from Mark to Matthew, and then Luke, and finally the apocryphal gospels and John: "This movement signals a constantly strengthening *secularization* of the gospels."[13] It fortunately advanced slowly enough to permit the canonical gospels to escape being corrupted. They remained faithful to the early tradition and to the earliest state of Christianity itself. "Primitive Christianity, in general, did not enter into the *World*."[14] "This state of affairs only began to alter on the fringes of primitive Christianity, and was associated with the hellenization, that is, the secularization, of the primitive Christian movement."[15] That secularization progressed relentlessly, and soon it became impossible for an authentic gospel to take shape. This distinctive form was replaced by alternative literary genres drawn from the surrounding Hellenistic culture, and disappeared, leaving only a few lucky examples behind, recurring thereafter only sporadically and imitatively. Matthew, Mark, Luke, and John are at once the flower and the epitaph of authentic *Urchristentum*.

The proper appreciation of the gospel form is accordingly not only a literary question. It is a theological one as well: "Thus the form critical perspective is a theological matter."[16] The uniqueness of the

---

[12]"Nicht nur bestimmten Autoren, bezw. Redaktoren eignet, sondern dem Volk selbst, das diese Überlieferung aus sich herausgesetzt hat" ("Stellung," 118).

[13]"Dieser Weg bedeutet eine immer stärker werdende *Verweltlichung* der Evangelien" ("Stellung," 131).

[14]"Das Urchristentum ist, aufs Ganze gesehen, nicht in die *Welt* eingegangen" ("Stellung," 134).

[15]"Dass dies erst an den Rändern des Urchristentums anders geworden ist und mit der Hellenisierung, d.h. Verweltlichung der urchristlichen Bewegung zusammenhängt" (*TCT*, 101; *RGG*[2], 114).

[16]"So ist die formgeschichtliche Betrachtungsweise eine theologische Angelegenheit" ("Stellung," 134).

gospel form not only symbolizes the distinctive nature of the Christian religion, as Bultmann remarked—it virtually incarnated it. The theological task is therefore to discern the esoteric tradition of Jesus embedded in the unique gospel form, a tradition that was the prime cause of the gospel's specific nature and the gradual loss of which was the major reason for the desuetude of the form.[17] "However, we who stand outside struggle to perceive in its structure an *esoteric tradition*."[18] But the form itself is not to be too much stressed, except as a larger exemplar of the cultic tradition: "what is crucial is the study of the oldest evangelist Mark, and the preliminary stages of the gospels."[19] The theological project is not to be easily resolved. "On account of the esoteric nature of the gospels, bound to the cult, much must remain in suspension."[20] But the theologian must bring what he can out of this suspension, through a sound appreciation of how the gospel came to be unique, just what sort of uniqueness it has, and just how and why it could not be sustained.

The gospels (says Schmidt) provide an authentic theological foundation because and insofar as they are the organic end-product of a natural and spontaneous tradition processed within the matrix of the believing community's cultic life. As Christian literature began to show the impact of other forces and adapted to literary modes of the surrounding secular culture, it began to yield to adulteration and deformation. The shift from the literary uniqueness of the gospel, in Schmidt's view, came about only through the weakening of the communal cultic life by which the authentic tradition was begotten and preserved in its integrity, the exposure to secular culture from which that tradition had been withheld because the community had been withheld, and the awakening of literary self-consciousness on the part of Christian authors who began to speak *to* rather than merely *from* Christian experience. The theologically authentic tradition remained

---

[17]*TCT*, 100; *RGG²*, 114.

[18]"Doch wir Draussenstehenden mühen uns ab, eine *esoterische Überlieferung* in ihrer Struktur zu erkennen" ("Stellung," 134).

[19]"Entscheidend ist das Studium des ältesten Evangelisten Markus und der Vorstufen der Evangelien" ("Stellung," 89).

[20]"Es liegt in der esoterischen Art der Evangelien, in ihrer kultischen Bestimmtheit, dass vieles in der Schwebe bleiben muss" ("Stellung," 123).

sound and healthy as long as it was gestated within the cultic womb, formed only by the powers of its heredity; once released into a worldly environment, it became corrupted beyond appropriate recognition. Theology is the proper rediscovery of gospel uniqueness.

A Shift from Schmidt's Hypothesis

Schmidt's view about both the fact and the significance of the gospels' literary uniqueness impressed both his contemporaries and his successors. Rudolf Bultmann claimed nearly sixty years ago that the gospels "are a unique phenomenon in the history of literature, and at the same time are symbolic of the distinctive nature of the Christian religion as a whole."[21] Much more recently, Norman Perrin wrote that "The literary form 'Gospel' . . . must be held to be characteristic of a distinctive element in early Christian faith."[22]

Uniqueness has come to be an important theological category; and the responses of Bultmann and Perrin indicate that this is what lies at the heart of the special appeal Schmidt's hypothesis has had for two generations of scholarly researchers. If the literary uniqueness of the gospels was in some way the embodiment of and a key to the religious uniqueness of Christianity, then the new style of gospel research held unusual positive promise. Even the followers of Barth, who had seen a similar promise in the work of Franz Overbeck (in whose wake Schmidt was gratefully and praisingly aware of steering),[23] could expect that no matter how much critical dismantling of the gospel tradition took place, the final truth of the gospels' uniqueness would ultimately support their position. It was the theological issue above all that gave Schmidt's hypothesis such attractiveness, despite its a priori literary implausibility.

And it was implausible, by the normal canons of procedure in literary history, where the usual presumption is against uniqueness.

There are two principal and interrelated reasons why the literary historian assumes nonuniqueness as a standard working hypothesis.

---

[21]"Evangelien," in RGG[2], Vol. 2 (Tübingen, 1928), col. 419; translated in TCT, 89.

[22]What Is Redaction Criticism? Guides to Biblical Scholarship (Philadelphia: Fortress, 1969), p. 75.

[23]The pedigree of course goes back much farther: most of the important points had already been registered by Johann Gottfried Herder before the close of the eighteenth century.

Both are rooted in homely self-understanding, and are constantly confirmed by research. The first is that both our needs and our capacities for genuine originality are quite limited. Most verbal expression consciously attends to content rather than to form, and seizes easily and instinctively on established unoriginal modes. The sense of how to go about it, what will do the trick, what words and phrases and idioms and tones and techniques of expression are appropriate, is deeply conditioned by what one is used to in the culture's habits. Americans tend, when poked by ball-point pens in their pockets, to say "Ow!" or "Ouch!" without realizing that Indians and Chinese make a different noise because of a different acculturation. We conform with natural ease to the received vocabulary and grammatical structure of our language, and we conform just as readily to the restricted set of formal options by which both the larger and the smaller units of our discourse are ordered in unselfconscious imitation of what we have learned to do. Even when one is self-conscious about literary composition, one can indulge in only so much of the unprecedented without beginning to feel (and expecting to be found) bizarre.

The other major reason for the literary historian's presumption is in part a reflex of the first one. It is that meaning can be offered and received in discourse only by passing through a matrix of shared conventions. I wish you to understand what I mean to say. I must therefore say it by means of strategies through which I believe I am raising some expectations and inhibiting others, establishing the notions and values I intend, disclosing their desired relationships with one another, and shaping the whole to a resolution that you will be able to accept as coherent and at least a respectable ending to what you have taken my task to be. If I fail to discipline my remarks to the techniques we share, you lose me; and whatever is left wild is disruptive and dysfunctional. If I fail to come to any conclusions, you will feel abused, because you know the genre of academic paper well enough to know that I can't get out decently without doing so. If it is my ambition to leave you with at least a couple of things that you have not thought of already, I can do it only by staying within the boundaries of the ways you are used to thinking.

Of course, sometimes one has a sassy point to make, and the best way to make it may be to violate or distort the established conventions. But even in such cases, the meaning takes place by an interaction

between the expectation and its pointed affront, a tweaking of convention that comes out as a kind of metaphor of form—and its intelligibility resides in your ability to recognize both factors. This maneuver is often overt and conscious for both sender and receiver, but it need not be so in order to be effectually operative. Shakespeare's *Othello* employs a number of conventions that were in his day far more at home in romantic comedy than in tragedy, from minor effects like an arranged eavesdropping to larger ones like the wedding-night conclusion. How conscious either the author or the audience might have been about this is impossible to determine; but conscious appreciation is not necessary in order for them to contribute a grotesque effect that both he and they would feel to be somehow appropriate in the representation of the distorted values that gradually corrupt Othello's sense of life and of truth. Conventions acquire functional properties of their own, and condition the meanings delivered through them, whether consciously or unconsciously, sometimes with pleasing effects, sometimes ludicrous, sometimes stunningly apt.

Thus the literary historian assumes generic nonuniqueness on both small scale and large, and recognizes that controlled conventionality is really the only way to set up an intelligible uniqueness at all—for an unintelligible uniqueness is of no use. This presumption operates on all levels, from the smallest—where a hapax legomenon should normally be suspected of being an odd survivor of a pattern of lost general usage, to the largest—where an unusual literary form may be prudently supposed to be substantially derived from antecedents that have not survived or from analogues that have not yet been properly appreciated. To shift from an emphasis on the uniqueness of the gospels is therefore to shift toward the normal procedures of literary research, and accordingly to invite the possibility of enhanced interpretive control.

My topic is the implications of a shift from the Schmidt hypothesis. It is not one of my tasks to comment on a shift to any particular alternative. But I wish to make two remarks in passing. One is to reemphasize that shared conventions need not be either obvious or programmatically consistent in order to make their mark. The interpretative relevance of another paradigm, such as an aretalogy or a cultic biography, does not depend upon one's being able to argue that the gospels conform consistently and rigorously to any extant exam-

ples or to any hypothetical abstract patterns derived from them. The relationship may be much less overt, much less pervasive, and still partially determinative of invested meanings. The second remark is that the absence of known antecedents should not lead to the assumption that there were none, though it often mistakenly does. Shakespeare's *Hamlet* has many enigmatic features. I suspect that we would know much better how to understand them if we had access to the earlier play on the same subject, now lost but known from a couple of pieces of evidence to have existed and to have been very much alive a decade before Shakespeare's version. I have no doubt that it formed an important part of the conventional expectations with which Shakespeare worked, usually by violating them pointedly. I suspect similarly that we would be much better off in grasping how the gospels are meant to be read if we had a better understanding of the sources from which they report John the Baptist's annunciation, birth, calling, words, deeds, imprisonment, execution, and interment.

Now, Karl Ludwig Schmidt did not content himself with the mere observation that no known literary examples allow us to account for the generic form shared by the four gospels. His hypothesis ran deeper than that, and offered not only the claim that the gospels are unique (apparently true, but perhaps only by default of survival), but an explanation of *why* they are unique, and what the significance of their uniqueness is. It is one thing to concentrate on the ways in which a form seems unprecedented and to neglect the pursuit of potentially illuminating analogues; but it is quite another thing to argue that the unprecedentedness is of the essence and that the possible analogues can only be misleading as an interpretive instrument. Schmidt's hypothesis is of the latter type, and deserves a seriousness that need not be accorded to the former. It claims that the gospels are what they are on account of a naive fidelity to an antecedent tradition for which the evangelists were little more than precipitating narrative catalysts—and the antecedent tradition was what it was because of its faithful cultic preservation of the esoteric tradition of Jesus. The gospel form is thus, in its literary uniqueness, a last stage of authentic contact with the uniqueness of basic Christianity, before its contamination by the things of this world diluted its literary originality and its cultic fidelity with the acquisitions of self-conscious literary craft. Schmidt's assumption that purest unique gospel is represented by Mark will

perhaps not wash well in the Dallas/ Fort Worth climate without fading, but his general position is not necessarily dependent on this. He saw the gospels as drifting steadily away, but still staying within the pale. What then does it mean to drift away from Schmidt?

To the best of my knowledge there has never been a searching critical blitz of the Schmidt hypothesis. If the Qumran caves had yielded a pre-Christian gospel about the Teacher of Righteousness, Schmidt's hypothesis would have been falsified. If an unanswerable critique of his argument had been registered in scholarly publications, it would have been discredited. Neither, as far as I know, has happened. Some new evidence has emerged since his day, but not such as to be automatically devastating to his case. He has not been torpedoed by a doctoral thesis known to me, though some have made inroads on his turf.[24] If scholars shift from the Schmidt hypothesis, it is not because they are compelled to do so. Why, then?

It is of course both why and whether—but my topic permits me to proceed without reference to either. I merely have to deal with the significance of *if*. But before I turn to the theological implications of *if*, I take the opportunity which the genre allows me to speculate on the side of my assignment.

The waters on which Schmidt floated his proposal have been much disturbed since then, and in ways that might possibly weaken scholars' ready assent to Schmidt's views. In addition, the history of scholarship shows a recurrent tendency for an important hypothesis to lose its command after being in high fashion for a generation or so. I will not suggest a Freudian-Oedipal explanation for the phenomenon. But I suggest as both cause and symptom the emergence of redaction criticism. On the one hand, its result—drawing acute attention to how Mark and Luke and Matthew, not to mention John, each has has own theological program—naturally erodes the peculiar satisfaction originally aroused by Schmidt's assurance that they were eventually all one and the same. On the other hand, redaction criticism really requires that such erosion have already taken place—for according to

---

[24]E.g., Philip Lester Shuler, Jr., "The Synoptic Gospels and the Problem of Genre" (Ph.D. thesis, McMaster University, 1975); David Lawrence Barr, "Toward a Definition of the Gospel Genre: A Generic Analysis and Comparison of the Synoptic Gospels and the Socratic Dialogues by Means of Aristotle's Theory of Tragedy" (Ph.D. dissertation, Florida State University, 1974).

Schmidt's view, an evangelist can have a significantly independent idea only where the pristine Christian consciousness has broken down and yielded ground to an authorial self-awareness that falsifies. To follow Schmidt closely means to rule out the possibility of redaction criticism, or at least of obtaining any really interesting results from it. The Schmidtian evangelist is a mere compiler, faithful to the community he records, leaving no personal stamp on the material he dutifully assembles. If he intervenes, he is insinuating into the record an individual mind that is at least technically alien to the authentically gospel-making communal cultic life, just as any independent individual consciousness is technically alienated from any collective in which it would otherwise be indistinguishably embedded. Such a consciousness would of course be subject to the judgment that it is culturally alienated as well, expressing itself through conventions other than those already established as communally kosher. In Schmidt's terms, an evangelist whose personal path can be tracked in the redactional snow has got in the way of the gospel rather than quietly bringing its inevitable pieces together.

Redaction criticism requires an adjustment of Schmidt's hypothesis, but not necessarily a large-scale shift from it. Schmidt himself saw the gospels in sequence, progressively drifting away toward worldly inauthenticity and authorial artistry. One might simply adjust a bit, and argue that the drift was more rapid and complete than Schmidt or Overbeck admitted, that even the canonical gospels already show signs of real decline, and are already invaded by an authorial self-consciousness that may have weakened the seamless transmission of the esoteric cultic tradition. But that is not the sort of argument that I hear being made by those who practice redaction criticism, convenient as it might be for holding Schmidt's values. Indeed, I sometimes marvel at the enthusiasm of redaction criticism, which has often received, on the basis of highly dubious arguments, a response that suggests that it was readily welcome whether or not it managed to pay its dues. It has weakened Schmidt's position; but surely its meteoric rise suggests that Schmidt's position was already somehow undermined. Not cause, but symptom. The shift had already taken place. Why?

The rude and obvious answer from a literary historian's point of view is that the trail no longer seemed worth tracking: the results had been disappointing. I so conclude. The unique gospels did not render

up their secrets to interpreters who respected them as such, or become transluscent vessels of a central and discernible Christian truth. Schmidt's own suggestion, that the Synoptic Gospels no less than the Fourth Gospel, "consist of numerous individual reflections on the theme of the *incarnation of the Logos*,"[25] does not appear to have been found generally persuasive. Competing attempts to pluck out the heart of the mystery and formulate the esoteric tradition of Jesus implicit in the gospels' structure had their day and faded. The attempt to do without the usual interpretive controls does not appear to have been successful. We wound up not much more skillful in reading a gospel than we had begun, not much wiser about how to understand what a gospel means to be. In the circumstances, one is naturally attracted to the routine supposition, suspended only by the hope engendered by Schmidt and his colleagues, that despite its evident dissimilarities to other known literary forms, a gospel may have sufficient kinship to be provided with interpretive clues.[26]

And now that the ice is broken, I would like to offer some suggestions about the appropriateness of the shift. There are weaknesses in Schmidt's position, probably protected from scholarly scrutiny because of the theological values involved, that I think deserve to be

---

[25]"Sondern in einer Fülle von Einzelspiegelung wird das Thema der *Menschwerdung der Logos* behandelt" (*TCT*, 101; *RGG*², 115).

[26]There has been considerable activity on this front over the last decade. I will cite a few titles, from which the reader may retrieve many more. William G. Doty offered a helpful survey, "The Concept of Genre in Literary Analysis," *SBL 1972 Seminar Papers*, vol. 2, ed. Lane C. McGaughy (Missoula MT: Scholars Press, 1972), pp. 413-48; in the same volume, J. Arthur Baird treated "Genre Analysis as a Method of Historical Criticism," pp. 385-411. A more pointed survey may be found by Robert H. Gundry, "Recent Investigations into the Literary Genre 'Gospel'," in *New Dimensions in New Testament Study*, ed. R. N. Longenecker and M. C. Tenney (Grand Rapids, 1974), pp. 97-114. The key study so far is undoubtedly Charles H. Talbert, *What is a Gospel?: The Genre of the Canonical Gospels* (Philadelphia, 1977). A good brief introduction to some of the leading theorists, with some helpful thoughts about how to make use of them, may be found in Mary Gerhart's article "Generic Studies: Their Renewed Importance in Religious and Literary Interpretation," *JAAR* 45 (1977): 309-25. The theorists whose names and works most frequently appear in the current conversation, in my limited experience of it, are Hans-Georg Gadamer, whose *Wahrheit und Methode* appeared in English as *Truth and Method* (New York, 1975); E. D. Hirsch, *Validity in Interpretation* (New Haven, 1967); and Paul Ricoeur, whose several works on the subject include *The Conflict of Interpretations* (Evanston, 1974), and *Interpretation Theory* (Fort Worth, 1976).

registered. It seems to me to depend upon a curiously romantic view of folk-traditions, rather reminiscent of Friedrich von Schlegel at his most *Volksgeistlich*. It assumes that a folk-tradition is notably faithful in its process of transmission, free of individual self-conscious invention, and significantly different from "literature" in its use of conventions for the communication of meaning. I do not think any of these assumptions justified. Deliberate originality is admittedly less common in folk-materials than in "high literature," but it is not absent—and it is further complicated by the indeliberate originalities that come about through blunders, lapses, misunderstandings, and inadvertent conflations. And if popular literature shows a notable neglect of the conventions of surrounding high culture, it has plenty of its own to substitute for them, whether or not we have a reliable way of isolating their functions and values. A personal letter that betrays an overt recognition of public norms only by beginning, absurdly enough, "Dear Shirley," and ending "Sincerely," is nevertheless dependent throughout on the author's expectations of how Shirley will respond to every turn of phrase and direction, all of which are either presumed on the basis of the genre or guided by conventionally shared clues—or both. What the letter *says* cannot be grasped apart from a fundamental understanding of the loose but definite literary form to which the initial and concluding signals declare it to belong—and Shirley is hopelessly naive if she supposes that the initial "Dear" or the concluding "Sincerely" necessarily carry weight beyond what has been conventionally established. In Schmidt's defense, I acknowledge that the cultic embedding of the folk-traditions of earliest Christianity undoubtedly produced their own special signals, probably less casual than in the forms of popular lore that he recognized to be legitimately analogous. But to argue Schmidt's position against the analogies entails a burden of proof which Schmidt and his successors do not seem to me to have shouldered.

A shift from Schmidt's hypothesis may be legitimately motivated by disappointment in the results it has produced, or by critical misgivings about the inner and outer weaknesses of his theory of gospel origins, or by a hope—partially encouraged by reassessment of earlier work that suffered eclipse during the apogee of Schmidt's views and further stimulated by more recent scholarship—that alternative ways of proceeding may lead to helpful results. I do not suppose that such a

shift means to challenge Schmidt's supposition that the gospels were
unique because they were "concerned with something unique which
forms more than simply a part of world history."[27] But in raising the
question of uniqueness, a shift from Schmidt implicitly denies that
such a thing can be established on literary grounds. If Schmidt's sense
of the necessity of the gospels' uniqueness leads him to say that "it was
not possible to make statements about Jesus of Nazareth such as are
made about other historical personalities,"[28] then a shift from
Schmidt's view implies, and may be motivated by, the restoration of
the possibility he denies.

But let me emphasize again that this is not a casual matter for
Schmidt's hypothesis. To his mind, it was not possible for the authentic
Christian community to present Jesus in accordance with the generic
literary modes used for the presentation of such other historical personalities. The Synoptic Gospels cannot, and therefore "do not contain
stories of an individual who was the founder and originator of Christianity,"[29] because "by the standards of primitive Christianity, to seek
to present Jesus in this sense as the originator of Christianity and the
founder of the Christian Church is a misleading and Pelagian idea."[30]
The proper mode of presentation was the one which took shape in the
gospels, one which both "preserves Christology from the perversion
found in docetism, and the watering down that is implied by venerating
him as an heroic figure."[31]

The paramount Christian theological question has traditionally
been one of genre: of what kind was Jesus? Schmidt found it intimately
connected with the issue of literary genre: what is a gospel? The grasp

---

[27]"Es handelt sich um den einzigartigen, in die Weltgeschichte nicht einzuordnenden"
(*TCT*, 168; *RGG*[2], 151).

[28]"So können über diesen Jesus von Nazareth nicht Aussagen gemacht werden wie
über eine andere Persönlichkeit der Geschichte" (*TCT*, 103; *RGG*[2], 116).

[29]"Keine Erzählungen von einem persönlichen Gründer und Stifter des Christentums werden dargeboten, sondern" (*TCT*, 101; *RGG*[2], 115).

[30]"In solchem Sinne Jesus als den Stifter des Christentums und Begründer der
christlichen Kirche hinstellen zu wollen, ist, an dem urchristlichen Bewusstsein
gemessen, eine abwegige, pelagianische Auffassung" (*TCT*, 102; *RGG*[2], 105).

[31]"Bewahrt die Christologie von einer Verflüchtigung, wie sie im Doketismus, und
einer Verkümmerung, wie sie in der Heroenverehrung vorliegt" (*TCT*, 168; *RGG*[2],
151).

of the uniqueness of the gospel was for him the way to apprehend the uniqueness of Jesus Christ. But the issue of what is misleading or Pelagian is not for literary criticism to decide, even if Schmidt thought the results to be the same. It is a theological question, not a literary one. And that takes me inexorably to the first and final portion of my assigned topic.

The Theological Implications

The Evangelists. There is a special tidiness to the Schmidt hypothesis as it applies to the theology of the evangelists themselves. If they were, as Schmidt maintains, essentially compilers without self-conscious literary presence, then the theology they disclose in the course of their compilation is nothing more or less than another facet of the complex but single jewel of the essential gospel. Quoting with approval the remarks of Goethe on the St. Roch legends, Schmidt remarked that both there and in the gospels there were "innumerable variations, which probably arose from the fact that each mind assimilated the story of his life, and its individual events, in a different way"—then adding that "anyone who attempts to portray the life story of Jesus from the gospels must first obtain a clear understanding of this unity in diversity, which is the very nature of the synoptic problem."[32]

Had the evangelists dealt otherwise with their material, attempting to cast it in a form borrowed from cultural resources other than the diversified but unified communal tradition, the theological implications would presumably, in Schmidt's view, have been to their disadvantage. Such interference would have been a diminishment and falsification as well as an arbitrary departure from the character of the communal treasure. To account for the evangelists' differences from one another, we need not appeal to their own theology, in which they did not diverge significantly. Difference was simply a minor situational given, and the fidelity of the evangelists is not compromised but rather confirmed by its appearance in their compilations. "From the very first

---

[32]"Unendliche Unterschiede, welche daher entspringen mochten, dass jedes Gemüt einen anderen Anteil an der Begebenheit und den einzelnen Vorfällen genommen.... "Wer es unternimmt, die Geschichte Jesu aus den Evangelien heraus darzustellen, muss sich von vornherein diese Einheit bei aller Mannigfaltigkeit—diese Mischung macht ja gerade das Wesen der synoptischen Frage aus—verdeutlichen" (*TCT*, 104; *RGG²*, 116).

there must have been *numerous and varied traditions*, all of which were intended to illustrate the one theme of Jesus Christ. It is only when this is understood, that we can see why the evangelists themselves were not conscious of the problem of the gospels. . . . They were aware of the *unity of theme* and did not object to *numerous variations in this theme.*"[33] The evangelists were mere compilers of a diversified but unified tradition; this is the very nature of the synoptic problem, and the reason why it could not have been a problem for the synoptists themselves; it is also the point of convergence between the synoptists and the Fourth Gospel, all recording their material from the "numerous individual reflections on the theme of the *incarnation of the Logos.*"[34] According to such a view, an attempt to isolate the theology of an evangelist is probably fatuous and certainly inconsequential, rather like trying to distinguish the theology of the Mass for the Feast of Saint Peter from that of the Mass for the Feast of Saint Paul.

What it means to shift from such a theory depends on where and how one shifts. One may, after all, maintain that the gospels are literarily unique but deny that their uniqueness derives from the genesis proposed by Schmidt—hypothesizing, for instance, that the genre *gospel* was the creative invention of Mark, or of Proto-Luke, or of some other candidate, and was simply imitated directly or indirectly in the four evangelists' final versions. Or one may postulate that the gospels came about through the convergences of different subgeneric forms, blended in one way by Matthew and in another way by John.[35] On the other hand, one may choose rather to stress the ways in which the gospels resemble other established literary types and argue interpretively from their nonuniqueness.

To accept Schmidt's hypothesis is to conclude automatically that any quest for the theology of Mark is not analogous but identical to a

---

[33]Am Anfang hat gerade eine *bunte Vielheit von Überlieferungen* gestanden, die alle ihre Abzweckung darin hatten, das eine J-Chr-Thema zu illustrieren. Von hier aus wird es überhaupt erst verständlich, warum der Druck einer Evangelienfrage, einer synoptischen, einer johanneische-synoptischen Frage von der Evangelisten selbst nicht gespürt wurde. Man empfand die *Einheitlichkeit des Themas* und stiess sich nicht an den *mannigfachen Variationen dieses Themas"* (*TCT*, 104; *RGG²*, 116).

[34]"Einer Fülle von Einzelspiegelungen wird das Thema der *Menschwerdung des Logos* behandelt" (*TCT*, 101; *RGG²*, 115).

[35]For this strategy, see especially James M. Robinson and Helmut Koester, *Trajectories through Early Christianity* (Philadelphia: Fortress, 1971).

quest for the theology of John, of Luke, of the primitive community. The gospels are unique not because of the originality and conscious decisions of the evangelists, but precisely the opposite—because of their faithful nonoriginality and their lack of self-consciousness about the task of compiling. This is the very heart of Schmidt's proposal, and I suppose that it must be the first point of compromise in virtually any historically responsible shift away from it: for if he is granted this assumption, nearly all else follows. To depart from Schmidt therefore implies that one accords to the evangelists some significant measure of originality or literary awareness, at least in their choice and use of literary forms.

Unfortunately, that does not in itself advance the problem much, because literary self-consciousness does not necessarily imply controlled and deliberate theological purpose, or even an assenting awareness of theological implications. The redaction of Genesis included the creative move of combining different accounts of the origin of mankind, the Abrahamic promise and covenant, the agreements with Noah. The redactional step of including these alternates within the same account resulted in what might fairly be thought a new literary form; but we have no way of knowing whether the step was taken with any theological reflection at all, let alone whether it involved an understanding of the potential theological implications. When E. V. Rieu chose to translate the *Iliad* in the form of a novel, on the decent grounds that it would be more readily accessible to the modern popular reader in this form than through the culturally alien peculiarities of epic verse, he may or may not have considered (let alone willed) that this decision considerably diminishes the text's theological force, so important to its first several centuries of readers.[36] Can we conclude anything about the theological views of the authors of *Godspell* and *Jesus Christ Superstar* from their having adapted the content of the gospels to the modern genres of musical comedy and rock opera? As George Gershwin observed about a different set of theological problems, it ain't necessarily so. We have no reason to suppose that these productions represent their authors' whole or even chief theological dispositions, and we certainly must allow for the possibility that certain turns of event and emphasis within them arise from a simple

---

[36]This shift is evident on the very first page of Rieu's translation.

surrender to the habits of the genre. Their playfulness does not mean that their authors did not take the content seriously. Earnest audiences sit through them pleased and unscandalized, because they are able to recognize that the very audacity of the undertaking entails an accommodation to a new set of proprieties and expectations that are familiar enough, even if not normally associated with this material.

I mean by these examples to suggest that there is a fallacy in supposing that we can calculate the theology of an author from the properties of his chosen genre. I do not mean to suggest that all such calculation is thereby excluded. My limit cases are faulty in various ways. From gospel to *Godspell* is a sizable leap into a very different medium with a very different mood, and is not an appropriate paradigm for the composition of the original gospel itself, however instructive it may be about general principles. Rieu's *Iliad* is closer to the mark; and although we cannot guess much about his theology from the novelistic changes he made, we can at least see that he did not take Homer's theology very seriously, which says at least something about his own theological position. He may or may not have been aware that he registered this fact in various ways, but there can be little doubt that this was the case. Let me offer one more example that seems to me to illustrate more representatively the general problem, the genuine possibilities of discovery, and the limits.

When I was a child, I bought a copy of the Classic Comics version of Genesis. I knew enough about the versatility of the comicbook genre not to expect Genesis to be funny. But I was not as aware then as I am now that a translation into comicbook form involves certain decisions that Genesis itself does not even invite, much less require. Many of these decisions have potential theological implications—for example, which of the two options about the origin of Eve does one select? The authors, who were obviously reverent and well-intentioned, made the obvious choice—the rib story, which is so consistently perceived as the more interesting that it has almost totally eclipsed the more theologically wholesome alternative over the last millenium. That choice certainly has theological reverberations, but what can we deduce about the *authors* from the fact that it was made? It would surely be unfair and inaccurate to presume that they *meant* to support a sexist position. This decision could have been the result of lazy inattention that failed to observe the potential theological implications, or a thoughtless

conformity to the history of art and thought, or an unreflective preference for the more dramatic, or even an agonized concession to cultural
habits, made on the grounds that a failure to make such a concession
here would damage a credibility they zealously wanted to preserve.

Close scrutiny may fairly calculate theological implications from
the changes made in adjusting to the new medium. But the locus of
theological responsibility is hard to assign—some credit or blame must
go to tradition, some to the surrounding culture, some to the properties
of the new medium, and it is not obvious how much may be laid at the
doorstep of the author's deliberate intention or habitual views. Often,
especially when the author does not expect to be held highly responsible or scrutinized exactingly, conscious and unconscious levels inter-
sect, compete, and fail to get resolved. I guess that the authors of the
comicbook assumed that God created Eve as a paradigm of what
women were meant to be. Did they then also assume that he created the
Eve they depicted, in all her luscious white blonde demure American
playmate femininity? If asked, I have no doubt that the artist would
have replied that he (I'm sure it was *he*) was only being conveniently
conventional for a delimited audience. On the witness stand, he would
probably have pleaded that he did not mean this to be prejudicial to
other possible ways of representing essential womanhood. Under
cross-examination, he may have confessed that he really hoped and
supposed that this is how all women would look in the resurrection.

The upshot is that we can indeed learn about theological implications from what authors do with a new genre, but with an uncertain
relation to the authors' real convictions. In some instances, we can
learn things that they intended us to learn, or would have been glad to
know that they had promoted inadvertently, out of lazy habit. We can
also learn other things that they would be embarrassed to discover that
they had disclosed. In still other cases, they might deny that the
implications are there, but would deny quite wrongly: they held and
revealed unconscious views that were inconsistent with their conscious
convictions. But in yet other cases, they would be innocent on even the
unconscious level, and might legitimately protest, "That is not it at all;
that is not what I meant at all." It is not safe to presume that what they
neglected they also rejected, or that they were aware of any appropriate
alternatives to their choices. I do not in fact remember whether there
was in my comicbook an opening panel corresponding to "In the

beginning." But if the authors naively offered one, it must have been a desperate choice, depicting little more than the debris resulting from the collision of the original uniconic theology of Genesis with the imperious demands of a pictorial medium. Whatever they did would be relatively uninformative about their theology: it is not only a no-win situation, but a no-place and no-show one as well. Wherever the artists and authors stood theologically, they had to make an arbitrary decision. Whatever decision they made would be potentially subject to endless theological recriminations. Even if the panel had been drawn with the utmost care for theological responsibility, its designers would not have disclosed much about themselves, and could not fairly be held accountable. The genre would have worked its will to their helpless disadvantage.

The weight of these illustrations, each of which captures parts of the overall problem, seems to me to be both encouraging and discouraging to the enterprise of discovering the theology of the evangelists. I find it encouraging insofar as it reminds us that a transfer from one genre to another produces a fresh range of decisions required by the new medium, and that these decisions will, if one has sufficient command of the context, not only reveal some special theological assumptions of the author (or authors) in a way that a close imitation of the old genre might not. For rediscovering the theology of the authors, it does not much matter whether we can discriminate conscious program from unconscious newsleak. What matters is to discover the theological attitudes, presuppositions, and notions of the mind in charge, along with hints about the theological position which its intended audience was supposed to occupy. All this is potentially present to the researcher's probe to the extent that the variables can themselves be known and specified.

That is the good news. The bad news is twofold. On the one hand, the gingerly and tentative language I have just used represents a limit beyond which I do not think we can responsibly go. Even in a well-controlled case, we are only making likely guesses. On the other hand, the news is even worse. Most of the instances I selected were deliberately cases in which we know in great detail just what the author faced in shifting genres. We know not only the particular content with which he (presumably) was working but even the literary form he found it in, and we know also a privileged range of popular responses over a long

history of the primary text's reception, plus most of what he could be expected to know about his own audience's potential—in short, we know most of the data by which his own decisions were both guided and indemnified. We can apply an unusually exacting literary micrometer to such cases. We still come up with ambiguous conclusions. With the formation of the gospels, it is no such matter. There, we have nothing like the special vantage point from which we can see the work of the translator of Homer, the confectors of musicals, or the daring entrepreneur of Christian comicbooks. In these latter cases, we know exactly what the authors were working with, and we know the expectations of their audiences by chapter and verse. Yet we still have to be cautious about any calculations concerning the authors themselves. By comparison, the situation with the gospels is nearly hopeless: we know only guessingly what they were assembling into a literary whole or omitting from the final product; we know almost nothing about how they understood others to be thinking about these preliminary materials; and we are desperately at sea when it comes to figuring out just what they supposed they were accomplishing, consciously or unconsciously. We no longer have access to the rules of the game they played: we cannot even be sure that *they* did.

Accordingly, if we depart from Schmidt far enough to allow the evangelists the chance of tinkering with literary possibilities not entirely endogenous to the Christian cult (which is the minimum level of departure), we simply do not know where we are. We are free to entertain options excluded by Schmidt, but this merely issues us into a vast and uncharted territory. We can suppose that the gospels may show the appropriation—even the conscious and deliberate appropriation—of presentational models that were not in fact derived from kerygmatic and cultic traditions. We are free to think that perhaps the gospels were trying to imitate the accomplishments of extant (and, alas!, nonextant) pagan literature of their own day. We are even free to entertain the thought that the gospels may have deliberately attempted to portray "an individual who was the founder and originator of Christianity," despite Schmidt's specific exclusion of this possibility. But the unhappy truth of the matter is that we do not know the nature of the situation; and that we never will; and that even if miraculously or serendipitously we should come upon it, we still wouldn't be much ahead in pinning down the theology of the evange-

lists. They were children of their time. We shall never know how they used their time, or quite what their time was. What they did was partly inevitable routine, and partly inventive. We can never know which was which—and even if we did, we would not know how to evaluate it.

Let me summarize the bad tidings of this part of my assignment. A firm shift from Schmidt is likely to result not so much in an increased precision of knowledge about the theology of the evangelists as in a growing realization that this new moon calls into question some recent tides. Within the rush to know how the evangelists thought, came an inappropriate and unjustified overconfidence about possible answers. Schmidt's goes first; but then, like dominoes, go the overstatements in the proposals of Conzelmann and Marxsen as well.[37] *Redaktionsgeschichte* has properly counterpoised the excesses of its predecessor, including the work of Schmidt, but has done so by a swing of the pendulum. It is not in equilibrium. I think it should go back to the center and start over. Whether or not this is a disappointing prospect from a theological point of view depends upon how largely one has invested in the stock of the evangelists relative to the grand enterprise of doing theology in general. And that takes me to the final issue, and to another aspect of the Schmidt hypothesis: what then do we do about theology?

Theology in General. If theology is no longer the queen of the sciences, neither is she their press secretary. The theological implications of Schmidt's views are processed by different theologies in different ways: Barthians did one thing, Bultmannians another. The theological results of straying from Schmidt are potentially even more various, falling all over the spectrum, according to the chosen theological prism. Some will conclude that we must abandon unrewarding historicity altogether and take refuge in the convenient doctrines of infallibility and inerrancy; others will conclude that there is after all nothing new under the sun and wait dispassionately for the next fashion to come and go. An attempt to deal with "the" theological implications of a shift from Schmidt's hypothesis is not only beyond

---

[37]I have never understood the respect that has been accorded these *Redaktionsgeschichtliche* landmarks. I would have scolded an undergraduate for putting forth an argument with such patent weaknesses in argumentation, and such disdain for sound evidence.

my capacities but out of my brief and well beyond my genre. I will therefore focus my attention on the theological implications which Schmidt himself tied to his views, and then move on to some further suggestions of my own.

The question of gospel genre can be taken to be theologically neutral, and has so been taken by our chairman at the end of his careful investigation of what a gospel is.[38] This is a sound stance, but it differs starkly from Schmidt's. For him, the literary issue of the uniqueness of gospel genre was ineluctably embedded in the theological issue of the uniqueness of the Christian dispensation. Indeed, it was embedded in the ultimate theological issue altogether. "The general philosophical question of content and form," wrote Schmidt, "crosses over into the theological question of God and World, of Christianity and Culture. The radical and positive view of the gospels is a function of the basic theological question."[39]

I concur with Schmidt's assertion that the question of God and World is the basic theological question, and I agree that the relationship between Christianity and Culture is a function of this basic question. In fact, I find it difficult to imagine how it can be thought otherwise. But the answers that may be offered to these questions by pious intelligence are quite varied. H. Richard Niebuhr has shown this with admirable lucidity and impartiality in his classic work *Christ and Culture*—for although it was not part of his undertaking to demonstrate that what was ultimately at stake in the thinking of those whose writings he surveys was really the question of God and World, it does not take much critical probing to discover that this was really the case. All theological roads lead here eventually; those that deal with Christianity and Culture lead here soon.

And so did Schmidt's. The uniqueness of the gospel genre meant to him two things of primary theological significance. Negatively (that is, in the gospels' abstention from the literary possibilities of the surrounding cultures), it meant that the content of the gospels had not been diluted and compromised by accommodation to alien modes of

---

[38]Charles H. Talbert, *What is a Gospel?*

[39]"Die allgemein philosophische Frage nach Inhalt und Form ist übergeführt in die theologische Frage nach Gott und Welt, nach Christentum und Kultur. Die radikale und positive Betrachtung der Evangelien ist ein Exponent der theologischen Hauptfrage" ("Stellung," 134).

expression and representation: Christianity had spoken in a way that was true to its separation from the world as an eschatologically cultic people. Positively (that is, insofar as the gospel form was born of an unsophisticated attempt to register Christian faith), it meant that the gospels provide a direct expression of faith, and thus (at least theoretically) an access to it.

These two notions are reciprocals of one another in Schmidt's case. They are not so inevitably—the spontaneous naive is sometimes compromised by being reformulated according to more sophisticated standards, but it is often improved in both its internal integrity and its expressive adequacy. Despite the faint reek of imperialism, I presume that an audience of professional educators is not likely to quarrel with that. Schmidt wanted to make the case of the gospels an important exception. There are of course important exceptions. But Schmidt's special appeal about the gospels, and his sense of the important reciprocity of the two principles I have cited, suggests the presence of three theologically important presuppositions, almost certainly held by Schmidt himself and clearly shared by many who have rallied to his cause. The first is that the gospels bear witness to a culturally unique and unified faith within the primitive Christian community. The second is that this faith not only was not expressed within the mental habits and literary modes of the surrounding cultures, but that it could not be thus expressed. The third is that this faith is theologically normative. Taken together, they locate Schmidt's implicit response to the *theologische Hauptfrage:* God and World, Christianity and Culture, are substantially at odds, and possibly incompatible.

Let me take these three presuppositions in order. The first, the presumption that the gospels show us a unique and unified Christian faith, does not seem to me to have been adequately established by those who have attempted to do so. Interpretations that try to see the gospels as prosecuting any one consistent prepossession, be it Schmidt's own notion of the incarnation of the logos or the more common modern supposition that they attest consistently to "the" kerygma, seem to me not only unpersuasive but negligent, foundering not only on their failure to account for some of the less cooperative of the individual pericopae but also on the puzzling features in the overall shape of the gospels' behavior. Recent scholarship has led to an appropriate measure of skepticism about the project of finding the alchemical philos-

opher's stone by which gospel genesis can be accounted for. The assumption of a unique, unified, and consistent early confession has yielded under scrutiny to the more temperate recognition of a variety of early Christian ways to understand and formulate what had taken place, and this had led in turn to the aptly hesitant observation made a decade ago by James Robinson: "in view of the plurality of kerygmatic trends in primitive Christianity, and their history-of-religious parallels, the view that one distinctive *Gattung* Gospel emerged sui generis from the uniqueness of Christianity seems hardly tenable."[40] This argument a priori is variously supportable and expandable from an a posteriori critique which may cite not only the interpretive inadequacies of various unitive proposals but also the force of relevant questions not often posed and still less often confronted. For instance: what *kerygmatic* point is being formally made by the peculiarly dilatory and rather routinely detailed way in which the trial and passion of Jesus are treated in all four gospels?[41]

Even an assumption of multiple *kerygmata* seems to me inadequate to explain the nature of the gospels as we have them. What is presented appears to be governed by several centers of differing interests, not all of which are clearly in the service of any form of proclamational intent, or directly derivable from one. In the present state of the art, I submit that we still have no good reason to believe that the gospels as they have come to us control, in any important sense of the word, or even consistently register, what it is that earliest Christianity understood to be, and wished to express about, the peculiar nature of its faith.

The second supposition, that the earliest Church was unable to express itself according to the cultural modes publicly available, has already been subjected to some criticism in the earlier stages of my discussion, and has been called into question by recent (as well as earlier and inadequately refuted) attempts to show that it did in fact do

---

[40]James M. Robinson, "On the *Gattung* of Mark (and John)," *Jesus and Man's Hope* (Pittsburgh: Pittsburgh Theological Seminary, 1970), 1:104.

[41]I do not remember ever seeing a satisfactory attempt to raise and deal with this issue. It has long been a commonplace of New Testament criticism that the gospels began with passion narratives, and added the words and works of Jesus as a preface. The point is not normally defended, and I cannot think how a good case could be made for it—or for the common assumption that the main motive behind the passion narratives is the expansion and development of the kerygma, which I should think would have produced a kind of writing very different from what was actually done.

so. Schmidt, with characteristic sagacity, observed that it is a procedural error to suppose that the very earliest states of gospel tradition were necessarily more on target than the later ones. Adequate understanding and expression were not given all at once and at the beginning; a measure of sifting experience and reflection were necessary before things fell into place. I suggest that this insight may legitimately be pressed farther than Schmidt would be inclined to authorize. Some very early states of Christian awareness had an uncertain grasp of what had taken place and of its theological significance. The same is plausibly true of some fairly settled later states. The progressive attempts to formulate an intelligible way of recording the nature and meaning of what was theologically significant—or to register the response of Christian faith—did not necessarily reach their natural and successful conclusion, or exhaust their theological responsibilities, at the point where they made the extant gospels possible. Nor were later developments necessarily a series of seductions into less appropriate worldly ways of expression. I therefore suggest that a shift from Schmidt's hypothesis means that we can and must give serious theological consideration to the possibility that the gradual abandonment of the gospel genre and its replacement by other forms was not a process of weakening and forgetting but an honorable attempt to make sense of what had not been quite adequately presented in the first place, a flight not from but toward theological responsibility. And I further suggest that if the gospel genre became literarily obsolete (which it largely did), this was not merely because it was perceived to be uniquely privileged as the foundation early witness to Christian faith (which was probably the case), but also because it was perceived to be an inadequate vehicle of Christian theological purpose—not just because it was no longer the mode in which Christian understanding could be satisfactorily presented, but because it never was.

The third of the presuppositions is the most theologically delicate: that earliest faith—or at least the state of faith that correlates with the gospels—is theologically normative. There are different ways of supporting this proposition. It can be endorsed on the grounds that the gospels preserve the historically most primitive witness. But no Christian theologian will argue that most primitive means most authentic: the gospels are themselves agreed in rejecting the adequacy of the understanding of Jesus' closest disciples before the crucifixion and

even just after the resurrection. Schmidt was more perspicacious than to fall into that fallacy. Alternatively, it can be taken as a point of constitutional law: sound theology is that which takes its point of departure from an obedient acceptance of the faith witnessed to by the gospels. This is a coherently manageable principle, but theologically it begs the question. In that sense, I believe that Schmidt was entirely right in claiming that his apparently literary hypothesis evokes the basic theological issue of God and World, and is finally dependent for its credibility not on how successfully one thinks he trounced Clyde Weber Votaw, or how persuasively he has put into play the analogies from the Faust legends, or even how impressively coherent with one another are his searching observations and arguments, but rather on how one deals with the *theologische Hauptfrage* of God and World.

It is my judgment that the Schmidt hypothesis is radically gnostic, in that it assumes that a specific esoteric and cultic way of responding to the foundational events and disclosures of Christianity was the sole theologically authentic way, untranslatable into and alien from the means by which available human culture—primarily then, but implicitly ever—might be prepared to receive the best revelational news. I acknowledge that some such gnosticism has, despite the repudiation of some of its forms, remained fairly close to the heart of Christian theology from its inception to our own day. I do not deny that brilliant and coherent theologies have been written under its influence. I am even willing to admit that it may possibly represent the truth of the matter. But I also submit that the logic pursued by the rejected versions of gnosticism was more theologically sound than the logic by which orthodox Christianity has traditionally protected its own brand of gnosticism. I think that the gnostic revelational principle is ultimately irreconcilable with the idea of the relationship of God and World represented by the doctrine of benevolent omnipotent creation, and I presently suspect that any program of theologizing that pledges allegiance to both will ultimately self-destruct if taken to a state of full responsibility.

Having already gone beyond the spaciotemporal bounds of my invitation, I will not try to press the argument further. Let me rather summarize: a shift from the K. L. Schmidt hypothesis of the literary uniqueness of the gospels has a wide variety of potential theological implications, depending on the theology employed and the locus and

nature of the shift. I have tried to engage what appears to me to be the most salient theological issue for Schmidt, for whose mind I have profound respect, and which happens also to be the most interesting for me. I do not remotely suggest that my own interest in the degnosticizing of Christian theology forms part of the program of those who have already rejected Schmidt's hypothesis. But I take the opportunity of this assignment to draw to their attention, and to the attention of all who are willing to listen, that this is at least one of the salient theological possibilities reopened by a shift from the views of Karl Ludwig Schmidt on the literary uniqueness of the gospel.

As you ponder whether this suggestion is worth considering, you will naturally, and properly, look first to the main theological tradition. It is of course inhospitable to such a proposal—that is one of the reasons for its ready acceptance of Schmidt. But the main tradition begs the question. We should survey the state of the union more broadly, and with a diagnostic eye. As we do so, I call our collective attention to one suggestive detail. Of all the traditional divisions of Christian theology, the most moribund is Apologetics. I remarked at the beginning of this paper that we can still learn from the first-known of the great early apologists, Justin Martyr. I further suggest that we can learn from all the apologists, and that the major lesson is the one that is institutionally and procedurally implied in the present enfeeblement of the discipline they founded. Traditional apologetics does not work. It may manage successes here and there, but not for the reasons traditionally presumed—that it makes better sense, that it unfolds a vision of God and World that is persuasively worthy of worship and belief. Having now gone more thoroughly into the World, Christian theology has met with sobering experience, and has learned new things. That is as it should be. It touches intimately the prime theological problem. I remind you that it was Schmidt himself who pulled out the stops about God and World. A shift from his views at least reopens the possibility of rethinking the issues which he so closely wedded to his hypothesis. That is my concluding theological recommendation. In making it, I am consciously alert to the appropriateness of the relativizing remark Schmidt once made in passing: "The scholar too is a function of his time: that is fate and good fortune—*Auch der Wissenschaftler ist ein Exponent seiner Zeit; das ist Schicksal und Glück.*"[42]

---

[42]"Stellung," 89.

Schicksal and *Glück*—conditioned response and lucky break. Just which is which is unfortunately not so easy to decide.

SEMINAR DIALOGUE WITH JOHN MEAGHER

Moderator: Thank you, John, for your presentation. We will have a very informal discussion here, and I wonder, David Barr, would you like to begin the raising of questions that we might put to Professor Meagher.

Barr: First, let me thank you and say that I at least can agree with quite a number of things that you suggest. The notion that uniqueness is a relative concept and not an absolute one, I think, I heartily endorse. The notion that genres are both conscious and unconscious and may even be more forceful if they are unconscious; that genres are channels of meaning that color the content that is poured into them—with all those things I agree. I find myself agreeing with a great deal of your paper, but in part I wonder if that isn't because there are some things you don't come down sharply on, like what a genre is, for example. You say you want to use the term rather broadly, that at one point it doesn't have to have shared conventions, they do not have to be either obvious or programmatically consistent. Can we begin by probing how you understand the genre concept?

Meagher: I would like to make a correction on your understanding of that passage. I evidently did not make myself adequately clear. What I

am saying there is that the application for interpretive purposes of a genre known from other literary history, does not stand or fall in its appropriateness on whether the work we are examining consistently pursues the program of that genre. What I am trying to do there is to validate the suggestion that, if we look at this passage in the light of that type of literature, not the whole gospel, but this passage or that feature, you can't rule that approach out of court on the grounds that the gospel itself doesn't consistently follow the program of an aretalogy or a cultic biography or whatever is the candidate. Now, in order to be called a genre at all, I would insist that it has to be programmatic in itself, that is, there has to be a consistent kind of structuring of some sort. Now I will allow that to be, in some cases, highly loose. I will use the example (which I did not try to absorb into the precis) of the popular letter which is bounded by "Dear Shirley" and concludes "Sincerely," and everything in between follows much looser rules though those are very strict. But it does signal something, [even if] it doesn't tell you exactly how the internal material is going to be pursued. It's one of the loosest of the genres we have. Others are much more strict. A limerick has much tighter rules, and you know exactly what is going to come up in its formal structure and [it] therefore creates a different set of expectations in [the context of] which you can make a different kind of point. So I do insist that to talk about a genre at all you are talking about the rules by which it behaves. . . .

I don't think that the present state of our understanding is such that anybody can fairly claim that we know what a gospel is as a genre. What I do think is possible, and to be encouraged is the application of other generic forms toward the interpretation of the gospel. Let me just give you a hypothetical instance. If, for instance, one troublesome pericope or a certain pattern of happenings that occurs seven times in a given gospel, appears to be interestingly similar to that type of happening or that type of pattern in a well-established kind of antique literature, then it is fair to try on the hypothesis that here the gospel may be intended to behave in a manner that is analogous to or identical to the generic behavior of this other more well-established form. And if we try reading those features of the gospel with that kind of interpretative assumption, then it may set up possibilities that will permit us to perceive other sorts of things.

In a way it is a kind of analogue of Ed Sanders's proposal that if we look at what in fact happened in Christianity, then it sets us up to look

back and see the antecedent implications of that and be alert to things we might otherwise miss. I am merely suggesting that you rule out the Schmidtian assumption that it can only be misleading to notice how the gospels in some respects resemble biographies or aretalogy, or folk literature, or this or that. Rather than insisting that it can only be misleading, it's time to try it out again more amply than we have been doing over the last couple of generations and see what we come up with. It offers the possibility of enhanced interpretative control. It may not pay off. We may come to the same kind of results that I judge to be the case of the Schmidt hypothesis, namely that after testing it out, it seems to be somewhat fanciful, not very well grounded and doesn't really produce much that is valuable even if it should be true. But it's worth trying. The possibility of an answer to interpretative control is there.

Hobbs: John, I want to say I found this one of the most delightfully written scholarly papers which I have encountered in many years. The style and flair are quite delightful. I must say you carried me along and I felt totally convinced by it, except that—and here would be my hesitation—it is a case of overkill, I suspect. Let me say what I mean by that. It may not be overkill for Schmidt, but I think it is overkill for any possible heirs of Schmidt. You tend in the paper to identify a "uniqueness" which we do find in Schmidt; with "distinctiveness" you make this move several times. For example, you quote Norman Perrin after quoting Bultmann. You say Perrin wrote that the literary form gospel must be held to be characteristic of a distinct development in early Christian faith. Uniqueness has come to be an important theological category, and so on. Now I would urge that uniqueness is not the same as distinctiveness. And I think that distinction is really quite crucial here. Total uniqueness, I suspect, in literature and anything else is probably nonexistent, except as meaninglessness. That is, if anything is totally unique to the human [mind] it would be incomprehensible. We can only interpret in terms of categories that are not unique. Distinctiveness, it would seem to me, would involve generally new configurations of comprehensible elements of some sort. One of the two examples I was going to give to breach into your field was the limerick. You just mentioned the limerick; the sonnet was my first choice. Now a sonnet, I would take it, is a distinctive form; a limerick is a distinctive form. Is it unique? Well, there is nothing else that is exactly like a

limerick or it would be called a limerick. I would suppose that if you said, well, over in Swahili culture they have a form where the poetry goes da da da da da da da A, da da da da da da da A, da da da da B, da da da da B, da da da da da da A. And I would say, well that's a limerick. They just don't call it a limerick; they call it something else. Now it seems to me, that [that] is a limerick and if uniqueness means that it is not exactly the same then that fits most of what we have to deal with in literature and everything else. But I think what is crucial to say is that distinctive items come up, distinctive configurations come up when comprehensible elements are reorganized, rearranged and so on. The limerick, after all, is rhyme. We know this is a very special rhyme scheme. We know that there is meter, we know there are lines of different numbers of feet and so on. These things are known. This particular configuration would be distinctive and whether we call it unique—meaning distinctive—then we shouldn't push the word unique to mean there is no parallel to it.

To the extent any claim of total uniqueness is made for the gospels or anything else by Schmidt or anyone else, this argues for incomprehensibility and I think your paper makes that abundantly clear. And I think what you have argued is that Schmidt's case on the face of it can't stand at all. I really wonder whether that is what is being said by many people on the contemporary scene who want to argue for the distinctiveness of the gospels. That is, that here is a new form. I can't believe that people say that Amos Wilder first proposed, for example, that the gospels are a distinctive new literary category. Surely he didn't mean an incomprehensible item. He surely didn't mean that there are no analogues whatever to this. Rather he means there is a new configuration, a new pattern that appears and this needs to be accounted for and in turn it accounts for other things. As I said, I am really persuaded, I am not sure but what you have done such an overkill job that the fallout in the contemporary scene is maybe too much.

Meagher: I have no problem with what you say about uniqueness and distinctiveness so I don't think that is the trouble. But what I perceived in the remarks of, for instance, Perrin, is a matter of two other very important things. One is that we are really not in a position to make that bold a claim about distinctiveness, about the novelty of the literary form. To do so would presume that we had control, a fairly exhaustive

control, over what had gone before. I just don't think we have that. So if there was a gospel of John the Baptist, for instance, put together by John the Baptist's disciples, quite independently of the Jesus movement, then we just have to say the gospel is not a new literary form as a Christian entity. So we are not in a position to say it is distinctive. That begs the question again. The second matter is that Perrin betrays this residual piece of Schmidt. He is much more modest and temperate than Schmidt was, but just as we can't really claim the distinctiveness of the gospel, if it had been distinct, what right have we to claim that it is somehow characteristic of Christian faith? I think that is an unargued proposition, or if argued it is usually argued from assumptions that are not very well defended. And that's where I think the Schmidtian thing characteristically breaks down. Perrin's words are the last avatar of the Schmidtian view temperately stated but bearing those crucial marks of a false assumption of what we can control in literary history and a false historical assumption about its being characteristic of some essential element in Christian faith. I don't think we can pull that off.

Hobbs: I won't argue with those points. Those aren't what I meant to bring out.

Ellis: I would like to come to the question of genre criticism, and I appreciate your comments. The question I have is where does this critical technique move from being a servant to being master. We see this in other areas, not only in genre criticism; I think we had an example of it this afternoon in rhetorical criticism where I had the impression that the letter of Galatians was being read as if this were a homework assignment for Rhetoric 101, so that the genre then became the touchstone for the interpretation of the document. And I wonder if there isn't this same problem when we do see analogies to gospel literature in other ancient literature; I think it's proper to look for them and to identify them, but I think we need to be aware (at least my impression is) that the gospel writers never feel themselves the servants of a particular form. Also I have some question as to when we begin to use this literary technique, as to the boundary where technique becomes the master for an interpretation of the text.

Meagher: I don't frankly feel very comfortable with language like servant and master. I think of genre and of other critical instrumentalities as techniques for making love to a text. And like all such techniques they have to be used with tact. Nobody gets to make the rules automatically. You have to find out what works, what kind of diplomacy is necessary in order to get the happiest response, and the one which provides the most lasting relationship between your intelligence and the text that you are working with, the one which is most finally and thoroughly understanding and honoring of what is there in that document and in the historical context from which it came.

Shuler: I would like to raise the question with respect to Schmidt that might hopefully clarify rather than muddle the water. As I recall, when I laboriously worked through Schmidt's article, the conclusion, what you seemed to focus on, namely the uniqueness—wasn't that the result of all that Schmidt was doing? It seems to me, if I recall correctly, Schmidt's thesis was a result that he inherited from Dibelius and other form critics who had already determined that there was no comparable parallel to the gospels as literature, and Schmidt went through the laborious task of verifying that conclusion; and he seemed to have gone through, at least in his own mind, the full gamut of literature available to him at that time, each time coming out with a negative factor. Consequently, what we talked about with respect to uniqueness is not the presupposition of Schmidt as intended in the paper, but rather an attempt to explain the absence of such comparable analogies.

Meagher: With respect to the procedure I think you are quite right. In fact, Schmidt was quite right to survey all the stuff that could be put out as an example of what the gospels were borrowing from in literary generic terms and coming to the conclusions that the gospels are significantly different, that there is a distinctiveness—whether or not we use the word unique, which I agree with you somewhat muddies the water—there is a distinctiveness from the other surviving literature that is very interesting as a problem. Now what Schmidt then went on to do, which I think is inadmissible and a false procedure, was to say that not only aren't there any other examples, there never were. It's not just a question of survival; he just declares that there weren't any antecedents, and then goes on to try to defend why there couldn't have

been. And [that] there couldn't have been depends on the relationship of the gospels to the tradition, in turn to the cult, in turn to the esoteric tradition of Jesus. At that point, he is maintaining that the uniqueness of the literary form is therefore bound up with the uniqueness of the Christian religion and this helps to explain why it was so important to him totally to neglect the possibility that there might have been some lost literature that would make the gospel seem a very nondistinctive literary form, and why it was important to him to disqualify all of the other, admittedly somewhat distant but still potentially relevant, literary forms by which we might still get some critical inroads.

Hobbs: Which seems to be a theological way of justifying the absence of parallels since he would probably admit to you and agree with you and all of us that to write something without pre-established conventions (or the use of conventions) is a rather extraordinary endeavor.

I wonder if I might at least probe a little in the form of taking some issue, and perhaps we could begin with the Genesis account as a kind of example. I kind of place in comparable relation the attempt with the Diatessaron. And I assume that we are at least in some degree of agreement with respect to the source criticism behind the Genesis accounts. The accumulation of various sources, is that what you have in mind with respect to Genesis in using that analogy?

Meagher: Let me briefly remark that not being very knowledgeable in the state of Old Testament scholarship and its literary background, I simply remarked that the book of Genesis builds in alternative accounts of the same event, such as the creation of humankind, dealings with Noah, promise and covenant with Abraham. And as far as I know, which is of course very limited, that may be the first time in the history of literature that a literary work was composed straightforwardly putting together two somewhat inconsistent, partially incompatible, alternative versions of the same account rather than preferring one and abandoning the other and simply not reporting it. Now, obviously from my own principles, I would not conclude that the absence of any known antecedent in that form means that Genesis invented it. But here is an example of a literary procedure that has to have properties of its own that are different from narratively systematic accounts.

Hobbs: But this account you would not want to say in its final form is void of theological implications that perhaps were not present in the singular form in which they existed beforehand.

Meagher: No, what I would claim is that whoever made the decision to keep both stories, may not have had the least clue about what the theological implications could eventually be seen to be in doing so. It may have been purely a political move. We'll keep both stories because if we drop this one it will alienate the Northern tradition, if we drop that one we will alienate the Southern tradition; to keep everybody happy we will make the diplomatic maneuver of keeping them both, because what does it matter anyhow?

Hobbs: Then would not the shift from Schmidt's position simply open the game really to what are the theological implications of the form that we now have? Or the end result that we now have? Would not at that point ascertaining of genre play a significant role with respect to what might be pointers in the direction—not definers, but pointers in the direction—of what might be drawn in terms of theological implications?

Meagher: Oh, absolutely, if we could do it. What I don't think we have any reasonable ground for hoping is that we will pin down what a gospel is meant to be read as. We are not going to find the other ones. I don't for a moment believe that that means that there never were any such; I think we simply have a gap in literary history that would be insuperable to us in research purposes, and the best we can do is make intelligent speculations from what we *do* have in evidence about what the lost immediate literary background of gospels might have been, so that we can get an edge on experimental interpretations as a result. So I fully concur with the implications of what you say. I just don't think that we can establish what genre a gospel is.

Dungan: I would like to thank you for the explication of Schmidt; I think that's well done. But this last statement I find really astonishing in view of the fact of what Talbert has been trying to say—that the parallels to the gospels are there. So has Shuler, and so have I. We have given all kinds of material to show what the parallels are and in fact what the genre is, or genres are. And I am surprised that you do this.

Meagher: No, I follow you as far as you talk about parallels. I just haven't been persuaded by a one of you in trying to say in fact what a genre is.

Dungan: Well, let's discuss some cases. What about Philo's *Life of Moses*. Wouldn't you say that that's a rather similar type of writing to both Luke and the Gospel of John.

Meagher: Rather similar, I'd go that far, yes.

Dungan: If Philo's *Life of Moses* is what Morton Smith said it is—a kind of sacred biography—then maybe that's a genre.

Meagher: Maybe I would go that far.

Dungan: Well, what more do you need? Do you need Philo to say I have read the Gospel of Luke and I agree it is a sacred biography? What would it take to convince you? Give me an idea of the evidence you need.

Meagher: The kind of evidence that makes a difference between circumstantial by default and the sort of thing that would really stand up in a court of law. Now, if you say, as far as I know, it is rumored that you were the only person in the room at the time that the deed was done, and in the absence of others since there is a certain potential plausibility that you were the one who perpetrated it, then sure I will go along with your "maybe's" and your "seems to resemble's" and so on. But if you are going to try to convict me on that, I will feel abused. However, there are other kinds of cases in which we have . . . well, let me just use the example we used about the limerick. Depending on how we want to go about defining limerick—and this is a tricky point— whether it is simply formal abstract or some culture-bound version, which in the case of the limerick in the Western world really means something about the characteristic content and handling, as well as the abstract verse form and rhyme pattern. Now, suppose we agree that we are talking just about Western limericks. Well, I can tell you how a particularly sly and sardonic limerick is meant to be understood, on the basis of its conformity to a type of which I have a lot of examples. Now, if all of a sudden, all of the limericks perish except four, and it wasn't

entirely clear from the four whether they were being ironic or simple-minded, whether they were being deliberately allusively erotic, or that was simply a coincident in language that the authors would have blushed to see, we wouldn't know. We would be able to make some hypotheses, but we would not know what the genre of the limerick really was in the way that we know it now. Obviously these things are degrees and it is a continuum of certitude about the properties of genre. But merely to seize upon the closest, most plausible, most promising examples neighboring this unusual piece of literature, I don't think is to establish that you have found the genre of gospel at all.

Dungan: Let me ask a slightly different question. When you say these are unusual—one of the statements in your paper is that the gospels ceased as a type—that implies that you know what they are. I suggest they didn't cease; they kept on being written straight on down through the Middle Ages and are still being written today. Could you say something about the *Gospel of Barnabas* that appeared in the ninth century or the *Helion* that appeared in the ninth century, some of these other gospels like the *Gospel of Peter*. Apparently you accept Schmidt's distinction between apocryphal and canonical gospels as indicating a genre distinction. I was wondering if you would comment on the *disappearance* of gospel genre.

Meagher: Here I was simply relying on other people's work. I am not sure that I ever knew—if I did I certainly thoroughly forgot—that the *Gospel of Barnabas* was a ninth-century piece. I was operating, trusting some other folks in a way which now you quite properly corrected me, and that part of the paper will be adjusted accordingly. As in the case of the *Gospel of Peter*, it was my assumption that it was close enough in time that it was within the boundaries of what I was trying to say. Now when you say that I think that I know what the gospel genre is—no, I certainly didn't mean to imply that and I will look at how I said those things to lead you to that unfortunate impression. What I was trying to say there is simply that people quit using the term "gospel" to describe a certain kind of literature. I am wrong in that and I now stand corrected. But I didn't intend anything more than that except to the extent that certain patternings that make the *Gospel of Peter* and the *Gospel of Barnabas* like Matthew, Mark, Luke, and

John in a way that say Grimm's Fairy Tales are not, or the *Epistle of Barnabas* is not, and so forth. It is a literary patterning that is patently similar. Now, I don't know the properties of this literary patterning, except to the extent that whatever kind of points the gospels themselves were making, obviously these other writings were trying to do similar sorts of things. But again, I don't mean in the least to belittle the already registered results or the further promise of the kind of research that you and Shuler and Talbert have been doing, but merely to confess that I don't think that you have unlocked the problem yet. You have given a great deal of help toward doing so, but I just sit back with the same kind of skepticism as I have held for some years about what seems to me the equally inplausible claim, now fading in popularity, that the gospels can be explained as simply an extension of the kerygma. I was never convinced by that and I am even less convinced by it now than I was then. I think it was a good idea to work with; I think yours are good ideas to work with, but I don't come to the conclusions that you come to. I don't think the case is quite satisfactorily established.

Robbins: I would like to start with the observation that Bultmann's first edition of *Die Geschichte der synoptischen Tradition* was written prior to Schmidt's essay. The second edition was written after it. And the effect of Schmidt's essay on the second edition was to cause Bultmann to make his statements more moderate to indicate, in fact, that there were some types of literature that bore analogy to the gospels more than he had thought they did. All right, now why did Schmidt take the position he did, then, if in fact he did cite enough material to convince Bultmann that he had to moderate the statements. I suggest the reason is that Schmidt was following the classical genre theory, which is prescriptive, which is normative, which says if you are going to write an epic, you must proceed in this fashion. Now, it seems to me in your paper, you are first of all attempting to follow modern genre theory. Modern genre theory is comparative and descriptive, not prescriptive and normative. However, as you work with this it seems to me when you do talk about the gospels and want to find parallels for the gospels to discuss the genre, then I think you slip into classical genre theory and you begin to talk normatively. So that you say, we have got to have something like a Gospel of Theudas or a Gospel of John the Baptist. First of all, then, I would like for you to see if you

would be willing to come clean on this in such a way that we might be able to begin to describe the gospels comparatively and descriptively so that we can talk about Luke as a particular kind of *bios*, maybe a sacred *bios*. Now, would you be willing for us to do that and what is wrong with that kind of generic description? We do not need to have a Gospel of John the Baptist to talk generically about Luke or Matthew, do we?

Meagher: Oh, no, I don't think that at all. We can still say that there they are and it's pretty clear that they resemble one another and they aren't very much like the *Iliad*. And that's a start. But it really doesn't resolve the problem. What we would have if we had a Gospel of John the Baptist is a demonstration that the Christian gospels are not the original, the distinctive, much less the unique literary accomplishment which Schmidt held them to be. That's all. It wouldn't necessarily put us a lot ahead in understanding. I think it probably would put us ahead if we had a fifth Christian gospel from around the same time that had been received by the overall church in essentially the same kind of way. And that might help out too. But basically, certainly, I agree with you that we can start out. We can do this simply by definition. So let us say that the Gospel of Luke is a sacred *bios*. How do we define a sacred *bios* and its properties? Well, we start doing so by our test case. It is something that behaves in the way that the Gospel of Luke behaves. And how does the Gospel of Luke behave? Well, then we are in a bit of a conundrum. Do we say that we can tell about the behavior of the Gospel of Luke in cases of doubt by appealing to Philo's *Life of Moses*? Well, we can try that out and see if it helps us—what kind of results it gives, whether it proves itself upon the pulse as persuasive and convincing. But it is not absolutely clear that this is a legitimate way of proceeding, because the distance between the Gospel of Luke and Philo's *Life of Moses* is just sufficient to make it possible that that's a misleading example. Now, I think probably more likely the reason that Bultmann was willing to change his mind is that once Schmidt came out with his ingenious explanation about how you can face the fact of ancient lives and legendary materials and rabbinic stories and so on, and still hold the gospel as unique, then Bultmann didn't have to feel so strongly about denying that the gospels had resemblance to other literature at all. He could still have his theological cake and make the

scholarly comparisons that Schmidt had faced up to. He could still say, yes, these are relevant—as Schmidt did—insofar as they suggest to us a typical kind of literary behavior in certain kinds of common situations, but all the same, the gospels are not copying them—there's no self-conscious literary awareness of that kind of happening. It's just that these are parallel happenings. Just as in modern theory one is ready to suppose that parallel sociological conditions will lead to similar kinds of developments without any suggestions that the one is imitating the other, or deriving it self-consciously from the other's having taken place.

Robbins: Now, just having made the statement about the sociological context, I can't correlate that with the previous statement about the distance of those documents from Luke. It brings me to the question of what is the purpose of genre analysis. I had thought we had given up the idea that genre analysis was to lead us to a clear definite classification which would be immovable but rather was to help us clarify dimensions of that document in relation to other documents. Now, I don't quite understand why if we could position Luke between Philo's *Life of Moses*, Plutarch's *Lives*, Philostratus's *Life of Apollonius*, Xenophon's *Memorabilia*, that we might not blend Deuteronomic history and the Book of Daniel, why we might not be able to describe the dimensions of the Gospel of Luke in such a way that the procedure would be satisfactory.

Meagher: Well, I think I follow that and I don't find anything, frankly, to quarrel about in it. Let me put the problem a slightly different way, now that I think I understand you better. Let me revert once more to the example of the popular letter. If we are dealing with a highly structured form like a sestina, for instance, we know something about the way in which meaning and value are managed and ordered within the sestina because of the intensity of the strict rules of that game. And therefore we know some things—we know how to deal with it interpretatively in ways that we wouldn't necessarily for, say, a casually written free-verse poem by someone who wasn't particularly adept at literary control. In the case of the personal letter, if we had, say, only four twentieth-century examples surviving, one of which starts "Dear Shirley," one "Dear Vincent," one "Dear Vernon," and one "Dear

David," all of which end "Sincerely," we would know we were on to something. And if they all started out by talking about the weather and then proceeded to say some things about family matters, we would be very sure we were on to something. And if we picked up some nineteenth-century examples that were generally similar in form, it would give us some potentially exciting possibilities of unlocking what the author of those four twentieth-century letters—or the authors— thought was going to be in the minds of the readers, and intended them to be read as. But it wouldn't be necessarily a safe calculation because it may turn out that the nineteenth-century examples we have are decorous love letters growing out of an unfortunate passion, but disciplined by the decorum that prevailed in Victorian times and might be extremely misleading as a paradigm of what these other letters were attempting to do. That we can say they are all letters, I think, is fine. I have no problem about saying that the gospels are *bios*; I think that is the most plausible category of the ones that are easy to have. But what that doesn't tell me is what we then learn from making the application. Now I want to make one correction, about where I agree with you. I don't think that the first instance in generic description here is for the purpose immediately of making application to other literary instances. The first thing, for the generic description of the Gospel of Luke, is to try to get a clearer coherent idea of how the Gospel of Luke itself behaves as we have it. And if it can be of some help to appeal to other analogies—literary instances—all the better. But the final test of the pudding is whether this really illuminates the Gospel of Luke's behavior in such a way that we can say, Aha, now I see why he made that move. Aha, now I feel the weight of this term. Now I get what he must have presumed his audience would have expected from his having started out this way and using this kind of general procedure. That is the point that I don't think we have reached.

Talbert: I would like to take chair's perogative here before the other two speak. If we work, John, with the analogy of the letter "Dear John," "Sincerely, Charles," there we have an external form. Well, if we look in the ancient world and we find a document that begins with a man's origins and ends with his death, and in between are his random deeds and sayings, there we have a form. But you say for a nineteenth-century love letter and a twentieth-century personal letter, it would be

misleading to interpret one by the other because they had different social functions. But if we found a document or documents that began with origins and ended with death and had anecdotes and sayings in between, that had similar social functions, then it seems to me we are overcoming the objections to the *bios* literature. But at the end you distinguished between two questions. Whether or not we can identify the gospels with the *bios* literature. I heard you treading water or even backing up at that point and retrieving to the second level of what difference would it make after all. That, I think, is the question that should be debated very seriously. But it seems to me that those are two different questions whether we can identify the gospels in terms of outer form, social function, and basic attitude, with the *bios* literature and then, secondly, if we can do that—which I think we can—then what difference it makes, if any, in the interpretative task?

Meagher: I think it's a potentially fruitful procedure to say, yes, there is nothing that is so obviously like a gospel that there can be no question about the patternization. And therefore start with the kind of prudently measured, initial assumption, working hypothesis that it will be fruitful to think of gospel as a special form of *bios*. And then see what we can then say about in what sense is gospel a highly distinctive form of *bios*, such that we can't generalize from *bios* as such to gospel as a distinctive particular version of it. And in response to the answer of that question will be determined how much difference it is going to make in part. And here again, I can simply reiterate that my perception—which I don't expect everybody else to share—is that it has not yet been persuasively established that the degree of distinctiveness by which gospel is a peculiar species of the genus *bios*. It is sufficiently little to allow us simply to forget about its being a distinctive version of, and say gospels are examples of, *bios* rather than a distinctive special category within. Now, with respect to your other problem, again, I come back to the recurrent point. I think you are absolutely right. When you have something that has formal characteristics, text A to text B, and we find that text A and text B have similar social functions, then we are on a very important trail, and we might snip off something really good. What mystifies me is that it seems to me that almost everybody but me takes for granted that we know much more about the social function of the gospels than I understand there

to be evidence to claim. I just don't see that we can really pin that down. If we could, then we would be on a much better track, I think, than we are. But it's not at all clear to me that we have that under control. We know something about the social functions that the gospels came to have at later stages, but whether this resembles the social functions they had at their original composition is entirely a different matter. We know, indeed, the kind of function that the gospels have for certain contemporary communities, but that doesn't mean that from that we can calculate the social functions of the gospels in the historical way that has been presupposed by this whole discussion. I don't think we have that under control. And until we do I don't see that an argument can be made from parallel social functions.

Hedrick: I actually have two questions, but I am going to ask one of them, a very general question; maybe I can come back later. I don't want to change the course of the discussion. I am curious to know— rephrasing the question in a different way than I had planned on asking it—if you accepted the description of gospel that Professor Talbert set out—that sort of a general thrusting home of the question—how do you conceive of the genre gospel formal characteristics when you read Matthew, Mark, Luke, and John? When I read those documents I discover a multiplicity of literary forms. To be sure, there are many similarities, some of them superficial, some of them may be innate to the genre, if I can use that term because we really haven't defined it, but what I am really interested in at this point is picking your brain about the formal characteristics of those four documents we call gospel.

Meagher: This obviously is a question to which I can't possibly give an adequate answer. But I will try within the sensible time limits which I will check myself on. I agree with you that there are multiple literary forms within the gospel. I think that's fine—now a virtually indisputable result of form critical achievement. . . .

Hedrick: If I can just interject, I meant the overall thing too, not only what was inside of it, but in the total form.

Meagher: As for the gospel as a whole, it also seems to me partly from the failure of the unitary proposals of the contrary, and partly from

what seems to me the phenomenology of the literary behavior of the gospels—it seems to me that we have to say that there are multiple centers of interest governing the literary form gospel itself. It is not prosecuting any single prepossession; it's not trying to do one single-minded thing all the way through. But the attention drifts here and there. There are different things that work. I am not talking simply about the possibility of there being multiple kerygmata underlying the gospels, but here again, I am very sympathetic to the enterprise previously referred to in the days in which—as far as I can tell—everybody I read insisted that there is no biographical interest in the gospels. I couldn't see what gave them the right to say that, because it seems to me quite clear that there is a biographical interest in the gospels, and I so timidly went on public record. Okay, I think that's going on. I think there are lots of things going on that form the gospel. But it seems to me the gospels are very uneven documents.

That the literary form and texture are highly uneven, and I'm really suspicious about whether we can develop a descriptive view of the gospel that will make fully satisfying and adequate sense to us about, for instance, why after a series of these choppy little stories through most of the body of the gospels they all carry on with a wanderingly detailed and sometimes desultory, sustained narrative account of the passion and death of Jesus. That's a behavior very different from what's gone on before and I haven't yet seen a proposal that makes me say, Aha, that's why it does that, that's why it's doing it. I don't see that the proposal, for instance, that this is because the kerygma made the death of Jesus an important point, is the least bit persuasive. If the acid test for just rule of thumb trial seems to me to be, if this is what you are trying to accomplish in writing the gospel, would you do it this way? Well, I sure wouldn't write the passion accounts in that way if what I was trying to do is to insist on the centrality of the death and resurrection of Jesus as the turning point in salvation history. I wouldn't do it. And if somebody submitted to me a gospel written as they are, saying that that was what he was trying to do, I would strongly suggest that we go back and re-edit the thing, because it's not going to make its point very effectively, if that's what it is attempting to accomplish. So at the moment I just don't know a thoroughly persuasive account that makes sense of, that accounts for the actual behavior that we see in the movement from verse to verse, from episode to episode, from one type

of literary texture to another, and the overall shape and sweep which is so curiously shared by four of them each with its distinctions from the other. Enough to make each in its own way distinctive and if you like, unique. But sufficiently resemblant to the others as to make it obvious that we have got to solve the problem in looking at them together if we are going to do so responsibly at all. It seems to me likely that we will also have to bring in *bios* literature, but that's not as obvious to me as that we will never really grasp the phenomenological behavior of Luke without facing up to what happens in Matthew, and so forth.

Hedrick: Just to pursue it a little further, at the risk of incurring everybody's wrath—when I look at the gospels, Mark begins abruptly, and I'm not going to recount the whole thing, but his account is radically different from Matthew, though they do have at least a couple of things in common and that is the passion narrative, and they both begin the ministry of Jesus with John the Baptist. And then beyond that point, they use the same materials, but the overall structure is radically different.

Meagher: Well, when you say overall structure, I can see how I could validate what you just said. But you surely can also see how it is easy to validate my perception that the overall structure looked at in other of the structural principles is very much the same. Namely, are you dealing with the report in a relatively unselfconscious literary narration with quotations and so forth of the workings leading up to a more detailed account, beginning with John the Baptist, leading up to a more detailed account than has previously been gathered of the final episodes, and then a somewhat surprisingly truncated account of the resurrection and the experiences deriving therefrom? The overall structure in that sense is very much the same. Now these may not be the elements of structure that seem to you most promising to pursue, and I certainly grant you that, though I think unless one contends with these resemblances in overall structure, one is doing a very incomplete job of dealing with either one of those gospels. I would certainly accept the alternative proposal that another set of patternings, disclosures that are very different in overall structure, are certainly at least possible.

Farmer: John, I would like to create a new genre for discussion by saying that I have no desire to match wits with you. I have reason to

doubt that I could if I would. I want to try to bring the seminar this morning into relationship with the seminar this evening. I know you weren't here this morning but I know that you know that it was on the topic of the synoptic problem. Now, in your book on Mark, you proceed without depending methodologically upon the reigning research paradigm in gospel studies. And you defend that procedure on the grounds that the present stage of the discussion of the source problem is such that would justify you in not disciplining yourself at that point and assuming at every point the priority of Mark or the existence of Q. I am not acquainted with the work of the participants around the table on the topic of genre. I am acquainted with Professor Talbert's work and Professor Shuler's work. And it seems to me that in comparison to where we were fifteen years ago, when it was widely held that Karl Ludwig Schmidt was correct—that the gospels are sui generis and that they have no meaningful relationship to contemporary literary form, certainly not the *bios* literature—it seems to me we are making some progress. And I am conscious of the fact that Professor Talbert, in regard to this matter of the source paradigm, has stated that anyone wanting to study the Gospel of Luke would be making as much sense if he assumed the priority of Mark and the existence of Q in trying to understand Luke as someone would be making sense if he tried to understand Paul by assuming the authenticity of Ephesians or perhaps Ephesians and Colossians. Now I am also aware of the fact that Professor Shuler has done his work with the consciousness of the problematic nature of the status of the two-document hypothesis. And I have come to the conclusion that not only Karl Ludwig Schmidt but Dibelius, were in part dependent upon the notion of Markan priority for their conviction that the literary form of the gospel and the literary forms within the gospels are sui generis. I am reminded of the argument of Dibelius—for example, with regard to the *chreia* form of the Markan paradigms which deviate from the *chreia* form in ways that the parallels in Matthew and Luke do not—I am reminded of the fact that he argued as follows: the Markan paradigms are unique because Christian religion is unique. And that what you have in Matthew and Luke is the tendency of these authors to conform the unique paradigm in Mark to the more literary form of the *chreia*. Now, a similar argument could be made on the Markan hypothesis. One could say that the Gospel of Mark is unique and sui generis because the differences between Mark and other *bios* literature are very noticeable. One

could argue that Matthew and Luke—that are not so different from *bios* literature as is Mark—represent the tendency of those authors to conform the unique literary form of Mark to the more conventional literary form of *bios* literature. Now, where I would like to invite you to share with us whatever your reflections might be, in a very free way, is what you think the implication for this discussion we are having tonight would be if in fact Mark were not the first in the genre that we think of as Matthew, Mark, and Luke, if any?

Meagher: I don't see frankly, Bill, that at the moment it would make any significant difference. I think the reason that Schmidt preferred— casually supposed—that Mark was first is that, in the first place, as you know, it is an old German scholarly tradition to make that assumption. It goes back at least into the eighteenth century. Wrede made a similar point about Mark being the first establishing a new kind of literature and so forth. And from Schmidt's point of view as he saw the disappearance of gospel form being part of a trajectory in which it added more and more decoration from an imitation of world cultural frames, it drifted away, and of course, from that kind of assumption you take it back to the gospel that seems simplest, farthest away from the literary elegance of the Hellenistic world, and so it's comfortable to say, Mark. I mean it fits his assumptions about why gospel ceased to be written eventually, though I now understand he exaggerated that even more than I knew an hour ago. But if Schmidt had been persuaded by undeniable external evidence that the Gospel of Matthew, say . . . or let me use my more favorite example because it's one to which nobody will assent. Suppose the Gospel of Luke, he concluded, had clearly been the first of the gospels. But that would have meant that he would change his theory somewhat about the progressive drift of the gospels away into the Hellenistic world and say, well, when we started out some people were tampering with Hellenistic stuff and after a while some of them got rid of that and tried to get down to basics and then they tampered with Hellenistic stuff again and finally it drifted off. I don't think it would have shaken his hypothesis at all. Because his hypothesis has to do really with gospel form itself. And Schmidt maintained that though there is a kind of small-scale continental drift visible within the four canonical gospels, from one another and from the center, still they all remained within the pale and therefore they are all still, for

him, authentic early Christian, faith-bound variants under one theme. So in what order they came wouldn't really be especially important to him. From his point of view the theological implications would be the same whether you juggle up the order or not. These are all variants and are essential, cult-bound, esoteric tradition phenomenon in which the evangelists may have strung things together but were here and there invaded at random by cultural by-products which they carelessly or deliberately absorbed to some extent.

Farmer: I would like to come back to this in just a moment, but now bring up another point. I think that the Gospels, Matthew, Mark, Luke, and John, are united in relationship to other gospels and perhaps in relationship to other *bios* literature by their being concerned with the flesh-and-blood martyrdom of the Son of God. Now assume for a moment that does characterize them in a way that would unify them from the point of view of the content; I think that one could say that, yes, that's unique. But I thought that genre had to do with form. Now, if you take the form of Matthew and Luke, and you take all of the topics that are dealt with, those topics are for the most part covered as topics that you are to deal with the encomia. So I am impressed with what Shuler has done at this point, and it would seem to me that if Matthew and Luke are the first members of this, in this sequence, that when it comes to Mark and John, there is where, formally speaking, you depart more radically from the rules of the encomia. Now, let me return now to my question. It seems to me then, that it does make a difference how you perceive the sequence of the gospels, if you are thinking about the form. Granting Karl Ludwig Schmidt's point that the content is unique, it seems to me the form is not so unique. I would like for you now to go back to the point you made about Karl Ludwig Schmidt and the tendency toward gnosticism or gnostic tendency, and ask you whether there isn't something at stake here, or did you imply that if you abandon Karl Ludwig Schmidt's notion somewhere that you are moving in an antignostic way? Would you amplify what you might have in mind there?

Meagher: Now, as briefly as I can, while remaining intelligible to your first point. Had Shuler established that the gospels are encomia and that's that, then there might be some things that would follow, which

from my present critical perspective do not follow. The best I can say is the gospels seemed—or the evangelists seemed, whether consciously or not—to have picked up certain habits and values which are characteristic of encomia. And that is an interesting clue about how we might profitably understand what the authors thought they were doing or how their audiences were responding to them and things of that sort. All right, now let's suppose that he had established that they were encomia, just plain and simple, that the distance wasn't what I now perceive it to be. Then what we could say about Mark and John is that their authors decided to jettison the encomium dimension of the previous undertakings. How would we understand the theological significance of their having done so? I don't think that would be an easy task at all. Does this mean that they decided that was a little bit too fancy part of it? Was it an act of simplifying humility? Was it an attempt to be alienated from the Greek cultural world? Was it an attempt to stress certain other features of Jesus that might be misleadingly thought of in encomium terms? We don't know. We wouldn't in that instance know what the theological value of the departure was. We wouldn't know how the communities were thinking, or how the evangelists were thinking. We would see a phenomenon that had interesting clues, and we could test these out and say, all right then, what do we get if we try reading it under the assumption that since it is one of the possible meanings of what has happened, this is in fact what happened. They were trying to simplify and abstract from elegant touches, back to sackcloth and ashes kind of thing. Well, then, we could think about that, we could say then it would follow that Mark was thinking in this kind of way. It would then follow more clearly that Luke and Matthew were thinking in a different way significantly, but I don't think that we could calculate theological implications with any great satisfactory results.

As for the question of gnosticism. What I meant by that point was essentially this: that when a theological position maintains that there is an esoteric tradition—which you just have to buy into or you miss out on what is important, especially if it's maintained that this is a radical condition, buying into it is a radical condition of salvation—then, I think the position is fairly characterized as gnostic. I don't mean to suggest by that, that it brings in the whole Valentinian package or any of the other specific versions of it. But just as a theological category,

gnosticism seems to be most helpfully used as a theological category as distinguished from an historical one to mean a theological position that supposes that there is an indispensable revelation which one simply must accept or be lost, and whose acceptance is given mysteriously through no ordinary or known human modes of apprehension and judgment. I think that Schmidt does this in the way that he deals with the question of the literary uniqueness of the gospels and in the way in which he ties a special theological significance to that uniqueness of origin and character. I wanted to point out one of the theological implications of shifting from Schmidt, and that is opening theology more than a binding to Schmidt would permit it to be opened, to a de-gnosticizing process in which theology becomes free to say, well, maybe they don't have the last word after all.

Petersen: I agreed ten years ago with where you are today. I hope you are further ten years from now than I am, ten years after that one. But I think we agree that the connection between medium and message is basic to your point: it is critical that the ultimately theological problem is to what extent does the medium help us to interpret, to understand, the message. I think that was the hope, not only of the task group on gospels, 1970, but also of the seminar on Paul and Pauline letters, where the same question of genre emerged and also the seminar on parables which began around the same time. There is a hope in all three cases that if we could learn more about the medium we would have a better chance of getting at the message. I think in one sense it is fair to say that we failed. Although, in the process, I think we haven't lost our hopefulness. And I speak because I have been in a couple of these seminars. For example, if we can learn to distinguish between parable and allegory as medium, we have gained something. If we can learn, let's say, that parables are not allegories, we have got a handle on how to deal with certain messages that are parables and not allegories. We aren't going to confuse E. E. Cummings's poem with the Greater Dallas-Fort Worth telephone directory. Or, the difference between Deissmann's notion of the Pauline letters as private letters and Bjerkelund who sees it more in terms of Hellenistic world correspondence is of great hermeneutical significance. I think there was this hope also for the gospels, and initially it was not the *bios* but the aretalogy, which I hope is not dead—which is one of the reasons I hope you don't find my

paper, because I was thinking a retalogy in those days. I don't anymore. But I do believe that the relationship between medium and message is incredibly important, and it has been so in a confusing way in the history of the tradition because the idea "gospel" has been attached to both the notions of the *medium*—the form, the cultural medium, the wave—and the *message*. When we have been talking about Schmidt who emphasized the form, the medium, in connection with the notion of gospel, we haven't mentioned the fact that Bultmann denied it. The gospel is a dogmatic category, not a literary category. He insisted on that. Dibelius in an ambiguous sort of way comes close to the same thing. I think that is the big difference. And if you follow up the Schmidtian interpretation of the significance of form criticism in the early thirties, he prepared the groundwork for the whole theological emphasis of redaction criticism by saying that by concentrating on the message—the gospels as message, or gospel as message—our task is to elaborate the kerygmata of the individual gospels. No question of the medium the same gospels have in the sense of articles coming out. Form was form, which is essentially what the form critics were saying. If we recognize that the idea of gospel as message is one thing and gospel as form is another, you can justify the proliferation of gospel according to titles that appear at the end of the second century in terms of message, not in terms of form. One of the things that I was asked to do in my paper, was to address the question of the implications of all these gnostic gospels with the question of gospel as genre. And the most obvious thing of all was that the only thing they had in common was "gospel" according to titles.

What I am saying is that if you followed the gospel as message, then you can accept the line of the gospel according to titles, all of which are formally irrelevant. But that returns us to the question: then what, if any, role does the medium or do the media of our gospel texts, canonical or uncanonical—what do the media do to help us understand the individual texts? And here I think we come to another problem, because if we take away the gospel titles—as I think we should have done long ago, because they are all irrelevant to the original compositions—then you come down to the question of more philological relationships between the texts that happen to have gospel titles and those other texts that look like them but don't. When you come to the canonical texts called gospels, we have a very peculiar

problem. We come to your question about sources. The fact that there exists some kind of source relationships between the four canonical gospels muddies the whole water about medium. Because in part, at least, in principle, what those four texts have in common may be the result not of medium but of source relationships. And, in fact, the differences may be due not so much to individual compositional proclivities or different sources as to different media. . . .

Features of Matthew do not look to me like encomium or biography, and certainly not aretalogy. And it is the common biographical features that the four gospels share, you see, that makes Matthew look like that. But where Matthew differs—again regardless of who uses whom—from the biographical common denominator, he starts doing things that look like manuals of discipline. Like the *Manual of Discipline* from Qumran, like 1 Corinthians, which I think is a Christian proto-manual of discipline and like some of the monastic orders.

Farmer: Could we agree that they are sub-genres?

Petersen: But what is that going to prove, though, Bill?

Farmer: Well, I agree with what you are saying about Matthew to the point that there are these collections of sayings that remind you of the *Manual of Discipline*, but it seems to me that the Gospel of Matthew, taken as a whole, belongs, along with Luke and Mark and John, within Christian literature as witnessing to the flesh-and-blood (this rules out the Gospel of Peter, you see) martyrdom of the Son of God.

Petersen: That's a theological abstraction. That's not a formal phenomenon.

Farmer: Well, I would say that that describes what Matthew is, if you are interested in seeing what unites it to Luke and what unites it to John, and what unites it to Mark. But I don't think that's going to solve the problem of genre. I think genre, once again, has to do with form. I was being taken through the library by our librarian with a class of students the other day, and we came to two pages of the Gutenberg Bible and he pointed out that the [printed text] closely resembles what Bibles copied by hand looked like at that time. In other words, the

printers made a conscious effort to create a type that was similar to what people were used to. All right, this, I think, is as close to a law of literature that we have: that, in the beginning, you have to communicate, and therefore you—if you are creating a new genre—have to take up a known pattern. If one of the gospels, if one of these four comes first, one would expect that that one would be more similar to *bios* literature, or whatever is being read by the people the author is trying to communicate with, and subsequently once a genre is created, once this has been accepted, it can be modified. So you can see the development of the genre in terms of its similarity in form to the existing literary forms of developing in a unique way, so that what you end up with are forms, are gospels which not only on the basis of content, but on the basis of form, are rather unique.

Barr: Well, I think we have come here to at least one of the hearts of the problem, that comes back to Vernon's point about whether genre is a descriptive or normative category. It seems to me that perhaps you played a trick on us here tonight. That is, you talk about abandoning Schmidt, but yet in much of your defense you have come back to the point that the gospels are, in fact, unique. We don't have anything else like them. And it seems to me that that evades the central issue that we are talking about. In your paper you make a point that it seems to me is crucial—and it comes to Norman's point also—that the payoff of genre insight has to do with something about the reader's expectation when he reads the piece of literature. Now you also mentioned Justin's remark about the gospels as memoirs and discount it because it won't stand up to modern critical study. And yet that is the closest we have come to an ancient person, familiar with ancient literature, much more than we are, who looked at the gospels and said, in fact, they are like memoirs. Now, that is his expectation that, from reading them, perhaps not the original one, but one much closer than ours, it had something to do with his memoirs. Which leads me to the point, we do have quite a body of ancient literature. We may take that body to be at least in some ways representative of the major kinds of literature people were reading in the ancient world. So we ought to be able to look around at that literature, whatever we have left of it and say, by looking at that we ought to be able to get some notion of what readers expected when they read gospel literature. When you say *Manual of*

Discipline, I find that incredible, because I can't think of anybody reading Matthew and saying, yes, I read something like that before, the *Manual of Discipline*. It just doesn't seem to me the kind of thing a reader would expect or you would expect a reader to say who's reading both of those kinds of documents. Now, admittedly there are points of *Manual of Discipline* in Matthew, but I think that same paper we have lost, said something about a lion who swallows a man isn't necessarily a man because of it.

Petersen: If it were biography you would also be surprised that having the Jesus of Matthew talking to teachers who are going to have to teach this stuff. If you take a biographical model for Matthew, *bios*, it is a little bit surprising to see Jesus making these particular points about having to be careful about what you teach, not only in what you do, and so on. There are all sorts of behavioral distinctions that are being made consistently—the commandments of the gospel.

Meagher: I want to speak to this. This is a very good illustration of the point that I was trying to make earlier, namely, that in order to say that the *Manual of Discipline* is a relevant paradigm for figuring out something that is going on in the Gospel of Matthew, you don't have to say that somebody picking up the Gospel of Matthew would say, oh, not another Manual of Discipline! You don't even have to say that the author of Matthew was explicitly conscious of doing anything like what a *Manual of Discipline* is doing. All you have to do is to say that some of the reflexes that went into the writing of Matthew, picked up from some of the things that go into the writing of manuals of discipline, and that therefore it is going to be worth some illumination to think about Matthew with the *Manual of Discipline* ringing around in the back of your head.

Two other points in response with what you said. Now, I tried as well as I could to forestall a big hangup on the question of uniqueness. As I mentioned at the beginning of my paper, though not in my precis, uniqueness is far overrated, theologically. And I think that that is a substantial problem that points to something that is pathological in Christian theology. I am serious about that, also a little playful, but serious. Now, uniqueness—literarily I tried in my paper, where I did not try to do it in the precis, to deal with that by saying it is unique and

the gospels are unique. The Gospel of Matthew is itself unique in its difference from Mark, Luke, and John. The gospel form is unique by comparison with other types of *bios* literature. The *bios* family is unique by comparison with epistles. You say unique, or distinctive, or whatever, and then try to do something with it that makes it a useful thing to say. What really counts is what we can find out about the nonuniqueness that helps us learn how to read these things that are unique, or what we can find about the intrinsic characteristics of those unique things that helps us to see what they are trying to pull off, what their internal rhythms are, what their internal structures are.

Now, sure, maybe Justin was right. It might be profitable to look at the gospels as some sort of memoir, but on the other hand, do we really think that Josephus was right in saying that the Pharisees, Sadducees, and Essenes are schools of philosophy? You have got to make certain kinds of accomodations. The first accomodation to recognize is that of Josephus trying to speak a language that the Greeks would understand, and it seems to me that it is highly plausible that Justin can't be credited with anything more than that kind of diplomacy—locating these things within the established literary landscape of the Hellenistic world. If he said the gospels were drawn from apostolic witness, who would know what he was talking about? If he said memoirs, then at least you get the general drift. Now, I don't mean by saying that to say that we should therefore pay no attention to what happens in the gospels, if we read them as if they were written to be and likely to be received as the memoirs of the apostles. Let's try that on. But I strongly suspect that if we do it more seriously than is being done these days, what we will discover is that it is not a very rewarding exercise. They don't really behave like memoirs. We don't learn much about the gospels from doing it that way.

Talbert: As chairman, I have the last word. We want to thank Professor John Meagher for his paper and each member of this group for a genial discussion—one that did not bog down, at least from the chairman's point of view, and a very happy one.

SEMINAR ON
PAULINE CHRONOLOGY

INTRODUCTION

John C. Hurd, Moderator

I<small>T MAY SEEM PARADOXICAL</small> that a colloquy concerned with "fresh approaches" should include a segment called "Chapters in a Life of Paul—After Thirty Years." John Knox's book appeared in 1950. There—as the reader will hear again!—Knox discussed the relative value of Acts and the Pauline letters as sources for our knowledge of Paul. Without using the actual terms he made the distinction between primary and secondary historical evidence which will be central to the discussion below. He affirmed the "obviously and incomparably" greater trustworthiness of the letters. On this point he observed mildly, "The truth in principle of this . . . statement no serious student of Paul's life is likely to deny, but its meaning in practice is not so widely or so clearly seen" (p. 31). Knox's words have turned out to be more prophetic than he intended. It is true that the chronology Knox proposed on the basis of this distinction has become widely known. Indeed it has become the practice among those who write on introductory matters to refer to it. But they refer to it only as a more or less eccentric alternative to the real options. The basic reason that they do not consider it more seriously is method. Most of these scholars indeed raise the problem of method themselves and include a sentence or two in which they affirm the superior value of the letters. But they then proceed to use material from Acts wherever it is not contradicted by the letters. Relatively few

New Testament scholars have tried to enter by the door which Knox opened. Thus, for most, Knox still represents a fresh approach and an untried possibility.

In order to understand fully the papers in this section and the seminar transcript concerning this debate the reader may need to refer to the relevant books by our three writers. In reviewing the entire discussion we will consider first the relationship of each author to the other two. Luedemann's work is the simplest to present. His paper follows closely the far more detailed argument of his book, and the correspondences are easy to locate. His relation to Jewett is consistently set out in his book, in his paper, and in the supplementary asides that punctuated the oral presentation of his paper. His relationship to John Knox is also clearly stated, and his development of Knox's position is, it seems to me, entirely in line with Knox's method and principles. This accounts for Knox's sympathy with and enthusiasm for Luedemann's work in spite of some differences over particular conclusions.

On the other hand, for two reasons in particular the reader may have difficulty in understanding Jewett's work. In the first place, the statements about his indebtedness to Knox are confusing. At first reading there seems to be a startling inconsistency in his treatment of this matter. At times—especially in his paper—he expresses warm appreciation of Knox; at times—especially in his book—he is sharply critical. The issue can be clarified somewhat by comparing his paper with Luedemann's. There is a basic difference in terminology which may mislead the reader. Luedemann and Jewett both say that they follow Knox, but they mean different things by this statement. When Luedemann speaks of following Knox, he means that he follows Knox's method. When Jewett says that he follows Knox, he seems to mean little more than that he has adopted a three-visit framework for Paul's ministry—in spite of some statements which give the impression of a closer relationship. That Jewett can associate himself with Knox is understandable from this point of view. In comparison to the multitude of those who write on Pauline chronology and adopt the five-visit pattern to be found in Acts Jewett is clearly on Knox's side. That Jewett can speak of Knox as having predecessors is also understandable: any scholar who at a date earlier than Knox proposed a three-visit pattern—for whatever reason—is a predecessor. But for Knox

"method is everything." To follow him must mean to follow his method. For him the three-visit framework was only a result of the application of his method. It was not the method itself. Jewett's lack of clarity in this regard helps to explain the puzzlement expressed by Knox at Jewett's professions of kinship.

The second matter is to some extent related to the first. Jewett seems unclear about historical method and his statements on this subject appear inconsistent. At some points he exalts the letters and professes himself opposed to accepting any material from Acts without confirmation. This principle, if consistently applied, would take him down the path traveled by Knox and Luedemann. But at other points he speaks of creating a "neutral data-base" containing all relevant information—a procedure which, if carried out consistently, would submerge any qualitative superiority of the letters. Thus Jewett "limps between two opinions": he follows the letters for the reasons proposed by Knox, but only as far as the three-visit framework. From this point on his method is actually the traditional one—in spite of the somewhat trendy way in which he describes it and again in spite of some protestations to the contrary. In practice he takes chronological information from wherever he can find it. He uses Acts as a major source and is willing to confirm items in it by other material from the same source. He is even willing, as Luedemann points out, to allow the cumulative weight of details from Acts to outweigh data from the letters. Clearly his method is not Knox's.

A factor contributing to Jewett's inconsistencies is the apparent haste with which he has worked on these issues. In 1966 not long after his dissertation had been completed, he was attempting to find a channel for its publication. He kindly sent me some of the introductory chapters—the ones concerning Pauline chronology. I read them with great interest, particularly the section concerning John Knox. Then, as he had requested and as I indicated in a footnote to his present paper, I wrote out my comments and sent them to him. Among other matters were several which related to Knox—two in particular. I pointed out (a) that he had overlooked Knox's discussion of the Gallio date and thus should not accuse him of ignoring it, and (b) that he was mistaken about Knox's dating of Galatians. As I said,

> You appear to be saying that if the fourteen-year intervals mentioned in Galatians and in 2 Corinthians are identified with each other, then

the two letters would be contemporaneous. This conclusion results . . .
from an "error in logic." It is, of course, 2 Corinthians and the
Apostolic Council (Gal. 2:1) which would be roughly contemporaneous. Galatians could have been written at any point after the Council.
Knox himself thinks that Galatians may have been Paul's last letter.

I was therefore surprised to find the same two mistakes still unchanged
when Jewett's book appeared in 1979 (pp. 79-80), particularly since a
third point that I raised in my letter had been rectified. It is disconcert-
ing, to say the least, that the two points at issue are described in the
book as "glaring mistakes" on the part of Knox. At my urging Jewett
has attempted to rectify this oversight by revising his paper, but in my
opinion he has been only partially successful. The reader is left with the
impression that it was Knox's lack of clarity which was responsible for
Jewett's misunderstanding. In actuality, when Jewett says, "inexactitudes like this are regrettable," he is referring quite correctly to his own
errors. But this statement, coming as it does after his criticism of
Knox's date for Paul's final visit to Corinth, may sound as though it
were directed at Knox. The above explanation should clarify the
situation. Jewett's retraction on these points removes his two sharpest
criticisms of Knox and is only just.

Something further needs to be said about Jewett's proposal of the
"experimental model" as useful in historical investigation. This way of
speaking, which he derives from the social and physical sciences, seems
of mixed value. His "neutral data-base" is intended to discourage
prejudgments about the way in which separate items of information
may become useful in the final scheme. This aspect seems to me to be
useful but also a matter of common sense. It is a somewhat self-
conscious way of speaking of a procedure that historians regularly use
when analyzing a complex problem: to keep open as many options as
possible before formulating the final hypothesis. The same "data-base"
procedure, however, also tends to conceal from the researcher the
origin of the data and its relative value.

It has, however, a much more mischievous result. In the case of our
problem we have two classes of data that are qualitatively different.
What this means in practice is that the two should not be considered
simultaneously, but one after the other. When as full an account of
Paul's life as possible has been reconstructed from the letters, then Acts
can be examined. To lump all the data into one mass obliterates this

distinction and leads to false results. Thus two "data-bases" are required.

And even two are not enough. Not all the material from either source is of the same degree of reliability or definiteness. Incontroverti- ble evidence from the letters should go into one collection, less definite indications into another, and so on through both sources. These nested "data-bases" then need treatment in the order of their historical weightiness.

From my own point of view as a former physical scientist there is a further objection. The selection from a single "data-base" of those items that mutually confirm each other seems a throwback to the dawn of science when experimenters regularly selected those of their experi- mental readings that most nearly fit the theory that they were propos- ing. Historians of science have shown that often the data finally recorded by those early scientists shows greater reliability than their instruments actually allowed. Accepting what fits and discarding what does not is no longer considered good scientific method. A better procedure is to come to a better understanding of the data.

We have examined at greater or lesser length the relationships that our three authors have to each other. It remains to comment briefly on the discussion that followed the summary presentation of the papers. The questions by Wilson and Farmer serve admirably to point up the differences between Jewett and Luedemann. My own position is also clear to the reader by now: I think that Jewett, by proposing as a hypothesis the three-visit pattern for Paul's career, made a hopeful beginning. But his rapid abandonment of the priority of the letters shows that he has not really understood the nature of the sources. Luedemann, on the other hand, sees the problem of method clearly, and I welcome his exploration of the implications of Knox's work. Later in the discussion, however, the possibility that Paul's theology developed during the period of the letters was raised. On this subject the seminar expressed considerable opposition. Luedemann was will- ing to go the farthest with his observations about the death of Chris- tians before the parousia. But he has reserved further investigation of the subject to his third volume which will follow those on chronology and on Paul's opponents. My own opinion is that he has moved too quickly from the letters to a consideration of Acts and to assigning absolute dates within the relative chronology derived from the letters.

Baird's question about the point at which Acts comes into the picture, had it been addressed, would have put this issue on the table. I think that the bare letters chronology needs to be fleshed out with further information about Paul's exterior life—for example, problems which confronted him in his ministry—and with analysis of his inner life, his thought. It is not just his treatment of deaths before the parousia that changed. Of course, there comes a point in this reconstruction where the basic picture becomes clear and where the remaining items of evidence are doubtful enough that they no longer serve to strengthen the major hypothesis. Luedemann believes that he has reached this point by the end of his first volume. I think that Paul's opponents and further elements in his thought could profitably be analyzed before the Acts material and the question of absolute dates comes into the picture. The location of this point, however, is a matter of judgment, and it is Luedemann who has written more on this subject than any of us.

The discussion never got to this important question, however, because the problem of the historical value of Acts loomed so large in the minds of many. We never reached agreement about the distinction between primary and secondary sources. The matter, as Ellis's question shows, is complex, involving as it does the possibility of sources within Acts. Again my conviction is that Paul's letters provide us with a unique opportunity to check the reliability of Acts and that this opportunity must be taken. Obviously, however, opinions differ. But because of this basic disagreement we were not able to move further. We argued whether Luedemann—or Jewett, for that matter—had gone too far. Thus we were not able to get to the question of how to proceed beyond Luedemann. In this regard the discussion as a whole accurately reflects the current state of opinion on Pauline chronology.

But while we were arguing, Knox was working. His essay provides a fitting close to the colloquy. In it Knox himself takes a first step in moving beyond current positions by making a "fresh approach" to the problem. It would be an appropriate tribute to Knox if his essay should serve to stimulate further work in this important area.

CHRONOLOGY AND METHODOLOGY: REFLECTIONS ON THE DEBATE OVER CHAPTERS IN A LIFE OF PAUL

Robert Jewett

IT GIVES ME PERSONAL satisfaction to be able to take part in this colloquy in honor of John Knox. Although I have never had the privilege of meeting him, his work on Pauline chronology was the decisive stimulus for my own reflections. I would like to begin by describing his impact on my work and then move on to discuss the significance of Gerd Luedemann's and my efforts to develop the Knox position further, touching on some of the recent assessments of the state of the discussion. Then I want to sketch the methodological and historical issues that should now be addressed.

I

In the summer of 1961, when I was working out the chronological premises for a study of Paul's anthropological terms, I found a copy of Knox's book in Tübingen. Although I had skimmed *Chapters in a Life of Paul* several years earlier while studying at Chicago, there was now an urgent need to provide a reliable basis for dating the Pauline letters. I decided to see if the hypothesis of a three-Jerusalem-journey framework could be correlated with a more extensive data-base consisting of time-spans ascertainable in Acts and the letters, seasonal contingencies, and estimates of travel schedules based on conditions in the ancient world. I began in an experimental manner by placing these

details on large calendar sheets so that the relations between overlapping time-spans could be calculated. Within a few days, it became apparent that Knox's elimination of Jerusalem journeys 2 and 3 relieved acute pressures within the data-base between the most firmly established date-frames and time-spans. In particular, a perfect correlation emerged between the Aretas datum, the Claudius edict, the Gallio inscription, and the 14 + 3 year spans mentioned in Galatians when one identified the apostolic conference journey, as Knox did, with Jerusalem journey 4 as reported by Acts. The pieces of the puzzle fit together so smoothly that I suspected my mind had overlooked some crucial contradiction somewhere.

I spent the next year and a half looking for some fatal flaw that ought to have destroyed my simple adaptation of Knox's hypothesis, checking out historical details and trying to master the history of the debate. Rather than disproving the hypothesis, each piece of additional data seemed to confirm it. In the process, I discovered several predecessors of Knox,* and gained a clearer understanding of why the various kinds of compromise chronology had exerted such pressures on the data-base.

By the spring of 1963 the material for a monograph on the problem of Pauline chronology was assembled, while my research on the anthropological terms continued to lag behind. I suggested to Otto Michel that the chronology chapters might be submitted as a dissertation, but he said he felt it was largely irrelevant for the understanding of Pauline theology as far as the German discussion was concerned, and that he wanted me to complete the investigation of the anthropological terms. So the chronology hypothesis based on Knox's theory was buried in a rather lengthy dissertation completed in 1964,[1] surfacing for the first time in the chronological debate in Alfred Suhl's monograph of 1975.[2] In the meanwhile I had spent the summer of 1966 revising the chronology chapters for publication, incorporating some of the extensive cartographic resources I found at the Yale University

---

*[On Knox's predecessors see his essay below.]

[1] *The Pauline Anthropological Terms: Their Use in the Struggle Against Early Christian Heresy*, completed for a D.Theol. degree in Tübingen, August 1964; oral exam on 2 February 1966.

[2] Alfred Suhl, *Paulus und seine Briefe: Ein Beitrag zur paulinischen Chronologie* (Gütersloh: Gerd Mohn, 1975), pp. 305-11.

Library. For various reasons, the manuscript was turned down by European and American monograph series. The hostility of some of the evaluations of the chronology manuscript led me to the conclusion that the times were unripe to build an experimental extension of the Knox hypothesis. I turned to other writing projects while continuing to gather materials on the chronology question, refusing to accept the verdict that my adaptation of the Knox analysis had led to undiscussable conclusions.

II

In the thirteen years between the completion of my chronology monograph in 1966 and its publication by Fortress Press in 1979, the Knox hypothesis was quietly gaining adherents on this side of the Atlantic. The conviction Knox shared with Riddle and others in the Chicago School* concerning the precedence that should be given to the primary evidence in the Pauline letters came to be widely accepted among younger scholars. There was an increasing acceptance of Knox's reduction of the number of Jerusalem journeys from the five recorded in Acts to the three reflected in the epistles. More and more scholars saw the point in Knox's elimination of the so-called "silent years" in the early portion of Paul's ministry and accepted his insistence that the "missionary journeys" radiating outwards from Jerusalem are a Lukan invention that distorts our sense of how Paul's work was actually conceived and organized. Admittedly, some of these contributions were disputed or inadequately understood.[3] For example, I was confused by a suggestion in Knox's earlier work that the fourteen-year span in Gal 2:1 might be identical with that referred to in 2 Cor 12:12, wrongly inferring that he concluded these letters were thereby written in the same year.[4] An additional imprecision has been called to my attention concerning my description of Knox's rejection of the usual coordination of Paul's initial Corinthian visit with the

---

*[On Knox's originality see his essay below.]

[3]Cf. Ernst Haenchen, *Die Apostegeschichte,*13th ed. (Göttingen: Vandenhoeck & Ruprecht, 1961) p. 60, n. 480; George Ogg, "A New Chronology of Saint Paul's Life," *Exp Tim* 67 (1955-56):120-123; Thomas H. Campbell, "Paul's Missionary Journeys as Reflected in His Letters," *JBL* 74 (1955): 80-87.

[4]Robert Jewett, *A Chronology of Paul's Life* (Philadelphia: Fortress, 1979), pp. 79-80.

Gallio inscription. Knox does not "disregard" this datum[5] but rather suggests it may relate to Paul's final visit to Corinth, which Knox places in A.D. 53. Since this is a year too late for actual correlation with Gallio's tenure in Corinth, which even Knox places in A.D. 52 and which I would date more precisely from 1 July 51 to 1 July 52, I drew a rather blunt conclusion. Inexactitudes like this are particularly regrettable in a field requiring historical and descriptive precision, but fortunately in this instance they did not have sufficient weight to overbalance an increasingly positive appraisal of Knox's contributions.

Several publications followed those of M. Jack Suggs, Robert W. Funk and Paul S. Minear[6] in forming a critical consensus favorable to Knox. John C. Hurd, Jr. made decisive contributions including his definitive article on chronology in the *IDB Supplement* that established a widely accepted framework of dates and events visible in the letters.[7] Full-length chronologies by John J. Gunther and Alfred Suhl gave heed to Knox's methodological breakthrough while remaining bound in some degree to compromise frameworks.[8] The increasing acceptance of redaction-critical insights about Luke-Acts sustained Knox's suspicion of the five-Jerusalem-journey framework, while studies by A. N. Sherwin-White and Martin Hengel suggested the usability of some of the incidental details in Acts.[9] These advances prepared

---

[5]Ibid., p. 80.

[6]M. Jack Suggs, "Concerning the Date of Paul's Macedonian Ministry," *NovT* 4 (1960): 60-68; Robert W. Funk, "The Enigma of the Famine Visit," *JBL* 75 (1956): 130-136; Paul S. Minear, "The Jerusalem Fund and Pauline Chronology," *ATR* 25 (1943): 389-96.

[7]John C. Hurd, Jr., "Chronology, Pauline," *The Interpreter's Dictionary of the Bible: An Illustrated Encyclopedia*, Supplementary Volume (Nashville: Abingdon, 1976), pp. 166-167; his earlier studies were "Pauline Chronology and Pauline Theology," *Christian History and Interpretation: Studies Presented to John Knox*, ed. W. R. Farmer et al. (New York: Cambridge University Press, 1967), pp. 225-48; and "The Sequence of Paul's Letters," *CJT* 14 (1968): 189-200.

[8]John J. Gunther, *Paul: Messenger and Exile: A Study in the Chronology of His Life and Letters* (Valley Forge: Judson, 1972); Suhl, *Paulus und seine Briefe*.

[9]A. N. Sherwin-White, *Roman Society and Roman Law in the New Testament* (Oxford: Clarendon, 1963); Martin Hengel, "Christologie und neutestamentliche Chronologie: Zu einer Aporie in der Geschichte des Urchristentums," *Neues Testament und Geschichte: Oscar Cullmann zum 70. Geburtstag*, ed. H. Baltensweiler and B. Reicke (Tübingen: Mohr-Siebeck, 1972), pp. 43-67.

the way for a reconsideration of the entire issue of Pauline chronology. The crucial requirement was to discredit the compromise solutions, for only when they were shown to be untenable would the question become vital. This is in fact what has occurred in the last several years.

A double blow in favor of the Knox approach came with the publication of monographs by Gerd Luedemann[10] and myself, and I think it is fair to say that neither of them would have made as much impact without the other. Coming at the issues from different starting points, and using different historical methods, we agree on three basic matters.

> (1) The compromise chronologies are untenable and Knox has shown the major reason why: the conflicts between Acts and the epistles in the number and placement of Jerusalem journeys.
>
> (2) Knox is correct in identifying the journey of Acts 18:22 with the apostolic conference described in Gal 2:1-10, which means that the conference followed rather than preceded the so-called second missionary journey. Luedemann came to his conclusion about the independent Pauline mission in Greece prior to the apostolic conference on the basis of exegetical analyses of Acts and the letters while I arrived at the same conclusion by an experimental approach to the problem.
>
> (3) There is a need to go beyond *Chapters in the Life of Paul* by assembling a more adequate data-base from Acts as well as the epistles, and this implies a willingness to discuss the incidental details as potentially useful.

It is my view that agreement on these basic points is far more significant than our differences in adapting the Knox hypothesis. With a couple of provisos, Lamar Cope recently concluded that "it may not be too strong to assert that Jewett's study has at last put Pauline chronology on a sound footing."[11] I would prefer to argue that the evolution of Knox's hypothesis in Luedemann's work and mine offers such a footing because it provides a basis for testability. Whereas the compromise chronologies resisted refinement, their internal tensions causing infinite variations that defied falsification, there is now a possibility of objective evaluation. I would not want to claim that either of our chronologies is definitive, but the basis is there to reach a more definitive answer. It now makes sense to argue over the individual historical details that go into the data-base because the possibility

---

[10]Gerd Luedemann, *Paulus, der Heidenapostel*, Studien zur Chronologie 1, FRLANT 123 (Göttingen: Vandenhoeck und Ruprecht, 1980).

[11]Lamar Cope, review of *A Chronology of Paul's Life*, in *ATR* 62 (1980): 178-79.

of progress is at hand. If we have done no more than offer this kind of "sound footing," I would be content. But even this, as far as I am concerned, would have been quite impossible without Knox's breakthrough.

III

The debate about our efforts to adapt the Knox hypothesis is not yet far enough along to allow a secure assessment. I had hoped to include a response to Luedemann's forthcoming review of my work in the *Journal of Biblical Literature*, and of course it would be appropriate at a later date to take into account the reviews that appear concerning his recently published monograph, and the translation of our books into German and English respectively. The reviews of my book that have appeared give the impression that the Knox hypothesis is gaining decisive headway.

As might be expected, the reviews in North America have been more positive than those that have appeared thus far in Great Britain. After sketching the theoretical basis for the new hypothesis in detail, David Granskou in *The Christian Century*[12] observes that with the deletion of extraneous Jerusalem journeys, "the Acts account of Paul is seen as amazingly accurate and informative. This interpretation allows Jewett to interlock time spans in Acts and Paul to a degree hitherto impossible." Granskou is critical of so positive a use of Lukan material and confesses "a certain scepticism about dating with Jewett's precision. His interlockings sometimes appear more like crossword puzzles than true historical reconstruction. Still, the overwhelming effect of the book is positive." He feels that the "study will set the stage for a new debate on the chronology" and that the reactions of specialists will be required to sift through the details.

Robert Holst in *Currents in Theology and Mission*[13] sketches my argument and method, mentioning Barnikol and Knox as important precedents. He concludes that the book can help people "understand the question better." George T. Montague's review in the *Catholic Biblical Quarterly*[14] describes the hypothesis in detail, notes its depend-

---

[12]David Granskou, review in *The Christian Century* 96 (14 November 1979): 1138-39.

[13]Robert Holst, review in *CurTM* 7 (1980): 254.

[14]George T. Montague, review in *CBQ* 42 (1980): 122-23.

ence on Knox, and concludes that it is "a convincing and well-argued case." Even more significant an indication of the way the wind is blowing is his conclusion that the issue cannot be denied by resort to the traditional chronologies: "Any further discussion of Pauline chronology cannot possibly ignore this significant work." Lamar Cope in the *Anglican Theological Review*[15] describes what I hope is an expanding consensus concerning Knox's insistence "on the primary value of the letters for both the life and thought of Paul." He expresses surprise that the interlocking of various kinds of chronological data in my chronology is so exact. Although Cope feels that some of the dates are "too precise and some of the external data rest on questionable tradition," he concludes that the application of the experimental method leads to a positive result: "Especially when there is a correlation between all three types of evidence, the probability that the dating is accurate is extremely high."

Barry Crawford's review in the *Journal of the American Academy of Religion*[16] provides an extensive discussion of the experimental method, concluding that "the precision of Jewett's chronology is deliberate and stems from his confidence that a methodical use of the sources warrants such exactness and his conviction that it is only when something is made specific enough to be falsifiable that it can ever be shown to be true." He shares an impression with John G. Gibbs, who writes in *The New Review of Books and Religion*,[17] that although the new chronology "has not settled the issues once for all, there can be no responsible discussion of Pauline chronology that does not take [it] into account." In a similar tone William Baird concludes in *Religious Studies Review*[18] that the chronology is "at main points reminiscent of John Knox" and is "a model of thorough research and careful reasoning."

Although some reviewers of the British edition have been quite positive, there is considerably more skepticism about my reliance on Knox as well as my effort to evaluate the evidence in Acts. Margaret

---

[15]Cope, review in *ATR*.

[16]Barry Crawford, review in *JAAR* 47 (1979): 667-68.

[17]John G. Gibbs, review in *The New Review of Books and Religion* 4 (December, 1979): 8-9.

[18]William Baird, review in *RelSRev* 5 (1979): 224.

Thrall's review in *The Expository Times*[19] refers favorably to the abandonment of the Lukan framework of five-Jerusalem-journeys as well as to my "forcible demonstration that the missionary activities which according to Acts take place between the Apostolic Conference and the arrival in Corinth cannot possibly be fitted into the eighteen-month period which is all that the seventeen-year span before the Conference, correlated with the Gallio inscription, would allow." In a similar vein, N. T. Wright in *The Churchman*[20] concludes that my study will become "a standard starting-point for future discussions of apostolic chronology." He recognizes it as a typically American approach, a modification of John Knox's work while bearing "the marks of its Tübingen origins" in being overly critical of Luke's historicity. Henry Wansbrough's review in *The Tablet*[21] is less concerned about Luke's reputation and expresses appreciation for the calculations that allow "Paul a reasonably leisurely rate of travel, and a reasonably long period of evangelising in each place, instead of frenetic rush which . . . demands from Paul the temperament of a Marathon runner." He insists, however, that other chronologies are equally plausible. Edwin Bannon in the *Catholic Herald*[22] concludes on a similar vein, that the new chronology must be accounted "a brilliant hypothesis rather than a convincing solution."

In the *Scottish Journal of Theology*[23] Ernest Best raises questions about several ascertainable dates and time-spans. "Jewett never mentions the tradition that Paul and Peter were martyred in Rome in A.D. 64," he asserts, having apparently overlooked the discussion of Clement's Epistle to the Corinthians on pages 45 and 132 which led me to establish a *terminus ad quem* shortly after July 64. He is sceptical of allowing full three- and fourteen-year periods in the chronology because "over such long periods no one attempts to make such exact statements." The difficulty is that since we lack an objective technique of estimating the degree of Paul's inexactitude in this instance, the best we can achieve is to place the detail in an experimental framework that

---

[19]Margaret E. Thrall, review in *Exp Tim* 91 (1979-1980): 122.

[20]N. T. Wright, review in *The Churchman* 93 (1979): 348-49.

[21]Henry Wansbrough, review in *The Tablet* (26 January 1980): 83-84.

[22]Edwin Bannon, review in *Catholic Herald* no. 4868 (24 August 1979): 6.

[23]Ernest Best, review in *SJT* 33 (1980): 487-88.

allows for verifiability by the degree of correlation with other data. This seems preferable to making subjective guesses about how many months more or less than seventeen years might have been involved in the time-spans about which Paul's memory was presumably so vague. But Best dismisses such methodological considerations as "pretentious scientific mumbo-jumbo." He does conclude, however, that "the method of the interlocking of periods . . . is a good tool for the solution of the problem" and concludes that the historical verdict about the feasibility of the "cogently argued" new chronology "will not be harsh."

G. B. Caird is the best known chronologist who has commented on the book thus far. His review in the *Journal of Theological Studies*[24] provides a positive assessment but raises two major questions: "This hypothesis is very carefully worked out and may well be correct. Like that of Knox, on which it is a vast improvement, it has the advantage of eliminating the 'silent years' between the first visit to Jerusalem and the first missionary journey. Yet it is not so wholly free from difficulty as Jewett believes." The first question relates to the Aretas datum, which he correctly perceives is "the cornerstone" of my hypothesis. Its correlation with Pauline chronology, he insists, is entirely dependent on "the Lucan framework" and thus would be discredited if that framework is abandoned. I would retort that this is one of those instances where Luke happens to parallel the primary evidence in the Epistles and thus does not need to be called into question. Gal 1:17 explicitly states that Paul returned to Damascus after his conversion and went from there to Jerusalem. Thereafter he traveled not to Arabia or Damascus but rather to Syria and Cilicia (Gal 1:21). Since this is Paul's only reference to Damascus aside from 2 Cor 11:32, the inference I have drawn about its correlation with the rest of his life would stand if there were no reference at all in Acts.* Moreover, if one accepts the principle of "multiple attestation" as a criterion of historicity, as one typically does in the discussion of synoptic parallels, the fact that the sequence is paralleled in Acts ought to augment the credibility of the correlation I have drawn. This is one of those instances where an undifferentiated skepticism about Acts gets one into unnecessary historical difficulties.

Caird's second objection reveals how little he is actually inclined toward such skepticism. He points out that Barnabas accompanied

---

[24]George B. Caird, review in *JTS* 31 (1980): 170-72.

*This answers the major objection raised by A. J. M. Wedderburn in "Keeping up

Paul to the Jerusalem conference: "Yet upon the evidence of Acts, confirmed by that of the Thessalonian letters, Paul and Barnabas had separated before the second missionary journey. Is it not much more likely that Paul and Barnabas would have made a joint visit to Jerusalem at a time when they were still colleagues?" This is actually an instance where Luke's report appears to be contradicted by a fragment of primary evidence that Caird has overlooked, because Paul refers in 1 Cor 9:6 to Barnabas as a missionary colleague with whom the Corinthians were intimately acquainted. Compared with this direct reference, the argument from silence concerning the lack of a greeting from Barnabas in the Thessalonian correspondence must surely recede into insignificance. Barnabas may simply have been engaged in other activities at the time Paul wrote to the Thessalonians. The new hypothesis actually offers the basis of a plausible explanation of the very real contradiction between Acts 15:39 and 1 Cor 9:6. If the apostle conference is placed *after* the so-called second missionary journey, then the tradition that Acts relays of a conflict between Paul and Barnabas after that conference would correlate chronologically with the report of their disagreement at Antioch in Gal 2:13. The contradiction between Acts and 1 Corinthians is therefore easily explained by Luke's mistaken placement of the apostolic conference *before* the travels that founded the churches of Greece. I would therefore agree with Caird that Paul and Barnabas were working together at the time of the conference, but would caution overhasty reliance on Luke when direct conflicts with the primary evidence are apparent. The methodological controls on the use of material from Acts should be applied in the same way for both of these questions that Caird raises, and when this is done, the evidence serves to confirm the plausibility of the Knox hypothesis about the correct placement of the apostolic conference.

The lengthy review by John W. Drane in the *Journal for the Study of the New Testament*[25] refers to my favorable use of John Knox but refuses to grant priority to the evidence in the Pauline letters or to make any distinction between Luke's editorial work and his sources. "If Luke amended details for theological reasons, could not Paul, at least in principle, have done the same, especially in Galatians 1-2 where he had very strong theological reasons for doing so? . . . It would surely

---

with Recent Studies, VIII, Some Recent Pauline Chronologies," *The Expository Times* 92 (1981): 103-108, esp. 105.

[25]John W. Drane, review in *JSNT* 9 (1980): 70-75.

be more consistent either to reject the Lucan material altogether . . . or to proceed on the assumption that it is broadly accurate . . . . The attempt to find a *via media* at this point certainly raises a number of methodological problems that are not resolved satisfactorily." Although Drane provides an impartial account of my use of the experimental method, his commitment to the credibility of Luke makes it impossible for him to accept its employment. Without offering precise historical evidence to the contrary, Drane simply disallows three of the details that make the compromise chronologies so untenable: the two year span of Aretas' jurisdiction over Damascus, the seventeen year span in Galatians, and the extensive itinerary on the so-called "second missionary journey." To counter my rather exhaustive sifting of the historical evidence and scholarly debate on these issues, he places these events in a paragraph illustrating "the same tendency to overlook or play down some of the evidence [that] appears repeatedly in Jewett's handling of the historical data." The principle that appears in such statements is that anything countering the traditional compromise chronologies or threatening the credibility of Luke is automatically to be categorized as irresponsible and biased. This principle appears to guide Colin J. Hemer's recent article[26] that dismisses John Knox's contribution on grounds that he makes "a Procrustean use of the evidence to accommodate his scheme." He finds my chronology "problematic" because it accommodates itself to the same three details that Drane would like to disallow. Their defense of total Lukan accuracy results in jeopardizing the credibility of a large number of incidental chronological details both in Acts and in the letters because they are irreconcilable with the five-Jerusalem-journey framework that Luke provides. Hemer concludes that my "varying use of Acts is a recurring focus of problems. The book is interesting, but its arguments and conclusions uncompelling. I have learnt much from reading it, and yet feel unconstrained to wish to alter materially any part of the substance of what I have written."

It is perhaps appropriate to conclude this account of scholarly reviews with the thoroughly sceptical if not hostile perspective of

---

[26]Colin J. Hemer, "Observations on Pauline Chronology," *Pauline Studies: Essays presented to Professor F. F. Bruce on his 70th Birthday*, ed. Donald A. Hagner and Murray J. Harris (Exeter: Paternoster; Grand Rapids: Eerdmans, 1980), pp. 3-18.

Michael Green. He writes in *Church Times*[27] that my rejection of evidence from the Pastoral Epistles, my critical use of evidence in Acts, and my placement of Paul's escape from Aretas between A.D. 37 and 39 are "exceedingly shaky, as any competent New Testament scholar knows." The experimental methodology which begins with a "modest" assessment of probabilities and concludes by anchoring details firmly in a precise chronological framework strikes Green as misleading and irresponsible. Such methodology ". . . turns a learned and in places sensitive and well-argued book into a very poor example of scholarship." He concludes in the following manner: "This is a book whose thesis will prove unconvincing to those who know their way round New Testament chronology, whose presuppositions are not only suspect but are used to buttress massive conclusions on the most frail grounds, and whose research lacks in places evidence of sufficient rigour."

IV

The methodological issues raised by the reviews that have appeared, and the ones likely to arise out of Luedemann's critique of my chronology, fall into three categories. First, there is the question of how best to carry out Knox's assumption of the methodological priority of primary over secondary evidence. This assumption appears to be generally acknowledged at this stage of the debate, but the question is how to apply it. Suhl and Gunther are surely sincere in adopting the principle, yet they appear bound to the Lukan framework of Jerusalem journeys with the result that their chronologies suffer from time compression. It is likely that both Luedemann and myself will be charged as vulnerable on similar grounds because we make such extensive use of incidental historical details from Acts. I establish the rule of eliminating such details whenever a direct conflict with the primary evidence is

---

[27]Michael Green, review in *Church Times* no. 6083 (14 September 1979): 6. It would be appropriate at this point to include reviews from the continent and the Third World, but only one is available at the time of completing this article. X. Jacques, S. J. provides a detailed summary of my thesis and its method in *NRT* 102 (1980): 908-10. He appears favorably disposed to my adaptation of the Knox hypothesis: "Cette élaboration nouvelle de l'hypothèse développée par Knox ne manque pas de séduction, d'autant plus que l'auteur excelle à lui donner les attraits de la rigueur, de la logique, de la clarté." Since the publication of the German edition, translated by Gisela Koester, had not appeared by September 1981, reviews from that quarter will not arrive until sometime in the future.

present, and further insist that redaction-critical insights should be taken into account. Whenever Luke's editorial hand appears to have distorted the evidence, the datum ought to be given at most a tertiary role in any chronology reconstruction. Finally I suggest that the historical details in Acts that survive this critical sifting should be granted only an experimental value that can be tested by inclusion in a larger framework that allows for their confirmation. If a detail can be successfully incorporated into a larger, experimental framework, it may then be granted a measure of plausibility. But no single detail from Acts, it seems to me, deserves to be raised to the level of independent credibility. This methodological insistence may be overly cautious, and it may be attacked as inadequately carried out in the work I have done. But the difference between Luedemann and myself should be rather sharply drawn at this point. He argues that the elimination of Luke's redactional overlay is sufficient to raise evidence in Acts to the point of independent credibility, as one sees by the decisive role he gives to the account of the Corinthian ministry in Acts. When such redactional cleansing occurs, Luedemann argues, the details in Acts "erreichen fast denselben historischen Wert wie die Primärquellen."[28]

A second, related area of methodological concern is whether the deductive-experimental method that is ordinarily utilized in the social and natural sciences is actually suitable for historical questions. I have yet to find other efforts along this line in the fields of classical, biblical, and historical studies. As a result the question has to be focused on the adequacy of the experimental concepts I have devised to cope with the issue of Pauline chronology:

> • the creation of a "neutral" data base, with chronological details calculated without reference to their bearing on a chronological hypothesis
> • the creation of time-spans for most historical events, designating their *termini a quo et ad quem*, but refraining from drawing premature conclusions about when the event actually occurred within that range
> • the comparison of overlapping date-frames and time-spans to reduce the "range" of chronological implications
> • the concept of chronological interlocking by which data from different sources are brought into correlation with a

---

[28]Luedemann, *Paulus, der Heidenapostel*, p. 203.

calendar of a person's life, assuming that the details allow only one sequence of unrepeated historical events, and that an alteration at one point in the chronology has implications for everything else

• the use of probability calculations to measure the likelihood of events interlocking in particular ways, and the use of seasonal and travel details concerning distances and road conditions or sailing schedules to evaluate the implications of an interlock

• the precise calculation of a chronological hypothesis so that each detail can be evaluated and thereby disproven if necessary

• the idea of systematic facticity, by which incidental historical details that have inadequate credibility when taken by themselves are raised to higher levels of historicity by their successful correlation with a chronological hypothesis

• the treatment of the history of research as an account of previous experiments whose success or failure can be objectively determined by their compliance with the database.

In these and other areas, my effort to apply the experimental method to a complex historical problem must be acknowledged as exploratory and provisional. The best that can be hoped for at this point is that a more precise grasp of the methodological issues may arise of the debate. But here again there are substantial differences between Luedemann and myself, as one can see by the criticism of his use of the laws of probability in reducing the time-spans of Paul's life from 14 and 3 to 13 and 2 years respectively. He defends himself by asking, "wie anders denn als mit Wahrscheinlichkeitsurteilen der Historiker sich seinem einzigartigen Gegenstand nähert."[29] The question is how such laws are to be applied, and my conviction is that a larger experimental framework is required to avoid subjective assessments.

V

If Gerd Luedemann and I have been successful in moving the discussion of Pauline chronology onto the "sound footing" that John

---

[29]Ibid., p. 197. [On this point see Luedemann's response in the seminar dialogue, below.]

Knox prepared, a series of historical questions will shift to the center of the discussion. For it is only in our assessment of the historical data that we are divided. Here is a brief accounting of the points of disagreement.[30]

(1) Did the expelling of Jewish-Christian agitators from Rome under Claudius take place in A.D. 41 as Luedemann insists or in 49 as I conclude? This question should be addressed within the larger context of Claudius' policies toward the Jews and his sensitivity about religious propaganda; it should also take account of historical trends that are independent from Pauline chronology, such as the evolution of both church and synagogue in Rome.

(2) How is the Aretas datum to be incorporated into Paul's life and how is one to correlate the detail about an escape over the wall of Damascus with the view Luedemann shares concerning the Ethnarch of Aretas's guarding of the gates from the outside? If my argument about the narrow time frame of A.D. 37-39 for Aretas's control of Damascus is accepted, Luedemann's chronology would require major revisions.

(3) The most complicated unresolved question is the date of the crucifixion. I am uneasy with the state of our knowledge of the discrepancies between John and the Synoptics and particularly about the reliability of calendric calculations of the date of the last supper. Although my chronology would remain intact with dates of A.D. 27, 30 or 33, the results of this investigation might have drastic effects for Luedemann. He opts for the earliest date, offering A.D. 30 as an alternative, but even this would provide serious problems for his chronology if reckoned out in detail. If the year 33 proves most plausible, the problem would be irresolvable for his chronology because then the founding of the churches in Greece would have occurred only 8 years after the beginning of the Christian movement. But whatever the bearing on our chronological theories, the problem demands resolution, and I suggest that the application of the experi-

---

[30]The following points are derived from my critical evaluation of Luedemann's hypothesis in *Chronology of Paul's Life*, pp. 81-85. My original plan for this article had been to respond to his reply to these issues in his *JBL* review announced for volume 99 (1980), p. 5 in the "Vorwort" of *Paulus, der Heidenapostel*. My inquiry to the editors of the journal in September 1981, indicated that the review still had not arrived.

mental method might be particularly promising in resolving the conflicts within the evidence.

(4) The question of the validity of the ascertainable dates and time-spans that Luedemann deletes is likely to remain troublesome. These include the references in Acts to the Festus/Felix transfer, the Egyptian rebel, and to Ananias as High Priest. The evaluation of the astronomical calculations underlying the dates for the departure from Philippi and from Fair Havens is an urgent desideratum. I suspect that some serious discrepancies lurk in the work that has been done in this area. Even more problematic is the detail about eighteen months of resurrection appearances. The origin and significance of this datum has not been thoroughly investigated since the time of Harnack, so far as I know. Finally there needs to be a critical evaluation of my effort to narrow down the time-span of the execution of Paul to the period from the spring of A.D. 62 to the summer of 64. A positive historical judgment on any of these issues would have serious consequences for Luedemann's hypothesis of an early close of Paul's ministry in A.D. 52 or 55, and refinement or adjustment of these dates would likely result in recalculations of my chronology as well.

(5) Perhaps the most significant historical and exegetical issue arising from Luedemann's work is whether the conflict between Paul and Peter reported in Gal 2:11-14 occurred prior to the apostolic conference described in Gal 2:1-10. It depends on how one understands the rhetorical structure of Galatians and how one reconstructs the conflict that led to that letter,[31] but the consequences reach very widely into the picture we have of the evolution of the debate over the law and the intercultural participation in the common meals of the early church.

I would like to close by insisting again that the points of disagreement between Luedemann and myself are far less significant than the common effort we have made, quite independently of each other, to sustain the Knox hypothesis and to turn the discussion of Pauline chronology away from the fruitless avenues of the compromise solutions. Despite our differences, we are allies in a common cause, and I am encouraged to have him contending alongside me in the fray. It is possible, of course, that we may experience the fate of inadvertent

---

[31] Jewett, *Chronology of Paul's Life*, pp. 82-84.

allies who become opponents the moment their original adversary has given way. But at the moment I cannot believe that the long dominance of compromise chronologies will dissipate so quickly as to make this likely, despite the tone of a few book reviews. A scholarly community that largely dismissed for decades the contribution of Knox's chronological studies can hardly be expected to find his successors less objectionable. Whatever else can be said about Gerd Luedemann and myself, we have produced some rather large and vulnerable targets. Granted the untoward use of this military rhetoric, I remain convinced that scholarly advances occur only when "conjectures" remain in tension with "refutations," to use the language of Karl Popper. The quest for truth must transcend the fate of any alliance or any individual contribution.

A CHRONOLOGY OF PAUL*

Gerd Luedemann

M ODERN RESEARCH INTO THE New Testament proceeds from a few basic presuppositions as, for example, the (modified) two-source theory for the exegesis of the synoptics and a standard chronology for Paul and primitive Christianity up to the year A.D. 70.[1] It is the task of historical research to draw such presuppositions into question whenever evidence to the contrary begins to emerge. In the following, I shall present a critical examination of the standard opinion on the chronology of Paul. This examination will show that the time is ripe for a new proposal about the order of events in Paul's life. I shall then offer such a proposal.

*The following article builds upon my book *Paulus, der Heidenapostel*, vol. 1: *Studien zur Chronologie*, FRLANT 123 (Göttingen: Vandenhoeck & Ruprecht, 1980). I want to thank F. Stanley Jones, Vanderbilt University, for substantial help in the preparation and writing of this article. Mr. Jones is also the translator of the forthcoming English translation of that book.

[1]Cf., e.g., M. Hengel's statement of the present relative consensus on New Testament chronology up to 70 A.D. in: M. Hengel, "Christologie und neutestamentliche Chronologie," *Neues Testament und Geschichte*, Festschrift O. Cullmann, ed. H. Baltensweiler and B. Reicke (Tübingen: Mohr-Siebeck, 1972), pp. 43-67, esp. p. 44, fn. 5.

I would indicate first, however, that neither my criticism nor my positive presentation is absolutely novel. A number of scholars in the past have questioned the standard view. I am especially indebted to the work of John Knox. Since Knox's writings have so often suffered misrepresentation, I shall attempt to describe briefly the essentials of his view.[2]

Knox proposes, first of all, a methodology that acknowledges the vastly inferior value of Acts as a source for Paul's career in comparison to the apostle's own letters.[3] He holds that the barest hint in the epistles is of more worth than even the most explicit statement of Acts. Any statement in Acts that conflicts with the letters should thus be deemed in error. Acts merits *full* credibility only where the letters provide a supporting statement; never, however, where an assertion is not confirmed by the epistles. Knox attaches particular suspicion to the statements in Acts that serve a special interest or purpose of the author. According to Knox, a rigorous employment of these methods can yield a coherent outline of Paul's apostolic career. The two key items in Knox's chronology are (1) a date for the Jerusalem conference much later in Paul's career than where Acts places it, and (2) a date for this conference just a few years before Paul's final visit to Jerusalem.

In my judgment, the redaction-historical investigation of Luke's two-volume work has achieved much that provides a basis for an amplification and improvement of Knox's chronology. Let us turn to the standard view on the chronology of Paul.

The Conventional View

The works that present the conventional view on the chronology of Paul may be broadly described as attempts to effect the most ingenious combination of the statements in Acts with the information in the letters. A consensus has nevertheless arisen as to how these two sources may be brought into harmony. One proceeds on the basis of the sole

---

[2]For this summary, I am indebted to John Knox who, in a letter of 17 September 1980, succinctly restated the essential elements of his position.

[3]Cf. the similar method, developed already by F. C. Baur, *Paul: The Apostle of Jesus Christ*, trans. A. Menzies, 2 vols. (London/Edinburgh: Williams & Norgate, 1875-1876) 1:4-5: "It would appear natural to suppose that in all the cases where the account in Acts do not altogether agree with statements of the Apostle, the latter must have such a decided claim to be considered authentic truth that the contradictions would scarcely be worth attention. . . . The comparison of these two sources leads us to

absolute datum for the life of Paul, the Gallio inscription. Since Gallio held office in A.D. 51-52, Acts 18:12 is taken as a sure indication that Paul stood trial before Gallio in this year. Further confirmation is then derived from 18:2, which mentions the arrival of Priscilla and Aquila from Rome after the expulsion of the Jews (the year is assumed, on the basis of Orosius, to be A.D. 49). Since these two dates confirm one another, it is held that Luke's report of Paul's *first* Corinthian mission in Acts 18 is historically accurate. With the date of the mission on European soil relatively set, other dates are reckoned both before and after this period. *After* the stay in Corinth, Paul traveled to Ephesus, then on to Palestine, and then back to Ephesus (Acts 18:18ff.). There Paul wrote the Corinthian letters and later traveled back to Jerusalem (by way of Macedonia) to deliver the collection. In Jerusalem, Paul was arrested and was eventually taken to Rome to meet his death as a martyr. *Before* the stay in Corinth, Paul had worked as a missionary in Philippi, Thessalonica, and Athens (an agreement of 1 Thessalonians with Acts 17ff.). Prior to this mission, Paul had traveled as a delegate of the Antiochene congregation, to Jerusalem for the conference (Acts 15:2ff.). One determines the date of the conference, fourteen to seventeen years after Paul's conversion, on the basis of Galatians 1ff. Confirmation of this view is then found in the reference to the ensuing conflict between Paul and Barnabas in both Acts 15:36-39 and Gal 2:13. For eleven to fourteen years prior to the Jerusalem conference, Paul had worked, as a missionary of the Antiochene congregation, in Syria and Cilicia (a combination of Gal 1:21 and Acts 13ff.).

I wish to emphasize at this point that if this view were correct, then all of Paul's letters would have been composed within about five years of one another. They would all have been written by a man who had already been a Christian for about nineteen years and who was a veteran missionary. Accordingly, one should expect the letters to be quite homogeneous; little room would be left for any theory regarding a development in Paul's thought reflected in the letters. The historian's exposition of the letters could rather proceed from the old theological principle, "scriptura ipsius interpres."

---

the conclusion that, considering the great differences between the two statements, historical truth must be entirely on one side or entirely on the other.... For the history of the Apostolic Age the Pauline Epistle must in any case take precedence of all the other New Testament writings as an authentic source."

A Few Critical Objections

Though the standard harmonization of Act and the letters has not been without important critical results—one may recall the rejection of the historicity of Acts 9:26ff., on the basis of Paul's own statements in Galatians, dissatisfaction with this view has continued to crop up. In the following, I shall mention a few matters which have provoked discontentment.

A. Paul, a Delegate of Antioch before the Jerusalem Conference and a Junior Partner of Barnabas?[4] In Gal 2:1ff., Paul writes that his reason for traveling to Jerusalem was a revelation. This seems to stand in tension with the (Lukan) view of Paul as a junior partner of Barnabas (Acts 11:25; 12:25). In 2:2, Paul stresses his intention to present the gospel that *he* preaches among the Gentiles; this statement allows one to conclude that, at that time, Paul had been operating an independent mission. In 2:3, Paul notes that he had taken Titus with him to Jerusalem. This action, which is never mentioned in Acts, witnesses to a considerable self-consciousness on Paul's part, for it accentuates the inclusion of Gentile believers in the eschatological people of God. Moreover, since we only know of Titus from Paul's mission in Europe, it is indeed plausible that Paul had conducted a mission independent of Antioch *before* the conference.

B. A.D. 49 as the date of the expulsion of the Jews from Rome is actually uncertain. This date derives from a late source (Orosius) and stands in tension with earlier sources: The witness of Suetonius and Dio Cassius points to A.D. 41 as the date of the expulsion (more on this below).

C. Luke strings together episodes in Acts by means of *loose chronological indications* (for example, 6:1, 12:1, 19:23). We shall therefore have to ask if Luke is not presenting selected episodes rather than a continuous history. One should note the difference of space allotted to the first thirteen to fourteen years of Paul's life as a Christian (Acts 11:26-15:1ff.) as compared to that allotted to the last few years of his life (fourteen chapters).

D. Luke's references to incidents in world history are often incorrect. I shall mention here only the following: Acts 4:6 and Luke 3:2

---

[4]The expression "junior partner" is taken from E. Käsemann, *An die Römer*, HNT 8a, 3rd. ed. (Tübingen: Mohr-Siebeck, 1974), p. 4.

incorrectly designate Annas, rather than Caiaphas, as the high priest during the ministry of Jesus and after his death; Luke 2:1ff. incorrectly dates the census by at least a decade; the census was also limited to Judea and Syria and was not, contra Luke, worldwide; Acts 5:36ff. incorrectly dates Theudas and blunders grossly by ordering Judas the Galilean *after* Theudas; the notion of a worldwide famine in Acts 11:28 contradicts both world history and chapter 11 itself, for there it is stated that the congregation in Antioch was able to send aid to Jerusalem.[5]

E. The chronological information offered by Luke *is often conditioned by Luke's redactional intentions.* Luke is concerned to demonstrate that Christianity is a politically safe religion; it is ready to be adopted as a world religion. It is well known that Luke thinks in terms of eras in the history of salvation. The last stage begins with the formulation and adoption of the apostolic decree at the apostolic conference (Acts 15): Paul is then free to operate his mission among the Gentiles. For Luke, this decree means that Paul stands in continuity with the primitive church. The placement of the Pauline mission *after* the adoption of the decree thus primarily serves interests that are dogmatic rather than chronological. Another point that I wish to emphasize under this heading is one that has seldom been noticed: though Luke may report several times on visits by Paul to a given locality, he presents information about the apostle's activity there in only one of these reports (Corinth: 18:1ff., cf. 20:2ff.; Thessalonica: 17:1ff., cf. 20:2; Philippi: 16:11ff., cf. the two visits in 20:2, 3-6). It is unlikely that Luke only had access to local traditions that were related to the first missionary journey; he seems rather to have gathered all the various information about a given locality into a single report.

The Task and the Method

These diverse objections reveal the dubious nature of the conventional harmonization of Acts with the letters. Historical and redaction criticism is showing us that we have been too gullible with respect to Luke's chronological references: Luke most often operates as a theologian and develops his chronology from proper dogma. The observation that Luke contradicts Paul at some points further renders it

---

[5]For more errors on Luke's part see Luedemann, *Paulus, der Heidenapostel*, pp. 26-32.

necessary to adopt a method for the establishment of Paul's chronology that proceeds solely on the basis of the letters and only afterwards attempts a critical evaluation of the traditions in Acts. This method[6] would be parallel to the present general consensus concerning the reconstruction of Paul's theology: we must first focus exclusively on the letters and only later, in the light of the achieved results, evaluate the statements of Acts.

On the other hand, Paul did not write as a historian, either. His statements require critical consideration, due weight being given to the circumstances in which he wrote and to the literary genre of his statements. We shall proceed, first, by analyzing Galatians 1ff. Second, we shall employ the collection as an external criterion for the arrangement of chronological data. Later, we shall return to Acts to see how the information there fits in with that of the letters, for by no means do we wish to deny *en masse* the reliability of all the information (=the traditions) in Acts. Our claim is that the answers to such issues as the existence of an itinerary and the actual chronological place of the traditions in Acts may only be approached *after* a careful evaluation of the letters.

A Reconstruction of the Chronology of Paul Solely on the Basis of the Letters

A reconstruction of the chronology of Paul solely on the basis of the letters must begin with an analysis of Gal 1:6-2:14, the central pillar of every chronology of Paul. Here, due to the invasion of the Galatian congregations by Palestinian Jewish Christians, Paul is forced to present a summary of his relations to the apostles in Jerusalem. The opponents maintain the inferiority of Paul's gospel to the gospel of circumcision. They probably claim that Paul's gospel is dependent on the gospel proclaimed in Jerusalem, and they say that Paul has fallen away from this true gospel: his gospel must be supplemented with observation of the Jewish law.

It is important to note that Paul uses a particular literary genre in answering the charges of his opponents. H. D. Betz has recently offered an appropriate characterization of Galatians as an apologetic letter

---

[6]Critical method means everything here. A. J. M. Wedderburn's objections to my book (cf. review in *SJT* 34 [1981]: 87-91) are based on an inadequate distinction of primary and secondary sources (cf. already my remark on p. 6 of my book).

that may be analyzed in terms of ancient rhetoric.[7] In the following, we shall presuppose Betz's analysis of the rhetorical pattern underlying Galatians 1-2. According to Betz, Gal 1:6-2:14 constitutes the *exordium* (introduction stating the factual reason for the address) and the *narratio* (a persuasive statement of the facts pertinent to the situation). While the precise subdivision of these components is not of direct concern for our argument here, we do need to ask, for the sake of an accurate judgment regarding the chronological information in Gal 1:13-2:14, if the *narratio* necessarily follows the chronological order of events. That is, does the order of events in Gal 1:13-2:14. necessarily correspond to the actual historical order? We know that, in general, the *narratio* followed the natural order of events.[8] Quintillian and others, however, document the view that the speaker could take the matter of special concern out of the natural order and place it at the end.[9] We shall thus have to keep this possibility in mind as we turn now to examine a few passage in Galatians 1-2.

A. Galatians 1ff. 1. The ἔπειτα in 1:18 and 2:1 has created some confusion in research. While all agree that the ἔπειτα in 1:18 refers back to the conversion (that is, three years after the conversion), opinion differs as to whether the ἔπειτα in 2:1 stands in reference to the conversion or the first visit to Jerusalem. The fact has been overlooked, however, that whenever Paul uses ἔπειτα in a temporal sense, he thereby joins up with what *immediately* preceded it (cf. 1 Cor 15:5, 6, 7, 23, 46; 1 Thess 4:17). Since this is certainly the sense of ἔπειτα in 1:21, the most natural reading of ἔπειτα in 1:18 and 2:1 would be as an adverb linking up with what immediately preceded: 1:18 means three years after the return to Damascus (we thus have no information about the length of the stay in Arabia); 2:1 means fourteen years after the journey to Syria and Cilicia.

2. *Syria and Cilicia* are mentioned in Gal 1:21 as the place to which Paul journeyed after his first visit to Jerusalem. The rhetorical rules for the *narratio* preclude all unneccesary information about persons, pla-

---

[7]H. D. Betz, *Galatians. A Commentary on Paul's Letter to the Churches in Galatia*, Hermeneia (Philadelphia: Fortress, 1979), pp. 14-25, and the works by Betz mentioned there on p. 14, fn. 96.

[8]See, e.g., Cicero *De Oratore* 2.80.329; *Rhetorica ad Herennium* 1.9.15.

[9]See Quintillian *Institutio Oratoria* 4.2.83-84; Dionysius of Halicarnassus *De Isaeo* 15.615.

ces, and events. It is a noteworthy observation that the only changes of locality mentioned by Paul in Galatians 1ff. concern travel either in the direction towards or away from Jerusalem. Thus, the point of the statement that Paul went to Syria and Cilicia is that he *left* the immediate vicinity of Jerusalem. Nothing is said of where Paul spent the fourteen years after the trip to Syria and Cilicia, and the flow of the argument itself prohibits any statement not concerned with traveling towards or away from Jerusalem.

3. The *occasion and content of the Jerusalem conference* may be determined through a careful evaluation of the historical and traditional nature of Paul's own statements.

a. *Gal 2:7-8* has often been taken as a direct statement about the conference. Research has reached an impasse in its attempt to determine whether these verses represent part of the protocol of the conference or a Pauline interpretation of this. Word statistics yield only an ambiguous result: it could be either.[10] It has never been asked, however, if 2:7-8 might be a tradition deriving from the time before the conference. This actually seems to be the case for there are great differences between vss. 7ff. and vs. 9: in vs. 9 (1) the opposition Peter-Paul is no longer mentioned; (2) Paul returns to his usual designation of Simon as Cephas; (3) Paul and Barnabas are mentioned together; and (4) James stands at the head of the list. These differences lead to the conclusion that vss. 7-8 cannot derive from the agreements formulated at the conference. Since vss. 7-8 do however contain traditional material (the opposition circumcision-uncircumcision and the notion of a division in the gospel), we must ask if it is possible to date this tradition. One indication that this tradition existed already before the conference is the aorist participle in vs. 7: Paul's mission among the Gentiles is both presupposed and recognized. The fact that the aorist recurs in vs. 8 shows that Paul and Peter had been entrusted with their respective missions at a moment which lay some time in the past. Further, the particle γάρ and the fact that vs. 8 consists of a parenthesis recalling information to the minds of the Galatians allow us to conclude that vss. 7-8. reflect a tradition current among Paul's Greek-speaking congregations (this alone explains the unusual designation of Simon as Peter) and that this tradition stems from Paul's first visit with

---

[10]See Luedemann, *Paulus, der Heidenapostel*, pp. 87-91, for an analysis of the vocabulary.

Peter in Jerusalem. The presentation of Paul and Peter as equals here is also best explained as a formulation either of Paul or of his followers.

b. *Gal 2:9* then presents us with the agreement formulated at the conference; it establishes an *ethnographical* division of the world mission. The purpose of the agreement was to eliminate problems that arose from the commingling of the two Christian groups, Jews and Gentiles. Now, Paul never mentions that he had a mission to the Jews, and all his letters are directed to Gentiles. That Paul never did have a mission to the Jews and that Titus is the representative of Paul's mission provide the best explanation for Paul's statement in vs. 6: "those who were of repute added nothing to me." The emphasis of the "me" indicates, however, that something may well have been added to Barnabas. Barnabas was the representative of a mixed community and would thus have been greatly affected by such an ethnographical division. The most likely conclusion is that something similar to the apostolic decree was formulated for the existing mixed communities; this decree would have been taken by Barnabas back to Antioch.

c. *Gal 2:11-14.* We mentioned above that, in the *narratio*, it was possible to diverge from the natural order of events to place special emphasis upon a particular occurrence. Now we want to ask if Paul actually did this, for there are a number of reasons for dating the controversy in Antioch *before* the conference: (1) the naive table fellowship pictured in 2:11-14. could have occurrred only before the conference; (2) a fundamental challenge to table fellowship between Jewish and Gentile believers would have been possible only before the conference; (3) the demands of the opponents in Antioch are similar to the demands of those who brought about the conference: Jewish Christians must separate themselves from Gentile Christians. It further seems likely that Paul would break the chronological continuity of the *narratio* in order to emphasize this incident, for here he is able to demonstrate his independence to a greater extent than in the report on the conference: at Antioch he even reproached one of the "pillars" face to face. The strength of these arguments leads us to affirm that Paul did indeed alter the order of events (notice the absence of ἔπειτα in 2:11). Further, it is likely, though not strictly provable, that the incident in Antioch was the direct cause for the conference in Jerusalem.

B. The collection as an External Criterion for the Establishment of a Chronological Framework. We are now ready to turn to the collection as an external criterion for the establishment of a chronological

framework, for the aorist in Gal 2:10 makes it clear that immediately after the conference, and *only after* the conference, Paul began an operation intended to provide continual support for the congregation in Jerusalem. Gal 2:10 further indicates that the collection was known to the Galatians and that it was still under way. Confirmation of this last statement may be found in the other letters. We shall now examine the information on the collection in the Corinthian correspondence and Romans, the only other letters mentioning the collection.

1. The first reference to the collection is 1 Cor 16:1ff. The Corinthians here ask Paul *how* the collection should occur. Their knowledge of the collection itself is clearly presupposed. The nature of their questions shows, however, that they had learned of the collection only recently.

2. Since 1 Cor 16:1 refers to the collection among the Galatians, we may ask whether the chronological place of Galatians can be determined. The following points speak for the chronological priority of 1 Corinthians over Galatians:

a. Rom 15:26 does not mention the Galatians as participants in the collection; it thus seems likely that the collection had fallen through in Galatia. (If at some point the collection did fall through in Galatia, then, at any later time, Paul would hardly have mentioned the churches in Galatia as a paradigm for the organization of the collection [that is to say, in 1 Cor 16:1].)

b. If Galatians had been written before 1 Corinthians one would have to assume that Paul, through his letter, succeeded in winning back the Galatian communities. Otherwise 1 Cor 16:1 would not make sense. However, in this case the absence of a reference to the Galatian churches in Rom 15:26 is difficult to explain. In addition, the lack of any Pauline tradition in Galatia in the postapostolic period contradicts the assumption that Paul was able to win back the communities.

c. The noticeable similarity of Galatians to Romans is best explained if Galatians was written shortly before Romans.

d. Galatians shares a number of stylistic and linguistic features with 2 Corinthians 10-12.[11]

Thus, virtually everything speaks for the chronological priority of 1 Corinthians to Galatians.

---

[11]See U. Borse, *Der Standort des Galaterbriefes,* BBB 41 (Cologne/Bonn: Hanstein, 1972), pp. 84ff.

3. The remarks in 2 Corinthians 8-9 allow us to assume that the Macedonia collection began around the same time as the Corinthian collection (cf. 2 Cor 8:1-4; 9:2).

C. Topographical and Chronological References in the Passages Concerning the Collection. 1. From the predominance of the passover motif in 1 Corinthians (5:7; 10:1ff.; 11:23ff.; 15:23), it is most likely that Paul wrote 1 Corinthians in the spring. Due to the references to the past in 1 Cor 15:32 and due to the time which must be allowed for the organization of the collection from Ephesus (the most probable location for the composition of 1 Corinthians), Paul probably spent at least one winter in Ephesus.

2. Gal 4:13 and the reference to Galatia in 1 Cor 16:1 make it probable that Paul had been in Galatia for a second visit. This, however, is not strictly provable.

3. The Corinthian correspondence allows us to follow the apostle as he travels, first, to Corinth for a short visit, second, back to Ephesus, and, third, again to Corinth by way of Troas and Macedonia. The numerous events that followed upon the composition of 1 Corinthians and the phrase in 2 Cor 8:10, "what you began a year ago," seem to be sure indications that a winter had elapsed between the beginning of the collection and the composition of 2 Cor 8. Paul stayed the next winter in Macedonia, travelled to Corinth in the spring, and remained through the following winter in Corinth, where he wrote Romans.

The entire period under consideration thus covered three to four years.

D. The Initial Mission in Macedonia and Greece. From 1 Cor 4:18 and the reference to a letter to the Corinthians prior to 1 Corinthians (1 Cor 5:9) it is most probable that, when Paul composed 1 Corinthians, he had not been in Corinth for a long time. Other passages also hint that the founding of the Corinthian congregation had not occurred in the recent past:

1. Apollo's stay in Corinth (1 Cor 3:6), and his later presence in Ephesus with Paul (1 Cor 16:12);

2. the manifold problems that had arisen in Corinth;

3. the fact that "many" have fallen asleep since Paul's last visit (1 Cor 11:30);

4. the announcement of a *sudden* arrival (1 Cor 4:19) and the reasons proffered for the delay (1 Cor 16:8).

whole[12] though this does not fit in with the standard view that Paul preached in Greece only after the conference. 1 Thess 2:2; 3:14 then supply the stations of Paul's first mission: Philippi, Thessalonica, Athens, Corinth.

The combination of all these facts renders it certain that Paul operated a mission in Greece *before* the Jerusalem Conference.

The Arrangement of the Traditions of Acts
into the Framework Developed Solely on the Basis of the Letters

We may now turn back to Acts to consider how the information there fits in with the chronology developed solely on the basis of the letters. We shall limit ourselves to a few passages which are directly related to the chronology constructed above.

A. Riddle of Acts 18:22. By its very brevity, *Acts 18:22* forms a riddle for exegetes. The absence of a direct reference to Jerusalem is a sure sign that we are dealing with a tradition, and not redaction, for Luke usually expresses special interest for trips to Jerusalem (cf. especially 11:27ff., which is a Lukan composition). The brevity of the report in 18:18-22 thus seems to be due to Luke's possession of an itinerary with the following stations: Corinth, Ephesus, Caesarea, Jerusalem, Antioch, Galatia, and Phrygia. While the work of the redactor Luke is perspicuous in the reports on Paul's earlier trips to Jerusalem, the unaffected simplicity of 18:22 points towards its traditional nature: Luke demonstrates no particular interest in this visit. Further, since the list of stations carries on after Jerusalem, it is extremely improbable that 18:22 is a doublet of 21:15 (the last visit).

We may therefore ask if 18:22 originally represented Paul's second visit to Jerusalem and if the visits postulated by Luke in 11:27-30 are not just Lukan creations formulated parallel to this visit. The linguistic evidence of these latter two passages points unmistakably to the hand of the redactor Luke, though it is also clear that Luke is employing some traditional material here: 11:27 mentions Barnabas together with Paul and also a collection; 15:1-4 also mentions Barnabas alongside Paul. There are, however, major differences between Acts 15:1-4, and Paul's own statements:

---

[12]Cf. M. Jack Suggs, "Concerning the Date of Paul's Macedonian Ministry," *NovT* 4 (1960): 60-68; Luedemann, *Paulus, der Heidenapostel*, pp. 141-47.

1. Acts fails to mention that Paul travelled to Jerusalem due to a revelation.

2. Acts overlooks Titus, an important figure for Paul; and

3. Paul himself does not state that he traveled to Jerusalem from Antioch.

These differences reveal a certain tendency behind Luke's report. Further, Luke has a particular reason for placing the conference in 15:1-29. For him, the conference represents the pivotal point marking the transition from the mission of Jerusalem and Antioch to Paul's world mission. After the continuity of salvation history between the earliest church and Paul has been established, Paul steps to the center stage; James, Peter, and the representative of the Antiochene congregation, Barnabas, are left to one side and (except for James: Acts 21) never reappear in Acts. Here we see Luke developing the appropriate chronology on the basis of proper dogma: For him, Paul's world mission *cannot* have occurred before it was legitimated at the Jerusalem Conference. Since Acts 11:27-30 is also Luke's work,[13] we conclude that 18:22 must represent Paul's second visit to Jerusalem.

This last statement receives verification from the letters, for the stations listed by Luke after 15:1-29 agree with those mentioned by Paul as his stops before the conference:

Acts: Antioch, Syria, Cilicia, Derbe, Lystra, Phrygia, Galatia, Philippi, Thessalonica, Athens, Corinth;

Paul: Syria, Cilicia, Philippi, Thessalonica, Athens, Corinth.

The additional stops listed in Acts derive, for the most part, from the redactor:

1. The visit to Antioch in 15:30-41 functions as the transition to Paul's independent mission (and also to the new source regarding this mission [15:40-41]). This passage does, however, reflect the historical dissolution of Paul's relations with Antioch.

2. The visit to Derbe and Lystra (16:1-5) serves Luke (a) to introduce Timothy (note the unhistorical reference to the circumcision of Timothy), and (b) to represent the continuity of the church (the transmission of the apostolic decree to the communities that were founded before the conference).

---

[13]For the redactional nature of Acts 11:27ff, see G. Strecker, "Die sogenannte zweite Jerusalemreise des Paulus (Acts 11, 27-30)," *Eschaton und Historie* (Göttingen: Vandenhoeck & Ruprecht, 1979), pp. 132-41.

3. The trip through Phrygia and Galatia (16:6-8) is a strange account of a nonmissionary journey. Verse 6 reflects the difficulties Paul encountered in Asia (cf. 1 Cor 15:32; 2 Cor 1:8). When Luke writes that "the Spirit of Jesus did not allow them" to go into Mysia and Bithynia, he is consciously creating a contrast to the European mission (cf. vs. 9). These strange notes do seem to indicate, however, that Luke is working here with certain traditions, the nature of which can no longer be precisely determined.

In summary, the correspondence of the stops in Acts 16-18 with those reconstructed from Paul's letters for the period between the first and second visits to Jerusalem provides a strong argument for 18:22 as the original chronological location of the second visit. Further support for this view is found in the stations mentioned after 18:22, for they correspond exactly with those which are reflected in the letters of Paul: Antioch, Galatia, Phrygia, Ephesus, Macedonia, Greece.

B. The Traditions in Acts 18:1-17. We suggested above that Luke combines all information about a given locality into one report. Now we want to ask whether Luke did this in his report on Corinth. Acts 18:1-17 contains three groups of traditions:

1. vss. 2-3: Paul meets Aquila and Priscilla in Corinth;
2. vss. 5-8: Paul's mission in Corinth; and
3. vss. 12-17: the Gallio episode.

From the Gallio inscription we know that Gallio held office in A.D. 51-52. The date of the expulsion of Jews from Rome is usually set in A.D. 49. This date rests, however, on the information supplied by Orosius (in A.D. 417-418). Now, Dio Cassius reports of an imperial command regarding the Jews in the year A.D. 41,[14] and the wording of the passage seems to indicate that Dio Cassius might be using Suetonius[15] as a source and, at the same time, correcting him;[16] it is also possible, however, that both reports rest on a common source. The historical kernel of these reports is the following: in the year A.D. 41, Claudius issued a decree regarding the Jews; it pertained to the disturbances that had arisen in a synagogue and had involved Chrestus; the

---

[14]Dio Cassius 60.6.6. The chronological report on 41 A.D. begins in 60.3. For more on this see Luedemann, *Paulus, der Heidenapostel*, p. 185, fn. 66.

[15]Suetonius *De Vita Caesarum, Claudius* 25.

[16]I am referring to Dio Cassius's denial that Claudius expelled (all) the Jews.

decree entailed the expulsion of those Jews who had been directly involved in the disturbances. One may, therefore, conclude that the tradition regarding Aquila and Priscilla could well derive from Paul's first visit to Corinth in about the year A.D. 41. This date fits in well with the chronology developed solely on the basis of the letters. Also, since 1 Cor 1:14 mentions Crispus, the second group of traditions indicated above (vss. 5-8), with its reference to Crispus in vs. 8, also derives from the first visit to Corinth. Further confirmation of this view is found in the allusion to the arrival of Silas and Timothy from Macedonia (vs. 5), for this corresponds exactly with 1 Thess 3:6 and 2 Cor 1:19. With the date of the first visit to Corinth set, it is readily apparent that Paul's last visit to Corinth could well have occurred during Gallio's tenure of office in A.D. 51-52 (though it is also possible that Paul's visit to Corinth in this year was the second, short visit).

Chronological Table

The above considerations allow us to reconstruct the following rough chronology:[17]

A.D. 27/30	The crucifixion of Jesus
30/33	Conversion of Paul in or near Damascus; stay in Arabia; return to Damascus
33/36	Paul's first visit to Jerusalem
34/37	Journey to Syria and Cilicia
	Mission there and in South Galatia together with Barnabas under the auspices of the Antiochene mission
From circa 36/39	Independent Pauline mission in Europe
41	The decree of Claudius regarding the Jews
Circa 41	Paul in Corinth: 1 THESSALONIANS
Before or after the mission in Greece	Founding of the Galatian congregations due to sickness; Incident in Antioch, which was perhaps the direct cause for:

[17]The two sets of dates in the following table arise from consideration of two possible dates for the crucifixion of Jesus.

47/50	The second visit to Jerusalem: the Jerusalem Conference, followed by the journey to the Pauline congregations for the organization of the collection
Summer 48/51	Paul in Galatia
Fall 48/51-spring 50/53	Paul in Ephesus
Fall 48/51	Sending of Timothy to Macedonia and Corinth; the previous letter to the Corinthians with instructions about the collection (or, the instructions were sent per messenger)
Winter 48-49/51-52	Timothy in Macedonia
Spring 49/52	Letter of the Corinthians with questions regarding the collection (or else, the questions were delivered orally)
Circa Easter 49/52	1 CORINTHIANS
Summer 49/52	After bad news about Corinth by Timothy, short visit to Corinth; precipitate return to Ephesus; letter of tears; sending of Titus to Corinth
Winter 49/50-52/53	Paul in danger of his life (imprisonment in Ephesus?)
Spring 50/53	Paul's journey with Timothy from Ephesus to Troas; further journey to Macedonia
Summer 50/53	Arrival of Titus in Macedonia from Corinth; bad news from Galatia; composition of 2 CORINTHIANS 1-9 2 CORINTHIANS 10-13/GALATIANS; sending of Titus to Corinth to deliver 2 Corinthians and to complete the collection
Winter 50/51-53/54	Paul in Macedonia; completion of the collection there
51/52	Gallio as proconsul of Achaia
Spring/summer 51/54	Journey of Paul with Macedonian escorts to Corinth; completion of the collection there
Winter 51/52-54/55	Paul in Corinth: ROMANS
Spring 52/55	Journey to Jerusalem in order to deliver the collection.

The Eschatological Statements in 1 Thess 4:13ff.
and 1 Cor 15:5ff. as Confirmation of
Paul's Early Macedonian Mission[18]

In our chronological reconstruction, we began with an analysis of the letters alone and turned only later to Acts to evaluate its traditions. It was our conscious intention to employ only external data in the letters of Paul and an external criterion, the collection, in the determination of this chronology and to leave to one side all arguments based on internal criteria. Now we want to ask if we can anchor our chronology through another external criterion: Paul's eschatological statements. We may employ these statements as an external criterion because we know that the earliest Christians laid down specific termini ante quem for the parousia: first it was held that the Christians would continue in life until the parousia (Matt 10:23); later this hope was modified to the belief that at least the majority of the first generation Christians would survive until the end (Mark 13:30); at a still later stage, it was held that at least *some* of the first generation would still be alive at the time of the parousia (Mark 9:1; John 21:23). We may thus say that whenever a text presupposes that Christians must not die before the Parousia, it most likely derives from the period that followed directly upon the death and resurrection of Jesus; a text that limits the number of those not to die or that presupposes the death of all should be considered as belonging chronologically either at the end of the first generation (A.D. 47-57) or to a later generation. This is thus an external criterion. Now Paul reflects on the issue of the death of Christians and on the date of the end in two passages: 1 Thess 4:13ff. and 1 Cor 15:5ff. Let us consider these passages.

A. In 1 Thess 4:13-18 we find the Thessalonians concerned because some Christians there have died; they are incertain what will become of these Christians. Indeed, their entire Christian hope has been threatened by these deaths (vs. 14). Since Paul indicates, with the phrase οὐ θέλομεν δὲ ὑμᾶς ἀγνοεῖν (vs. 13), that he is about to teach the Thessalonians something new, it seems most probable that the Thessalonians had not previously (or, at least, not adequately) been instructed about

---

[18]For the detailed arguments behind the following analysis, see Luedemann, *Paulus, der Heidenapostel*, pp. 220-71; idem, "The Hope of the Early Paul: From the Foundation-Preaching at Thessalonike to 1 Cor. 15:51-57," *Perspectives in Religious Studies* 7:3 (1980): 195-201.

the resurrection of dead Christians at the time of the parousia. Paul corrects this situation by affirming the resurrection of dead Christians at the time of the parousia (vs. 16); Paul emphasizes that "we" the living will not precede the dead and that the dead will suffer no disadvantage. It is, however, the clear presupposition of vs. 15 that the majority of Christians would still be alive at the time of the parousia ("*we* who are alive").

These observations lead us to the conclusion that Paul did not deal with the resurrection of Christians during his initial mission in Thessalonica. Even at the time of the composition of 1 Thessalonians, Paul viewed the death of Christians as the exception rather than the rule. When the criterion stated above is applied, the importance of these observations for the chronology of Paul is apparent: The initial mission in Thessalonica must have taken place, at the latest, at the end of the 30s; the composition of 1 Thessalonians cannot have been much later. Thus, this provides a strong confirmation of our chronology based on an early Macedonian mission.

B. In considering 1 Cor 15:51-58, we want to ask primarily about the relationship of the number of the Christians that are presupposed to be still alive at the end to the number that are presupposed to have died. We shall also take a short look at the conception of the resurrection expressed here.

First, it is apparent in this passage that, compared with 1 Thess 4:13-18, the proportion of living to dead is inversed. It is now held that those who live on until the parousia are the exception rather than the rule: "We shall not *all* sleep, but we shall all be changed" (vs. 51b). That this is the correct reading of this statement is confirmed by other passages in 1 Corinthians: 11:30 ("*many* have fallen asleep"); 6:14 (death is presupposed as normal); 15:6 (the admission that *some* of the 500 have died); 15:18 (Paul speaks of "those who have fallen asleep in Christ" as a matter of course).

Second, this passage refers to a transformation which will take place at the end (vss. 51, 53) whereas 1 Thess 4:13-18 does not contain the vaguest hint of such an occurrence. We know that the Corinthians wrote to Paul and asked him about the nature of the resurrection body (1 Cor 15:35). Paul answers this question with a christological argument about the nature of this body (vss. 45, 47, 48, 49). The point that we want to emphasize is that these statements reflect a later stage in Paul's thought about the events of the eschaton: Contra the situation

pictured in 1 Thessalonians, the resurrection of Christians has now become an autonomous theme in Paul's theology. It is clear that considerable time has elapsed since the composition of 1 Thessalonians.

C. We may now indicate the results arising from these observations: The situation of 1 Corinthians, which presupposes that the Christians who have died before the time of the parousia will outnumber those who will still be alive, is best explained if 1 Corinthians was written at the end of the first Christian generation, i.e., circa A.D. 50; the situation pictured in 1 Thessalonians reflects a date much earlier, well within the first generation. Further, the differences of imagery in 1 Thessalonians and 1 Corinthians (the introduction of the notion of a transformation) is also best explained if a period of eight or eleven years separated the composition of these two letters. An examination of Paul's eschatological statements thus offers strong confirmation of the central thesis of the chronology[19] of Paul developed in the preceding part of this paper.

The consequences of the above chronology for the study of Paul's thought should be clear: We may now deal with the question of the early Paul on the basis of 1 Thessalonians and may pursue the question of the development of Paul's thought by comparing 1 Thessalonians with the later letters.

---

[19]Cf. now the adoption of this chronology by K. Rudolph, *Die Gnosis Wesen und Geschichte einer spätantiken Religion*, 2nd ed. (Göttingen: Vandenhoeck & Ruprecht, 1980), pp. 322, 416; H. H. Schade, *Apokalyptische Christologie bei Paulus* (Göttingen: Vandenhoeck & Ruprecht, 1981), pp. 173-75, 290-92.

SEMINAR DIALOGUE WITH ROBERT JEWETT AND GERD LUEDEMANN

Moderator: With this seminar, we arrive at the part of the program that has to do with John Knox. The title I gave this section is "*Chapters in a Life of Paul* after Thirty Years." What we hope to do is not only to honor John Knox, but also to see whether we can delineate some options or even agreements on the basis of which further work can be accomplished. That is, it's not simply a matter of looking back to what has been published and whether we agree with this point or that point. In particular, it is not a pair of reviews of the two major works that have just been published by our two speakers. That's part of it, but that's not the end of it. We need to keep before us the question of where do we go next and on what basis. In case you have not seen them here is Bob Jewett's *A Chronology of Paul's Life* in an eye-catching cover, Fortress Press; and Gerd Luedemann's *Paul the Apostle to the Gentiles,* volume 1, *Studies in Chronology,* Vandehoeck and Ruprecht.

We begin with thanks to our two paper writers. Each of them is involved in publishing obligations this fall, and it took a separate set of arm twistings on my part in order to obtain what you have before you, and the promise of amplification of that material before all of this material goes to publication in the symposium volume. The two speakers are going to emphasize the main points of their own papers, and introduce, if they wish, topics which they want treated in the later discussion. We begin, then, with Bob Jewett.

Jewett: Thank you, John. It's a real pleasure for me to take part in this consultation, particularly in view of the fact that my own work is so heavily indebted in the area of chronology to the contribution of John Knox. In order to work with the fifteen minute limit, and offer something that those of you who have not had a chance to read the paper would find useful, I would like to rapidly read several sections of the paper, expand several sections where additional reviews have come to light, and then concentrate in the end on the major methodological questions that I think might be pursued. For those of you who have a copy and wish to follow, I'm going to start the rapid reading on page 3 toward the bottom, in which I describe—about five lines up—the earlier fate of the chronology monograph: it was turned down by European and American monograph series for being audacious, ridiculously precise, and too disrespectful of the consensus of great scholars.

The intense hostility of the written evaluations of the chronology manuscript led me to the conclusion that the time was unripe to experiment very seriously with the Knox hypothesis. But I continued to gather materials and to reflect on the chronology question. I still have not been able to come to a satisfactory answer as to why a contemptible hypothesis can suddenly become discussable after the passage of a dozen years. But at least part of the answer is that gradual acceptance of Knox's analysis has emerged, at least on this side of the Atlantic. The conviction that he shared with Riddle and others in the Chicago school concerning the precedence that should be given to the primary evidence in the Pauline letters came to be widely accepted among younger scholars. Hurd's studies, and in particular his definitive article in the *IDB,* helped to form a critical consensus about the framework of dates and events visible in the letters. Full-length chronologies by Gunther and Suhl gave heed to Knox's methodological breakthrough. And the increasing acceptance of redaction insights about Luke/Acts sustained Knox's suspicion about the five-Jerusalem-journey framework. All this prepared the way for a reconstruction of the issue on Knox's grounds. The crucial requirement in my view was to discredit the compromise chronologies, for only when they were shown to be untenable would the question become vital. And this is in fact what has occurred in the last two years. The double blow in favor of the Knox approach came with the publication of monographs by Gerd and myself. And I think it is fair to say that neither of

them would have made as much impact without the other. Coming at the issues from differing starting points and using differing historical methods, we came to agreement on three basic matters. One, the compromise chronologies are untenable and Knox has shown the reason why. Two, Knox is correct in identifying the journey of Acts 18:22 with the apostolic conference described in Galatians 2, which means that the conference followed rather than preceded the so-called second missionary journey. And three, there is a need to go beyond *Chapters in a Life of Paul* by assembling a more adequate data base from Acts as well as the epistles and this implies a willingness to discuss the incidental details as potentially useful.

It is my view that the agreement on these basic issues is far more significant than the differences between Luedemann and myself in adapting the Knox hypothesis. With a couple of provisos, Cope recently concluded, "It may not be too strong to assert that this study has at last put Pauline chronology on a sound footing." I would prefer to argue that the evolution of Knox's hypothesis in Luedemann's work and mine offers such a footing, because it allows testability. Whereas the compromise chronologies resisted refinement, their internal tensions causing infinite variations that defied disconfirmation, there is now a possibility of more or less objective evaluation. I wouldn't want to claim that either of our chronologies is definitive, but the basis is there now, I think, to reach a more definitive answer. It now makes sense to argue over the individual historical details that go into the data base, because the possibility of progress is at hand. And if we've done no more than offer this kind of sound footing, I suspect that Gerd and I would both be content.

The debate about our efforts to adapt the Knox hypothesis is not yet far enough along to allow a secure assessment. I had hoped to include a response to Luedemann's review and of course that would be appropriate to take into account at a later time. The four reviews of my book that have already appeared may lead to an overly optimistic assessment. And, by the way, last night as I unpacked some more boxes in the place I am moving into, I found, belatedly, six additional reviews and I'd like to incorporate them at this point. But taking these reviews at face value, in fact, would lead to the impression that the Knox hypothesis is gaining decisive headway. Holst sketches my argument and method mentioning Barnikol and Knox as important precedents; he adds that the book can help people to "understand the question

better." Something of the same tone is struck, rather surprisingly in my view, by Margaret Thrall in her review in the *Expository Times* which says the investigation is a fascinating piece of detective work in itself and a useful contribution to Pauline studies in general. Montague's review in *CBQ* describes the hypothesis in detail, notes its dependence on Knox, and concludes that it is a convincing and well-argued case. Even more significant an indication of the way the wind is blowing is his conclusion that the issue cannot be denied by resorting to traditional chronologies. Something of the same note perhaps has been struck by N. T. Wright in the *Churchmans* who notes that the chronology I offer is, and I quote him here, "substantially an American solution, that of Knox, with several modifications which Jewett reaches after a fascinating piece of detective work that cannot fail to provoke both admiration and disagreement." But he goes on to talk about the suspicions my work arouses and he says with very doubtful countenance, no doubt, the work bears "the marks of its Tübingen origins." Apparently I studied under F. C. Baur or something. "A clear-headed mastery of detail alone will make it a standard starting point for future discussions of apostolic chronology," he concludes. And the review that I found last night by Henry Wansborough, whom I also don't know, writing in the *Tablet* in Great Britain, notes some of the advantages of this hypothesis, picks up the John Knox background, noting that (here I read from his review) "the author adopts the solution of Barnikol and Knox." He talks about some of the advantages of the hypothesis but says that he feels that Benoit's chronology offers just as much advantage.

Lamar Cope in the *ATR* describes the consensus concerning Knox's insistence on the primary value of the letters and expresses surprise that the interlocking of various kinds of chronological data is so exact. Although he feels that some of the dates are too precise and some of the external data rests upon questionable tradition, the application of the idea of probability leads to a positive result. He writes, "especially when there is a correlation between all three types of evidence, the probability that the dating is accurate is extremely high."

I passed over the review by Barry Crawford, which appeared in the *JAAR,* which explicitly lays out the use of the deductive experimental method describing the method in some detail and then pointing out, by the way, some of the embarrassing typos in the book; and some of the mistakes, by the way, in the printed version of the book on pages 97

and 98, are in fact, the unforgivable sin for chronologists, namely to get my own dates fouled up which I did manage to do. But he concludes that it is only when something is made specific enough to be falsifiable, that it can ever be shown to be true, showing, I think, considerable sympathy for the experimental method. John Gibbs, in his cumulative review of several books, speaks in a positive way about the carefully constructed chronological interlock.

Caird is the best known chronologist who has commented on the book thus far. His review in the *JTS* provides positive assessment but raises two major questions. "This hypothesis is very carefully worked out and may well be correct. Like that of Knox, on which it is a vast improvement, it has the advantage of eliminating the 'silent years.' . . . Yet it is not so free of difficulty as Jewett believes." The first question relates to the Aretas datum, which he correctly perceives is the corner-stone of my hypothesis. Its correlation with the Pauline chronology, he insists, is entirely dependent on the Lukan framework and thus would be discredited if that framework is abandoned. I would retort that this is one of those instances where Luke happens to parallel the primary evidence of the epistles and thus does not have to be called into question.

I ought, I think, to point out the one really hostile review by Michael Green in *Church Times,* who argues that this is terrible research and the methodological problems turn "a learned and some-times sensitive and well-argued book into a very poor example of scholarship. This is a book whose thesis will prove unconvincing to those who know their way around New Testament chronology."

I think probably the methodological issues are the most significant to discuss: (a) the question of how to carry out the distinction between primary and secondary evidence, and (b) the question of how to adapt the experimental methods normally used in the social and natural sciences to historical problems. I have laid out some of the methodo-logical suggestions. And then on the final pages, I sort of sketch the major historical issues that arise from a consideration of Luedemann's and my books: number one, the dating of the Claudius edict; number two, the Aretas datum and how it is to be incorporated; number three, the date of the crucifixion; number four, the validity of the ascertain-able dates and time spans that Luedemann deletes; and then, number five, the question of conflict between Peter and Paul and its relation to the apostolic conference.

I would like to conclude with the final paragraph. I would like to close by insisting again that the points of disagreement between Luedemann and myself are far less significant than the common effort we have made, quite independently of each other, to sustain the Knox hypothesis and to turn the discussion of Pauline chronology away from the fruitless avenues of compromise hypotheses. Despite our differences we are allies in a common cause, and I can think of no one I would rather have sitting beside me than Gerd.

Luedemann: I think that all historical critical scholars have a common cause to do and it is in such a context that I have a common cause to do with Robert. Let me make some autobiographical remarks which are not in my paper, but they are in Bob's paper, and they are as interesting as his.

I came to this country in 1974-75 as a research assistant of W. D. Davies at Duke University. The first time I became acquainted with John Knox was when Davies warned me against the excessive skepticism of my friend John Knox. Well, it is very interesting when a British scholar calls somebody an excessive skeptic. So I read through Knox's books and articles and thought that he wasn't and that most Americans and Germans had not taken him seriously enough. And after returning to Germany, I started to write a chronology on the basis of John Knox. I assume that most of you have read this paper and I cannot read all of it to you. Let me just read the introduction which, as you will see, has a slightly different picture of John Knox than Bob offered, and that, I think, accounts for our remaining differences.

Modern research into the New Testament proceeds from a few basic presuppositions—in Germany, for example, the modified two-source theory for the exegesis of the Synoptics and the standard chronology for Paul and primitive Christianity up to the year A. D. 70. It is the task of historical research to draw such presuppositions into question whenever evidence to the contrary begins to emerge. In the following I shall present a critical examination of the standard opinion on the chronology of Paul. This examination will show that the time is right for a new proposal about the order of events in Paul's life. I would indicate first, however, that neither my criticism nor my positive presentation is absolutely novel. I am especially indebted to the work of John Knox and Riddle, in this order. What about Knox's methods? Knox proposed a methodology which acknowledges the vastly inferior value of Acts as a source for Paul's career compared with the apostle's

own letters. He holds that the barest hint in the epistles is of more worth than even the most explicit statement of Acts. Any statement in Acts which conflicts with the letters should thus be deemed in error. Acts merits full credibility only where the letters provide a supporting statement, never, however, where an assertion is not confirmed by the epistles. So that when Bob tries to show that he has presumed the Knox chronology, that's not precise. This has been said by some reviewers— that it is Bob who carries out Knox's program; but in view of this, it is not quite precise, because he starts with the sources and adopts to a certain extent the chronological statements of Acts. So that is what John Knox would not do because of his principle. Knox attaches particular suspicion to the statements in Acts which serve a special interest or purpose of the author. It is Knox's opinion that rigorous employment of these methods can yield a coherent outline of Paul's apostolic career. The two key items in Knox's chronology are, first, a date for the Jerusalem Conference much later in Paul's career than where Acts places it, and secondly, a date for this conference just a few years before Paul's final and third visit to Jerusalem. I have then criticized the standard view of scholars who give preference to the dates of Paul's letters but who nevertheless harmonize a little bit and end up with the outline of Acts. That means they hold with Acts that Paul's missionary enterprise in Greece started after the conference. So, though criticizing Acts, they nevertheless adopt this scheme.

I have raised some critical objections to such a view. I think that on the basis of the Pauline letters it cannot be established that Paul was a delegate of Antioch or junior partner of Barnabas. I also questioned the accepted date for the expulsion of the Jews from Rome (A.D. 49). I do not think this date can be substantiated by the sources. The one source doesn't date it, Suetonius, and the other source, Dio Cassius, who I think has a literary relationship to Suetonius, dates it explicitly in the first year of Claudius. So I have raised some objections to the method and unfortunately, I did not discuss the more conservative views of British and other scholars. I only mention Sir William Ramsay. My sole partner was the semicritical chronology of German scholarship. That does not mean that I haven't read Ramsay. So the task and the method was then contrary or different from what Bob does. First to establish the chronology on the sole basis of the epistles. That's my chapter two.

Then in chapter three I turn to the evidence of Acts to see whether

information of Acts fits in with this chronology. So I think these two steps have to be distinguished from each other. Otherwise, once you combine Acts with Paul, then your method is not critical enough. So I started, of course, with the outline Paul gives in Galatians 1 and 2 about his life: the three years, the fourteen years, and the places and dates where he has been. I left the absolutes—the question of the absolute dates—open and the main exegesis was then, of course, the exegesis of the apostolic conference. I asked whether we can develop a criterion which helps us to establish a sequence of the letters, a relative sequence of the letters. And this criterion I have found in the agreement made at the conference, the agreement to organize a collection in the Pauline communities, "which very thing I was eager to carry out." This sequence—which had been done already by Buck in his article, "The Collection for the Saints"—led me to a chronology for the three or four years after the conference. And I combined this question of the sequence with chronological and topographical questions.

The result was that, apart from Philippians and 1 Thessalonians, all the other authentic Pauline letters could be dated, or could be put in a certain order and so that gives room for three or four years after the conference. Whereas 1 Thessalonians, I think, has to be dated before the conference because of Philippians 4:15, which is a reference to the early Macedonian mission. There are other reasons why I think that Paul was in Greece before the conference. Let me just tell you one counter-argument that I do not accept: that because Paul doesn't say that he was there, he wasn't there. Some people argue that because Paul says, "then I went to Syria and Cilicia," that excludes an early Macedonian mission. I don't think that is a substantial counter-argument. So I end up with the relative chronology. And then I come to the evidence of Acts and the only absolute date which I accept is the date for the crucifixion of Jesus, 30 or 27, and I just guess that the conversion of Paul must have happened around 32. From that I start and then try to fit the thirteen years, not fourteen years, and the two years into this scheme.

Now I go to Acts. I look at the absolute dates, find the date of the expulsion of the Jews from Rome in Acts 18 and the date for Gallio and realize that these dates have some importance or can be substantiated by the chronology gained on the basis of the letters. So that's what I did. I reached, then, by looking at Acts, some absolute dates, but I

must emphasize that this just helped me to test the value of Acts. I do not claim, as Bob does, that I have settled the question whether Paul was in Macedonia in October or September. So I am not concerned with that. I am only concerned with probable dates.

The last question I had, or my contribution to the chronology, apart from working out and proving the Knox chronology, was then an exegesis of 1 Thessalonians 4:13. I asked the question, Are there any other criteria by which we can date letters or date beliefs? I began with early Christian expectation not to die while waiting for the parousia, and I thought that if we find a source in early Christianity which reflects this belief at the stage of the redaction, as 1 Thessalonians does, then it cannot have been written twenty or twenty-five years after the resurrection of Jesus. And on the other hand, we find in 1 Corinthians 15:51 a passage which reflects many deaths—clearly a big difference from Paul's expectation in 1 Thessalonians. I concluded that there must be more than one or two years between these letters.

All in all, I hope that I have made some suggestions about Paul's chronology and have at least made a possible proposal about an early date of Paul's Macedonian ministry which, of course, has immediate hermeneutical and theological consequences. That would mean that for the first time, the question of the development of Paul's thought can be asked; in that case, we would have one letter from the first decade of Paul's life and theology, whereas the old attempts by Dodd had to work with the fact that all the letters they dealt with were written within five or six years. This question of development will be dealt with in volume three of my *Paul*; volume two will deal with the opponents of Paul. It is at the press right now.

Hurd: I hope that those in the back can hear. If you can't, just stick your hand up so I can see you. I can't keep asking you, of course, but I am concerned that you are able to follow what is going on. I would like to have from members of the panel topics which they would like to see discussed. I will give you a rundown of the four areas that I am proposing.

(1) The first is simply the question of method, that is, to reflect on Knox's basic insight that primary sources and secondary sources are to be dealt with in a different manner. Now both our papers, both the books refer to this insight, build on this insight. This is obviously a topic which we need to discuss.

(2) Then I would like to move to the question of what kind of a chronology it is that we are looking for when we talk about Pauline chronology. There are really two different points of view. By chronology one can mean the absolute dates in Paul's life—which appear for the most part in Acts. Or alternatively one can talk about the relative sequence of events in Paul's career. This second perspective involves, of course, reconstructing the order in which the letters were written and the sequence of the various events which impinged on his ministry.

(3) Next I would like the Seminar to look at the sort of evidence we might expect to find in the letters. This question connects with the area that Gerd opened up at the end of his paper: the possibility that in addition to explicit references by Paul to external events in his career there may also be implicit chronological evidence concerning letter sequence, laspe of time, and changes in his thought in reaction to events in his career.

(4) Finally we should discuss the source criticism of Acts. At this point we get to Acts itself as a document in relation to the Pauline chronology.

Now if there are other areas under which you want to subscribe yourself that is fine. But what I think we might do is simply begin with methodology and run the rest of this first hour, then have a break which would allow me to collect the bits and pieces, and plan for the other three areas in the second hour. The thesis which I am laying before you is not stated as such by Knox; it is something that seems to me to be implied. For our discussion Knox's work serves more to lay out the questions rather than to provide the final answers. The value of his book, it seems to me, lies more in the delineation of the problem than the specific set of answers that he gave to the problem. Now to put the matter in as black and white a way as possible, I'd say the distinction between Acts as a secondary source and Paul's letters as primary sources is a qualitative not a quantitative difference.

Do you want to begin by reflecting as to whether that seems to you to embody what Knox is getting at or is he saying something different? Then we can get to the question of whether you agree with it or not.

Wilson: Just a point of clarification for me: I haven't had a chance yet to read Gerd's book, but I have read Bob's book. On page 11 Bob's paper (p. 000 above) seems to me to imply that Gerd has an opinion of the validity of Acts, the chronology of which he is in fact denying by his

own statement—the quotation which you have here—that when redactional cleansing has occurred, the details of Acts can stand as a primary source. In Gerd's own outline here, he seems to me to be saying that he will only use Acts where it is confirmed by something in the epistles and he will not go beyond that, thereby following what he understands to be Knox's principle. By reverse, if I might turn to Bob, the way you are wording it here is to imply that you are more skeptical about Acts as a source than he is and yet at least on reading your book I find you to be not so skeptical about using data from Acts, especially data that are unconfirmed by anything else.

Jewett: I think Gerd needs to respond as to whether the claim made on page 11 is appropriate. Is that, in fact, a citation from your book? Is it wrongly cited? Have I misunderstood it, or what?

Luedemann: Let us first turn to page 5 (p. 275 above), where Bob says under point two, "Luedemann came to his conclusion about the independent Pauline mission to Greece prior to the apostolic conference on the basis of exegetical analyses of Acts and the letters." That is right and wrong at the same time. In chapter 2 I reach that conclusion and then in chapter 3 I go to Acts, from the letters to Acts, so the argument from Acts doesn't have as much force as the argument from the letters has. I think one has to watch this order. Acts can only be used on the basis of the letters so that my chronology breaks off with Paul's plan to go to Jerusalem. I do not speculate about Ananias and I cannot accept any dates there. For example, when we look only at Acts 5 at the confusion about Theudas, yes, it is the blunder that the author of Acts makes that excludes the possibility of using the Egyptian rebel or such things for the dating of Paul. Yes, that was my principle. Then what you quote on page 11 I say in chapter 3 of my book, page 203. I compare the evidence of Acts with the evidence of the letters and I claim there that the tradition which the author of Acts has used has almost as much value as the evidence of the letters. But you can reach this only in this order—letters, Acts.

Wilson: But it has equal value only because it is confirmed by the epistles in the first place?

Luedemann: Yes, but on the other hand, once the value is established, it allows some more conclusions.

Jewett: It seems to me that it is a question here of methodology and my preference is to develop an experimental framework that allows you to see, in fact, whether any of the details in Acts are usable. My belief is that none of the details in Acts can be independently confirmed. And that only by placing an experimental framework together which is primarily framed on evidence within the epistles, namely, a three-Jerusalem-journey framework as Knox has done it, and only through an experimental framework can you in fact determine whether a particular date fits in or not. So I would say that's a major difference between the two of us.

Luedemann: I don't want to talk too much, but I want to speak to it because this is an important point that divides the two chronologies. Bob starts with a chapter on the methodological use of sources and, for example, accepts Luke's talk about three months as good information. He uses that for the time spans as you can see on page 60 of his book. I look at my concordance and find now that the word "three" is a word which Luke likes and I dismiss that as redactional; I cannot use that. So that's a different procedure and there are other examples. For example, when Luke pairs the expression ἡμέραις ἐκείναις in Acts, I look again in my concordance under ἱκανός and see that it's typical in Luke and Acts, and I dismiss it. So I have a selected use of Acts. But that's a difference of method.

Hurd: Let me sharpen the distinction here—to get back to the thesis as I put it. The issue is whether or not you can take information from the letters and information from Acts simultaneously and lay them on the same table and shuffle them around and try to come up with a solution. That's to make, perhaps, a quantitative difference between Acts and the letters. One may give more weight to one than to the other or the same weight to one and the other. But what I suggested is that there is a qualitative distinction implicit in Knox's opening up of the problem, which means that you do not put the same information on the same table, but rather you first take the letters and squeeze all the information out—Gerd's chapter 2 perhaps—and then subsequently come back to that other historical source, namely, Acts. Now I don't want to get into the whole area of what can we believe in Acts versus what can we believe in the letters because that will take us forever. But it's this distinction, how do you go about using material from Acts and material from the letters, simultaneously or seriatim?

Luedemann: You see this method leads me to a very—for some people—strange exegesis of Acts 18, where my conclusion is that this chapter really reflects two different visits of Paul to Corinth and not one as the author of Acts has it. At first this sounds rather strange, but, on the other hand, it is not so strange. You see, Luke never talks about Corinth again; he just mentions it. From this I conclude, well, it may be that it was his habit to put the traditions together.

Baird: It seems that, in my judgment in hearing the papers, there is no doubt that one is a primary source and the other is a secondary source, and that a primary source takes priority over a secondary source. The issue seems to be, How does one use the secondary sources? And I don't see any of the chronologies in front of us that do not make some use of the secondary sources. Knox, for example, thinks that the Festus accession is very important to his argument for crowding of details at the end of a career. Gerd, if I understand him correctly, thinks that the edict of Claudius at 41 is extremely important, but we know about the edict of Claudius as important for Paul's career exclusively out of Acts. So the real question, I think, is how do we use that secondary source? Everybody seems to be using it. Bob seems to me to use his a little more heavily than Gerd does. I like his rationale, but I haven't read Gerd's book, only the paper. I like Bob's way of saying we have got to deal with it on the basis of sources and redaction. Admittedly, John, you say that we are not going to be able to solve that problem; I know we aren't, but it seems to me that that is a crucial issue.

Vardaman: I'm not so sure that we can say that the book of Acts is not also primary. You have a great deal of personal documentation in the book of Acts. Now, perhaps you can if you want to date the book of Acts very late, but it seems to me you have to presume and make some assumptions to say this. And my own feeling is that to take personal letters, epistles, theological encouragements, pastoral letters, and say we are going to assign them to the pedestal of authority as far as being authoritative, and taking a carefully documented work such as the book of Acts and say, now, we will not take this evidence seriously, or at least we will not take it on the same level of authority as the epistles, is itself a questionable type of approach.

Ellis: Can I supplement that? When we talk about primary source, secondary source, we have to ask, primary source for what? secondary source for what? And I think one reason that Jewett has taken a more

serious view of Acts and the weight of Acts at least, is that (if I remember in his book) he takes the author of the "we" sections to be the author of the book. Is that not correct? Whereas Knox's book, *Chapters in a Life of Paul*, came after his *Marcion and the New Testament*, where he concluded that Acts is a document that comes from about 150. So I think that these introduction questions are important for the way in which one weighs the two documents; even if you regard Acts as secondary, we have to say secondary in what sense? If it's a century away, that's different than saying that it's from a sometime companion of Paul. And to underscore what Vardaman has said, the nature of the letters is occasional, and the nature of Acts is (on the face of it) a writing which is attempting to give us some kind of a sequence in Paul's career. In Paul's letters apart from Galatians 1, I don't know that there is any place where that is the case.

Vardaman: I would just say simply that if you have pastoral letters and you try to find chronology in there, you are going to find personal names or encouragement or theological ideas that are bounced around. But the book of Acts is purportedly a historical document tracing the history of the church, giving specific names of individuals that are involved and these names, where they can be documented from Josephus, have simply shown themselves to be quite accurate. Now, you mentioned the Theudas problem; I don't think that the Theudas that is mentioned in Gamaliel's speech in Acts 5:36, 37 is the same Theudas by any stretch of the imagination that is mentioned as living under Cuspius Fadus in 45-46. Gamaliel simply has to come earlier than this period by any chronology that you want to find in the book of Acts or early Christian history. By another type of approach I have gotten some new material on this Theudas that is mentioned. Time would fail me to go into this in great detail, but this is why I can speak so very fully and so very strongly about this, that Theudas is one who lived in 12 B. C., was put to death by Quirinius in 11 B. C., and came also from Galilee. I won't carry this on more in detail, but to make an assumption that because you have the same name in Josephus, a Theudas who is also mentioned in the book of Acts, and say that these are *ipso facto* the same persons, it seems to me itself is not quite following a very sound procedure.

Hurd: I don't really think we can get very far today if the issue becomes, Shouldn't we be following Sir William M. Ramsay? Our agreed starting place is John Knox's book, *Chapters in a Life of Paul.* Now it may

be that you consider that Knox was wrongheaded, in which case it can be discussed elsewhere, but we haven't got time to decide whether or not he should have written that book. We are commenting on where the discussion which begins there and has been elaborated now in two longer works is going and can go. Now I am glad that Earle Ellis made the point over which I was too brief, namely, that you cannot decide what is a primary source until you also settle the question "for what?" Acts is of course a primary source if what you are interested in is the point of view of its author. Now you may have a view that the author is a highly creative writer or you may have the view that he is an extremely reliable, dedicated passer-on of tradition, but nevertheless the material flowed through his head and out his pen. That makes his work a primary source for the knowledge of the point of view of that writer but a secondary source for knowledge of information about Paul. Whereas Paul's letters come to us (to the extent that we agree that the words in our Greek testament are written by him and not significantly modified in transmission, without mediation, directly from his mind to ours. They are our primary source for Paul. Now again, one may have difference of opinion about how reliable Paul is. That is, it is perfectly possible for Paul to lie. The fact that he says something makes it a primary piece of evidence; whether one believes it to be historically true is another question that one goes on to. So primary and secondary as distinction is not a distinction between reliable and unreliable. There are many primary documents that are highly unreliable and many secondary documents like first-class history books which are very reliable. That's not the distinction we are talking about. The distinction that I am pointing you at, and I hope to keep you at, is a distinction between what goes from one mind directly to our mind—that is, primary—and what goes indirectly, that is, from the original events through another mind which arranges the material and then presents it to us—that is secondary. They are two different things.

Orchard: I would like to throw another bolt into the works. I don't believe that the passage in Galatians 2 has yet been properly understood. There is another interpretation, which in fact is being adopted by F. F. Bruce in his commentary on Galatians coming out, which ought to be noted and which has not been noted by commentaries. They don't understand what Paul meant.

Hurd: But is this to do with the distinction between primary and secondary? I have you down later on in the agenda for next hour on that issue, because that is important.

Gunther: To the extent that Luke was present with Paul he is certainly a primary source, so once you acknowledge that he is part of the "we," then he becomes primary. Just as primary as if two people go together somewhere they become fully aware of the events that transpired during that period. Now Luke is a secondary source when you are dealing with the life of Jesus if he wrote the book of Luke, and if you are talking about the first ten or twelve chapters of Acts. Now the "we" begins in 16:16 (or 11:28 according to the Western text), and if Luke were a native of Antioch as is often claimed, or of somewhere in the area of Greece, he was certainly privy to what was going on.

Hurd: The particular theory that Acts incorporates a document by an eyewitness of course does complicate the issue of what is primary and what is secondary. If Luke tells you what Paul thought, then of course he is secondary. If Luke tells you what the two of them did together, then he is a primary source.

Koester: I wonder, though, whether one should not say that Bob Jewett in his book has in a certain way overcome that problem, and that's at the same time a question to Gerd Luedemann, because Bob has essentially said it isn't that important, even if you have an eyewitness to an event. The court will still try out and say whether the pieces of evidence from that witness fit the general whole. If they can be fitted into the general whole it makes sense. In that respect even the primary source or witness could be subject to criticism. What Bob has done is to say that the final test lies in whether it is possible to put all the pieces of evidence from both Acts and Paul, where one could evaluate them equally, into one final framework that is possible and satisfies all information that we on critical grounds can accept as possibly reliable information. And here my question is whether we are not talking about something that is unnecessary when we try to make the distinction between primary and secondary beforehand. The second thing is to ask Gerd Luedemann, why, if you have established that as a method which you can use experimentally, why can you not go beyond Acts 18 and continue in the same way also with the data of Acts, particularly if you established some way in which earlier data of Acts can be harmonized

(in fact that I think Bob Jewett has tried to do) with what Paul is saying?

Luedemann: Before I answer the question let me make a comment. I think indeed that the question of whether the author of Luke was an eyewitness is a very important one. If he was an eyewitness then we would indeed have somebody who was present, and we would indeed have a primary source. The other question is whether the "we" points to a tradition, to a source of an eyewitness, and my opinion is that I regard the "we" as a stylistic device. If you read through Acts it doesn't make sense that suddenly with a "we," the new source begins, all the more since the vocabulary is identical with the rest of Acts. So that's my opinion about that. But I do think that this is a very important question which we tend to neglect. The other question is now what about the dates of Acts which fall outside of the realm which the Pauline letters cover?

Bob reaches the conclusion that the Festus-Felix date is 58. I reach the conclusion—or not yet the conclusion—but my chronology gained on the basis of the letters would favor a date of 55 which is equally possible. The study of the sources suggests both possibilities. So here we have an example of priority of methods. From my study of Paul I would be immediately skeptical of this possibility and for me this question of how to use Acts, that is, a tradition of Acts (we can talk only about the traditions) is an open one. The historian has to ask the question but I just want to avoid the seduction which is presently involved in Bob's work that we can gain some vantage point from which we can control Acts. That would spoil, I think, the purity of my method.

Hurd: Well, we have been going about an hour and we have discovered that on the thesis that I proposed there are those who think it's essential, those who think it should never have been put that way, and those who think it doesn't really matter and that one can get along anyhow, which is more or less what I expected. That covers the range of opinion I would think. If we could break for five minutes then I could have in writing from the panel items on which they would like to comment.

* * * * *

Hurd: Well, we got a bit of everything. We are not quite out of the

woods yet with respect to my first topic. I don't want to go on at great length, but I want to make one thing perhaps even clearer than I made it before. Namely, that what I am putting in front of you for discussion means that one deals with the letters on their own terms first of all and that is by no means a guarantee that all the questions are going to be answered. So it's no good saying, "What about this?" and "What about that?" that we find in Acts. "How will we ever know about it if we don't use Acts?" The question to ask first is, "What can we learn from Paul's letters taken all by themselves?" And that's exactly the way Knox puts it. Now Knox does actually slip back later get into the game of matching the visits to Jerusalem in the letters with those in Acts. But his initial question is the more important one: "What amount of information can we note simply from the letters?" Then having ascertained that as fully as possible, one takes up the book of Acts and asks, "Now, what do we make of this as a source of information?" And that's what is meant by the sequence primary followed by secondary. Professor Metzger would like to add a complication, a helpful complication.

Metzger: I would like to suggest that in addition to primary and secondary sources there may be also tertiary sources that ought to be looked at, though they contribute doubtless very little, but they might contribute a little something. First, the later editors of the Pauline epistles added at the ends of them notes that we know today as subscriptions. These are included in any edition of the King James Version. They are considerably later than the dates we are currently interested in, but how far are these retaining, and doubtless greatly modifying, earlier traditions is a question that perhaps, if we make a complete survey of sources, we ought to ask.

Secondly, and a little more in the realm of possibility of actually being tertiary materials, what about the *Acts of Paul* which a few scholars a century ago were thinking would contain some historical recollections about Paul and other materials, perhaps not so much chronological as biographical, in the life of Paul. My comment, then, is that in addition to looking at these really important things, for a full range survey of source material we ought to go beyond primary and secondary to tertiary and subsequent levels if we are going to do a fully *wissenshaftlich* piece of work.

Hurd: Yes, let's gather up all the fragments lest any be lost, but I am suggesting we keep them in different baskets for awhile. I think we

should move along. The second thesis that I proposed is as follows. The primary importance of Pauline chronology for Pauline studies is as a relative chronology of his ministry which means in practical terms, a relative chronology of his letters. As I said earlier there are really two ways in which one can talk about Pauline chronology. One can talk about datable events in the book of Acts that relate to Paul and by extension, datable events that relate to other persons as well. That's a whole set of problems in itself. And we can also talk about Pauline chronology as the attempt to deal with the primary sources on their own terms and there the problem comes down to the question of how can we understand the order in which the letters were written? To put it still more sharply, suppose that you had by divine intervention an absolute chronology of Paul's life signed, sealed, and guaranteed, what would you use it for? I suggest you would use it as a relative chronology on the basis of which to understand Paul's thought. Now, that distinction between two different kinds of chronology, it seems to me, is important to the next stage of our discussion. Bill Farmer has a question he would like to bring at this point.

Farmer: If I understood what was implied in something that Gerd Luedemann had to say about Bob's book, it is this, that there's a question as to when and in what manner any consideration of the absolute dates is to be taken up. And, as I understood Gerd, he felt that Bob brought these in earlier than he would feel was appropriate. First of all, I would like to know whether or not I understood the implication of his comment.

Luedemann: Yes, and the most famous example is Aretas. Bob says between 37 and 39 A. D. that he had control over Damascus. That is the cornerstone which can never be used as safe evidence.

Farmer: I understand that you would prefer to work with the letters and continue to try to infer as much information as you can from the letters before bringing in absolute dates.

Luedemann: Yes, I think that here the evidence for absolute dates is just ambiguous and cannot be used.

Farmer: My question therefore is whether we have not pinpointed an important issue. Bob, I would like to have you respond to this implied criticism.

Jewett: Well, it's essential in an experimental method to create a

neutral data base, and that is why I, so far as possible, try to ignore chronological implications when setting *termini a quo* and *ad quem*. I think part of the difficulty that we have had in ascertaining these dates and time spans in the past has been that we have asked too quickly if a given date can be fitted into a chronology. The pressure on the dates is due, in my view—and here I am acting as a Knox chronologist—to the internal pressures within the system itself, caused by the insertion of additional and extraneous Jerusalem journeys. Now, when one has created a data base that is more or less neutral, one still has not confirmed that any of the time spans is in fact usable. And so in an experimental system, one creates a series of dates and time spans and then starts experiments. And so the experimental method is why I have to urge that the time spans and date frames be established independently without reference to their chronological implications.

Farmer: But as a matter of procedure, do you agree or disagree that one should work with the letters as long as possible, inferring as much as you can about their chronology before bringing in the question of absolute dates?

Jewett: Well, yes. The framework of Paul's ministry must base itself on the letters, period. And none of the evidence from Acts can be allowed to insert itself there. That's why I follow the Knox hypothesis of a three-Jerusalem-journey framework, because those three journeys are in fact visible in the book of Acts. And at that point I think I am being loyal to the Knox legacy.

Luedemann: If I may comment on that. I agree to the three-visits pattern. But in criticism of my work Bob says in his book (p. 85), "None of these details derived from Acts bears decisive weight in and of itself, but the cumulative weight of discrepancies...." Here he is arguing that the cumulative weight of secondary materials can be used to dismiss chronological data from the primary sources. That separates us; I cannot concur.

Hurd: Perhaps Dr. Gunther would like to ask his question at this point?

Gunther: The basic problem as a historian is to determine the reliability and usefulness of the sources. Now there are two elements involved here. There's a primary versus secondary, and on the other hand, an implicit or explicit. To the extent that Acts often has explicit state-

ments, they have to be given greater value sometimes than a statement in Paul's letters which is ambivalent and open to half a dozen interpretations—if you will dig the commentaries out. And if you claim this one interpretation, a chronological interpretation of a certain statement in Paul's letters, as the one by which you exclude an explicit contrary statement in Acts, you are not being very historical in your method.

Sanders: I don't want to respond before the principal presenters; they want to respond to that. There are histories and then there are histories, and there is evidence to be derived and then there is evidence to be derived. Now if we suppose that Luke was as good a historian as Josephus, then we would suppose that if he wrote Acts a second time, the dates would be different and a lot of the events would be different. And furthermore, the motives would be different. And that is being a pretty good historian in the first century. I think that Acts has to be dealt with very carefully and precisely because the author did have the intention of presenting a chronological development running from Jerusalem to Rome. His first-century historical (not modern historiographical) intention is precisely what makes it difficult to use Acts. Although Paul's evidence on the number of trips to Jerusalem and other such things on which chronology is based does arise in a polemical context, it does not mean that the matters of fact which one may infer are wrong. On the contrary, as in the court case, one may take a testimony that is written for one purpose and employ it for another. That is, one may derive information from it and that information may be in fact more securely based than the information that would occur in a book such as Acts. I don't see that the so-called historical intention of Acts settles the question at all.

Hurd: I think we should move on now to a matter raised in both the papers but more perhaps in Gerd Luedemann's paper. The thesis: In Paul's letters evidence for relative dating can be found not only in Paul's explicit references to external circumstances of his ministry, but also in the reactive unfolding of his thoughts—development—and in the implications of individual letters as to sequence and lapse of time. Now, it is notable that at this point we are some distance beyond where Knox stopped. As I said earlier, he lays out the principle; he then goes back to dealing with visits of Paul to Jerusalem in the letters and in Acts; he doesn't follow through the implications that are in his original

program as to what can be discovered in the letters more than just simply the three-visits pattern. And then he ends his book by giving you a kind of biographical reflection on Paul, but that's not chronological; it's just what sort of things can we know about him on the basis of the letters alone.

Now, Steve Wilson wants to ask a question having to do with the way in which the letters are placed relative to one another.

Wilson: One way in which you can approach this is illustrated in Gerd Luedemann's paper where he used the development of thought as part of the evidence of chronology. And the question I had (which is to ask both of you for information) is, in the resulting chronology in Gerd's paper today and in Bob's book, one interesting feature is that Bob Jewett places all the epistles in a short time span of five to six years. In Gerd's projection that is doubled in fact and possibly even tripled. You have a span of something like ten to fourteen years. I wonder if both of them would like to give us their reflections on the effect this has upon interpreting the question of development in Paul's thought, as an implication of their chronological conclusions.

Jewett: I would be happy to speak to that point. First, a brief biographical statement. When I set about to try to explain the evolution of Paul's use of anthropological terms, I explored very extensively the developmental schemes. And I found that, first, the developmental schemes all contradict each other, and, second, the evidence as far as anthropological terms are concerned cannot be tallied because Paul's use of many of these terms seems so situational. I became, therefore, extremely skeptical about developmental schemes, and I must confess great skepticism on Gerd's hypothesis. I lay this out in chapter four in the book, particularly dealing with the Buck and Taylor book. Simply put, what is a theological advance for one scholar is a regression for the next; I find an element of subjectivity in these evolutionary schemes that is absolutely impossible for the chronologist to work with. Now, unfortunately, my chronology book does not contain the ten chapters originally intended to date the individual Pauline letters and what one has in my framework here—dates and time spans—are simply the result of what is going to be, in effect, volume two. I try to date the letters strictly on the basis of internal evidence about travels, numbers of visits to particular locales. I would prefer, therefore, to eliminate all developmental criteria from dating the letters. In my view, that puts the

cart before the horse. Once one decides the sequence the letters are in, then one can take up the question of the evolution of Paul's thought. And that to me is a very significant theological task, and I think we are going to find very interesting results. And as far as the anthropological terms are concerned—as I said earlier—I think we have a very creative thinker who adapts his thought and then moves back in many instances to terminology which has been his at an earlier time. You do not have a nineteenth-century pattern of gradual evolution and progress in Pauline theology.

Hurd: You wrote, of course, before my article which showed that the suggestions which scholars have made about the sequence of the letters from internal evidence all agree with one another. Further, no one is talking about a straight-line evolution. Steve's question is excellent; it really identified a difference.

Luedemann: I must say that I do not use the term "development" to confirm my chronology. I look for another criterion to make chronological statements about the relationship which the letters have to each other, and I start with the very simple assumption, namely, that early Christian preaching implied an imminent parousia (Mark 9, John 21, Matthew 10). That is an insight the history of religions school has gained. I tried to find a reflection of this belief in Paul's letters, and I estimated that one generation would last thirty years. If we find a belief that assumes the survival of most of the people, it must be quite close to the death and resurrection of Jesus; if we find a reflection of many deaths that called for new theological solutions, then we can put it at the end of the first generation, that is, between fifty and sixty. So much for the criterion. I did not use the term "development," but I did say that if my chronology is true, then, for the first time in scholarship we can ask this question with some hope of getting results. Because for Bob Jewett, if he is right, the span of chronology doesn't allow one to press for development: all the letters were written within four or five years. And I think that, whether or not you agree with my exegesis of 1 Thessalonians, you have to answer that question, and in addition, look at the evidence I have presented concerning the relationship of 1 Thessalonians 4:13 to 1 Corinthians 15:51 where we have some similarities. But as Barrett pointed out, the groups that are going to survive or to die just have shifted. This article, which John wrote, dealt with that, and I indeed think that 1 Thessalonians implies the survival of most of

the Christians; whereas, at the time of 1 Corinthians the death of most of them is presupposed, and this is the criterion to make an assumption about an early or late dating of 1 Thessalonians. Development has to be rethought. Paul was writing in different situations; the situation may have made him rethink something. So this naive idea that Paul was progressing like an evolutionist is wrong anyway. However, what we can do is to see whether there are changes in Paul due to particular situations or perhaps to some new insights or ideas.

Hurd: I have lined up two people who want to jump you on that particular point. Professor Ralph Martin.

Martin: I was interested in this precise question of the time span in relation to a traditional view. It seemed that you were criticizing that view because it brought the letters of Paul together within a five-year time period, and you suggested that if the letters were composed within that limited time frame, we would expect more homogeneity to exist between them. And my question was really related to that, namely, Is it not the case that homogeneity would only be expected if the letters were written to churches facing the same or similar problems? And I am really asking you, Have you taken into account the nature of the diversities within the Pauline mission churches that evoked Pauline responses? The question of eschatology would be a case in point where the situation in Thessalonica might be quite different from that at Corinth. You could extrapolate from the evidence the matter of what was wrong at Thessalonica, given the persecution in the church which is singularly absent from the Corinthian communities, and the notion of an idea of a baptismal resurrection which may be prevalent at Corinth which raises the whole question of incipient gnosticism and the problem of death to which Paul was responding. I am asking you to consider now the adversaries, whether internal or external, that are in the mix to which Paul then is responding.

Hurd: Could I restate the question to see if I understand it correctly? There are admittedly differences among the letters. Are these differences to be attributed to differences between church situations, or are they due to differences in Paul's thought at different stages in his career?

Luedemann: Well, I can agree to everything that you said, but one thing remains constant, and that is that everybody has to die. This fundamental experience had to be dealt with sooner or later, given the

early Christian expectations. That provides me with the criterion. On everything else, concerning the diversity and so on, I could not agree with you more. But death is fundamental. That allows me to take seriously the fact that we have in different Pauline letters quite different views of death and expectation of the relationship of one's own death to the parousia (2 Cor. 1:8; 5:1ff.). So I think that I don't want to deal with development and that this is a difficult or dangerous term. But I would restate my point that Paul—whatever the differences of the communities were—had to deal with the fact of death. And, secondly, his early preaching in Thessalonica and Corinth implied the survival of most Christians. If you could agree to that then we have taken one step together. I think everybody has to agree to that.

Koester: Very briefly, I don't find this persuasive because as you move closer to the parousia, that is, the later it is in time, the fewer people you would expect to die. So you could just turn it around and come to the opposite result.

Hurd: If the parousia is tomorrow, then most of us who are here will be there for the parousia.

Koester: Ten years before the parousia you would expect that quite a few will die, but one day before the parousia you would expect that everybody would still be alive.

Hurd: Well, eschatology is not an exact science, is it! It breaks out unexpectedly. Jack MacGorman had a question in the same area.

MacGorman: It was directed to Luedemann, but I think he has already probed very much the question that I was going to ask. I am mindful of the fact that in Dodd's treatment of development in Paul's letters, not only does he appeal to eschatology as a criterion, but also to Paul's attitude to social institutions, such as courts of law, marriage, and the like. It is interesting that in his treatment he lumps the eschatology of 1 Thessalonians and 1 Corinthians together. And he uses 1 Corinthians as a kind of base in attitude toward social institutions from which to measure development toward a being more at home with social institutions in the later writings. So I suppose that the comment deals with the fact that attitude toward social institutions in 1 Corinthians was used in his hypothesis as a base from which to measure the development. In your presentation you have eight to eleven years difference in the times for the writings of 1 Thessalonians and 1 Corinthians upon the basis of

whether or not one would be alive at the parousia. I would like to hear you respond to that, if you will, please.

Luedemann: Well, I am skeptical of Dodd's argument because it has been based on Ephesians and Colossians, and I cannot regard these letters as authentic.

MacGorman: What about the attitude in Romans, for example?

Luedemann: Romans 13 is a tradition, and I don't see how one could argue like that. Let me just say one more thing to Helmut Koester, because I think that he missed my point. The question then is whether Paul's soteriological model, the way he thinks of Christian salvation as happening, reflects this model of death or survival, and I would indeed argue that Paul's experience with death is reflected in a different model. You do not yet have in 1 Thessalonians the model, like Christ, so the Christians; this model is developed in 1 and 2 Corinthians. So here, indeed, that's the only point where I can see the theological model which takes this shift or this different situation into account. Whether Paul expected to be alive at the parousia or not is difficult to say. He knew that children, of course, would be alive at the parousia. But I would indeed say that in 2 Corinthians 1:8 we have clearly the belief that he may die, that he has undergone an experience. I think one should take that seriously.

Hurd: I have always thought that Dodd was right for the wrong reasons. He believed that no sensible person could believe the sort of thing that you read in 1 Corinthians 15 or 1 Thessalonians 4-5 and that therefore Paul, being a sensible person, must see the error of his ways and change. As I say, right for the wrong reasons, perhaps.

I think we should move ahead, then, to our fourth topic; maybe we don't want to talk about it particularly. I am simply proposing that there have been many source analyses of Acts. A number of scholars have concluded that it is a game no one can win. If you are making a chronological use of Acts, then almost inevitably you have to talk about sources, because you must have pericopes in sequence and sequence implies source, a document. Whereas another way of going at Acts is to take it from the point of view of form criticism and say there's a lot of useful material about Paul; it falls into separate pericopes, and we will deal with these traditions in the same way that we deal with traditions found in any of the basic Synoptic documents. This occa-

sional use of Acts poses no problem of method. But if any sequence in Acts is to be relied on, one must show how the individual traditions retained their relative order in the oral period prior to the appearance of written records. Any response? We have touched on "we" already; perhaps that is a major source we are talking about. There is, of course, the obvious evidence in the text itself.

Let's move on, then, to an area which a number of you have expressed interest in, and this gets us right into an absolutely endless sequence of problems. So I'll open the door and stand back. Well, for example, exegesis of Galatians 2, Ramsay Michaels and Bernard Orchard both want to say something on this particular point. Let's begin with Professor Michaels.

Michaels: It's not so much a matter of wanting to say something as just suggesting that the exegesis of this passage is obviously very important. And the question that comes up especially as to whether [Galatians] 2:11 follows sequentially after 2:1-10, or whether it represents some kind of a flashback. 2:11-14 does seem to be the kind of transition between these two rhetorical portions of Galatians—the end of the *narratio.* Obviously when Paul says, "When Cephas came to Antioch," he has abandoned the ἔπειτα . . . ἔπειτα scheme, and it's not fixed in time. It seems to me that prior to that point, Paul has been talking about contact, very limited contact, between himself and the Jerusalem church, specifically, James and Peter and insisting that he is independent of them, that they added nothing to him. And he does this in terms of journeys to Jerusalem. In 2:11 it's a matter of a journey in the opposite direction. Cephas coming to Antioch, and there again, that confrontation seems to be told not in order to say definitely what the outcome is, because there doesn't seem to be any definite outcome, but it seems to me to simply again assert Paul's independence of Cephas. That leads to his own further reflection on that in verses 15ff., which then leads over into the next part of Galatians. I do think that whole context needs very careful assessment, exegetically.

Luedemann: I agree that's very important, and it is clear that one has to explore the function of 2:11 in the whole letter. Since the section addressed to Cephas leads to the crux of the whole letter, it must have some rhetorical function, and one should not say that because it is at the end of the narration it belongs there chronologically, whether it belongs there or not. However, I think that for chronology as such

(even if I am wrong, I may be wrong) the Knox chronology is not destroyed. However, it would explain, Bob, why Barnabas and Paul went to Jerusalem; that's what Professor Caird asked you. A setting like that would really explain that here Cephas, Barnabas, and Paul attack each other and they decide to go to Jerusalem in order to settle that. Which then had as its results (and now I am speculating a bit, but there's no history without speculation) that a situation like that in Antioch where Gentiles and Jews are eating together, would be prevented in the future, because now the missions would separate.

Orchard: There has been the general assumption throughout this discussion that there is nothing more to be said about the exegesis of the very difficult and critical passage in Galatians 2:1-10. This is the really critical question to decide whether Luke and Paul are clashing or not. I would like to suggest that the exegetes have not really properly understood this passage, and it's because of the peculiar way in which Paul uses ellipses and parentheses. This passage clearly refers to two situations. One is the situation in the first three verses and verses 7-10, when Paul goes up to Jerusalem with Titus and has the discussion with the three pillars. In the middle, verses 4 to 6, there is a parenthesis which is out of keeping with the other verses I have referred to. Now I believe this is a parenthesis which shows the situation which was in fact at the Council of Jerusalem. No time to get into it now except to say that there is, I believe, a complete distinction to be made between verses 4 to 6, which are a parenthesis which Paul introduces to explain why he has written the letter at all. I would recommend that those who are interested in it look into this because it does, I believe, avoid all these problems of a clash between Acts and Galatians. What it really amounts to is this: Paul wrote the epistle to the Galatians possibly on the way up to Jerusalem—we are told in Acts that the journey took a long time—and he got the message about the Galatian situation on the way. Because of the situation immediately facing him this parenthesis appears in the letter. But in 2:1-3, 7-10 he refers to a situation some years before when he and the three pillars met. So, thank you very much for allowing me to intervene.

Hurd: I want to thank particularly all the members of the panel. It seems a long time ago now that I was on the phone to you last summer making arrangements, and now they have come to be. This is just a beginning; there will be a transcription of the proceedings. In particu-

lar I want to thank our two paper readers, Bob Jewett and Gerd Luedemann who have borne the brunt of it all and taken us through to some very useful reflections.

CHAPTERS IN A LIFE OF PAUL— A RESPONSE TO ROBERT JEWETT AND GERD LUEDEMANN

John Knox

THOSE RESPONSIBLE for the planning of the Colloquy of whose proceedings this volume has been a record conferred on me a distinction I do not deserve, but of which I am very proud, in making me the recipient of special honor. The only reasons I can think of for their generous action are the dubious one of the Colloquy's date roughly corresponding with my eightieth birthday and the somewhat more valid one of its devoting one of its sessions to a discussion of a book of mine published thirty years before[1] and to scholarly work done by others in the field of the Pauline chronology which has followed upon, and to some extent perhaps has been influenced by, that publication.[2] These are hardly adequate reasons for the honor done me; and therefore I thank the president of the Southwestern Baptist Theological Seminary and members of its faculty, especially Professor Corley, for what I can regard only as an act of gracious good will.

---

[1]John Knox, *Chapters in a Life of Paul* (New York: Abingdon-Cokesbury Press, 1950).

[2]In particular, the recent publications of our speakers: Robert Jewett, *A Chronology of Paul's Life* (Philadelphia: Fortress Press, 1979); and Gerd Luedemann, *Paulus der Heidenapostel. Band I: Studien zur Chronologie* (Göttingen: Vandenhoeck und Ruprecht, 1980).

I have been asked to write the concluding essay in this volume—an additional ground for gratitude. I am permitted to write on any topic I wish so long as it is not unrelated to subjects dealt with in the Colloquy; and I have decided on the same topic as that discussed in the particular session to which I have referred.

This decision has not been merely a matter of choice; it is a decision dictated by necessity. I have read with great interest the papers on current Synoptic Gospel research—those of Professors Dungan, Meagher, and Koester—and have learned much from each of them. But anyone who knows me or is acquainted with my work will also know that I am utterly incapable of commenting usefully upon them, much less of making any contribution of my own to the research of which these papers represent distinguished examples. Like most New Testament students of my generation, I soon became convinced that Mark was the earliest Gospel. When William R. Farmer's book, *The Synoptic Problem*,[3] questioned this common conviction about Mark, I was shaken by the recognition that some of the arguments for this view had little or no weight and that the question of Mark's priority, as of the two-document hypothesis as a whole, was a more nearly open one than I had thought. Although (I hope this remark is not too personal!) I *wanted* very much to agree with Farmer as he continued to develop his position and was joined by others, I have not been able to do so, at any rate on this point of Mark's priority. But I should be the first to acknowledge that I have no right to an expert opinion on this subject, nor am I qualified to take any part in the current important and widening debate on Synoptic Gospel relationships in general.

This being true, I hope the three authors I have named, as well as Professor Sanders, will understand my concentrating my attention on the subject of the Pauline chronology. I do so, not only for the negative reason I have given, but also because I welcome the opportunity of reflecting again on my work of thirty years ago, especially after reading the books and papers of Professors Luedemann and Jewett, and of stating my present views on its subject. I am well aware that many of these views need defense against alternative or opposing views; but severe limitations of space, as well as other limitations, preclude my

---

[3] *The Synoptic Problem: A Critical Review of the Problem of the Literary Relationship between Matthew, Mark, and Luke* (New York: Macmillan, 1964). [Dedicated to John Knox.]

offering it. But I hope to present these views with appropriate tentativeness.

1

When my book, *Chapters in a Life of Paul*, was published in 1950, I had no thought of ever writing again about the chronology of Paul's life. I had given no little attention to this subject a decade earlier, and two articles recording or reflecting the results of my study of it had appeared in 1936 and 1939,[4] the emphasis in both articles being upon what I deemed to be correct method in using Acts and Paul's letters in this connection. But other interests had already begun to engage me, especially some speculations and growing convictions about the earliest history of the New Testament canon—an interest which had issued in my work on Marcion, published in 1942.[5] And after that date my study and reflections had been more and more concerned with the theology of the New Testament and, more particularly, with problems in Christology.

But when Emory University invited me to give the Quillian Lectures in 1949, I decided to attempt a restatement of my views of method in using our sources for Paul's life. I decided on this attempt for several reasons. First, and most generally, I did so because I hoped to find a wider audience for my proposals than had been found, or could have been expected, from their earlier publication in the two "learned" journals. Secondly, I wanted to revise my earlier statement in several minor ways. And, thirdly, the two articles had sought to apply the proposed method only to the problem of chronology, whereas I believed it would be worthwhile, particularly for the "average" student of Paul, to see its applicability to the life of Paul in all of its aspects and to have some of the results of this wider use of the method pointed out to him.

Probably it is not necessary at all, so far as the readers of these pages are concerned, for me to indicate what that method was (especially since Professor Luedemann has excellently summarized it in this

---

[4] "'Fourteen Years Later': A Note on the Pauline Chronology," *The Journal of Religion,* "16 (1936): 341-49; and "The Pauline Chronology,"*Journal of Biblical Literature,* 58 (1939): 15-29.

[5] *Marcion and the New Testament: An Essay in the Early History of the Canon* (Chicago: The University of Chicago Press, 1942).

very volume),[6] but for the sake of adequacy and coherence in this essay, I shall briefly give my own summary.

There was nothing new in my proposal that Paul's own letters were a better source for Paul than Acts could be; I suppose no one could deny so obvious a fact. Any novelty my proposal could claim lay in my conception of the dimensions of the superiority. I argued that this superiority was immense, and that it obtained, not only as regards Paul's personality, thought, and inner experience (here again there will be no dispute among those who have seriously reflected on the matter), but also as regards the events and the general course of his career. The incomparable value of the letters in this latter respect, I urged, is such (a) that the merest hint in the letters is to be deemed worth more than the most explicit statement of Acts; (b) that a statement in Acts about Paul is to be regarded as incredible if it conflicts directly with the letters (as many statements do) and is to be seriously questioned even if a conflict is only suggested; and (c) that statements about Paul in Acts are to be accepted with confidence only if such statements are fully and explicitly confirmed in the letters. In a word, it was argued that we can rely only on the letters for completely assured biographical information. The acceptance of these propositions does not mean the outright rejection of Acts as a valuable source for the life of Paul. There can be no doubt that it contains true traditions of facts and episodes in Paul's life, but these traditions can never have the certitude which data obtained from the letters possess. Even when a datum in Acts, unconfirmed but uncontradicted in the letters, is in all respects plausible or bears the marks of a primitive origin, it can be accepted only tentatively. Furthermore, even if the critic is disposed thus tentatively to accept such a datum in Acts as an isolated fact or episode, he must still closely question whether its order and context are also to be trusted.

Moreover, it must be said that in estimating the historical value of every biographical statement in Acts which is neither supported nor placed in doubt by the letters (whether the statement is being looked at in isolation or in its context), we must make due allowance for Luke's special tendencies and interests. One of these is his pride or pleasure in associating incidents in his story with well-known persons or events in general history. The palpable and gross errors he makes in many, if not

---

[6] See Luedemann's essay above.

most, of these references and, as we shall see, in other respects as well, raise doubts about his credibility in general. Furthermore, his theological or ideological interests must be taken into account, as, for example, his interest in the continuity of primitive Christianity with the true Israel, his related tendency to emphasize the importance of Jerusalem both in the life of Jesus and in the life of the early church, his concern to see the church as united under Jerusalem-centered apostolic direction, and his apologetic interest in representing it as politically innocuous. Luke was very far indeed from being what we would call an objective historian.

Such conclusions as these about a proper methodology in the use of Acts and the letters led me to ask what its application to Paul's apostolic career would mean as to the chronology of it, and I devoted chapters 3-5 of *Chapters* to answering this question. I bespeak your patience as I ask it again, even though the answer I shall make is not substantially different from my answer then. Still, the differences arising from thirty years of reflection, some of it stimulated by scholars who have taken part in this Colloquy, are sufficient perhaps to justify me in stating it. Besides, I shall venture to apply the method in greater detail.

II

Before beginning this supplementary statement, however, I should like to discuss as briefly as possible the question of originality as applied to my work in this area—a question which is bound to be raised by several remarks in Professor Jewett's book (for example, "Although unmentioned by Knox, there are several predecessors who identified Gal 2:1 with Acts 18:22. . . .")[7] and which, aside from personal considerations, is undoubtedly important and relevant.

I can say—or perhaps I should put it, I must confess—that my proposal was first made entirely on the basis of the study of the sources. To be sure, I had read rather widely in the secondary literature on Paul during my work as a student at Chicago and earlier, but I had never read anything suggesting or supporting the thesis of my first article or of any part of it, except in the negative sense that my dissatisfaction with current "harmonizing" efforts provided a certain stimulus. The

---

[7] *Chronology*, 80.

article was written while I was teaching at a small and rather isolated college, and I had no opportunity to search into the history of earlier research on the specific problem of chronology. But I must also say that I did not then, or ever, presume that in the long, rich history of New Testament study there may not have been partial anticipations— possibly more than that—of the methodology and the general type of chronology which I adumbrated. I presumed only that this methodology and this kind of chronology had never been commonly or generally accepted among scholars. A more thoroughgoing presumption of novelty I have never made for any particular proposal I have ever made on any subject. I would not have entertained such a presumption for I had even then learned its dangerousness. To cite one instance: when during my work on Philemon I first recognized on the basis of long reflection on Tertullian's and Epiphanius's accounts of Marcion's canon that Paul's letters (after Galatians) were arranged in the order of length, I thought I had made a "discovery" of my own, but my accidental reading a little later of an inconspicuous footnote in Harnack told me that he had "discovered" it long before.

But when the second article was written, I was at the Hartford Seminary and did make an effort to find out whether others had preceded me, whether in whole or part, and I had learned that several scattered German scholars had at some point anticipated my views (I mentioned C. Clemen as an example);[8] but I found none who had come even close to stating my overall conception, as to either method or the results of its use. I am sorry I did not "find" Barnikol's treatise[9] (cited by Jewett[10] and also by Luedemann[11]), and I am amazed that I did not. After reading Jewett's book, who properly emphasizes the importance of Barnikol's work, I made an effort to locate this treatise of his (*Die drei Jerusalemreisen des Paulus*, 1929), and through the kindness of a friend I was able to secure and read it. I am much impressed with the similarity between his manner of presenting the Jerusalem-journeys data in the letters and Acts and my own way of presenting the same

---

[8]"The Pauline Chronology," p. 18, n.6.

[9]Ernst Barnikol, *Die drei Jerusalemreisen des Paulus. Die echte Konkordanz der Paulusbriefe mit der Wir-Quelle der Apostelgeschichte,* Forschungen zur Entstehung des Urchristentumns des Neuen Testaments und der Kirche 2 (Kiel: Muhlau, 1929).

[10]*Chronology,* pp. 80-81.

[11]*Paulus,* p. 165, n.27.

data in *Chapters*. But here the resemblance ends. Barnikol's method of using Acts and the chronological results he arrives at bear no resemblance to mine. I am sorry I did not know of his book, but if I had seen it, nothing in it would have changed my position in any manner or degree.

It is in this second article—alone, I believe, among my writings—that I used the term "new chronology" in speaking of my total proposal, but after this thoughtless and over-bold use of that phrase, I hastened to add: "I say 'new chronology,' not in the sense of a chronology never suggested at least in part before, but in the sense of a chronology radically different from that ordinarily adopted."[12] The truth of *this* claim for it and for the method used in arriving at it is, I believe, confirmed to a degree by developments in this field of research which began in 1936-39. The appearance of my articles attracted some favorable response. I think offhand of D. W. Riddle, C. H. Buck, and Paul Minear, but I am sure there were others. And after 1950, when *Chapters* was published, this kind of response increased. A small and distinguished group—J. C. Hurd, Jack Suggs, H. L. Ramsey, E. P. Sanders, and others joined Buck, Minear, and me. Our number has always been, I think, on the increase, although it is still probably only a small minority among New Testament scholars. And just recently we have been joined by Gerd Luedemann with a magnificent contribution, the first full-length, full-bodied, fully documented chronology based only on the letters. There has never been complete agreement within this group on chronological details, but we have all agreed on methodology, which is the principal thing.

III

I now return to chronology itself. There will be general agreement among all students of the Pauline chronology that an interval of approximately three years lay between Paul's conversion (the revelation in Damascus) and his first subsequent visit to Jerusalem and that a period of around fourteen years separated this visit from his second. This conclusion follows from the most natural reading of Gal 1:15-2:10. We thus arrive at a roughly seventeen-year interval between his conversion and call to the apostolate—for in the letters these are inseparable—and the second, the so-called conference, visit. We cannot be sure of the seventeen years as an exact figure both because the

---

[12]"The Pauline Chronology," p. 18.

ἔπειτα in 1:18 and 2:1 may mean "after three [or fourteen] years" or "in the third [or fourteenth] year" and also because we cannot know whether in 1:18 the term refers to the conversion experience or to Paul's return from Arabia to Damascus. Still, since it appears likely that his stay in Arabia was relatively brief, our estimate of seventeen years can with a fair degree of certainty be regarded as correct— approximately correct at least. Perhaps to say sixteen to seventeen years would be safer.

But where and how were these years spent? We know that he spent the first few of them in Damascus (and Arabia), and, from Gal 1:21, that after a very brief visit in Jerusalem he went to Syria and Cilicia. But the absolute absence of references in his letters to churches established by him in these areas or to his having any continuing influence or authority there, taken together with his strong assertion in Rom 15:20 that he has been faithful in not building on foundations laid by others, would suggest that any labors of his in these regions were of relatively short duration. What happened then? What happened after his brief stay in Cilicia? I believe that *if we had only the letters as sources* (and we are assuming for the moment that such were the case), the consensus of scholarly opinion would be that his course continued in a westerly direction and, since he can speak later of his preaching in Macedonia as being "in the beginning of the gospel" (Phil 4:15), that after no long period he reached that province. This consensus, however, although supported by no explicit statement in the letters, would not rest only, or even chiefly, on the Philippians passage. It would rest also on the impression the letters give of the character of the man himself and of the nature of his calling. With the very beginning of his experience as a Christian came the assurance that he was called to preach the gospel to the nations, which for Paul would have meant the Mediterranean world. His resolution on such a mission, with Europe as the immediate goal, would have been taken early. It may indeed have been part of the motivation for his first visit to Jerusalem to talk with Peter and James (Gal 1:18). He may well have felt that he should not embark on it without some contact and, he might hope, some common understanding, with the earlier apostles. If he did, in fact, make his decision so early, his departure from Jerusalem for Syria and Cilicia was the beginning of its execution.

As to his route from Cilicia to Macedonia or as to events on the way, the letters alone would give us no clue. But his most direct route

would have been through or near the cities of Iconium, Derbe, Lystra, Antioch, and perhaps other places in southern Galatia and it would not have been unreasonable to suspect that the gospel was planted there in the course of Paul's journey across Asia Minor early in his ministry. All of these conclusions as to probabilities would have been based only on what the letters suggest. It may be noted, however, that Acts 15:41-16:12 tells us that Paul reached Macedonia by way of Syria and Cilicia and the cities of southern Galatia; and it may not be irrelevant in this connection to observe that it is toward the end of this account of Paul's journey from Cilicia to Philippi that the so-called "diary" makes its first appearance.

IV

"But," a critic may say, "what about the 'first missionary journey' (Acts 13-14)? Time for it must surely be allowed before this departure westward from Cilicia." My answer to this question is implicit in *Chapters* (see especially pp. 40-41), where I reject the whole "missionary journey" scheme.[13] But if a more explicit and specific answer is asked for, I should say that the "first missionary journey" did not occur at all—*that is, as a part of Paul's career*. That there was an Antiochene mission I should not be disposed to question, although whether it went so far beyond Cyprus as to include the cities of southern Galatia can plausibly be doubted for reasons I shall shortly give. But whatever the extent of this possible, even probable, mission, I should be inclined to deny that Paul had any connection with it. I would feel serious doubt about such a connection simply for the same reason I would question anything in Acts involving Paul which is not explicitly or by clear implication indicated also in the letters; and in this case the letters are completely silent. But my "doubting" moves toward "denying" because the silence does not stand alone. Other considerations point in the same direction.

Up to this point (that is, Acts 13-14) every statement of Acts about Paul can be demonstrated to be either inaccurate or highly improbable. Paul is mentioned first in Acts 7:58 as consenting to the murder of Stephen and in 8:1-3 as participating in the persecution of the church in Jerusalem which followed. But Paul clearly denies in Gal 1:22 that

---

[13]*Chapters*, especially pp. 40-42.

either of these statements is true. Luke's next mention of Paul is in Acts 9:1-30, which in its entirety is irreconcilable with Paul's Galatians account of his Damascus experience and its aftermath. Barnabas's finding Paul in Tarsus and bringing him to Antioch (11:25-26) is not, it is true, provably false, but in the context it is improbable. For these actions seem little more than the necessary prelude to the involving of Paul in an offering visit to Jerusalem (11:27-30); but we know from an implicit denial in the letters that if such a visit occurred at all, Paul had no part in it. And the same denial can be made of the truth, as regards Paul, of 12:25, whether the disputed reading is ἐξ or εἰς. Thus we are brought to chapters 13 and 14. But if all the Acts statements about Paul up to this point are either demonstrably inaccurate or of extremely doubtful accuracy (and the same can be said of the following chapter 15:1-35), why should we believe without any supporting evidence the statements in these chapters?

Moreover, in view of all the letters reveal of Paul and his sense of calling—"an apostle not from men or through men"—can we really "see" him going forth ordained and instructed by the elders at Antioch on a mission as Barnabas's subordinate? I find it impossible to do so. I do not doubt that some ancient and true traditions lie buried in Acts 13-14, some of them associated with Cyprus and others with the Galatian cities. But I believe I have given good reasons for our questioning, to say the least, Paul's being associated with Barnabas in either locality. Perhaps traditions about Barnabas in Cyprus and Paul in southern Galatia have been fused into a single story by the final author of Luke-Acts or by one of his sources. It is my opinion that, so far as Paul is concerned, that author had only sparse, scattered traditions and his own historical imagination to depend on up to the point represented by Acts 15:40. Only from that point on, did he have sufficient source material for anything like a consecutive account of Paul's travels, possibly because it was at that point that Paul's travels really began. I see Acts 15:41 as answering to Gal 1:21.

Whatever one's estimate of the argument I have been making in the last several paragraphs, I believe there may be general agreement that it is improbable that such cities as Iconium and Antioch, Hellenistic cities located in the very heart of southern Asia Minor, were not reached by the gospel fairly early. I concede readily that this fact cannot be proved. Conceivably Christianity was planted in the remote cities of ethnic Galatia to the north, as well as in the Greek peninsula

and even Asia before it was brought to these cities. But is this intrinsically likely? So long as we trust Acts 13-14, this question does not arise and therefore it has rarely, if ever, been considered. But if we distrust these chapters and still believe the gospel reached these southern Galatian cities quite early, is it not reasonable to suspect that it reached them while Paul was making his way from Syria and Cilicia to Macedonia?

One may further ask whether, if this is true, it is not probable—indeed, more than probable—that the churches established in those cities were among the "churches of Galatia" which were instructed about the collection for Jerusalem (1 Cor 16:1) some years afterward and were addressed under that same name in his letter later still. I say "included among" for it is quite incredible that if in cities which Luke describes as situated in Pisidia and Lycaonia but which could equally aptly be described as located in Galatia—if in these cities a vital beginning was made for the gospel, whether by Paul alone or by Barnabas and Paul—it is incredible that in a decade it would not have reached northward, possibly even as far as ethnic Galatia. But if this is true and Paul has in this later time occasion to refer to, or to address, the whole group of congregations, how shall he do so except as "the churches of Galatia"(Gal 1:2)? (Witness Paul's references to the "churches of Asia" [1 Cor. 16:19]? Actually, all of his geographical references, except to cities, are in terms of the Roman provincial system of his day.)

But if one takes this position and recognizes that these southern Galatian churches were a part—indeed, probably the "center"—of Galatian Christianity as Ephesus was of the movement in Asia, then one can no longer believe, not only that Paul participated in the "first missionary journey," but also that this "journey" (now seen as a journey of Barnabas and Mark) extended as far as the cities of Antioch, Iconium, and the rest. For the Epistle to the Galatians makes indubitable that it was *Paul* (not Paul and Barnabas) who first brought the gospel to the churches being addressed. The letter, throughout and in the most emphatic way, identifies them as *his* churches. *He* founded them; *he* has nurtured them; he has made two visits to them (4:13). And if it is asked: "*When* did he found them and *when* did he visit them a second time?", the natural answer is: he founded them on his way from Syria and Cilicia to Macedonia (Gal 1:21=Acts 15:41 [?]), and he visited them a second time on his way back to Ephesus after the conference (Gal

2:1-10) seeking their cooperation in the collection which he had just now undertaken (1 Cor 16:1).

The fact that this first visit to the cities of Galatia was connected in some way with bodily illness or disability (Gal 4:13) throws little, if any, light on where they were located, whether north or south. Nevertheless, it would seem much more likely that the illness was the occasion of an interrupting of a planned itinerary than that it was a reason for the itinerary itself. And if this is true, surely the South Galatian cities come nearer to being indicated than, say, Pessinus to the north. Galatians 4:13 may well mean that in his haste to reach Macedonia he might have passed south Galatia by if illness or disability had not stopped him. It would appear less probable that he could have gone to north Galatia without having intended to go there. This is, needless to say, little more than guessing. We simply cannot know. But certainly this reference does not require the "north Galatia hypothesis." Neither does any other reference ("so quickly" [Gal 1:6], "O foolish Galatians" [3:1], or any other) require it. I forbear traversing familiar ground in justifying this denial.

However questionable some, or all, of my proposal may be as to Paul's route from Syria and Cilicia to Macedonia (and no proposal can be demonstrably true), once he reached that province, there can be no doubt as to the direction of his next moves—from Philippi, to Thessalonica, to Athens, and eventually to Corinth. This movement southward 1 Thessalonians and Philippians make altogether clear and certain, and the fact that the Acts story agrees in this respect adds nothing to our assurance. But as to how long he stayed in these cities we have no definite indication. One would gather that he may have remained in Philippi and Thessalonica a year at least—perhaps several years in both of the Macedonian cities—and, from silences, that he spent a shorter time in Athens. These, again, are hardly more than guesses, as anyone's estimates must be. Such also is any setting of time limits to his first stay in Corinth. But the reader of the Corinthian letters is likely to gain the impression that it was a more extended one—a real *residence* as contrasted with later *visits*.

But it certainly would not have lasted indefinitely long, or indeed longer than necessary, for Paul could not have forgotten that Ephesus, hitherto unevangelized, had been left in his wake: and he would have wanted to see the gospel established there before he proceeded, as he intended, to Italy and beyond. There are indications in the letters

(Corinthians, Colossians, Philemon) that his stay in Ephesus was a prolonged one even as compared with that in Corinth. This conclusion receives some confirmation from Acts (compare 18:11 and 19:10). And such sources as Ignatius's letter to the Ephesians and the anti-Marcionite prologues suggest that Paul was later thought of as residing longer in Ephesus than in any other city. It is probable that the conference journey to Jerusalem began there, and it is plausible to surmise that it was on his way back to Ephesus that his promised visit to the churches of the Lycus valley (Phlm 22), as also his second visit to Galatia, occurred (compare Acts 18:23). The imprisonment in Ephesus for which Colossians, Philemon, and Philippians offer some evidence could have occurred before the conference (2 Cor 1:8-9 does not necessarily imply an imprisonment); and although 1 Corinthians and 2 Corinthians (certainly for the greater part) were obviously written after the conference, one cannot exclude the possibility that the earlier letter, referred to in 1 Cor 5:9, belonged to the prior period, once the possibility of such a period is acknowledged.

V

We have been dealing thus far with the sixteen- to seventeen-year period between Paul's conversion and the Jerusalem conference. We now turn to the question of how long a time must be allowed for the events between this conference and Paul's third, and presumably final, visit to Jerusalem. Almost all we know of these events is reflected in the Corinthian letters, and they present a confusing picture, which I shall not try to clarify, although it is pertinent to observe that it involves one, perhaps two, visits of Paul to Corinth before his final visit there and some exchange of correspondence. The crisis in Galatia which called forth his impassioned letter may also have occurred during this period. (My own strong inclination, however, is to date it later.[14])

The conference in Jerusalem had ended with the "pillars," James, Peter, and John, acknowledging the validity of Paul's mission and asking only that his churches should make an offering to the Jerusalem church. This "collection for the saints" Paul saw as a very important and urgent undertaking and immediately set about it ("which very

---

[14]See Knox, "Letter to the Galatians," in *The Interpreter's Dictionary of the Bible*, ed. G. A. Buttrick, et. al. 4 vols. (New York and Nashville: Abingdon Press, 1962) 2:338-43.

thing I hastened to do" [Gal 2:10]). We hear of it several times in the Corinthian letters as being in progress; and in Rom 15:25-26, apparently written in Corinth, we learn that it has been finally completed and that Paul is on the point of leaving Corinth for Jerusalem to deliver it.

This third journey, thus bound as it is to the second, could not have occurred long after it. To be sure, the collection was no small undertaking, for Galatia, Macedonia, Achaia, and Asia were involved in it. Besides, some very troubling difficulties at Corinth, and perhaps also in Galatia, claimed Paul's attention. But, on the other hand, the whole symbolic significance of the offering effort would have been lost, or significantly impaired, if the request for it and the Pauline churches' response had been long separated. An apparently reluctant gift would not have had the reconciling effect Paul had set his heart on. Furthermore, it is unmistakably clear that Paul is impatiently eager to see the end of the tiring project, for its completion alone is delaying a long wished for departure for Rome and regions farther to the West. I suggested in *Chapters* a period of not more than three years.[15] In doing so, I can now see that I did not take sufficiently into consideration the travel time factor. I would now propose an interval of four years between the second and the final Jerusalem journey—or, let us say, *three* or four years between the second and his departure from Corinth on the third.

I must repeat what has been said a number of times that the time estimates made in this paper are for the greater part very tentative. The only interval of which we can be virtually sure is the thirteen to fourteen years separating Paul's first Jerusalem visit from the second. The interval of approximately three years between his conversion and the first visit can be almost as certain. We can thus be fairly well assured of a sixteen- to seventeen-year period between his conversion and the conference visit. And now I have proposed an additional three or four years before his departure on his last visit to Jerusalem—a total of twenty or twenty-one years between his conversion and the last glimpse the letters give us of him.

Before raising the question of what happened to Paul after this final departure from Corinth and the even more vexed question of absolute

---

[15] *Chapters*, pp. 58, 80, 85.

dating, it may be useful to make a schedule of relative times in accordance with the suggestions which I have ventured to make.

PAUL'S CAREER .... DATE

a. Conversion and Call to Apostleship x

Residence in Damascus with journey to Arabia and a stay of
uncertain but probably short length there.

b. First Jerusalem Visit .... x + 3

Syria, Cilicia, Southern Galatia.

c. Arrival in Macedonia .... x + 6

Residence in Philippi, Thessalonica. Work in Macedonia.
Stay, probably short, in Athens.

d. Arrival in Corinth .... x + 9

Residence there with work in Achaia.

e. Arrival in Ephesus .... x + 12

Prolonged residence there, marked by various missions,
possibly by an imprisonment, and, most important, by his

f. Second Jerusalem Visit (Conference) .... x + 17

Activity based in Ephesus concerned chiefly with collection
and involving one or more visits to Corinth.

g. Departure from Ephesus for Corinth
   to Complete Collection .... x + 20

h. Departure from Corinth on Third Visit
   to Jerusalem to Deliver Collection .... x + 20-21

VI

This final journey to Jerusalem (h in the foregoing schedule) is spoken of by Paul only in prospect. But his letters give ample grounds for some fairly confident expectations about it—notably, that he will not go alone but will be accompanied by delegates from the churches which have participated in the collection effort. Luedemann's surmise (pp. 116ff.) that, since only Macedonia and Achaia are mentioned in Rom 15:26, the effort in Galatia had failed, and that therefore no Galatian representatives were included in the company,[16] becomes less plausible when we note that Asia also is not mentioned in that passage. Yet, can there be any question but that the Asian churches, particularly the church at Ephesus, were involved? To be sure, Luedemann thinks there is such a question and, consistently with his opinion about the Galatians, holds that the Ephesians, too, "organized no collection

---

[16]*Paulus,* p. 117.

because the apostle could not (longer?) gain a footing there.''[17] He cites 1 Cor 15:32 and 2 Cor 1:8 in this connection. I must differ from him at this point. There would be no disagreement between us, I feel sure, as to the fact that Paul worked (himself and through his aides) for a considerable period in Ephesus and in other parts of Asia (witness Colossae, Laodicea and Hierapolis: no doubt there were other cities) and that his relations with these churches were warm and close, even in the very period when the collection effort was being made (1 Cor 16:19). And there is nothing to indicate that they had altered for the worse when he left Ephesus finally (so far as we know) for Troas, Macedonia, and Corinth. It is not at all necessary to understand the crisis suffered there (2 Cor 1:8f.) as involving an alienation from the Ephesian church or even that the occasion of the suffering had any connection with that church at all. Besides, from this trouble, whatever it was, Paul can say that he was delivered. He did fight wild beasts in Ephesus, whatever that means, but again there is no hint that any alienation from the Ephesian church was entailed. Indeed, he speaks of this experience in the very letter in which cordial relations with that church are unmistakably reflected (1 Cor 16:19). I have said in discussions of the date of Galatians that it is difficult to understand Paul's being able to speak so complacently in Romans 15 about his work from Jerusalem to Illyricum if he was at that very time in a state of alienation from the churches of Galatia;[18] but that diffculty is enormously increased if Asia, too, was estranged. In considering the fact of Paul's silence about the collection in Asia, it may be well to reflect that we should know little about Paul's effort in Macedonia and Achaia if it were not for the Corinthian letters. But there *is* no letter to the Ephesians! And may not this fact itself point to his having his base or headquarters there? In addition to such considerations as these in support of the view that Paul's relations with Ephesus were close and cordial, I find impressive evidences of a tradition to that effect of which I have made earlier mention in this essay.

Luedemann makes the point that there was Christianity in Ephesus before Paul began his work there.[19] But as compared with the

---

[17] *Ibid.*, p. 118.

[18] "Letter to the Galatians," 2:343.

[19] *Paulus*, p. 161.

question of Paul's relations with the Ephesian church and other churches of Asia, especially in the period of the collection, the question of whether he can be spoken of as the "founder" of these churches is unimportant. Paul says nothing to indicate that he was not, and his affirmation in Romans that he had sought always not to build on others' foundations (Rom 15:20; cf. 2 Cor 10:15-16 and 1 Cor 3:10-15) should lead us to conclude that he at least was able sincerely to feel that he had not done so in this case. It is true that Acts speaks of the earlier presence in Ephesus of a John the Baptist movement and represents Prisca and Aquila, through the conversion of Apollos to the new Way, as having formed a brotherhood, although apparently it was still attached to the synagogue. Paul on his return from a journey is said to have made additional converts from among these disciples of John. Eventually these Christians were forced to separate themselves from the synagogue. This whole story in Acts (18:18-19:9) is confused, obviously represents a fusion of probably conflicting traditions, and can hardly be understood, much less trusted. There is evidence in 1 Cor 16:19 and (for what it may be worth) in Rom 16:3 of Paul's close association with Prisca and Aquila, and any work they may have done in Ephesus before Paul's arrival would have been regarded by both him and them as being basically Paul's, just as the work of Epaphras in Laodicea and Colossae was. But, as I have said, I cannot see this whole question, actually unanswerable in detail or with assurance, of the remote origins of Christianity in Ephesus as bearing in any significant way on the matter of the obligation of the Ephesian church to partici- pate in the offering or of its willingness to do so. It may be worth noting that the group which, according to the "we-source," accompanied Paul to Jerusalem to deliver the offering included the Asians Tychicus and Trophimus, as well as the Derbean (?) Gaius (Acts 20:4).

So, on the whole, despite the problem which Rom 15:26 presents, I am inclined to adhere to my view that both Galatia and Asia were participants in the collection effort and that Paul was able to present the offering to "the saints" as a gesture of gratitude and loyalty, not on the part of some of his churches only, but on the part of them all.

Besides the testimony the letters bear to the fact of this "final" journey to Jerusalem and to the fact that Paul was accompanied by representatives of these churches, they provide us with one other important fact. They let us know that Paul was expecting to encounter serious threats to his liberty and even his life at the end of the journey.

That he knew of, and feared, these threats Rom 15:30-32 says clearly, even eloquently; and once we are made aware of them, we can hardly fail to see a hint of them in 1 Cor 16:3-4. There we learn that Paul wants to avoid this journey. Undoubtedly, one reason for this wish is his impatience to be off to Rome and regions farther westward. But, in the light of Rom 15:30ff., can we doubt that another and probably even more poignant reason was his fear of dangerous developments in Jerusalem which might not only further delay his going to Rome, but conceivably prevent it altogether? But so important does he regard the offering in healing the threatened breach in the church that he finally reluctantly decides that he cannot simply delegate the delivery of it to others; he must go to Jerusalem himself. Thus the letters alone would prepare us to learn of his arrest there. But for an actual account both of the journey and its sequel our only source is Acts, and the necessary cautions apply.

Luke devotes a very substantial part of his second volume to this journey and its aftermath, from 20:3 to 28:30—almost a third of the entire book and more than one-half of that part of the book in which Paul is the dominant figure. How much confidence can we have in the truth of these final chapters? Looked at from this point of view, they constitute a very "mixed bag." Luke begins with Paul in Corinth—a good beginning, as we have seen. The route by way of Macedonia and Troas is not at all improbable. Paul's being joined there by persons from Macedonia, Derbe (Galatia?), and Asia is entirely in line with Paul's allusion to his having companions on his journey. I see no reason to question the itinerary from Troas to Jerusalem, by way of Tyre and Caesarea. The fact that this part of the narrative has its source in the mysterious travel diary confirms to some degree its truth.

But there are many reasons to question the accuracy of much of the following narrative. To be sure, the fact that conflict arose involving Jewish enemies of Paul and eventually the Roman authorities is not at all unexpected in view of what Paul himself has told us of his fears; and the fact of his eventual arrest is not surprising. But under what conditions and for what reason the authorities took this action we cannot, in the light of what we know of Luke's interests and method, avoid being more doubtful. A great deal of space is devoted to Paul's speeches, most of them his own apologetic explanations of his actions—speeches which deserve no more credence than all the speeches previously

attributed to him. And our knowledge of Luke is bound to make us suspicious that the creator of the speeches had some part in creating the occasions for them. He tells of Paul's eloquent addresses before Felix, Festus, and Agrippa (not to mention earlier speeches to "the people" and the Sanhedrin), and of the favorable impression Paul made on all three. How fortunate that his arrest took place at such a propitious time! Could Paul—or Luke—have wished for a happier juncture of circumstances and personages? Thus grave doubt is thrown on the only chronological datum in the account—namely, that Paul's arrest took place not long before Festus succeeded Felix as Procurator of Judea.

VII

Before turning directly to some attempt at absolute dating, I should like to point out the unimportance of such dating as compared with the task of determining the length of Paul's career as an apostle and the course of events within it. For the understanding of Paul it matters little, if at all, just when, in terms of calendar years, his work began or just when it ended. What matters is what happened in it—the order of events and the intervals between them. In other words what I called "a schedule of relative times," which I suggested earlier in this paper, is far more important than the schedule of "absolute" dates which I shall later propose—far more important and, I should say, considerably less uncertain. But this statement of mine would be incomplete without my making some such proposal, so that with this understanding of its comparative unimportance and with very great tentativeness, I shall proceed.

We may begin by observing that on this matter Paul himself gives us very little help. Indeed, his only reference to a possibly datable event is found in 2 Cor 11:32-33, where he tells us that when he left Damascus on some unidentified occasion: "The governor under King Aretas guarded the city of Damascus in order to seize me, but I was let down in a basket through a window in the wall and escaped his hand." Acts 9:23-25 alludes to this same incident. Since Paul leaves us to suppose that he did not go back to Damascus after leaving it for his first Jerusalem visit, it is probable that in the 2 Corinthians passage he is alluding to that same departure. It could not have occurred later than A.D. 40, when Aretas' reign in Arabia (or Nabatea) ended. Jewett believes he has established as quite solidly assured a date within the last

two years of Aretas' regime, that is, in 37-39;[20] but I do not think many scholars would share his assurance. To say this is to say that Paul's letters alone, except within broad limits, provide us with no clue as to the date of his conversion. We can be quite certain, needless to say, that it occurred after Jesus' crucifixion and, with great probability because of the Aretas reference, not later than 37 (that is, 40 less the three years of Gal 1:18). But as to how long after the crucifixion it took place is a very open question, and even the date of the crucifixion itself is subject to dispute, estimates ranging from 27 to 33. The conversion, then, may conceivably have occurred in any year between, say, 32 and 37.

If it is impossible for us to settle with any closeness on the date of the *beginning* of the twenty- to twenty-one-year period we are concerned with, it is natural to ask: "Can we succeed any better in establishing the year in which it *ended*?" Obviously, if the conversion can be dated between 32 and 37 and if our estimate of a twenty- to twenty-one-year interval between that event and his last journey to Jerusalem is true, we should be forced to conclude that this journey and his arrest occurred somewhere between 52-53 and 58. And as for myself, I should be willing to leave the matter thus indeterminate. But if it should be true that we had to make a more precise decision, however tentative we knew it to be, I should propose that Paul's arrest took place at about the time of the Felix-Festus succession, that this succession occurred in 55, and that therefore his conversion happened twenty to twenty-one years earlier, that is, around A.D. 34. This date for the conversion, it may be said incidentally, is precisely the same as that settled on by Jewett and is only one year later than that offered as one of two alternatives by Luedemann. It now becomes possible to suggest approximate dates for the several events mentioned in our schedule a few pages back:

a.	Conversion and Call to Apostleship	A.D. 34
b.	First Jerusalem Visit	37
c.	Arrival in Macedonia	40
d.	Arrival in Corinth	43
e.	Arrival in Ephesus	46
f.	Second Jerusalem Visit (Conference)	51

---

[20] *Chronology*, pp. 30-33.

g. Last Visit to Corinth
   (Completion of collection)   54
h. Last Visit to Jerusalem   54 or 55

I attempted in *Chapters* a less detailed account of Paul's career than I have ventured to make in this essay, but the emerging schedule of dates is not substantially different from that proposed in that book,[21] it being assumed that a sixteen- to seventeen-year (rather than a fourteen-year) interval lay between conversion and conference. The major difference, which concerns the date of Paul's final Jerusalem journey, has been explained by my recognition that I probably did not allow enough time for the interval between visits two and three.

On the basis of the Acts account I have tentatively accepted the fact, not necessarily that Paul was tried before Felix and Festus, but that his arrest and presumably his trial took place somewhere close to the date of Festus's accession. A reference, at least, should be made to two other statements of Acts in which the author connects events in Paul's career with datable historical incidents. One is its statement that Claudius's edict expelling the Jews from Rome accounted for the arrival of Prisca and Aquila in Corinth not long before Paul's first stay in that city, and the second is its allusion to Paul's trial before Gallio during that same stay. Both of these data, found only in Acts, have been cited in objection to the chronological reconstruction herein proposed. To these objections I would now make the same response as is made in *Chapters*.[22]

VIII

It remains for me to comment on the two papers of Professor Luedemann and Professor Jewett, respectively, which were read at the Colloquy. I shall attempt no adequate review of either, much less of their books, in which the results of their important researches in the Pauline chronology are fully stated. As for Professor Luedemann's *Paulus, der Heidenapostel*, vol. 1, *Studien zur Chronologie*, I have spoken of it earlier in this essay with great admiration and gratitude, hailing it as the most impressive exposition and defense so far of a chronology based entirely on the letters. He associates himself closely

---

[21] *Chapters*, p. 85.

[22] *Ibid.*, pp. 81-83.

with others of us who have adopted in principle the same methodology, although the work of none of us has approached his in comprehension and detail. My own book *Chapters* and this essay will indicate the large extent of my agreement with him. A comparison of his "chronologische Übersicht"[23] with my own brief summary in *Chapters*[24] and the somewhat fuller schedule presented in this paper will show a striking similarity if his second optional dating is adopted. This resemblance holds from the dating of the conversion through that of the second (or conference) Jerusalem journey. He presents a more elaborate schedule than I do of Paul's career from the time of this visit and the beginning of the collection effort to that of its completion and his final departure for Jerusalem, but we are not far apart as to the date of that departure, just as we are not far separated in our estimate of the date of Paul's first arrival in Corinth. Our procedures in arriving at our dates are sometimes different, but these differences enhance to a degree the significance of the fact that the final results are as near together as they are. My way of understanding what probably happened, so far as Paul is concerned, between his first Jerusalem visit in 37 (Luedemann, 36) and his coming to Macedonia diverges somewhat from Luedemann's, but we are in virtual agreement as to the date of the latter event—I suggest 40 and he, 39. We clearly differ as to the identity of the "churches of Galatia." I take a larger risk than he (perhaps wisely) is willing to take in fixing, even tentatively, on the date, or even the fact, of Paul's arrest in Jerusalem.

I can see no basis in the letters for Luedemann's statement that it was the activity of the Judaizers particularly in Galatia which occasioned Paul's second Jerusalem visit for the conference;[25] Philippians, not to mention parts of Corinthians, indicate that the threat to the church's unity created by this activity was widespread. As I have said in this essay,[26] I can agree with Luedemann in his interpretation of Gal 2:7-8.[27] I can also believe with him that instructions were perhaps given to Barnabas at the conference which were not given to Paul—the

---

[23] *Paulus*, pp. 272-73, and his essay above.

[24] *Chapters*, p. 85.

[25] *Paulus*, pp. 101-105.

[26] See section III, above.

[27] *Paulus*, pp. 86-94.

former working chiefly in mixed communities and Paul among Gentiles—and, moreover, that the locale of Barnabas's work was expected to be different from that of Paul.[28] There is really no evidence in the letters that Paul and Barnabas ever worked together, although they shared in many opinions and attitudes. (First Cor 9:6 and Gal 2:1 cannot be pressed into meaning more than this mutual sympathy; only in Acts are the two represented as being actual collaborators and even there only at the very beginning of Paul's career.) As to Gal 2:11ff., I leave open, as I did in my book,[29] the question whether the incident recorded there occurred before or after the events of Gal 2:1-10. To Luedemann's view that it occurred before them I offer no determined opposition—he may well be right—although the description of the conduct of Barnabas in 2:11ff. and the indication of Paul's strong hostile reaction hardly prepare us to find him accompanying Paul to the conference. There are other points where I question Luedemann's conclusions, one or two of which I have earlier mentioned. But I recognize the brilliance, the originality, the thoroughness of his work, and, as I have said, find myself in close sympathy with it. I am also indebted to it and grateful for it. It has enlightened me with new insights as often as it has supported me in opinions I had already formed.

On Professor Jewett's significant work in this field, I have greater difficulty in commenting. Needless to say, I am deeply grateful for the appreciative remarks he makes in his Colloquy essay about my earlier work and its importance to him. But at the same time, I am somewhat surprised, and a bit perplexed by those same remarks. For in reading his book, *A Chronology of Paul's Life*, I had received the impression that he was not, and did not consider himself to be, at all positively related to what I have earlier in this paper referred to as "the developments in this field of research which began in 1936-1939." I had gathered that his acceptation of the hypothesis of a "three-Jerusalem-journeys framework of Paul's life based on evidence in Paul's letters," affirmed at the end of the introduction,[30] rested on his own reflection, later confirmed by Barnikol's treatise. And the fact that none of the

---

[28] *Ibid.*, pp. 94-101.

[29] *Chapters*, p. 59.

[30] *Chronology*, p. 5.

participants in the largely American discussion of proper method in the use of Acts and Paul's letters—that none of these is mentioned in his chapter on "The Methodical Use of Sources" led me to believe that he conceived of his method as not having been influenced by them and as being distinctively different from theirs. This impression was confirmed by the book as a whole.

He devotes a large part of chapter 4 to "Epistle Oriented Chronologies," in which he reviews very quickly (I cannot but say, sometimes too quickly and not always quite fairly) the work of Riddle, Hurd, Buck, and Taylor, my own work, and that of Luedemann, but the multitude and weight of his adverse criticisms prevented my supposing for a moment that he thought of himself as standing within this group, or even on its edge, or as having any direct, much less dependent, relationship with it or with anyone within it. To be sure, something less negative is said in the final paragraph of the chapter,[31] but hardly enough to diminish the impression that he regards his methodology as being almost entirely his own and as not to be classified with the "Epistle Oriented" ones he has been discussing. If this impression is true—and I believe that most readers of his book will receive it—my surprise and gratification on reading the paper published in this volume will be understood—and my perplexity as well. Obviously I misunderstood his book, at least to some extent.

As a matter of fact, however, I believe that Professor Jewett is quite right in placing himself at some distance from the group of American scholars I have referred to and, in doing so, from Luedemann also. I cannot "see" him standing at Luedemann's side in any current or prospective "fray" over the Pauline chronology.[32] Their differences in methodology and in the resultant chronologies are too wide. I shall not presume to defend Luedemann's views as against Jewett's or Jewett's as against Luedemann's. Both scholars are quite able to defend their own positions. But that they have different views as to the proper method in using Acts is, it seems to me, quite obvious.

In defining his own method Jewett can say: "A general rule therefore is that material from Acts is usable in the chronological experiment only when it does not conflict with the evidence in the letters."[33]

---

[31] *Ibid.*, pp. 86-87.

[32] See Jewett, "Chronology and Methodology," above.

[33] *Chronology*, p. 24.

But, one might ask, if Acts can be shown to be wrong at so many points where the letters happen to provide a "check," what assurance can one have that it is right when the letters do not provide a "check"? In his essay Jewett seems to answer that question by saying (I believe, very truly): "No single detail from Acts, it seems to me, deserves to be raised to the level of independent credibility."[34] But is this principle consistently applied? As I read Jewett's book, I do not get the impression that it is, and I believe the earlier quotation gives a more accurate clue: He follows Acts, provided Paul's letters do not clearly preclude his doing so, the one notable exception being his association of the conference with Acts 18 rather than 15. This method accounts for what I regard as flaws in his chronology itself.

I, like him, am inclined to put Paul's conversion in A.D. 34, but I can do so only because I can consider the year 30 as the more probable date for the crucifixion than 33, Jewett's preferred date; an interval of only eighteen months between the two events seems to me, for a number of reasons I have stated elsewhere,[35] very much too short. Because of the agreement on the conversion date, we can agree on 37 as the date of Paul's first visit to Jerusalem. But I can see no grounds whatever in the letters—or in Acts, for that matter—for an interval of five years before Paul entered the mission field he was to make his own, namely, the territory beyond Cilicia. According to Jewett, Paul began his own significant independent work in 43, but I can see no reason, even in Jewett's own exhibit, for the belief that he did not begin it as early as 38. The fourteen-year "silent" period is an obvious major fault in the traditional chronologies. The estimate of a "silent" period of five years is clearly to be preferred. But why have any "silent" period at all? The letters do not suggest it—rather, the contrary—and surely do not require it. Nor is there any reason provided by the letters why some of the events which Jewett must crowd into the period after 51 (where both he and I would place the conference) could not have happened *before* 51, the assumption being made that some of them happened at all (for example, *two* Asian imprisonments). If these events were thus distributed, the period separating the beginning of the collection from its completion would not need to be extended to what seems to me a

---

[34]See Jewett, "Chronology and Methodology," above.

[35]*Chapters*, p. 65.

most improbable six years; and a 55 date for Festus's accession would not be so absurdly impossible, so far as a rational Pauline chronology is concerned, as Jewett considers it to be.[36] About the "missionary journeys" scheme (including the first), which rests entirely on Acts data and serves important Acts interests, I have spoken sufficiently elsewhere.

IX

I am sorry to conclude this essay—and unfortunately this book—on so controversial a note. But how can it be otherwise if one has chosen to discuss so controversial a subject? And if I had elected to write, and had the qualifications for writing, on the subject of Synoptic Gospel criticism, the same regret would undoubtedly have had to be expressed and the same justification offered. For a consensus on neither subject is to be expected nor, as things are, even desired. So far as the subject of the Pauline chronology is concerned, not only is it highly controversial, but it is almost surely destined to be such for a long time. But I trust the reader to recognize that although in this essay I have often been adversely critical of others' views, I am under no illusion that my own are always, or especially as regards details, even usually valid. Too much of Paul's life is completely hidden from us (as 2 Cor 11:23-27 alone would remind us) for any of us who have worked, or are working, in this field to be overconfident.

On a few things perhaps we *can* agree. We recognize the incompleteness and often the unreliability of the Acts account of Paul's career and the fact that his letters represent our primary and only wholly reliable source; and that, while the letters, when minutely examined, yield far more biographical data than we might at first suspect, these data are, after all, relatively meager and are often subject to more than one interpretation. We can also agree that although our search for a valid chronology is very much worthwhile and has yielded valuable results, the comprehensiveness, clarity, and certainty we seek are still far beyond our reach and, unless some fresh and abundant evidence is miraculously discovered in some new Qumran or Nag Hammadi, will probably always be.

---

[36] *Chronology*, p. 79.

Index

The history of the economic development that has brought the world to its current state of prosperity and enlightenment is a history of many technical adjustments to our financial system, of innovations inspired by financial theory but also based on realistic assessments of human nature. This part of the book indulges in extrapolations of past trends that have resulted in better and better financial systems; it also puts forth a number of concrete ideas for how the system can be improved in coming decades.

The epilogue offers some final thoughts on how power is actually wielded in finance, on our negative feelings about the concentration of power we see in the financial world, and on how in a financial democracy such power might be managed and reconciled with basic human values.

Part One

Roles and Responsibilities

An old saying holds that while the problem with socialism is socialism, the problem with capitalism is capitalists. Some of the headlines of the past decade—from the exploits of the executives of Enron and Satyam to those of the likes of Bernard Madoff—would seem to confirm that the problem with financial capitalism is indeed financial capitalists. But achievement of the good society is dependent on a healthy and robust financial sector—including the people who occupy the roles that enable the financial system to run, and thus help the economy to run. If finance is the science of goal architecture, those who work in the field are the architects who structure these goals and manage the risks of small businesses, families, school systems, cities, corporations, and all the other vital institutions throughout society. If finance, properly understood in the good society, is the stewardship of society's assets, it is these same people who are entrusted with the management and cultivation of those assets.

In this part of the book we review a full array of roles played by financial professionals, from CEOs through accountants and philanthropists. The idea is not to biopsy these roles for their flaws. Rather it is to get to the heart of their value; to understand their functions; to better appreciate how factors such as rewards, reputation effects, and codes of conduct promote best professional practices; and also to predict how these roles are likely to change in the future. And it is also to try to understand why so much of the public does not seem to appreciate the value of these roles, and why there is so often hostility toward those who fill them. For all the talk of critics and apologists alike about Wall Street, a clear, succinct account of the various roles and relationships that actually make it work has not existed until now. But any discussion of the future of finance and its connection to the goals of the good society presumes an understanding of these roles, so we begin here.

Chapter 1

Chief Executive Officers

The CEO of a company is in a very special position, because he or she stands for an idea—the core idea behind the company's activities, a way of thinking that defines the work of all the company's employees, and a culture that includes its corporate values, connecting the company to the larger society.

The CEO is responsible for the formulation of short-run goals that promote that very idea. The CEO embodies the purpose of the company. This responsibility has to be put, to a significant extent, into the hands of an individual and not a committee of equals, just as the writing of a novel usually has to be put into the hands of one individual. Human society has natural tendencies that can coordinate the activities of teams of people in performing routine tasks; teams seem to form naturally, but they are also vulnerable to conflict and to being sidetracked by the individual goals of their members. We still need the prefrontal cortex of one individual—however it may work—coordinating the activities of large groups of people. Large groups of people cannot be strategic or purposeful if they are leaderless.

A Succession of CEOs

That said, the corporation has a fundamental problem: it has to deal with a succession of CEOs. Companies, with luck, may live for centuries. CEOs, subject to human mortality, cannot.

The essence of a corporation is its longevity. Successful corporations have no termination date, no shelf life, no inherent limits on how long they can operate. The succession of CEOs of a corporation is like a succession of kings of an empire, each one of whom takes up the flag from a fallen predecessor and reinterprets and further develops the cause. Except CEOs cannot relax to enjoy the lives of kings: they have to work especially hard.

A CEO typically serves for only a few years, during which time she or he has to set goals for a company that is much longer lived than the CEO's own tenure. Thus there has to be an effective reward system that focuses the CEO on the long term. And this is a problem that lends itself to financial solutions.

CEOs have egos and personal interests that do not necessarily coincide with the long-term interests of the firm. Companies must find ways to keep their leaders focused on their jobs, attending to the boring and often unappreciated tasks that take up much of their time. A corporation needs a leader who will do an inspired job of keeping everything running over the long term, anticipating trends and shifts and providing a vision for the company, while putting his own needs and wants second.

The ego of a CEO is most naturally satisfied if he or she is the *founding* CEO of a company, for being first in any succession carries with it the greatest ego gratification. The founding CEO of a company is of special importance. If the company endures, the founding CEO may well become a legendary figure to later generations. Years or even centuries later, the founding CEO may be remembered by employees as an almost mythic figure.

Anthropologists have noted a human universal called a creation myth—a story that everyone in a given society knows, one that describes their origins.[1] Such a myth is typically humanized by the identity of a major leader. A founding CEO is part of the creation myth for a company. The founding CEO knows this and instinctively pursues such legendary status, living out a new version of that same ancient story. But that is only the *first* CEO.

Behind the succession of CEOs lies a financial structure, which indeed makes each CEO's employment possible. The CEO of a modern corporation is technically just an employee, serving at the discretion of the board of directors. He or she is defined by a financial contract, with terms relating compensation to the performance of the company and its stock. The CEO depends on a certain financial structure, a financial invention, for motivation.

Even though the CEO is usually not the founding CEO, he or she is still expected to be a visionary. The modern corporation must be reinvented again and again, in response to new information and new market demands.

Success in reinventing the company is reflected in financial prices. When the CEO is successful, the price of shares in the company goes up. When the CEO fails, the price falls. A CEO avidly watches the company's share price—it is like a continual report card on his or her activities, issued minute by minute. It is the reward signal for the cognitive center of the company, and there is an analogy to the reward system for the decision-making apparatus in the human brain, a point to which we shall return later in this book. In the corporation, as in the brain, the reward system is imperfect but essential.

The financial arrangement for the typical CEO is carefully human engineered, designed to incentivize that person to stay in the position long enough and prominently enough that his or her relationship to others as their leader becomes firmly established in everyone's minds.

The dispensation to CEOs of stock or options on the company's own shares is a method of aligning the CEO's incentives with those of the company. An option to buy a share in the company at a specified price is valuable only if the actual market price is higher, and so granting options to the CEO creates an incentive to take actions that will boost the firm's share price.

A share of stock does not have a termination date, as does the CEO's tenure. Assuming that the stock market price of a share in the company is a good indication of its true *long-term* value, then the change in the stock price is a measure of the CEO's contribution to the long-term value of the company. The stock price signals a reward only if there is good news. It responds to actual news, and it does not encourage gloating over past successes. The CEO is thereby incentivized to be the bearer, to attentive investors, of good news about the company's long-run potential—news about the long run, but news that is delivered today, *right now*—and thus to plan for the indefinite future, not just his or her own tenure.

Incentivizing by stock options can be a lot better than awarding bonuses to the CEO for achieving high profits: profits-based bonuses might encourage the CEO to merely milk the company in the short run, neglecting longer-term problems and leaving a disastrous situation for his or her successor. With stock-price-related incentives, on the other hand, the CEO is encouraged to steer the company toward opportunities that could improve its *long-term* value.

Setting the Level of the Reward

The salaries and bonuses of CEOs are the subject of many news accounts, owing to their extraordinarily high levels, especially in recent decades and especially in the United States. The anger and resentment over executive compensation account for much of the public hostility toward financial capitalism in general.

But sometimes a high level of compensation for a CEO is readily understandable. Consider the example of a man who was the very successful CEO of Corporation A, who has turned the company around, taking it from the brink of failure to success. Along the way he handled numerous unpleasant tasks like firing key people, waging policy battles against entrenched forces within the company, and shutting down operations—and he did so in such a politically deft way that those who remained in place were not resentful, and indeed were motivated to take the company to new levels. He was paid handsomely for his work, and he now presides over a well-managed, successful company. He may be thinking about retiring early and enjoying some of his fortune.

Now suppose the board of directors of Corporation B feels it needs to take those same drastic actions. It is entirely plausible that they would ask our CEO to quit his present job and become their new CEO. They *could* ask someone with no such experience to do what he did, but that other person would not have the same personality, the same judgment. They want *him*.

It is entirely possible that our CEO will respond that he has had enough of this unpleasant business and in fact has more money than he could ever spend. No, he doesn't want to go through all that again.

So it is plausible in turn that the board of Corporation B would offer a really attractive package to lure the CEO—a package that might, say, offer options on the company's stock potentially worth $30–50 million if he is successful. That amount is not enormous relative to the earnings of a large company. A diligent board exercising its fiduciary responsibility in presiding over a company with billions in revenue might consider a highly qualified, proven CEO worth all of this.

Running, or turning around, a business all over again, after one has already done it, may not seem all that glorious in and of itself the second or even third time around—yet it is precisely those who have done such an important job before who have the best credentials to do it again. CEOs, even those of Fortune 500 companies, are not usually particularly beloved or famous, with only a few exceptions. Thus high compensation is the best way to attract qualified candidates to such jobs.

It is often observed that in decades past, when CEO salaries were much lower, companies still found people who were willing to do the job. As president of American Motors from 1954 to 1962, George Romney, Mitt Romney's father, turned down huge bonuses.[2] In 1978 Lee Iacocca offered to serve as the CEO of Chrysler, to save it from bankruptcy, for a salary of only one dollar.[3] These are fine examples, but they do not mean that companies can always cheaply hire the CEOs they want. Romney and Iacocca were rare exceptions: each had a strong public moral persona, and for them such symbolic gestures may have been especially important. Romney later became governor of Michigan, and Iacocca later wrote three best-selling books about his business philosophy. At one time or another both showed signs of running for president.[4]

Moreover, the growth in high salaries that we have seen in recent decades might in part be explained as the result of improvements in our capitalist system, as the system comes to recognize the importance of qualified leaders and refuses to be bound by arbitrary pay conventions.

This is why the Squam Lake Group (a nonpartisan, nonaffiliated group of fifteen academics who offer counsel on financial regulation, of which I am a member) advised in its 2009 report that the government should not regulate the *level* of CEO compensation. Some CEOs are, and always will be, worth a great deal to their firms. On the other hand, the group *did* believe that regulation of the *structure* of CEO compensation is called for.[5]

Moral Hazard and Deferred Compensation

There *is* a reason for the government to intervene in the process of determining executive salaries: to mitigate a specific moral hazard that seems to have played a substantial role in causing the financial crisis that began in 2007—at least for big and so-called systemically important firms. This moral hazard arises because the CEOs and other top officers of such key firms have incentives to take extraordinary risks. They believe that their companies are too big to be allowed to fail. Because the failure of their companies would be simply too disruptive to the economy as a whole, they reason that the government will not allow that to happen.

Given such a mindset, the CEO may not very much care about the risk of precipitating an international financial crisis. He may on the other hand be very interested in taking a gamble that gives him a 50% chance of achieving a huge increase in the stock price and so reaping a windfall on his stock options—even if that same gamble has a 50% chance of wiping out the company and taking much of the global economy with it. In the one case, he ends up rich. In the other, well, his options are worth nothing—but they might have been worth nothing *for sure* if he had not taken the gamble.

Moreover, a CEO with a stock-option-based compensation scheme has an incentive to manipulate the flow of information out of the company and to doctor financial reports—to delay the release of unfavorable information until after he has received his compensation. And such practices do not conflict with the efficient markets theory—the theory, to be discussed in various places later in this book, that market prices efficiently and quickly incorporate all public information about a company. The CEO is a company insider and knows things that are being deliberately kept secret from the market.

Therefore, the Squam Lake Group recommended that government require that systemically important firms defer a substantial part of their CEOs' compensation for an extended period, say, five years.

The 2010 Dodd-Frank Wall Street Reform and Consumer Protection Act in the United States contains terms that resemble the Squam Lake Group's recommendation. Notably, the act includes provisions that require a CEO to give back "erroneously awarded compensation" that was the result of "material noncompliance of the issuer with any financial reporting requirement under the securities laws."[6] Yet the Squam Lake proposal is more far-reaching, in that it would deprive the CEO of the rest of the compensation if ever there were a bailout or failure of the company.

Cronyism in the Boardroom

Of course there are different circumstances under which a CEO might receive an especially high salary. It could be fraud. It could be that the board of directors votes in favor of a high salary out of a sense of professional courtesy or class sympathy. There may even be individual expectations of being repaid in kind later on.

Lucian Bebchuk and Jesse Fried, both professors at Harvard Law School, have argued in their 2006 book *Pay without Performance* that the growth of top executive salaries has largely been the result of a breakdown in the arms-length bargaining process between boards of directors and the top executives they hire. When the "bargaining" is among close friends, it may have only the appearance of being fair: "Directors have had various economic incentives to support, or at least go along with, arrangements favorable to the company's top executives. Various social and psychological factors—collegiality, team spirit, a natural desire to avoid conflict within the board team, and sometimes friendship and loyalty—have also pulled board members in that direction."[7]

Thus it is ultimately psychological tendencies that underlie the problem of cronyism in the boardroom. There has been public awareness of this problem, and reforms strengthening director independence have already been introduced by lawmakers. But the problem persists.

The issue, Bebchuk and Fried argue, is not with financial capitalism, but with certain details of its implementation. To reduce the problem of board favoritism, they propose reform of the election of board members, measures to make it easier to replace a board, and procedures to give shareholders the power to initiate changes in corporate charters.

The rise over the second half of the twentieth century of venture capital firms—which specialize in providing funding to unproven startup companies that have a high probability of failure, hoping to profit from the few that succeed—has helped deal with such problems, at least for startup or early-stage firms. They have replaced many of the angel investors—independently wealthy individuals who have supported startup firms in the past, investors who are not investment professionals and who, through inexperience, are vulnerable to error.

Venture capital firms have learned some things about CEO talent and compensation over the years. They have learned that the talent and dedication of the CEO and top executives make an enormous difference to the success of the firm, but that these talented people--at the stage in their lives when they are most hungry and most energetic—are not necessarily expensive to hire. Venture capital firms do make sure that the top executives in the firms they fund will participate substantially in the possible success of their companies; the firms have learned how to structure contracts, typically including stock options, that motivate executives well and protect them against the high risk of failure. A venture capital firm almost always demands a seat on the board of directors—a vantage point from which it will stop in its tracks any non-arms-length deals excessively rewarding CEOs. Venture capital firms also are more likely than angel investors to replace the founder with an outside CEO when things go badly.[8] Unfortunately, venture capital firms typically sell their shares and exit the business as firms in which they have invested succeed and grow larger.

Institutional investors—portfolio managers, to be discussed later—can sometimes enforce similar limits on executive overcompensation. Yet there is still a need to improve their methods and organization to help them do a better job of this.

Another ultimate cause of excessive CEO compensation is a public failure to understand the problem that Bebchuk and Fried have described. The general public, at least in the United States, cannot really appreciate all the issues surrounding the extremely high salaries paid to some executives, and the public has therefore been excessively willing to acquiesce in those salaries.

Failure to recognize the problem of non-arms-length negotiations between their boards and their top executives was a sign of the times in the late twentieth century, when there was excessive complacency about the ability of an unregulated free-market system to work perfectly. The late twentieth century was the era of the "charismatic CEO," overvalued by the public and incentivized to take excessive risks to perform miracles to justify his or her salary.[9] Indeed there was a bubble in executive salaries that mirrored the bubbles in home prices and stock prices.

The Universality of the CEO Incentivization Problem

The fundamental nature of the problem of CEO compensation can be seen from the fact that the same issues arose even in communist countries.

Yugoslav economist Milovan Djilas, in his 1957 book *The New Class: An Analysis of the Communist System*, showed frank parallels between executive behavior in communist countries and that in western countries.[10] His criticism of the communist system derailed Djilas' hopes of succeeding Josip Broz Tito as leader of Yugoslavia. It candidly exposed problems, including the reward system for government executives—a system that resembled the bonus system of western corporations. Government officials would receive an expensive house and other perks if they performed well. Communist managers form a crony system to milk the enterprise to their own advantage, just as certain managers do in capitalist countries.

David Granick, in his 1960 book *The Red Executive*, pointed out many more parallels between the Soviet *nomenklatura* and the western financial class. Business management in the Soviet Union relied on party committees, city committees, and regional committees who had an interest in the success of an enterprise and who played much the same role that stockholders and their appointed boards of directors do in western countries: choosing, motivating, and sometimes disciplining managers.[11] The Soviets had rediscovered the advantages of a system that awarded incentives to executives who would work hard to make an enterprise successful.[12]

The problem of motivating CEOs is a basic one, and difficult to solve. But as our understanding of the workings of the economy evolves, we find ourselves somewhat freed from the mistakes of the past. The roles of top managers (as well as their titles) are bound to change over time as we discover better ways to find and incentivize people to take on leadership roles and to take to heart the deepest goals of the organizations they lead.

In the future, we will still hear about some CEOs with extraordinarily high(-sounding) salaries and benefits. That will be part of the story of financial capitalism, but we can hope that there will be more sense to the process of awarding these benefits and so better public acceptance of them. This—and a better public appreciation of the principles underlying the corporation—would better align the interests of the corporation with those of the larger society.

Chapter 2

Investment Managers

Investment managers—those who manage portfolios of shares in companies, bonds, and other investments—are among the most important stewards of our wealth and thus vitally important players in the service of healthy and prosperous market democracies—in the service of the good society. They are employed by all kinds of organizations, from multinational corporations and union pension funds through city governments, universities, libraries, and churches. The funds they manage are of many different types and legal forms, with names like "mutual funds," "unit investment trusts," "exchange-traded funds," "hedge funds," or "private equity funds." In this chapter we lump the managers of all these different kinds of funds together according to their common purpose: they determine the composition of portfolios of investments on behalf of their clients and buy and hold those portfolios for those clients, the ultimate investors.

These managers provide many services to the investors who entrust their money to them, including such routine services as safekeeping of securities; spreading out investments into broadly diversified portfolios; recordkeeping; and minimizing the tax impact of investments in consideration of the client's particular tax status. They also deal with clients' special concerns, related to their long- or short-term goals; their needs for liquidity; risks they face, such as regional or political risks; and their priorities in terms of "green" or ethical investing. But they do much more than that, for they are a guiding force in the economy. When they actively select investments, they are directing capital toward particular uses at the expense of others, and they have an incentive to

27

try to direct capital to its best uses. Investment managers serve millions of people worldwide, including those with special needs: the retired, the sick, teachers, police, the dependent, young students. They are of fundamental importance.

And yet investment managers are, like the CEOs discussed in the previous chapter, subject to public hostility. This hostility comes in part from the same public sense that they are overpaid, that they are making "obscene" incomes. But public hostility toward investment managers also arises from another source: a sense that they cannot in fact do what they claim to do, to achieve better-than-average returns on the investments they manage. Hence the lack of trust between investment managers and the public they serve.

Beating the Market

Despite the wide variety of services investment managers provide, most advertise themselves as achieving superior returns, through active management of their portfolios and picking stocks that they predict will do well in the future. For much of history, most investment managers have *really* been in the business of "beating the market."

The popular efficient markets theory that has taken hold in academia is seen by many as implying that such investment managers are in fact, to put it bluntly, frauds. If statistical evidence proves that no one can outperform a strategy of choosing investments randomly, then their attempts to claim that they do so must be fundamentally dishonest. There is an element of truth to this academic view: many investment managers have succeeded in creating false impressions as to their superiority as investors.

Evidence in the academic finance literature shows that actively managed stock market mutual funds have generally been worse investments in recent decades than funds that follow a passive investment strategy and merely invest in all shares in the stock market. For example, Martin Gruber found in 1996 that mutual funds underperformed a diversified investment in the stock market by about 1.5% a year.[1] This underperformance reflected the regularly scheduled management fees imposed by the mutual funds on their investors, but not the load fees (large one-time-only fees that are collected when money is invested or taken out), so the actual performance of mutual funds was even worse.

Professional investment managers do not seem to do particularly well in selecting their own personal portfolios either. A 2011 study by Andriy Bodnaruk and Andrei Simonov obtained data on the personal portfolios of mutual fund managers in Sweden.[2] (It is possible to get these data in Sweden because the country levied a wealth tax until 2007, and so wealthy people had to report their entire personal portfolios to the government.) They found that the investment managers did no better on their investments than the average investor, nor were they more diversified.

And yet, in the past half century, investments in actively managed funds have grown dramatically. It would seem that investors, by entrusting their assets to these managers, must have been irrational. In his study Gruber concluded that not *all* mutual fund investors were irrational, since there is *some* persistence through time in mutual fund investment performance, and some investors, who are quick to follow the best mutual funds with their money, exploit this situation. But most people who invest in mutual funds are not so sophisticated, and they stay in poorly performing mutual funds. In many cases they do so because their mutual funds are held in retirement plans that do not give them a free choice of funds.

The basic diversification and portfolio services provided by mutual funds still make sense for many, and it is not that investors are terribly served by the current system. Certainly there may be many investors who do not choose their investment managers well—an issue to be addressed and remedied in the future. But we should not reach the unwarranted conclusion that investment managers, like mutual funds, are not providing a service to the public.

Modern academic finance sometimes seems to take the evidence on underperformance of investment managers as proof that no one should be leaving their assets in the hands of a professional investment manager since, given extremely efficient markets, there is nothing for these managers to do. Carried to its logical conclusion, this same efficient markets theory also appears to imply that *anyone* who trades in financial markets is making a mistake. By this logic, one should just buy a diversified portfolio and be done with it, except perhaps for periodic rebalancing to keep the portfolio diversified. It would mean there is nothing investment managers can do to beat the market.

The modern theory, which has held great influence in recent decades, asserts that there is no way to be smart about investment returns. In the words of Andrew Redleaf and Richard Vigilante, who are themselves hedge fund managers, "If the ideology of modern finance had a motto, it might be 'thinking doesn't work.'"[3]

But this cannot be the right conclusion to draw about investment managers. Surely professional attention to the investment of individuals' wealth cannot in the long run be detrimental to society. These professionals are paid to think about what should be done for investors.

There are problems with the efficient markets theory, and in particular with the notion that the market is so perfectly efficient because smart traders have made it so. If everyone is so rational, then why is there so much trading in these markets? If you can't make a profit trading, how can it be rational that there is so much trading going on?

Maybe the trades are made because some traders have inside information that others do not. But in a much-talked-about 1982 paper financial theorists Paul Milgrom and Nancy Stokey argued—assuming perfectly rational markets that incorporate all public information into prices—that even people with private information, information not known to the public, would not trade. Reducing their argument to its simplest form, they said they would not trade because they could not find trading partners among people who do not share their information, and they could not find trading partners because any potential trading partner would refuse to trade with someone who was motivated to trade only because of superior information.[4]

We *do* observe trading in financial markets—massive amounts of trading—and so, leveraging from Milgrom and Stokey, one might conclude that all this trade is ill advised from the standpoint of at least one of the two trading parties. One is led to wonder if psychological principles, such as overconfidence, are the dominant reason for trade in financial markets—or if those who profit from such trades, including stockbrokers and others, are not making suckers out of at least half of their customers.

But perhaps the Milgrom and Stokey theory is not really evidence that such overconfidence dominates. We might instead regard the theory as a reductio ad absurdum for the efficient markets theory. How can markets become efficient if that very result would imply that nobody trades?

If markets are going to display prices that efficiently incorporate all information, there has to be some activity. Part of this activity would involve trading, and other parts of it would involve information gathering. All this takes time and effort, and costs money. Who would undertake such activities if all markets were perfectly efficient? This viewpoint is reflected in another classic paper in financial theory, "The Impossibility of Informationally Efficient Markets," written by financial theorists Sanford Grossman and Joseph Stiglitz.[5] They frame their conclusion in terms of the "nonexistence" of an efficient markets "equilibrium." In other words, it just doesn't make sense to suppose that markets are really generally completely efficient.

Persistence of Investment Manager Performance

It is of course a truism that the average investor can never beat the market since the market is itself the definition of the average investor. And, as professional investors increasingly dominate trading, the average professional investor is fast becoming that average investor. But still there remains something useful for society in a competition among these professionals—a competition that eventually rewards the smartest institutional investors—for this competition leads to the best people rising to the top of the investment management world and taking control of the allocation of capital in our economy.

This theory relies, however, on the assumption that the smarter investors do tend to win. There is nothing in financial theory to deny that smarter investors should tend to win. There are only doubts that the financial system really rewards the smarter investors—doubts based on empirical research that some interpret as saying that financial outcomes are really just random, like the tossing of dice.

Casual observation indeed suggests that smarter investors do tend to win. The investment endowments at top U.S. universities have performed exceptionally well. My own university, Yale, leads the pack, with a 14.2% average annual return on its endowment portfolio under David Swensen in the twenty-six years since he began managing Yale's endowment in 1985, even including the years of the financial crisis since 2007.[6] Other universities have done nearly as well in recent years, notably Harvard and Princeton. Yet these universities haven't always done so well with their endowments: it was not until they established modern finance departments and cultivated a real sense of intellectual discipline about investing that their trustees would allow such thinking, rather than permitting traditional investing by conventional wisdom to dictate the composition of their portfolios.

But these isolated examples do not constitute proof that smarter investors tend to do better. It is hard to find out if smarter people generally can beat the market since it is hard to measure who is smarter. But we can find the names of the colleges investment managers attended, and there are data on average Scholastic Aptitude Test scores for students entering those colleges. Judith Chevalier and Glenn Ellison found evidence that smartness does generate performance for mutual fund managers.[7] Haitao Li, Xiaoyan Zhang, and Rui Zhao found similar results for hedge fund managers.[8] Mark Grinblatt, Matti Keloharju, and Juhani Linnainmaa found that individuals in Finland with higher IQ scores (measured when they first reported for that country's mandatory military service) showed evidence of better performance on their choices of investments, after correcting for risk.[9]

Another tack is to look at the *persistence* of performance of professional investors. We can measure their intelligence indirectly by looking at their investment performance up to a point in time, and see whether their subsequent investment performance is similarly high or low. That will allow us to determine whether investment success is just random from year to year or instead related to some characteristic, presumably intelligence, of the manager.

A number of studies have found modest persistence of mutual fund managers' performance, though the persistence seems to last no more than a year.

Harry Kat and Faye Menexe studied hedge funds. They found a small degree of persistence in hedge fund average return, though their ability to measure it was swamped by the enormous variability of their returns.[10]

Steven Kaplan and Antoinette Schoar studied private equity firms, firms that invest in stocks that are not publicly traded on stock exchanges. They concluded that "General partners . . . whose funds outperform the industry in one fund are likely to outperform the industry in the next and vice versa."[11] In judging the amount of persistence, which often seems small, one must consider that for an investment professional managing a large portfolio of a billion dollars, the extra return that this manager must earn to justify compensation of a million dollars a year is only 0.1% a year. Standard economic theory implies that competition among investment managers should drive them to the point where they just earn their keep, and so the excess return that they generate might be driven down to such a small number that it would be hard to detect among all the noise—yet they are earning their compensation. Competition should drive their returns down to the level at which they are on the point of looking for a job in another line of business. Part of the competition takes the form of new investment managers arriving in the business, hoping to compete with the existing ones, and thereby depriving the existing ones of investment opportunities. Another part of the competition takes the form of investors asking a successful existing portfolio manager to invest more money for them; faced with an ever larger portfolio to manage, the manager runs out of good investment opportunities and sees fund performance decline.[12]

Bubbles in Investment Manager Remuneration

Are top investment managers smart enough that they could routinely expect to earn a million dollars a year in another line of work? If so, and if the alternative incomes are predictable, they will have an incentive to leave investment management after their investment returns sink to this level or below, and the million-dollar-a-year income for investment managers will tend, by basic principles of economics, to be conserved. Workers' arbitrage across occupations will tend to keep the returns to skilled investing down to this level, and not let it fall below this level either. If investment managers' ability to earn excess returns through investing fell below this level, some of them would exit to their alternative jobs.

However, there is a complication: one cannot know exactly what the prospective excess return one can earn as an investment manager will be in the future, and one cannot easily move into another million-dollar-a-year occupation. Both learning about prospective excess returns and preparing for an occupation take so many years that the process of equilibrating alternative career earnings may take a generation or more.

In the meantime, there may be speculative bubbles—both positive and negative—in investment managers' salaries. If at any point there has been a shortage of skilled investment managers, then those who are in the business will earn high returns. It will be hard for others, in other lines of business, to train themselves quickly to perform at the pinnacle in investment management, and it will take years for new young people to come into the business to compete with them. It will likewise take years before the potential competitors appreciate that the existing managers really have achieved high returns by investing intelligently.

Eventually many more people will attempt to move into the investment management business. The field will become overcrowded, and investment returns will become disappointing. Then, after more years have passed, investors will become less willing to pay high compensation to investment managers and the bubble will burst; the compensation trend may even overshoot in the downward direction.

Bubbles in investment manager compensation may tend to occur in synchrony with bubbles in the markets themselves, to the extent that investors who allocate funds to investment managers are confused and assume that returns due only to the market are attributable to manager skill. We apparently have seen such a bubble in investment manager compensation in the bubble years of the late 1990s and early 2000s, when the stock markets of the world did very well. The bubble has generated such significant anger among the general public that there have been many calls to restrict the earnings of investment managers, along with those of top executives.

But it is perhaps not necessary for governments to put any caps on the salaries that investment managers earn, for the market forces needed to bring them down may already be in place. If we are seeing the bursting of a bubble in investment manager compensation, we may see relatively lean times in coming years for people in this line of business. Anyone contemplating going into this line of work must take such considerations into mind.

In his book *Enough! True Measures of Money, Business, and Life*, the founder of the Vanguard Funds, John C. Bogle, laments that many in the financial community are milking society based on their false hopes of extraordinary profits. There must be some element of truth here, but the true magnitude of this "milking" is hard to pin down, as Bogle himself recognizes: "I know of not one academic study that has systematically attempted to calculate the value extracted by our financial system from the returns earned by investors."[13]

It will be just as hard to measure the benefit that the financial community provides in improving the allocation of resources and incentives to achieve business success. Taking a simple approach, one might note that the United States and Switzerland are the two countries with the highest per capita income, and are also among the countries with the most advanced financial sectors. Ross Levine has taken such comparisons to a higher and more systematic level, comparing many countries.[14] But it is hard to sort out real causality. Are the more advanced countries successful because of their advanced financial markets, or is their success the cause of the financial development?

The real problem is that it is difficult to prove to what extent things would be different if the financial community did not exist. It is possible to compute how much those in the financial community are paid, and the combined impact of that compensation on investor returns has been documented.[15] Yet the aggregate benefit of all these people, offsetting this cost, is hard to measure. Much of this benefit is in a form that is external to the individual investor's decision: the process of investment management makes markets more efficient and thus directs resources in a better way.

Deceptive Games Investment Managers Play

Financial theorists have developed a substantial literature on how to evaluate the success of portfolio managers. An important fundamental problem is that investment managers can appear to do very well for a long time by investing in assets that other investors shun because of perceived risks, so long as there is no current news about such risks. The manager can take home high management fees for all the years that the risks do not show up, and then walk away when the catastrophe finally comes.

For years, finance students have been taught to use the Sharpe ratio to evaluate whether a portfolio manager is really beating the market. The Sharpe ratio, named after Stanford University finance professor William Sharpe, is the average excess return over the historical life of the manager's portfolio above the return of the market of all possible investments as a whole divided by the standard deviation of the return over the historical life of the manager's portfolio. A high Sharpe ratio is taken as a sign of a good investment manager. If the manager is outperforming the market consistently, then the numerator of the ratio should be large. But if the manager is taking significant risks to achieve a high return relative to the market, that will show up in the denominator as high variability in the manager's portfolio return, and thus bring down the Sharpe ratio.

But the Sharpe ratio is not necessarily a reliable indicator of a manager's performance, as the risks do not necessarily show up in a high standard deviation of returns for the portfolio over most of its life. If there is no news about the risks, then prices will not change, until the catastrophe comes.

Consider for example the risk of investing in politically unstable economies. Those investments are inherently very risky. But suppose the country was Egypt under Hosni Mubarak. The end of his regime came with shocking suddenness in 2011. It can be traced to an outbreak of riots in neighboring Tunisia. Within a month the quick fall of the Tunisian government had encouraged similar rioting in Egypt by those who sensed that Tunisia marked an important turning point and that the time was ripe for a popular revolt against Mubarak.

Investment managers can seek out investments like those in Egypt under Mubarak, ones that will blow up only in the future. If their sole objective is to pocket management fees right now, and they have no sense of integrity or commitment to their clients, they have a strong incentive to do just that. They know they cannot be prosecuted for negligence: who could really be blamed for not predicting something like Mubarak's overthrow? So if they are cynical they won't give such risks a moment's thought.

William Goetzmann and some of his colleagues in the Yale finance group have calculated the optimal strategy for a manager of an investment fund who wishes to deceive investors by producing good returns for a number of years, and then to take the investment fees and run in that rare year when the fund does very badly for its investors.[16] Such a nefarious strategy generates "tail risk," risk in the tails of the probability distribution of investment returns, or, in other words, "black swan events" that are so rare that investors may not see them coming, even though they are huge when they do occur. In the meantime, the investment fund can profit from the appearance of good and safe returns. The optimal strategy involves adding options to the portfolio, in such a way as to sell off the benefit of any (rare) unusually high portfolio returns (sell out-of-the-money call options on the portfolio) and also to profit in the short run by redoubling any (rare) unusually bad portfolio returns (sell out-of-the-money put options on the portfolio).

Investment companies can legally engage in such shenanigans if they disclose them. The private investment company Integral Investment Management, managed by former biologist Conrad Seghers, advertised, according to a *Wall Street Journal* story, an extremely high Sharpe ratio but disclosed that it was pursuing some unusual derivatives activities.[17] According to Goetzmann and his co-authors, Integral was coming close to the optimal Sharpe ratio manipulation because of massive sales of out-of-the-money puts on U.S. equity indices and a short call position implicit in the hedge fund fees. The manipulation worked, and Integral managed to persuade the Art Institute of Chicago to invest $43 million of its endowment in Integral and related funds. After the stock market collapse in 2001, and at least a $20 million loss on its investment, the Art Institute sued Integral. Integral was caught on a number of securities law violations, but it was not penalized for its unusual Sharpe ratio strategy.[18]

This example illustrates why investing cannot be done by the numbers alone. Integral Investment Management looked great in terms of the numbers. But the advantages were illusory. Other firms that pursue similar strategies that are not based on options trades may be even more successful at the same game Integral played. That is why one cannot merely allocate funds to the investment company that has had the highest historic returns or Sharpe ratios or any other statistic. These high numbers may be evidence of something very different than the competence of the managers. One must judge the integrity of the people who run the fund by the broad picture of their actions over time, and by other clues to their behavior. Character matters, and it is reflected in the reputation of certain firms, for better and worse.

Regulations can make it more difficult for retail investment companies to pursue such tricks. Securities laws in the United States and other countries prohibit investment companies from failing to state a material fact if such an omission would make their report of past returns misleading. These regulations are, however, necessarily imperfect. What "material fact" before 2011 could a fund have been accused of omitting that would have predicted the overthrow of Mubarak? The regulations were unsuccessful in preventing the deceptions that contributed substantially to the severity of the financial crisis that began in 2007.[19]

Integrity in Investment Management

The efficient markets theory works as well as it appears to because the theory is most routinely tested with assets that are heavily traded—assets that professional managers have done their best to price accurately, and hence have effectively endorsed as honest investments at the current price. In this way, the investment profession—including its self-regulatory organizations, which work with government regulators—is collectively responsible for the integrity that exists in our financial markets. We trust the market prices of investment-grade assets not just because they have had a market test but because we trust the integrity of the many analysts who evaluate them.

As Henry Kaufman, a managing director of Salomon Brothers, concluded in his 2001 book *On Money and Markets:* "Trust is the cornerstone of most relationships in life. Financial institutions and markets must rest on a foundation of trust as well."[20]

It is also a conclusion reached by Anna Bernasek in her 2010 book *The Economics of Integrity.* She refers to the "constant temptation to cut corners to save money or exploit the trust of others." But businesspeople with moral standards resist that temptation: "Integrity works to create wealth by making the economy more efficient."[21]

Ultimately, the idea that investment managers as a group are "frauds" because they cannot as a group outperform the market is mistaken. They are providing a multitude of services, including honestly watching over portfolios with sympathy for the needs of their clients—and the better among them apparently *are* outperforming the market. The intellectual community that they provide also constitutes an externality that benefits society, in directing resources and incorporating information into market prices. In the future, better regulation and better financial advice for general investors can help improve the overall state of the investment management industry.

Chapter 3

Bankers

Banks—and bankers—have survived centuries of financial evolution, and thus have found an important ecological niche in the economy. The form taken by banks evolves steadily; their function remains much the same. Their activities are fundamental to the economic environment; notably they provide transaction services and contribute to the money supply, which in turn facilitates commerce. They are so involved in our daily lives that they are known by everyone, and banking is a concept integral to modern world culture.

And yet there is immense hostility today toward bankers. The word *bankster* (rhymes with *gangster*) has come back into vogue to describe them. The word was first coined amidst the anger of the Great Depression of the 1930s, and it has returned with the public anger directed toward the financial community today. Much of this venom is directed at bankers because they were bailed out by the government, their compensation continuing at high levels while the economy remained in the doldrums.

Governments have put in place elaborate sets of laws and regulations to make it possible for such institutions to minimize the faults that have generated such ill will. In particular governments want to prevent instabilities in the banking system from creating economic recessions and depressions, as they have many times in history. And yet banks themselves are constantly and fundamentally changing, becoming much more sophisticated and universal in their activities—a trend that makes the problem of their regulation tougher and tougher, to the consternation and despair of bank regulators.

It is a curious fact that while there is much criticism of bankers, people do not carry over to them the criticism they aim at investment managers for their claims that they can beat the market. Of course, bankers are in much the same business as investment managers: when bankers make loans they are in effect making risky investments, just as investment managers do. But somehow it is thought that bankers must know what they are doing. This distinction must in part have to do with the fact that bankers typically stay out of the most volatile, headline-grabbing markets. But perhaps too it is because bankers, in contrast to hedge fund managers and the like, are following a long and time-honored tradition, extending back hundreds of years, which has evolved to solve certain problems—including liquidity, moral hazard and selection bias, and transaction service problems—to the satisfaction of most people most of the time.

The anger toward bankers takes a very different form. It seems to be anger at their power and presumption, at their single-minded pursuit of money. And the anger flares up whenever there is a banking crisis and the governments of the world come to the rescue of these wealthy interests.

But the public also has a sense of the centrality, sobriety, and safety of banks, and they must know that those who manage banks are highly influential in determining the economic outcomes in our society. The people who run banks indeed find themselves in a guidance or management role for the whole community.

Banking has historically been a pillar-of-the-community line of business, one that provides a degree of extra-monetary reward for those who go into it, at least in normal times when things are going well. But these days—at least as of the time of this writing—that feeling of reward is not so apparent.

The Origins of Banks

The current metaphor for a bank is a safe or vault for storing gold or money. The metaphor has become so ingrained in our thinking that the bank is thought of, viscerally, as providing a safe and practical investment option. In reality, the modern word *bank* was derived not from the word *safe* but, by the fifteenth century, from the Old Italian *banca*, related to the English word *bench*, referring to the tables on which bankers counted money in front of their customers. Still, metaphor counts for more than etymology in popular culture, and part of the ecological niche that banks occupy is still as a perfectly safe place to put one's money.

There will always be anxieties about money and a demand for the safest place to put it. Protecting wealth from theft or loss is a fundamental problem that has animated people from the very beginnings of the exchange economy. Even in today's anti-finance climate, people remain grateful for the services banks provide, and they still trust them.

For thousands of years, the best way to safeguard precious metals, jewels, or money was actually not to put them in a bank but just to bury them in an unmarked spot in a yard. Unfortunately burying valuables in a yard has drawbacks, too, as illustrated in Moliere's play *The Miser*, in which the rich man Harpagon has buried his fortune in his garden. His continual worries about whether it is still there eventually cause him unwittingly to reveal its location, and it is stolen. Moreover, burying gold is no longer as safe as it once was, as modern metal detectors can find it. We can't go back to ancient ways. We all need a modern provider of safety in saving.

The metaphor of the bank that developed after the Renaissance was the ancient citadel, or fortress, in the center of a city, like the Acropolis in ancient Greece. The wealthiest and most influential people could put their money there for safekeeping. That is part of the reason why bank buildings for centuries were built to resemble the Acropolis and other such classical buildings of a type found in citadels.

Bankers as Providers of Safe Return with Liquidity

A problem with burying gold or storing it in the citadel is that it earns no interest. People thus learned to trade off some safety for return, and even in ancient times they would leave some of their gold with money lenders. In ancient Rome, these establishments were called *tabernae argentariae* (literally, shops of money). They would pay interest on deposits left with them and make a profit by charging a higher interest rate on loans they made. About seven first-century examples of these *tabernae argentariae*, little more than small storefronts along a street, were found (with some of the coins still there) near the Pantheon in the ruins of ancient Pompeii. These were simple shops that housed a money lender with a few assistants; they were not large organizations like banks today. Pedestals for the oblong tables on which the money lenders counted the money are still visible. With so many to choose from, a depositor of the time could easily diversify the risk and deposit with several of them.

So banks are managers of investments on behalf of clients, just like other kinds of investment managers, but with greater claims to safety. The defining characteristic of banks has generally been that their investments take the form of deposits which pay a fixed interest rate, rather than an uncertain return, and that the deposits are usually liquid; that is, the money can be withdrawn with no more than short notice. Bank deposits are thus as freely available as money buried in the garden, but they improve on that approach in terms of safety and expected return.

The safety and return that banks offer bear further examination. How is it that they can offer a respectable return with great liquidity and little risk? Is it just because they are backed by the government, which won't let them fail out of concern for the economy? Banks flourished long before governments were generally involved in insuring their deposits or bailing them out when they were in trouble.

Banks solve a fundamental problem potentially encountered by anyone who seeks a return on an investment. If you as an individual loan money to another individual, who in turn uses the money to start or expand a business, or to buy a house, you can't demand it back with interest at a moment's notice. You have to wait until the business matures and starts yielding profits, or until the house can be sold at a profit. You probably can't easily sell your loan to another investor either. So in terms of ready cash flow you are in a bind—you are illiquid.

Banks also can't get their money back quickly from most of their investments. But banks achieve liquidity for their depositors by another means: pooling the investments of many depositors. They do not invest all the money that is deposited with them in illiquid investments. They keep in liquid form an amount of capital sufficient to cover the normal volume of withdrawals. So everyone can make deposits that are backed by illiquid investments yet have their individual deposits remain highly liquid. It seems almost a miracle.

This system usually works as intended, though it is vulnerable to sudden panic or bank runs: if people begin to distrust the bank, too many of them may ask to withdraw their money at one time and they will exhaust the bank's supply of liquid funds.[1] Even then, and even if there is no deposit insurance, if the government allows the bank to suspend liquidity temporarily, then depositors will still in all likelihood eventually get paid most of what they were owed, as the bank converts some of its illiquid holdings into cash.

Bank regulators in modern times attempt to further reduce the problem of bank runs by demanding that banks maintain an adequate amount of reserves (cash in the vault or deposits at other banks, to make good immediately on any sudden withdrawals by depositors) and of capital (the total cushion of assets, after subtracting liabilities, available to make good on promises to depositors), so that they will not put the government in the position of having to bail out the banks. In the United States, explicit reserve requirements date back to the early days of the Federal Reserve, in 1917.[2] Capital requirements for banks began to be enforced by the United States in 1982.[3] International capital agreements began with the Basel Accord in 1988, and they were reformed by the Basel Committee in response to the financial crisis that began in 2007, to avoid more government bailouts in future crises. Bank regulation becomes more and more complex as the years go by, as does the banking business itself.

In addition to providing liquidity, banks address another problem that individuals seeking a return on their investments face if they try to invest directly—a moral hazard problem. If individuals invest directly in companies, by lending money to them or buying their securities, they may in effect be robbed by the people with whom they invest. There are numerous ways for the managers of a business to funnel money out of the company and into the hands of friends, thereby in effect stealing money from their investors. They may pay inflated invoices from supplier companies run by cronies, enriching them and expecting a kickback later. They may deliberately destroy the business (in which they may never have really believed in the first place), liquidating its assets in the interest of redirecting the money to associates. Or the business could simply launch especially risky activities, with but a small probability of gain and a much larger probability of loss. The company may not care about the losses since they will be visited on the "sucker" investors.[4]

On the other hand, many banks have been in business for a long time—sometimes centuries—and thus have a reputation to uphold. (Reputation is still important even with deposit insurance, for many of the deposits in a successful bank will be above the statutorily insured limit.) The public perception is that banks are adept at sniffing out and avoiding such bad investments. And even if they do make the occasional bad call, they have numerous other investments in their portfolios, a strategy that generally helps them maintain their integrity and reputations—except for the occasional severe financial crisis, during which, admittedly, some may fail or be bailed out.

Banks solve yet another problem that less-skilled investors face: a selection bias problem. Those who are paying less attention to researching their investments will tend to be the more easily victimized; they will wind up with the "lemons" among investments because more skilled investors will snap up the better ones.

Most individuals have no way of evaluating the trustworthiness of businesses in which they might invest. They can try to read published reports on the businesses in newspapers or magazines, or reports issued by rating agencies. But these reports tend to be reliable only for the biggest of companies: there is little incentive for reporters or investment analysts to get into the nitty-gritty of really evaluating every business that is looking for money to expand. Such reports are not profitable for their providers because they are not really of interest to a broad audience, only to those actively looking for investing tips. Moreover, any time one of those reports is issued, there is a free-rider problem: people will spread investing tips gleaned from the report to others (the free riders) who did not even pay for the report.

Companies, at least large companies, do issue debt directly to the public, and some people try to avoid the need for bankers as intermediaries and invest directly in such company debt. They may find such investments safe enough because they know that many other investors, supposedly in the know, are investing in the same companies. But here again *they* are free-riding on the vigilance of other investors in the debt, and so there is the risk that the other investors may be free-riding too. It can turn out that *none* of the investors is really paying attention to the machinations of a company in which they are all investing, and this fact will become apparent only later—and alarmingly quickly—during a crisis.

A bank, on the other hand, stays connected, and it usually has branches in the communities in which it does business. The officers in those branches deal on a personal basis with the businesses to which they lend money, and they collect detailed information about what is really going on with these businesses, right down to evaluating those who run the companies—their trustworthiness, their real motivations and likely future behavior. There is no free-rider problem associated with the collection of this information since the bank does not publish it. Bankers traditionally make short-term renewable loans and demand regular reporting from the companies to which they lend, and the managers of these companies know they had better maintain a good relationship with their bankers or risk having their loans called.

These bank procedures have endured for centuries because, in normal times at least, they work. And they work especially well, relative to direct borrowing from the public, in less-developed countries, where there are fewer analysts, rating agencies, and newspapers and magazines to provide evaluation of investments. Hence banking plays an even bigger role in the economies of less-developed countries.[5]

In contrast, the role of traditional banks in the economies of more advanced countries has been in decline for decades: the fraction of these countries' debt that is accounted for by traditional bank loans has been falling.[6] This is so because the quality of publicly available information about securities is improving, and so the moral hazard and selection bias problems are reduced.

Banks will increasingly be transformed into more complex institutions, but their traditional banking business will not go away entirely. Such banking meets too many of society's needs, and banks' public persona—current events notwithstanding—is too strong.

The Evolution and Future of Banking

Indeed the severe financial crisis that began in 2007 was not due to any failures in the traditional banking business model, but instead to certain new kinds of business models, in which loans made to homeowners were not retained on the books of banks and other mortgage originators but bundled together into securities and sold off to other investors, including other banks—reintroducing the very problem of moral hazard that banks were supposed to solve.

Regulators, notably in the United States, have been increasingly permissive of alternative forms of banking. Over the past generation they have allowed an unregulated "shadow banking" system to develop, which is not subject to the same regulatory oversight as the commercial banking system. Shadow banks are merely financial institutions that manage to escape banking regulation by designing themselves so that they do not fit the definition of commercial banks. They do not literally accept deposits, but instead get the money they lend in slightly different ways.

Examples of shadow banks include the now-failed Bear Stearns and Lehman Brothers, which were called investment banks but were not regulated as commercial banks, since they did not accept deposits. They became shadow banks when they began to *act* like commercial banks. Another example is the structured investment vehicle (SIV), which was created by commercial banks before the financial crisis of 2007; they hoped to escape regulation by putting some of their business into the SIVs, which were considered separate (and unregulated) entities.

Shadow banks may obtain commercial securitized loans or mortgages and enter into repurchase agreements with institutional investors, using the securities as collateral. That business creates liquid investments for institutional investors, which resemble deposits, and so the shadow bankers are in effect creating money as well. Thus their activities may involve a risk of collapse of the entire economic system, just as with commercial banks.[7]

A bank's business—which may have had significant "charter value" because of barriers to entry into banking that serve to inhibit new competitors—is adversely affected by these new competitors. Thus traditional banks may feel an imperative to branch out, and they may start behaving like the shadow banks if they can, entering unconventional new lines of activity like originating subprime mortgage securities and thus creating risks to the economic system that may not be noticed by regulators of traditional banks.[8] That is what led to the current financial crisis.

New regulations, notably the Dodd-Frank Act in the United States, are designed to put many of these shadow banking activities under stronger regulation, to help prevent a repeat of the crisis. But that process has been slow and cumbersome. And it will be difficult to develop regulation to keep pace with, and prevent problems with, new kinds of shadow banks as they are invented. Critics of the financial system are right to be wary of this situation.

The Democratization of Banking

The business model that bankers have evolved over the centuries is a great idea, and people who know this well have sought to encourage a broader and broader application of this model. That is, they have been trying to democratize banking, moving it beyond its original role in serving primarily the wealthy and the financially sophisticated. This initiative stands as an excellent example of finance performing its role in the stewardship of society's assets.

There have been a number of historical movements to democratize banking. In the early nineteenth century there was the savings bank movement in Great Britain, followed by a similar one in the United States. These banks were initially set up as mutuals by philanthropists to give those with low incomes the means and incentive to save; hence they were nonprofit. That same century saw the beginnings of the building society movement in the United Kingdom, followed by the savings and loan association movement in the United States, both of which were aimed at providing people the wherewithal to buy a home.

Postal savings banks arose in that century and in the early twentieth century to provide savings vehicles to every town that had a post office. The twentieth century saw the microfinance movement, exemplified by Muhammad Yunus's Grameen Bank, which specializes in making very small loans to people who traditionally have been ignored by banks.[9] Evidence from randomly assigned individual liability loans shows that lending programs like those of Grameen Bank "increase ability to cope with risk, strengthen community ties, and increase access to informal credit."[10] Today microfinance loans are further promoted by a web site, kiva.org, that allows individual lenders all over the world to lend small sums via microfinance institutions to individual entrepreneurs in poorer regions and, through the power of the Internet, to deal one-on-one with the very people who benefit from their loans.

The democratization of banking is a slow process, occurring over centuries, benefiting from technological progress of various sorts, and still far from complete, even in advanced countries. A Federal Reserve study based on 2007 data showed that 25.1% of U.S. families in the bottom fifth of income have no transactions accounts at all.[11] Because of the absence of elementary banking services, these families find it difficult to save, thus undermining their ability to acquire important skills, send their children to college, and plan for their future.[12]

A number of government policies to encourage the democratization of banking have been proposed, including explicit incentives to banks to provide services to low-income people and the automatic opening of bank accounts for tax refunds and welfare payments.[13] We should also consider another drive to encourage more people to avail themselves of financial services: a repeat of the nineteenth-century savings bank movement for the twenty-first century.

For the better part of two centuries there has been an effort to deliver the full range of banking services to the broadest cross section of society, but the job is not yet complete. The democratization of finance is a route to the good society, and the democratization of banking is a trend—admittedly slow and long-term—that should play an important role in that process. Further democratization of banking is also the best means of dealing with the hostility currently felt toward bankers.

Chapter 4

Investment Bankers

Investment bankers are the people who help organizations sell new securities. In particular, they arrange for companies to issue shares to investors. If it is the first time the company has sold shares to the public, investment bankers help with what is called the initial public offering (IPO). If the company wants to raise yet more money by selling even more shares to the public, investment bankers help organize what is called a seasoned offering. Either way, the investment banker is facilitating the acquisition of capital by the company, dividing up the company into shares that appeal to investors, and helping manage risk.

Investment bankers, in their pure form, differ from conventional bankers in that they do not accept deposits and do not make loans. They specialize in *underwriting* securities, such as new shares, which means they perform due diligence on the issuing company, design the terms of the issue, place the shares with long-term investors, put their own reputation behind the new issue, and perform a variety of other tasks necessary to meet administrative and regulatory requirements.

Because the general public does not usually deal directly with investment bankers, the bankers are largely invisible to them and therefore do not usually elicit as much public hostility as other financial professionals—until there is a crisis that spotlights their activities. In the current financial crisis, major investment banking firms—such as Bear Stearns, Goldman Sachs, and Lehman Brothers—became objects of loathing for some. But in fact investment bankers are really responsible for the origins of our securities markets, including stock markets. Without them, we would not have these markets.

The stock market is a wonderful invention. It is important that companies be able to sell shares to the public, for that process engages a large number of people in their economic undertakings. It allows people to indulge their naturally adventurous spirit but also allows them to choose how much exposure they can tolerate. It decentralizes the allocation of capital, potentially to involve any member of society. And, in the case of corporate acquisitions, it allows individuals or entities to take control of an enterprise and run it as they see fit.

The idea of issuing shares in an enterprise is probably so old that it cannot be dated. It is known that shares (Latin *partes*) in corporations (Latin *publicani*) were traded near the Temple of Castor in the ancient Roman Forum. Records of the share prices do not survive, but evidence that these prices were talked about does.[1]

We know even less about what sort of investment bankers may have existed back then. Perhaps an important reason why there were so few shares in companies in ancient times is that the profession of investment banker had not yet developed very far. Modern methods of investment banking were as yet unheard of.

Shareholding gained momentum in Renaissance Italy, but even then it was not well developed. A notable advance occurred in 1602 with the founding of the Dutch East India Company in Amsterdam, for this corporation soon had a market designed to facilitate daily trading of its shares. The company opened its books to record new shareholders only once a year, but the law allowed for trading of these shares every day. Effectively people could buy shares and hold ownership in what is now called "street name," meaning that the shares are really in the physical possession of and recorded in the name of the broker, on behalf of the beneficial owner. The ownership was guaranteed by a broker, even though the company at first knew nothing about it. The daily trading of shares in a corporation had a profound psychological impact. The price fluctuations from day to day were widely noted, and this in turn generated increased interest in the investment. The freedom to get in or out of the investment day by day built a sense of excitement. This advance both democratized and humanized finance: it brought many more people into the market even as it respected their demand for liquidity and need for pride of ownership while they held shares.

The Amsterdam stock market became regulated when short selling (the sale of borrowed shares, not even owned by the seller) in 1609 led to market turmoil and the temporary abolition of that practice. The invention of the newspaper came soon after, and it was not long before the prices of the East India Company's shares were reported regularly, spurring immense public interest in the investment.

The issuance of shares in joint stock companies (companies owned jointly by a number of people through shares) was limited at first. To mount an IPO, each corporation needed its own special charter, which was hard to get. The Bank of England was chartered as a joint-stock company in 1694, but at the same time it was given a monopoly on joint stock banking. No other bank could have more than six partners, making it virtually impossible to compete with the Bank of England.

A quarter century later, in 1720, Parliament further restricted joint stock companies by mandating—in what later became known as the Bubble Act— that no joint stock company could ever be started without a royal charter. Perhaps this was an effort to support the rise in the price of shares in the South Sea Company, which was at the time soaring in an obvious bubble.

But as time went on pressures to democratize finance prevailed, enabling more corporations to be formed. Parliament restricted the Bank of England's monopoly to an area within sixty-five miles of London in 1826, and in 1844 the monopoly was eliminated altogether. This led to an expansion of banking activities, and within two decades England had seen bank offices proliferate to even small towns.[2]

The Democratization of Investment Banking

Investment banking received further impetus on the other side of the Atlantic in 1811 with the passage of a corporate law in New York State that made it clear that anyone who satisfied minimal requirements could set up a corporation, without special action by the government, and that clearly established limited liability for corporations. The law further democratized finance. By clarifying that shareholders would never be held liable for the debts of the corporation, the law made it possible for the first time for an investor to hold a diversified portfolio, consisting of stocks in many companies. Prior to the advent of limited liability, one could not have done such a thing, for fear of a lawsuit from any of the companies held. This development created a ready pool of investors with whom investment bankers could place newly issued shares. After seeing how steady a supply of capital for new businesses this innovation produced, countries all over the world copied it.

The framers of the New York law probably did not see themselves as the inventors of a brand new kind of market. Instead they apparently thought of themselves as merely responding in an imaginative manner to an economic crisis. The U.S. Congress had imposed an embargo on trade with Britain starting in 1807, citing grievances related to British behavior toward the United States as Britain fought a war with France. By 1811 the extended trade embargo was causing massive economic pain at home, for America had been an exporter of cotton and other fibers to British textile mills. There was a need to finance U.S. textile mills, but few wanted to start a local mill, thinking it would be hard to compete with Britain when the embargo was eventually lifted. The provisions of the bill were thought of merely as expedients to deal with this crisis. The bill followed a 1784 measure granting automatic incorporation to religious congregations, and similar measures for colleges and academies in 1781, municipalities in 1788, libraries in 1792, medical societies in 1806, and turnpikes in 1807.[3] Yet only by 1811 did general business have the status within New York society to win the same right. Equally important, the bill clarified that stockholders in these new corporations had limited liability: they could not lose more than the money they had put in in purchasing their shares.

The full name of the act was "A Bill to Encourage the Manufacture of Woolen Cloth, also Cotton, Hemp and Flax, and for other Purposes." As it turned out, it was the "other purposes" that would have lasting importance. Once again, dealing with a short-term crisis led to a financial innovation that would change the world, for the 1811 New York law became the model for new corporate law all over the world.[4]

Underlying the concept of free incorporation and the unrestrained trading of shares is a hoped-for result: an imaginative application of capital to new ideas and new business directions. Even if most of these ideas fail, some will succeed.

It has been argued by many that share trading is little more than gambling. Contributing to this idea is the "fact" that most entities traded on stock exchanges are big companies that do not regularly issue new shares. Stewart Myers offered a theory of corporate finance according to which there is a pecking order of new capital sources, and new issues of shares are last in the order. Seasoned issues of shares are, Myers asserted, relatively unimportant sources of capital for corporations.[5]

But it turns out that Myers's evidence was not as impressive as one might think. Eugene Fama and Kenneth French argued that, at the time Myers wrote, issues of seasoned shares *were* rare. But that merely reflected the situation in the economy at that time. At other times, including more recently, share issuance is a more important source for new capital.[6] Since Myers wrote, share issuance has also tended to come about as part of incentive packages given to employees of firms. Even though those shares are issued in special circumstances, they are still shares issued. The firm continues to depend on market valuations to maintain its ability to raise capital.

How Investment Banking Keeps Incentives Up to Date

As anyone who has ever lived in a family knows, there are profound difficulties in motivating everyone to do their work. Usually one person in the household shoulders most of the work and is responsible for keeping things running. The same would tend be true in any business organization. Fortunately, ever since fractional interests in corporations were developed, there has been a better way: allocate shares in the corporation, or bonuses or options paid in shares, to key people to reward them directly for bearing responsibility.

Facebook was founded by Eduardo Saverin and Mark Zuckerberg. According to recent news accounts Saverin currently owns only about 5% of the company, down from about 34%, while Zuckerberg's share has fallen from 66% to 24%. Why did their ownership stakes both decrease? They did so because Saverin and Zuckerberg needed to bring in other investors to grow the company. Why did Saverin's share fall more? Certainly no one took Saverin's stock away from him. He lost much of his percentage share of the company by dilution: new shares were issued to incentivize newly hired employees, and still more shares were awarded to Zuckerberg. Why? This is a sensitive subject, and one of the determinants of his share was a legal settlement. In part it—quite logically—has to do with the board of directors' opinion that Saverin needed less incentivization than Zuckerberg in order to move the company forward.

The process of issuing new shares in a company that unevenly dilute the ownership stakes of existing shareholders can become one of the fiercest battlegrounds in modern finance, as fortunes are wiped out, rivalries are created, and political machinations are indulged. There is no way to make this process appear fair to all involved. Lawyers may smooth some of the rough edges and ruffled feathers, but it is still a killing field where the absurd and the tragic often go hand in hand.

But the overall process of share issuance and incentivization is far kinder and gentler than armed conflict, and it provides a civilized outlet for human aggression that can ultimately lead to more productive corporations and thus beneficial outcomes for society as a whole. Investment bankers in a sense serve as diplomats negotiating an understanding between contentious powers—an understanding that ultimately allows them to cooperate and get on with their business. In the corporate world, investment bankers are, in the final analysis, keepers of the peace and promoters of progress.

Chapter 5

Mortgage Lenders and Securitizers

Housing is one of the most fundamental of economic needs. The need for housing tends to come at an early point in the life of a family, when it first has children or sees the immediate prospect of them, yet when resources may be low. There is a strong motive for the financial industry to help with this fundamental problem. Society, as we have already noted, regards the subsidizing of homeownership as beneficial, and so sees a public good in promoting mortgage lending.

And yet, particularly in the United States, public disgust has been directed toward mortgage lenders and securitizers today. They are seen as the instigators of the financial crisis that has spread from America around the world. The crisis began with the collapse of the subprime mortgage securities market in the United States, and so anger about the crisis has generalized to anger directed at those who made those loans initially.

Mortgage lending is a process of dealmaking among three major parties: the home buyer, the ultimate lender, and the government, which typically wishes to promote homeownership. Each of these three parties has different needs, concerns, and time horizons. Efficiently selecting and matching among all these parties is a problem that can benefit from financial innovation. It is also a process prone to error and even catastrophe.

A method for mortgage lending developed in the United States was being increasingly copied in other parts of the world until the advent of the severe financial crisis that began in 2007. The first stage of the process is mortgage origination, in which a local office works directly with the home buyer to arrange the terms of the loan and get the contract signed. The mortgage originator then sells the mortgage to a mortgage securitizer, who in turn bundles a large group of mortgages into a residential mortgage–backed security (RMBS), which may then be sold to investors.

Mortgage Origination

The process of originating mortgages is perhaps the most delicate link in the chain, for it involves crafting a deal between the least financially informed party, the future homeowner(s), and sophisticated professional financial representatives. The potential for neglect of the real needs of the borrowers, or even outright abuse, is high.

Most mortgage originators operate with integrity, and indeed they find that maintaining their reputations is part of what keeps them in business. The mortgage origination process works well when they feel part of their communities and are motivated to do well for their clients by that personal sense of integrity. But the process does not always work well.

The financial crisis of 2007 can in part be traced back to abuses of the mortgage origination process. Borrowers were given mortgages they couldn't afford or the wrong kind of mortgages.

The problem was not a new one, and the U.S. Congress had already tried to remedy the situation over the years. The Riegle Community Development and Regulatory Improvement Act of 1994 created a new legal entity, the community development financial institution, to ensure that people seeking home mortgages would be protected, and there are now over a thousand such community organizations. Congress also tried to help with its Home Ownership and Equity Protection Act of 1994, which established standards for mortgage lending—but its provisions were too easily evaded. Mortgage brokers at that time were not subject to licensing, and the industry had no professional code of ethics. Brokers would often talk clients into buying large homes with adjustable-rate mortgages, without clearly informing them that the rates would likely go up and the homes become unaffordable. State governments in the United States have now instituted licensing for mortgage brokers. The Dodd-Frank Act of 2010 forbids mortgage companies from incentivizing their loan officers to steer borrowers toward profitable mortgages that are not right for them, and it also requires mortgage originators to verify their borrowers' ability to repay.

Nevertheless all these government efforts have been only partly successful. There remains so much in the process of issuing a mortgage that simply cannot be seen and policed by the government. The weaknesses in the mortgage origination market—and in the behavior of certain market participants—reflects a genuine deficiency in the modern financial system and a prime site for innovative solutions.

Nonprofit organizations like the Center for Responsible Lending and the Center for Community Self-Help offer advice to homeowners, but they are just not big enough to reach most borrowers. Properly reforming finance means that at the very least we have to think about how such grass-roots assistance organizations can be expanded in the future.

Mortgage Securitization

The next step in the mortgage lending process, as we have seen, is that the mortgage originators sell their individual mortgages to a mortgage securitizer so that they can be bundled into a form that will allow them to be placed in investor portfolios. At this point there has often been another step in the process. The RMBSs will in turn be placed into a trust to allow a set of collateralized debt obligations (CDOs) to be issued based on the mortgage pool. The CDOs are divided up into pieces known as tranches, according to the perceived repayment ability of the holders of the underlying mortgages; in case of default on some of those mortgages, the senior tranche is paid first, followed by the second tranche, the third tranche, and so on. The various tranches, with their different levels of risk and accordingly varying pricing, are designed to appeal to different kinds of investors. The last tranche—the residual tranche, known colloquially in the industry as "toxic waste"—is paid last, and holders of it receive no income at all unless very few of the underlying mortgages default. All of these tranches, except for the last, the toxic waste, which is retained by the securitizer, are sold separately by the securitizer to investors.

According to the logic, the first tranche, the senior tranche, is very unlikely to default, and so securities rating agencies routinely gave these tranches AAA ratings before the financial crisis. They were easy to sell to the ultimate investors.

Yet the whole process became suspect after the collapse of the securities that were backed by subprime (low-quality) mortgages, resulting in a domino effect around the world. Something was indeed wrong with the process as it had developed by the early 2000s.

Many of the AAA-rated CDOs ultimately lost substantial value. The rating agencies—like so many lenient teachers who give out too many As—had grown complacent and distributed too many high ratings. The ratings were faulty, and so was the whole system based upon them.

And yet the tranching system and the rating system have nevertheless functioned fairly well so far in this crisis—a little-known fact. Research by Sun Young Park, recently a graduate student at Yale and now at the Korea Advanced Institute of Science and Technology, found that, contrary to popular belief, only a very small fraction (0.17%) of the principal of U.S. AAA-rated subprime mortgage–backed security tranches issued between 2004 and 2007 had experienced losses owing to underlying mortgage default as of 2011.[1]

News accounts of a few AAA subprime securities that suffered major default losses, of the significant default losses in the lower-rated tranches, and of major market price declines have all left people with a faulty impression of the failures of the tranching system.[2]

Mortgage securitization was all part of a design by—indeed was an invention of—the U.S. government. Mortgage securities were first issued by government-sponsored enterprises (GSEs): the Federal Home Loan Mortgage Corporation (Freddie Mac) in 1971 and the Federal National Mortgage Association (Fannie Mae) in 1981.[3] The process appeared to go well at first. Yet the mortgage credit risk of Freddie and Fannie together rose 16% a year from 1980 to 2007.[4]

But both enterprises later went bankrupt and came under U.S. government conservatorship in 2008, after the collapse in home prices left many mortgages in foreclosure and brought on the financial crisis. These GSEs had never thought a home price decline of such magnitude was possible, and so they did not plan for it. In common with the so-called systemically important private firms considered earlier, they enjoyed "too big to fail" status. The government could never let them fail as that might bring down the whole economy; it was therefore clear that the government would inevitably bail them out with taxpayer money. There was faulty oversight of their aggressive pursuit of advantages from their implicit government guarantee.[5]

Why did this system crash so terribly? The crash appears to have been the result of a combination of factors. The first and foremost was the near-universal assumption that home prices could never fall. If you believe this, then you will conclude that mortgage securities are a pretty safe investment: if anyone fails to repay a mortgage, the lender can simply foreclose and sell the home to recover the loan balance. Actually, in most cases there would not even be a foreclosure, since the homeowner who can no longer pay on the mortgage can, with a little prompting from the lender, just sell the house and avoid foreclosure.

I myself wondered, in the years just before the financial crisis, why so many people thought home prices could never fall. To me, the extraordinarily rapid ascent of home prices from around 1997 to 2006 suggested there was a housing bubble, which might burst, producing rapid price declines. But practically no one in the mortgage industry seemed to think that was even a remote possibility. I asked some of these people why they thought prices could never fall. They would sometimes reply that home prices had never fallen since the Great Depression. And the Depression was so long ago that it just didn't seem relevant anymore. Needless to say, they were wrong about that.

Another puzzle also presented itself in those days: why did the RMBS market become so important, when people had seen no need for it before the 1970s? We know that securitizers were creating new investment vehicles based on mortgages. But what is the difference, really, whether one invests in RMBSs or in shares in banks that own mortgages, as was the practice before Freddie and Fannie started issuing these?

Securitization was indeed never really popular in most parts of the world. The movement toward securitization of home mortgage debt became particularly strong in the United States thanks to powerful impetus from government support. But, lacking the subsidy effectively given by the U.S. government via Fannie Mae and Freddie Mac, mortgage securitization has not been common anywhere else.[6]

Before the crisis of 2007 finance theorists saw clear innovation in mortgage securitization. Securitized mortgages are, in the abstract, a way of solving an information asymmetry problem—more particularly the problem of "lemons." This problem, first given a theoretical explanation by George Akerlof, refers to the aversion many people have to buying anything on the used market, like a used car. They worry that they can't judge whether the item has defects, and that they will get stuck with a lemon. The seller knows whether a particular item is of good quality or not, but the buyer does not—at least not without expending a good deal of costly effort to find out.[7] In a nutshell, Akerlof's theory holds that if you think that the seller is going to pass off the bad stuff on you, you won't pay more for it than the lowest price. So the seller won't even try to offer the good stuff to the market, and the market becomes a repository for only the bad stuff. That is why people tend to keep (what they perceive as) good used cars in the family, but to dump the lemons onto the used market.[8] This all makes for a poorly functioning market.

Claire Hill, in her article "Securitization: A Low-Cost Sweetener for Lemons," written before the crisis, argued persuasively that an important reason the securitization and CDO market can function well is that it helps solve the lemons problem.[9] Bundling mortgages into securities that are evaluated by independent rating agencies, and dividing up a company's securities into tranches that allow specialized evaluators to do their job, efficiently lowers the risk to investors of getting stuck with lemons. They should be able to trust the higher-tranche CDOs more than any pool of mortgages or any share in a complex and difficult-to-understand mortgage-lending institution.

So there was a valid theory as to why the splitting of securitized mortgage debt into tranches was a good idea. Of course it turns out not to have worked superbly well in practice, but this is largely because of the erroneous assumption noted earlier—that everyone, including the rating agencies, thought home prices just couldn't fall. That mistake, and not any flaw in the logic of Claire Hill's theory, was the real problem.

And that is the problem that so often plagues finance. We can build beautiful models and theories about what kinds of financial products to provide, but thanks to human foibles we are always vulnerable to bubbles and their bursting.

The enormous growth of mortgage securitization in the United States also arose in part from regulatory arbitrage, that is, from businesses trying to please the regulators as efficiently as possible, and from bureaucrats who were not thinking deeply about the rules they were enforcing.

Ever since the Basel I agreement in 1988, which set the first important international bank regulatory standards, banks around the world have been subject to capital requirements that are tied by a formula to their so-called risk-weighted assets. Banks have to hold more capital, to hold back on their lending, if their investments include relatively risky assets as measured using this formula. But a neat trick on the regulators is possible: a bank that originates mortgages (which have a high risk weight and so significantly increase their risk-weighted assets) can bundle them into a security and sell them off in exchange for any other asset—even for more mortgages. Selling off the mortgages frees up the bank from its capital requirements and enables it to issue more mortgages. Under U.S. law, the bank can even go out and buy highly rated RMBSs with the money, on the assumption that these are nearly riskless. It may end up holding essentially the same mortgages as it started out with, but the regulators' formula quantifies the change as meaningful, and so banks that pursue this strategy are freer to lend.[10]

Part of the motivation for the creation of RMBSs was essentially to allow banks to escape capital controls. In 2001 the Federal Deposit Insurance Corporation, the Federal Reserve, the Comptroller of the Currency, and the Office of Thrift Supervision promulgated a new regulation, called the Recourse Rule, that offered special incentives for banks to hold securitized mortgages rather than mortgages themselves. For computing risk-weighted capital, an input in determining the capital requirements for banks, any securitized mortgages rated AAA or AA would qualify for 20% risk weighting, rather than the 50% risk weighting typically applied to mortgages. Consider what this means, for example, for two banks, both making most of their loans in the form of mortgages. Imagine that the banks are virtually identical, and that both have lent out about as much money as the regulators allow them to, given their current capital. Suppose they each package part of their mortgages into AAA securities and swap the securities with one another: each thus holds mortgages that the other originated—in the new, securitized form. You might think that nothing essential has changed. But think again. Because capital requirements are based on risk-weighted assets, and because the securities fall into a different asset class than the underlying mortgages, the effect is to loosen regulation and allow the banks to lend more.

You might ask, how could regulators be so stupid as not to see the potential for disaster here? They were not stupid. But they were operating on the assumption that the rating agencies were infallible—an assumption that they did not feel it was within their purview to examine, as they did not regulate the rating agencies. They were also politically constrained, following rules that had to be agreed upon nationally, and rules ultimately based on international agreements. Ultimately the problem was not stupidity; it was rather a problem of assigning responsibility to and coordinating the efforts of a diverse group of people.

And yet not everything was flawed: many features of the mortgage lending process will be corrected and developed into better institutions for the future. In principle, if the ratings of the RMBSs had been accurate, if they had taken accurate account of a possible collapse in housing prices, and if regulators had not given any special advantages to holders of those securities, then the system would have worked.

The defects of the mortgage securitization process were very visible in this crisis, and they will now be corrected. The benefits to society of mortgage securitization were hard to see because they take the form of lower borrowing rates for homeowners. People have no clear knowledge of what the rates might have been without the benefit of securitization. Certainly they have not thought about the possibility that they might not be living in a house at all, and that certain things that they value in life (e.g., having a home of one's own from the time the children are young) might have been made possible by it.

It is important to encourage financial innovation to proceed, to develop new and better mortgage institutions, despite the debacle with the innovative mortgage products associated with the financial crisis. Creative people in mortgage finance have a good deal of work ahead of them to make for still better deals between the parties to mortgage contracts. The mortgage contract could be made more flexible for the homeowner, with a preplanned workout.[11] Other kinds of mortgage financing innovations are possible, such as shared equity arrangements like the home equity fractional interests promoted by John O'Brien, which allow homeowners to sell shares in their homes, or the housing market partnerships promoted by Andrew Caplin and his colleagues, which allow homeowners to become partners with an institution in purchasing their homes.[12]

The rocky road that mortgage lenders have trod during the financial crisis is ample warning that we may yet experience further dislocations. But the jobs of mortgage originator and mortgage securitizer will still be with us, if perhaps in modified form, because they do help solve a basic economic problem. Next time, we won't believe that home prices can never fall, and we will do better. That is the painful process of learning that we see in financial markets—but it is a process that ultimately leads us to better financial institutions.

Chapter 6

Traders and Market Makers

The classic example of a trader is the specialist on a traditional stock exchange, who stands at a post where certain stocks are traded on the floor of the exchange, and who buys and sells from his personal inventory of these stocks in order to maintain an orderly market. But the specialist is only one of many people whose job involves trading minute by minute. In addition to market makers, there are also execution traders, who help others make transactions efficiently at good prices without disturbing the market to their own disadvantage, and proprietary traders, who trade on their own account to profit from short-run price movements, including doing risk arbitrage, that is, profiting from price discrepancies across markets. As the stock markets of the world become increasingly electronic, the majority of traders never even see the floor of an exchange, and mostly they feel no commitment to maintaining an orderly market. But together they do in general have the effect of making markets more orderly and prices more reflective of true value.

In the current environment the greatest hostility is often reserved for the traders, since they usually do not present themselves as helping society in any direct way. They are just buying and selling to try to make money for themselves. Their activities remind people of gambling—and the successes of some who excel in trading can be galling.

Traders are very different from investment managers who manage large portfolios of investments, who set portfolios on their course for years on behalf of clients and their long-term goals. Traders put themselves at risk every minute of every day, and for no one's benefit but their own.

Each of us gets involved in short-run trading to some extent at some point in life. One discovers a certain unpleasantness in confronting other people and having to bargain with them. It leaves one wondering: Are we on good terms or not? Am I concealing information, taking advantage of this other person? Yet traders have to specialize in doing just that all day long.

Of course, society needs traders. A market economy needs people who stand ready to buy and sell necessary items. We need traders in the same way we need used furniture dealers and scrap metal dealers.

People who trade for much of their lives learn a sort of bland professionalism that guides them, a sort of practical ethics that allows them to consistently stop just short of actions that would anger others. As Charles de Montesquieu observed in his 1748 book *The Spirit of the Laws*, "The spirit of trade produces in the mind of man a certain sense of exact justice, opposite on the one hand to robbery, and on the other to those moral virtues which forbid our always adhering rigidly to our own private interest, and suffer us to neglect it for the advantage of others."[1] Having long since thought through their own practices, traders find boring the anger that some of their counterparties show at what they perceive to be mistreatment; to experienced traders, it is business, pure and simple.

Those who spend a lifetime trading develop an expertise that involves an intuitive appreciation of market forces. Other financial professionals respect traders; they consider them a breed apart and often consult them for their insights in important decisions. That traders should have such expertise in no way contradicts the notion that markets are basically efficient. There is no respectable theory according to which there is not a normal return to be had in trading. Trading is a necessary activity for a market economy, and so there should be a normal return to expertise in trading.

Part of traders' expertise will be in the form of knowledge about how to "take advantage" of others. Only if they understand such things can they survive. Traders' professionalism may dictate that they not talk too freely about such things. Any profession develops certain dark secrets about behavior that, while not really unethical, is difficult to justify to outsiders.

Traders as Managers of a Financial Reward System

The existence of traders allows financial markets to respond almost instantly to new developments. When the price of a share of stock goes up, those who had bet on that stock are rewarded. Because of traders' activities, the reward is virtually instantaneous, and it serves to encourage similar activities again and again.

The markets that traders make are a "valuation machine" that assesses the value of various actions in a constantly changing environment and that gives nearly instant feedback and corrections in the form of meaningful price movements.

According to neuroscientist Read Montague, "Once life started to move, valuation mechanisms were an inevitable consequence."[2] Even the simplest motile microorganisms have a valuation mechanism and an impulse to pursue value. Montague points out that single-celled *Escherichia coli* bacteria have a mechanism to estimate the concentration in their fluid environment of the amino acid L-aspartate, which they consume, and a mechanism to propel them toward higher concentrations of it. The human brain is vastly more sophisticated, but its basic units are essentially similar to single-celled animalcules like *E. coli*. How does it achieve such masterful coordination of all these agents?

One theory about how it does this, called the dopamine gating hypothesis, has been proposed by quantitative psychologists Randy O'Reilly, D. C. Noelle, Jon Cohen, and Todd Braver.[3] The theory involves the dopamine system, which is in the brainstem but sends signals over long axons to many parts of the brain, notably the prefrontal cortex, which in turn sends signals back to the dopamine system.

The dopamine system responds to rewards and makes estimates of how advantageous the environment is. It is well known that this system sends signals to many areas of the brain, including the prefrontal cortex, which is an information integration center and helps in the maintenance of goals and associated actions.[4] It has recently been learned that the dopamine reward system also permeates "the gray matter in nearly every subdivision of the brain."[5]

The neuroscientist Wolfram Schultz has monitored the signals sent by the dopamine system and shown that it responds only to surprises—only to *unanticipated* rewards.[6] Furthermore the system responds not when a treat (say some food) is actually experienced, but when information about it is received. Thus if the brain gets an unanticipated signal that a treat is expected, the dopamine system broadcasts a stronger set of signals. It does not send out a stronger signal when the treat actually comes; it continues to fire at its normal background level. If on the other hand the brain is expecting a treat and is disappointed, the dopamine system's signals drop to an unusually low level at the moment the deficit is discovered.[7]

The reward stimulus from the dopamine system, according to the dopamine gating hypothesis, has the effect of turning off an information shield, and in response the prefrontal cortex selects a certain pattern of neural activity. The prefrontal cortex stabilizes the selected pattern into a goal and then uses the goal as the basis for a signal to other brain regions.

Since the dopamine system records rewards in much the same way the stock market does, it functions analogously to the stock market. When a company announces that a new special dividend will be paid to shareholders, traders bid up the stock in the market immediately after the announcement. They thereby send out a signal to the whole world that the stock is more valuable, just as the dopamine system sends out a signal to the whole brain. When the company actually pays the dividend on the stock at a later date, there is no higher return on the stock on that day. Just as with the dopamine system, the market reacts when the information about a future reward comes, not when the reward is actually received.

There is an uncanny resemblance between the plots Schultz has made of the signals fired by the dopamine system from a few seconds before to a few seconds after the time information appeared that a reward was coming and the "event study" plots produced by financial researchers of the daily returns on stock prices from just before to just after the time a special dividend is announced.[8] Just as with the dopamine reward system, the stock returns jump when an extra dividend is announced, not when it is paid. And that kind of instantaneous response to new information is exactly what is needed to make a reward system function well—whether in the brain or in the economy.

So-called parallel evolution may lead to the development of similar mechanisms or structures in different species. For example, there were sabertooth tigers and sabertooth marsupials, who developed similar tooth structure entirely independently. Another such example is that of ants and termites, insects that evolved separately but that share a complex colony structure and that build their own habitats. The reinvention in the course of economic evolution of a reward system similar to that in the brain may be regarded as a type of parallel evolution.

High-Frequency Trading

Rapid-fire electronic trading has been a source of concern for much longer than one might think. In 1847 a newspaper article lamented the fact that "Orders . . . were received by magnetic telegraph from New York to sell, and the consequence was a fall, the market closing unusually heavy—many sellers and few buyers."[9] As far back as the middle of the nineteenth century, information could be communicated at the speed of electricity.

And that was only the beginning of the apparent anomalies due to what we now call high-frequency or millisecond trading. There are certainly some more recent examples as well. On May 6, 2010, the Dow Jones Industrial Average suddenly dropped 9%, only to rebound within minutes. According to a postmortem of this "flash crash" by the Commodity Futures Trading Commission and the Securities and Exchange Commission (SEC), the crash followed a single $4.1 billion sell order, executed using an automated sell algorithm, and the sudden cessation of buying by high-frequency traders.[10] But events like this are merely among the growing pains to be expected whenever new technology is being adopted; they should become less frequent as market participants gain more experience and as regulators learn how to reduce their probability.

The real change that electronics has brought to trading has been more in the organization of information than in the speed at which trading is carried out. Once computers are involved, it is much easier for people to collect, col-late, and store information about investments. A related but much less significant benefit is the enhanced speed at which trading can take place. In a competitive world, speedy trading becomes a necessity to maintain competitiveness, but it does not change the basic activities of the participants. They are still serving clients who do not think in milliseconds. The advent of this form of trading may be compared to engineers' move from slide rules to calculators: high-frequency trading helps traders do their job faster, but it is still the same job.

High-Scope Trading

Far more important than high-*frequency* trading is trading of a broader *scope*—trading of more different kinds of things. The scope of trading has been gradually increasing over the past century. But progress has been slow, and still there are some extremely important assets for which there are no liquid markets. With the advent of high-scope trading, many more things are traded.

An example would be the "prediction markets" that set prices based on the probabilities that a specified event will transpire. The earliest prediction markets, dating back to 1988 at the Iowa Electronic Markets, traded contracts that paid out according to the outcome of a specified event, such as a candidate receiving a certain share of the popular vote. The price of such a contract turns out to be a useful estimate of the probability of that outcome.[11] Since prediction markets focus on a well-defined event in the near future and give quick feedback to participants, they are probably less likely to be influenced by speculative excesses than other markets, such as stock markets. Today there are many such prediction markets, including Intrade.com, Lumenogic at newsfutures.com, and the Foresight Exchange at ideasphere.com.

There have been attempts to start markets for macroeconomic aggregates.[12] In 1985 the U.S. Coffee, Sugar and Cocoa Exchange launched a market for the U.S. consumer price index, and in 2002 Goldman Sachs launched a market for nonfarm labor force statistics. Analogous markets have since been trading at the CME Group in Chicago.[13] The European Investment Bank in 2004 attempted to start a market for longevity risk—the risk that, because of developments in medical research and changing environmental conditions, people will on average live longer than expected (a problem for defined-benefit pension funds, which have to make payments for as long as retirees live) or less long than expected (a problem for life insurance companies, which will have to pay benefits early).[14]

Many of these markets have not yet achieved liquidity, and there is little volume of trade. Often, as in prediction markets, the volume is so low that the market seems more a game among enthusiasts than a significant economic institution. This problem poses a challenge for market makers, and it is instructive to understand the role they play in launching such markets.

For example, there was, until recently, no derivatives market for residential real estate prices, for single-family home prices. There are markets for commercial real estate prices, but not for the much bigger category of real estate represented by our homes. The subprime crisis, which triggered the severe financial crisis that began in 2007, was caused by a bursting bubble in U.S. home prices. Perhaps this crisis could have been averted if there had been a market that revealed public opinions about future home prices.

My colleagues and I worked with the Chicago Mercantile Exchange (CME) to launch a futures market in single-family home prices.[15] Futures market prices of single-family homes for ten U.S. cities—Boston, Chicago, Denver, Las Vegas, Los Angeles, Miami, New York, San Diego, San Francisco, and Washington, D.C.—as well as a market for an aggregate index of all ten of them together were launched at the CME on May 22, 2006. Options on futures were also offered at that time.[16] We had every reason to think that these markets would be fundamentally important, for real estate was a significant risk for which there were at the time no risk management vehicles.

I talked with some of the market makers for these contracts, and I was impressed by their spirit. They seemed genuinely committed to creating an important new market, excited by the prospect. These encounters confirmed for me once again that the vast majority of financial professionals are not in the business just to make money.

On the other hand, they had to be careful, for as market makers they were committing their own capital. If they were to make a market too aggressively— that is, fill large orders in such a way as to leave them exposed to market risk—they would put themselves in danger of sudden and catastrophic loss.

The problem at the time was that our contracts didn't become liquid enough to attract attention. I spoke to portfolio managers who might have taken a position in these markets, and they told me that the number of shares they could trade without causing large moves in market price was just too small to be worth considering.

It was a classic "chicken-or-egg" problem. To start an important new market, you need liquidity. To have liquidity, you need an important market. Market makers can sometimes create new markets, despite the chicken-or-egg problem, if they have enough capital and courage and commitment to make the market work. But it is a slow process, and we still have relatively few markets for individual fundamentals.

In this connection I would advocate tax incentives for market makers—at least market makers in fundamental and important new markets. They are providing a public good when they create such markets and sustain the liquidity in them. They need to be further encouraged in this, and also recognized publicly for their contribution to society.

I often encounter resistance to the notion that we should expand our array of derivatives markets, and that we need more active trading of derivatives for such things as consumer prices, GDP, longevity, and real estate risks. The public disgust with financial machinations is enormous right now, and such ideas are met with great skepticism. Many of those who object seem to think that such new markets would only create opportunities for bad behavior. But I find it ironic that no one (that I have ever heard) advocates shutting down trading in the major markets that *already* exist, like the stock market or the bond market. They don't suggest this because the importance of this type of trading in our existing economy is just too great. So how does one draw the line between "good trading" and "bad trading"? If trading of claims on corporate profits (trading stocks) is a good thing, then why isn't trading for claims on GDP likewise good? Corporate profits are, after all, just a (small) component of GDP.

Here is where the impulse for conventionality and familiarity, to be discussed in Chapter 22, is so powerful. People seem to want to return to their moral roots after a crisis, and that seems to imply, to a certain extent, a return to old ways of doing things. We believe that the trading in which we *already* engage is proper—as long as we send those who abuse the system to jail. All financial progress to date—or at least up to just before the start of the current financial crisis—was acceptable, as we have become used to such developments. But progress has to stop there.

Those who express such views do not seem to appreciate that financial trading creates, as we have seen, a reward system, similar to the reward system in the brain, that drives all manner of coordinated human activity. They do not seem to appreciate that the ongoing revolution in information technology is creating massive new opportunities for better-coordinated economic activities, and that financial trading should be expected to evolve with those opportunities. They do not seem to realize that the financial crisis was not primarily caused by a spontaneous outbreak of moral turpitude, but by a failure to appreciate and manage risks (notably real estate risk). They fail to realize that setting up a government committee to guard against financial excesses and bubbles, while probably helpful, cannot really solve the problem—at least not without destroying many of the positive advantages of our market system. They fail to realize that expanding the scope of our financial trading is in its essence a route to democratizing finance—by making financial markets more representative of and responsive to our needs—and thus to advancing the central objective of the Occupy Wall Street movement.

As we have seen, markets—and the people who make them and trade in them—are the vital link that allows financial capitalism to respond to developments in the larger society. It is through markets that we appreciate the value of that which is traded and, in many cases, have a sense of larger trends in our world. We need traders and market makers if we are to transform and improve our system of financial capitalism.

Chapter 7

Insurers

The insurance industry has been extremely important in reducing the impact of both major and minor tragedies on our lives. Most people simply do not appreciate what insurers offer, for the total value of the services they provide can be hard to grasp. In this respect the news media seem to see tragedy in the wrong places. Take for example the 2010 BP oil spill in the Gulf of Mexico, when the *Deepwater Horizon* oil rig exploded and spilled oil into the gulf for three months. The news media described this as a greater tragedy than it was, disregarding that much of the loss was insured. In fact the truest tragedy here was the initial loss of life, including the eleven crewmen who died in the explosion. No insurance policy can bring back life. But the other tragedies of the spill could be—and largely were—dealt with by insurance.

The media described the dislocations to local businesses, the temporary closing of beach resorts, and the loss of local jobs as tourists stayed away, as if they were all uninsured. But to the extent that all risks were insured properly, to the extent that the beach resorts had full insurance against oil spills, that workers and employers had appropriate unemployment insurance or business interruption insurance, then there was no real and lasting suffering. Tourists just went elsewhere until the beaches were cleaned up, and they later returned. To the extent that shares in BP and its insurance companies were held by international investors in well-diversified portfolios, then the losses were spread out worldwide, and then, except for the initial loss of life, the whole event had minuscule effects overall. The truth of a world with insurance is decidedly level and even—a truth that many news reporters would like to ignore in their zeal to write engaging and attention-grabbing stories.

About five million barrels of oil were lost, and at $77 a barrel at the time of the spill that approaches half a billion dollars. That may sound like a lot of money, but it is virtually inconsequential for the world as a whole. If the risks had been fully diversified around the world, major portfolio investors would have been only minimally affected by the lost barrels of oil, to an extent well below the threshold that would provoke any loss of sense of well-being. As regards risks that can be insured, there is no tragedy experienced by individuals—not one that is discernible to any of the individuals involved. This outcome reveals one of the ironies of finance, difficult as it may be to express given our natural emotional response: except for truly planet-wide catastrophes, the amount of total damage hardly matters.

If risks are shared appropriately and comprehensively, then, in the BP example, the clearest economic impact on happiness—on what economists refer to as utility—might come from the ultimate effects on the world economy of the loss of oil. A small part of the world's oil reserves has been wasted, and so the world might run out of oil, say, a few days sooner a century hence. But no—the impact is more abstract than that, as the world will never actually run out of oil. As supplies are depleted, the price of oil will be forced up to encourage economizing and also create an incentive for the development of alternative forms of energy, which will phase in as oil supplies wane. Therefore such an oil spill, in a world with complete insurance, means only incrementally higher prices over the next century—a fact of life that society will certainly learn to tolerate.

The general public should be eager to see fundamental progress in insurance, for all the ways in which it would improve their lives. But for the moment the public does not seem to understand fully the potential benefits of better insurance. The possibilities for future risk management from better insurance seem too abstract and remote. Yet the benefits of insurance—and of expanding insurance to cover many more risks than are covered today—are very substantial and real.

The Democratization of Insurance

The history of insurance in centuries past has been one of gradual extension of coverage to more and more people and to more and more risks. If we are to achieve the good society, we must continue this trend.

Life insurance was invented in the 1600s, but initially only a few financially sophisticated people bought it. The same was true of fire insurance. It was not until the nineteenth and twentieth centuries that these kinds of insurance became widespread in advanced countries. And they *still* have not penetrated to many poorer regions of the world.

The first imperative is to get a far broader segment of the public covered by existing, well-understood policies. For example, the fundamental tragedy of the Haitian earthquake of 2010, even including the loss of life, was that few buildings were insured there. This meant not only that there was no compensation for damage but also that there had been no insurance companies overseeing building codes in years past—a practice that certainly would have reduced damage and loss of life. The Caribbean Catastrophe Risk Insurance Facility had since 2007 tried to establish better property insurance practices in Haiti, as well as other countries in the region, but it had made little headway when the earthquake of 2010 struck. This magnitude 7.0 earthquake caused at least fifty thousand deaths. In contrast, the magnitude 6.7 earthquake in Northridge, California, in 1994—similarly significant in its proximity to an urban center and in its effects—resulted in only thirty-three deaths. The much better developed insurance industry in California as compared to Haiti is a major part of the explanation for this discrepancy.

The World Bank has been launching programs to better protect poor farmers against weather risks that might seriously damage their crops, causing massive hardship or even starvation. It has been estimated that about a billion people in the world have an income of less than one dollar a day, and that three-quarters of them live in rural areas that are heavily dependent on agriculture.[1] For these people the risk of crop failure is paramount, and this risk can be a life-or-death one. Foreign emergency aid tends to reach them too late, after they have already been forced to sell off their meager assets and slaughter their livestock just to survive. Primitive societies try to manage the risk of crop loss by risk sharing within the family.[2] But in practice all members of a family may be affected by the same crop failure, so this approach to risk management is far from ideal.

In the past, insurance companies have tried to help manage this risk by selling crop insurance—insurance directly aimed at crop failure on a given farm. But this kind of policy invites moral hazard: either shirking by the farmer or outright fraud to reduce the apparent yield of the crop. In response, insurers have recently tried to tie their payments not to the crop itself but to the weather conditions that would bring on a bad crop. After all, farmers can't influence the weather. This idea has also met with difficulties, since the kind of weather conditions that bring on a bad crop may be subtle and local or may be very closely dependent on the timing of the bad weather relative to planting and seed germination. But with better information technology and better agricultural science, weather insurance has improved to the point that it is now being actively promoted by the World Bank.[3]

Another problem with weather insurance—and one that underlies the penetration of insurance into less-developed countries generally—has been that poor farmers may not understand the insurance concept and may mistrust the institutions that provide it. They are thus reluctant to pay the premiums that are necessary to make the concept viable. The same problem is encountered with earthquake insurance in poor countries. The solution has to be a better marketing of insurance in such regions and an effort to win the trust of their residents. This is what is meant by humanizing insurance, and it is part of the same process involved in humanizing any area of finance.

Dealing with Long-Term Risks

If the insurance industry is to become more humanized, it has to deal better with the real risks that trouble people, and many of these are long-term risks that reveal themselves only slowly over time. Long-term risks—especially the kinds that reveal themselves slowly instead of catastrophically and suddenly— are still poorly managed.

One of the biggest concerns that people have is about their livelihoods, their ability to earn income. Disability insurance policies cover some of the risks to livelihoods, namely those that occur because of accidents or disease. But in the future insurance can and will do much more.

Livelihood insurance is one possibility.[4] This would be a long-term insurance policy that an individual could purchase on a career, an education, or a particular investment in human capital. One could choose to specialize far more narrowly than is commonly done today—say, on a particularly interesting career direction—developing the expertise for such a career without fear of the consequences if the initiative turned out badly. The insurance policy would pay off with a supplement to one's lifetime income if it turned out years or decades later, based on verifiable data, that there was less of a market, or even no market at all, for people with this career.

Someday there also could be marketplaces, like futures markets, for career incomes by occupation. If the markets were long term, they would entail price discovery for the career decisions individuals made. Promising careers would be indicated by high market prices.

Sometimes when a family member becomes ill, the disability is devastating for the remaining members of the family. Insurance could also be expanded to better cover many of these risks. Long-term care insurance is already privately offered, but the take-up rate for such policies is abysmally low so far.[5] Welfare and unemployment programs will sometimes cover such eventualities, but only on a temporary basis. The illness of a family member can last for many years, even a lifetime. It will take financial innovation to achieve such improvements, to overcome the real barriers to such insurance that we see today.[6]

As another example, hurricane risk in the eastern United States has shown signs of increasing over recent decades, and if weather patterns are changing so as to make hurricanes much more likely in the future, there may be a devastating impact on property owners in those areas. But hurricane insurance policies as currently offered are overwhelmingly short term. Thus there is nothing to insure against the risk that the long-term danger from hurricanes will increase. A new kind of insurance, long-term catastrophe insurance, which effectively insures against the risk that risks will increase, is an innovation we can expect to see in the future.[7]

The Process of Improving Insurance

The process of financial development includes broadening the scope of insurance. And in this area, it is clear that much remains to be done.

Moreover, extending insurance to larger segments of the population is not exclusively a challenge for the poorest regions of the world. Even in the most advanced nations, there are still risks crying out to be insured. There is a clear need for home equity insurance (which insures people against a drop in the market value of their homes) and, as we have seen, livelihood insurance. These seem no closer to reality today.[8]

Pushing the concept of insurance to new horizons can be inspiring work. The intelligent response to stories of human suffering in the BP oil spill or the Haitian earthquake or agricultural famines around the world is to recognize that the real costs of these disasters could be met by better risk management—by better insurance. There is certainly a role for those who wish to enter the field of insurance to make this happen.

Chapter 8

Market Designers and Financial Engineers

Market designers, sometimes called mechanism designers, start with a problem—the need for a market solution to some real human quandary—and then design a market and associated contracts to solve the problem. They are using financial and economic theory to create "trades" that leave people better off. In so doing they are humanizing finance and making it more relevant to human welfare. Sometimes these people are called financial engineers, since what they do seems analogous to what mechanical or electrical engineers do. At their best, market designers have the same practical common sense and drive to create, and the same grasp of basic science, that successful engineers have.

Alvin Roth is a professor specializing in market design in the Economics Department at Harvard University. One of his most notable achievements was constructing a simple market for kidney transplants. Many thousands of people in need of a transplant die each year for failure to find a suitable donor. The problem has been that few people would volunteer to donate a kidney: the operation is painful and the result may pose complications. The only people willing to donate would usually be close relatives or a spouse. But these people usually do not have the right genetic match.

Roth and his colleagues, inspired by a mathematical model of an ideal housing market devised by mathematical economists Lloyd Shapley and Herbert Scarf, worked out a new market for kidney transplants that solves this problem.[1] They founded the New England Program for Kidney Exchange, which is now operated by the Federal Organ Procurement and Transplantation Network.

The design of the market is incentive compatible. A spouse, brother, or sister of a kidney patient is asked to donate a kidney, not to his or her own relative but to someone who is a genetic match. The market tries to find a trade wherein everyone gets a kidney, though not necessarily from the relative. This process sometimes involves as many as six steps. In the three-step case individual A donates a kidney to the relative of individual B, who donates a kidney to the relative of individual C, who in turn donates a kidney to the relative of individual A. Making this happen requires sorting through a large pool of people to find such a circle of matches. It also effectively requires that all the operations occur simultaneously, lest one person back out after his or her relative has received a kidney. Avoiding that possibility meant putting together a kidney transplant center that could perform many operations simultaneously. Roth's creation of a kidney transplant market is a true step forward in finance, for it deals with risks, incentives, moral hazard, and production by means of a complex contractual arrangement.

Before Roth, people dying for lack of a transplant were almost invisible to society. Since it seemed nothing could be done for them, they simply passed out of our attention. The beauty of creating market solutions to problems is that the markets themselves, once they are up and functioning, steadily generate exactly the right kind of focused attention among people who can actually provide solutions.

Even so, the limits of Roth's kidney transplant market are still apparent today, for such markets have not reached most of the people in need of transplants. The slowness with which financial developments take place again reflects a demand for conventionality and familiarity and an overreliance on tradition, both of which continue to inhibit financial innovation.

The Variety of Market Design Objectives

Market design is becoming a lively field. There are now, for example, mechanisms in place to help reduce the problem of global warming in an efficient manner, internalizing (making the emitters of greenhouse gases pay for) the damage they cause by contributing to global warming. The "cap and trade" system forces producers of CO_2 emissions to buy permits to emit, as measured in certified emission reduction (CER) units, on an open market. Thus a price is set on emissions, and those producers that can most easily sell will do just that, transferring their permits to others who need them more, for a profit. This mechanism ensures that those businesses that can most efficiently make the adjustment to lower CO_2 emissions will be the ones that do so, minimizing the cost of reducing the emissions.

There are now six climate exchanges: the Chicago Climate Exchange, Commodity Exchange Bratislava, the European Climate Exchange, the European Energy Exchange, NASDAQ OMX Commodities Europe, and PowerNext. Analogously, the World Bank has sponsored "cool bonds," which pay out to investors in response to CER units produced.

There have been numerous proposals for other such markets. Michael Kremer and Rachel Glennerster have proposed a solution to the problem of pharmaceutical firms showing little interest in developing drugs for major diseases of the poor like malaria, preferring instead to concentrate on luxury drugs for wealthy people, like wrinkle-reducing creams. Governments would promise to buy and distribute for free drugs for major diseases, thereby creating market forces to motivate private enterprise to find drugs that would cure the diseases.[2] Ronnie Horesh has proposed "social policy bonds," issued by governments, that would pay out more if certain social policy objectives were met, thereby creating a financial incentive for free-market participants to buy the bonds and then figure out how to meet the objectives.[3]

Market-Design Solutions to Even the Most Personal Problems

To appreciate the importance of market design, and how it can really contribute to the good society, it is helpful to think of a very personal problem that creates untold anxiety, yet for which a mechanism can be designed.

Consider finding a mate, someone to live with in a close relationship, usually as husband and wife. It is indeed a sort of market problem, in that the issue is not just finding a satisfactory person but also finding someone, confronted with the same search problem, who is willing to consider you as his or her best choice. Finding a match between husband and wife is like finding a trade in a financial market. It entails learning a market price (in the marriage market it is one's attractiveness to certain kinds of potential spouses) and finding the best deal at that price. This analogy is not meant to put a commercial slant on a very personal problem, but instead to start us thinking about how we can design a better solution to the problem.

Finding that special someone is, for most people, essential to the deep meaning of life. The search for a compatible mate is very difficult, as one may have to sort through many different people and it may take months or years to get to know what one has found. One of the most serious problems is confronting disappointment in a relationship, and in many cases having to break off the relationships after "wasted" years together. Help with finding the right person at the start of one's search is essential, but it has not been thought of by economic theorists as a problem for the economic system—until recently.

Even with full information, the problem faced by those who would offer such help, such as dating services or matchmakers, is daunting. The romantic notion of "falling in love at first sight," happening randomly as part of every-day life, cannot be the logical basis for matching people. As far back as 1825, a newspaper article noted the profound importance of the search problem: "Experience proves that thousands lead a life of celibacy, not from choice but prudence, and the reason is obvious: it is because of a limited circle of acquaintance, persons of suitable age, disposition and circumstances cannot be found. We daily hear of unhappy differences after marriage, owing to the great disproportion of age, disposition, & c., which, if there were more facility afforded to become acquainted, would almost invariably be obviated."[4]

Companies that allowed for at least a preliminary search for a potential spouse based on set characteristics (including availability) were early creations of capitalism. For example, a matrimonial plan in England and Wales in 1801 invited persons desiring a spouse to subscribe a sum of money to the plan and send a self-description. The plan offered several suggested examples of what one might include in the self-description. One for a man was "A clergyman, thirty years of age, dark eyes and hair, robust and healthy, enjoys three curacies, keeps a small school, of which he is heartily tired, and wishes for a more active department, and is of a very affectionate disposition." Another for a woman was "I am tall and thin, auburn hair, one eye rather brighter than the other, active and conversible, having had a good education, and am 24 years old and live with my father, who can give me 1500l. down, if I marry with his approbation."[5] Readers of such short descriptions will certainly find some information worth pondering—even, in the case of the woman, a price. Subscribers to the plan could read a list of such self-descriptions and communicate their interest to the plan. If there was a match, the plan would arrange an interview. This was indeed a sound business idea, one that enabled improved searching for a spouse.

Even these early businesses must have helped people with the market problem of finding a *matched* trade, that is, finding a person who not only is suitable but also thinks *you* suitable in turn. Indeed, finding a coincidence of wants is one of the most painful and difficult aspects of dating. Perhaps the administrators of these plans could have helped people lessen the pain and speed the conclusion if they had used their experience in matching in a way that did not force people to search slowly and sequentially through a list of those who were for the most part uninterested.

Finding a match is an intrinsically difficult market problem. Depending on the relative abundance of those with certain characteristics, people may search for years for a suitable match when their problem is simply not knowing what level of success to expect. They may remain celibate their entire lives not just because, as the newspaper article cited earlier suggests, there is a shortage of available acquaintances, but also because they may have misjudged the available supply of people with the characteristics they desire. That problem might be called, in purely financial terms, a problem of price discovery. Market designers can certainly help with this problem.

But then, once we try to design a technical solution to this problem, and to develop algorithms to provide such a solution, we will discover that there are deeper theoretical issues. For the number of possible matches is very large, and the criteria for sorting through them present some challenges.

Suppose we have a dating service with a hundred male and a hundred female applicants. Even using a computerized database with information about all of them and seeking to assign them to couples, one would find the task daunting. There would be 100 factorial possible pairings of all these people—a number difficult to comprehend, for 100 factorial is approximately 1 followed by 158 zeroes, a number unimaginably in excess of our existing digital storage options. Some of those pairings would undoubtedly be vastly superior to others, but how can we proceed to evaluate them systematically?

The complexity of the marriage problem has been explored by economic theorists. David Gale and Lloyd Shapley defined a particular marriage problem in a 1962 publication in the *American Mathematical Society Monthly*.[6] Let us imagine that each female has given the dating service a ranking (based on her own personal preferences) of all one hundred males and that each male has given a ranking of all one hundred females. How would we write a computer program that chose actual pairings of couples based on these rankings?

The problem, even when so well defined as in Gale and Shapley's terms, presents some complexities. Not only is the total number of possible pairings astronomically large, but it is hard even to decide what should be the objectives of the pairing. Given a candidate for an optimal set of pairings, how would we even decide whether it is in fact optimal?

The first thing that should happen, according to Gale and Shapley, is that the pairings should be "stable." That is, no couple would want to switch places after the fact. There would be no man who wanted to leave his assigned match for a woman who also wanted to leave her assigned match for him. Gale and Shapley provided an algorithm for the dating agency that would find a pairing and ensure that the pairing was stable in this sense. But, as they showed, there are generally many different stable pairings among the hundred men and hundred women. So the dating agency would have to consider which of these was in some sense optimal. They showed a pairing system that could be used to write a computer program for the dating agency that would yield a set of stable pairings that was optimal for the men, and another set that was optimal for the women. But they could not find a system that was in any appropriate sense optimal for everyone.

We need a system to surmount this problem, and that system is not easy to design. Governments that do not encourage entrepreneurial enterprises that actively look for problems to solve won't be very helpful. For example, dating agencies apparently came late to the Soviet Union. For decades, the best help the Soviet economy could provide was the free vacations to Black Sea or Baltic Sea resorts that Soviet enterprises offered their best workers as a reward for achievement. These vacations were intended to help fulfill the narrow objectives of the current five-year plan. Helping people meet others was not part of the plan. Liaisons were nonetheless an unintended by-product—but unfortunately these were mostly short term, as the people one met tended to be from far away.

The central planners of the Soviet Union did not have a reward system in place that focused their attention on the needs of the people. There was no force to allocate capital to enterprises that might provide dating services. Today, in post-Soviet, market-oriented Russia, dating services are well established. This trend reflects the emergence of financial and economic sophistication in that country and illustrates once more the human benefits of financial capitalism.

The point of the dating service example is to provide a real sense of the mathematical and theoretical complexity of even our most intimate problems, and to help us appreciate that financial theory ought to be involved in the future solution of these problems. In the future—thanks to improvements in information technology as well as economic science—we can expect to see more and better mechanisms to help us make all manner of economic decisions.

Financial engineers can help us solve such problems in the future just as mechanical engineers have designed the artificial heart or electrical engineers have designed the mobile phone.

Chapter 9

Derivatives Providers

In recent years, the term *derivatives* has become a dirty word, blamed by many for real evils, including the severe financial crisis that began in 2007. But a derivative is merely a financial product that derives from another market, and it is not inherently good or evil. Those specialists who drive the derivatives market may have gained a bad reputation, but in fact they are involved in some of the most creative and sophisticated aspects of finance.

One example of a derivatives market is a forward market for a commodity, in which one can sign a contract to buy from another a commodity or a property for future delivery at a specified date at a specified price. Another example is a futures market for a commodity, which is the same as a forward market except that it occurs on an organized exchange with established standards for quality, margining, and so forth. There are also markets for options: with an option one can purchase the right to buy something, say a stock or a bond, at a specified future date for a specified future price. Yet another example is a swap market: in a swap, such as a foreign exchange swap, two parties agree to exchange financial instruments (in this example two currencies) at a specified time in the future at a prespecified exchange rate. There is a derivative price in each of these markets: the price of the forward, future, option, or swap.

We have to ask why so many view the people who participate in such markets as evil. Who uses derivatives and why? Does derivatives trading fulfill a constructive purpose? As with other speculative activities, the purchase and sale of derivatives seems to many people to be a form of gambling, or worse, a vehicle for the exploitation by the clever of the less so. Certainly it is gambling to some. But is that all it is?

The Origins of Derivatives

Derivatives go back a long, long way. One of the earliest mentions of derivatives, by Aristotle (384–322 BCE) in his *Politics*, describes the successful trading of the noted Greek philosopher Thales (mid-620s to mid-540s BCE), the man who is sometimes described as the world's first real mathematician for having conceived of mathematics as the practice of formal deduction from stated assumptions with rigorous proofs. Apparently mathematicians were interested in finance from the very beginning!

Aristotle describes Thales as giving earnest money, *arrabon* (ἀρραβών), for the use of olive presses at an agreed rental rate for a later harvest. Earnest money and option premium are really the same thing. The word *arrabon* has taken on a different meaning (that of an engagement to marry) in modern Greek, but in ancient Greek we can say that it referred to a sort of option.

Actually, an engagement to marry *is* a kind of option—and so is marriage itself, as investment theorists Avinash Dixit and Robert Pindyck have argued: both involve nonmonetary commitments that resemble earnest money. As part of their argument that options theory is of ubiquitous importance in everyday life, Dixit and Pindyck offer many examples in which option-like possibilities occur naturally. Consider the exhaustion of natural resources or the destruction of tropical rainforests. Until they are exhausted or destroyed, there is an option to exhaust or destroy them, or to choose not to exhaust or destroy them. The choice itself has option value, before the decision is finalized—something that one must consider before making the choice.[1]

The exact nature of the contract between Thales and the farmers who owned the olive presses is not known. Perhaps the contract gave the presser the right to a fraction of the oil produced in compensation for the costs he incurred in pressing the olives. Thales was buying what we now call options on olives because he could later choose not to buy, and sacrifice his earnest money, if the value of olives fell instead of rising. His contract differs from a typical derivative today in that it appears to be based on total value rather than price, but that distinction is not essential to a discussion of options theory. He was making an asymmetric bet on olive values, benefiting fully if the olives had value above the contract rent but losing only the earnest money if not. That asymmetric bet on prices is the essence of an option.

According to Aristotle's story, the value of olives in fact went up as Thales had predicted. Hence "he gave deposits for the use of all the olive-presses in Chios and Miletus, which he hired at a low price because no one bid against him. When the harvest-time came, he let them out at any rate which he pleased, and made a quantity of money. Thus he showed the world that philosophers can easily be rich if they like."[2] Aristotle's intent in telling this story appears to have been merely to show that scholars can be effective in the real world. The story does not convince us that options markets in and of themselves are a good thing. Indeed it sounds rather like a story of a smart operator taking advantage of the broader public.

But we learn from this story that olive press owners were open to the sale of options. Presumably they had made such trades before. Why were they willing to do this? Clearly the pressers got the worse of the deal in this instance. Were they deceived by Thales?

In fact it is easy to imagine why olive pressers were willing to sell options on use of their presses when Thales came to them with an offer. Here was an offer of money on the table for the chance—which the pressers must have regarded as small—that olive values would increase to a high level. They must have assumed that Thales did not know that olive prices would be higher, so they were trading the "upper tail" of possible performance for a sure thing today. The payment would help them offset their possible losses if olive prices *fell* far below the contracted price. The pressers might have preferred insurance against massive falls in olive prices, if the terms were right—but Thales was apparently not offering that.

Were speculators like Thales, who wished to buy olive options, irrational? Not if they, like Thales, had some way to predict olive values. But we have seen that pressers wouldn't sell to them if they knew that the options purchasers *knew* that olive values would increase. This is a fundamental dilemma for financial theory, one that was discussed previously in connection with the work of Paul Milgrom and Nancy Stokey.[3] It seems from their theory that trade in such markets requires some kind of irrationality, such as overoptimism on the part of the purchaser of a call option or underoptimism on the part of the seller.

On the other hand, trade in olive options markets makes perfect sense if we consider that buyers of options are people who have reason to be concerned about the risk of changes in the price of olives. For example, retail olive oil merchants might wish to sell options on olive values, for if there were a short crop of olives they would expect to have a bad year. Buying the options might offset the damage to their profits. In this case, an options trade between pressers and olive oil merchants would benefit both even in the absence of information about future olive oil prices.

The options market must be working much better today than it did in the time of Thales. Then there was perhaps only one mathematician / option trader in the entire world; with no competition, he could make a fantastic profit. But now such practitioners are so numerous—look at all the graduate programs in mathematical finance, or attend one of the Institute for Quantitative Research in Finance (Q Group) conferences—that they compete heavily against one another, thus bringing options prices closer to their fundamental values.

Justifications for Derivatives Markets

In a classic 1964 article, economic theorist Kenneth Arrow argued that a major source of economic inefficiency is the absence of markets for risks.[4] Financial theorist Stephen Ross made Arrow's theory the raison d'être for options markets. In his 1976 article "Options and Efficiency," he argued that financial options have a central place because an immense variety of useful complex contracts can be " 'built up' as portfolios of simple options."[5]

But in fact only a small fraction of our risks are traded in any derivatives markets. The ancient example of Thales notwithstanding, it is a curious fact that in modern times, until just a few years ago, no olive oil derivatives were traded on any organized markets in the world.[6] More importantly, there are few or no derivatives for such key economic variables as GDP, wage rates, real estate prices, health care expenses, or average lifespans.

Behavioral finance scholars Hersch Shefrin and Myer Statman have argued that much of the demand for options trading is not for the high-minded purpose of managing risks to our livelihoods but is instead irrational. The demand is created by careful framing—by salespeople exploiting the psychological weaknesses of their customers. They argue that the most significant source of interest in options trading is not on the part of people like Thales who think they can predict the market, but from those on the other side of the market who may misunderstand options and see more value in them than really exists. As evidence, Shefrin and Statman quote a manual for options brokers who are seeking out customers willing to take the side of Thales' olive pressers. The manual offers a script for these would-be brokers:

> JOE SALESMAN: You have told me that you have not been too pleased with the results of your stock market investments.
> JOE PROSPECT: That's right. I am dissatisfied with the return, or lack of it, on my stock portfolio.
> JOE SALESMAN: Starting tomorrow, how would you like to have three sources of profit every time you buy a common stock?
> JOE PROSPECT: Three profit sources? What are they?
> JOE SALESMAN: First, you could collect a lot of dollars—maybe hundreds, sometimes thousands—for simply agreeing to sell your just-bought stock at a higher price than you paid. This agreement money is paid to you right away, on the very next business day—money that's yours to keep forever. Your second source of profit could be the cash dividends due you as the owner of the stock. The third source of profit would be in the increase in price of the shares from what you paid, to the agreed selling price.[7]

The argument is apparently effective but ultimately deceptive, for it emphasizes only the number of income sources, but does not suggest a comparison of the price received for the option with the expected loss in those cases when the stock price exceeds the agreement price. If the customer's attention is diverted from consideration of this price, or if the customer has no idea how to price options and thus cannot estimate whether the offered options price is a good one, then the customer could be lured into a bad deal. Others who understand options will be more than happy to

take the other side of this deal even if they have no idea where the underlying stock price is going, expecting to make money on average if the prices
they pay for the options are low.

Although Aristotle did not suggest it, it seems in fact conceivable that Thales
was doing just that, even if he never developed any formal theory of options
pricing. He may have had enough intuitive quantitative insight to sense when
an option was underpriced, and would buy it just because he thought it was
underpriced. He would then do well on average. If this was in fact the case,
then Aristotle had a point: mathematicians *will* win when pitted against naïve
counterparties.

Fred Schwed Jr., in his 1940 book *Where Are the Customers' Yachts?*, describes
other sales tactics of options brokers. One of them is suggesting to clients that
they buy out-of-the-money put options (options to sell at a price below the
current market price) on stocks that they already hold, thereby putting a floor
on their losses:

> There is no denying the fact that the above procedure supplies the speculator
> with definite insurance, "term" insurance, actually. But like all other forms
> of insurance it costs money to buy. Thus the simple question is set: is the price
> of the insurance commensurate with the amount of protection attained? Un-
> fortunately this problem cannot be solved mathematically. It can be attacked
> empirically, but this method of research is likely to be costly.[8]

It may seem strange that a well-developed options trading industry existed
in Schwed's day and yet there was still no theory of options pricing—a prerequisite that would seem essential to trading in that market. Actually a service-
able options pricing theory had been published in 1900 by the French
mathematician Louis Bachelier.[9] But there is no evidence that anyone in the
options market had even heard of his paper. That did not change until 1964,
when the mathematical treatises of A. J. Boness and Case Sprenkle appeared.[10]
Boness remarked on the strangeness of this: "Investment analysis is largely in a
pre-theoretic stage of development. Security analysis, narrowly defined, consists
chiefly of naïve extrapolations from ratios based on accounting data."[11]

Why, if the pricing of options was of such central importance to these
markets, did no one care about the mathematical theory behind it? That indeed
suggests that these authors are right—that much options selling is fundamentally exploitative. This fact ought to be remembered when we ponder whether
markets are really efficient.

There was also, in 1940, no exchange anywhere in the world for the trading
of options, so there was no way even to know whether the price a broker
quoted was indeed a market price. The first options exchange, the Chicago
Board Options Exchange, did not open until 1973.

The lesson is again that our financial system is not nearly a finished product.
If traders in 1940 had no mathematical theory whatsoever for options, but

were trading them every day nonetheless, it is indeed unlikely that our financial markets have reached perfection today.

The Regulation of Options

Stockbrokers around the world strive to maintain ethical standards against blatantly manipulative practices. In the United States the Financial Industry Regulatory Authority (FINRA) is the self-regulatory organization that represents a variety of investment professionals, including stockbrokers. In preparatory materials for their Series 7 licensing exams, prospective "registered representatives" are warned that in selling options they are constrained from certain unethical practices. But it seems that the Joe Salesman option-selling script is not proscribed. It is difficult for a self-regulatory organization to forbid such subtly misleading arguments, for it is hard to formally define when an argument is misleading.

Firms that value their reputation will avoid having their reps read from the Joe Salesman script, for their savvier clients will see through such a ploy, and they may communicate their dissatisfaction by taking their business elsewhere and telling others. But, in the end, brokers do not really need such a script, for, as Shefrin and Statman argue, many of their clients will fall into this trap of reasoning on their own with no help at all.

The sense of sleaziness associated with options has pervaded the public consciousness, perhaps because of such past bad practices. Most people do not trade options, for they are not on the usual lists of useful financial products recommended in investor advice columns, in the news media, or in investment advice books. Disreputable sales practices for options persist, but by now they have a limited, and declining, audience.

These practices could be reduced further if we could provide the kind of disinterested financial advice to the broad public that is the subject of the next chapter. The fallacy in the Joe Salesman argument is readily apparent to anyone trained in finance. Legal and financial advisers who are committed to serving their customers' interests will easily see through such a sales pitch, and will in fact warn their clients away from it.

If we move to a world in which people have access to better financial advice, then the options market could move closer to the ideal market initially envisioned by theorists like Kenneth Arrow and Stephen Ross. The market might even expand further in its usefulness, by aligning itself more squarely with the real interests of real people. Options could be created that represent genuine, personally significant risks to individuals, like the risks of a decline in home prices or a decline in career incomes. This would make derivatives such as options, even more clearly than they are today, instances of finance in the service of the good society.

Chapter 10

Lawyers and Financial Advisers

Lawyers and financial advisers are fundamental to financial capitalism because they provide information that is tailored to their clients' complex needs. Richard J. Murnane and Frank Levy, whose theory of the role of labor in modern society was discussed in the introduction, chose law as a prime example of an occupation that will not be replaced by computers. They chose it because the practice of law essentially depends on both expert thinking and complex communication. The same is true of financial advisers.

Efforts to create expert-thinking web sites to help people make financial decisions have not entirely succeeded. The mechanization of financial and legal advice with online expert systems is a new and important trend. As our online community continues to expand, as social media take increasing account of the financial community, we may expect to see help with financial problems provided to individuals via this channel. But it will not eliminate the need for more and better human help. The challenge for information technology is to provide an interface to allow people to more readily access both electronic and human help.

Even the celebrated site financialengines.com—created by financial theorists William Sharpe and Joseph Grundfest in 1998, initially to provide financial advice with no human intermediation—has brought human advice back into the loop. Although they do not override its algorithms, the system now provides for human advisers, who help customers determine how best to interact with the site. For the foreseeable future, no computer will fully replace developed human intelligence in helping other humans with their financial needs.

Integrity is still a human force, and even sites that provide automated financial advice, such as financialengines.com, are only as good as the people behind them. If people were ever to rely wholly on machines in making their investment decisions, the shift would open up a huge set of opportunities for investment products lacking in integrity to prey on them.

Quite to the contrary: the value of *human* financial services is so essential that the provision of such services to those of modest incomes needs to be encouraged and subsidized, either by the government or by philanthropic organizations. Certainly financial software will develop further, and it will become an even more important part of an adviser's toolkit. Social media will help advisers disseminate their advice to more and more people. And yet one-on-one human financial counseling will always be an essential prerequisite for satisfactory financial capitalism.

Lawyers

Lawyers are fundamentally involved with finance. Every financial device—including stocks, bonds, futures, and options—is represented by a long and complex legal contract, and typically by multiple legal filings with government regulators as well. In an important sense, the lawyers are the real engineers who construct financial devices.

Yet the boundaries between purely financial and other legal matters may be ill defined; indeed most of the contracts with which lawyers deal have financial elements, including employment agreements, leases, and divorce settlements.

Lawyers who specialize in securities law, corporate law, bankruptcy law, and contract law are rather controversial figures, for they are viewed by many as helping the rich make even more money. Lawyers who help with contracts are, of course, protecting their clients, who represent special interests of one sort or another. And of course their clients are not always rich. When a lawyer writes a bond indenture, the benefit will accrue to anyone who receives income from the security—a group that may include poor people as well as rich.

The role that lawyers play in a society depends on the resources of the people who hire them. If only the rich can afford lawyers, then lawyers will tailor their careers, and their advice, to the needs of the rich. But it does not have to be that way.

The Availability of Lawyers Generally . . .

There are enormous differences across countries in the number of lawyers per capita. Among countries for which data are available, the country with the highest number is Israel, with one lawyer per 169 people. Brazil is second with one lawyer per 255 people, and the United States third with one per 273 people. Next in line are various advanced European countries. At the other extreme are various Asian countries, with Japan at one lawyer per 4,197 people, Korea with one per 5,178 people, and the People's Republic of China with one per 8,082 people.[1] There are nearly fifty times as many lawyers per capita in Israel as there are in China!

Why these huge differences? There does not appear to be a scholarly literature that explains them, but they are no doubt related to complex cultural and institutional differences.

Consider Israel. There are many jokes about Israeli litigiousness. One describes a scene during the Six-Day War, when an Israeli tank and an Egyptian tank accidentally collide in the desert. The Egyptian tank driver jumps out and shouts, "I surrender!" His Israeli counterpart jumps out and shouts, "Whiplash!"

The culture in Israel, which encourages legal action, must certainly be affected by the tradition of Halakhah, the Jewish law. Perhaps it is related to the degree of attention to business issues in that legal tradition, extending back for millennia, and to the focus of that law on the resolution of business disputes.

The presence of a large number of lawyers may also reflect a burdensome legal tradition. For Brazil, writes Belmiro V. J. Castor in his book *Brazil Is Not for Amateurs*, "The judicial system is of limited help, given the unbelievable complexity and formalism of Brazilian laws. Appeals, reviews and suspensions are the delight of lawyers and the despair of plaintiffs. Bringing a lawsuit to right a wrong or repair some damage is invariably complex and expensive. . . . In some cases the situation borders on the absurd."[2]

According to Castor, the complexity of the Brazilian legal system is in turn rooted in deeper aspects of Brazilian culture. There is an aspect of the Brazilian national character, referred to by the word *jeitinho*, which describes a sort of impulse to improvise, to not rely on rules, to find some devious way to get things done in spite of the rules—and hence to make the rules doubly hard to navigate. The resulting atmosphere can be very conducive to lawyers' business.

Explaining differences across countries in the number of lawyers will not be easy. But it is worth noting that in countries such as Israel and the United States in particular, entrepreneurship has flourished in part because the relatively large number of lawyers permits people to undertake much more complex actions, and with more certainty about the outcome.

. . . and for Low- and Middle-Income People

There is an even more serious problem throughout much of the world, in that low- and middle- income people do not have adequate access to lawyers. This dearth affects them in numerous ways, including an inability to readily understand simple financial documents, like home mortgages or credit card contracts. The severe financial crisis that began in 2007 was made worse by the failure of most low- and middle-income people to get anything more than perfunctory legal and financial advice.

Legal advice for low-income people, at least in some minimal form, is subsidized by governments in most countries. Some do this more comprehensively than others. In the United Kingdom a Legal Services Commission provides legal advice to those with low incomes. Its annual budget is £2 billion, and about two million people a year are served, implying an expenditure of about £1,000 per person served, or about £40 per person in the United Kingdom. These services are augmented by the Citizens Advice Bureaus, which give broader-spectrum advice. Questions persist as to whether this is really enough, but the situation is clearly far better in the United Kingdom than in most countries.

In Canada government-sponsored Legal Aid Ontario offers legal services on something like the scale of the United Kingdom's Legal Services Commission.

In most countries a limited amount of free legal advice is offered on a pro bono basis. As such it is surely in short supply. As a result low-income people cannot easily make financial contracts and cannot expect contracts to be honored. The overall effect is to exclude these people from the very financial technology that has brought prosperity to so many.

Financial Advisers

Financial advisers, like lawyers, are very numerous in advanced countries with a tradition of financial sophistication. In the United States, according to the Bureau of Labor Statistics, there were 208,000 personal financial advisers in 2008, or about one for every 1,500 people.[3] But, once again, there are not enough of them.

Government subsidy of financial and legal advice can be justified on the basis of the externality provided by having a society that functions well, without some feeling that they are excluded from the financial world and later finding themselves punished for their mistakes.

In this country we already have *some* government subsidy of legal and financial advice, since these are deductible on personal income taxes. But such a subsidy benefits only those with higher incomes, who are therefore in high tax brackets and who itemize their deductions. We need to democratize the government subsidy of legal and financial advice so that it really benefits everyone, not just the wealthy.

Government subsidy of such advice would be a great democratizer of finance in that it would give people the information they need to make informed financial decisions.

Many countries now support financial literacy programs, and the web sites of government regulatory bodies now often have financial education materials on them. These are cheap and easy to produce.

But individuals need more than just web pages to look at. They need real expert financial advice—advice that is individually tailored and dedicated to their welfare. And this is very costly to provide.

Salespeople for financial products fill an important information-providing role in the modern market economy. But we should not have to rely exclusively on salespeople for financial advice. An adviser, if he or she is to receive any government subsidy, should sign a statement, a code of ethics, agreeing not to collect commissions for steering the client toward financial products that pay such commissions.

In the United States, the commitment required of all members of the National Association of Personal Financial Advisors (NAPFA) can serve as a model:

> NAPFA defines a Fee-Only financial advisor as one who is compensated solely by the client with neither the advisor nor any related party receiving compensation that is contingent on the purchase or sale of a financial product. Neither Members nor Affiliates may receive commissions, rebates, awards, finder's fees, bonuses or other forms of compensation from others as a result of a client's implementation of the individual's planning recommendations. "Fee-offset" arrangements, 12b-1 fees, insurance rebates or renewals and wrap fee arrangements that are transaction based are examples of compensation arrangements that do not meet the NAPFA definition of Fee-Only practice.[4]

But NAPFA advisers are costly to hire: they charge between $75 and $300 an hour, an amount beyond the budgets of many, even those in the middle class. A legitimate case can be made for government subsidy of any financial advice given under a commitment to the client like that required of NAPFA members.

Most people can't afford heart surgeons when they need them either: that is why we have government subsidies of health insurance for low-income people. It is commonplace for governments to subsidize medical advice. We can see—especially in the financial crisis that continues as of this writing, particularly in the United States—that many people have made errors in the purchase of their homes and the selection of their mortgages—errors that could have been prevented had they had proper *financial* advice as well. Avoidance of a financial crisis such as the one in which we now find ourselves offers a perfect example of the kind of externality that justifies government subsidy of financial, as well as legal, advice for everyone.

Legal and Financial Advisers as Key Elements in Financial Capitalism

Increasing access to legal and financial advice—access that affords people a patient and sympathetic adviser—is one of the key factors in developing a truly responsive financial capitalism for the future.

If people have good legal and financial advisers who really *represent* them, who are committed to nothing more than helping them, they will make better decisions. They can sign contracts and take on investments that involve the creative application of financial theory to their individual problems. In evaluating financial products, they will no longer need to fall back on conventionality as an indicator of quality. They will not feel the need to seek safety in numbers by attempting to do whatever they have the impression everyone else is doing. They will be less likely to be victimized by operators who try to appear conventional.

There are some who argue that financial and legal advice would not have prevented some of the errors that led to the current financial crisis. This may be true—most lawyers or financial advisers were not immune to some of the basic errors that led to the crisis. Before cracks in the financial system began to appear in 2007, they probably were victims of the same kind of errors, such as thinking that home prices could never fall and that an AAA rating on a security is a good indicator that it is safe.

But even so, legal and financial advisers who sat down with their clients and patiently talked through the issues would most likely have reduced the extent of the errors that so many made just before the crisis erupted, such as thinking that they should buy the biggest possible house, or even two houses. When one borrows a large sum of money to make an investment, one leverages the risks, as only a small drop in the value of the investment can wipe out the investor—and any competent adviser should know this. Advisers are trained to see the full array of possible investments and to have better knowledge of the risks inherent in leverage.

The further development of legal and financial advisers, including government support of their services to clients with lower incomes, will also create a different culture in our society. It will foster an expanded public discourse that might in turn help change the conventional wisdom, and better connect the knowledge base with the real problems people face, as well as make it more timely and relevant. The more people have access to those with useful knowledge, the more intelligent will be our approach, as a society, to financial capitalism.

Chapter 11

Lobbyists

One of the most troubling aspects of finance in modern society is that it often appears that the financial community now has the ability to take control of the government. They can hire lobbyists to present their case and persuade lawmakers to take their side. The "bailouts" and the favoritism apparently shown to some financial interests during the current financial crisis are widely seen as evidence of this.

The Unbalanced Power of Lobbyists

Arthur Levitt, the chairman of the SEC from 1993 to 2001, wrote about his experiences in a 2003 book, *Take on the Street*. He remarks as follows:

> During my seven and a half years in Washington, I was constantly amazed by what I saw. And nothing astonished me more than witnessing the powerful special interest groups in full swing when they thought a proposed rule or piece of legislation might hurt them, giving nary a thought to how the proposal might help the investing public. With laserlike precision, groups representing Wall Street firms, mutual fund companies, accounting firms, or corporate managers would quickly set about to defeat even minor threats. Individual investors, with no organized lobby or trade association to represent their views in Washington, never knew what hit them.[1]

The financial dealmaking that we have been considering among business-people is augmented by dealmaking among businesses and organizations and elected government officials, or among businesses and organizations with the

support of government. These deals can be productive, but they tend sometimes to lean toward the sordid. Bribery is illegal, but bribery can take subtle
forms. For example, a congressman who supports business interests can
often expect to be rewarded with a lucrative private-sector job *after* his term
of government service is done.

Levitt details how businesspeople recruited congressmen to battle the
regulations imposed by the SEC, and even to threaten him personally for failing to accede to their demands. The appendices of his book contain actual
threatening letters to him from congressmen (couched, of course, in idealistic
language that disguised their real meaning). He singled out Congressman
Billy Tauzin, a Louisiana politician who started out as a Democrat and later
became a Republican, as the most no-holds-barred supporter of business
interests. Tauzin did not seek reelection in 2004, and he then became head of
the Pharmaceutical Research and Manufacturers of America (PhRMA). PhRMA
offered him over $2.5 million per year, outbidding the Motion Picture Associa-
tion of America, which had offered him only $1 million.

There was nothing illegal about what Tauzin did, although it would be
illegal today, now that Congress has tightened its own rules regarding lobbying. The Honest Leadership and Open Government Act of 2007 (HLOGA),
signed into law by President George W. Bush, specifies that members of the
U.S. House of Representatives must now wait one year after leaving their jobs
before they can lobby the federal government. Tauzin could still become a
lobbyist, but now he would have to accept a slight delay before starting his
new job.

Certainly no one can prove that Tauzin wasn't entirely sincere in the causes
he took on. Yet it appears that there is at the very least a potential (even with
the one-year wait) for abuse when this kind of career path is normal. Ultimately
government works as well as it does because people of integrity refrain from
actions—or from being coerced into actions—that tarnish their reputations.

This pattern of influence of business on government has changed over
decades as financial interests have grown more sophisticated in their lobbying,
and reforms like HLOGA can never completely offset that. The amount of
money behind special-interest lobbying is now far greater than that behind
genuine public interest groups.

For example, Americans for Financial Reform is a lobbying group that
represents a coalition of consumer rights, civil rights, investor, retiree, community, labor, religious, and certain business groups. It has an annual budget
of $2 million. Its own 2011 analysis of what it is up against, based on public
disclosure of lobbying records, shows that the finance industry spends $1.4
million *a day* in the United States to advance its interests.[2]

Lobbying by financial interests is certainly not entirely selfish. Lobbying
groups sometimes come to lawmakers with important new ideas. For example,
in 1933 the National Association of Real Estate Boards (NAREB, whose suc-

cessor is the current National Association of Realtors) presented to the U.S. government a proposal for what was in effect to become the Home Owners' Loan Corporation (HOLC).[3] Congress followed this advice almost immediately, passing the legislation to establish the agency that same year.

Undoubtedly NAREB acted out of a degree of self-interest. The HOLC did help the industry with its bad mortgages. But it also helped troubled homeowners who were about to lose their homes, and the latter outcome was extremely important at a time when high unemployment and desperately bad times made home foreclosure a difficult loss for families to bear. Listening to the real estate lobbyists' proposal was certainly a good thing for government to do back then. But was their proposal really biased in favor of the mortgage industry? It is not obvious that it was, and it appears that the "bailouts" the HOLC offered did not cost taxpayers any significant amount of money.[4] Its founding represented a deal whose outcome could not confidently be predicted but that turned out well, for both mortgage lenders and their customers.

Lobbyists do transmit expertise about financial markets to lawmakers, and often enough they help them avoid serious policy mistakes.

But the increasing influence that major financial interests can buy by hiring lobbyists has some troubling consequences. According to the U.S. Congressional Budget Office, for the 1% of the population with the highest income, average real after-tax income grew 275% between 1979 and 2007—quite a dramatic increase. Over the same interval, Americans with income in the bottom 20% of the population saw only an 18% increase.[5] Clearly there has been a dramatic increase in the concentration of income among the most affluent.

Jacob Hacker and Paul Pearson, in their 2010 book *Winner-Take-All Politics*, argue that the increased number and professionalization of lobbyists for financial and business interests since 1979 is a good part of the reason for this increase in the after-tax income of the wealthy. While they do not prove a causal relation between the income increase and the increased number of lobbyists, they offer some compelling circumstantial evidence.

But Hacker and Pearson do not present evidence that a worsening of this situation can be expected in the future. It is not that the increasing sophistication of the financial community will make it better and better over time at exerting control over government regulation. Instead their view is that circumstantial events play a large role in the increasing power of lobbyists. They argue that the increasing number of individuals willing to pay for lobbyists to press cases related to social issues like gay rights or abortion rights has left a vacuum, a shortage of lobbyists willing to argue for the causes important to low-income Americans.

Hacker and Pearson's proposed solution to the problem of the excessive power of financial lobbyists is "the creation of organized, sustained pressure on legislators to make American politics more responsive and open to citizen engagement."[6] Democratic societies have shown a history of legislation to limit the power of wealthy special interest groups. Money does not uniformly buy influence over the government. Indeed studies that try to find an effect of campaign contributions on election outcomes have typically found surprisingly little.[7] It is hard to buy an election because voters will realize what is afoot, if only by observing the number of advertisements thrust in their faces. It does not take a great deal of sophistication to be suspicious of a candidate who is buying massive amounts of advertising. According to Robert Guest, business editor for *The Economist*, "The strongest force shaping politics is not blood or money, but ideas."[8] That is why the wealthy often prefer to sponsor partisan think tanks rather than lobbyists. But even think tanks are successful only insofar as they can make their ideas work in practice.

The history of legislation regarding lobbyists in the United States is full of examples of efforts to curb excessive influence for special interest groups. In particular, the Federal Regulation of Lobbying Act of 1946 required lobbyists to register with the Clerk of the House and the Secretary of the Senate, the Lobbying Disclosure Act of 1995 required lobbyists to write semiannual reports detailing their activities, and in 2007 HLOGA further strengthened disclosure requirements. Congressmen, aware of the potential for scandal, are now far more cautious in accepting any gifts from financial lobbyists. HLOGA has created a web site at which lobbying activity can be monitored by the public. Few other countries have established such extensive lobbying laws. Besides the United States, Australia, Canada, Taiwan, and Ukraine have lobbyist disclosure laws.

Another tactic to control lobbyists is to adopt "clean money" or "voter-owned" election rules that disallow all large campaign contributions. Such campaign finance reform would considerably weaken the power lobbyists could exert on behalf of wealthy vested interests. A number of countries have such laws; indeed in the United Kingdom they date back to the nineteenth century. In the United States several states have them, and a movement is under way to enact them in other states. But vested interests are likely to block such initiatives. In his 2011 book *Republic Lost: How Money Corrupts Congress—and a Plan to Stop It*, Lawrence Lessig, a Harvard Law School professor, suggests tactics that a grass-roots campaign could use to make such a movement a success.[9]

And Yet Lobbyists Can Benefit Society

The problem isn't that financial interests attempt to influence legislators. There is a need for *every* major group in society to help lawmakers reach their decisions, and of course, there is a legitimate reason for forming groups to defend special interests. According to opensecrets.org, financial, insurance, and real estate interests accounted for less than 15% of all lobbying activity in 2011.[10] There are also lobbyists for churches, charity groups, and the helping professions.

Legislators need lobbyists, for there is no way that they can fully assess how their legislation affects various interest groups in society unless informed representatives of these groups convey the appropriate information to them. Ethical lobbyists help make good laws. Lawrence O'Donnell Jr., who served on the U.S. Senate staff from 1988 to 1995, recalled, "There are honorable lobbyists. I dealt with them every day. By honorable lobbyists I do not mean just the ones who did pro-bono lobbying for charities."[11]

What kind of person becomes a lobbyist for an interest group? He or she is per se no less ethical than the general population. Presenting a case for an interest group is not in itself unethical, just as it is not unethical for a lawyer to represent a client in a criminal case, even if that person might be guilty.

Lobbyists tend to be people who are interested in public affairs; they find the profession a way to become involved with issues that interest them and to earn a good income while doing so. It is usually as simple as that. Often a lobbyist is a former lawmaker. Or a lobbyist may be someone who is interested in politics but reluctant to make the sacrifices required by public service. Lobbyists may find the behind-the-scenes action exciting and personally rewarding. One lobbyist, Joseph Miller, who wrote a book about his experiences, *The Wicked Wine of Democracy: A Memoir,* spoke of it this way: "I had experienced big-time politics up close for five years, but I still clung to the notion that my principles had an essential nobility about them and that the real purpose of it all was the betterment of humanity. If that sounds hopelessly naïve, I plead guilty."

But he also described falling for the temptations of a lobbyist: "When I expressed my misgivings to a business-lobbyist friend, he laughed and said: 'Just wait until you make a hundred thousand for getting an innocuous amendment or little clause added to an obscure bill. You'll get hooked. It's like hitting the jackpot. You get addicted.' He was right." Yet the temptations never completely got the better of him. When he was paid to try to influence Stewart Udall, a prominent member of the U.S. House of Representatives, for a less than idealistic cause, Miller ended up changing his mind and refunding the money: "Stewart Udall was my friend, and I was expected to use my influence with him. . . . It turned out that I couldn't. It was just too crass."[12]

Lobbyists are often held in low esteem in modern society, because they are viewed as mercenaries defending wealthy interests. But in fact as a group they are probably more public spirited than most. To function well as a lobbyist in a democratic society one must be fully conversant with the real issues that lawmakers are debating.

To be sure, there was some public anger when it was learned that lobbyists had managed to persuade the U.S. Congress to exempt automobile dealerships from the scrutiny of the Consumer Financial Protection Bureau. And they still manage to win subsidies for farmers that make little sense. But it is not clear that such actions outweigh the benefits of all the information lobbyists convey to government decision makers. The elation that Miller reports on getting a change enacted into law reflects just how hard it is to achieve that goal.

Lobbyists are not all powerful. It used to be thought that there would always be high tariffs protecting domestic producers. It was considered inevitable since the benefits to raising any single tariff rate redound to a small group of producers, while the costs are spread out over all of society. Hence it was believed that lobbying on behalf of tariffs would always be successful. In fact, however, the General Agreement on Tariffs and Trade has reduced most tariffs over most of the world to nearly zero. The same can be expected for financial lobbyists. The level of citizen concern we are seeing today at the excessive influence of financial lobbyists has already set in motion a process to limit this very influence.

Financial lobbyists, if they are properly regulated, are essential, for only the financial community has the expertise to understand the financial marketplace and the ability to evaluate policy regarding it. They must of course be monitored and regulated, but a healthy modern economy will necessarily involve such lobbyists.

Reforming Lobbying and Lobbyists

There is an ongoing process of improving the disclosure of information regarding lobbying and political contributions. Yet more remains to be done; for example, there could be better rules regarding disclosure of the actual force of the lobbying effort. In the United States today, companies can make their political contributions to intermediaries whose actual activities are not disclosed.[13]

Furthermore, if poorer people are not as effectively represented by lobbyists, social inequality will only increase. Indeed there is evidence from voting records that the opinions of the wealthy are taken into account to a disproportionate extent. Political scientist Larry Bartels, in an analysis of data on opinions and incomes collected by the National Election Survey, found that people in the bottom third of the income distribution have virtually no impact on the voting of their representatives in the U.S. Congress, compared with those in the middle and top thirds.[14]

Labor unions have in the past been the most likely lobbyists for lower-income people. But their influence has been waning throughout much of the world.[15] Symbolically important changes came with the aggressive moves of Ronald Reagan, who broke the U.S. air traffic controllers' strike in 1981, and Margaret Thatcher, who broke the U.K. coal miners' strike in 1985. Unions' traditional source of power, collective bargaining, has been weakened by international competition and new labor laws. We as a society must devise other, possibly very different, ways to energize lobbying efforts on behalf of neglected interests.

We need lobbyists as representatives for *all* groups in our society, including the "other 99%" with which the Occupy Wall Street protesters identify. The laws that provide for disclosure of lobbyists' activities do not themselves restore balance to lobbying efforts.

We need somehow to encourage lobbying activities on behalf of under-served groups. And subsidizing public interest lobbying on behalf of the currently voiceless is a good cause for philanthropists, as many of them already know.

Chapter 12

Regulators

Regulators as people with vision and purpose are typically omitted from discussions of financial markets. We hear a lot about energetic and effective entrepreneurs, but rarely about the people who work for regulatory agencies, whether they regulate government or industry. But in fact regulators and their intellect are fundamentally important to the financial system. It is they who make and interpret the all-important rules of the game.

Just as in sports, people in business want referees who will enforce the rules. Everyone has an interest in the game being fair. The fact that players try to push the limits of the rules or argue with referees doesn't mean they don't want them. In the same way, businesspeople very much want regulators, for regulations imposed on all players do not generally work to their individual disadvantage—quite to the contrary, they typically work to the advantage of all. Without effective rules one is forced to do things that one finds personally questionable to stay in business. That is why businesses set up their own self-regulatory organizations, which impose rules that are usually (though, to be sure, not always) in the public interest.

But there are some who think that regulators are not doing anything of the sort. Milton Friedman, following his 1954 study with Simon Kuznets of occupational incomes and regulation, made a strongly worded argument against regulation, particularly occupational licensing, in his 1962 book *Capitalism and Freedom*.[1] He thought regulation was little more than a cynical ploy to limit the supply of services so as to keep their prices high. Friedman's book turned out to be very influential, creating a measure of public distaste for regulation.

His University of Chicago colleague George Stigler carried the theme forward, writing in 1971 that "as a rule, regulation is acquired by the industry and is designed and operated primarily for its benefit."[2] Stigler believed that the principal goal of regulation, whether government regulation of an industry or self-regulation by the industry itself, is to deny entry to competitors.

Despite Friedman's and Stigler's arguments, the scope and extent of regulation have only grown in the United States. Morris Kleiner and Alan Krueger find that the purview of occupational licensing has grown dramatically in the United States, from only 5% of the labor force licensed in the 1950s to 29% in 2008. The increase in the percentage of the labor force that is licensed more than fully offsets the decline in the percentage of the labor force that is unionized.[3] That same trend may not be observed elsewhere in the world, and of course the trend around the less-developed world has been toward greater reliance on free markets. For example, a major part of the Indian economic reforms in the 1990s was a massive cutback in industrial and trade licensing.[4]

The Friedman complaint was taken up again by other University of Chicago economists, Raghuram Rajan and Luigi Zingales, in their 2003 book *Saving Capitalism from the Capitalists*. But now the argument is more nuanced. Rajan and Zingales recognize the need for appropriate regulation in many places and also believe that society can exert oversight over regulators to help prevent their capture by private interests. It isn't that we need "more" or "less" regulation, but that regulation must not be commandeered by selfish special interests, and that it needs to be done right.[5]

Indeed, whereas there should be some prudent concern lest regulators be captured by the industries they regulate, we need not take that as a foregone conclusion. At least in today's developed countries, regulation has not been totally captured by business interests. In the United States, we have had a civil service since 1872 (copying many other countries going all the way back to China in the Han Dynasty), which prevents hack political appointees from taking control. Regulators are now trained professionals. Although an elected politician could in theory try to divert civil servants from their responsibilities, it would be much harder to order them to formulate regulations designed to create monopoly power on behalf of some special interest. In today's climate of media alertness, such behavior would soon be revealed and lead to a scandal.

In his 2010 book *No One Would Listen*, stock market analyst Harry Markopolos argued that government regulators can be deaf to evidence of financial excess, even fraud, if the culprit appears to have legitimacy and prestige. The regulators quickly go after small-time crooks, Markopolos argued, but when it comes to large companies, they are "captive to the companies they are supposed to regulate." Markopolos uncovered substantial evidence that the massive hedge fund run by the respected Wall Street figure Bernard Madoff was nothing more than a Ponzi scheme, a fraudulent investment scheme built on a plan for social contagion of enthusiasm among investors. The fund was eventually exposed in 2008. But Markopolos had complained about Madoff's scheme to the SEC as early as 2000. In 2005, three years before the ultimate collapse of the scheme, Markopolos presented a twenty-one-page document to SEC New York Branch Chief Meaghan Cheung and explained his findings. According to his account of their meeting, she told him she had read his report, but she did not have a single question for him. "The strongest impression that I got from her was that I was bothering her. There was no excitement, no enthusiasm, no recognition that I had just put in her hands the biggest case she would ever have in her career."[6]

Ms. Cheung, in an interview with the *New York Post* after the book was published, responded that she was not at liberty to discuss the SEC's deliberations regarding Madoff, but that she was distressed by the Markopolos accusations: "I was not influenced, and I don't believe anyone in the New York office was influenced, by any other desire than to find out the truth. . . . There is no other reason to work there for so long, except that I love what I do. No one in my office had any incentive to miss something like this."[7]

Of course there is no way we can reconstruct exactly what happened, but I am inclined for the most part to believe Ms. Cheung. What influence could Madoff have had to induce the SEC to cover up a massive fraud that, according to Markopolos, would eventually be discovered and create a national scandal? If influence by Madoff was indeed a factor, it must have operated at a subtle, interpersonal level, in much the same way that confidence men influence their sometimes-too-credulous victims.

People are quick to blame regulators. The mistake of not prosecuting Madoff earlier can probably be traced largely to mistakes by overworked regulators or to faulty administrative procedures. A significant error will naturally occur in any system from time to time, and the major sources of that error can be corrected. Despite the arguments of critics like Markopolos, regulators—at least in the United States, both those appointed by industry itself and those in the government—are much more often well meaning and substantially more effective than is commonly acknowledged.

Self-Regulatory Organizations

In the United States, as we have seen, FINRA is a nongovernmental self-regulatory organization funded by the securities industry that works to set professional standards and encourage ethical behavior among practitioners. Originally it was called the National Association of Securities Dealers (NASD), and it launched the NASDAQ trading system and stock price index. The NASD merged with the member regulation, enforcement, and arbitration functions of the New York Stock Exchange in 2007. Today FINRA regulates some 630,000 registered representatives in nearly five thousand brokerage firms.

Other countries have similar agencies, such as the Investment Industry Regulatory Organization of Canada and the Securities Investment Institute in the United Kingdom.

To become a registered representative in the United States—that is, to be licensed to sell securities and have the power to act as an agent—FINRA dictates that one must pass the Series 7, Series 24, and Series 63 examinations, which heavily emphasize standards of ethical dealing, and also demonstrate a level of general knowledge about securities. In the preparatory materials for these difficult exams, prospective stockbrokers, or registered representatives, are warned against using deliberately misleading sales tactics, such as "selling dividends," that is, pressuring a client to buy a stock so as not to miss a dividend check, without pointing out that the price of a share generally falls after a dividend is paid. They are forbidden from "front running," that is, buying shares on their own account just before filling a large customer order, to profit personally from the price rise the large order will create. They are warned against "churning," deliberately advising a client to make many purchases and sales merely to generate commissions. Registered representatives are at all times required to communicate with their supervisors, who are expected to uphold an even higher standard of conduct.

FINRA also requires registered representatives and their supervisors to participate in regular continuing education programs. During some of these, the reps are shown video clips of actors portraying real-world situations in which temptations can arise.

It is hard not to come to the conclusion that the activities of FINRA are fundamentally well meaning and effective in improving the climate of the financial industry.

Government Regulators

The "bureaucrats" who run government regulatory agencies are rarely appreciated publicly. There is no room in our public imagination to view them as of any interest, let alone as heroes. We hear about pitched battles among elected officials, and about the often dramatic activities of lobbyists and powerful corporate interests, but little or nothing about the everyday activities of the final arbiters who actually deal with all the details.

It is hard for most of us to know with certainty whether these regulators are doing a good job for the citizens who depend on them. Of course we can count the number of regulations they promulgate, but we cannot say with any certainty how our society would be different if they weren't in place. The rules they make have numerous effects on our lives, but it is difficult to quantify or summarize these effects. We are left for the most part with only vague impressions of what regulators do.

In 2002 I visited the SEC with my colleagues at a firm I had co-founded, MacroMarkets LLC. Going there on business was unusual for me, for I was (and still remain) a full-time professor devoted mostly to education and research. We went to the SEC to gain approval for a new and unusual security that we wanted to launch: MacroShares, which were intended to make previously untradable risks tradable, and in so doing to provide price discovery for basic economic values for which there was at the time no such discovery. In truth I did not have particularly high expectations for the kinds of people we would meet at the SEC.

We were accompanied by representatives from the American Stock Exchange and our lawyers from Skadden, Arps, Slate, Meagher & Flom. I was impressed by the team we had assembled on our side. But I remember sitting there thinking that many of those representing the SEC were equally impressive—knowledgeable, enlightened, sympathetic. It seemed to me, as an outsider to such things, that together both sides represented a community of intelligent, public-spirited, sincere people.

The sense I got of the SEC that day is another reason why I am inclined to believe Meaghan Cheung when she denies being influenced in the Madoff case.

On another occasion, when I was visiting a second U.S. government regulatory body, the Federal Deposit Insurance Corporation, I asked some of the regulators at lunch: Why do you do it? What drives you to take a job like this? Many of them feel that a stint as a government regulator is an important part of a career in finance. Individually they seemed to have a well-thought-out sense of their own careers, of their places in the financial community, and of a broader mission. Collectively there seemed to be a sense not only of self-advancement but also of social purpose.

I invited Laura Cha, former vice chair of the China Securities Regulatory Commission and a member of the Executive Council of Hong Kong, now non-executive deputy chairman of the Hong Kong and Shanghai Banking Corporation, to talk to my Financial Markets class about her experiences as a regulator. She reflected as follows:

> So, I had a total of 14 years of experience as a regulator. And I have to say that it has been hugely gratifying, because as a regulator and a policy setter I was able to facilitate the development of markets in Hong Kong. In the early days— I mean in the '70s and the '80s—Hong Kong was largely a local market. The international players like Goldman Sachs and Morgan Stanley, they came and they went, they took a look and decided the Hong Kong market was too small for them. All that took a change in 1992, when the Chinese government decided that they wanted to use the Hong Kong market as a way to help transform or reform the state-owned enterprises.[8]

I believe she is speaking honestly here—a career as a regulator can be highly gratifying, quite apart from any personal financial profit. To effect changes in a market as she did is to be part of history—in her case, part of the historic advance of the Chinese civilization.

Of course, things don't always go so swimmingly well in negotiations with regulators, and I am told that many of the people who pay visits to the SEC can be manipulative and adversarial. There is also, among those who work at the SEC and at other regulatory agencies, a degree of frustration with political interference, inadequate budgets, and overwork. Because it is the regulators who make and enforce the rules that govern financial capitalism, they must be given adequate resources to do so, as well as the respect and appreciation that they deserve.

Chapter 13

Accountants and Auditors

For an economic organization to function, it must have its own memories and its own way of storing, accessing, and communicating those memories. Accountants manage the repositories of financial memories, whether of an organization or of an individual client. Auditors evaluate and interpret their work. Accountants—particularly those who are chief financial officers of companies—are essential to finance because they preserve the integrity of essential financial structures.

People who are actively involved in managing and running a business will typically have fine short-term memories, but, like most of us, they may not always be able to remember details over time. They are best at remembering the specifics of their *own* employment contracts, their own options, their own incentive compensation. More typically, their memories become fuzzy when it comes to remembering promises made to *others* in their organizations, or to dealing with the minutiae imposed by tax authorities or regulators. CEOs have loftier goals in mind, and they can't be expected to know all the details.

We have compared CEOs to the prefrontal cortex of the brain. In the same way, we could compare accountants or chief financial officers to the hippocampus, which converts short-term memory into long-term memory and connects different memories in the brain. An organization draws inspiration from its CEO in terms of vision and goals, but it also needs a different kind of inspiration, no less lofty than that expected of a CEO: a drive for orderliness and consistency.

Accountants have to determine what is important to remember, to document, to publish. The term *bookkeeper*—with its suggestion of dusting off old documents in a basement archive—gives a misleading impression of what they do. Their responsibilities are far more central, for they are essential to the stewardship that should be the central mission of our financial institutions.

Responsible for storing essential information, accountants are upholders of consistent moral standards, since consistency of standards is a prerequisite for remembering commitments and details. They must have a strong sense of their own standards. They tend to be hired by those who want or need to prove to others that they are honest—but who sometimes behave as dishonestly as possible within that constraint. This fact creates a moral challenge for accountants, a major theme in their everyday lives. But the best, and over time the most successful, in the accounting profession are those who embrace this moral challenge.

In her book *Confessions of a Tax Accountant*, Noelle Allen reveals a long list of dishonest tax dodges that her clients have asked her to approve. Reading her account reminds one of the deceptive side of human nature. She tells a story: "I was called for jury duty recently. As a part of the process of jury selection, the prosecuting attorney in the case asked me if I thought I could tell when someone was lying. I replied 'Sir, I'm a tax accountant. People lie to me all the time.' His response: 'Ms. Allen, you're excused.'"[1]

An accountant has to keep an emotional distance from the people and organizations he or she serves, so as not to be drawn into any of their machinations. Of particular importance, a corporate accountant must feel a general sense of sympathy for the various claimants to the organization's purse, so as to remember all of them and treat them all fairly.

A CEO cannot double as the accountant or chief financial officer of an organization. Human impulses to be manipulative and self-dealing are too strong. There is necessarily a degree of conflict of interest between the CEO and the accountant—a conflict that is built into the very model of the modern organization. The CEO is supposed to be a visionary, looking to the future. The accountant remembers commitments and resource limits, with an eye to the promises of the past and the realities of the present.

There are a large number of self-regulatory organizations in the accounting profession. The International Accounting Standards Board (IASB) (a successor to the International Accounting Standards Committee) traces its history back to 1973, when it was created by a number of accounting organizations: the American Institute of Certified Public Accountants (AICPA), the Canadian Institute of Chartered Accountants, the Ordre des Experts-Comptables et des Comptables Agréés in France, the Institut der Wirtschaftsprüfer in Germany, the Institute of Chartered Accountants in Australia, the Institute of Chartered Accountants in England and Wales, the Japanese Institute of Certified Public Accountants, the Instituto Mexicano de Contadores Públicos in Mexico, and the Nederlands Instituut van Registeraccountants in the Netherlands. Many other countries' groups representing accountants have become involved since then. The U.S. Financial Accounting Standards Board signed a memorandum of understanding with the IASB in 2002, with the goal of converging accounting standards around the world.

These professional organizations set and enforce standards for the activity of their accountant members, notably their practice in auditing corporate books. They discipline members who do not meet these standards. And they serve as lobbyists for accountants' interests.

Some of these organizations have come under criticism during the current severe financial crisis. In the United States, AICPA's performance has been the subject of some dispute. AICPA performs a number of important regulatory functions that are essential to maintaining an honorable profession. It administers the Uniform Certified Public Accountants Examination for licensing accountants, and the exam includes detailed questions on ethics and responsibilities. But AICPA was chastised for doing nothing to prevent Arthur Anderson & Co., then one of the so-called Big Five accounting firms in the United States, and the auditor for Enron Corporation, from conspiring to manipulate that company's earnings statements. Arthur Anderson was convicted on criminal charges in 2002 and went out of the accounting business.

Arthur Levitt, the former chairman of the SEC, pointed out in 2003 that AICPA has disciplined few accountants and that no Big Five firm had ever failed a peer review. He was annoyed by what he saw as the institute's aggressive lobbying on behalf of its members, to the exclusion of the interests of ordinary investors. He concluded that "AICPA has fallen down on the job."[2]

And yet examples like the Arthur Anderson fiasco are rare. The accounting industry does have a reliable sense of professional ethics, which it imparts to its members and which forms the backbone of our system of financial capitalism. Accountants are responsible for ensuring that financial appearance matches reality, and it is ultimately through their efforts that we trust our businesses enough to find it motivating and even inspiring to work for them or invest in them.

Chapter 14

Educators

At this point we have discussed the most central roles and responsibilities in the financial world, and we now move to some of those on its periphery. But peripheral does not mean less important, merely less involved in day-to-day operations. Educators are of central importance to the functioning of the financial system. Delicate as the proper functioning of the system is, it requires some understanding of the origins of its institutions, its practices, and their purpose, and a sense of how one's own career can fit into that picture.

Errors by educators in recent decades seem to have played an important role in the severe financial crisis that began in 2007. In particular, the efficient markets theory was oversold to students, and this helped contribute to the formation of speculative bubbles. Many teachers seemed to inculcate the extreme view that markets are perfectly efficient. From this view many of their students drew the conclusion that it hardly matters ethically what one does in business, since nothing one could do would ever disturb this magnificent equilibrium.

But educators are also responsible for the rapid expansion of financial sophistication in the financial markets in recent decades and for teaching the method and mission of financial stewardship. These roles will continue to be fundamental to financial institutions in the future.

The Historical Mission of Business Education

There has long been tension about teaching finance and business in colleges and universities. There has been a sense on the part of some in academe that these disciplines are somehow beneath other areas of study in the arts and sciences curriculum that has dominated higher education. Many colleges have long resisted starting an undergraduate business major and may offer very few business-related courses. Business education tends to occur only in separate business and law schools, which tend to be viewed by some as "vocational" schools which are not quite as intellectually strong. These attitudes are by no means new; they relate to the negative attitudes about those in business and finance that have characterized our society for centuries.

The fight against these negative prejudices has been most evident in the United States, which has always placed great emphasis on practical education. This practical focus is a long-standing trait of the United States. Benjamin Franklin, in a 1787 article for Europeans thinking of moving to the United States, described it thus:

> According to these opinions of the Americans, one of them would think himself more obliged to a genealogist, who could prove for him that his ancestors and relations for ten generations had been ploughmen, smiths, carpenters, tanners, or shoemakers, and consequently that they were useful members of society; than if he could only prove they were gentlemen doing nothing of value. . . . There [in America] they may be taught and practice mechanic arts, without incurring disgrace on that account; but on the contrary acquiring respect by their abilities.[1]

Even so, even in America, it would not be for another hundred years that a college business school would open its doors. The first such school was founded at the University of Pennsylvania in 1881, and the first graduate school of business (offering a master of science in commerce, essentially today's masters of business administration or MBA) at Dartmouth College in 1900. No other country followed suit until Canada's University of Western Ontario did so in 1951, half a century later.

Joseph Wharton—who made a fortune with the Bethlehem Steel Company, was the author of scholarly papers on metallurgy and other scientific topics, and later became a philanthropist—founded the business school at the University of Pennsylvania. It was at first called the Wharton School of Finance and Economy, a name that has since been shortened to the Wharton School. It was dedicated to teaching business as a noble calling. According to an 1881 summary of its prospectus, its purpose was "to inculcate, among other things, the immorality of acquiring wealth by winning it from others rather than by earning it through service to others."[2] Here Wharton was on to a fundamental truth about finance: it is not, and should not be, merely a zero-sum game, but rather an adjunct to, and a means toward, a productive life.

Wharton's was not the first business school in the United States, but its predecessors were not university-affiliated and were strictly vocational, teaching only basic business skills. An even older example of a business school was Bryant and Stratton College, founded in 1854 and incorporating the earlier

Folsom Business College. It claimed some prestige in its day and later included among its illustrious students John D. Rockefeller Sr. and Henry Ford. The college still exists today, offering associate of applied science degrees in accounting and other business fields, bachelor of science degrees in financial services and other fields, and preparation for certification examinations for financial planners, registered representatives, and others. The difference between Wharton and Bryant and Stratton remains the same today as it was at their founding: Wharton is more broadly intellectual while Bryant and Stratton is focused on teaching important basic business skills.

In 1890 Joseph Wharton gave a speech about education at the Wharton School in which he described his motives in founding the school within a college. He made it clear that one of the measures of a college should be the marketable skills its students receive. The speech was received with a chorus of negative comment from the presidents of the elite universities of his day. Francis Amasa Walker, the president of the Massachusetts Institute of Technology, declared, "I exceedingly dislike to see the question of college education put upon such low ground. A young man who would allow his decision between going to college or staying away to be determined wholly or mainly by the prospect of pecuniary return is unworthy of the benefit of a liberal education." Franklin Carter, the president of Williams College, said, "I have believed that the business men of the future are to come from the colleges. But then they must be trained men, disciplined and developed in all mental directions, not overfed mollusks."[3]

The same views, only slightly transformed, were still in evidence a hundred years later. In his 1991 book *Creating Academic Settings*, the economist John Perry Miller detailed the arguments he had to make for founding a management school at Yale University while he was dean of the graduate school there. Yale did not get its management school until 1976 because of the objections of many alumni who thought such an addition too vocational. Miller on the other hand believed that management and finance are indeed intellectual disciplines, which potentially offer their own intrinsic rewards to everyone in the intellectual community:

> Equally important is the impact of such a program on the life and vision of the faculty and students in other parts of the University. The horizons of faculty members and their educational programs are affected significantly by the various professional schools which surround the central Faculty of Arts and Sciences. Yale's faculty members are different and, I believe, better for living in an environment of colleagues pursuing research and education in the various professions. The effects are subtle but real. The perspective of faculty and students is broader, their vision of man and woman and their ways richer.[4]

By the time Miller wrote, the field of finance had become transformed from a discipline of description and rote memorization into a mathematical and empirical science considered by many worthy of becoming part of a true liberal education.

Our colleges and universities are where finance starts, where the people who make the decisions are first exposed to the theory and philosophy of business. They need to understand both the abstract theory and the practical applications and issues of morality that underlie a life in business.

Economic Education and Morality

It is in school—starting with the education of children and teenagers, and leading next to undergraduate programs and MBA, JD, and PhD programs—that young people have their only real, unhurried opportunity to examine the underpinnings of their future professions, to talk to others unhampered by nondisclosure requirements and professional loyalties. This is where the moral decisions that will guide later life are really made, and educators have a responsibility to see that they are made well. There is unfortunately a so-called agency problem, particularly in our colleges and graduate schools, where academic faculty often see themselves as having no purpose other than to train scholars like themselves. Their teaching may become too focused on the frontiers of research and on research methods, rather than on preparing their students to be participants in the real-world practice of financial capitalism.

Business education must to some degree be vocational: it should not avoid teaching basic skills. But it should also integrate this knowledge into a broader intellectual framework. This is particularly important for those students who will become business leaders. Our educational institutions have an obligation to present a view of the true workings of financial capitalism, and to cover both the mathematics of finance and its human, practical, and moral side.

Chapter 15

Public Goods Financiers

Public finance, the financing of public goods and causes, is curiously considered a very different profession from "straight" finance. Courses in public finance at the university level are generally offered in the economics department, not the business school, and it appears that the professors in the two fields rarely talk to one another. Communications between the fields seem to be improving, and recognition is growing that they are, or at least ought to be, closely related. They deal with essentially similar problems, differentiated by the fact that public finance confronts a special "public goods" problem. Yet there still remains an unfortunate division between the fields, one that adversely affects their intellectual content.

The fundamental problem for public finance is that public goods are not naturally provided in a free-market system. A public good is an economic activity that automatically benefits the public, including all those who choose not to pay for the activity. Roads and scientific knowledge are public goods, as are clean air and cities free from crime. If one thinks the air is not clean enough, or that the streets are still too dangerous, one cannot go to a store and buy these things for oneself. The provision of these goods has to be public, the result of a collective decision to embark on certain costly activities. Individual and corporate philanthropy is usually inadequate to deal with the full range of public goods opportunities that present themselves. Indeed the primary justification for having a government is that it provides public goods.

A problem with public goods provision is that information about what can be done is neither visible nor comprehensible to most voters. A candidate for public office extolling some new plan to clean the air or reduce crime will be met with incomprehension by most individuals. They might know how much cleaner they would like the air to be and how much they would pay for that, but such awareness does not translate for them into specific knowledge of how they should vote on the issues.

Most individuals do not have the imagination to conceive of what might possibly be done. They tend to have some understanding of public goods *already provided*, for they observe their benefits. But they are unlikely to have any sense of what to do next.

General-mail postal services, provided on a mass scale for the public, have a public goods aspect since they furnish an economic infrastructure— something like an older version of what the Internet does today. This infrastructure, when it was introduced long ago, changed the playing field for everyone and made possible whole new lines of business activities that people could not even have imagined until the infrastructure was in place. Postal services may not be provided adequately by the private sector, without government support, because private markets do not take into account the value of the public good and because of the monopolistic pricing problems that may be associated with the natural monopoly of a massive delivery system.

Before effective and economical postal service was provided extensively in the nineteenth century, most people probably did not regret its absence. They knew that they could get something delivered, at considerable expense, through private couriers or through an expensive government mail service, and they probably did not imagine that they would ever find much reason to want to have something delivered cheaply by mail. They could not have known that the development of an infrastructure for cheap and efficient delivery would launch a million other economic activities. They could not have known that creation of a national postal service with post offices in every town would change the economic layout of the nation, creating jobs and opportunities, improving land use, and resolving congestion problems.

It was not until after a persuasive 1837 pamphlet was published by Rowland Hill in London that there came to be an extensive and effective postal network in England, a "Penny Post" with the rule "for every letter a penny." Hill argued that the British government was charging too much for postal services in an effort to maximize government revenue. Considering the cost of delivering mail, the government was, he argued, in effect putting a tax of at least 200% on postal services. This tax came at the expense of (though he did not use the term) an important public good:

> When it is considered how much the religious, moral, and intellectual progress of the people, would be accelerated by the unobstructed circulation of letters and of the many cheap and excellent non-political publications of the present day, the Post Office assumes the new and important character of a powerful engine of civilization; capable of performing a distinguished part in the great

work of National education, but rendered feeble and inefficient by erroneous financial arrangements.[1]

Even after the Penny Post was fully implemented, it would have been hard to *prove* quantitatively that it had become a "powerful engine of civilization"—but people believed just that. It was soon copied all over the world. Nevertheless it is something of a miracle that, thanks to the calculation of public financiers like Hill, extensive postal networks got started in the first place.

The provision of public goods is essentially a deep financial problem. It is subject to the same constraints seen in the provision of private goods. We need to encourage organizations of people who together can be productive in providing public goods. We need to identify genuine public goods and to assign a priority ranking to them. We need to see that the people charged with providing them are appropriately incentivized and not corrupted. We need to deal with the fact that information about what might ideally be provided as public goods is dispersed among many people and somehow has to be pooled. And so the financial technology that we have put in place for providing private goods carries over to the provision of public goods.

There have been several major milestones in the provision of public goods—milestones that are significant for the spur they gave to creativity in this area.

In 1932, in the depths of the Great Depression, President Herbert Hoover created the Reconstruction Finance Corporation. A key idea underlying effective public goods finance is that it does not have to be the government that comes up with ideas for public goods through a political process, and it does not have to be candidates for national office who dream up such ideas. The Reconstruction Finance Corporation listened to ideas from the private sector and actively sought private-sector advice. And the strategy worked: even in the midst of the Great Depression, almost all of the loans it made to private businesses were repaid.

Another key idea is that the government can finance organizations of individuals rather than hire single individuals as employees of the government. In that way, expenditure on public goods is entirely analogous to expenditure on private goods, except that the customer is the government.

In 1950, at the suggestion of Vannevar Bush, former dean of engineering at the Massachusetts Institute of Technology, the United States created the National Science Foundation. Bush had written a short book in 1945, *Science, the Endless Frontier*, and presented it to President Franklin D. Roosevelt. The book argued that scientific research was a profoundly important public good, which up until then had been supported primarily by private benefactors and private universities. Bush had clear ideas about how government should facilitate the advancement of science. Grants should be made to organizations outside the federal government, which should never operate its own laboratories. Decisions to award funds would be made not by bureaucrats but by real scientists, outside the government, who would volunteer to evaluate research proposals.[2]

The National Science Foundation would thus operate more like an investor in a venture capital firm, specializing in science, than a typical agency of the government. The foundation would provide the funds that would enable risk management and incentivization, but beyond that, market forces would be allowed to operate. Bush's model has been a spectacular success, and it has been copied by virtually every developed country in the world.

Public finance will always need arrangements like this, to stimulate public creativity in the realm of public works, just as the private sector stimulates creativity through commercial enterprises.

There is widespread public concern about the continued provision of public goods and a tendency to think apathetically, to believe that nothing can be done. Popular singer-songwriter Joni Mitchell's song "Big Yellow Taxi" had the famous refrain, "They paved paradise and put up a parking lot." The song offers no ray of hope. But what are the concrete complaints that she aired in that song? She mentions the unnecessary cutting down of trees to make way for "a pink hotel, a boutique, and a swinging hot spot" and the destruction of birds and bees by farmers' insecticides. It is the job of public financiers to provide the resources to enable projects to protect the trees, birds, and bees and to manage land use.

Fortunately, we do have public works, and we do have environmental protection agencies that fund specific environmental projects. Problems like those in Mitchell's song are being addressed—albeit not as creatively, extensively, or quickly as we might like. The challenge is to create more effective strategies for public finance to allow us to continue to achieve such goals in the future.

Chapter 16

Policy Makers in Charge of Stabilizing the Economy

Financial capitalism is far from a perfect system, and one of its fundamental problems is that it is vulnerable to booms and busts, recessions and depressions. These events have happened so many times in the past that one can predict with certainty they will happen again. So it is widely appreciated that we need policy makers whose duty is to counteract such instabilities and reduce their impact.

But preventing these episodes presents a difficult problem: the reasons for them have never been well understood. The causes of economic booms or busts are multifaceted, and understanding them requires human judgment—judgment of people's motives, of their patterns of thinking, and of the changing political climate.

There has long been hope that forecasting and stabilization of the economy can be reduced to a science. To a significant extent this hope has been fulfilled: there *is* a science of economic forecasting. My own research with Ray Fair, the author of FairModel, an econometric model of the world economy, confirms that his and other prominent models of the economy do have some ability to forecast. The model makers have learned how to extrapolate economic data, and moreover their models do more than just extrapolate plots of data: their underlying economic theory appears to be sound as well.[1]

But the value of these models is limited. The forecasters are somewhat good at predicting the time path of run-of-the-mill recessions, the kind of relatively short-run fluctuations that they have seen many times. But they are not at all good at predicting the kind of rare and severe economic crisis that started in

111

2007—a crisis of a severity that has not been seen since the Great Depression of the 1930s. It is no surprise that the forecasters are not so good at predicting events that come along very rarely and that fracture key financial institutions. And yet it is these severe economic crises about which we care the most.

For the foreseeable future, economic stabilization will require dedicated people to use their intuitive judgment, as well as formal models. These policy makers often resemble politicians more than scientists, for the kind of judgments they must make not only are constrained by politics but also depend on social and political forces. The success of expert judgment in the social and political sphere has been notoriously hard to verify and quantify, and that problem is very much with us in evaluating the efforts of policy makers tasked with economic stabilization.[2]

Monetary Policy Makers

Central bankers have been the first line of defense against economic instabilities ever since the Bank of England evolved from a private bank into the world's first central bank. As we have seen, it was founded, initially with no clear economic-stabilization responsibilities, in 1694. Though it was initially a private bank, over the centuries it gradually assumed a stabilizing function for the broader economy. It became the primary issuer of paper money in Britain, and it could use its power of credit to lean against excessive booms and to support the economy when it was flagging. The success of the Bank of England was noticed all over the world, and it became the model for many other central banks, including, in 1913, the Federal Reserve System of the United States.[3]

Central bankers' role is substantially to try to manage the major driving force of the economy, business confidence, or its close analogue, credit. As Walter Bagehot, then the editor of *The Economist,* put it in the 1896 edition of his book *Lombard Street: A Description of the Money Market:* "Credit—the disposition of one man to trust another—is singularly varying. In England, after a great calamity, everybody is suspicious of everybody; as soon as that calamity is forgotten, everybody again confides in everybody. . . . The Bank of England is bound, according to our system, not only to keep a good reserve against a time of panic, but to use that reserve effectually when that time of panic comes."[4] The job of trying to manage such things as suspicions and panics is inherently difficult for anyone—more akin to the work of a psychotherapist than a scientist or an engineer. It is a fundamentally human task—so much so that it is very difficult to conclude in hindsight whether the task has been done well or to draw really useful lessons for future interventions.

In a best-selling biography by Bob Woodward published in 2001, Alan Greenspan, the chairman of the Federal Reserve System from 1987 to 2006, was nicknamed "Maestro" for his ability to guide the U.S. economy. The book appeared near the very end of the spectacular stock market rise and economic boom of the 1990s.[5] Greenspan was widely admired, even considered a genius. But it turns out that he was presiding over an unsustainable boom, one that devolved into a severe financial crisis soon after he left his post in 2006. Suddenly he was no longer a genius.

The financial meltdown tested the stabilization abilities of the world's central banks, and they were forced to improvise and try altogether new policies. Yet even these were not adequate to prevent a precipitate world financial crisis. The interconnectedness of the world financial system caused an initial crisis in the housing market and the market for subprime mortgages in the United States to set off a chain reaction around the world.

At the root of the difficulties central bankers face is the difficulty of anticipating crises or preparing for them. In its May 10, 2006, statement, the Federal Open Market Committee of the U.S. Federal Reserve System—which is the committee of the U.S. central bank that is most directly in charge of stabilization of the economy, through its control of interest rates and credit—had no clue of the coming crisis: "The Committee sees growth as likely to moderate to a more sustainable pace, partly reflecting a gradual cooling of the housing market and the lagged effects of increases in interest rates and energy prices. . . . The Committee judges that some further policy firming may yet be needed to address inflation risks."[6]

In his July 26, 2006, introductory statement to the European Central Bank's interest rate announcement, bank head Jean-Claude Trichet wrote, "Global economic activity remains strong, providing support for euro area exports. Investment is expected to pick up, benefiting from an extended period of very favourable financing conditions, balance sheet restructuring and accumulated and ongoing gains in earnings and business efficiency."[7]

The International Monetary Fund, an international agency that works closely with central banks, also saw little of the problems that would bring on the crisis. In its April 2006 *World Economic Outlook* the fund said: "Notwithstanding higher oil prices and natural disasters, global growth has continued to exceed expectations, aided by benign financial market conditions and continued accommodative macroeconomic policies. Looking forward, the baseline forecast is for continued strong growth, although . . . risks remain slanted to the downside, the more so since key vulnerabilities—notably global imbalances—continue to increase."[8]

Concern with "global imbalances" is a long-standing refrain of the fund's, describing such things as the U.S. trade deficit and the Chinese trade surplus, having nothing fundamentally to do with the severe financial crisis that began in 2007. There was a brief mention later in the report of a "key uncertainty" for the United States in its inflated housing market.[9] But the reader of this summary surely came away expecting "continued strong growth" thanks to "benign financial market conditions."

The Bank for International Settlements in Switzerland, which also works closely with central banks, in its June 2006 *Quarterly Review*, would say only that there were "hints of trouble ahead" in highly priced asset markets.[10]

The fact is that *no* central bank saw the crisis coming, even on its very eve. A 2006 study by Martin Čihák of the International Monetary Fund of the then-most-recent financial stability reports issued by forty-seven central banks around the world concluded that "virtually all (96 percent) have started off with a positive assessment of soundness of the domestic system, characterizing the health of the system as being, e.g., 'in good shape,' 'solid,' or at least 'improving.'"[11]

This total failure of central bankers to anticipate the crisis is related to the politically involved nature of their jobs, the importance of political judgment to their jobs, and the difficulty political forecasters have always faced. The bankers, being professionals, no doubt wanted to avoid sounding any alarms until they had objective evidence—but what evidence there was of a coming crisis required personal intuition to judge, and there was no politically correct consensus that would have encouraged them to use such intuition publicly.

Forecasting the crisis would have required making judgments about such things as the wishful-thinking bias that led to the housing bubble, the moral lapses that many leaders showed in failing to criticize the bubble, the political reasons for the failure of regulatory authorities or securities raters to confront the bubble, and the convenient opportunity the bubble gave to politicians to make use of the "let them eat credit" strategy (to use a term coined by Raghuram Rajan after the collapse of the economy) to deal with worldwide rumblings of discontent resulting from increasing social inequality.[12]

Reforms in the wake of the financial crisis have included the creation of new government agencies charged with learning more about financial instabilities and recommending policies to deal with them. In the United States the Dodd-Frank Act of 2010 created the Financial Stability Oversight Council, and in the European Union the European Parliament created the European Systemic Risk Board, initially under the auspices of the European Central Bank.

But these agencies face difficult tasks going forward. Somehow they must figure out in advance that trouble is coming so that they can take action to deal with it—action which itself is politically difficult. Given that central bankers already had prodigious research departments at their disposal and regularly attended international conferences, yet had hardly any clue about the present crisis, there is plenty of room for skepticism that they will succeed.

The severity of the world crisis suggests that the efforts of the central banks, though rather late in coming, were nevertheless helpful in staving off real disaster. But they alone are not enough to prevent severe dislocations arising from economic contractions. The other main tool for stabilization of the modern economy is fiscal policy, the tax and expenditure policy of the government.

Fiscal Policy Makers

Starting with the Great Depression in the 1930s, the idea took hold that government policy makers need to stimulate the economy from time to time, when central bank policy has proven inadequate, by means of appropriate fiscal policies, that is, by cutting taxes, raising government expenditures, or both. Such policies were called "pump priming" during the Great Depression, the analogy expressing a wish that a little fiscal stimulus might make a big difference to the economy.

The problem with this notion—discovered during the Great Depression and again in the economic crisis of the 2000s—has been that while it seems easy to cut taxes, cutting taxes without cutting expenditures increases the national debt. If the depression continues for a number of years, the burgeoning national debt becomes a concern, and the public is likely to call for a period of fiscal austerity—a possibly premature reversal of the stimulus.

In theory the economy may be boosted by a balanced-budget stimulus, increasing both taxes and expenditures by the same amount, so as not to increase the national debt. Economists in the 1940s asserted that the "balanced budget multiplier" was equal to one, at least when interest rates were stuck at rock bottom, as they were in the Great Depression and are in the United States today. That means that GDP goes up dollar-for-dollar with the increase in government expenditures.

But the problem here is that the tax increases weaken the impact of the fiscal stimulus, so that the policy effect is not so much "pump priming" as it is "commandeering." If one wants to boost the economy with balanced-budget expenditures, one has to use a lot of such expenditures.

Then there comes the problem of finding suitable causes on which to spend the government money. It is very difficult to come up on short notice with quality government expenditure projects on a large scale—projects that can also be fairly quickly shut down if the economy improves.

This difficulty limited the ability of government policy makers to stimulate the economy in the Great Depression as well as in the economic crisis of the 2000s. If the projects are not well chosen, there may be extensive public complaints that they benefited only special interest groups, and public support of the stimulus program may not last. That is indeed what we saw in the later years of the Great Depression and also, at the time of this writing, in the current financial crisis.

During World War II there was talk in the United States about this problem, since many people feared another Great Depression once the economic stimulus of wartime expenditures was removed. In 1941 the U.S. government formed the Public Work Reserve, which was to create a "shelf" of high-quality, turnkey public works projects that could be started any time the economy faltered.

According to a 1943 analysis of its operations by Benjamin Higgins, the control of that organization was divided between several agencies, and "a struggle for control developed in which the agency that established jurisdictional rights turned out to be the agency which had no funds to continue the project."[13] The operations of that agency were also inhibited by the distractions of the war itself, and it was disbanded in 1942, its responsibilities distributed among other agencies, and soon forgotten.

The short life of the Public Work Reserve does not necessarily prove that such a program could not be a success. We need agencies that are more for-ward looking, as the National Science Foundation has been. Martin Shubik has proposed re-creating something like the Public Work Reserve in a new form that he calls the Federal Employment Reserve Authority.[14]

It is likely that fiscal policy will need to be deployed in future economic contractions, and one way or another we should develop a system of more responsive fiscal policies, to prevent the implementation problems encountered in the past.

Developing Financial Institutions to Reduce Economic Fluctuations

We have seen that stabilization policy makers are essential to the success of modern financial capitalism, and that their job is inherently difficult. We can, however, make their job easier if we develop better financial institutions to manage the risks of these largely unpredictable crises. Financial markets, despite their vulnerability to excesses and speculative bubbles, at least have the advantage that their activities are not overly influenced by political cor-rectness: the markets attract independent-minded people who are not shy about taking action depending on their intuitive—and perhaps unprovable—theories.

We ultimately cannot completely prevent major economic fluctuations with monetary or fiscal policy, but we can still lessen the impact of those fluctua-tions on individuals by setting up appropriate financial institutions. These are known as automatic stabilizers—institutions that relieve the policy makers of the burden of making politically difficult stabilization moves.

Unemployment insurance, as government policy, dates back to 1911 in the United Kingdom. It lessens the impact of economic fluctuations on vulnerable individuals. A progressive income tax is another automatic stabilizer, since tax collections automatically decrease in an economic downturn and increase in a boom, thus dampening the fluctuations.

In the future, such automatic stabilizers should, and probably will, take many new forms. There could be insurance policies against declines in home prices or home equity, which would protect homeowners against declines in the value of their homes, or there could be risk-managing forms of mortgages like the continuous-workout mortgages that I have proposed.[15]

Governments should issue shares in the nation's GDP or other similar measures of its economic success.[16] This would be like issuing equity—shares in the nation's economy—rather than debt. Thus debts would be made more flexible, and the repayment of debts would become more contingent on economic outcomes. For example, the GDP-linked bonds would automatically become less onerous to the government in an economic crisis. Countries could issue shares in their GDPs to investors around the world. If one share was equal to one-trillionth of total GDP, these might be called "trills."[17]

Perhaps governments should issue *leveraged* shares in their GDPs to international investors, shares that go up and down by more than one-for-one with GDP. Think of the collapse of the Greek national debt that the world has been expecting since 2009. Had the Greek government, whose debt nearly collapsed in 2010–11, substantially financed its borrowing before the crisis with such debt, its indebtedness would have dropped sharply with the crisis—and in fact there might not have been a crisis at all.[18]

Stabilization in the Future

Our ability to insulate people from the vagaries of booms and depressions still seems to be one of the most imperfect aspects of our financial system. A good part of the reason why we have found it so difficult to manage such instabilities is that they arise from a higher-order system, a complex system that involves people and their emotions. People must be incentivized to do good work, but such incentivization, by reason of its emotional component, becomes hard to design to perfection. One cannot do controlled experiments with national economies to learn their dynamics. But we must do the best we can, developing a better understanding of the instabilities in a modern financial economy and being as creative as possible in our application of this understanding.

The current major tools of stabilization policy—tax and expenditure policies by the government and monetary policy by the central bank—have been standards around the world since the middle of the twentieth century, and their significance surely increased with the financial crisis of 2007. But a changing environment will see these policy tools evolve in the future, and they may one day even be obsolete and largely forgotten, like the clearing house loan certificates, the nineteenth-century technology for dealing with bank failures.

The information technology revolution, coupled with innovations in financial technology, is even now changing policy. Central bank policy, traditionally focused on managing the money supply, is already relying on tools that were unknown a short while ago, such as large-scale asset purchases, currency swaps, and quantitative easing. The scope and complexity of the financial system are fundamentally changing.

And even more fundamental changes are in the offing, like the elimination of money in favor of electronic units. The change could be the occasion for a new system of economic units of measurement, like the *baskets* described in Chapter 22 of this book. It is likely that there will be a fundamental change in the nature of our central banks in coming decades—if they are even called central banks anymore. Central banks are an invention that served its purpose at a certain time in history, in a certain kind of environment. Their time may have passed.

Stabilization policies around the world are being reinvented right before our eyes, in response to the current financial crisis, and they will continue to be reinvented. Yet their defining purpose—the stabilization of a naturally unstable economy—is likely to remain unchanged. The real story of the central banks is not their current array of tools and procedures but their lasting commitment to real-world application of sophisticated financial tools for this purpose.

Chapter 17

Trustees and Nonprofit Managers

Trustees manage portfolios to support others' causes—causes that tend to outlive their clients, the people who defined them. Nonprofit organizations make grants or undertake activities in support of a cause. They enable people to see to it that their purposes are carried forward on a large scale and over a long time frame, though not always as perfectly as they might have wished. Defining such institutions is a difficult financial problem, but one with which we, at this point in history, have had some success.

Trustees Make Long-Term Purposes Achievable

Most human goals have an implicit time frame, and many goals cannot be achieved without consistent activity over a long period of time.

Trust companies, and trust departments in banks, outlive individuals and so make it possible for people to manage causes for the ages. To take a familiar example, parents with a special-needs child may set up a trust to support that child. They will do this since they expect the child to outlive them, and they need someone to help manage their child's future life. In so doing, they can extend their activities in support of the child far beyond their own lifetimes. Trusts are a remarkable invention of modern finance, allowing people to extend their lives of purpose and even, under certain circumstances, making them "immortal."

The system works well in many ways, though there is a difficult agency problem: the world changes, the nature of the cause changes, and the people who finance the trust find it difficult to define how future trustees should respond to such changes.

The Shakers, officially called the United Society of Believers in Christ's Second Appearing, is a religious sect originating in North America that was founded by Ann Lee in the eighteenth century, based on the concept that celibacy is the route to salvation. Since members had no children, the community could not grow through reproduction, and they hoped to prevail by recruitment, partly through orphanages they ran. But their hopes were in vain, as U.S. laws began to look askance at church-run orphanages and recruitment success fell, and the Shakers exist now primarily as a financial legacy, only because of the trusts they set up. The Shaker Trust with the state of Maine now maintains a Shaker community at Sabbathday Lake Shaker Village in that state, but today the people there are almost entirely non-Shakers. As of this writing, only three living Shakers remain in the village.

And yet the Shaker tradition lives on through their financial arrangements. The United Society of Shakers, Sabbathday Lake, Inc., is a nonprofit corporation, devoted to promoting the Shakers' beliefs—but now run by non-Shakers. The board of a nonprofit is constrained by its corporate charter to fulfill its stated mission as they see fit, and to hire and pay appropriate salaries to the people who do so (including themselves). Since there are no longer any young Shakers to fill that role, the board members must interpret their mission in light of present-day conditions as best they can. Perhaps the board members are not overly sympathetic to the aims of the trust, and they may not be doing all they can to reestablish the religion. But the religion lives on in the financial sphere, long after the ecstatic spiritual motivation for it has faded. Hope for a rebirth of the active religion may not run very high, but with the help of the nonprofit it survives financially. We can imagine that the founders of the religion would not be entirely pleased with this outcome, given the intensity with which they apparently held their religious beliefs. But a good society has limited ability to make everyone's dreams a reality—and finance is all about reality.

The financial arrangements that trusts make possible are the best device that society has yet come up with to make life's goals and purposes immortal. They are not perfect institutions. But they far surpass any other institution for allowing us individually to fulfill our personal goals over a long time frame. The alternative—lobbying the government specifically for funding for our goals—can work, but only if those goals are "politically correct" and have at least some legitimacy among the majority of the population. The Shakers certainly could not pass that test, and there are myriad other people with causes that would fall into the same category.

Nonprofit Organizations

A nonprofit organization, as the name implies, distributes no profits. It has no stockholders who can expect dividends. In some cases a nonprofit may be nothing more than a charitable trust. But it often runs a business, such as a nonprofit hospital or university. Some nonprofits even engage in controversial business practices, in competition with the for-profit sector. For example, according to a study by Total Compensation Solutions, a human resources consulting firm, in 2007–8, 42% of nonprofits in the United States have put formal executive bonus plans in place to incentivize their top managers, and the percentage is increasing.[1]

A nonprofit differs from a for-profit organization in that it does what it does on behalf of some cause rather than to achieve a return for investors. The nonprofits represent an important "third sector" of the economy (after government and for-profits).

U.S. law is unusually focused on the concept of for-profit companies as existing solely for the benefit of shareholders. Ever since Adolf Berle and Gardiner Means wrote their classic *The Modern Corporation and Private Property* in 1932, U.S. law has emphasized protecting shareholders (who are too dispersed to oversee the companies in which they have share ownership) from selfish boards of directors and giving them rights to sue directors if they do not uphold the shareholders' interests.[2] U.S. corporate law, through a sequence of state court decisions, has evolved the concept of "duty of loyalty" of board members into a duty of loyalty to shareholders.

In contrast, in Europe (where share ownership has traditionally been less dispersed), corporate boards have less to fear if they interpret their duties more broadly than making money for shareholders.[3] Institutional structures encourage less focus on shareholder value. In Germany, for example, the supervisory board (*Aufsichtsrat*) of a corporation must by law, in most kinds of companies, have members representing labor, and boards often include representatives of labor unions.[4] Surely such boards will be less focused on maximizing shareholder value.

There is of late a movement under way in the United States to persuade state governments to create what is envisioned as a "fourth sector," comprising a new kind of corporation—called a benefit corporation—that includes in its charter acknowledgment of some broader cause, beyond simply making a profit. A benefit corporation is not legally obligated to maximize return to shareholders and so does not need to worry about lawsuits from those shareholders if it does not single-mindedly pursue profits. The articles of a benefit corporation may stipulate a specific public purpose, which would make these corporations more clearly publicly oriented than are European corporations. A benefit corporation does not enjoy the tax advantages of a nonprofit.

To date seven U.S. states have passed legislation to make possible these corporations. Maryland was the first, in April 2010, followed by Vermont, New Jersey, Virginia, Hawaii, California, and New York. Still more states have legislation pending to enable them.[5] This seems a healthy development, for many investors in private companies really do not want them to pursue profits single-mindedly. So-called ethical investing has a clientele, and the odds are that this clientele will be growing and that they are likely to be interested in investing in benefit corporations. In Chapter 28 I argue that there could be still another kind of corporation—one that I call the participation nonprofit, different from a benefit corporation—that might enable social purposes even further.

Benefit corporations are still a new concept and remain inconsequential to the financial system as a whole, but true nonprofits are already very important. It is remarkable that we have as many nonprofits as we do. In the United States in 2010 there were 1.6 million of them.[6] Why have so many people set these organizations up when they derive no profit from them? The answer is that people really do have purposes other than making money for themselves.

Of course, one can still make money from helping set up a nonprofit or working for one, for nonprofits pay salaries to their employees. The difference is that these salaries are expected to be in line with market salaries for comparable jobs in the for-profit sector. By creating a nonprofit one can create jobs for oneself and others. One is just not supposed to get rich doing so.[7]

This is not to say that a nonprofit does not *make* profits. It simply does not *distribute* them; it keeps them in its endowment for the furtherance of its causes. Many nonprofits find themselves really *trying* to make a profit as they compete alongside often similar for-profit organizations. They may even start to look very much like the for-profits. But they are fundamentally different because they exist to serve an institutional cause rather than the individual causes of their owners, and so their organizational identity can have a stronger element of corporate idealism.

The economist Joseph Schumpeter wrote about these organizations in his classic *Capitalism, Socialism, and Democracy* in 1950. He gave the example of a nonprofit hospital, an important institution in a capitalist society but one that is in a sense not capitalist since it does not have the profit motive. He wrote, "It is nonetheless the product of capitalism not only, to repeat, because the capitalist process supplies the means and the will, but much more fundamentally because capitalist rationality supplied the habits of mind that evolved the methods used in these hospitals."[8] Indeed, nonprofit hospitals have financial arrangements as complex as those of any for-profit entity— with their donors, with their employees, with their creditors, and with the government.

Institutional Accumulators

Many nonprofit institutions accumulate money over many years, with little thought as to what will eventually be done with the accumulated wealth. Universities typically grow their endowments with no plan to spend them down, living only off part of the income. This seems irrational: if the money is never to be spent, then why have it?

There is evidence that nonprofit hospital corporations do not respond as well to declining demand for their services as do the owners of for-profit hospitals. They continue to plow their profits back into new hospitals even when this does not represent a wise allocation of resources. In a sense, the profits are converted to "trapped capital" that continues to stay allocated to the same purpose even after it is no longer needed.[9]

Universities sometimes amass huge endowments from their activities. To what purpose do they put them if they never spend them down? One argument is that the endowment is a buffer, to be used in emergency situations. But, as economist Henry Hansmann has stressed, most universities typically have not drawn down their endowments—not in any historically known contingency.[10] The severe financial crisis that began in 2007 did not cause universities to spend any substantial amounts of capital from their endowments; instead they tended to curtail activities.

This accumulation of endowments for no apparent purpose is the institutional counterpart of individuals accumulating wealth far beyond their ability to benefit from it. Indeed it seems at least in part driven by some sense of immortality. By maintaining a large endowment in perpetuity, a university is able to appeal to alumni donors, who see their own mortality and look to the university as a means of transcending it.

The Future for Trusts and Nonprofits

The jobs performed by trustees and nonprofit managers are fundamental to financial capitalism because they extend our economic powers beyond the promotion of immediate consumption and direct them to our nobler purposes—and do so in an individualistic and democratic way. In the future, the structure of our nonprofits might be improved to help deal better with the problems discussed in this chapter, including loss of focus among trustees and trapped capital in nonprofit entities. I discuss some specific remedies later in this book.

That structure can and should be improved, to allow trustees and nonprofit managers to be more effective in achieving their ultimate goals. As our understanding of human psychology and of behavioral economics improves, we can expect to see further refinements in the structure and management of nonprofit institutions.

But even as they stand today, trusts and nonprofits have emerged as important vehicles that allow many to fulfill the purposes that give meaning to—and in some cases transcend—their lives.

Chapter 18

Philanthropists

Philanthropists are essential to the market economy. Indeed there is only so much a purely selfish individual can do with the large amounts of wealth that our financial system can bestow on successful people. One can drive (or be driven in) only one car at a time. One can eat only so much food, or wear only one set of clothes at a time. Virtually all of the things one can buy are based on products that are made available to the great mass of people, and hence are not that dissimilar from the products everyone else consumes. One can buy the finest wine, but in truth it is only incrementally different from other wines produced for the multitudes. Certainly some wealthy people do strive to own multiple large homes, expensive cars, and other luxury items, but we must assume there is diminishing satisfaction in amassing such possessions.

This fact was noted by Adam Smith in his *Theory of Moral Sentiments*:

> It is to no purpose, that the proud and unfeeling landlord views his extensive fields, without a thought for the wants of his brethren, in imagination consumes himself the whole harvest that grows upon them. The homely and vulgar proverb, that the eye is larger than the belly, never was more fully verified than with regard to him. The capacity of his stomach bears no proportion to the immensity of his desires, and will receive no more than that of the meanest peasant. The rest he is obliged to distribute among those, who prepare, in the nicest manner, that little which he himself makes use of.[1]

The Little Prince (in Antoine de Saint-Exupéry's classic 1943 children's book of the same name) met, in his space travels from asteroid to asteroid, a businessman who claimed he owned the stars. The man was scrutinizing a large sheet of

124

paper that had them all listed, all 501,622,731 of them. But, the Little Prince asks, "What good does owning the stars do you?" The businessman answers, "It does me the good of being rich. . . . It lets me buy other stars, if someone discovers them."[2] Ownership of most other things is just as meaningless—a bit of basic wisdom that Saint-Exupéry felt the need to instill in children.

Seeing the futility of amassing large fortunes, most people choose not even to try. Many choose another kind of benevolent behavior that is akin to philanthropy: they enter occupations that are relatively low paying but that give them the satisfaction of helping people and seeing the results directly. Teachers and nurses are obvious examples, but one might argue that *most* people's jobs are philanthropic in this sense.

The Fundamental Economic Role of Philanthropists

The philanthropists that are the subject of this chapter are those who do their work with the objective of making money and then giving it away in support of causes; charitable, religious, artistic, scientific, environmental, educational, and so on. Because they spend much of their lives focused on making money, they may, as they live their lives, miss the opportunity to see directly the good that they are doing and enjoy the gratitude of their beneficiaries—but they may also be able to multiply the amount of good they are doing. For people of considerable managerial or financial talents, and possessed of an ability to think ahead to the future benefit to others, there is a moral obligation to do just that.

People who amass large fortunes *have* to plan to give it away, whether to their children, to friends or relatives, or to philanthropic causes. There is no other sensible end to their story. But that ultimate disposal of the fortune should not be just an afterthought for them. There is a natural mission for a person who amasses great wealth. The kind of person who is able to earn a fortune in business is also most likely well suited for managing philanthropic endeavors.

Andrew Carnegie argued this in his article "Wealth," published in the *North American Review* in 1889 and soon renamed "The Gospel of Wealth."[3] The article immediately attracted great attention and controversy, and there has been a revival of interest in the article in recent years, over a century later.

It is not that those successful in business are necessarily smarter than other people. In fact they may be relatively insensitive to the real needs of the poor and, because of their specialization in business, to many intellectual pursuits as well. It is rather that they are specialized in a particular kind of intelligence: the ability to put human talents and business opportunities together. This same talent can and should be used for human benefit.

Carnegie wrote in his article that "men possessed of this peculiar talent for affairs, under the free play of economic forces, must, of necessity, soon be in receipt of more revenue than can be judiciously expended upon themselves; and this law is as beneficial for the race as the others."[4]

Carnegie's article was a theory of capitalism as an arena for competition: the business world is a stage for "survival of the fittest."[5] Those who are most fit in practical managerial skills will tend to rise to the top and become wealthy. But for Carnegie it is not simply a vicious Darwinian competition, for a moral duty stands over it. The moral duty of the winners in the economic struggle is to retire from their business careers when they are still young enough to retain the skills that got them where they are, and to begin managing the disposal of their wealth for the public good.

His own life embodied this ideal. His philanthropic endeavors began, seven years after the publication of "Wealth," with the founding in 1896 of the Carnegie Museum of Natural History, an institution that led numerous pale-ontological expeditions. He did this at age sixty-one. He founded the Carnegie Institute of Technology (now Carnegie-Mellon University) in 1900. He sold Carnegie Steel to J. P. Morgan in 1901 and retired, at the age of sixty-five, to embark in full on his life of philanthropy. There followed the Carnegie Institution (dedicated to scientific research) in 1902 at age sixty-seven, the Carnegie Endowment for World Peace in 1910 at age seventy-five, and the Carnegie Corporation of New York (to advance education) in 1911 at age seventy-six. He died at the age of eighty-three.

In our own time, perhaps inspired by Carnegie, Bill Gates and Warren Buffett, currently the two richest men in the United States according to the Forbes 400 survey, have begun advocating what they call the "giving pledge."[6] Wealthy people are asked to pledge half of their wealth to philanthropy before they die. In 2010 they both traveled to China and invited fifty of the wealthiest people in that country to meet with them to hear about the pledge.

The Bill and Melinda Gates Foundation gives to a number of international causes. It does this in a different way than governments, which are often hampered by having to justify their activities as being in the national interest. For example, the foundation gave a grant to the Liverpool School of Tropical Medicine to find a cure for river blindness, a disease that is a scourge in poorer regions of Africa and Asia. Government support for such a cause is too weak, for there is little political capital to be gained by helping poor people in foreign countries—and there would certainly be political difficulty were the U.S. government to propose funding a U.K. university to benefit people in far-off countries. Yet a private foundation can simply sweep past all such obstacles to make it happen.

Egotism and Philanthropy

Philanthropy often seems to be egotistical—but of course much of it is. There is a generous side to human nature, but it is not the only side. Yet it is still philanthropy even if the donors insist on putting their names on it and enjoying the rewards of earning a reputation for generosity.

One comes to the realization that the satisfaction great wealth might bring lies almost entirely in enhancing one's own self-respect, and hardly at all in either the consumption of wealth or the gratitude or admiration of others. A newly wealthy person has most likely already received praise for his or her many achievements, from a distance, from relatives and associates, and the actual making of the money is only the last in the long string of those achievements. These same relatives and associates are unlikely to know much about, let alone praise, the individual's philanthropic contributions. After the initial thrill, wealth provides at best a lonely pleasure, and each discovers for him- or herself that it brings neither fame nor friendship. Contemplating one's wealth may in fact lead to an empty feeling.

Reflecting on what to do with one's fortune becomes at once a realization of the limits of property. One can win in the capitalist game and indeed own something very substantial, but one soon realizes that this ownership is merely a set of specific rights that are limited by law, and ultimately even more starkly limited by one's own frailty and mortality. Wealth enables one to obtain others' help in tasks one has deemed significant. But one is left wondering what tasks one really wants done—and whether one can in fact use the wealth to persuade others to do those tasks constructively, and not end up spending the money on something very different from what one wanted.

In the end, for all of us who strive to achieve, whether in business or in other walks of life, the end of life is a disappointment. The personal pleasure over a lifetime was mostly in the striving and in one's friendships and interactions. The pinnacle of achievement does not bring happiness, but at best the reflection that the striving achieved some benefit for others, unappreciative and unrelated though those others may be.

The quandary that people feel when they contemplate giving away most of what they have accumulated over their lifetimes is an important example of the discontents experienced under financial capitalism. Our satisfaction with our lives—under whatever economic system we live—can never be perfect. We have an instinct for heroism and a yearning for the eternal achievement of fundamental goals, and yet we find that realistically we have to live out most of our lives at best as minor specialists in specific occupations—not unlike those we have considered in this part of the book.

In the next part of the book we will focus in on a number of these discontents and their relation to principles of human psychology. We will then be able to consider how—even if the simple psychological reality is that we can never be fully happy—we *can* find a meaningful place in one of the occupations supported by financial capitalism. We *can* improve the system so that it makes such meaning more genuine for us. We *can* contribute to a financial system that better enables whatever long-term goals we may decide upon in our most focused contemplation.

Part Two

Finance and
Its Discontents

In his 1930 book *Civilization and Its Discontents*, Sigmund Freud described a "profound long-standing discontent with the existing state of civilization" and a widespread popular view that "civilization itself is to blame for a great part of our misery, and we should be much happier if we were to give it up and go back to primitive conditions." He attributed the popular appeal of traditional communism to such a view: "By abolishing private property one deprives the human love of aggression of one of its instruments."[1] But Freud ultimately concluded that civilization, with its complex psychology, is not so easily improved.

Our discontents reflect fundamental human nature and are refractory. The human spirit is not just aggressive; it yearns for something more. Eliminating private property under traditional communism was like treating anxiety with a lobotomy.

Indeed we cannot go back to a simpler, older, kind of civilization. We can only move forward. And to be successful at that, we have to come to a better understanding of these discontents. We must also ask: What are our inspirations? What kinds of innovations, financial or otherwise, should we focus on developing?

The next phase of our civilization—with an expanded scope of our financial markets and an information technology vastly superior to the one we have today—will cause the financial roles and responsibilities that were discussed in Part One to evolve into something perhaps very different. Yet there is no clear roadmap to this future. Any proposed remedies for our discontents are not obvious or without their own risks.

Chapter 19

Finance, Mathematics, and Beauty

Financial theory, as well as economic theory more generally, can be beautiful. I was struck by remarks to this effect at a retirement dinner for my colleague Herbert Scarf, a distinguished mathematical economist. A number of speakers at the dinner noted that his lectures were "elegant." They of course meant that the field itself had an inherent beauty, and that Herb was a master at expressing it.

The fact that the real world of financial capitalism is so often messy and inhuman, and that it involves so much hypocrisy and manipulation, may detract from this sense of beauty. But the same is true of nature: for all its beauty, it produces ugly things as well.

Symmetry

"Beauty is bound up with symmetry," wrote mathematician Hermann Weyl in his assessment of beauty in mathematics and other fields.[1] He thought that the sense of beauty we find in mathematics was related to the sense of beauty we derive from art, and he analyzed works of art and architecture to reveal an underlying similarity in the achievements of fields that at first seem completely different.

That symmetry is perceived as beautiful has been proven experimentally. Psychologists have shown, in experiments in which subjects are asked to judge the beauty of human faces from photographs, that people respond more favorably to photographs that have been digitally altered to be more perfectly bilaterally symmetrical than to the originals, and yet they seldom realize that they are so affected by symmetry.[2]

But the reaction to symmetry goes far beyond the mere assessment of balance. It is about the *discovery* of hidden and important symmetries. "Comprehending the universe means understanding its symmetries," wrote physicist Leon Lederman.[3] Symmetry in physics goes beyond the obvious things such as particle-antiparticle pairs. Conservation laws in physics are one example of the broader application of the symmetry principle in that field. And mathematics is the language of conservation laws. What is conserved is namable and reflects a deeper reality. Though the word *energy* is ancient in its origin, it had only a vague meaning until mathematical physicists gave it a precise definition. With that definition, we see that energy takes many different forms—forms which can be seen as expressions of the same fundamental reality only if we understand the language of mathematical physics.

There is a fundamental concept of symmetry implicit in the concept of market efficiency. This is the idea, fundamental to financial theory, that prices in different markets are just different manifestations of a deep underlying truth. The apparently meaningless jiggles in financial market prices are reflective of powerful forces. The accumulation through time of these small price changes amounts to a result that is not random but that instead provides discovery of true economic value—a value that is highly useful in the allocation of economic resources and in generating our livelihoods.

The discovery of a mathematical law to describe the price of a stock option in terms of the price of the underlying stock (as exemplified by the famous mathematical formula derived by Fischer Black and Myron Scholes) is an example of a conservation law in finance.[4] The option price is driven by exactly the same shocks as affect the price of the underlying stock, but with a nonlinear transformation of effect, a transformation that is at first challenging to comprehend but that, upon sufficient reflection, seems almost obvious. The same kind of conservation laws can be found throughout the field of financial derivatives pricing.

The so-called Modigliani-Miller theorems reveal another fundamental conservation law in finance. The theorems showed, at least for an idealized world in which we abstract from the intricacies of tax law, that there is a fundamental irrelevance to a firm's dividend payouts or to the choices firms make between financing through equity and financing through debt.[5] Once again a scholar has to learn how some values and returns are transformed by financial decisions, so that total value is exactly conserved.

The impulse toward perfection in framing any theory has been behind the widespread acceptance of efficient markets theory, the theory that financial markets efficiently incorporate all publicly available information, so that their price movements are not the result of any human error but, on the contrary, of some grander design that is essentially perfect. Implicit in much efficient-markets theorizing by economists is the notion that those who trade in markets are perfect rational calculators. Such a belief gives economic thinking a solid core.

Yet our belief in the perfect applicability of the efficient markets theory goes even further than that, to an impulse to simplify the mission we expect businesspeople to pursue, and hence to moral implications. For example, consider the theory that corporate executives should take as their sole goal the maximization of shareholder value. If that is what executives do, it greatly simplifies the theory. One single objective, measured by the price of a share, becomes the driver of everything, just as energy in physics is the driver of everything, and this objective manifests itself, subject to mathematical transformations, in every other financial variable.

As another example, our faith in efficient markets seems to have given rise to the notion of Ricardian equivalence, as expounded most notably by Harvard economist Robert Barro, refining the work of nineteenth-century economist David Ricardo, who had suggested the concept over a century earlier.[6] The principle is that government deficit spending to stimulate the economy is in a sense a trick, for savvy taxpayers will know that any such expenditure needs to be followed by increased taxes to pay back the debt. A simple mathematical expression called the present value relation equates the future tax increases to the present stimulus. Here again there is a conservation law at work, and one of some value—though of considerably less practical value than many economists perceive.

There is a very human tendency to be a bit too attracted—perhaps distracted —by the symmetrical and the beautiful. The conservation laws of finance are only as valid as their underlying assumptions, and their applicability to real-world phenomena has been overrated. And yet the sense of beauty pervading the theory, tempered with reality, remains part of the satisfaction for practitioners of this or any other science.

The Beauty of the Economic Activity Supported by Finance

Beyond the beauty of the theory, there is even more beauty in finance for what it *creates*. For finance is about human desires and human possibilities, and it facilitates all the day-to-day activities that constitute our working lives. These purposeful activities are themselves beautiful, and one can stand back and marvel at them, as did Walt Whitman in his 1892 *Leaves of Grass:*

> A Song for Occupations!
> In the labor of engines and trades and the labor of fields I find
>   the developments,
> And find the eternal meanings.
> Workmen and Workwomen![7]

It is in the facilitation of the full variety of human activities—of an active human society with a richness and diversity shared and appreciated by all people—that finance manifests its most genuine beauty.

Chapter 20

Categorizing People:
Financiers versus Artists and Other Idealists

One of our feelings about economic inequality is that high incomes in our society seem often to reward selfishness and narrow-mindedness rather than idealism and humanity. People naturally categorize other people, and we place them into groupings that take on exaggerated significance in our imaginations. We tend to think that those in careers other than our own are fundamentally different kinds of people. Personality and character differences are indeed somewhat associated with occupations. But this overly strong tendency to categorize people is related to what psychologists have dubbed "the fundamental attribution error."[1] It is a known fact that we tend to attribute the behavior of others to personality differences far more often than is warranted.

We tend to think of the philosopher, artist, or poet as the polar opposite of the CEO, banker, or businessperson. But it is not really so. The idea that businesspeople have personalities fundamentally different from those in other walks of life is belied by the fact that people often combine or switch careers. Let's consider a few examples.

Walt Whitman is one of our most revered poets, and his poetry is among the most spiritual. How did he achieve his success? He wrote notable poems, of course. But first he had to free himself from the economic necessity that forced him to write his first major work, *Franklin Evans, or, The Inebriate: A Tale of the Times,* a mass-market novel that made money but was an embarrassment to him. The first edition of his classic work *Leaves of Grass* in 1855 was self-published. That means he had somehow managed to convince a printer to support the idealistic endeavor. Whitman offered to set his own type as part of his deal with the printer. He himself arranged for booksellers to take a chance on his book. Although the book gradually gained acceptance, each subsequent edition of *Leaves of Grass* was not published without additional business struggles, and getting his poetry into the hands of readers became a lifelong passion for Whitman. His third edition was long delayed, and then the publisher's bankruptcy caused the printing plates to be put up at auction, so that Whitman lost profits that could have helped finance his further writing. Such are the financial travails of a successful poet, but they are not something that we hear much about.

Charles Ives, thought by some to be America's greatest symphonic composer, was first a highly successful insurance executive. He graduated from Yale in 1898, and in 1907 he and a partner founded a life insurance agency, Ives & Myrick. Ives wrote a finance book, *Life Insurance with Relation to Inheritance Tax*. Ives & Myrick, which by 1929 had grown to be the biggest life insurance agency in the United States, made him a fortune of over $20 million.[2] His wealth gave him the ability to produce, and subsidize the performance of, his idiosyncratic and not immediately popular music. We do not know exactly how such a fortune enabled him to persist over a lifetime with genuinely important but mostly still unpopular compositions, but we can take some clues from a biographer, in a discussion of the making of one of Ives's phonograph recordings: "Once again, probably with a sigh or a curse, Ives pulled out his checkbook and tried to make everybody happy. He would pay for another conductor for Ruggles but insisted on Slonimsky for his own pieces, and he would pay Nicolas the same as if he had done both sides."[3] Surely, aided by his fortune, Ives was better able to produce only the kind of music in which he truly believed. He did not have to take hack composing assignments just to support himself. The composer Arnold Schoenberg said of Ives, "There is a great man in this country who solved the problem of how to be true to oneself. His name is Charles Ives."

Two of the most highly regarded—and highly priced—contemporary artists, Jeff Koons and Damian Hirst, both sometimes sell their works for over $10 million apiece. Koons holds the world's record auction price for a living artist: $25,752,059 for his sculpture *Balloon Flower (Magenta)* when it was auctioned at Christie's in 2008. Koons and Hirst are not just solitary artists; they are both financial sophisticates. Both run businesses with numerous employees, and both are aggressive marketers of their own works. Koons started out as a commodities trader at Smith Barney and used his profits there to finance his art.

Christie's, on its web page for *Balloon Flower (Magenta)*, includes a disclaimer that reveals just how tight has become the nexus between art and finance:

Special Notice: On occasion, Christie's has a direct financial interest in lots consigned for sale which may include guaranteeing a minimum price or making an advance to the consignor that is secured solely by consigned property. This is

such a lot. This indicates both in cases where Christie's holds the financial interest on its own, and in cases where Christie's has financed all or a part of such
interest through a third party. Such third parties generally benefit financially
if a guaranteed lot is sold successfully and may incur a loss if the sale is not
successful.[4]

It would appear that the lawyers had a hand in writing this disclaimer, in
anticipation of the possibility of litigation by other financial interests. The
image of a struggling artist devoted exclusively to art for art's sake, waiting
to be discovered by an influential art critic, thus to achieve success, hardly
describes Koons—or many other artists, for that matter.

Even those in the most spiritually minded professions—in the church, in
the arts, or in philanthropy, for example—find themselves routinely involved
in managing financial resources and executing financial contracts that immerse
them in calculations and dealmaking.

Even revolutionaries have to involve themselves in finance. In *Walden: Or
Life in the Woods*, Henry David Thoreau described how he spent the years
1845–47 completely apart from modern society in the woods at Walden Pond,
contemplating nature and spirituality. But he was not really an advocate of
dropping out, and in fact in his own life he did not do so. Throughout most
of his life he was actually involved in managing his family's pencil company
and even invented a new way of making pencil leads. So he was actually a
businessman; he just thought that making money should never be the over-
riding purpose of his life. "To have done anything by which you earned money
merely is to have been truly idle or worse." The key word in this sentence is
merely.[5]

The *British Quarterly Review* wrote of Thoreau in 1874, "Still it is a vital error
to lead in any way to the idea that Thoreau was a hermit, or that he perma-
nently banished himself to Walden Wood to study trees, and beasts and fishes,
and to map out the land like a surveyor. . . . And yet with us in England he is
too much conceived of in this light."[6] In fact, Thoreau was able to take his
time off at Walden because the income from his family business gave him the
leisure to do so. It was in reality a well-earned vacation to a beautiful spot.
Today he would likely be posting his vacation photos on the Internet. Moreover, the Harvard education his family had purchased for him probably helped
him conceive and execute the wonderful book about his vacation that has
come down to us today.

We can even add political revolutionaries to this list. Jerry Rubin was an
antiestablishment political radical, author of *Do It! Scenarios of the Revolution*,
who was sentenced to four years in prison for inciting protesters to riot at the
1968 Democratic National Convention in Chicago. Sometime after the sentence
was overturned by an appeals court, he joined Wall Street to work as a market
analyst for the brokerage firm John Muir & Co. The press thought his two
careers, "from yippie to yuppie," a fundamental contradiction, but Rubin

himself insisted there was no contradiction. In 1980 he said, "The fact is money has always been power. But in the 1960s a picket line made a difference. The Eighties are much more hierarchical. Picket lines don't get much attention. Accountants have more power. Money is more the pressing social issue of our day."[7] The point here is not whether Rubin has a coherent moral philosophy. Rather it is that the very same person could be either on the picket line or on Wall Street, depending on personal proclivity or historical circumstance.

This may not be the world about which young artists, philosophers, and poets fantasize, but it is reality—and a reality we must learn to accept. Self-promotion and the acquisition of wealth, whether by financial or other means, is no crime. In fact, some of our greatest human achievements have their origins in just such behavior.

Chapter 21

An Impulse for Risk Taking

Economic theory presents people as substantially risk averse, rationally avoiding uncertainty. And yet there is a side to people that impels them to do just the opposite—to put themselves in risky situations. This natural impulse, which is connected with our sense of adventure as well as our self-esteem, is part of what drives entrepreneurship, what drives animal spirits in the real world. It is also part of what causes speculative bubbles and ultimately crashes.[1]

This side of human nature has not been adequately recognized in much of financial research—even in much of the work of behavioral finance researchers, who often measure risk preferences by asking people to choose between hypothetical risky prospects on paper, in situations where well-defined probabilities are laid out. When we consider the real functioning—and malfunctioning—of the financial system, we need to keep in mind the visceral impulse for risk taking that shows up in real-life experiences.

Wolfram Schultz, whose classic experiments with the dopamine reward system in the brain were described in Chapter 6 on traders in Part One, has shown that the reward signals from dopamine neurons respond to uncertainty. He found that uncertainty that takes the form of a chance of a future reward is itself stimulative.[2] Nature has built into our brains a tendency to savor the *possibility* of future rewards, and to put ourselves in a position where such a possibility is real.

Apparently there has been some evolutionary advantage to such deliberate risk taking. Schultz and his colleagues speculate that the dopamine signals in a time of uncertainty trigger attention and learning responses in the brain that are appropriate to the situation. But there is a side effect of these signals. The mere presence of uncertainty in a positive direction creates a pleasurable sensation, and so the reward system creates an incentive to take on risky positive bets. Maybe that side effect is also advantageous from an evolutionary point of view. It helps people not just to focus on the predictable and the known but to be visionaries.

This human tendency helps explain why people like to gamble, and why many people will return every day to bet a small sum in a lottery. It also helps explain why people are willing to speculate aggressively on investments.

Not everyone is the same in his or her attunement to risks. Psychologists have identified a personality trait—which differs measurably across people—called sensation seeking. Psychological testing can reveal those who have more of a sensation-seeking personality.[3] A substantial psychological literature on sensation seekers exists. High sensation seekers are restless people, those who want excitement in their lives. They seek excitement per se rather than pleasure. They want novelty for novelty's sake. They are more prone to alcoholism and drug abuse, to having multiple sexual partners, and to engaging in unsafe sex. They may also be useful to society, more likely to be entrepreneurs.

Neuroscience is just beginning to explore the neural origins of sensation seeking.[4] Neuroscientist Sarah Martin and her colleagues have found that high sensation seekers tend to have larger hippocampus regions in their brains.[5] Jane Joseph and her colleagues found that when subjects were subjected to sensation-arousing stimuli while under observation with functional magnetic resonance imaging, high sensation seekers showed more activity in the insula region, while low sensation seekers showed quicker responses in the anterior cingulate cortex.[6] Thus sensation seeking appears to reflect physical properties of the brain, something that we cannot change by the mere exercise of "free will."

Risk Taking Becomes a Calling

Human culture has also evolved to respect and admire risk taking, within limits. Adam Smith recounts an ancient story of a man whose highly spirited horse became uncontrollable and accidentally killed a slave. But, Smith notes, the rider was not criticized for keeping and riding such a horse: "That timid circumspection which is afraid of every thing, is never regarded as a virtue, but as a quality which more than any other incapacitates for action and business."[7] Indeed for some, risky pursuits are a moral imperative.

We instinctively respect people who take risks, so long as they are not antisocial in so doing. One result of this is our tolerance for social inequality. Despite all the anger that inequality can generate, it actually does so only

when it is thought of as ill gotten; great wealth is even admired. All our financial arrangements are focused on eliminating ill-gotten and fortuitous inequality, leaving the respect for the real winners.

Inequality is not in and of itself a bad thing, so long as it is not accompanied
by crushing poverty and resentment.[8] Correcting inequality will have economic costs, and doing so may make it harder for us as a society to achieve
other ends. Most of us value many of the achievements of our admittedly
unequal society, such as those in the arts and sciences and in sports. We are
fascinated by thinking of the wonderful things the future will bring. But such
things come about only with a vibrant economy—which seems to necessitate
a degree of inequality.

Beginning in the past few centuries, the idea has gradually taken hold in
human thinking, or at least in western thinking, that finance, among other
occupations, can be pursued as a calling—a noble call to duty. Max Weber
argued that the concept of a calling—meaning a life's purpose defined by
participating in any of a wide array of occupations—initially took form with
Martin Luther and the protestant Reformation and continued to have great
influence in the evolution of capitalism.[9]

Disquiet and Inequality

The problem with a life in business is the focus it gives to attention to serious
risks—risks that can be disquieting—rather than to spiritual fulfillment. Yet a sense that one is fulfilling a calling in life—a calling to take on
certain challenges—can be deeply rewarding, even if the challenges are
disquieting.

A career that involves one with financial risks, like a career in the military,
has at its heart a sense of the uncertainty created by adversaries who would
do you harm. The need to take measures against them can be an everyday
event, and in some people that can lead to a feeling of stress and emptiness.
In others, it can lead to a sense of calling, a sense of satisfaction in having met
risks and dealt with them in a masterly way.

People have to find out who they are—whether they are sensation seekers,
and whether or not they can find meaning in a life that is filled with risks.
Modern society allows us to sort ourselves into occupations according to our
self-assessments, and this self-sorting is one of the reasons for the success of
financial capitalism.

The economic inequality that we tend to observe is in part a consequence
of this sensation seeking. In this respect, inequality that is the outcome of
constructive risk taking, as long as it does not become excessive, is not altogether a bad thing: it is a consequence of some of our natural proclivities.

But sensation seeking is not directly a desire to make one's lifetime well-
being uncertain, though it can have that consequence. A well-designed finan-

cial capitalism should allow outlets for sensation seekers, in the form of stimulating opportunities, while at the same time making it possible for people to avoid meaningless uncertainty. Risk management needs to be a fundamental principle in our financial system, even though many people will ignore or try to circumvent it.

Chapter 22

An Impulse for Conventionality
and Familiarity

Standing in opposition to the impulse for risk taking described in the preceding chapter is a nearly opposite impulse for conventionality and familiarity. This impulse can take many forms, but for our broad purposes here it is important to consider how it can push people toward reliance on old-fashioned financial institutions and outdated economic structures.

Financial concepts, as abstract as they are, are difficult for most people to comprehend. They fear being manipulated or cheated by others who are more facile with these concepts. And yet people readily understand that financial arrangements are terribly important to their lifetime well-being, as individuals, or for the long-run success of their enterprises, as managers. They fear surprises, years or decades down the road, that may do real harm.

There is thus a tendency to rely slavishly on traditional financial forms, to want to copy time-honored institutions, and often to do so based on outward appearances. People are naturally drawn to financial forms that appear to be steeped in long tradition and that are thought of as characteristic of the successful. These forms even become viewed as elements of a system of justice: the traditional financial arrangements are associated in our minds with the eternal rights of mankind.

There are a number of reasons for this impulse for conventionality and familiarity. Partly it is just habit. If one looks at newsstands, one will find that they are for the most part selling the same brands of candy bars they were thirty or fifty years ago. We just tend to grab for the familiar.

Partly it is because of concerns about liquidity: we do not want to get into an unconventional financial instrument because we think we might have difficulty selling it, for other investors would not be familiar with it. Partly it is because we fail to take into account the often-subtle special factors (e.g., legal restrictions, the state of information technology) that once made older forms of finance necessary, factors that may no longer be relevant in modern times; thus we tend to conclude, incorrectly, that those older forms have a still-relevant essential wisdom behind them.

Partly it is because we think that it is always risky to experiment with new things (such as new medicines) because their problems will be revealed only with time. Partly it is a problem with government financial regulators, who may feel restricted by bureaucratic structures and the perceived need to respect past law, created in an earlier environment that did not anticipate a particular financial innovation. Partly it is because of a free-rider problem: there is little incentive for the provider of a new financial instrument or service to expend resources to educate the public on its value if that value will just go to other providers who will hop onto the bandwagon after its worth has been proven.

For whatever reason, conventionality is a major factor inhibiting the application of financial principles to the design of new financial institutions. Financial modernization has been a very slow process, and the latitude for financial innovation is circumscribed. Often important new financial ideas are adopted by only a small fraction of the population who have better understanding—or who are more trusting of others who understand. Thus the democratization of these innovations proceeds at a snail's pace, often over centuries. Progress in finance can seem excruciatingly slow.

The invention of corporate shares, as we have noted, dates to ancient Rome. But the shares were used only for certain limited purposes then, and corporations did not reappear until the seventeenth century. The invention of insurance, in its simplest forms, likewise goes far back into ancient times, but the first modern forms of insurance did not recur until the seventeenth century. Even so, well into the twentieth century most people in developed countries still did not have either life insurance or fire insurance. Most people in less-developed countries are still not adequately insured.

The amortizing mortgage—in which the borrower pays the same amount each month, and, after a specified number of months, is done paying and has no more principal to repay—sounds like a very simple, commonsense concept. Such mortgages have an advantage in that the borrower does not have to have the foresight and self-discipline to accumulate the money to pay off the principal when it comes due. But amortizing mortgages did not become well established in the United States until the government stepped in to encourage them, well into the twentieth century.[1]

Inflation-indexed bonds were invented in the eighteenth century, but there were virtually no issues of them until the second half of the twentieth century.[2]

Even today most people do not appear interested in replacing their fixed-income investments with inflation-indexed ones, let alone in adopting some more complex investment vehicle that is tailored to their particular risks and designed to share these risks effectively.[3]

The first mutual fund—an investment vehicle that treats all participants equally and that is transparent about its methods of investing—was set up in the 1920s. But mutual funds did not become a significant part of the market until the late twentieth century.

Progress is certainly made, but fundamental progress in finance seems to be measured in lifetimes rather than years.

People seem to want to persist in using the same tried and true financial technology that was used by their grandparents—even though there may be memories of major economic dislocations in their grandparents' times. We are very happy to adopt the newest automotive technology, or the newest kind of computer or smart phone, and so we see rapid progress in those areas. But progress in financial technology is another matter altogether.

This slowness to innovate has to do with our difficulties in handling basic financial concepts, which are unfamiliar abstractions, and our reliance instead on the familiar concepts that are already built into our thinking.

Taking Words for Things

The philosopher John Locke, in his 1690 work *An Essay Concerning Human Understanding*, discerned a human tendency to err in "taking words for things." He noticed that we tend to imbue concepts that are associated with words in our language with an objective reality that causes us to exaggerate their importance. When concepts are dignified by a word, they start to seem "so suited to the nature of things that they perfectly correspond with their real existence."[4] Opinions, once given names, seem more than opinions; they seem to take on an objective and tangible reality, so much so that they make our thinking more rigid. This human tendency, Locke believed, encourages schools of thought, which in turn encourage an obstinacy in thinking that is related to the language of the particular schools of thought.

The names of political parties or approaches to philosophy seem to reflect an objective, not just a transient human, reality. But the names and slogans of political parties in other countries seem baffling to us. So too do the names of financial instruments. Innovative financial instruments often seem to be tied to the culture of one country; thus we have securitized mortgages in the United States and, in a somewhat different form, covered bonds in Europe. From the U.S. perspective, covered bonds seem inscrutable—in the same way securitized mortgages do to those in Europe.

Psychologist Paul Bloom refers to such a tendency as "bad essentialism."[5] The brain categorizes things by their presumed essentials, and concepts are filed away with these essentials as filenames—making it very difficult for the mind to avoid taking these presumed filing categories as essentials in every respect. The dominance of word and metaphor in our thinking has been an important object of inquiry for the field of linguistics.[6]

It appears that neuroscientists are just beginning to find a physical basis for this practice of "taking words for things." Neuroscientist Friedemann Pulvermüller has studied the neuronal architecture that represents individual words—arrays of neurons that he calls "word webs" because they are not located in a specific isolated region of the brain but consist of webs of neurons scattered around the brain. He finds that these webs are hardwired into regions of the brain associated with the meaning of the particular word: "If the referent is an object usually perceived through the visual modality, neurons in the temporo-occipital areas should be included in the web. If a word refers to actions or objects that are manipulated frequently, neurons in fronto-central action-related areas are assumed to be wired into the cortical representations."[7]

There is still no agreement among neuroscientists on just how words are processed in the brain.[8] But the evidence for word webs in the brain does seem to enliven the idea, due to the linguistic philosopher Ludwig Wittgenstein, that words stand for family resemblances—series of overlapping similarities in which no one similarity is common to all the meanings of the word.[9] With such complex neural circuitry corresponding to individual words, it is inevitable that cognitive errors will be made that have the effect of "taking words for things."

The highly familiar words we have for money and currency impose a structure on our thinking.

The scientist Simon Newcomb noted the confusions related to the word (or metaphor) *money* in 1879. Remarking that people tend to measure wealth in terms of currency units, such as dollars, even when the buying power of the currency unit in terms of commodities swings wildly, he noted that "Even when the facts are understood, the idea that the change is in the value of the commodities measured, and not in that of the dollar itself, is so natural that a long and severe course of mental discipline is necessary to get rid of it."[10]

As a result, people seem to strongly prefer contracts denominated in currency, and thus lay themselves open to financial disaster should the value of the currency swing widely. They show relatively little interest in inflation-indexed bonds, wherever they are offered, substantially because of the "taking words for things" phenomenon and the resulting belief in currency as a standard of value.[11] Throughout history hyperinflations have repeatedly wiped out the value of bonds into which people put their life savings, and yet most of them never learn, at least not for more than a generation. The 1923 hyperinflation in Germany—which virtually wiped out the real value of all bonds and contributed to the social unrest that brought Hitler to power—left a generation or so of Germans strongly opposed to inflation, but by now that resistance is fading among younger Germans.[12]

Financial innovation is never going to be just a technical challenge, for part of the innovation must lie in the reframing or re-marketing of familiar concepts. We correct or reposition such concepts by inventing new words for them— words that, once they gain a foothold in our language, gradually grow in familiarity. Thus, for example, following the failure of investment funds after the bubble years of the 1920s, we needed to invent a whole new word for such vehicles, and out of that need came the mutual fund. The word *mutual* lent the necessary democratic and benign quality to the name.

We can correct the aforementioned problems with inflation by devising a system of economic units of measurement that provides new words for essential concepts. In some countries, such new words have already been invented to help people correct their thinking. In fact, ancient Rome had the *denarius communis:* a unit of account, not represented by any physical coin, whose exchange rate with the silver denarius coin was announced periodically by the government. Wages and prices were set in terms of this unit, whose real value could instantly be adjusted by the Roman government.

More to our point, Chile has since 1967 had a *unidad de fomento* (UF), a nonmonetary unit of account indexed to inflation. In Chile money is often no longer used for specifications in contracts and quoted prices. Prices are quoted in UFs, though transactions are executed in Chilean pesos, according to a published exchange rate.[13] For example, the rent on one's apartment is likely to be quoted in UFs, and so there are no fluctuations in its real value. Every month one pays a different amount in pesos. It makes sense to do this, but in most countries of the world apartment rents are quoted in currency units, and so the real value of rents declines steadily with inflation for a while until the landlord takes the painful step of announcing a rent increase in currency units. Thus, in most countries, the real value of apartment rents describes a sawtooth pattern through time, an absurdity that reflects problems with our language.

I have argued that something like the UF should be adopted all over the world, and with a simpler name.[14] I would call consumer price index units of account *baskets* to refer to the market basket of consumer goods and services that statisticians price each month to produce the consumer price index that is used to measure inflation. People would then understand that, for example, when their rent is quoted in baskets, they are in essence paying with a fixed number of real baskets of goods and services that matter to them, and not in terms of some arbitrary and unstable unit. With modern electronic technology, it ought to be possible to make payments directly in baskets without even bothering to look up the exchange rate. There could also be other kinds of units of economic measurement, representing consumer prices for subgroups of the population (such as the elderly), or representing income flows, or for the special purpose of wage setting.

Simple financial words like *debt* have profound implications in our language. If it is government debt, it seems to be associated with our patriotic faith in our government. But if it is our own debt, then the word is immediately, reflexively, judged as aversive, even though debt plays a fundamental role in the modern economy. Renaming the debt incurred to buy a home as a *mortgage* changes the whole frame of thinking, for now the debt is thought of as in some sense part of the home, and therefore acceptable to people who would never otherwise think of going into debt. Those who approach debt in that way are likely to want the terms of their mortgages to correspond to traditional forms.

Debts are a traditional contract, almost always fixed in terms of currency units. Experimentation with alternatives tends to fizzle out. For example, in the late 1970s, when inflation in the United States reached double-digit levels, mortgage lenders began introducing price-level-adjusted mortgages (PLAMs). But after the inflation rate started coming down in the 1980s, public interest in these faded. And yet, even today, PLAMs would be a great idea, since mortgages tend to be long term, often up to thirty years, and the uncertainty about inflation over a period that long remains very high. But—having experimented in recent years with alternative forms of home financing, often to unhappy effect—people now seem to be drifting back to the familiar conventional mortgage.

One would think that debts should be tied to a variety of economic outcomes, not just the inflation rate, from the start. Debt should be flexible, should respond to economic circumstances. For example, mortgage borrowers should have, in the initial debt contract, a preplanned workout. The continuous-workout mortgage that I have proposed would specify changes in the terms of the mortgage in the event of an economic contraction or a fall in home prices.[15] We would probably not have experienced the financial crisis of 2007 if such mortgages had been the norm. But few attempts have been made to implement anything like them. One reason is that people have a strong cultural tie to the simple notion that one should promise to repay another in the simplest possible terms when viewed from the perspective of our existing language.

Regulators and lawmakers find themselves attached to traditional forms, such as nonindexed straight debt, even if they are presented with logical arguments that it is not ideal. They may fear that their reputations might be harmed by backing a new product that looks a little odd. They are fearful that new forms will not be liquid—that is, will not have a ready market—if others are unfamiliar with them. Tradition in financial contracts is a surprisingly powerful force.

Declarations for change by the government tend to come only during an emergency—a war or a depression, for example. Financial progress can hap-

pen at such times—although it is then unfortunately hampered by the distractions of the crisis itself, which discourage thinking about how to implement
the innovations in the best possible way for the long term.

Part of the reason for this rigidity of thought is that people maintain in their
minds certain stereotypes, or personas, of how one should behave. Becoming
part of the financial profession is a profound choice, one that in turn cuts off
other choices, and it seems to require hewing to a conventional standard of
behavior that has at least some superficial acceptability.

Yet all of these biases can be reduced if we introduce new words, and new
units of measurement, to help shift patterns of thinking. Such seemingly
inconsequential matters as changes in wording must actually be part of how
effective financial innovation proceeds.

Entitlements

There are ancient traditions behind the framing of our ideas of the *rights* of
humankind, and while these ideas have enormous positive force in our world,
the traditions behind them sometimes conflict with financial reality. That is,
the rights of man are set down in financially inconsistent ways that are the
result of arbitrary or traditional framing of concepts, rather than in terms of
some sensible philosophy. The word *right* is of great force in human discourse,
and it can trump any other words of societal advantage or compromise.

The Universal Declaration of Human Rights adopted by the United Nations
in 1948 provides some examples. It says in Article 25 that "Everyone has the
right to a standard of living adequate for the health and well-being of himself
and of his family, including food, clothing, housing and medical care and
necessary social services." Article 26 proclaims that "Everyone has the right
to education. Education shall be free, at least in the elementary and fundamental stages."[16]

The declaration is well intentioned. But it neglects to consider how these
activities will be financed: who will pay for them and what should be the
economic situation of those who pay. The declaration does not build in any
flexibility or compromise. The rights that people have ought instead to be
defined in terms that respect the well-being of *all* people, in terms more carefully crafted to represent the concerns of *all* segments of the population.

Social security systems around the world defend the rights of the elderly—
usually without regard to the situation of the working people who must
pay for those entitlements. The right to a standard of living in old age is framed
in an absolute manner, and so the provision of pension benefits becomes
stuck in an ancient system. Government pensions should instead be indexed
to some indicator of taxpayer ability to pay, such as GDP, but this is rarely
done. This and similar policies would promote intergenerational risk sharing,

allowing people of all ages to share the major risks to our society, without piling those risks onto any one generation.[17] But reliance on conventional entitlements works against such risk sharing.

The "living wage" that many reformers have been advocating, often for government employees, is again described in absolute terms—as if it were a right to dignity and respect that somehow has become incarnated in a fixed amount, the living wage, without regard to the situation of those who will pay for it.

We need to reframe the wording of "universal human rights" so that they represent the rights of *all* people to a fair compromise—to financial arrangements that share burdens and benefits effectively.

In the future of financial capitalism, we ought to see better development of our covenants regarding these "rights," as financial contracts that are more democratic and nuanced, with the rights of mankind redefined in more basic terms.

This means that our business world should be less constrained by pre-written, standardized financial contracts and be more imaginative in its definition of such agreements. As we have seen at various places in this book, the process of improving our financial arrangements will involve new concepts, new language, and new information technology—inviting conflicts but at the same time laying a path to their resolution.

Chapter 23

Debt and Leverage

The impulses described in the preceding two chapters can interact to create a dangerous situation regarding debt and leverage. The impulse toward risk taking can cause people to disregard danger signals and run with crowds and bet on bubbles, taking on too much debt to do so. The impulse toward conventionality and familiarity can mean that they take no steps to protect themselves from the risks they assume. When the calamity comes, they are in serious trouble. It is no surprise that people have done such things repeatedly throughout history, given the primacy of these basic impulses.

When one has borrowed a considerable sum, using conventional debt, any slight decline in one's economic fortunes can lead to disaster, for the decline is leveraged against the existing debt, which does not decline. Moreover, when there is less inflation in consumer prices than expected, as tends to happen in an economic crisis, the real value of the fixed debt actually goes up, making the situation even worse.

Such mistakes have happened readily throughout history because the institution of debt, in some form, is such a simple and natural one. Every modern society has mechanisms for borrowing and lending. These institutions reflect the fundamental purpose that these markets serve. People have special needs when they are young and have not yet accumulated assets: children must be educated and young adults may wish to buy a house. So they borrow, they become indebted one way or another. And in so doing, with conventional debt, they become leveraged—that is, they begin to suffer the problems of life as a debtor.

151

Their best earning years tend to come rather late in life. This presents a fundamental economic problem that has been solved since time immemorial through family relations, not by means of formal borrowing and lending. Because of instincts to care for their young, parents naturally provide for their children and even help them to purchase homes, thus keeping some indebtedness within the family.

In a modern economy, we recognize that this primordial system of transferring resources from old to young is imperfect. Some parents—and some children—are irresponsible. Even if they are responsible, their means vary. Children typically do not want to borrow from their parents these days because of the conflicts that may result from such an arrangement. But the children will likely need to borrow from someone. So they become indebted, and their indebtedness and the associated leverage become a public policy problem.

Businesses likewise have needs when they are young or have expansion plans, and just as with individuals their best earning years tend to be later, when they are mature. Businesses cannot get started without funds. This problem has also been solved since ancient times by the family, which may lend the resources to start a family business—but the family is even less well suited to providing funds to launch such a substantial enterprise. In modern times, businesses have acquired the ability to raise funds by selling shares in themselves. But even this method of raising funds has its limits. Simple borrowing by businesses, and the financial institutions to support that process, have appeared in parallel with the issuance of shares. But indebtedness creates a danger for the firm, leaving open the risk that a going concern could be forced into liquidation by its creditors.

Governments also have need to borrow, notably when they too are young and at other times as well, when they foresee greater needs ahead. For example, a new city may need to build roads and a sewage system in expectation of a later population influx, since putting the whole system in place at once is the most efficient approach. It would be sensible for the city government to finance these infrastructure needs by borrowing: the current population of the city cannot afford them, and they ought to be paid for by the subsequent residents, who will actually use them and be resident in the city when the debt comes due. Governments may also need to borrow during an economic crisis, again in expectation of better times ahead. Yet the indebted government may run into problems, for example if the anticipated future population does not arrive or if the economic crisis lasts longer than expected.

Human Errors Regarding Debt

People and businesses have trouble living up to the standards of rationality presupposed by the economic theorists who model and quantify these fundamental economic issues.

First of all, as discussed in the previous chapter, people—individuals and to a significant extent those in corporations and governments as well—seem to blandly accept the kinds of credit vehicles that are put before them by salespeople, and that have been sanctified by conventional wisdom or popular opinion. As discussed in Chapter 10 on lawyers and financial advisers, most individuals do not usually have experts available to help them with such decisions. Financial engineers—who might help reduce the problems associated with leverage—are by and large not listened to in public policy discussions. So people often find themselves faced with serious leverage problems.

To behave rationally, in accordance with theory, those involved in financial decision making must keep in mind the long-term wealth management problem: initially borrowing, then eventually tapering off their borrowing and saving enough wealth, given interest rates, to provide a good long-term outcome.

Yet individuals, as well as businesses and governments, often have difficulty in fully understanding—at least before a crisis develops—that when they borrow heavily they become leveraged, so that any otherwise small problem becomes magnified by the debt. If debt becomes too large relative to resources, there is a "debt overhang," which inhibits any form of positive action. People, and firms and governments as well, feel pinned down by their debt. Few of the individuals presented with this problem have the quantitative skills to understand and resolve the underlying issues without the help of financial advisers.

Lenders may step into this situation, hoping to make a profit, and sometimes with little regard for the real interests of the borrowers. The extent to which they can advertise and the kind of lending schemes that regulators allow differ significantly from one country to another. Hence there are massive differences across countries in average levels of indebtedness, and in propensity to save and build wealth.

Leverage in the U.S. Financial Crisis of 2007

During the boom in the United States just prior to the severe financial crisis, between 2001 and 2007, household debt, including mortgage debt and credit card debt, doubled from $7 trillion to $14 trillion. Household debt as a fraction of income rose to a level not seen since the onset of the Great Depression. After the decline in home prices began, strapped households began to curtail their consumption, setting a course toward a severe recession.

The United States has in recent decades had a low savings rate, and in the years just before the crisis the personal savings rate was just about zero. At the same time the personal savings rate in China was approaching 25%. This enormous difference cannot be justified in terms of different economic fundamentals; it is concrete evidence of a failure of our financial institutions to reliably address fundamental economic problems. It is a sure sign that our financial institutions remain imperfect.

In the years leading up to the crisis, U.S. mortgage loan-to-value ratios soared. The boom in home prices that preceded the financial crisis was intimately tied up with increasing leverage. Mortgage lenders, caught up in the same psychology as the home buyers, were willing to accept lower and lower down payments as the boom progressed. The lower down payments made it possible for people to afford increasingly expensive housing.[1] When the boom came to an abrupt end, mortgage lenders became worried and started demanding higher and higher down payments, making it impossible for home buyers to buy homes, even at reduced prices, and thus contributing to a downward cycle. The contraction led to a large number of foreclosures on houses, and the states with the strictest laws enabling foreclosures tended to have the steepest economic declines.[2]

In the United States in 2008, on the eve of the crisis, there were five credit cards per person, while in China there were thirty-three persons per credit card. Credit cards in the United States were, until the financial crisis, widely advertised, even sent out unsolicited to households, accompanied by glossy, flattering advertisements informing the recipient that the card was an honor and a recognition of achievement, thus overcoming natural skepticism about borrowing. Relatively few people in China received such a credit card or advertisement.

Overreliance on credit cards has been a serious problem. Those U.S. counties which had shown the greatest increase in credit card debt before the crisis likewise showed the sharpest contraction afterward.[3]

There has in recent years been recognition of the problem of aggressive credit card promotions leading to overburdening debt. In the United States, this recognition is behind the development of the Consumer Financial Protection Bureau, created by the 2010 Dodd-Frank Act, which has jurisdiction over lending services, including credit cards. If these beginnings set a path for further discussion about changing our patterns of leverage, we can start reformulating our debt institutions to work more effectively in the public interest.

Leverage and the European Debt Crisis

The European debt crisis that came to widespread attention in 2010 has occurred substantially because of similar problems, related ultimately to the impulses toward risk taking and conventionality. The political process does not naturally bring to the public's attention financial advisers and economic theorists who might present sound advice about the quantity and form of debts. During a time of complacency, as before the crisis, there is a natural tendency to underestimate the risks of indebtedness. At such times politicians do not generally want to focus on the issue, for fear of being accused of harming public confidence in business. They do not find it advantageous even to raise the issue of overindebtedness, so few citizens give it any thought.

In Europe the problem of excessive government debt in some countries was compounded by European bank regulators, who imposed zero capital requirements on banks' holdings of euro-denominated government debt. This regulatory decision meant that government defaults could also bring down banks. Why did the regulators decide that government debt was riskless? Probably they did not really believe that, but they did not want to disturb confidence by signaling their concerns through capital requirements. It was a case of burning the bridges behind us to force ourselves to keep marching ahead: a sense that they did not want to destroy confidence by calling attention to risks. Moreover, almost no one was paying attention to the problem, and, given the social basis for human attention, it was natural that most people would simply not think about debt overhang.

These are powerful psychological motivations *not* to fix the fundamental problem, and as of this writing European banks still have zero capital requirements against euro-denominated government debt, although a new temporary capital buffer has been imposed, and a European Banking Authority was created in 2010 to impose new procedures to evaluate banks.

The European Systemic Risk Board was also created in 2010, to provide oversight intended to minimize the risk of another such crisis. Creating such a board does not in itself alter the political impulses that brought on the crisis, but it begins a cycle of research and dialogue that may ameliorate the problem.

The outcome of the crisis is still not apparent as of this writing, but it is clear that it has had the potential for major repercussions. The crisis may result in the fragmentation or loss of the euro, the very name of which had come to symbolize European unity. The loss of that symbol may indeed be disastrous in the long run, given the human tendency to take words for things.

The Leverage Cycle

There is a leverage cycle that extends over the whole world. The cycle is not of fixed length, and there may be a long interval between crises. But everywhere one looks, overindebtedness seems naturally to develop during boom times, and it leads to collapse after the booms are over.

The same pattern is seen when one compares countries. In a study of sixteen countries, those that saw larger increases in leverage from 1997 to 2007 tended also to show larger increases in home prices. Moreover, the countries with larger increases in leverage during the interval 1997–2007 tended to show larger drops in consumption expenditure in the depths of the crisis, the years

2008–9.[4] Clearly a leverage cycle was at work on a global scale in producing this financial crisis.

In such cycles the overindebtedness can be individual, corporate, or governmental—or a combination of all three. The idea that such a cycle is fundamental to economic fluctuations has received only limited attention from economic theorists, perhaps because economists tend to focus on the relatively small fluctuations—the recessions that occur frequently and that provide a great deal of data—rather than the infrequent major depressions or near-depressions.

The economist Irving Fisher wrote in 1933 that a cycle involving leverage was the major factor leading to the Great Depression of the 1930s.[5] When prices fell after 1929, the real values of all debts were magnified. This change benefited creditors at the expense of debtors, but the net effect was negative. The augmented debt overhang led to cutbacks in expenditure that persisted as long as did the overhang problem.

Recently economic theorist John Geanakoplos has expanded on Fisher's theory; he argues that although there has not been significant deflation during the severe financial crisis that began in 2007, the crisis is indeed well thought of as a debt overhang problem.[6] When people's debts exceed their assets, many problems are created for the economy: Geanakoplos lists nine troubling "externalities" caused by the debt overhang. These include troubles in the construction industry, setbacks for small business, rising inequality, loss of productivity, and damage to collateral.[7] Thus there is a clear role for government regulation of leverage.

A boom period tends to be a period of overoptimism and complacency. There is a sense that "the government" will fix any problems that might occur, and a feeling of safety in numbers as millions of people increase their indebtedness. After the boom, during a time of severe debt overhang, there is still a tendency to regard the government as the ultimate savior, and to circle in a holding pattern, hoping for help. The holding pattern itself generates economic distress.

The debt overhang problem is remarkably refractory. People, corporations, and governments who have accepted higher leverage in boom times may be unable to rid themselves of its adverse effects for years to come.

Evidence for the persistence of a debt overhang problem can be seen in the events that typically follow a change of government in a country. When there is such a change, one might think that the new government would readily disavow the debts to foreigners incurred by its predecessors. In fact there are only limited circumstances under which international law allows such repudiation of debt.

Not only are new governments often unwilling to cancel financial debts incurred by previous governments, they may sometimes even restore indebtedness that was repudiated by an earlier government. Hitler repudiated

Germany's World War I reparation debt when he took power in 1933, but part of that debt was recognized again after World War II by the German government, wishing to reestablish trust after the atrocities of the war. A final payment of $94 million was made in October 2010—over ninety years after the debt was first incurred.

The nations of the world are more aware of such problems in the current financial crisis, but they still have not found a reliable way to fix them. As we have noted, new government regulators have been created, including the Financial Stability Oversight Council in the United States and the European Systemic Risk Board. The Financial Stability Board in Basel and the Basel Committee on Banking Supervision are involved in studying leverage problems on a global scale. But regulatory organizations have in the past not done enough to prevent the problem of the leverage cycle from recurring. The truly effective actions lie not with regulators alone, but also in the development of better financial procedures and instruments—instruments that do not rely on our current rigid mindsets and traditions but change the fundamental ways in which we do things.

Lasting solutions to the problems of the leverage cycle and the debt overhang have to balance the benefits of freely available credit against the cyclical and systemic problems that debt can create. Designing these solutions will be a challenge to the development of new financial institutions and techniques—a task for many minds and for the most creative financial innovators.

Odious and Salubrious Debt

The idea that there is something evil about money lenders extends back to ancient times. The Catholic Church took a clear stand against the charging of interest with the First Council of Nicaea in 325, and that prohibition lasted until the time of John Calvin and Henry the Eighth in the sixteenth century. The Koran contains passages that appear to condemn the charging of interest, and Sharia, the religious law of Islam, effectively blocked Muslim banking until the 1960s. Halakhah, the Jewish law, has forbidden money lending by Jews to other Jews, and orthodox Jews today continue to condemn the practice.

There is a legal concept according to which not all debt is evil, only so-called odious debt: debt that does not originate in free and informed contracting between the parties, or debt that is not managed in a humane way. For example, in the United States in the years leading up to the crisis that began in 2007, excessive mortgage debt was cynically issued to low-income, ill-informed families, who were not told of its consequences. This debt may be considered odious, and it may therefore give the debtors some later moral claim to help with their predicament. If a country with a dictatorial government borrows money without any implied consent by its public, and does not use the money to benefit the public, then a subsequent government can disavow that debt as fraudulent and not binding on the new government. Unfortunately there is as of now no international body that defines in an orderly manner which debt is to be considered odious.

More attention must be paid to the problem of odious debt, and that attention must be paid early, before massive problems appear. Economists Seema Jayachandran and Michael Kremer have argued that an international authority like the United Nations should declare the future debt of certain governments—governments that it might wish to punish for unacceptable behavior—as odious. These measures would make it harder for them to borrow, even from lenders who themselves had no scruples, since the lenders would have no moral authority to demand repayment from a successor government. Such sanctions will be less easily evaded, Jayachandran and Kremer argue, than the conventional trade sanctions typically used today to influence rogue governments.[8]

The opposite of odious debt—let us call it salubrious debt—is debt that is designed by the lender to have a salutary effect in terms of social welfare. Such debt has conditions, either as part of its covenants or in associated agreements and understandings, that are designed to provide healthy incentives to borrowers or other relevant parties.

An example of such salubrious debt is the loans (along with grants) that the United States made to various European countries after World War II through the Marshall Plan (officially the Economic Recovery Program). As argued by economic historians Helge Berger and Albrecht Ritschl, these loans stipulated conditions to correct a dangerous tendency in Europe at that time.[9] They came as European countries were demanding heavy reparation payments from Germany—demands that were being met by the dismantling and exporting of much of the German capital stock, demands based on deep-seated anger and antagonistic feelings that were hard to set aside. The Marshall Plan envisioned an open European marketplace, including a Germany restored to its traditional industrial prowess. Of course, U.S. motives were not entirely selfless, for America had an interest in a stable and prosperous Europe. But the ultimate outcome—a reunited Europe with a once-again-prosperous Germany—certainly benefited all.

In ensuring that more debt is salubrious rather than odious, and that debt is used to solve basic human problems, financial regulators face a long road ahead. Achieving this state of affairs will mean encouraging financial innovation that allows debts to be defined more flexibly, as in the continuous-workout mortgage or the GDP-indexed national debt described earlier, or other indexation schemes that really work in the interest of the borrower. Achieving better management of debt and leverage—more enlightened debt—will require a change not only in the lending institutions themselves, but also in the way they hedge, securitize, and bundle debt.

Chapter 24

Some Unfortunate Incentives to Sleaziness Inherent in Finance

There is a widespread sense that there is something sleazy about the business of finance, or the people who populate it. This impression is probably behind the commonly voiced opinion that it is a shame so many young people today are going into finance-related occupations, when they could be doing something more high-minded in other fields.

Many people in business do seem to feel rewarded, for the short run at least, in putting salesmanship ahead of purpose, in cutting corners on the law or the intent of the law; they seem to be focused on the money above all else and to have little moral purpose in their business affairs. Yet if one lives in the real world one has to work with, or even for, such people. They are a reality. There may be a slippery slope, as one is obligated to carry out their orders, wrong though they may seem.

The reality is that battling against the slippery slope is an ongoing challenge, a part of living in all walks of life. Certain finance-related fields are among those that often put people in positions offering more than the usual temptation to be manipulative or less than honest. Some of them are aware at some level that they are doing this, and cognitive dissonance (as we shall see below) may push them to develop a mechanism to defend their self-esteem and justify such behavior. Their perceived self-righteousness may in particular rankle those who have dropped out of a similar life situation.

Finance may seem to have more than its fair share of sleazy practitioners because it is a profession that offers, at least to the lucky few, astronomically high incomes. On occasion we may even ask: why would anyone with a sense of personal morality go into finance?

Finance may also seem corrupt because the management of information is so central to success in the field—and that immediately means that there are opportunities for providing misinformation to others. To make the best deal in a financial transaction, there is always the temptation to withhold information.

What other occupation offers such temptations to manipulate others' thinking by selective release of information? A schoolteacher's neglect of students, a sin of omission rather than commission, can evoke negative emotions in parents—but emotions not nearly as anger-producing as those in response to deliberate financial deception. Not only is the latter case viewed as outright theft, it is also ego-wounding to those who have lost money, challenging their sense of self-worth as they feel foolish to have been duped.

A Comparison with Gambling Casinos

Gambling casinos offer a revealing example of the commercial exploitation of patterns of recurring errors in judgment. How is it that casinos, considered by some to be the epitome of sleaziness, are able to induce many people to make investments (in the form of bets) that have a negative expected return—and to do so repeatedly, so that, by the law of averages, losses become a virtual certainty?

The "gaming industry," as it styles itself, defends its activities as a form of entertainment. Certainly it is that, but it is unique among entertainment forms in that it cultivates and amplifies to a considerable extent human risk-taking impulses, sometimes with disastrous consequences.

The puzzle comes down to why one would be willing to place even one single bet at a casino. Research by psychologists Daniel Kahneman and Amos Tversky has shown that people exhibit a tendency toward loss aversion.[1] They are pathologically avoidant of even small losses. If offered an asymmetrical bet on a coin toss—to win $20 if it comes up heads, to lose $10 if it comes up tails—most people will turn down the bet, even though it has a positive expected return of $5. How then are gambling casinos able to induce people to place bets with a negative expected return, and to do so again and again despite having experienced repeated losses?

Part of the answer has to relate to the impulse for risk taking described earlier, which is context specific. The casino context is expressly designed to deflect attention from the reality of the actual gamble and to place that gamble in a context that encourages risk taking. Casino operators are usually not psychologists, but they experiment with different settings, and they replicate anything that works for them. They tinker with many seemingly minor details of the gambling environment—things that one might not even consciously notice, but that affect the willingness to gamble. Survival of the fittest among casinos has resulted in casino environments that are exquisitely designed to overtake risk aversion.

Casinos arrange their environments in certain particular ways, some of them very obvious, to lower inhibitions. They freely serve alcohol. They also cultivate the notion that those who frequent the casinos are rich and success-ful. This confuses some people, who lose sight of the reality of their repeated losses at the tables.

Psychologists Joseph Simmons and Nathan Novemsky have noted that casino gambling differs from the psychological laboratory settings of Kahne-man and Tversky in a number of subtle ways.[2] In casinos people see others making large gambles, which makes their own potential losses less salient. When there are maximum wager amounts, the amounts are set at a high level, which makes the bet actually placed seem small. People are asked to generate their own wager amounts while subject to a minimum allowable wager. Sim-mons and Novemsky replicated some of these features in their psychological laboratory setting, and they found that such factors indeed encourage risk taking.

Left to unregulated market forces, many brokerage services would closely resemble gambling casinos. We know this from observing the nature of securi-ties establishments before regulation was effective. The "bucket shops" of the late nineteenth and early twentieth centuries, where customers bet on com-modities and prices, were not that different from casinos. They allowed patrons to make many very small bets, in a social atmosphere and while watching others bet—not unlike a casino of today. One patron described a bucket shop in the financial district of New York in 1879 in these terms: "The bucket shop always reminded me of a horse-pool room—in fact, there is very little difference—and I would never be surprised to hear dead and gone 'Doc' Underwood's resonant voice crying, 'Now gentlemen, Falladeen has gone as the favorite for six hundred dollars; what am I offered for second choice?'"[3] (The horse-pool room was a place for an early form of parimutuel betting, and Doc Underwood was a well-known promoter of such betting.)

It is hard to see how people could make good investment decisions in such an atmosphere. For quite a while, reports of police raids on illegal bucket shops were regular newspaper fare. In the progressive era in the United States, in the first two decades of the twentieth century, these bucket shops were eliminated by state regulators.

But outside these casino-like establishments, sleazy brokerage practices persisted. In the 1940 book *Where Are the Customers' Yachts?* stockbroker Fred Schwed Jr. vividly called attention to this problem, with enough amusing accounts of the tricks and hypocrisy at brokerage houses to gain his book a wide readership. He focused on the showmanship of these brokers, who were attempting to project an impression of wealth (with many rich customers) and confidence (with carefully crafted but largely phony advice), all the while surely knowing that their investment advice was practically worthless. Schwed describes a typical stockbroker or adviser:

> And, if you ask Mr. Big on what he predicates his fifteen-year opinion, he will give you so many reasons you will wish you had not asked. But he ought to know better. If he should ever lift his nose out of the minutiae of his fascinating business and view its history whole, he would be forced to admit the sad truth that pitifully few financial experts have ever known for two years (much less fifteen) what was going to happen to any class of securities—and that the majority are usually spectacularly wrong in a much shorter time than that.[4]

Although Schwed's book was anecdotal and presented no statistical evidence, it was an early and effective statement of the efficient markets theory.

Cognitive Dissonance and Hypocrisy

Cognitive dissonance, a term coined by social psychologist Leon Festinger, is a negative emotional response, a feeling of psychological pain, when something conflicts with one's stated beliefs—an emotional response that may lead to something other than a rational updating of the beliefs.[5] In particular, when a person's own actions are revealed to be inconsistent with certain beliefs, he or she often just conveniently changes those beliefs. Hypocrisy is one particular manifestation of cognitive dissonance, in which a person espouses opinions out of convenience and to justify certain actions, while often at some level actually believing them.

The evidence that Festinger and his successors presented is solid: cognitive dissonance is a genuine phenomenon and leads with some regularity to human error—or at times to what we would label sleaziness. And yet there remains skepticism about cognitive dissonance in many quarters, particularly among people who feel committed to the fully rational model of human behavior.

Recently a new form of evidence has appeared in support of Festinger's theory. It has been found that brain structure is fundamentally tied to cognitive dissonance. Neuroscientist Vincent van Veen and his colleagues put human subjects in an experimental situation in which they were paid or otherwise incentivized to lie about their true beliefs as they were observed by functional magnetic resonance imaging. The researchers found that certain regions of the brain, the dorsal anterior cingulate cortex and the anterior insula, were stimulated during this experience. These are regions of the brain that are known to be stimulated when people lie. When van Veen and his co-workers measured the extent of stimulation in these regions, they found that some subjects showed more stimulation in these regions than did others. Importantly, those subjects with more activity in these regions showed a stronger tendency to change their *actual* beliefs to be consonant with the beliefs they were made to espouse.[6] We thus have evidence of a physical structure in the brain whose actions are correlated with the outcome of cognitive dissonance, and that thus appears to be part of a brain mechanism that produces the phenomenon Festinger described based solely on his observations of human behavior.

If hypocrisy is built into the brain, then there is a potential for human error that can be of great economic significance. A whole economic system can take as given certain assumptions, such as, for example, the belief in the years before the current financial crisis that "home prices can never fall." That theory was adopted by millions of people who would have experienced cognitive dissonance had they not done so, either because they were involved one way or another in a system that was overselling real estate or because they themselves had invested in real estate.

For another example, there may even have been an element of cognitive dissonance behind the decision of European bank regulators years ago to put zero capital requirements on euro-denominated government debt. The decision had already been made, and widely affirmed, that an end to the euro was unthinkable; hence any later decisions that recognized the risk of failure would have created dissonance. So European regulators adopted what in retrospect seems a hypocritical stance—that euro-denominated debt was completely safe—thus setting the scene for a potential disaster in the banking sector.

This kind of psychological problem is perennial and fundamental. But the finance professions also attract people who are relatively invulnerable to hypocrisy. It attracts those who become traders or investment managers, who delight in the truth that is ultimately revealed in those markets. They are often people who are troubled by hypocrisy. They seek vindication by being proven right, not by sounding right.

A financial system that lets them take a stab at doing just that will generate some economic inequality. But they do collectively offer a benefit to society in leaning against conventional and politically correct thinking. The presence of people who will respond in this way to financial opportunities is part of the success story—poorly understood by most of the public—of modern financial institutions.

For financial theorists, it is often difficult to comprehend the real reasons we have the financial institutions that we do and the reasons that they contribute so well to a good society. Many theorists have tried to represent people as merely profit maximizers, perfectly selfish and perfectly rational about it. But people really do care about their own self-esteem, and profit maximization is at best only a part of that self-esteem.

Moral Purpose

It might appear that the sleaziness constantly pursued by the regulators is a real taint on the entire profession of finance. But in fact the practice of finance does not universally incline its practitioners to such behavior. It also seems to reward people with a certain kind of moral purpose—one that may be visible to outsiders only intermittently. Even high-minded financial professionals may appear superficially sleazy because of those with whom they associate, and whose orders they may be required to carry out.

The moral purpose inherent in helping one's clients is hard to see on a day-to-day basis, and it is easy to conclude that such moral purpose does not even exist among those in finance. But in fact the human spirit, among most people, naturally projects such purpose onto the day-to-day routine. It appears that most people need such moral purpose, such a spiritual direction, in order to carry out all the activities that define a job. Most of us instinctively want to be helpful and good, within certain limits, to those around us.

The moral calculus of accumulating large sums of money over a lifetime and dispensing them near the end of that life is extremely opaque for most of that period, since one cannot appreciate the purpose of such accumulation until it is over. We will for the most part never have a true reckoning of our own moral purpose, let alone the moral purposes of others, as no one is keeping score; not many here on earth are ranking people after their deaths with an accounting of the moral purposes that drove their lives.

One makes a moral decision knowing that there is virtually no one evaluating whether one has made the right decision, for no one is really paying attention except superficially. The news media like to gossip about the rich, but the stories they love the best are those that depict their moral lapses. The general public has very little interest in the good deeds of the wealthy.

We have an inherent desire to think of ourselves as good people and to live up to this self-image. But the desire, if followed through logically, seems to put us in a lifelong loop in which we do that which often does not appear inspiring, with no clear moral vindication, no clear end, no final judgment.

John D. Rockefeller Sr., himself the son of a small-time huckster and bigamist, was a ruthless, take-no-prisoners aggressor in his business life. In her 1904 book *The History of the Standard Oil Company*, Ida Tarbell made a scandal of his business practices.[7] But in his later life he became a philanthropist in the mold of Andrew Carnegie. His actions in business may have appeared sleazy, but his life had a noble conclusion, including his founding of the Rockefeller Foundation, the University of Chicago, and Rockefeller University. Moreover he bequeathed much of his fortune to his son John D. Rockefeller Jr., who continued his philanthropy and in turn trained his six children, five sons and a daughter, in the ways of public service. All of them played important public and philanthropic roles. One of them, Nelson Rockefeller, became vice president of the United States. The fourth generation includes John D. Rockefeller IV, who is a U.S. senator from West Virginia and has been in that position for over a quarter of a century.

So what ultimately motivated the Rockefellers? Was it mere ego gratification and the drive to found and perpetuate a family dynasty? Or did their philanthropy serve some deeper moral purpose? It was most likely a little of both. Some will see inspiration in the century-long philanthropic tradition carried on by members of a family that emerged from controversial business origins and matured into a positive social force, each generation picking up the torch from the previous one. Such a story indeed suggests to some a model for living. Unfortunately, stories like that of the Rockefellers are rare, for the intergenerational transmission of purpose and values is usually far from perfect.

I have sometimes been struck, when talking with wealthy people who have family foundations, how important the foundation appears to be to their sense of self. They can become genuinely emotional in discussing it. It gives them a sort of moral superiority. Something like this sense may also come, for example, from having donated to a college and having a building named after oneself. The behavior appears to be at once egotistical and altruistic, both motivations coexisting in the mind.

And yet the rest of the world generally takes little note of family foundations or the names on campus buildings. We all would probably acknowledge, if our attention were ever drawn to the people behind the foundations or the buildings, that they are good people for having made these gifts. But we almost never meet these people and so do not think about them. Thus they are able to achieve a sense of public praiseworthiness, and achieve their own moral purposes, without inciting direct envy or hostility.

Being Mistaken for the Sleazy

One problem with the attractiveness of financial dealings for the genuinely sleazy has been that they discredit the entire profession, even those who are scrupulously honest. At one extreme is the inherent risk, even for the most ethical, that they will be indicted for crimes and misdemeanors they did not commit and thus suffer a permanent loss of reputation.

Those in finance and business management acquire genuine power—power to make things happen that perhaps only *they* individually *want* to have happen. Even a top elected official with a budget in the billions has less power because, at least in democratic countries, he or she is subject to checks and balances and holds power for only a limited time. The essentially unlimited power achieved by the very successful in business (and their heirs) is almost unknown in other walks of life.

For males (and most financiers are male) this also means power over women, and this is a source of resentment among both women and other men. In parts of the world today, their status brings with it the power to command multiple wives, at the expense of other men who will have no wives—a situation sure to cause resentment among those men. Some women in these polygamous marriages might be even more resentful. In much of western society, ever since ancient Greece and Rome, polygamy has been illegal or at least widely opposed. But even with those conventions, wealthy men find it much easier to have affairs outside their marriages or to hire the most sought-after prostitutes.

More concretely, the power that the rich obtain is the power to engage in what the economist Thorstein Veblen termed conspicuous consumption, which, when indulged in by men, is instinctively recognized by the general public as a possible ploy to attract the opposite sex—even if the plan is never consummated. Underlying the desire for wealth is a sexual and social-status impulse. This applies as well to women, whose desire for wealth may arise from somewhat different, though equally strong, motives.

The hostility that is felt against the rich is partly in recognition of that power. Even if people plan to give away all their wealth eventually, no one else knows for certain what their ultimate intentions may be, and thus others are naturally suspicious of those intentions. Such suspicion may express itself in a tendency to brand all of the rich as sleazy.

People Are Certainly Conscious of Sleaziness

As we have just discussed, attitudes toward top businesspeople are often negative. Yet quantitative research suggests that such negative stereotypes are pervasive but not universal.

In 1990 Maxim Boycko, a Russian economist, Vladimir Korobov, a Ukrainian economist, and I did a questionnaire survey comparing American (specifically New Yorkers') and Russian (Muscovites') attitudes toward business.[8] We asked, "Do you think that those who try to make a lot of money will often turn out to be not very honest people?" In both countries many people answered yes. But more felt that way in Russia: 59% of the Muscovites said yes, compared with only 39% of the New Yorkers.

We then asked a more personal question: "Do you think that it is likely to be difficult to make friends with people who have their own business (individual or small corporation) and are trying to make a profit?" In Moscow 51% of the respondents said yes, compared with only 20% in New York.

It is significant that the perceptions of sleaziness were higher in the country that had had no experience with *legal* businesspeople. It would appear that part of any country's process of becoming financially advanced involves getting over exaggerated perceptions of sleaziness. And, with some 20–40% of Americans perhaps still holding a low opinion of businesspeople, there is clearly still work to do in dealing with the problem in our own country.

Avoiding Overreaction to Sleazy Behavior

The further success of financial capitalism once again depends on people adopting a more nuanced view of human nature as it is expressed in a financial environment. We have to accept that some less-than-high-minded behavior may be the product of an economic system that is essentially good overall.

Financial speculation, the subject of the next chapter, is associated in many people's minds with sleazy behavior, since it takes place in an economic environment that brings out the selfish and manipulative. It is hard to judge the role of speculative markets in the good society without thinking of this less-than-inspiring behavior. But we must take a careful look at just what constitutes that behavior, and what its overall consequences are.

Chapter 25

The Significance of
Financial Speculation

There has long been a negative feeling among the general public about speculation in markets. To them, the activity doesn't seem to contribute to society. It seems to many to be a form of recreation for the rich or for those who really just want to be rich, an activity that is fundamentally selfish and egotistical—and, on top of that, often delusional. In a 1904 essay Charles Conant observed that

> One of the most persistent of the hallucinations which prevail among people otherwise apparently lucid and well informed is the conception that operations on the stock and produce exchanges are pure gambling. A moment's reflection, it would seem, might convince such persons that a function which occupies so important a place in the mechanism of modern business must be a useful and necessary part of that mechanism; but reflection seems to have little part in the intellectual equipment of the assailants of organized markets.[1]

Certainly, Conant was right about public opinion. Many thought leaders have said as much. He must have known that Karl Marx thought speculation was akin to gambling: "Since property here exists in the form of stock, its movement and transfer become purely a result of gambling on the stock exchange, where the little fish are swallowed by the sharks and the lambs by the stock exchange wolves."[2] And among the critics of speculation we have also to count the most important and influential economist of the twentieth century, John Maynard Keynes: "It is generally agreed that casinos should, in the public interest, be inaccessible and expensive. And perhaps the same is true of Stock Exchanges."[3]

The controversy between those like Conant on the one side, who think that speculation is an essential economic activity, and those like Marx and Keynes on the other, who have grave doubts, has continued for more than a century and remains unresolved to this day. The reason it has not been resolved is that there is an element of truth to both sides—or perhaps both sides are speaking half-truths. Moreover, the extent to which speculation lives up to Conant's ideal depends on our financial institutions—which can either encourage or discourage healthy and productive speculation, and can either attract or repel the kinds of people who are naturally and productively speculative.

Speculation Contributes to Market Efficiency

The term *efficient markets* has long been used with various meanings, but it was given its specific modern meaning by University of Chicago economist Eugene Fama in 1965:

> In an efficient market, competition among the many intelligent participants leads to a situation where, at any point in time, actual prices of individual securities already reflect the effects of information based both on events that have already occurred and on events which, as of now, the market expects to take place in the future. In other words, in an efficient market at any point in time the actual price of a security will be a good estimate of its intrinsic value.[4]

The "competition among the many intelligent participants" clearly refers to speculators, for if the intelligent advice were to *avoid* speculation, and just diversify broadly, then there would be no force pushing prices to the right, "efficient," level.

Long before Fama, many besides Charles Conant had expressed similar ideas about the perfection of financial prices. The difficulty in forecasting changes in prices (as we noted in quoting Fred Schwed Jr. in the previous chapter) has often been interpreted as attesting to their perfection. Moreover, statistical research—as in the work of Holbrook Working in 1934 and Maurice Kendall in 1953—had already found evidence, years before Fama, that short-run changes in prices in speculative markets are hard to forecast.[5] But Fama raised this theory to the status of a broad new scientific paradigm and likened to astrologers the old-fashioned analysts who looked to patterns in stock market data for trading opportunities. Fama believed that market prices were too perfect to be predictable, to show any pattern other than a random walk.

Fama used a data set that had recently been compiled by the Center for Research in Security Prices (CRSP) at the University of Chicago, founded in 1960 with a $50,000 grant from Merrill Lynch. The center's initial purpose was to put a huge set of monthly (later daily) stock prices, and associated information about capital changes and dividends that would allow accurate computation of returns, on magnetic tape so that the data could be analyzed with a UNIVAC computer. The CRSP directors obtained the cooperation of the New York Stock Exchange. But they soon found that the exchange had never organized these data and was in no position to get the data ready quickly and accurately. The extent of their unexpected woes revealed that no one else had ever organized such a data set before, in the United States or anywhere else in the world. When the information was finally prepared, the tapes mounted on the computer, and the data processed, the authority of the idea that speculation makes for perfect market prices was much enhanced.

That same "CRSP tape," considerably updated, is still the major source for daily prices of individual stocks going back to 1926. By bringing financial analysis into the computer age, the efficient markets hypothesis gained the status of an icon, and as a result it led people to infer much—in fact too much—about the perfection of markets.

The discovery that day-to-day fluctuations in stock prices are difficult to forecast should have come as no big surprise: if there were a simple trading strategy that consistently offered a profit of as little as a tenth of a percent a day, it would yield annual returns of over 30%. Clearly someone would already have been onto such a trading strategy, and its adherents, competing against each other, would have the effect of eliminating the opportunity in the market. That would have to be the effect, since we can't all get rich by trading with each other. Having daily data on the CRSP tape made it possible to produce voluminous studies confirming the obvious: that it is not very easy to get really rich really quickly through short-run trading.

A great deal of the horsepower of academic research was focused on testing one aspect of the efficient markets hypothesis: whether it is easy for smart traders to beat the market. Another aspect of the hypothesis—whether prices behave the way they ought to if markets are indeed working so well—is much harder to test.

As the enthusiasm for the efficient markets hypothesis after Fama's watershed 1965 paper reached excessive levels, it brought forth an unhealthy degree of credulity in people trusting their money to financial markets. Investors lost the sense that markets are a matter of opinion and that their fluctuations represent, in substantial part, changing public moods.

In fact, when one considers the aggregate stock market, it appears that price changes in the United States have been *mostly* due merely to changes in moods or attitudes or something else unrelated to the actual changes in real underlying value to which the changes are constantly ascribed. In my 1981 paper "Do Stock Prices Move Too Much to Be Justified by Subsequent Changes in Dividends?" I presented evidence, using stock market data for the United States since 1871, that the fundamentals corresponding to the aggregate stock market just never changed very much from year to year.[6] If people had known the future perfectly and priced appropriately, then the stock market should have behaved pretty much like a stable upward trend. So it doesn't make sense to think that all those fluctuations up and down around the trend could be attributed to "new information" about the future. Instead there is excess volatility in the stock market.

Thus, for example, the stock market crash of 1929 was not justified by the depression that followed. Even if people in 1929 had known that an economic collapse was imminent, even if they had had a perfect crystal ball, they still should not have marked down the price of the U.S. stock market by very much. For in fact U.S. companies fared much better in the Great Depression than is commonly suggested by our embellished stories. Not a single company of the thirty in the Dow Jones Industrial Average went bankrupt. In fact large U.S. corporations generally did quite well overall. They lowered their dividend payments for just a few years, and then they were back on trend. The value of a share in a company ought to be related to the present value of all future dividends, and not just the next few years' dividends. So if the 1929 crash was a reaction to information about the future, it was an egregious overreaction.

For a more recent example, consider the market reaction when a conference of European Union leaders in Brussels announced, on October 27, 2011, a broad package of measures to deal with the ongoing financial crisis. They said they would increase their bailout fund, recapitalize the banks, and reduce Greece's debt load. The German DAX stock price index rose 5.3% in one day. The news media suggested, by the way they quoted people and referred to economic "facts," that the price changes made some basic sense. On subsequent days the volatile price changes were interpreted as reevaluations of the news about the European economy. Suggestions that all the aggregate price changes are, at their core, psychological in origin are usually omitted from news stories—as if there were a common and unquestioned consensus that markets are efficient.

Most financial writers have apparently never heard of excess volatility, and they continue to write their stories about the day-to-day fluctuations in the stock market as if the market were dominated by traders with razor-sharp minds and fast computers who have a deep understanding of the economy and grasp the import of every nuance in today's economic news. Writing in this way flatters their readers, and most of these writers are not in the business of challenging comfortable conventional wisdom.

Many traders do indeed have sharp minds, but the game they are playing is not generally to involve themselves in macroeconomic forecasting. They are instead playing a game against each other—a game of guessing each other's psychology.

This excess volatility of the aggregate U.S. stock market, despite some controversy about it, is, in my opinion, an established fact.[7] This does not mean that the fluctuations in the Chinese or Indian stock markets, where underlying fundamentals are changing much more rapidly, are as irrational. This does not mean that all speculative markets are as crazy as the aggregate stock markets. In the next chapter we shall see that fluctuations in *individual firm* stock prices make somewhat more sense. If the efficient markets controversy teaches us anything, it is that we have to consider more carefully what *really* drives aggregate markets.

Animal Spirits

The success of our financial markets in producing prosperity has much to do with the way in which they guide animal spirits—our inner stimulus to action, something John Maynard Keynes described as "a spontaneous urge to action" rather than careful and deliberate calculation. He believed that real business decisions are emotional, not "the outcome of a weighted average of quantitative benefits multiplied by quantitative probabilities. . . . Thus if the animal spirits are dimmed and the spontaneous optimism falters, leaving us to depend on nothing but a mathematical expectation, enterprise will fade and die;—though fears of loss may have a basis no more reasonable than hopes of profit had before."[8]

My colleague George Akerlof and I were so convinced of the importance of these fluctuations in animal spirits, and of their importance in the world economic crisis, that we wrote a book about it, entitled *Animal Spirits.*[9] Fluctuations in animal spirits that are shared by large numbers of people are, we argued, social phenomena, the result of epidemic social contagion, which makes these fluctuations very hard to comprehend and predict.

Some of the inherent fragility of our decision-making process can be appreciated if we look introspectively, as we consider our own decisions about whether to launch some risky and time-consuming endeavor. There is a distinct emotional flavor to any such decisions.

Ultimately human judgments are driven by emotions, and their origin is largely subconscious. Marcel Proust, an introspective novelist, gives, through the voice of his protagonist, a sense of these inner storms. He reflects on the mystery of his own fluctuations in animal spirits: "And I begin asking myself again what could it be, this unknown state which brought with it no logical proof, but only the evidence of its felicity, in reality, and in whose presence the other states of consciousness faded away?"[10]

A decision not just to tell friends about an interesting investment whose fundamentals can't be verified but to actually raid one's life savings and put them at risk to make the investment is an emotional decision that cannot be taken lightly. It must be influenced by the social milieu and by the psychology of others.

Looking back on Eugene Fama's original formulation of the efficient markets theory, as discussed earlier in this chapter, it seems from our vantage point a little glib to take it for granted that "intelligent participants" know how to reflect new information, as it arrives, in financial prices, and that they are perfectly logical and ready to stake their fortunes on this knowledge. Such a world view presumes that they have a solid economic model that tells them just how much prices should change due to any new information. In reality it is not always easy to say in which direction a bit of business news should move a stock price; beyond that, it is nearly always extremely difficult to know by how much the price should move and, even more confounding, whether the price was even anywhere near right *before* the news came. Any model of stock values is really just a matter of opinion, and the model must be subject to change. Moreover, the structure of the world and the economy is always changing in new and different ways, and so past statistical analyses of stock prices are of questionable relevance. Thus no one really knows how to do the reflection that Fama presumes. There is no escaping the role of animal spirits in driving prices and financial activity.

Selection and Speculative Behavior

Countries and cities that seem to be highly successful in generating healthy animal spirits and entrepreneurship are the objects of imitation around the world. Less successful places wonder how to achieve the same results—a problem of the greatest importance.

A realistic assessment of the situation, however, suggests that such animal spirits will never be successfully exported, in fullest form, everywhere in the world. For in fact those regions of the world where such spirits are predominant may have gotten that way by in effect selecting the kinds of people who will go there to live.

John Gartner, a psychiatrist at the Johns Hopkins University Medical School, alleges that countries with a significant share of self-selected immigrants in their populations have attracted a large number of manic as well as "hypomanic" (a subdued version of manic) people.[11] The United States, Canada, and New Zealand, he points out, are, according to studies published in psychiatric and medical journals, the three countries with the highest proportion of people who have mental illnesses that fit the medical definition of bipolar disorder. Hence they probably have a high proportion of hypomanic people as well. They are all nations of self-selected immigrants who had to overcome hurdles to reach their shores. I would think that other centers of business, like Dubai or Hong Kong or Singapore, have been favored by similar selection. People who emigrate from the comfortable environment in which they grew up are thus naturally selected for certain traits, both genetic and cultural. These hypomanic people are naturally more entrepreneurial.

I have wondered about the validity of Gartner's theory in light of the fact that all countries of the world, and especially all countries outside Africa, were the result of immigration at some point in human history. But those ancient migrations were more like emigrations of whole populations, rather than of isolated individuals—and even to the extent they were of isolated individuals, the migrations may have been random, rather than the result of an adventure-some quest to set out for a better life alone or as a small nuclear family. Modern society makes it possible to emigrate much more freely as an individual, and thus heightens the selection effect.

I think of my own family history. All four of my grandparents came to America over a hundred years ago from Lithuania as single individuals. My paternal grandfather George Shiller emigrated alone, as he told me, to avoid conscription into the Russian army, by those he regarded as occupiers of his country. My paternal grandmother Amelia Miller emigrated alone to America at age eighteen, hardly speaking English, to avoid an arranged marriage to a man she loathed. Doing that no doubt took some spirit. My maternal grand-father Vincas Radziwil came to pursue an education at the Cleveland Institute of Art. My maternal grandmother Rosalia Šerys never told me her reasons for emigrating alone, but I know she suffered some difficulties on the trip, includ-ing being stranded alone in London for two years. All of them might be regarded as at least a shade hypomanic for launching on such independent adventures, and I wonder what such selection tells me about my own makeup.

The stories I have heard about illegal emigration from China to Hong Kong in the time of Mao Zedong—including swimming for miles down the Pearl River at night, only to be apprehended and punished by guards and then, weeks later, try it again—top even my grandparents' stories.

And I wonder how much the liveliness of urban areas around the world may have to do with hypomanic selection, for leaving the quieter countryside for a remote yet exciting big city suggests a similar self-selection process.

Limited Liability

Some forms of business also involve the selection of people. Financial institu-tions in economically successful countries have been designed to be conducive to the constructive expression of a speculative personality trait. The institu-tions themselves can select for hypomania, even within a single country, by bringing together hypomanic people into a single organization, where they form a larger hypomanic whole.

It is commonplace around the world today that investors in shares in pub-licly traded stocks are assured limited liability, which means that the investors cannot be sued for any transgressions of the firm. The investor can rest easy: the most that can be lost is the amount initially paid for the shares. For many it makes investment in shares almost a pleasurable experience, like buying a lottery ticket: having already paid for the experience, one can just sit back and savor the possibility that the investment will make a lot of money. In fact the inventors of general limited liability, centuries ago, understood this psychol-ogy, and it was part of their motivation for enacting limited-liability laws.[12]

Limited liability is an example of a financial institution designed to get people to express their animal spirits. The financial markets, with their limited liability, encourage a sort of gambling spirit that, while often unsuccessful, may on some rare occasions result in major entrepreneurial achievements. The idea that one can participate in a speculative venture with no other consequences than the loss of the money originally put up to purchase shares inspires a sense of playful excitement. Indeed the game one plays may likewise be acceptable to one's spouse, because the risk is plainly and unequivocally limited.[13]

That is why, ultimately, countries all over the world have seen fit to put in place limited liability laws that make it as clear as possible that there are no unexpected negative consequences to participating in the stock market. That is why we need such laws. True, firms could individually give their shareholders limited liability, even in the absence of a limited-liability law, merely by purchasing insurance for the shareholders against any losses beyond their initial investment, just as they currently buy insurance for directors against lawsuits brought against them individually. But such a move would never provide 100% coverage for shareholders, as they would have to check whether the insurance policy was sound, whether it had deductibles or exclusions, and whether the firm was keeping the policy in force as time went on. When we have shareholder limited liability as a fundamental, universal, and time-honored principle, then shareholders can bask in their fantasies of unlimited upside potential and sleep relatively easily at night since they have limited their losses.

A Shift Away from Partnerships toward Public Corporations with Limited Liability

The partnership is a natural structure in which a small number of people together go into a business in which reputation and integrity are of particular importance. Traditionally professional firms—whether in investment banking, law, consulting, or accounting—have taken the form of partnerships. The partners themselves are the owners, and they lack limited liability. But, particularly in investment banking, the partnership form has been dying out in recent decades, raising concerns that some of the factors contributing to the integrity of our financial markets are being lost, that careless speculation is being encouraged, and that this change may have contributed to the severe financial crisis that started in 2007.

Until 1970 the New York Stock Exchange required member firms to be partnerships because of the members' belief in the superiority of this form of organization (and probably for anticompetitive reasons as well).[14] Eventually, however, changes in the technology of business that encouraged large-scale enterprises led the exchange to relax this rule, and after the rule change there was a wholesale move away from the partnership structure in finance.

Donaldson, Lufkin & Jenrette changed its partnership structure and went public in 1970. It was followed by Merrill Lynch in 1971, Lehman Brothers in 1984 when it was acquired by Shearson/American Express and then spun off, Bear Stearns in 1985, Morgan Stanley in 1986, and Goldman Sachs in 1999. Among major Wall Street firms in the United States, only Brown Brothers Harriman retains the partnership structure, with its partners still suffering the burdens and risks of that structure.

In a traditional partnership, the partners' investment in their business is highly illiquid: they cannot easily get out, and its value is opaque, as shares are not traded minute by minute. They *are* their business, and tax law routinely accepts them as individual taxpayers, with no profits tax on the organization. They do not have limited liability; they are liable individually if the partnership is sued. They could lose everything if the partnership fails.

The partners are stuck with this investment, and this risk, for much of their lives, and therefore the partnership structure may be conducive to hard, cooperative, and effective work. Since they cannot exit easily by selling shares, when they discover problems in the firm they must endeavor to fix them. Thus the partnership form is widely thought to select for a different kind of person, to encourage partners to be very selective in finding new partners, and to create a strong sense of commitment among partners.

The most often cited problem with the partnership structure is that it is difficult for a firm to grow while adhering to that structure. Economies of scale for investment banks and broker-dealers are important. It is hard for partnerships to bring in new partners because partners, fearing the consequences of unlimited liability, feel they need to know everything about their peers. They need to know their character—which may take years to ascertain. Beyond that, they must have some sense of their wealth, for if one comes into a partnership with more wealth than the other partners, one is more vulnerable than they to the effects of unlimited liability.[15] The price of a share in the partnership is thus in effect different for each new partner, and the information-collection problem is significant. In contrast, with a corporation, all shares have the same value to everyone, and one need look only at the cash flow of the corporation in deciding whether to invest.

The decline in the partnership structure on Wall Street may have contributed to the severe financial crisis that began in 2007, as it would appear to have reduced the incentives to manage long-term reputation and long-term risks in favor of a structure that encourages rapid growth of the firm. Certainly speculative appetites are whetted by the spectacle of the rapid fluctuations of the stock market prices of firms that were once partnerships, and the ultimate collapse of firms such as Bear Stearns, Lehman Brothers, and Merrill Lynch—

and of the economy as a whole—may be related to the changes wrought by the end of the partnership structure.

Encouraging the Good in Financial Speculation

Charles Conant, quoted at the beginning of this chapter, was certainly right: speculative activity is central to the functioning of the modern economy. It is central because of conventional economic factors: the information that speculative markets reveal and the spurs to action that those prices generate. It is also central in the stimulus such markets give to animal spirits, in helping people of suitable risk-taking mien to come together and work together.

Some behavioral economists have embarked on efforts to channel the speculative impulse constructively, to help people make better financial decisions. For example, Peter Tufano and Daniel Schneider have proposed "lottery-linked savings," an alteration of government-sponsored lotteries so that they transform the gambling impulse into an impulse to save.[16]

But that is not to say that channeling every activity to speculative markets is necessarily a good thing. In retrospect, viewed from the vantage point of our severe financial crisis, it seems that investment banks might better have remained with the partnership structure, rather than having their shares traded on a daily basis in public markets, even if that structure diminished the flow of information and the rate of the firms' growth.

Every change in financial institutions is an experiment, and only after many years of experience with any institution do we know how well it will work. There is no simple answer as to what form our economic institutions should take. Designing financial institutions is difficult, for the designs have to accommodate a wide array of human foibles, and we have to consider such issues as the kinds of people who are selected into alternative forms of financial institutions and how the institutions would interact with each other in a financial crisis.

The next chapter considers the most salient of these foibles—the troubling tendency for markets to run into bubbles, the likes of which have caused numerous financial crises in history, including the most recent one. But, as we shall see, there can be comparable, or even bigger, analogues to speculative bubbles associated with economic activity even where we do not have speculative markets. We shall see that the problem with bubbles is a problem in dealing with the universal behavior of *people*, not the behavior of the abstract entities called markets.

Chapter 26

Speculative Bubbles and
Their Costs to Society

Economic history is peppered with stories of speculative bubbles, their bursting, and the resultant economic dislocation. There are more such stories than any of us can remember. Even before we had stock markets, there were economically important fluctuations in speculative asset prices. There are vague stories of housing booms in ancient Rome, in the time of Julius Caesar and in the time of Hadrian. Large swings in land prices wrought great distress even before we had stock markets of any size. After the invention of the newspaper in the early 1600s, stories of bubbles began to take on their modern form, and the intensity and frequency of reports of bubbles jumped significantly. The intermittent occurrence of these bubble stories seems an integral part of living in a system of financial capitalism.

Just What Is a Speculative Bubble?

When I wrote the second edition of my book *Irrational Exuberance* in 2005, I was struck by the fact that there didn't seem to be a good definition of a "speculative bubble." Dictionaries gave only vague general definitions for the word *bubble* in this context, as something insubstantial or filled with air. Finance textbooks in the efficient markets era generally did not even mention the term. It has, at least until recently, seemed a term used by writers for the popular news media rather than scholars. So I wrote my own definition, which seemed to capture what people typically mean when they refer to bubbles:

I define a speculative bubble as a situation in which news of price increases spurs investor enthusiasm, which spreads by psychological contagion from person to person, in the process amplifying stories that might justify the price increases and bringing in a larger and larger class of investors, who, despite doubts about the real value of an investment, are drawn to it partly through envy of others' successes and partly through a gambler's excitement.[1]

Looking back on this definition years later, I am struck by the fact that it contains many psychological, or emotional, terms: *enthusiasm, psychological contagion, doubts, envy, gambler's excitement*. Most economists would not put such words in the definition of any economic term, for they suggest the primacy of raw emotions in an economic decision. But it seemed to me then that the presence in large numbers of people of these emotions is what identifies a bubble.

Perhaps it would be better to define a list of symptoms of a bubble. Bubbles are a phenomenon that may be compared to a social mental illness, and not all bubbles are identical. We need something like the diagnostic criteria that the American Psychiatric Association has provided in its *Diagnostic and Statistical Manual of Mental Disorders*, now in its fourth edition (*DSM-IV*). Psychiatrists seeking to diagnose a patient's mental condition usually cannot rely on concrete factors like the bacterial cultures or x-ray images that other physicians use in diagnosis. *DSM-IV* provides a numbered list of the possible symptoms for all known mental disorders, and a required number of these symptoms from the list for a diagnosis to be valid, thereby allowing a diagnosis that should be replicable across different psychiatrists, and also allowing for useful statistical measures of the illness.

Social Epidemics

Yet a speculative bubble is different from a mental illness in that it is a social phenomenon, the result of an interaction among large numbers of mostly normal people. A positive bubble occurs when people observe price increases in some speculative market and the observation generates a feedback loop. Price increases attract attention, both in the news media and in popular talk, to theories—often so-called new era theories, inspirational stories of why the future is going to be dramatically better than the past—that justify the price increases, and more people decide to buy, thereby bidding up the price even further. At each stage of the loop prices have to be bid up enough that some existing holders of the asset will start to think that the price is too high and thus sell, preserving for the moment the equality of supply and demand. At each stage of the loop the contagion of the new era theories brings new demand and is in turn enhanced by the public attention generated by the price increases. As the loops repeat, the stories become ever more prominent and the price deviation ever larger.

In a negative bubble, it is the same, except that falling prices generate negative stories—catastrophe stories—that encourage selling. The feedback loop means that falling prices encourage the catastrophe stories, the greater public attention to them in turn leads to further price declines, and on and on. At each iteration of the loop prices have to fall far enough that some investors will buy the assets others are selling, despite the increased prominence of the negative stories.

Bubbles generate profit opportunities for those who see and understand what is happening, and the activity of such people tends to be stabilizing. Still, such activity tends to be limited, as it is never known just when the bubble, whether positive or negative, will end. Frequent short-run market reversals seem to mark ends to the bubble—spurious though these are—which only confuse people. Betting against a bubble is a risky business. And it all remains a matter of opinion; there is no way to prove that there is indeed a bubble, for bubbles cannot be well quantified. Changes in ratios, such as price-earnings ratios, are never proof of a bubble. There are not enough major bubbles in one market or country relative to a person's active professional lifespan to allow one to establish a secure reputation as an exploiter of bubbles. Nor are there enough to allow institutions or government organizations to gain the reputation that would allow them to convince investors or taxpayers to provide massive capital to lean against nascent bubbles and so prevent them from developing.

Sociologists have told us in the past about social epidemics, though most of these are not related to finance and hence technically are not speculative bubbles. Yet we have to rely on the understanding that modern sociology gives us of these epidemics if we are to comprehend speculative bubbles.

We have to rely on modern neuroscience as well in understanding bubbles. The coordination of all the different agents that make up the brain is imperfect, for the evolutionary processes that shaped the human brain have not made it into a perfect machine. In our evolution the mammalian brain was built "on top of" the reptilian brain, and there is a degree of duplication and contradiction within our brains. Like a house to which new wings have been added over the years, the structure is not a truly unified whole, and there are cold spots and drafty areas. There still are "brain bugs"—similar to bugs in computer programs—as neuroscientist Dean Buonomano has characterized them in a book with that title: "Simply put, our brain is inherently well suited for some tasks, but ill suited for others. Unfortunately, the brain's weaknesses include recognizing which tasks are which, so for the most part we remain blissfully ignorant of the extent to which our lives are governed by the *brain bugs*."[2]

Speculative bubbles are the effect on the entire financial system of a number of these brain bugs. I listed a number of them in *Irrational Exuberance*. The bugs include

- *Anchoring,* a tendency to be influenced by extraneous cues when in ambiguous circumstances,
- A tendency to be overly influenced by *storytelling,* particularly human-interest stories,
- *Overconfidence,* particularly in ego-involving judgments,
- *Nonconsequentialist reasoning,* a difficulty in thinking through the array of hypothetical events that could potentially occur in the future, and
- *Social influence,* a tendency to adopt the attitudes of others around us without realizing we are doing so.

All of these factors create a vulnerability to thought viruses, or memes—ideas that spread across the population the same way disease viruses do.

There is also cognitive dissonance, which we discussed earlier. During a bubble, it operates on both an individual and a cultural level. At the cultural level, it contributes to the proliferation of a conventional wisdom that justifies the bubble-enhancing activities in which we are already involved. There are people who actively feed this conventional wisdom, as anything that disrupts the conventional wisdom will evoke cognitive dissonance in those who have internalized it—and who, moreover, may have made business arrangements or placed bets that are predicated on this wisdom.

Nonfinancial Investment Bubbles

It is important to recognize, when we think about how to regulate or prevent them, that speculative bubbles are just one particularly frequent and salient example of social epidemics. The above description of a social epidemic that creates speculative bubbles presumes the existence of financial markets that reveal the prices of speculative assets and news media that disseminate information about those prices, so that the price movements can accelerate the contagion of bubble thinking. But the process of a social epidemic involving the economy can proceed even in the total absence of financial markets—though the process would then necessarily be different.

To find clear examples, we have to look at economies that have no financial markets at all. Consider the centrally planned economies during the age of communism in the twentieth century. These examples are not normally referred to as "bubbles," since the central command of the economy did not involve a large segment of the population. The bubble thinking underlying these economies was less visible and less remarked on—but no less intense and disastrous.

In the Soviet Union, the collectivization plan of 1929 has aspects of a speculative bubble. The plan called for a massive reorganization of agriculture from small individual farms to giant collectives, which would be given modern farm equipment to increase productivity. The Soviet government promoted the plan to the general public to encourage its enthusiastic implementation. The initial forecasts for its success were as outlandish and wildly inflated as those in any financial bubble. The public participated in the enthusiasm, and it even became the fashion to name babies "Traktor," "Electrifikatsiya," and the like.

There was no way to buy shares in the collectivization schemes, though one could indirectly invest in a collective farm by throwing oneself into its workforce with hopes of promotion and rewards. More significantly, there was no price for such an investment recorded in any market, and no tempering forces for the bubble through comparing prices with alternative investments or making short sales. There was no broad publication of balance sheets and profit statements, and there were no independent analysts who could openly criticize the new enterprises. The bubble was ultimately proven to be a disaster. Eleven million people died in the famine of 1932–33, which was directly related to the disruption in agriculture that collectivization had produced.

The Great Leap Forward in communist China from 1958 to 1961 was another such investment bubble that took place in the absence of financial markets. The plan involved both agricultural collectivization and the aggressive promotion of industry, notably of the iron and steel industry. Once again there were no market prices, no published profit and loss statements, no independent analysts. Steel production was to be carried out in backyard furnaces that would be considered laughable by knowledgeable steel industry analysts, but those who understood that had no influence in China at the time. Of course there was no way to short the Great Leap Forward. As a result of this bubble, agricultural labor and resources were rapidly diverted to industry. The result was massive famine, with tens of millions of deaths.[3]

The Great Leap Forward also has aspects of a Ponzi scheme. There are reports that Mao Zedong, on visiting a modern steel plant in Manchuria in 1959, became doubtful that the backyard furnaces were a good idea. According to his personal physician and later biographer Li Zhisui, "he gave no order to halt the backyard steel furnaces. The horrible waste of manpower and materials, the useless output from the homemade furnaces, was not his main concern. Mao still did not want to do anything to dampen the enthusiasm of the masses."[4] The Great Leap Forward, as well as the Cultural Revolution that followed it, was essentially a calculated scheme to create a social contagion of ideas.

Accounting fraud played a major role in the disaster created by the Great Leap Forward, for the event created an incentive for collectives to overstate their harvest, and there were no regulators to ensure that the reports were honest. When the central government demanded its share of the reported produce, there was little left to feed the producers.

Some may object that these events were not really speculative bubbles because the activities were imposed on the population by totalitarian governments, and the deaths reflect government error more than investment error. But they nevertheless have aspects of bubbles. The simple fact that in each case the government was able to have its plans carried out for so long and on such a massive scale must mean that there was enthusiastic public support for the underlying ideas.

Fortunately no speculative bubble in any advanced financial country has ever had the disastrous consequences of Soviet collectivization or the Chinese Great Leap Forward. The presence of free markets, analysts, and balance sheets and income statements at least limits the magnitude of such disasters.

Wars and Bubbles

World War I was in a sense a bubble. As with many conflicts, the precipitating event, the assassination of Archduke Franz Ferdinand, became less significant as events progressed through a sequence of reactions and counterreactions—a feedback loop that no participant could seem to stop.

Emil Lederer, a sociologist, remarked in 1915 that he was struck by the transformation of society wrought by the war. The practice of universal conscription, he wrote, made the prospect of war an immensely personal matter, touching almost every family, which then invaded everyone's thinking and led to a change in interpersonal relationships. As he put it, *Gesellschaft* (society) was replaced by *Gemeinschaft* (community), which made it impossible to be detached from the feedback.[5]

World War I was so obviously a destructive feedback loop that it led to international mechanisms to curtail such feedback in the future. These included the League of Nations, which, after it failed to stop World War II, was replaced by the United Nations. An essential function of the United Nations is the mediation of disputes and the placement of peacekeeping forces to interrupt such feedback loops as close to their origins as possible. We could have analogous advances in curtailing speculative bubbles—though they will never be curtailed completely.

The Good Society

As with the founding of the United Nations in the twentieth century, the twenty-first century is seeing progress toward the achievement of the "good society." One example has been the development of the association of nations known as the Group of Twenty (G20), formed in 1999, as an effective economic policy institution. This development builds on centuries of progress in developing agencies of international cooperation among the great powers, starting with the Congress of Vienna in 1814–15. The League of Nations and the United Nations were important milestones, as were the Group of Seven and its successor the Group of Eight. The Economic and Social Council of the United

Nations, and the Second Committee of its General Assembly, did have some impact on economic policy formulation. But before the G20 no body of international agreement was effective in coordinating economic policy.

In the group's first summit statement, dated November 15, 2008, the leaders of the G20 nations committed themselves to ensuring "that all systemically-important institutions are appropriately regulated."[6] In their September 15, 2009, statement they announced their commitment to "policies designed to avoid both the re-creation of asset bubbles and the re-emergence of unsustainable global financial flows."[7]

Steps are being taken in the nations of the developed world to comply with these policies. In the United States, for example, the Dodd-Frank Act has set up, along with the Financial Stability Oversight Council, an Office of Financial Research, which is charged with collecting data that will allow informed decisions about systemic risks. In the European Union, the European Systemic Risk Board has an Advisory Technical Committee charged with helping it figure out how to deal with bubble-like problems.

But preventing speculative bubbles and overleverage in an economy is inherently difficult for any government agency. One wonders how well these agencies will succeed. Past examples are not uniformly encouraging. In 1987, right after the biggest one-day stock market crash in U.S. history, President Ronald Reagan created such an agency, the President's Working Group on Financial Markets, which consisted of the secretary of the Treasury, the chairman of the Federal Reserve Board, the chairman of the SEC, and the chairman of the Commodity Futures Trading Commission. It was similar to today's Financial Stability Oversight Council but had fewer members. That body apparently took no measures as a group to forestall the present financial crisis. On October 8, 2008, near the peak of the crisis, it issued only a weak statement that consisted of descriptions of the various actions that each of the four agencies constituting the working group had already undertaken, without offering any evidence that the existence of the group itself had been of any benefit.[8]

Descriptions of the activities of these agencies tend to be technical in nature, couched in terms of data on capital ratios, crossborder capital flows, and the like. They do not usually include the word *bubble*. The problem seems to be that accountants can often conceal the real meaning of the numbers. Recognizing a bubble is essential to preventing a financial crisis, but recognizing bubbles is as much a question of judging, from their actions, people's intentions and motives as it is of looking at the numbers themselves.

That is why formulating plans for new agencies to prevent bubbles is so difficult. And that is why the dislocations that we have seen during the present financial crisis will tend to recur.

Regulators play an important role, but they are human. Designing financial institutions around the imperfections of regulators—as much as that can be done—is just as important as designing financial institutions around the imperfections of market participants.

The Significance of Bubbles

Assuming all this is true, what good are prices in financial markets? What else can they do *besides* create bubbles and crashes? There is widespread talk among apologists for speculative markets that the markets provide price discovery, implying that they create important information. But what is the nature of the information the markets are revealing? What are the markets "discovering" in their prices?

The answer has to be that even though the fluctuating level of aggregate stock market prices over the past century has generally discovered little more than changing market psychology, stock prices still mean something. Notably, at the very least, *individual* stocks' prices clearly carry useful information.

The economist Paul A. Samuelson opined that stock prices are "micro efficient" and "macro inefficient." He meant that there is more truth to the efficient markets hypothesis for individual stocks (micro in the sense that we are talking about tiny parts of the aggregate market) than for the stock market as a whole (the macro side of the market). We call this Samuelson's Dictum.

In a paper I wrote with my former student Jeeman Jung, we found evidence that gives some support for Samuelson's Dictum.[9] We noted that excess volatility is most apparent for the aggregate stock market. For the aggregate market, there has never been much fluctuation in earnings or dividends; they have always followed a trend—with only short-run interruptions that tend to reverse themselves in a matter of a few years—and so should not have a significant impact on stock prices. There has thus never been much genuine information predicting substantial future movements in economywide earnings or dividends away from the trend. So, for the stock market for an entire country, the bubbles have dominated.[10]

But when one looks at individual stocks, and not just at the aggregate stock market, one finds that the percentage movements in dividends are much larger. Even if these stocks are just as vulnerable to booms and crashes, the large movements in the fundamentals, to some extent forecastable, provide a justification for fluctuations in the price-earnings ratio.

For example, Jung and I looked at those stocks that have never yet paid a dividend, typically young stocks, issued by relatively new companies that hope to reward their investors later with dividends. Efficient markets theory predicts that, while they are not paying dividends, these stocks will show higher price increases over time than other stocks, to compensate investors for the lack of dividend income. For stocks that pay no dividend, we find that in fact there *is* a higher capital gain on average. The market must know something; it somehow puts a value on these stocks, knowing that they will appreciate at a higher rate, and they in fact *do* tend to appreciate at a higher rate. So that valuation is meaningful.

In a research study titled "What Drives Firm-Level Stock Returns?" financial analyst Tuomo Vuolteenaho looked at the valuations of a large sample of U.S. stocks using over 36,000 firm-year observations over the years 1954–96. His conclusions imply that about two-thirds of the variability of individual company stock prices stems from responses to genuine information about the expected future cash flows of the firms, and only about a third of the variability can be attributed to changes in investor attitudes toward risk and time. He did not enumerate what might change these attitudes, but influences probably would include speculative bubbles, or possibly other factors that change investor willingness to pay, such as fashions or fads in investing, changing liquidity, publicity for individual stocks, market manipulation, or changing availability of shortable shares. But since these account for only about a third of the variability of individual stock prices, Vuolteenaho confirms that individual stock price movements mostly do make basic sense in terms of information about the future.[11]

Fischer Black, the co-author of the Black-Scholes option pricing theory, wrote in his presidential address to the American Finance Association that the efficient markets theory of the stock market "seems reasonable" if we adopt the right definition of "efficient." He defined "efficient" to mean that individual company stock prices are between half true value and twice true value almost all of the time. And he defined "almost all" to mean "at least 90%."[12] That judgment seems roughly to correspond to Vuolteenaho's assessment.

As I interpret the evidence, financial markets are not perfect, and a substantial fraction of the variation in individual stock prices is not explainable in terms of anything that makes good economic sense—at least not sense that we can discern today. Bubbles are frequent and, when they occur, salient. But enough of the variability of individual stock prices, or other individual asset prices, *does* make sense that the market remains an extremely important source of information for directing resources.

Chapter 27

Inequality and Injustice

We have ample reason to believe that financial markets are quite useful. And yet our wonderful financial infrastructure has not yet brought us the harmonious society that we might envision. There remains the ugliness of extreme economic inequality, of some who endure hardship while others are pampered. While some inequality is actually in many ways a good thing, for the motivation and stimulation it provides, arbitrary and extreme inequality poses problems.

The public aversion to inequality is deep seated and ancient. It has been shown that even our distant relatives, nonhuman primates, share with us an aversion to inequity.[1] It is an imperative that people feel society is basically fair to them.

We see this aversion most clearly today in the worldwide protests associated with Occupy Wall Street and its variants. The unfairness of the allocation of resources under financial capitalism is a major theme. Rising inequality is certainly a valid concern, and one that must be addressed. But financial capitalism does not *necessarily* produce unjust wealth distribution. Public policy can allow us to enjoy the benefits of modern finance without producing such inequality. We must examine the relationship between finance and our problems with inequality before we jump to unwarranted conclusions.

Finance and Injustice

We seem able to live with, even admire, wealthy people. There is no sense of injustice if we believe that the wealthy in some sense earned or deserve their wealth. Public awareness of inequality itself does not seem to be strongly associated with overt signs of anger, such as terrorism or antisocial acts.[2]

A college student with a good business idea who drops out, founds a company, raises the financing for it despite being an outsider to the system, and quickly becomes a billionaire does not seem to inspire resentment. To most people, that is just an interesting story. The greatest resentment is reserved for the social classes who focus their attention exclusively on amassing fortunes and keeping them from the eyes of the tax collector, year upon year and generation upon generation.

There is widespread skepticism that those who become extremely wealthy through financial dealings, or very high executive compensation packages, are sufficiently deserving of their wealth.

How the Rich Are Connected to Finance

If we define finance as broadly as in the introduction to this book, then most of the richest people in the world may be classified as connected to the field of finance. Looking at the Forbes 400 list of the richest Americans, all of them billionaires, one sees that the great majority of them have some real connection to finance, in the sense that they are in charge of large enterprises that participate frequently in markets and deal making.[3] Finance is usually not listed as their specialty: for only a quarter of them is the source of wealth given as investments, hedge funds, leveraged buyouts, insurance, or other distinctly financial businesses. But, though they may run a business with a specialized nonfinancial product, they do so on such a scale that they are surely involved in finance.

Forbes also maintains the Celebrity 100 list, the members of which are selected based not on their wealth but on other factors indicating their public presence, as well as their income.[4] Only three of those on this list—Oprah Winfrey, Donald Trump, and Steven Spielberg—are also on the Forbes 400 list. They are on both lists only because they are leading double lives as managers and entertainers—and big-time, as each manages a massive entertainment empire. Being famous is not at all the same as being rich, and finance is not by itself a route to celebrity.

The Forbes 400 billionaires have usually made use of some kind of specialized knowledge to achieve their wealth, but they rarely stand out for important contributions in any intellectual or creative fields. There appear to be no distinguished scientists on the list. There does not appear to be a single Nobel Prize winner on the list—though of course the Nobel Foundation might see little purpose in bestowing a mere $1.5 million on one of these billionaires.

There are only a few best-selling authors on the list, and even they are on the list because of their business ventures. If one searches Amazon.com for Oprah Winfrey, Donald Trump, or Steven Spielberg, many books come up, with numerous co-authors, but these books appear to be part and parcel of their media and entertainment enterprises.

Their wealth appears to be related to large-scale financial activities, not just artistic creativity. For example, Oprah Winfrey now has her own cable network, the Oprah Winfrey Network or OWN, and her own magazine, *O, The Oprah Magazine*. Donald Trump is more squarely situated in finance, with his Trump Organization and Trump Entertainment Resorts. Steven Spielberg has not been just a producer and director of films; he was a co-founder in 1994 of DreamWorks Studios, which has financed and distributed films, video games, and television shows. DreamWorks was sold to Paramount Pictures in 2005 for $1.6 billion.

As we have discussed, finance is a powerful tool because it has the ability to amass capital, pool information, and coordinate and incentivize people. It is no wonder that it is so central to the lives of the wealthiest. Their wealth comes not solely from their own efforts and talent, but often from their ability to form and lead huge and effective organizations composed of many other talented people.

Possible Bubbles in Financial Compensation

Still it remains a puzzle that those connected to finance can become so fabulously rich to the seeming exclusion of everyone else. Wouldn't you think that at least one scientist could come up with a patentable idea that would top all their successes? But that never seems to happen—not even close. Why is that?

Part of the answer might be that finance in recent decades has been going through an anomalous period. Perhaps the compensation that those in finance earn is going through a speculative bubble or an adjustment to new technology and will be corrected in the future. Indeed finance salaries have increased dramatically in recent decades, as a 2008 study by Thomas Philippon and Ariell Reshef has shown.[5] These authors found that the compensation of those in finance was also unusually high around 1930, just around the time of the 1929 peak in the stock market, and then fell dramatically for the next half century. In that interim period there were many low-paying jobs in finance. Philippon and Reshef also pointed out that the average education level of people in the finance professions was likewise high around 1930, after which it decreased; it has recently returned to a high level. These findings suggest that the path of financial salaries was not just a bubble—that it reflects an actual change in the composition of the financial labor force. In any event, their results encourage caution in making the assumption that because the compensation of people in finance is high now, it will always be high in the future.

But Philippon and Reshef were talking about the rank-and-file members of the finance professions, not the richest ones. It seems likely that finance will continue to produce a small number of super-rich people unless public policy changes the landscape.

And in considering the super-rich we have to come back to the fundamental nature of financial dealmaking, which enables the power of the dealmaker to be multiplied via his or her command over vast numbers of people. Scientists are, in their capacity as scientists, not dealmakers, and they depend largely on collegiality and professional courtesy to make the research progress they so value.

Although there does often seem to be injustice in this situation, in and of itself it is not extreme. The scientists are mostly living comfortably doing what they really want to do, and their everyday life is enriched with products that are provided by others doing less essentially gratifying work. The situation can still be improved, but it would not be without cost to eliminate inequality entirely from our society.

Family Dynasties

Part of the reason for a sense of injustice at the unequal distribution of wealth is that some of the inequality seems to be the result of family dynasties, through which the children of successful businesspeople become rich, whether or not they are deserving. Some of these children, for example Donald Trump, keep working in the family business. But in fact only about a third of family businesses are continued by the children of the founders, and only a tenth of them by the grandchildren.[6] Still, the later generations remain rich.

Having one's children and grandchildren become wealthy and perhaps continue the family business is a source of great meaning to many of those who have founded businesses. This sentiment endures despite the fact that studies have indicated that children who inherit large fortunes tend to feel a degree of meaninglessness in their later lives. According to one authoritative study, children of the very rich show "elevated disturbance in several areas— such as substance use, anxiety, and depression."[7]

And yet the dream of the family dynasty persists. Even though Karl Marx and Friedrich Engels cried "Abolition of the family!" in their *Communist Manifesto*,[8] today's hard-line communist countries pursue this dream. For example, in North Korea it drove Kim Il Sung to anoint his son Kim Jong Il and he in turn to anoint his son Kim Jong Un as leader of North Korea. It has even motivated Fidel Castro, who is a true communist, to bequeath his role as ruler of Cuba to his brother Raúl.

Positional Consumption

The tendency for wealthy families to annoy others by "showing off"—by spending extravagantly and wastefully on themselves—is often a cause for resentment. Consuming conspicuously feeds their ego. It may also help them convey social status to the next generation, by securing for their children a head start in the pecking order.

This tendency toward consumption for show has been dealt with for centuries, going back to ancient Greece and Rome, by means of sumptuary laws, that is, laws that directly forbid specified forms of wasteful consumption. For example, in seventh-century BCE Greece, women were forbidden by the Locrian code to wear extravagant clothing or jewelry unless they were prostitutes. Similarly, sumptuary taxes are special excise taxes on items of conspicuous consumption.

Sumptuary laws and taxes, however, have difficulty in actually preventing spending that invites the resentment of others. As one eighteenth-century observer sized up these laws, "they are null, because luxury employs itself upon objects which the laws have not foreseen, and could not foresee."[9] The laws' details were commonly ridiculed, and in modern times they are thought to be inconsistent with individual freedoms. They did, nevertheless, reappear again and again for thousands of years, reflecting the persistence of public disgust with the extravagance of the rich.

There is an economic theory that would seem to justify something akin to sumptuary laws or taxes. The theory was described by Thorstein Veblen in his 1899 book *The Theory of the Leisure Class* and the economic part of the theory was expanded by George Akerlof and other economic theorists.[10] Many people spend lavishly on consumption that they do not really even enjoy merely to signal to others their status—a practice called positional consumption because its value to the consumer depends on how it establishes his or her position relative to others. As argued convincingly by social psychologist Leon Festinger, with his 1954 "theory of social comparison processes," people are instinctively constantly comparing themselves with other people, and they delight when they are doing better.[11] They tend to compare themselves with others close to them in the social ranking and who are attempting to achieve similar things, and disregard those who are doing very much better or very much worse or who are very different in their measures of success.

The comparisons are substantially subconscious, and since such comparisons are generally frowned upon, many people deny to themselves as well as others that they are making them. From Festinger's other theory, of cognitive dissonance, we see that people often manage to convince themselves that they enjoy the positional consumption goods because the items consumed are intrinsically good; they experience a sense of enjoyment as if the enjoyment were intrinsic rather than positional. This is not to say that people cannot make value judgments independent of status considerations, just that such considerations impose a bias that affects their judgments, often subconsciously.

This theory has always been controversial, and even repugnant to those who dislike being accused of such low motives, even if the accusers recognize their good side as well. We should not overstress the theory of social comparisons, for people have sympathetic and communal aspects as well, but the theory is by now well established. A 2007 study even identified a region of the brain (the ventral striatum) that is stimulated especially strongly after a reward if others nearby are seen as not receiving the same reward.[12] There is thus a physical basis for the social comparison theory.

A modern version of sumptuary laws calls for progressive consumption taxes: taxes based on the amount one consumes rather than the amount one earns, and with higher tax rates on higher levels of consumption. Such a tax was proposed in the United States Senate by Democrat Sam Nunn and Republican Pete Domenici in 1995. Adding a progressive consumption tax is like adding a sumptuary tax, but one that is broadly applied to overall levels of consumption, not just consumption of particular items. Recently economist Robert H. Frank has advocated replacing the income tax with such taxes, to help reduce the problem of positional consumption.[13]

Switching from a progressive income tax to a similarly progressive consumption tax might be a good idea, for such an approach does not penalize one from earning a large income; it simply discourages excessive spending from that income, and it might encourage saving, philanthropy, or both.

However, there are serious implementation problems that make progressive consumption taxes difficult. For example, in implementing such a new tax regime, it would be hard not to effectively reduce taxes on the highest-income people, and it would be hard to manage withholding on income, since responsible withholding would have to depend on unknown future consumption.[14] Neither a sumptuary tax nor a progressive consumption tax is an easy and obvious solution to the problem of wasteful and resentment-inducing positional consumption. We need to keep such ideas in mind, though, as fodder for public financial innovation, possibly in some altered form or through reliance on future advances in information technology.

Estate Taxes

Whether or not rich people actually feel any sense of connectedness to others in their country, their countrymen will feel that they ought to. Upon their death, distributing their estates to their own children seems selfish, especially as their children may not seem particularly deserving, at least in the eyes of others. Levying estate taxes is one of the most effective ways of restoring a sense of fairness in society. Many countries tax estates heavily at the time of death.

If estate taxes were pursued aggressively, they would do much to reduce economic inequality. But there remains an issue: often the most important reason people try to make money is to pass it to their children. Such desires to promote the welfare of one's children are in some ways instinctive. Leaving a financial estate for them may not be the most fundamental expression of such instincts, but it is a desire that crops up repeatedly in human societies.

Estate taxes can seem extremely onerous to some. In late 2010, when a law abolishing the federal estate tax in the United States was set to expire on January 1, 2011, bringing the maximum estate tax rate up from 0% to 55%, the media told unconfirmed stories of elderly people in poor health asking their doctors to cut off further treatment so they would die before the year was over.[15] Representative Cynthia Lummis of Wyoming said, "If you have spent your whole life building a ranch, and you wanted to pass your estate on to your children, and you were 88-years-old and on dialysis, and the only thing that was keeping you alive was that dialysis, you might make that same decision."[16]

She makes a good point: some people do spend their lives trying to promote their children's welfare—a goal that, one has to admit, is far from evil. But here we have an essential conflict, for their doing so very successfully can create a situation of social resentment.

There is no way to eliminate this essential conflict, and so the best solution would seem to be setting estate taxes at some intermediate level, neither confiscating wealth at death nor allowing its complete transition. In fact, most people think about the issue in this way. Most believe that society should give in somewhat to the natural desire to make one's children rich, but simply limit the exercise of that desire. A 1990 survey that Maxim Boycko, Vladimir Korobov, and I conducted found that people in both the United States and the Soviet Union—people from two very different economic traditions— thought that the estate tax should take about a third of an estate.[17]

We may consider tragic the stories of people losing the family farm—having to sell the farm and move to an apartment in the city just to pay the estate tax, thus upending a family's whole way of life, possibly for generations to come. But we also have to consider the resentment caused by wealthy children holding such wealth indefinitely, and the feelings of society as a whole.

In fact, the form of estate tax favored by most people actually allows wealthy people to leave their children a ranch or a family farm. In this case parents are perceived as transferring not just wealth but also a set of responsibilities, and meaningful work, to their children. But transferring responsibilities and work does not *require* a massive transfer of wealth. The people that Representative Lummis talked about could probably have paid any higher estate tax in 2011 by taking out a mortgage on the farm and paying it off through time. Finance offers many flexibilities, and if the ranching lifestyle is important to a family, they can probably find a financial strategy that will allow them to continue it.

Inequality Indexation or Inequality Insurance

Besides estate taxes, one of the most important weapons society already has against economic inequality is the progressive income tax system. Progressive income taxes have higher tax rates on higher levels of income, and so revenue is raised disproportionately from high-income people, and much of the benefit of the proceeds is directed to, or at least shared by, the poor. Moreover, government expenditures on many things (education, public goods) are shared among all people. Over the years, income tax systems have become more sophisticated in managing inequality. For example, the tax systems in the United States and other countries have forms of the "earned income tax credit" that in effect gives low-income workers a negative income tax on their wages.[18]

But, strangely, the income tax system has never been expressly designed with the objective of managing inequality. The word *inequality* does not seem to be in the tax code. So the system deals with economic inequality in a haphazard way purely as a by-product of its stated goals, and tax law is not written in a way that allows it to respond to economic inequality.

I have proposed that in the future nations should *index* their tax systems to inequality.[19] Under inequality indexation (which I have also called inequality insurance) the government would not legislate fixed income tax rates for each tax bracket, but would instead prescribe in advance a formula that would tie the tax rates to statistical measures of pretax inequality. If income inequality were to worsen, the tax system would become automatically more progressive. This is a "financial" solution to the problem of inequality in the sense that we impose the indexation scheme *before* we know that income inequality will worsen, and *before* people know who might effectively be highly taxed by it. So the indexation scheme is dealing with a *risk*, the risk of rising inequality, before it happens, much as insurance contracts do. In fact, inequality indexation could be considered a kind of insurance—inequality insurance.

The inequality indexation scheme could be designed either to gradually reverse the level of inequality, to bring it eventually to a more acceptable level, or to merely freeze it at the present level, so that it does not get worse. The latter course may be the most politically acceptable. A scheme could be designed that would allow substantial income inequality to persist forever, that would merely be aimed at preventing a serious *worsening* of income inequality. It would after all be easier to accustom people to inequality indexation of taxes if such a system had no immediate impact, and no chance of changing the current social order. People would still be able to get rich, as they can today, but we would plan in advance not to let income inequality get much worse. If inequality never worsened, then the inequality indexation scheme would have no effect.

The combined wealth of the Forbes 400 in 2011 was $1.5 trillion, or 2.6% of the national household net worth.[20] As the percentage of total societal wealth is small, and as most of these people are seen as contributing to society by running large businesses, this degree of inequality may be acceptable, or at least there may not be the political will to address it. But the inequality could get worse. How much of a concentration of economic blessings do we really want to allow? The possibility that the 400 could come to have a much greater—perhaps an extraordinary—share of our national wealth, in return for a contribution to society that is not at all proportionate, seems odious. If such changes were to occur, it would not be because the distribution of talents or skills in their genes had suddenly changed. The change would no doubt be widely perceived as an injustice.

It would be easier to legislate contingency plans in advance against any future worsening in income inequality than to wait until the inequality became a reality. It is much easier to insure a house *before* it burns down. The same principle implies that it is easier to construct a tax system that deals with increasing inequality before it happens. If the day should come when we have a much larger class of wealthy people, then these people will tend to feel entitled to what after-tax income they already have and will have the economic clout to lobby forcefully to maintain that status. We need to put mechanisms in place now, not later, that will prevent that cycle from ever starting, and this is one route to limiting the power of the lobbyists who were discussed in Part One. It will seem unfair if we change the tax laws after the fact. So we should deal with the potential problem now.

An inequality indexation formula might be enacted as a political quid pro quo for some pro-growth policy that is controversial because of its possible consequences for income inequality. The formula would promote average economic well-being as well as deal with risks to that well-being.

Leonard Burman at Syracuse University and I did a historical analysis of the possible effects of inequality indexation, had it been imposed many years ago.[21] We found that if an inequality indexation scheme had been legislated in 1979 that would have frozen after-tax income inequality at the then-current level, the marginal tax rate on high-income individuals would have increased to an extraordinarily high level, over 75%. This finding provides stark evidence of how much economic inequality has worsened since 1979. We were concerned that full inequality indexation might be too much to be accepted, and so we also proposed partial inequality indexation, as part of a broader attack on random economic influences that create inequality, using other insurance and hedging schemes. An inequality indexation scheme also has to be designed, and constrained, to minimize effects that encourage welfare dependency or provide strong incentives to immigrate or emigrate.

The Need to Be Systematic and to Apply Financial Theory

Progressive income taxes and estate taxes—and possibly also progressive consumption taxes—are important tools for dealing with excessive economic inequality. Real public concerns about inequality have already made some of these taxes common around the world.

But societies have great trouble dealing with the issue of inequality in a systematic manner. The principle has never been articulated that some degree of inequality is a good thing, that there should be some who are richly rewarded for their business success (or their parents' success), but that society has to systematically put some limits on this inequality. Because that principle has never been established, the effects of various tax laws are never considered systematically and holistically. Thus the wealthy instinctively oppose any increase in their taxes, fearing that acquiescing even to a limited extent might leave them open to a haphazard series of tax increases that, in combination, could amount to confiscatory taxation.

Measures to deal with economic inequality should be implemented holistically and articulated clearly, in terms of achieving some appropriate level of inequality. The inequality indexation scheme described here is one trial balloon for such an idea. It may not ultimately prove to be the right course, but it is at the very least illustrative of the principle that we should be considering more complex systems of tax rates that are grounded in risk management theory and behavioral economics. Our tax system is still hampered by that old impulse for conventionality and familiarity. But given our rapidly advancing information technology—in an age when computers are increasingly calculating our taxes and we are increasingly filing our taxes electronically, and looking forward to the day when tax paying can be automated even further—we can introduce quite a bit more responsiveness and nuance into the tax system to help achieve a better society—a society in which people feel that basic economic justice is assured.

Chapter 28

Problems with Philanthropy

Why is it that gifts to causes (charitable, religious, artistic, scientific, environmental, educational, and so forth) are not more common? In the United States in 2010 only 2.2% of national income was given away by individuals and organizations.[1] It would seem that people would give more. With just a little thought one naturally concludes that we suffer what economists would call diminishing marginal utility of consumption; that is, one cannot really consume a large amount of wealth. Certainly there are always others who are in greater need. So why don't people see this and do something about it?

Giving as we observe it today seems often to be a distinctly unrewarding experience. People often give merely in response to immediate social pressure.[2] They seem to respond better to charities that offer them some kind of prestige in return for the giving, as if that were all that mattered.[3] It is hard to imagine that such giving, apparently motivated by the wish to avoid opprobrium or to impress others, can be as rewarding to the giver as giving intended to fulfill his or her own moral purpose.

One challenge to motivating donations without external pressure or rewards may be that there is a lack of fulfillment when those who give to philanthropic organizations do not feel any real gratitude from the recipients, for they never meet the people who benefit from their contributions. Psychologists have shown that people are not well motivated in their charitable giving by mere statistics about human suffering: they have to see a suffering individual and put a human face on the need.[4]

Many of the hopes that are expressed for philanthropy seem to take the form of a national sense of community. One feels a responsibility toward others in one's own country, as if the *country* were one's family. Political scientist Benedict Anderson has asserted that the modern nation-state is an "imagined community," standing in place of family.[5] But it is only an *imagined* community, since the people in it have never met most of the other people in it and have no relationship whatsoever with them.

Those who advocate sharing with others face a problem: generosity seems to require a sense of community. Friedrich Hayek, in his 1944 book *The Road to Serfdom*, discerned a "universal tendency of collectivist policy to become nationalistic."[6] The imagined community has to be elevated to people's constant attention to encourage their sympathy with or acquiescence in the collectivist policy. Of course, when Hayek wrote in 1944 his prime example was the German National Socialists, the Nazis. But he argued that promotion of the idea of a national community was a universal tendency. Socialists may pay lip service to the notion that theirs is an international movement, but underneath it all the appeal they make to their constituents is distinctly nationalist.

In many ways modern political leaders have created a sense of family for a whole nation, and people are up to a point willing to sacrifice for the nation as if it were their family. But there are definite limits to the satisfaction one may obtain by considering the nation as one's family. One is repeatedly reminded of the stark reality that all those millions of other people in one's country do not know or care about you.

Philanthropy in today's world is made doubly unrewarding by the typical giving process. A paid caller for some philanthropic organization telephones at dinner time, beginning to read from a script that has been carefully worded by professional marketers. The paid consultants who write these scripts have years of experience with telemarketing. The scripts are such a powerful force that local governments in the United States require that charities register their scripts with the attorney general or the charitable trust division.

The script is designed to elicit a cash contribution, by one tactic or another. Readers are likely very familiar with the typical response when one hesitates to promise a particular dollar amount: "I need to enter a minimum amount that you are prepared to give," perhaps with the additional explanation that the organization needs to set its budget. Obviously the real reason for this line in the script is that organizations have found that asking the potential donor to come up with a number that will be put down in black and white on a pledge card is motivational. Even when one supports the organization's cause, the tactics used to collect donations typically leave one feeling manipulated.

The sense that, in contributing to a philanthropic organization, one is giving in to manipulation puts a chill on the whole process, detracting from the sense of fulfillment and purpose in earning an income and giving a portion of it to good causes. One would rather feel that one has been creative in supporting causes that are personally meaningful, that are congruent with one's sense of identity. It is not just a question of personal satisfaction. It is also a matter of principle. People, whether of modest or high income, who justifiably want to see their lives as building or creating something of value might best focus on making substantial (relative to their own incomes) gifts to no more than a few causes. For it is only in this way that one can have the time and energy to think carefully about and truly identify with these causes, and fulfill the moral imperative of actually directing one's own resources, on one's own terms, to a cause one considers meaningful.

The *Gospel of Wealth* by Andrew Carnegie, discussed earlier in this book, has become an inspiration for many, notable among them Bill Gates and Warren Buffett, who modeled their "giving pledge" on it.[7] Recall that Carnegie considered it the moral duty of those who achieved great financial success to retire from their business careers early enough to begin managing the purposeful disposal of their wealth for the public good. But what if anything has been the lasting effect of Carnegie's theory?

Carnegie's theory, now over a century old, has still not succeeded in convincing most wealthy persons to take personal charge of giving their wealth away. A 1995 study concluded that there are 35,000 active family foundations in the United States with combined assets of $190 billion. That may sound like a lot. However, it is but a fraction of 1% of U.S. household net worth. Another study estimated that the annual giving of the top one hundred family foundations in 2008 was $7.049 billion in the United States, £1.174 billion (US$2.198 billion) in the United Kingdom, and €725 million (US$920 million) in Germany—each amount representing a tiny fraction of 1% of the countries' respective national incomes.[8]

Improving Incentives for Philanthropy

The emptiness that is often felt in making philanthropic contributions—and that may underlie the low national charitable-giving figures just cited—could perhaps be remedied by improving the process whereby it is managed. For example, it is well known, and controlled experiments have confirmed, that giving is enhanced if the solicitation involves a promise that the donor will be identified to his or her peers, along with a broad indication of the amount given.[9] The desire for publicity for one's gifts is an understandable human impulse; not only do people enjoy recognition for having made substantial gifts, but they may also want the publicity for their gifts to influence their friends to give to the same or similar causes, which they consider important. Further research may reveal that there are yet better ways, not in the current repertory of charity solicitors, to fulfill this desire for recognition—perhaps recognition that is longer term or more personalized.

Research has shown that giving can also be increased if the giver is made to feel that the charity is not all one-way. One study demonstrated that a seemingly generous promise to refund the contribution if the goal of the drive was not met substantially improved the level of giving.[10] Also, a reward for giving also appears to heighten the incentive to give. A field experiment showed that people give more to a charity if they are primed by first receiving a gift from the organization.[11] Human relationships are normally reciprocal— even if the exchanges are not equal in monetary value—and designs for charitable campaigns might better reflect that fact.

The advent of social media should offer new means for promoting giving by creating a sense of community and providing for more personal recognition. Child sponsorship is a significant example. Save the Children, established in the United Kingdom in 1919, led the way by assigning a single child in poverty to each contributor, who would correspond by mail, giving the contributor a sense of personal relationship. Save the Children is now an international organization, and a number of other such organizations have followed. Some now employ more advanced communications tools, such as Skype calls between donors and recipients, to allow a closer bond to develop. One can look the child in the eyes and feel empathy as never before.[12]

It seems that we are gradually learning more about how to make the giving experience more meaningful, and that current strategies are not the final word in encouraging such giving. Perhaps new kinds of social organizations— relying on innovations in social media—could lend a better sense of a shared experience, and of true community between the giver and the receiver.

Tax Laws Favoring Giving

To help humanize finance, and reduce inequality of incomes without destroying incentives, it may also be helpful to change the nature of our tax laws regarding charitable contributions, so that people will find it more rewarding to give their wealth away themselves, to disperse it widely and on their own terms. Even though consideration of tax implications seems to appeal to our self-interest, appropriate redefinitions of the tax laws might still have the effect of encouraging altruistic behavior. The tax deduction itself stands, psychologically, as a kind of affirmation and recognition that helps make one's generosity personally meaningful.

There is a precedent for increasing the deduction for contributions as a sweetener for the wealthy when tax rates on them are sharply increased. It was in fact such a quid pro quo that was responsible for the contribution deduction in the United States in the first place. There was no contribution deduction in the first year of the U.S. income tax, 1913. It was not until 1917 that such a deduction was introduced. That was the same year that, because of the need to finance World War I, the top federal income tax rate was raised to 67% (from 15% in 1916 and 7% in each of the years 1913, 1914, and 1915). At that time Senator Henry F. Hollis of New Hampshire argued successfully for adding the deduction. He quoted a letter from one of his constituents, Felix Warburg, who represented a Jewish philanthropic organization: "I fear that with heavy taxes rightly placed upon the people during this war, if no allowance be made as suggested above, many institutions will be forced to close their doors and the State will have to carry the burdens in their stead, which will be most deplorable."[13]

Before the increase in tax rates went into effect, philanthropic contributions had been rising sharply.[14] It was a time when the suffering associated with the war was prominent in people's thinking, and U.S. soldiers were dying abroad. It was also a time when U.S. allies in the war were suffering horrendous losses, indirectly on behalf of the United States. It thus seemed only appropriate that the nation acknowledge and encourage generosity closer to home.

The same thing happened during World War II, when the war pushed the maximum federal income tax rate up to 94% in 1944 (after the highest marginal tax bracket had been lowered to 25% between the wars). Because of continuing war anxieties caused by the cold war, including the revolution in China in 1949 and the Korean War from 1950 to 1953, the top tax bracket remained very high: it was still 91% in 1963, when tax cuts were enacted under President John F. Kennedy. The reaction to these high tax rates—which must have been expected to continue for the foreseeable future—began around 1948, when a number of U.S. national leaders began to ask for an increase in the 15%-of-income limit on charitable deductions that had been in place since the beginning in 1917.

J. K. Lasser, best known as the author of a series of popular tax guides, asked that the limit be raised drastically or abolished altogether; he saw it as "penalizing the public-spirited individual who has a social conscience."[15] The limit on contribution deductions was raised, to 20% in 1953 and to 30% in 1954, and in 1956 an unlimited deduction was given to those whose donations plus income tax payments exceeded 90% of their income for eight of the past ten years.

All of these changes in the law, intended to encourage philanthropic contributions, were made in response to high tax rates. When tax rates were cut—after the Kennedy tax cuts in 1963 started a downtrend in the top marginal tax rate, to 77% in 1964 and then all the way down to 35% by 2003—the limit on contributions was also cut. In 1969 the unlimited contribution deduction was abolished, though the limit on contribution deductions was raised to 50% for some kinds of contributions.

Thus it is entirely plausible that if we raise the top tax bracket again there would be public support for some extension of the tax system's mechanism for encouraging charitable contributions. That must be part of our plan to deal with even worse economic inequality, should it arise.

At this point some more ambitious changes to our tax system might help reduce income inequality and also serve as a sweetener for any proposed increase in income tax rates. Here I propose a number of ideas that may be controversial; they would certainly need to be considered carefully. I do feel we need to be more creative in thinking about how to achieve a more just and equal society, and our tax laws potentially provide us with useful tools to achieve that goal.

There Is Less Need Today for Tax Simplification

Incentives for giving in the United States took a big hit in 1944 when Congress passed, and President Franklin D. Roosevelt signed, a new law that aimed to simplify tax preparation. That law introduced a "standard deduction," which anyone could claim even if he or she made no contributions. The standard deduction was put in place so that most people would not have to go through all the effort of assembling the paperwork to prove their various deductions. Today, about two-thirds of U.S. taxpayers avail themselves of the standard deduction, and so for them there is effectively no tax benefit from donating.[16]

The standard deduction was enacted in 1944, when paperwork really was paperwork. Certainly we do still need to keep tax preparation simple. But today, when computers are at hand to calculate taxes on our behalf, we should not have to resort to tax simplification methods that eliminate important charitable incentives.

Today a system could be set up so that philanthropic organizations would themselves be responsible for reporting to the tax authorities individual contributions they receive. The system would automatically make the necessary adjustment to the individual's tax form, even if the individual chose the standard deduction. There would be no need for a standard deduction to simplify taxes, and the taxpayer would need to do nothing to obtain the benefit of the deduction. Moreover, a truly comprehensive automated system could immediately adjust withholding for income tax purposes, and thus the donor's paycheck would immediately rise in response to the charitable contribution.

We must always bear in mind that our existing tax system was created taking into account computation limits that are no longer relevant. All its various "simplifying" measures should be reexamined with the goal of building real incentives into the system.

More Finely Focused Contribution Deductions and Tax Credits

The contribution deduction as an active tool in achieving a better society has not been much considered in public discourse. Usually contributions either do or do not qualify as deductible—it is all or nothing. In the United States, there are no gradations in the rate of deductibility, no responsiveness to changing public needs for charitable activities, nor is there active use of tax credits instead of deductions. There are different deductibility limits for different kinds of philanthropies (for example, a private foundation may have only a 30% limit, while a private operating foundation may have a 50% limit), but these differences do not appear to have been motivated by any sense of public purpose. A better-thought-out system of contribution deductions and credits could lead to an improved society, one in which people feel more purpose in their economic lives and in which government policies are fulfilled in more creative ways.

The government could give special tax incentives for contributions to organizations designated as filling particular national needs, instead of just raising taxes to pay for government expenditures for those needs. This would be an alternative form of public financing of important activities. For example, in a time of recession, directed contribution tax incentives could be implemented that would encourage donations to organizations helping to create jobs for the unemployed. Or, at a time of rising inequality, there could be a special tax incentive for donations to organizations that embrace the concerns of the poor or that help to foster a sense of community between rich and poor. The tax breaks would be much bigger than the usual contribution deduction. They could take the form of a partial tax credit, rather than just a deduction, so that the gift-giving would be just as meaningful for people in lower tax brackets.

The government could afford such high tax incentives if the specifications for the qualifying organizations were written so as to encourage them to carry out work that the government itself would otherwise have to do. And the resulting complexity in the tax code could be dealt with by suitable improvements to the information technology infrastructure.

Such tax breaks would allow people to put their own mark on these causes, giving their own personal direction to the expenditures while at the same time promoting the public-goods programs of the government. They would give the wealthy a sense of personal satisfaction and at the same time allow them to feel the gratitude of others for their contributions. Such a plan might receive far greater public acceptance than one to merely "tax the rich and give to the poor."

Tax Incentives for Interpersonal Gift Giving

We ought to consider giving people at least a partial tax deduction when they disperse some of their income irrevocably to others, even if the recipients are individuals and include friends or relatives.

Such giving is in fact already commonplace, even without a tax break. According to one study, 40.8% of U.S. households made substantial gifts to relatives not living in their own homes, and 26.2% made direct gifts to friends, neighbors, or strangers.[17] But even though such interpersonal gifts should tend to reduce income inequality, there is generally no encouragement in the tax law to support this form of giving.

I have seen firsthand some examples of such charitable giving. A close friend and colleague of mine and his wife often give away or loan substantial sums of money to students. The institution where he teaches assigns all entering students from outside the United States a "host family." Over the years he and his wife have hosted more than two dozen such students; many of them experience financial difficulties at some stage in their lives. My friend has provided personal emergency assistance to them. He has thus far financed seven automobile loans, three graduate school tuitions, countless trips home, and at least three dental procedures. In one case, a student needed several crowns and root canals totaling about $12,000 which were not covered by her dental insurance. The dentist agreed to do what was needed for half the price, and my friend picked up the rest.

If the tax law's progressivity is intended to reduce inequality, governments might consider giving some kind of encouragement to such generosity, including tax breaks. If gifts to other individuals (excluding one's own children) were made fully tax deductible for the giver, but taxable for the receiver, then in any given case there would be no effect on total government tax revenue unless the two persons' tax brackets were different. With progressive taxes, a total government revenue effect would occur only when an individual in a higher tax bracket gave to someone in a lower tax bracket, thus promoting income equality. If so much giving from higher to lower tax brackets went on that total government tax revenue was too low, the government might have to raise tax rates overall to achieve the same level of revenue—but we would have achieved a degree of social equality with the same overall amount of taxes collected.

The principal concern about such a scheme for tax encouragement of interpersonal gifts would be tax fraud, if an individual made a gift and got the money back under the table. The gifts might also be disguised payments for services. But in our informationally advanced society, it should be possible to create surveillance mechanisms to verify large such gifts and to limit tax fraud. All tax systems are subject to fraud, and governments learn to limit it.

There are some who doubt that there should be any such interpersonal gift giving, for doing so may create an expectation of such gifts and therefore some uncomfortable situations. Indeed this may be an unavoidable consequence of the proposal. But offsetting that would be the atmosphere of social connectedness and caring that would be engendered.

Instead in the United States today we have a gift tax. The gift tax was created by the U.S. Congress in 1932 to prevent evasion of the estate tax by those who gave their wealth away to their heirs before their deaths. Gift tax rates mirror those of the income tax, currently up to a maximum of 35%. Currently one can give up to $13,000 annually as a gift to any one individual before that person is requited to pay the gift tax. It should be just the opposite: instead of a gift tax we should have a gift *deduction* from current income, designed to encourage small- to moderate-size gifts to many people, without making it possible for the clever to completely frustrate the estate tax.

To some extent the current tax treatment of contributions already supports a form of such interpersonal giving. Taxpayers are allowed to deduct contributions to religious organizations, and it is no surprise that the biggest single component (35%) of contributions in the United States today is to churches.[18] People typically give to their *own* church. It is not just because they are religious; it is also because they know some of the people who will thus benefit and have a sense of family and connection with them. Such giving allows them to be appreciated by those whom they know. The second biggest category of contributions in the United States is to schools and colleges. Again most people give to their *own* schools, not to others'. And again there is a sense of connection to these people.

The Participation Nonprofit

There could be instituted a new kind of organization that I will call a participation nonprofit corporation. It would be a nonprofit, aimed at a public purpose such as running a hospital, but in a different sense. The participation nonprofit would raise money by issuing shares, but buying shares in it would be a charitable contribution for tax purposes. Selling shares in it would have no tax consequences as long as the proceeds were donated to other charitable causes, such as by buying shares in other participation nonprofits. The shareholder could sell the shares and consume the money from the sale, but such actions would be subject to a substantial tax penalty. The organization would distribute profits to shareholders with the stipulation that they could use their share of the profits only for charitable purposes, including possibly investing in other participation nonprofits. By distributing its profits, the organization would solve the "trapped capital" problem to which I alluded in Chapter 17: the profits would come back to the participation nonprofit itself only if the shareholders saw value in that.

If one donates to a cause, such as a new nonprofit hospital or a new college, by buying shares in a participation nonprofit corporation, the story is not over after one makes the donation, as it is with conventional charitable contributions. One now has a psychological stake, akin to ownership, in the nonprofit. One can look forward to receiving dividends and watching one's stake in the organization grow. One can watch the market price of the nonprofit rise and fall; those price changes are (admittedly imperfect) indicators of the underlying success of the nonprofit. With their dividends, shareholders can even set up their own private foundations (with their names on them), though they cannot consume the dividends without incurring a serious penalty.

If the investment proves highly successful they can use their dividends to underwrite new buildings with their names on them, or they can make other charitable donations with their names attached. They might also be allowed to spend the money on themselves, without incurring a tax penalty, in the case of a certified family emergency. Allowing investing in such a participation nonprofit might be a way to generate more widespread interest in public causes, since it would give people a sense of participation and accumulation, allow for memories of one's past largesse, provide what would in a sense be a "playable game" to occupy time, and allow for more ego involvement in a chosen cause. We saw earlier that the invention of tradable common stock shares in for-profit corporations was an important innovation because, by making investing in companies fun, it increased the amount of capital available to them. The establishment of participation nonprofits may well offer the same advantage.

And yet the participation nonprofit will probably still be viewed by most people, such as patients in a hospital or students at a new school, as a nonprofit, and so they will be likely to have the same goodwill toward it. They may even have greater goodwill, if they are connected to institutional or other shareholders in the participation nonprofit.

Other Ways to Improve the Effectiveness of Philanthropy

Many wealthy people may see a problem with the contribution deduction in its present form, in that donations have to be made every year during the period that one is earning the income to accumulate a fortune. If one does not make contributions regularly each year, one misses the deduction almost completely. If one defers giving, one has paid heavy taxes on the income and does not recoup the past taxes upon finally making a gift. U.S. tax law allows up to a five-year carryforward of deductible contributions, which means that amounts contributed in any year that exceed the percentage-of-income limit can be deducted in subsequent years—but there is no carryback.

Most wealthy people would like to accumulate a huge fortune first and then give it away later when they have had time to think about what they will do with the fortune—time to think carefully about the mark they are making on the world. If marginal tax rates were much higher, we might rule out altogether the possibility of the wealthy accumulating a fortune at the same time they are busy making a living and then undertaking a major philanthropic project like funding a school or research foundation with the accumulated money after they retire. This problem is purely one of timing—and if not addressed, it may make higher-than-current income tax rates seem far more onerous than they would really be.

In fact, current U.S. law allows people to substantially solve this problem, by giving away a significant share of their income while they are young to a private foundation or donor-advised fund, which will accumulate their fortune for them tax-free and then allow them, years later, to choose (within certain limits) how to give it away. (Donor-advised funds are like private foundations without the hassle: they are designed for the general public and even allow people to put their names on their charitable contributions.)

So one may think that donor-advised funds eliminate the timing problem. Even if income tax rates for high-income individuals were raised substantially, wealthy people could still have the satisfaction of accumulating large fortunes (within their private foundations or donor-advised funds, to which we might also add participation nonprofits) and still see their names in the Forbes 400 (if Forbes decides to include such funds in their calculations, which would be a logical step)—even though in effect they would have already given the bulk of their wealth away. Problem solved? Not quite.

Tax provisions on private foundations and donor-advised funds are still not well designed from a behavioral economics perspective. People plainly enjoy accumulating wealth, even if it is only symbolic. Yet at the present time under U.S. law these funds are required to distribute 5% of their assets to qualifying contributions each year (with some exceptions for special projects, but then too only a five-year exception). This means that in most cases increases in the assets of the foundation or fund will be small or nonexistent. And there is a limit—currently 30% of income—for deductions made for contributions to donor-advised funds that delay spending contributions for more than a year.

Something isn't working well with these funds. The five largest donor-advised funds in the United States together have total assets of less than $10 billion, and so they represent about two-hundredths of 1% of the national wealth. Private foundations and donor-advised funds should be allowed to accumulate.

Presumably something could also be done to make these funds more convenient, such as offering a check-off on the tax form that would automatically create a donor-advised fund account to enable a last-minute deduction for the tax filer, thereby dramatically lowering his or her tax liability.

We can imagine other advantages to amassing a large fortune that is dedicated to helping others. For example, there could be a new provision in the law that the founder of a private foundation could withdraw any amount of the money, before it is spent on philanthropy, to pay medical expenses for anyone of the founder's choosing. Paying a family member's (or anyone's) medical expenses directly is not currently considered a deductible contribution. If this were changed, then a wealthy person who had contributed his or her fortune to a private foundation would still be perceived as wealthy and as a pillar of strength on whom others could rely. This change would further encourage giving.

There should be no limitation on the share of income that could be given away—unlike the provisions of current U.S. law, under which contribution deductions are limited to 50% of income (in some situations to 30% or even 20%) and the deduction appears to be in danger of being reduced even further.[19] Moreover, deductions for gifts abroad should also be allowed, as philanthropy knows no borders. Gifts made directly abroad are now deductible in the United States only when the gift is to certain organizations in Canada.

The law could also be changed to permit new kinds of organizations devoted to the public good that may be better able to reward their donors. The benefit corporation, described previously, is an example of such innovation. We need to experiment with such new organizations, and to continually improve their structure in light of our knowledge of human nature and our experience with existing organizations.

Goals and Our Lives

We all need to think more about the ultimate purpose of our wealth. The basic theme of this book is finance as a means for achieving goals. But we have seen that most of us have trouble with the final step of actually realizing a basic goal. We become involved in the steps along the way, and some of us may accumulate large fortunes, only to see our grip weakening as the goal comes into sight, so that the fortunes are never spent constructively.

Psychological research has shown that when people act altruistically, they are happier, less likely to be depressed.[20] Altruistic acts in a social context are an effective antidepressant. Showy houses and luxury cars do not bring happiness. Individual fulfillment depends on a sense of meaning and purpose, and society should act so as to encourage individual actions that reinforce such meaning, including encouraging the giving away of accumulated wealth.

There is a positive externality for all of us in seeing a society in which altruistic acts are common, and so governments should encourage such acts, even if the encouragement might be interpreted by some as appealing to selfish motives. There is often a fine line between selfishness and altruism, but a tax law that encourages people to accumulate wealth in order to gain recognition for giving it away should have the effect of promoting the general sense of a good society.

The real risk, if we do not set up policies that encourage philanthropy, is that many may be left with meaninglessness, individually and collectively. Finance concerns itself with risk management—but not with the risk of meaninglessness. Dealing with that risk is left to our conscience and to our human spirit.

Chapter 29

The Dispersal of Ownership of Capital

The history of financial capitalism is to a substantial extent a history of deliberate government policies to disperse financial interests, to disperse ownership across a wider segment of the population. Such policies have helped democratize finance.

People seldom realize to what extent we live in a society that is structured by financial design to become better and better over time. The history that brought us to certain financial arrangements is often forgotten, and it is useful to remind ourselves of some of that history. Here I offer some examples of past progress that is unseen and unappreciated today.

A modern market economy seems to many observers increasingly to be run by a relatively small number of business leaders who are, by virtue of their financial and general business savvy, excessively influential. To these same observers it may seem at times that the more free-spirited among us will not want to participate in top management at all, for such a role seems to entail a mindset that they find repugnant. The wealthiest and most influential people in our society may come to seem like ensconced feudal lords, lacking in essential humanity, who set the pace for society as a whole. Then the majority of us may feel as if we are mere serfs in a society that puts the ambitious and inhumane at the top.

William O. Douglas, the second head of the SEC and later a U.S. Supreme Court justice, wrote as follows in 1940:

> In big business, management tends to become impersonal. The huge aggregations of capital of big business mean that the number of public security hold-

ers is large. These investors are largely scattered. Management acquires a sort of feudal tenure as a result of the utter dependence of the public security holders on them. . . . There can be no question that the laxity in business morals has a direct relationship to the size of business. Empires so vast as to defy the intimate understanding of any one man tend to become playthings for manipulation.[1]

Douglas was part of President Franklin D. Roosevelt's New Deal: Roosevelt nominated him to the Supreme Court in 1939. The New Deal was a relatively humanizing social force, even as it retained the real strength and integrity that characterize the best financial solutions.

This loss of a sense of individual participation in society was the concern that occupied Friedrich Hayek in his 1944 book *The Road to Serfdom*. He tended to focus on excessive *government* intervention as the source of the problem, rather than the practices of big business, but he also spoke of government being captured by big business.[2] Excessive reliance on such large controlling entities, Hayek believed, leads to a defeated attitude, the attitude of serfs.

It may seem odd that his major treatise on capitalism was published near the end of World War II, a time when one might think society would have been occupied by much more pressing concerns. But the timing is not as surprising as it might seem, for World War II was also a time of struggle between economic systems, and a time when people wondered how the Nazi leaders could command such outrageous crimes from some of those they governed— even going so far as to carry out the orders that resulted in the Holocaust. Hayek wondered at the deeper underpinnings of support for such a party, or for any organization. The serf mentality of which he spoke was a social phenomenon of the utmost interest.

The modern capitalist system with all of its regulatory machinery may, if power within it does not become too centralized and institutionalized, be *liberating* from just such a serf mentality. If the right rules are in place, they may pave the way for the development of a multitude of creative organizations that can achieve far more than any individual, however free, ever could. The set of rules and assumptions that allow orderly businesses to be initiated and then to proceed represents a kind of social capital that is enabling for creativity.

The dispersal of *information* about the economy and its opportunities across millions of people—with their different situations, different locations, different eyes and ears—is a given. Hayek emphasized this.[3] We need also to facilitate, on top of that arrangement, a dispersal of *control*. This can be done by encouraging broader public participation in shareholding in corporations, or by giving tax preferences to small firms, or by other means to encourage the dispersal of property holding throughout the population.

Collectively we can make a deliberate decision to plan a more broadly based financial capitalism. Such a plan can be compared with traditional communism, which similarly sought to equalize ownership. But that system had control over property, if not its actual ownership, centralized in the government, in the hands of a bureaucracy. This centralized model has been falling out of favor around the world, since such centralization of control does not allow truly broad participation and does not allow people to use their diverse information actively to direct the use of capital.

The term *ownership society*, referring to a society in which citizenship and responsibility are encouraged by the widespread ownership of and control over individual properties, is attributed to President George W. Bush; he popularized the term in his 2004 reelection campaign. It is an expression of the desirability of the democratization of finance. But the idea goes back much further in history than that.

Land Reform

In centuries past, when agriculture constituted the bulk of national product, policies to disperse ownership of capital were concentrated on land. Land reforms that encouraged (or forced) landlords to give up their holdings and that distributed farmland took their impetus from the French Revolution at the end of the eighteenth century, which transferred ownership of land from the ancien régime to individual family farms.[4] Following this example, there were numerous land reforms in the nineteenth and twentieth centuries, in Albania, Bolivia, Brazil, Bulgaria, Canada, Chile, China, Colombia, Croatia, Cuba, Czechoslovakia, Denmark, Egypt, El Salvador, Estonia, Ethiopia, Finland, Germany, Greece, Guatemala, Hungary, India, Iran, Ireland, Japan, Kenya, Lithuania, Mexico, Namibia, Nicaragua, Peru, the Philippines, Poland, Romania, Russia, Slovenia, South Africa, South Korea, Syria, Taiwan, Venezuela, Vietnam, and Zimbabwe.

These land reforms, while sometimes imposed harshly, did usually represent real social progress, and they helped economic growth. For example, the South Korean postwar economic growth miracle has been attributed to that country's land reform and the resulting lessening of income inequality after the Japanese occupiers were expelled with the end of World War II. The South Korean Agricultural Land Reform Amendment Act (ALRAA) of 1950 specified that anyone could own agricultural land but only if he or she actually farmed it, set at three hectares the maximum amount of agricultural land that any one individual could own, and prohibited tenancy arrangements and land-renting. Landlords were forced to sell their lands in exchange for government debt, the land to be redistributed to smallholders.

Even before the ALRAA took effect, after World War II the rich landlords were already selling much of their land to small owners at relatively low prices. The landlords' position in Korean society was growing untenable because they were generally viewed as having been complicit with the Japanese occupiers, and many even began to fear for their personal safety. The end result was that wealth was extracted from the South Korean landlords (in a more peaceful way than in China or North Korea after the communist revolutions there) to lower inequality, effect a modernization of Korean society, and launch that country's economic miracle.[5]

The United States has a long and unusual history of land reform since it had available vast undeveloped public lands. Andrew Johnson, Horace Greeley, and others argued that ownership of one's own farm was healthy for democracy. Their efforts led to the passage of the Homestead Act of 1862, which divided up public lands and sold small farms to individual families. The act was passed during the U.S. Civil War, after southern votes representing the plantation system had been removed from Congress. The rationale underlying northern support for individual small farms was succinctly explained, just before the war, by the *Chicago Press and Tribune:*

> It should be the policy of our government to encourage the multiplication of landed proprietorships. The history of the world proves that the larger the proportion of land-owners in any given country, the greater is the degree of personal liberty, the greater the progress in civilization, and the greater the security of the nation from external attack. Slavery is impossible, as a permanent institution, except where the ownership of the soil is confined almost exclusively to the slave-holding class. . . . A prosperous non-slaveholding class, identified with the country by the ownership of a portion of it, would soon become powerful and dangerous opponents of slavery.[6]

A good part of the sense of equality and common good feeling that exists in America today probably owes its origin at least in part to this democratic nineteenth-century land reform.

Homeownership

Government policies to encourage urban individual home ownership, instead of just farm ownership, tended to come later, as the world became urbanized. These policies have discouraged the development of huge corporations that might have operated rental properties for the general public. Instead we have a large home-owning population in the United States and other more developed countries. This did not happen by accident.

The concept of a "property-owning democracy" was developed by Conservative British member of Parliament Noel Skelton in the 1920s and 1930s. His cause was taken up by Prime Minister Harold Macmillan in the 1950s, with a home building program, and Prime Minister Margaret Thatcher in the 1970s, with a program to sell council houses (public housing managed by local councils) to their renter inhabitants.

In the United States major policies to promote homeownership came in the 1930s with President Franklin D. Roosevelt's New Deal. The Federal Housing

Administration was created in 1934 to provide for government insurance of new mortgages, and the Federal National Mortgage Association (later called Fannie Mae) was created in 1938 to buy mortgages from their originators to support the housing market.

China, with its communist ideology, came late to the ownership society concept. But the Chinese government eventually made homeownership a priority. In 1998 China created a Housing Provident Fund for all its citizens, a compulsory saving plan with employer matching. The government also created an affordable housing program that subsidized construction of low- to moderate-income housing. Associated with these initiatives has been a rapid expansion of the Chinese home mortgage market (although it is still relatively small). As of 2004 total mortgages in China amounted to US$1.6 trillion, or a little over $1,000 per capita. Total mortgage value then was only 5% of total urban residential property value, but it was growing fast.

The idea of encouraging homeownership pops up everywhere. Noel Pearson, an Australian aborigine who has campaigned for the rights of indigenous peoples, in 2004 founded an advocacy organization for them, the Cape York Institute. On their web site we find a plea for public policy to encourage homeownership:

> There is now an inter-generational expectation within Indigenous communities, that governments will provide, maintain, and in the end replace their housing. Like other forms of passive welfare over the past three decades, public housing in Indigenous communities has promoted dependency and passivity. The Institute believes that we must break this dependency and reintroduce personal responsibility. This must entail moving towards home ownership solutions where families make sacrifices to acquire or build a home of their choice and take ongoing responsibility for its maintenance.[7]

Homeownership, in contrast to land ownership or stock ownership, does not usually directly involve people in any specific business. But it has been widely thought of as helping to create a market-oriented psychology that encourages other kinds of property ownership as well, and as encouraging a feeling of participation and equality in society.

In some other countries—notably Switzerland, which recently has had a low homeownership rate (only 35% of households, per its 2000 census, compared with 65% in the United States)—it is apparently the ownership of stocks and bonds that contributes to a feeling of participation. In Switzerland—where the mountainous land is considered a common heritage of all Swiss, and where the banking system and financial sophistication are elements of national pride—it is rather natural that the ownership society would take this form. Swiss laws regarding rentals make the rental market work to a high level of satisfaction among the renters. Because of a high level of confidence in their financial system, the Swiss have not supported government subsidies of their owner-occupied housing.

In other countries—such as Spain, in which over 90% of households owned their own homes before the recent severe financial crisis—the high ownership rate is substantially the result of government policy. Spanish rental policy, instituted after the Spanish Civil War of 1936–39, had made it very difficult to evict renters, and hence few properties in that country are offered for rent. Starting in the 1950s, Spanish laws facilitated the conversion of apartment buildings into condominiums suitable for purchase.[8]

Government policy should not overemphasize homeownership, for the overreaching of the ownership society concept has in the past led to government policies that tried—particularly in certain countries, notably the United States and Spain—to get too high a fraction of the population into homeownership. This in turn helped feed a housing bubble that eventually burst and served as a prime cause of the severe financial crisis that began in 2007. But in general a degree of government support for individual homeownership, particularly targeted at lower-income and marginal households, will contribute to a better society.

Ownership of Investment Portfolios

A real sense of participation in society and the economy may be promoted more broadly by policies that encourage more business-oriented ownership, notably ownership of broad portfolios representing the real productive assets of the country.

Singapore, under Lee Kuan Yew, led the way to an ownership society with its Central Provident Fund, a mandatory saving plan for its citizens, with both employer and employee contributions, that allowed them to purchase both international investments in stocks and bonds and also housing for themselves in Singapore. He reflected: "The CPF has made for a different society. People who have substantial savings and assets have a different attitude toward life. They are more conscious of their strength and take responsibility for themselves and their families."[9]

Defined contribution pension plans, which began in the early 1980s in the United States, also encourage people to become owners of investment portfolios, ostensibly to provide a pension for them, an income in retirement. They do not serve pensioners optimally in their present form, for they leave them open to making mistakes in planning for their retirement. But they do get people involved in financial decision making and allow them to feel more a part of a society that takes so much of its structure from finance.[10]

All of these policies, in many different countries around the world, were efforts to democratize and humanize finance, to make finance serve people and to encourage people to consider themselves participants in a society built on the principles of finance.

Policies That Promote Employee Ownership of Business

Louis O. Kelso (the founder of the private equity firm Kelso & Co.) and Mortimer J. Adler (who created the Syntopicon series of great books), in a pair of best-selling books, *The Capitalist Manifesto* in 1958 and *The New Capitalists* in 1961, presented a plan aimed at achieving more dispersed ownership of business. These books are probably almost totally forgotten today. And yet they have left a legacy of better employee morale.

The books were published at a time when people were troubled about the state of relations between labor and management. In the 1950s, when the labor movement in the United States was gaining strength, there was much concern about the unfortunate "dual loyalty" of workers.[11] It was claimed that no one could be loyal to both labor union and firm. To achieve good morale and high effectiveness in the workplace, it is helpful if the worker feels loyalty to the employer. On the other hand, when there is a contentious labor-management situation, the worker may feel greater loyalty to his or her union. The conflict creates stress for workers and may lead to perplexing ethical quandaries.

There is a basic tribal instinct to be loyal to a group with which one associates on a daily basis. Membership in the group becomes a source of identity. George Akerlof and Rachel Kranton, in their book *Identity Economics*, stress that this identity is fundamental to economic behavior.[12] A psychological experiment they describe randomly divided boys into two groups. The experiment showed that even though everyone knew the groupings were random, there was a dramatic change in the boys' behavior as group identities began to develop: the groups became rivals and the boys became intensely motivated by the rivalry. We form these identity-defining relationships casually, almost randomly, based on who we encounter, and our beliefs then tend to conform gradually to those of the group. Akerlof and Kranton stress that this all makes for a rather absurd element of the human experience.

The development of modern communications technology and means of transportation, and the rise of multinational corporations, have tended to change tendencies toward loyalty in unpredictable ways. The general tendency may be to reduce national loyalties. The automobile allows the formation of separate enclaves of rich and poor. The Internet allows people to define for themselves the subgroup from which they will learn and with which they will communicate every day.

Both of the Kelso and Adler books envisioned changes to our financial institutions that would improve our sense of loyalty to our business colleagues. And while they didn't completely "solve" the problem of dual loyalty, they have helped lead us to a better form of financial capitalism.

The first of the two books was a plea for what are now called employee stock ownership plans (ESOPs), whereby companies encourage their employees to participate in the ownership of the firm by obtaining stock in the firm.

The authors argued that such a plan would motivate employees to work more effectively and help create a capitalist culture.

The ideas in the book may at first have seemed rather unlikely to be implemented, but sixteen years later the U.S. Congress enacted tax incentives for such plans with the Employee Retirement Income Security Act of 1974, which institutionalized the ESOP.

It took many years before serious research was done to see whether the Kelso-Adler proposal for ESOPs had really had any of the intended effects. It has been learned that indeed, as Kelso and Adler predicted, on-the-job shirking is common in businesses everywhere, and that when such plans are introduced they reduce the tendency of workers to shirk. This happens even though rational-person economics implies that ESOPs would have virtually no such effect, except in the tiniest of firms. Under that calculation, each worker would rationally conclude that he or she might as well shirk, even with an ESOP in place, because the positive effects of an individual worker's efforts are divided up over all stakeholders in the enterprise, while the negative feeling of effort is experienced by just the worker, and thus effort has a negative effect on just that worker. Yet apparently, in a firm with an ownership plan, an anti-shirking culture develops.[13] It has also been found that employees of firms with ESOPs have higher wealth overall, perhaps because the ownership plan encourages a more capitalist culture.[14] The intuitive foundations on which Kelso and Adler built their theory were shown to have some validity, based on latter-day behavioral economics research, even though they could not articulate their vision in terms that would have been taken seriously by the mainstream economists of their time.

In their 1961 book *The New Capitalists*, Kelso and Adler proposed a Capital Diffusion Insurance Corporation that would guarantee loans to encourage the founding of small businesses, thereby increasing the diversity of such businesses and allowing for new startups that might someday grow into bigger businesses. This is another proposal that would serve to bring more and more people into the process of financing business, while creating positive externalities in terms of a better business culture.

At the time, this proposal was greeted by some as just another strange idea. But once again Kelso and Adler were simply ahead of their time. Their argument actually convinced some congressional leaders to effect change. The U.S. Small Business Administration (SBA) had been created in 1953 to replace the Depression-era Reconstruction Finance Corporation, and it was then a maker rather than a guarantor of loans. The SBA, in its original form, might well have been shut down because of its excessive quantity of bad loans, which ultimately defaulted, at cost to taxpayers. To follow Kelso and Adler's proposal and involve the public in the selection of loans to be made, it became evident that the SBA should leave the actual lending to the public. Thus the SBA was transformed from a lender into a partial guarantor of small business loans.

Today the public has an incentive to participate in the risk-taking, relieving the taxpayer of the full burden.[15] The activities of the SBA as they are today are useful, but they could be further improved by placing more emphasis on subsidizing the most innovative small business ideas.[16]

Concentration Limits

Competition law, which dates back to ancient times, has long attempted to reduce the power of large monopolies. The development of modern capitalist institutions brought with it newfound opportunities for very large organizations, and in response competition law has become more aggressive in antitrust policies, in breaking up (or preventing the formation of) companies that are so large that they seriously inhibit competition. Lobbyists for these companies will try to derail such efforts and argue that much is lost by such breakups. But there can be many advantages as well.

The current financial crisis has generated calls for preventing the increased concentration of economic power, but so far the response has not been very effective. In the United States the Dodd-Frank Act of 2010 introduced a concentration limit for financial firms: subject to some discretion and with a few exceptions, no financial company may merge with, consolidate with, or acquire another company if the resulting company's consolidated liabilities would "exceed 10 percent of the aggregate consolidated liabilities of all financial companies."[17]

The motivation for creating this concentration limit was ostensibly to reduce the "too big to fail" problem, the concern that some financial companies had become so central to the economy that they would have to be bailed out by the government in the event of pending failure. But this limit plausibly had something to do as well with some of the issues emphasized in this chapter— those of making our financial markets more democratic amidst widespread resentment of the concentration of wealth and power.

This is a significant, though rather weak, limit on the size of financial companies. According to a 2011 study by the U.S. Financial Stability Oversight Council, based on currently available data sources and definitions it is difficult to ascertain just how many financial firms are already near or over this 10% limit; however, there may well be some to which the Dodd-Frank provision would apply.[18]

It may be that the framers of Dodd-Frank settled on a limit of 10% because it seemed just beyond a situation that would require action today. And indeed no actions have been taken, or appear to be in immediate prospect, to reduce the concentration of power in U.S. financial firms.

As an alternative to concentration limits, the government could merely impose an incentive system to discourage large concentrations of power in financial firms. The corporate profits tax in the United States today is progressive; that is, it taxes large corporations at a higher rate. But the tax brackets are set so that only the smallest of firms have lower tax rates. The tax laws could be arranged differently, so as to discourage the formation of really massive financial firms in favor of less-dominant ones. Moreover, as suggested by the Squam Lake Group, capital requirements on large and systemically important financial institutions could be systematically raised.[19]

The Combined Effects of Policies to Disperse Capital

The policies of the past to disperse ownership of farms, homes, and companies are part of the reason we have a sense of equality and participation in our society today. The policies themselves are largely unknown to most people, but they see their effects. We often seem inclined to think that the current ownership structure happened naturally. In fact the widespread ownership of farms, homes, and companies and the various forms of employee participation plans that we see today are all part of a public policy that has as a tangible benefit a significant improvement in public morale. These are not best described as "government plans," for, though they were in fact implemented through government action, the ideas come from the people themselves and in response to popular concerns.

In the future we will need to be vigilant to prevent the concentration of economic power, and we should work to disperse the ownership of capital even further. Doing so effectively and efficiently, so that the net results are beneficial and not destructive of productivity, and in ways that take account of new developments in finance and information technology, will require continuing attention and innovation.

Chapter 30

The Great Illusion,
Then and Now

In 1910 Norman Angell, a British member of Parliament, documented a widespread and dangerous misconception through his best-selling book *The Great Illusion: A Study of the Relation of Military Power to National Advantage*. The great illusion was, in Angell's words, an "optical illusion" that stood as "an all but universal idea": the belief that

> a nation's financial and industrial stability, its security in commercial activity —in short, its prosperity and well-being, depend upon its being able to defend itself against the aggression of other nations, who will, if they are able, be tempted to commit such aggression because in so doing they will increase *their* power and consequently *their* prosperity and well-being, at the cost of the weaker and vanquished.[1]

In short the illusion was that military conquest brings economic advantage. This misconception persisted despite Angell's book and, quite arguably, led to uncompromising and provocative actions by governments, and ultimately to World War I. Despite the fact that the book did not bring about peace, in 1934 Angell won the Nobel Peace Prize for it.

Angell argued that this "universal idea" was without merit, and yet he saw evidence that people deeply believed in it, in numerous speeches, newspaper articles, and books. It was a politically destabilizing meme that had spread throughout society. The idea became widely and uncritically accepted that human nature is inherently warlike—that we should not lament that reality but understand that we who are alive today are descended from the victors in previous wars, and accept that military victory is an expression of human excellence. The idea, and the assumption that other nations thought similarly, led to expectations of future attack and a justification for preemptive strikes—strikes that might start a war.

Today we no longer widely share this once-commonplace illusion. Few people in the twenty-first century think that it would be economically advantageous for Europe to attempt to conquer the United States or the reverse, or for Japan to conquer Korea or the reverse.

But we still suffer from an analogous illusion: an illusion that those in the business world will stand to benefit from business conquest, from aggressive and inhuman business tactics. Thus people *think* that the wealthy in our society —among them the financiers—have a real and genuine incentive to use devious means to attack and subjugate, economically, the majority of the population.

To take a concrete example, people widely assume that it was in Goldman Sachs's interest to deliberately double-deal its clients, as it allegedly did in 2007, urging securities on them that Goldman thought would eventually fail, because the securities were designed to benefit a different client, Paulson & Co.—a fact not disclosed to the clients. At the same time Goldman Sachs was effectively taking short positions in these same securities.[2]

As another example, people widely assume that Countrywide Financial Corporation deliberately issued and securitized mortgages that they believed would ultimately default. It has been claimed that the subprime mortgage collapse that brought on the current financial crisis was a deliberate plot by Countrywide and other mortgage lenders.[3]

There may well have been some moral lapses behind these events, but it is not correct to claim that these institutions acted deliberately in full knowledge of the actual outcome. To the extent that they misbehaved, it was not really in their ex ante interest to do so.

The assumption today, analogous to Angell's great illusion, often seems to be that businesses have a real incentive to behave in an aggressive and evil manner. This assumption, if left unchallenged, will create resentment toward business that will inhibit its proper functioning, thus threatening to slow the advance of the world's prosperity in coming years.

The Great Illusion, 1910

Concerns about the possibility of war were widespread at the time Angell wrote, just before World War I: the arms race among the countries of Europe was taking on alarming proportions. The race created an unsettled psychology throughout the continent. It appeared that every country was arming itself because of a fear of attack by another. But that situation was absurd on its face, since no government was in fact threatening to attack. They were all only talking about defense. The fear of attack came not from their words but from the great illusion.

The great illusion, the belief in the primacy of human aggression, must have seemed plausible to many in the years before World War I and World War II because of a careless and loose extrapolation of Darwin's theory of evolution to the affairs of modern states. Yet the extrapolators of Darwin's theory typically paid little direct attention to his works, and one of the most influential of them, Friedrich Nietzsche, actually labeled himself as "anti-Darwin." But even Nietzsche adopted something akin to a survival-of-the-fittest frame of reference.[4]

Humankind has been in a perpetual state of warfare, it was argued by many at the time, as with all living things. We who are alive today, it was thought, are the survivors of a bitter struggle, and our very intelligence and talents are the result of that struggle.

Angell argued that it would be absurd for any country to attempt to conquer another, for in the modern economy no conceivable economic advantage could accrue from such an attack. Armed warfare may have made sense in ancient times, but no longer. According to the synopsis at the beginning of the 1910 book,

> wealth in the economically civilized world is founded upon credit and commercial contract (these being the outgrowth of an economic interdependence due to the increasing division of labour and greatly developed communication). If credit and commercial contract are tampered with in an attempt at confiscation, the credit-dependent wealth is undermined, and its collapse involves that of the conqueror; so that if conquest is not to be self-injurious it must respect the enemy's property, in which case it becomes economically futile. Thus the wealth of conquered territory remains in the hands of the population of such territory.[5]

Angell emphasized that there is nothing really to be gained by conquering another country because the victor could find little of value that could actually be taken from the conquered. He provided an analysis of the reparations payments imposed by the victor, Germany, on the vanquished, France, after the 1870–71 Franco-Prussian War, and he concluded that, paradoxically, the French who were making the reparations payments fared better than the Germans who were receiving those payments. The problem, as Angell emphasized in a chapter entitled "The Indemnity Futility," was that countries by and large do not have large amounts of gold or other transferable things of value—far too little to pay the huge reparations demanded by the victors in modern warfare. So the reparations must take the form of exports of new goods and services. The paying country must somehow develop a huge export industry, of unnatural proportions, to pay the reparations. Making the payments must entail something like the "dumping" or "unfair competition" that free traders deplore. And receiving the payments drives out the businesses in the same sector in the receiving country, thereby depressing that country's economy. So there can in fact be no benefit to the conqueror:

> For a modern nation to add to its territory no more adds to the wealth of the people of such nation than it would add to the wealth of Londoners if the City of London were to annex the county of Hertford. It is a change of administration which may be good or bad, but as tribute has become under modern economic conditions impossible (which means that taxes collected from a given territory must directly or indirectly be spent on that territory), the fiscal situation of the people concerned is unchanged by the conquest.[6]

Another element of this great illusion is taken up by Angell in a chapter entitled "The Psychological Case for War." Advocates of military aggressiveness argued that military victory, by demonstrating heroism, hardiness, and tenacity, reinforces national morale, and that it has a psychological benefit to the victorious country in stimulating its economy. It is hard to quantify such an effect, but, Angell argued, we do know that against these presumed advantages of a warlike philosophy there is the perpetual burden of maintaining a military force, and of occupying a sullen and angry vanquished country. The resentment of the oppressed ultimately proves so costly, in terms of emotional ambience and risk of future war, as to wipe out the psychological advantages gained from victory. This is the burden of empire, noted many times throughout human history.

Angell's book was for the most part misinterpreted in its time. People thought he was asserting that because the economies of the modern world were so interconnected, war was no longer possible. So the sudden outbreak of World War I in 1914 discredited the book in the eyes of many. It was widely derided and was cited by some commentators as evidence of great naïveté among intellectuals about the real prospect of war in the modern world.

But Angell's book did not actually assert that war was no longer possible. In a 1933 edition of the book, lamenting that the great illusion was still very much with us, Angell explained that he had, when he first wrote the book in 1908, actually suppressed his fears of something like World War I:

> To have given the very first emphasis to the fact that war was certainly coming unless we changed our ideas and our policy, would have had with the ordinary reader of 1908 just one effect—to make him shout for more Dreadnoughts. The author saw and expressed this difficulty. . . . But in clarifying the fact of avoidability he may have allowed an impression of improbability or "impossibility" to grow up in some reader's mind.[7]

As had happened many times before and has happened many times since, even the most thoughtful discussions are curtailed by considerations of their effects on public confidence and the possible results of talking openly about worries for the future.

The Great Illusion as the Ultimate Cause of World War I

The fears generated by the arms race before World War I created a state of mind that led to a startlingly swift descent into war in 1914. There were countless proximate causes of this descent; we have to drill down to the ultimate causes. The war began with a seemingly minor event, the assassination of Archduke Franz Ferdinand of Austria in Sarajevo by a small fringe group, on June 28, 1914. The assassination would not at the time have seemed significant on a worldwide scale. The assassin, Gavrilo Princip, explained his motives after his capture: "I am a Yugoslav nationalist and I believe in unification of all South Slavs in whatever form of state and that it be free of Austria."[8] Most people around the world, occupied with their own concerns, wouldn't have cared one way or another about his cause, and so it may seem a puzzle that this event was the immediate trigger for World War I.

But a feedback loop took its first turn when Austria demanded that neighboring Serbia take action against an underground railroad that supported the terrorists. Serbia, whose relations with Austria were strained, acceded to only some of the demands. Austria in turn invaded Serbia on July 28, 1914. Both countries had military alliances with other countries, who were thus drawn into the conflict. The events drew public attention to long-standing animosities among these other countries as well, and a war fever erupted that proved unstoppable. Politicians, after mobilizing their armies in response to the public's appetite for war, could not realistically demobilize for fear of the internal political consequences. According to historian Gordon Martel's 2008 assessment of the public spirit at the very beginning of that war,

> It may now be difficult for us to imagine a time and a place in which war was not only acceptable but popular. . . . The kind of thinking that led people to rejoice at the prospect of war is now difficult to recapture—but rejoice they did: there was dancing in the streets and spontaneous demonstrations of support for governments throughout Europe; men flocking to recruitment offices, fearful that the war might end before they had the opportunity to fight; there was a spirit of festival and a sense of community in all European cities as old class divisions and political rivalries were replaced by patriotic fervor.[9]

That fever pitch was not purely psychological, for it was ultimately informed by an idea—the idea that Angell had called the great illusion, which inspired a genuine feeling of individual self-actualization through war.

The Great Illusion in Business Today

The great illusion lived on long enough in public discourse to pave the way for a second world war, just as Angell had suggested in the 1930s.[10] But by now we are much less afflicted by his illusion—as it applies to nation-states.

Yet we still must deal with the popular notion that corporations and wealthy individuals have an interest in "conquest," just as states were once thought to have. The idea is widely held that extremely wealthy people in our society have an interest as a group in aggressively preventing even the most modest redistribution, through taxes or regulation, that would tend to diminish their extreme wealth.

Amassing a large fortune may seem to many to be a real way to boost one's self-esteem; many of the honors that are routinely awarded for achievement are considered suspect, as they may have been awarded carelessly or for ulterior motives. But we tend to feel that when someone amasses a significant fortune it is proof of some real talent associated with genuine business acumen. There appears to be no "nonsense" about such an undeniable achievement. The winner was not announced by an effete intellectual society or obscure government bureaucrat. But people are admired for such an accomplishment only if they stay within certain limits in their business dealings. Being too zealous in acquiring and defending wealth does not inspire admiration, and so we should not expect most wealthy people to engage in such behavior.

Something similar to the indemnity futility that Angell described between nations also applies between social classes in business. If the wealthy do somehow manage to economically subjugate the majority of the population, thus angering them, what then can the majority still transfer to the wealthy that is of real value to them? Once again, it cannot be gold or other tangible goods, for the subjugated majority will no longer have much of such things. It must take the form of services provided to the wealthy. Yet in providing these services, they would be taking away those industries from the wealthy themselves. The wealthy and the members of their families would lose a sense of involvement and purpose.

The "psychological case for war" that Angell described is another part of the great illusion that is used to argue that people and social classes derive an inherent advantage from having, and maintaining a tight grip on, great wealth. It is true that acquiring great wealth does appear to provide an ego boost to the members of a wealthy family. And, within some limits, it permits them to achieve more by granting them better education and time to devote to pursuits beyond earning a living. But it does not give them a boost in terms of their overall psychological well-being, and it does not appear to motivate them, or their children, to achieve on a higher level.

Such an illusion threatens to halt the very kind of financial development that the world desperately needs. Just as the news media perpetuated Angell's great illusion before the world wars, doing so because it made for an attention-grabbing story, so too are they perpetuating the great illusion today.

The great illusion that Angell discerned was an *idea*—and there can be great danger in ideas, such as this one, that sow mistrust. This particular idea may have, for all practical purposes, caused two world wars. There is similar danger in the idea that people will relentlessly pursue wealth in business, for it too sows mistrust, which in turn diminishes the possibilities for constructive business.

Life Satisfaction

Most of the real satisfaction one gets from business is not really closely related to the level of profit. One derives pleasure from making a fine product or from helping customers, from providing jobs to employees. And one simply enjoys being involved with others in a shared activity and shared business interests.

There is absolutely nothing in financial theory that says that people should value making money to the exclusion of all other rewards. On the contrary, the theory holds that people can have preferences regarding anything and everything, and it is perfectly consistent with people's natural willingness to sacrifice some income for quality of life. It is true that those in fiduciary positions, such as managers of investment funds or businesses, outside of nonprofits or benefit corporations, may be under some obligation to focus exclusively on making money for their clients or shareholders. But even then they are under such an obligation only to the extent that their principals have so informed them.

It may seem hard to believe that one might go into finance for reasons other than making money. It seems that the scorecard for this game is the money earned, and one naturally falls in with the idea that amassing the biggest possible fortune is everything.

But if one looks at the lives of *real* people in finance, the impression one gets is quite different. For example, in his autobiography, John L. Moody, the founder of Moody's Investors Service, spoke of his mission in founding the company. He admitted that he had the dream of making millions, but he also recounted that he was following a "literary or writing bent," even though it may seem implausible that there is anything literary about publishing investment manuals.[11] His motivation wasn't quite profit maximization: it was indulgence of himself in a certain pursuit that gave him personal satisfaction—and this led him ultimately to success in finance.

Many people interested in finance go into regulation. Here there is no sport in making money. Some may be surprised to learn that there are those who actually *prefer* a job in regulation, dealing with finance without the possibility of making a fortune. They find finance inherently interesting and understand that it offers satisfactions other than profit.

The futility of conquest in business mirrors the futility of conquest in war about which Angell wrote. Angell noted that it is impossible to extract much wealth from conquered countries. It is likewise impossible to extract much happiness from wealth that has been earned by antisocial financial means. There is little that one can do personally with a large fortune that is really satisfying, except to give it away. Owning a mansion or mansions is not intrinsically satisfying, as the law of diminishing returns soon sets in. One also suffers a degree of emotional distance from most people, as well as a sense of selfishness and social isolation when one is conspicuously wealthy and not sharing with others, to say nothing of fears about kidnapping or extortion.

And yet there is a common presumption, replicated constantly in the news media, that business is relentlessly selfish—and ready to attack us all, if we ever let our defenses down. This presumption leads to an atmosphere of excessive suspicion, and that atmosphere has some of the same social costs that Angell envisioned.

Just as that great illusion led in substantial measure to the world wars, so too does that same illusion in business lead to economic inefficiency and disappointment. There is a significant role for people of influence, including educators, in working to correct this illusion, and making that correction will be a fundamental step toward building the good society.

Aggression in Life and in Business

A financially sophisticated economy provides an outlet for aggression that is substantially constructive and does not result in loss of human life. That is what Montesquieu wrote about in his *Spirit of the Laws* in 1773: "The spirit of commerce is naturally attended with that of frugality, oeconomy, moderation, labour, prudence, tranquility, order, and rule. As long as this spirit subsists, the riches it produces have no bad effect. The mischief is, when excessive wealth destroys the spirit of commerce; then it is that the inconveniences of inequality begin to be felt."[12] Montesquieu did not have the benefit of knowing Darwin's theory. Nor is it clear how we should understand the word *spirit* in this context. But perhaps we are not far amiss in inferring that he is talking here about a social environment, a unique construction of the human species, that can induce changes in our aggressive tendencies.

Ethologist Konrad Lorenz, in his 1966 book *On Aggression*, concluded that most animals have evolved inhibitions against attacking their own species—inhibitions that prevent unnecessary destruction of the species. The effect of the inhibitions depends on the environment, and throughout the development of species evolution has made these inhibitions work in the environment as it is usually encountered. But alter the environment and these inhibitions may fail to function normally. Lorenz points out, as an example, that even though doves are to us the symbol of peace, if one cages two of them close together, putting them in an artificial environment where they cannot separate from each other, the stronger of the two will torture the other to death, without the arousal of any inhibition.[13]

Another ethologist, Frans de Waal, in his 1990 book *Peacemaking among Primates*, detailed how four different species of primates—chimpanzees, rhesus monkeys, stump-tailed macaques, and bonobos—all separated from humans by millions of years of evolution, have methods of reducing conflict among themselves after an argument—methods that sometimes resemble and sometimes differ significantly from analogous behavior patterns among modern humans. The exact forms of controlled aggression and reconciliation behavior are specific to the species. Chimpanzees tend to uses kisses, putting fingers in one another's mouth, and love bites, while stump-tailed monkeys tend to present their rear ends, followed by genital inspection. But all these behaviors serve a common purpose as "buffering mechanisms" to reconcile conflicting interests.[14] De Waal wonders why patterns of limited aggression, in the context of the patterns of reconciliation that follow aggression, are not seen by more people today as a good thing, worthy of appreciation as promoting a stable and effective society. Unfortunately, these patterns of aggression and reconciliation evolved in small groups, and they do not always function well on a national or international scale: human institutions must be built that exploit these behavior patterns in a constructive manner.

Steven Pinker, in his 2011 book *The Better Angels of Our Nature: Why Violence Has Declined*, reviews a number of studies showing that in the past few thousand years human society has evolved into one that makes better use of these built-in behavior patterns to reduce aggression, and that violence has dramatically subsided since the hunter-gatherer days of our species. He notes that the brain has built-in patterns of aggressiveness. For example, a sudden fit of anger can be artificially stimulated by current to an electrode implanted near the "rage circuit" of the brain, and it can be stopped by merely cutting off the current. The brain even appears to have a program that can launch a rampage, or "forward panic." The program facilitates joining a group to commit carnage against another, vulnerable, group, if a particular circuit is triggered. But Pinker argues that such violence "is not a perennial urge like hunger, sex, or the need to sleep," and that people can go through their entire lives without seeing a forward panic triggered. These "inner demons" can be controlled in a society that encourages "gentle commerce," an "expanding circle" of connections, and other socially constructive institutions.[15]

Modern society is the result of centuries of thinking about how to manage human aggressive tendencies and avoid situations in which people are confronted with others' selfish behavior, resentments become intolerable, and aggression turns into open violence. This progress has done much to sustain financial capitalism, and among its products are restraints on the inconveniences of inequality of which Montesquieu spoke. We have a tax system and a system of public goods provision that work against human aggression leading to vexing inequality—albeit, as we have noted, somewhat unsystematically and haphazardly.

Finance and Conflict Management

Albert O. Hirschman, in his 1977 book *The Passions and the Interests*, traces a history of thought about human evils and of the origin of the concept of capitalism.[16] Hirschman traces the idea that man "as he really is" is driven by passions that often create conflict. There is no escaping these passions. They are part of the natural human condition. Indeed one of the results of these passions is that the history of the world has in large measure been a succession of wars and rebellions. But, Hirschman argues, starting around the 1600s the idea gradually emerged that the best hope for reducing the damage from the unconstrained expression of these passions was to create a situation in which people have interests that countervail these passions. A modern economy, in which complex business interests develop, is just such a means of restraining passions.

Hirschman traces this train of thought from Francis Bacon to Thomas Hobbes to Niccolò Machiavelli to Charles de Montesquieu and to James Steuart. He sees the development of capitalism in terms of a gradual decline in the concept of military glory as an end that might justify the expression of angry passions, and a recognition of the imperfectability of humankind, an understanding that human passions need to be controlled to prevent war. Given this imperfectability, the concept arose of setting up a structure that would provide "countervailing passions," that is, one within which people have "material interests" that work against these passions. Material interests usually means financial interests: ownership of property, of shares, and of bonds, and long-term employment contracts.

Some academic articles have attempted to test the hypothesis that economic interconnectedness helps prevent wars. The political scientists Bruce Russett and John Oneal, in their book *Triangulating Peace*, have presented a statistical analysis of data on wars around the world from 1886 to 1992.[17] They conclude that three variables, measured for any given pair of countries, help explain the likelihood that those countries will be at war: economic interconnectedness, democratic traditions, and membership in international organizations. All three factors help prevent wars, and when all three are at their most favorable, the probability of war is reduced by 71%.

Among these factors, Russett and Oneal found economic interconnectedness to be the most important. Of course, there are difficulties in interpreting just why interconnectedness fosters peace. International economic activity may foster international communications and hence a "transnational identity," to use a term due to political scientist Bruce Cronin, or an "imagined community," to use a term from political scientist Benedict Anderson.[18] The relation could also be spurious: perhaps friendlier countries are more likely to trade with each other in the first place.

But Russett and Oneal have interpreted the effect of economic inter-connectedness, measured by volume of trade flows relative to GDP, as supporting the line of thought described by Hirschman. Economic trade creates an interest in maintaining peace. While other interpretations are possible, it appears that trade raises the cost of conflict and thus raises the benefits of maintaining peace.[19]

Montesquieu argued centuries ago that "movable wealth" prevents wars by creating a sudden and intense consequence for any military action. If countries are financially free to invest in each other, and have done so but have the freedom to withdraw their investments, then this situation creates an incentive for the owners of that capital to use their influence to prevent war.

Most studies of the incidence of war have, like Russett and Oneal, used trade flows to measure economic interconnectedness. But another study by Erik Gartzke, Quan Li, and Charles Boehmer found that *financial* inter-connectedness, namely capital flow, is a better predictor of war than any of the factors studied by Russett and Oneal.[20] They showed, using world data for the interval 1951–85, that foreign direct investment as a percentage of GDP helps explain militarized interstate disputes between pairs of countries: the higher the percentage, the lower the probability of a dispute, even after controlling for the variables used by Russett and Oneal.

Financial interconnectedness may help prevent war for deeper reasons than those associated with the perceived risk to capital movements. Financial interconnectedness provides another outlet for aggressions, a civilized stage for the playing out of aggressive impulses and an environment in which exposure to risk is carefully chosen by each player, not determined arbitrarily by a military commander. Creating a large and varied playing field for business may be like giving Lorenz's two doves, closely caged together and fighting as a result, a larger environment, one in which their conflictual tendencies have space to roam. Thus financial development may lead to a kinder and gentler—if not altogether kind and gentle—society.

With the development of modern weapons of mass destruction, the corresponding development of means for limiting aggression becomes an imperative. It is not unrealistic to suppose that we can achieve such a mechanism, and that we will achieve it by improving financial capitalism, democratizing and humanizing it, and putting a final end to the "great illusion" and its consequences.

Epilogue:
Finance, Power, and Human Values

There is one more aspect of financial capitalism, not fully dealt with in this book so far, that bothers many people deeply. And that is the economic power that some in the financial community attain. Their power in itself rankles. It offends our sense of participation in a society that aspires to respect, appreciate, and support everyone. The pursuit of power that so often seems to drive financial capitalism seems contrary to the concept, promoted in this book, that finance is all about the stewardship of society's assets.

If one searches the bookseller Amazon.com today for the phrase "wealth and power," one finds that almost eighty-five thousand books come up.[1] People may be reading these books to learn how to *achieve* wealth and power, but a good fraction of the books seem to regard the existence of the wealthy and powerful as a scandal that deserves our contempt.

Yet part of the reason successful societies develop power elites is that they need a leadership that has the power to get things done. We have to make it possible for a relatively small number of people—a management—to use their personal judgment to decide on the direction of our major activities. One of the themes of this book has been that despite rapid advances in information technology, we are still just as dependent as ever on the judgment of individual human beings. The faculties of "complex communication" and "expert thinking" that Levy and Murnane found to have survived the information technology revolution are needed as much as ever for coordination of the economy, and a system of financial capitalism will eventually imbue those in possession of such faculties with wealth and power.

But there is still a reason that the level of resentment of the wealthy and powerful is so high: a free capitalist system can support an equilibrium in which some kinds of social *conspiracy* pay off. George Akerlof, in his 1976 article "The Economics of Caste and of the Rat Race and Other Woeful Tales," has provided an economic theory of the human tendency for certain social groups to form a sort of business conspiracy against outsiders.[2] He takes the caste system—most notorious in traditional India, but in fact to some degree a part of human society everywhere—as a long-standing example of this. People who belong to a higher caste realize the immense economic advantage provided by their membership in that caste. Fearful of compromising that status, they adhere to the caste's social norms—which include ostracizing fellow caste members who fail to adhere to the norms. They favor their own caste in business and reject those who do not belong to the caste or who *do* belong but flaunt its norms by offering jobs and business to outsiders. Akerlof's point was that an economic equilibrium with castes can be stable, and that no business that flaunts caste norms can outcompete the caste businesses, so there is nothing to upset the equilibrium.

Business communities can be caste-like if there is a suitable culture and there are leaders who encourage exclusionary behavior. Those who have gained admittance to such a community value their connections and favor others in the caste in their business activities and financial dealmaking. In modern society a "caste" may be defined in terms of connections to a specific business culture, or in racial or sexual terms, or it may take form among graduates of elite colleges. If one is in a position of power and uses this opportunity to make an important deal with someone who is not connected with the business group, a member of a minority group, a woman, or merely a nondescript outsider, this behavior may cause one to lose power or even become an outcast. So, instinctively, one shuns outsiders and reconfirms the existing concentration of wealth and power.

But these are problems that we associate with finance only because advanced finance is used as a tool by some who wish to preserve their special status. It is not the financial tools themselves that create the caste structure, though their mechanisms are part of the equilibrium. The same financial tools can also, if suitably designed and democratized, become a means to break free from the grip of any caste equilibrium. Truly democratic finance can enable one to escape outcast status.

Financial capitalism is a work in progress. It is not yet perfected, but it is gradually improving. As we have seen, it is defined by a long list of financial practices and specific roles and responsibilities for people within those practices. Watching most of these people in operation from day to day, one comes to feel that in our modern society caste-like behavior has been much attenuated.

Even the caste system itself has never been accepted by the Buddhist, Christian, and Muslim religions, though caste-like behavior nonetheless continues among many of their adherents. It has survived in the Hindu religion, at least in some of its schools of thought, which have incorporated the notion of caste into their fundamental concepts, so caste loyalty is still very much alive. But even there the system—which was deplored by Mahatma Gandhi and other spiritual leaders—is now declining.

The same distaste for castes or their analogues was promoted by Vladimir Lenin in Russia, Kemal Atatürk in Turkey, Yukichi Fukuzawa in Japan, Sun Yat-sen and Mao Zedong in China, Eva Perón in Argentina, and Nelson Mandela in South Africa. These thought leaders couldn't be more different from each other, but together they provide evidence of a worldwide trend that finds castes or their analogues repugnant. Just as these beliefs represent a trend toward greater social enlightenment, there is a parallel trend toward enlightenment about caste-analogues in the business world.

I have been teaching at Yale University for some thirty years. Even my own university has seen a gradual transformation over the centuries from a training center for elite American families to an educational institution serving the people of the world. It has also become a financially sophisticated institution, given its success in investing its endowment. It is private and internationally focused, not connected with the U.S. government—a nonprofit, with its own goals. Those goals are substantially social and benevolent, and reflective of the views of a unique intellectual community.

The concept of an aristocracy or "high society," so strong in the nineteenth century, is fading around the world. The *Social Register* is a publication listing the wealthy and socially prominent families in the United States. Inclusion in it was once a coveted symbol of membership in the elite. Today it is largely a list of the descendants of the same families who were wealthy and prominent a century ago, and it has largely been forgotten by mainstream society.[3] Much the same has happened to *Burke's Peerage* in the United Kingdom and its European counterpart, the *Almanach de Gotha*, which ceased publication in 1944.[4] In China the national records of degree-holding literati and the local gazetteers died out before the end of the Qing dynasty in 1912. There is a more egalitarian spirit abroad in the world, and this spirit is supported by democratized finance.

Partly it is the presumption, the arrogance, that accompanies economic power that rankles. And the fact that so many people seem to admire the wealthy and powerful bothers us. Why do people think the wealthy are so special? Even presidents wonder about that. Franklin D. Roosevelt once said,

> I am simply unable to make myself take the attitude of respect toward the very wealthy men which such an enormous multitude of people evidently feel. I am delighted to show any courtesy to Pierpont Morgan or Andrew Carnegie or James Hill, but as for regarding any of them as, for instance, I regard . . . Peary, the Arctic explorer or Rhodes the historian—why I could not force myself to do it even if I wanted to, which I don't.[5]

Most of us might think that Roosevelt himself was rich. After all, in the 1940s his family was the most prominent of all in the *Social Register*, with no less than a page and a half of entries.[6] But he was not among the extremely rich, and apparently he did not *feel* that he was one of them either.[7] He seems to have considered himself at the same distance from these people that most of us do, and this mindset must have been a factor in his New Deal policies, which helped democratize U.S. financial markets.

At times we seem to be stuck in an economy that arbitrarily elevates a small number of the undeserving and forces the rest of us to pamper and flatter them. Resentment of such circumstances can suddenly build up to an intense level. For example, in 2011 the board of the Miami Art Museum announced that the museum would be renamed the Jorge M. Pérez Art Museum of Miami-Dade County in recognition of a donor, a real estate developer, who had given $35 million to the museum in the form of his personal collection of Latin American art, valued at $15 million, and a pledge of another $20 million.[8] A storm of protest followed. The museum had been funded mostly by tax-payers, and a $220 million capital campaign relying on numerous small donors was under way. It appears that the acknowledgment to Mr. Pérez was mis-applied. Perhaps the board should have offered only to name a wing of the museum or an auditorium within the museum after him, and then refused his gift if that was not enough for him. The granting of recognition in exchange for gifts has to be handled sensitively.

But we are usually not so sure that we bear any resentment toward such wealthy donors, for sometimes they *do* seem deserving. Often we set aside our social comparison processes because these donors do not seem in any way comparable to ourselves, and sometimes we imagine that we or our children could actually be as successful as they are

It has always been a source of satisfaction to me that Yale University, where I teach, has not followed a policy of selling naming rights to the high-est bidder. For example, the names of all twelve of its residential colleges are those of distinguished alumni, not merely wealthy donors who "bought" their way onto the colleges' walls. The Yale Law School and the Yale School of Management are not named after anyone—yet. If one or the other is someday named after a philanthropist donor, there will have to be general agreement within the university community on the worthiness of that person.

Part of this acceptance of wealthy donors is just the natural human willing-ness to live and let live. Each of us has other ways of maintaining self-esteem besides achieving wealth. So we want an economic system that allows for the attainment of human potential in various forms; we want it to be basically fair. Most of us will choose not to try to get rich, and we will pursue meaning in our lives in our own ways. We realize that we can't build an economic system that allows most of us to be prosperous and healthy and able to pursue our own individuality without producing some unusually successful, and possibly arrogant, people

The democratization of finance entails relying more on effective institutions of risk management that have the effect of preventing random redistributions of power and wealth—a system of financial contracts. Finance is supposed to *reduce* randomness in our lives, not increase it. To make the financial system work well, we have to further develop its inherent logic, its own ways of making deals among independent and free people—deals that leave them all better off.

The democratization of finance as spelled out in this book calls for an improvement in the nature and extent of participation in the financial system, including awareness of fundamental information about the workings of the system. The public needs to have reliable information, and that can only be provided by advisers, legal representatives, and educators who see their role as one of promoting enlightened stewardship. When people can benefit from such help, they will come to feel less strongly that our economy is run by a power elite. At present most people have little or no such information. Instead they are routinely confronted by salespeople for financial products, who have inadequate incentive to tell them what they really need to know. But it could be different, under a truly enlightened system of financial capitalism.

We have seen that some government interventions are needed, including redistributions through a progressive income tax, and this could be done more deliberately and judiciously than at present, without raising alarms that wealth might be unfairly confiscated. There needs to be a social safety net, and this safety net has to be continually improved and reworked. But under financial capitalism many of our best protections, and inspirations, come not directly from the government but from our own private financial arrangements. The government can merely be a facilitator.

The democratization of finance works hand in hand with the humanization of finance. To that extent it is important that finance be humane, and that it incorporate our increasingly sophisticated understanding of the human mind into its systems, models, and predictions. The rise of behavioral economics and neuroeconomics in recent decades provides a foundation for such an approach, for understanding how people really think and act. People are not inherently and uniformly loving to their neighbors, but our institutions can be changed to reward the better side of human nature.

One of these better sides is the philanthropic impulse, and the tendency, at least in the right social environment, for wealthy people to give much of their wealth away constructively. As we have seen, such a tendency ought to be considered central to financial capitalism. The gifts of the wealthy might in some respects be self-serving or motivated by ego, and they may in some cases generate resentment rather than gratitude, but financial capitalism makes full sense only when we recognize the importance of their gifts.

A problem with philanthropy is that, in the words of Craig Calhoun, president of the Social Science Research Council, there is a "loss of dignity for workers and citizens to feel they are dependent on charitable gifts—rather than on protections rightly available to them."[9] Yes indeed, the financial power that some achieve is resented, even if they eventually give away much of the wealth from which that power derives. But wealth accumulation followed by charity will still play a fundamental role in the good society, for, as we have seen, allowing or even actively encouraging people to amass wealth and give much of it away creates a system that motivates them to do good things. The loss of dignity that Calhoun notes can be minimized, and it may be more than offset by the overall beneficial results of such a system.

This conclusion is perhaps more sobering than inspiring. From what we know of human nature, we must continue to perfect a system that provides outlets for people's aggressive nature, that allows them to be egotistical. The system must also give them the opportunity to express their better natures at some point in their lives, for the good of society as a whole.

In my Financial Markets class, I ask students to read the philosopher Peter Unger's 1996 book *Living High and Letting Die*.[10] The book remarks at the widespread indifference—not just among the rich, but among the majority of the population—to the true suffering of poverty-stricken people we do not see every day. Unger tells us that it is not so easy for those of us in developed countries—or in the advanced parts of less-developed countries—to justify this neglect. He takes apart the moral arguments we use to justify this indifference, concluding that they are self-serving and specious. However, there is something futile about his exhortations, for relatively few people read Unger's book or change their behavior after having heard his message.

Other philosophers have taken the view not only that it is futile to ask people to be charitable, but also that human nature is essentially focused on a quest for power. Friedrich Nietzsche was very influential in promoting this view, and he was an inspiration for aggressors in both World War I and World War II. He wrote in *The Will to Power* (1901) of his theory

> that the will to power is the primitive form of affect, that all other affects are only developments from it; that it is notably enlightening to posit *power* in place of individual "happiness" (after which every living thing is supposed to be striving): there is a striving for power, for an increase of power;—pleasure is only a symptom of the feeling of power attained . . . that all driving force is will to power, that there is no other physical, dynamic or psychic force except this.[11]

Nietzsche seems to a modern ear almost to be saying that the brain is hard-wired for a lust for power.[12] However, he overstates his case: neuroscience shows many patterns of behavior in the brain, including altruistic impulses, which cannot all be derived from any unitary "psychic force."[13]

One singularly important human impulse, which Nietzsche did not seem to appreciate but that is emphasized by Adam Smith in his book *Theory of Moral Sentiments*, is not a desire for power per se but a desire for *praise*.[14] We see this desire plainly in the behavior of the youngest children and the oldest and weakest people, those with no hope of attaining "power" over others.

There is an enormous literature in modern psychology confirming the importance of self-esteem. But Smith gave his discussion of the desire for praise a different slant, one perhaps more closely aligned with the contemporary psychological literature on essentialism,[15] and one still not as appreciated today as it ought to be. Smith wrote that in mature people the desire for praise is transformed into a desire for *praiseworthiness:*

> The desire of the approbation and esteem of those we live with, which is of such importance to our happiness, cannot be fully and intirely contented but by rendering ourselves the just and proper objects of those sentiments, and by adjusting our own character and conduct according to those measures and rules by which esteem and approbation are naturally bestowed. . . . We are pleased not only with praise, but with having done what is praise-worthy.[16]

He seems almost to be saying that this craving is inherent in the human psyche and that our brain wants to categorize the praise we receive by its essential truth, by the real category of people into which it places us. Smith notes that most people would find it unsatisfying to be praised by mistake, for something they did not do. No one is satisfied merely to *look* praiseworthy. One wants to *be* praiseworthy. This is an aspect of human nature that is essential to the success of our economic system.

It is human to view a forged painting in entirely different terms than a genuine one, even though in many cases no one but an expert could tell the two apart. One might think that we would be just as happy to have a nice forgery hanging on the wall—after all, it gives us the same visual gratification. But we most certainly are not. In the same way, one does not want to be a forged *person*. Even criminals who commit frauds and violent crimes probably do not either. They merely imagine that they are praiseworthy within the confines of a moral philosophy that they perceive as sharing with their social group.

Economic development is in substantial measure the development of a social milieu in which it is harder and harder to find others who will truly feel that corrupt behavior is actually praiseworthy.

Pablo Escobar, the notorious Colombian drug lord, had hundreds of public figures, including a presidential candidate, assassinated, and he even had a commercial passenger airliner bombed, killing 110 people. When he was finally hunted down and killed by Colombian security forces in 1993, his mother, Hermilda Gaviria, demonstrated a strong conviction that her son, however brutal, was a good man because of what he had done for his family and the poor people in his community. At his funeral, amidst adoring throngs of his supporters, she said, "Pablo, you're in heaven, and the people acclaim you. The people love you. You have triumphed, Pablo."[17] Escobar probably did have a generous side. Had his business been legal and run within a system of financial capitalism, his aggressive instincts might have been channeled into mostly productive directions.

When a society is fragmented into fiefdoms run by primitive warlords, it is easier to feel praiseworthy for one's antisocial activities. The same society may in time evolve to a higher level at which the warlords are gone, but the government and business sectors remain filled with corruption, bribery, and caste-like behavior. Once again, those involved may still feel praiseworthy because there is a viewpoint—which they view as well entrenched in their society—that the laws they are breaking are meant to be broken and that one must do so to support one's friends and family.

As we mature we come to have the inner sense that we are praiseworthy, and not just superficially so. That, as Adam Smith observed, is a fundamental aspect of human nature that makes human society, and the economy, work as well as they do.

Ultimately, a well-constituted financial capitalism creates a safe venue for power struggles without violence. Achieving such a system requires appropriate innovations that humanize finance, taking account of our increasing knowledge from behavioral economics and neuroeconomics. There is no known economic system that can perfect aggressive human impulses—but they can be softened.

Financial institutions and associated regulations are like the rules of war. They lessen the unnecessary damage from human aggression, and they work to encourage the expression of other, more charitable, human impulses. We have seen that alternative economic systems work less well than a developed financial capitalism in their handling of the more difficult aspects of human nature.

Before modern financial capitalism, power was wielded in much more stark ways. For example, throughout most of human history, hostage exchange was used to guarantee agreements between governments.[18] A king might be forced to give up his son to spend years in the land of a rival leader, with the understanding that the son would be killed if the king did not live up to a treaty or other bargain. Because of the outrageous inhumanity of such a practice, it is now eschewed by respectable governments the world over.

Many of us will remember Brendan Behan's 1957 play *The Hostage*, which tells the story of an eighteen-year-old British soldier who is taken hostage by the Irish Republican Army. He strikes up a romance with an Irish woman of the same age who has been given the job of taking care of him in captivity—

and then he has to be killed. The play vividly reveals the inhumanity of war and its tactics.

But modern finance has not done away with all forms of hostage exchange to seal deals. The term for modern-day hostage exchange is *collateral*, and the hostages are financial assets instead of people. The practice was elevated to a high level before the severe financial crisis that began in 2007, with the widespread use of repurchase agreements, or repos, to carry financing farther forward. Even the home mortgage is in essence a hostage exchange, one in which the home (and the sense of equilibrium and well-being it provides to its inhabitants) is the hostage. The foreclosure on a house for failure to make the mortgage payments has its human consequences too, and it may lead to tragedies not entirely unlike that described in Behan's play. But the home mortgage could not have been made in the first place without such a collateral arrangement.

Many of our hopes for the future should be pinned on further development of the institutions representing financial capitalism. We are easily dazzled today by advances in information technology, and these advances can certainly interact positively with financial innovations. But the advances in our economic institutions may ultimately be more important than those in our hardware and software. The financial system is itself an information-processing system—one built out of human, rather than electronic, units—and the field of artificial intelligence is nowhere close to replacing human intelligence.

The key to achieving our goals and enhancing human values is to maintain and continually improve a democratic financial system that takes account of the diversity of human motives and drives. We need a system that allows people to make complex and incentivizing deals to further their goals, and one that allows an outlet for our aggressions and lust for power. It must be a system that redirects the inevitable human conflicts into a manageable arena, an arena that is both peaceful and constructive.

Notes

Preface

1. Videos of the complete set of lectures for my course Economics 252, Financial Markets, can be found on http://oyc.yale.edu/economics and a number of other web sites that collect such lectures. The lectures for 2008 and 2011, two different versions of the same course, are both available free to the public. When they are fully up on the site, the 2011 lectures (which were given while I was writing this book) will include problem sets and their answers, final exams and their answers, and self-scoring questions and answers. However, there is no provision for obtaining credit at Yale for taking this course online.

2. National Commission on the Causes of the Financial and Economic Crisis in the United States (2011): 188.

3. This trend, visible in many individual countries, has been offset for the world as a whole by the rise of the emerging countries. See Sala-i-Martin (2006).

4. Smith (1776).

Introduction: Finance, Stewardship, and Our Goals

1. Edwards (1938).

2. Nicolas Sarkozy, from his speech at the symposium "New World, New Capitalism," Paris, January 8, 2009, http://www.gouvernement.fr/gouvernement/ouverture-du-colloque-nouveau-monde-nouveau-capitalisme.

3. Tony Blair, from his speech at the symposium "New World, New Capitalism," Paris, January 8, 2009, http://www.tonyblairoffice.org/speeches/entry/speech-by-tony-blair-at-the-new-world-new-capitalism-conference/.

4. Yavlinsky (2011): 48.

5. http://www.imf.org/external/pubs/ft/weo/2011/01/, Figure 1.6 data, "Global Outlook."

6. Marx (1906): Volume 1, Chapters 13 and 26, pp. 365, 785–86, 786.

7. Duflo (2011): 4.

8. Government subsidies for small businesses are used today to help solve the problem. Social programs to provide early education have been the subject of some experimentation, and effective methods of developing talent among the poor are starting to be implemented. See Heckman and Carneiro (2003).

9. A living history of this revolution can be seen on my behavioral finance web site (http://www.econ.yale.edu/~shiller/behfin/index.htm), which shows a list of the seminars that Richard Thaler and I have organized since 1991, and my behavioral macroeconomics web site (http://www.econ.yale.edu/~shiller/behmacro/index.htm), which shows a list of seminars that George Akerlof and I have organized since 1994. Books about behavioral economics include Shleifer (2000), Shefrin (2007), and Thaler and Sunstein (2008).

10. Laird (2009).

11. http://www.research.ibm.com/deepqa/deepqa.shtml.

12. Levy and Murnane (2005).

13. Gilpin and Wallace (1905).

14. U.S. National Income and Product Accounts, Table 1.14, "Gross Value Added of Domestic Corporate Business," http://www.bea.gov/national/nipaweb/SelectTable .asp?Selected=Y. This figure excludes many finance-related activities, which are not directly part of financial corporate business.

15. According to the U.S. Bureau of Labor Statistics, 20.3% of the total employed U.S. population in 2008 was engaged in finance and insurance (activities related to credit intermediation, plus other investment pools and funds, insurance agencies and brokerages, other insurance-related activities, and insurance and employee benefit funds). National Employment Matrix, http://www.bls.gov/data/#employment.

16. Food services: Purchased meals and beverages was $528 billion or 3.7% of GDP in 2009. National Income and Product Account Table 2.4.5, "Personal Consumption Expenditures by Type of Product," http://www.bea.gov/national/nipaweb/TableView .asp?SelectedTable=70&Freq=Year&FirstYear=2009&LastYear=2010.

17. Jayadev and Bowles (2006) also report international estimates excluding police and private security personnel (for which they were unable to find reliable data in many countries). By this definition, the United States ranks quite high in terms of guard labor as a fraction of the population, but even the countries with the lowest fraction of guard labor, notably the Scandinavian countries, still have about half the U.S. level of guard labor.

18. *The Federal Reporter: With Key-Number Annotations . . .*, Volume 160, p. 467, http://books.google.com/.

19. Ibid., p. 472.

Chapter 1. Chief Executive Officers

1. Long (1983).

2. "Romneys Reported $3 Million Income from 1955 to 1966," *New York Times*, November 26, 1967, p. 46.

3. Iacocca (1984).

4. Iacocca said afterwards that he had only "kidded with" reporters when he expressed interest in running. Ibid., p. 291.

5. French et al. (2009).

6. Dodd-Frank Act, H.R. 4173-579, Section 954.

7. Bebchuk and Fried (2006): 4.

8. Hellman and Puri (2002).

9. Khurana (2004).

10. Djilas (1983 [1957]).

11. "In fact, the Party committees are extremely active in their 'protection of the stockholding interest,' far more than is the case of their counterparts in American business. With the duty and obligation of 'supervision' over industrial management, they have in fact injected themselves deep into the management function." Granick (1960): 203.

12. "Both in Russia and in the United States, managerial incentives are very strong. Since top-management posts are not restricted to candidates qualifying through family or friendship connections, junior executives have opportunities for major advancement. Income differences are sharp, and promotion up the managerial ladder can lead to sharp rises in income." Ibid., p. 130.

Chapter 2. Investment Managers

1. Gruber (1996).

2. Bodnaruk and Simonov (2011).

3. Redleaf and Vigilante (2010): 8.

4. Milgrom and Stokey (1982).

5. Grossman and Stiglitz (1980).

6. This 14.2% is based on a geometric average of gross returns, as it should be.

7. Chevalier and Ellison (1999).

8. Li et al. (2008).

9. That is, among the individuals inducted into the army between 1982 and 2001, those who had higher IQ scores had higher Sharpe ratios for their 2000 portfolios, controlling for other factors, reflecting greater exposure to small-cap and value stocks and better diversification. Grinblatt et al. (2011).

10. Kat and Menexe (2003).

11. Kaplan and Schoar (2005).

12. Berk and Green (2004).

13. Bogle (2009): 47.

14. Levine (1997).

15. French (2008).

16. Goetzmann et al. (2002).

17. Dugan et al. (2002).

18. Dugan (2005).

19. Acharya et al. (2010).

20. Kaufman (2005): 313.

21. Bernasek (2010): 48.

Chapter 3. Bankers

1. Diamond and Dybvig (1983) lay out the issue of bank runs as a problem of multiple equilibria in a model of banks as creators of liquidity, thereby providing both a clear rationale for the existence of banks and an understanding of their vulnerabilities.

2. http://fraser.stlouisfed.org/publications/bms/issue/61/download/130/section10 .pdf, Table 130.

3. There were some forms of capital requirements before 1982, but no national systematic and regular enforcement of them for banks until then. See Gorton and Winton (1995).

4. Akerlof and Romer (1994).

5. Mayer (1990) and Mishkin (1996).

6. Gorton (2010): Chapter 5.

7. Gorton (2010) argues that the Federal Reserve was mistaken to have stopped calculating and publishing the M3 measure of the money supply, which included some repurchase agreements, in 2006, just before the severe financial crisis that began in 2007. They should instead have expanded the coverage of repurchase agreements in M3, which might have helped them see the origins of the speculative bubbles and the risks of a crisis.

8. This trend was seen long before the beginnings of the financial crisis in 2007. See Marcus (1984).

9. Yunus (2003).

10. Karlan and Zinman (2011). Banerjee and Duflo (2010) report that microcredit has numerous effects, including promoting self-control and saving on the part of the borrowers.

11. Bucks et al. (2009): Table 6B, p. A18.

12. Barr (2004).

13. Blank and Barr (2009).

Chapter 4. Investment Bankers

1. Malmendier (2005: 38) quotes Cicero referring to "partes illo tempore carissimae" (shares that had a very high price at that time).

2. "Modern Banking in Europe," *Bankers' Magazine and Statistical Register* 14(3): 183–214 (1864), p. 188.

3. Seavoy (1972): 89.

4. Moss (2004).

5. Myers (1984).

6. Fama and French (2005).

Chapter 5. Mortgage Lenders and Securitizers

1. Park (2011). Of course, the market value of these securities took a greater hit because of the possibility of more losses in the future. The U.S. Financial Crisis Inquiry Commission, in its final report, emphasized that 83% of Moody's Aaa-rated mortgage-backed securities tranches were eventually downgraded to lower ratings—downgrades that affected their market price. But downgrades do not necessarily represent much in the way of losses because of actual defaults. National Commission on the Causes of the Financial and Economic Crisis in the United States (2011): xxv.

2. A lucid account of the nature of the disparity between actual default losses and market turmoil can be found in a review by Gary Gorton (2011) of books by Michael Lewis (2010) and Gregory Zuckerman (2009). See also Gorton and Ordoñez (2012).

3. Some mortgage securities had also been issued by the Government National Mortgage Association (Ginnie Mae) as early as 1968. See Fabozzi and Modigliani (1992).

4. Acharya et al. (2011).

5. Ibid.

6. Canada has an entity similar to Fannie Mae and Freddie Mac, the Canada Housing and Mortgage Corporation (CHMC), which insures mortgages and buys pooled mortgages and resells them to the public as its bonds. It is not bankrupt, as there was no comparable collapse in Canadian home prices, but the possibility that there could be problems with CHMC in the future, like the problems experienced by Fannie Mae and Freddie Mac, has been the subject of some concern in Canada. The Japan Housing Finance Agency also pursues mortgage securitization, but on a relatively small scale. In much of the rest of the world, although there has been some limited attempt at mortgage securitization, investors have mostly held mortgages indirectly by owning shares in the mortgage originators.

7. Franco Modigliani and Merton Miller (1963) assumed that investors did not have to expend any resources to acquire information about the assets they invest in. George Akerlof shared the 2001 Nobel Prize in economics for a 1970 article that detailed how information asymmetry sometimes prevents markets from existing.

8. Akerlof (1970).

9. Hill (1997).

10. National Commission on the Causes of the Financial and Economic Crisis in the United States (2011): 196.

11. Shiller (2008).

12. Davis (2006) and Caplin et al. (1997).

Chapter 6. *Traders and Market Makers*

1. Montesquieu (1773 [1748]): Volume II, Book XX, Chapter II, p. 2.

2. Montague (2007): 119.

3. O'Reilly et al. (2002).

4. It has been discovered that some dopamine neurons, which are part of an anatomically distinct second dopamine system, are stimulated by aversive, rather than rewarding, events. See Brischoux et al. (2009).

5. Vickery et al. (2011): 166.

6. Schultz et al. (1997).

7. Schultz (1998). See also Glimcher (2011).

8. Compare Brickley (1983) and Schultz (1998).

9. "Commercial Summary," *The Sun* (Baltimore), February 13, 1847, p. 4.

10. U.S. Commodities Futures Trading Commission and Securities and Exchange Commission (2010). For broader perspectives, see Melamed (2009).

11. Berg et al. (2008).

12. Wolfers and Zitzewitz (2004).

13. The Eurozone HICP futures settle on the harmonized Index of Consumer Prices, http://www.cmegroup.com/trading/interest-rates/interest-rate-index/eurozone-hicp-futures_contract_specifications.html. The CME Group nonfarm payroll futures were delisted on December 5, 2011. See also Labuszewski et al. (2010).

14. Thomsen and Andersen (2007).

15. The real estate futures settle on the S&P/Case-Shiller Home Price Indices, http://www.cmegroup.com/trading/real-estate/. See John Dolan's homepricefutures.com.

16. See Fabozzi et al. (2010) for a discussion of options on real estate prices.

Chapter 7. Insurers

1. Chen and Ravallion (2007).
2. Townsend (1994).
3. Barnett and Mahul (2007).
4. Shiller (2003).
5. Scharlach and Lehning (2012).
6. O'Leary (2012).
7. Jaffee et al. (2008) and Kunreuther and Useem (2010).
8. Shiller (1994, 2003, 2008).

Chapter 8. Market Designers and Financial Engineers

1. Shapley and Scarf (1974) and Roth et al. (2005).
2. Kremer and Glennerster (2004).
3. Horesh (2008).
4. "A New Matrimonial Plan," *New England Galaxy and United States Literary Adverttiser*, May 13, 1825, pp. 8, 396.
5. "New Matrimonial Plan," *The Port-Folio*, November 7, 1801, pp. 1, 45.
6. Gale and Shapley (1962).

Chapter 9. Derivatives Providers

1. Dixit and Pindyck (1994).
2. Aristotle (1977): 16.
3. Milgrom and Stokey (1982).
4. Arrow (1964).
5. Ross (1976): 75.
6. MFAO in Spain first began trading olive oil futures in 2006.
7. Gross (1982): 166, as quoted in Shefrin and Statman (1993).
8. Schwed (1940): 140.
9. Bachelier (1900).
10. Boness (1964) and Sprenkle (1964).
11. Boness (1964): 163.

Chapter 10. Lawyers and Financial Advisers

1. The sources for the figures, all for 2010, are as follows: Israel—Israel Bar Association, http://www.israelbar.org.il/english_inner.asp?pgId=103336&catId=372. Brazil—Ordem dos Advogados do Brasil (Brazilian Law Board), http://www.oab.org.br/relatorioAdvOAB.asp. United States—American Bar Association, http://www.americanbar.org/content/dam/aba/migrated/marketresearch/PublicDocuments/2011_national_lawyer_by_state.authcheckdam.pdf. Japan—Japan Bar Association, http://www.nichibenren.or.jp/ja/jfba_info/membership/index.html. Korea—Korean Bar Association, http://www.koreaherald.com/opinion/Detail. jsp?newsMLId=

20101209000705. China—inferred from information supplied by the Chinese Ministry of Justice, http://www.moj.gov.cn/index/content/2010-05/27/content_2157168.htm.

2. Castor (2002): 189.

3. http://data.bls.gov:8080/oep/servlet/oep.nioem.servlet.ActionServlet.

4. http://www.napfa.org/membership/OurStandards.asp.

Chapter 11. Lobbyists

1. Levitt (2003): 251.

2. http://ourfinancialsecurity.org.

3. "National Realtors Call for Reforms," *Washington Post*, January 29, 1933, p. SP19.

4. Harriss (1951).

5. U.S. Congressional Budget Office (2011): 1.

6. Hacker and Pierson (2010): Kindle edition, location 5089.

7. Stratmann (1991).

8. http://www.thedailymaverick.co.za/article/2011-05-26-how-really-powerful-are-the-people-with-brains-and-money.

9. Lessig (2011).

10. http://www.opensecrets.org/lobby/top.php?indexType=c.

11. "Good Lobbyists, Good Government," *Los Angeles Times*, January 13, 2006, http://articles.latimes.com/2006/jan13/opinion/oe-odonnell13.

12. Miller (2008): 158, 157, and 163.

13. Committee on Disclosure of Corporate Political Spending, Petition for Rule-making, August 3, 2011, http://www.sec.gov/rules/petitions/2011/petn4-637.pdf.

14. Bartels (2005).

15. Visser (2003).

Chapter 12. Regulators

1. Friedman and Kuznets (1945) and Friedman (1962).

2. Stigler (1971): 3.

3. Kleiner and Krueger (2009).

4. Bhagwati and Srinivasan (1994).

5. Rajan and Zingales (2004).

6. Markopolos (2011): Kindle edition, locations 270, 2589–96.

7. Mongelli and Mangan (2009).

8. Laura Cha, lecture to Shiller Financial Markets class, March 23, 2011, video and transcript available online as part of Shiller's 2011 course, http://oyc.yale.edu/economics.

Chapter 13. Accountants and Auditors

1. Allen (1993): 58.

2. Levitt (2003): 266.

Chapter 14. Educators

1. Franklin (1787): 212–14.

2. "Education in Finance," *Friends' Intelligencer*, April 16, 1881, p. 140.

3. "A College Education," *Washington Post,* June 15, 1890, p. 9.
4. Miller (1991): 207.

Chapter 15. Public Goods Financiers

1. Hill (1837): 6.
2. Bush (1945): Chapter 6.

Chapter 16. Policy Makers in Charge of Stabilizing the Economy

1. Our study compared the out-of-sample performance of large-scale structural econometric models, single-equation autoregressive models, vector-autoregressive models, and a form of autoregressive model that we called the "autoregressive components" model. See Fair and Shiller (1990).

2. Efforts to confirm that expert political judgment can result in useful forecasts have yielded results that are hard to interpret, reflecting the essential ambiguity of their forecasting problem. See Tetlock (2006).

3. In the United States, the Federal Reserve was also in part modeled on another U.S. institution. For more than half a century before the founding of the Federal Reserve System, temporary interruptions of liquidity in bank accounts were made more bearable by a private institution, owned by its member banks, that issued clearing house loan certificates to member banks. The Clearing House Loan Committee of the New York Clearing House decided on the loan policy, and in doing so it was performing a task analogous to that carried out today by the Federal Open Market Committee of the Federal Reserve Board, although it was an entirely private, not a government-associated, committee. See Gilpin and Wallace (1904). This was a private-sector financial invention, of some utility, that is by now virtually forgotten. Although it served its purpose in its time, its principal flaw was that the system did not protect against bank suspensions of payments to the public, which were associated with sharp recessions.

4. Bagehot (1896): 131, 189.
5. Woodward (2001).
6. U.S. Federal Open Market Committee, Press Release, May 10, 2006, p. 1, http://www.federalreserve.gov/newsevents/press/monetary/20060510a.htm.
7. Jean-Claude Trichet and Lucas Papademos, "Introductory Statement," July 6, 2006, p. 1, http://www.ecb.int/press/pressconf/2006/html/is060706.en.html.
8. International Monetary Fund, *World Economic Outlook,* April 2006, p. 1.
9. The IMF *World Economic Outlook* for April 2006 did mention concerns about the U.S. housing market, calling it a "key uncertainty" (p. 17).
10. Bank for International Settlements, *Quarterly Review,* June 2006, p. 6.
11. Čihák (2006): 19.
12. Rajan (2010).
13. Higgins (1943): 188.
14. Shubik (2009).
15. Shiller (2008).
16. Shiller (1994, 2003, 2008, 2011) and Athanasoulis and Shiller (2001).
17. Kamstra and Shiller (2010).
18. Shiller (2012a).

Chapter 17. Trustees and Nonprofit Managers

1. http://compforce.typepad.com/compensation_force/2008/02/bonusincentive .html.

2. Berle and Means (1932).

3. Salacuse (2003).

4. The requirement to have labor representatives on the *Aufsichtsrat* is codified in German Corporate Law (*Aktiengesetz*) Section 96, http://www.gesetze-im-internet.de/ aktg/BJNR010890965.html. This same German law, Section 88, forbids board members from competing with the company, but it has no explicit provision for a duty of loyalty, no stipulation that the board's exclusive responsibility is to the shareholders.

5. http://www.bcorporation.net/publicpolicy.

6. http://nccsdataweb.urban.org/NCCS/V1Pub/index.php.

7. Sometimes nonprofits do produce millionaires. See Buettner (2011).

8. Schumpeter (1950): 125–26.

9. Hansmann et al. (2003).

10. Hansmann (1990).

Chapter 18. Philanthropists

1. Smith (1761): 272–73.

2. Saint-Exupéry (1943): 38.

3. The concluding sentence in Carnegie's original 1889 article was "Such, in my opinion, is the true Gospel concerning Wealth, obedience to which is destined some day to solve the problem of the Rich and the Poor, and to bring 'Peace on earth, among men Good-Will'" (p. 664). The article was republished in London that same year as "The Gospel of Wealth," and it was later altered by Carnegie to include that title when it became a part of his book of collected essays (1901).

4. Carnegie (1889): 656.

5. "The price which society pays for the law of competition, like the price it pays for cheap comforts and luxuries, is also great; but the advantages of this law are also greater still, for it is to this law that we owe our wonderful material development, which brings improved conditions in its train. . . . It is best for the race, because it insures the survival of the fittest in every department." Carnegie (1889): 655.

6. Buffett (2010) and http://givingpledge.org/.

Part Two. Finance and Its Discontents

1. Freud (1952 [1930]): 776, 788.

Chapter 19. Finance, Mathematics, and Beauty

1. Weyl (1952).

2. There is an extensive psychological literature on how people judge facial beauty. See Rhodes (2006).

3. Lederman (2004).

4. Black and Scholes (1973).

5. Miller and Modigliani (1961) and Modigliani and Miller (1963).

6. Barro (1974).

7. Whitman (1892): Book XV, "A Song for Occupations!"

Chapter 20. Categorizing People: Financiers versus Artists and Other Idealists

1. Ross (1977).

2. Swafford (1996).

3. Swafford (1996): 403.

4. http://www.christies.com/LotFinder/lot_details.aspx?intObjectID=5101408.

5. Thoreau (2008 [1863]): 4. See also Shiller (1994): 79.

6. From a book review (of William Channing, *Henry Thoreau, The Poet-Naturalist*, Boston: Roberts Brothers, 1873) reprinted from the *British Quarterly Review* in *Littell's Living Age*, March 14, 1874, pp. 643–71; quote on p. 643.

7. Kasper (1980): B1.

Chapter 21. An Impulse for Risk Taking

1. Akerlof and Shiller (2009). See also Chapter 25.

2. Fiorillo et al. (2003).

3. Zuckerman et al. (1978) and Arnett (1994).

4. Patoine (2011).

5. Martin et al. (2007).

6. Joseph et al. (2008).

7. Smith (1761): 183.

8. For an elaboration on this point, see Krueger (2003).

9. Weber (2010 [1905]).

Chapter 22. An Impulse for Conventionality and Familiarity

1. The Federal Farm Loan Act of 1916 established amortizing mortgages for farms, amidst opposition from those who thought the government was overreaching in making farm mortgages a "compulsory savings fund." See "Finds Flaws in New Loan Plan," *New York Tribune*, January 30, 1916, p. B10. An example advocating amortizing mortgages is Davis (1917). Amortizing mortgages for homes did not become common in the United States until Congress established them with the Home Owners' Loan Corporation in 1933.

2. Shiller (2005a).

3. Shiller (1997).

4. Locke (1841 [1690]): 352.

5. Bloom (2004): 49.

6. Mac Cormac (1985) and Lakoff and Johnson (2003).

7. Pulvermüller (2002): 59.

8. It has been found, for example, that the brain stores words as "unique objects." Neuroscientist Laurie Glezer and her colleagues used functional magnetic resonance imaging to study the "visual word form area" in the visual cortex of the brain, and they found that words have nonoverlapping neural representations there. Glezer et al. (2009).

9. Wittgenstein (1953): Part I, Sections 164–65.

10. Newcomb (1879): 230.

11. There are other factors to consider in understanding the lack of interest in indexation. See Shiller (1997).

12. Ibid.

13. http://valoruf.cl/.

14. Shiller (2003, 2009).

15. Shiller (2008), Kroszner and Shiller (2011), and Shiller et al. (2011).

16. United Nations (1948).

17. Gollier (2008).

Chapter 23. Debt and Leverage

1. Adelino et al. (2011) confirmed that access to mortgage credit has significant effects on house prices in the United States by using changes in conforming loan limits as instruments to detect exogenous changes in credit supply.

2. Mian et al. (2011).

3. Mian and Sufi (2010).

4. Glick and Lansing (2010): Figures 3 and 4.

5. Fisher (1933). See also Shiller (2012b).

6. Geanakoplos (2009).

7. Geanakoplos (2010).

8. Jayachandran and Kremer (2006).

9. Berger and Ritschl (1995).

Chapter 24. Some Unfortunate Incentives to Sleaziness Inherent in Finance

1. Kahneman and Tversky (1979).

2. Simmons and Novemsky (2009).

3. "Mr. Prowler Discourses This Week on One Kind of Bucket Shop," *National Police Gazette*, June 14, 1879, p. 14.

4. Schwed (1940): 19.

5. Festinger (1957).

6. Van Veen et al. (2009).

7. Tarbell (1904).

8. Shiller et al. (1991).

Chapter 25. The Significance of Financial Speculation

1. The essay "The Functions of the Stock and Produce Exchanges" was reprinted in Conant (1904): 83–116; quote on p. 83.

2. Marx (1906): 440.

3. Keynes (1936): 159.

4. Fama (1965): 56.

5. Working (1934) and Kendall (1953).

6. Shiller (1981). My paper was followed by some others, with John Campbell, that made significant improvements in the analysis (Campbell and Shiller 1988a, 1988b). See also LeRoy and Porter (1981) and Summers (1986).

7. For a discussion of the controversy see for example Cochrane (1991).

8. Keynes (1965 [1936]): 161, 162.

9. Akerlof and Shiller (2009).

10. Proust (2002 [1913]): 46–47.

11. Gartner (2005).

12. Moss (2004).

13. Andrew Hertzberg (2011) has shown how households composed of partly altruistic and partly selfish individuals can behave very differently from a rational single individual.

14. Morrison and Wilhelm (2008). Professional organizations and professional norms are the dominant explanation for the prevalence of the partnership form in law, consulting, and accounting. See Nordenflycht (2008).

15. Esterbrook and Fischel (1985).

16. Tufano and Schneider (2009).

Chapter 26. Speculative Bubbles and Their Costs to Society

1. Shiller (2005b): 2.

2. Buonomano (2011).

3. Becker (1997).

4. Li (1994): 291.

5. Lederer (1915).

6. http://www.g20.utoronto.ca/summits.htm, http://www.g20.utoronto.ca/2008/2008declaration1115.html.

7. http://www.g20.utoronto.ca/2009/2009communique0925.html.

8. http://www.treas.gov/press/releases/hp1177.htm.

9. Jung and Shiller (2005).

10. Shiller (1981).

11. Vuolteenaho (2002). See also Cohen et al. (2003).

12. Black (1986): 533.

Chapter 27. Inequality and Injustice

1. Brosnan (2009).

2. Krueger (2007).

3. The analysis here refers to the thirtieth annual Forbes 400 list, the cover story of the October 10, 2011, issue of *Forbes*. The list can be found at http://www.forbes.com/forbes-400/list/.

4. http://www.forbes.com/wealth/celebrities/list.

5. Philippon and Reshef (2008).

6. Stanley (1991): 271.

7. Luthar and Latendresse (2005).

8. Marx and Engels (1906 [1848]): 39.

9. De Lazowski (1788): 689.

10. Veblen (1899) and Akerlof (1976).

11. Festinger (1954).

12. Fliessbach et al. (2007).

13. Frank (2011).

14. Graetz (1979) lists eight practical problems with a progressive consumption tax and concludes that until these problems are solved "a progressive personal tax on consumption should remain low on the list of political priorities" (p. 1661).

15. In fact, the U.S. Congress passed an act on December 16, 2010, that reinstated the estate tax but also gave a new stepped-up basis for capital gains, so that after the fact there was no unambiguous tax advantage to dying in 2010 rather than 2011.

16. Quoted in Tarlow (2010).

17. Shiller et al. (1991).

18. A wage subsidy could be used to augment and regularize the earned income tax credit. See Phelps (2007).

19. Shiller (2003).

20. *Forbes*, October 10, 2011, p. 218. Household net worth was $57.4 trillion in the fourth quarter of 2011, according to the Federal Reserve Flow of Funds Accounts, Table B-100, http://www.federalreserve.gov/releases/z1/Current/z1r-5.pdf.

21. Burman et al. (2007).

Chapter 28. Problems with Philanthropy

1. The Center on Philanthropy at Indiana University (2011) reports that $290.89 billion was given to charity in the United States, which is 2.2% of U.S. third-quarter national income, as seen from the National Income and Product Accounts, http://www.bea.gov/national/nipaweb/TableView.asp?SelectedTable=43&Freq=Qtr&FirstYear=2009&LastYear=2011.

2. Della Vigna et al. (2011) constructed an experiment in which potential donors in an experimental group were allowed to opt out of even having to confront a representative of a charity. The total giving by the experimental group was significantly lower than that of a control group not given the option.

3. Harbough (1998).

4. Small et al. (2007).

5. Anderson (1991).

6. Hayek (1944): 161.

7. Carnegie (1901), Buffett (2010), and http://givingpledge.org/.

8. Pharoah (2009): 9. Data are for the most recent year for which information was available in 2009 for each foundation.

9. Karlan and McConnell (2009) showed experimentally that such publicity increases the amount given. The desire for recognition may be evidence that gift-giving is at least in part a form of disguised exchange. See Stark and Falk (1998).

10. List and Lucking-Reiley (2002).

11. Falke (2004).

12. One such Skype call, complete with smiles and kisses, is shown at "Meeting Our Compassion International Sponsored Child OVER SKYPE!!!" at http://www.youtube.com/watch?v=tT3CY8Lwiak.

13. "Except Gifts from Income," *New York Times*, June 17, 1917, p. 3.

14. The *Chicago Tribune* estimated in 1920 that $4 billion had been given to war organizations, the Red Cross, religious and educational movements, and other causes since 1915. "$4,000,000,000 to Philanthropy," *Chicago Tribune*, April 25, 1920, p. 8.

15. "Tax Revision for Charity," *New York Times*, February 11, 1948, p. 26.

16. Prante (2007).

17. Toppe et al. (2001): Table 1.7, p. 35.

18. Ibid., p. 6.

19. The U.S. National Commission on Fiscal Responsibility and Reform (chaired by Alan Simpson and Erskine Bowles), in its 2010 report to President Obama and the U.S. Congress, recommended replacing the charitable deduction with a 12% tax credit. There were public concerns that Congress's Joint Select Committee on Deficit Reduction (the "Supercommittee") would in 2011 propose the weakening of the charitable deduction, but in fact the committee reached no agreement on the question.

20. Post (2005).

Chapter 29. The Dispersal of Ownership of Capital

1. Douglas (1940): 16.

2. "It should be noted, moreover, that monopoly is frequently the product of factors other than lower costs of greater size. It is attained through collusive agreements and promoted by public policies." Hayek (1944): 2.

3. "Today it is almost heresy to suggest that scientific knowledge is not the sum of all knowledge. But a little reflection will show that there is beyond question a body of very important but unorganized knowledge which cannot possibly be called scientific in the sense of knowledge of general rules: the knowledge of particular circumstances of time and place. It is with respect to this that practically every individual has some advantage over all others." Hayek (1945): 521.

4. Sargent (1961).

5. Jeon and Kim (2000).

6. "Land for the Landless," *Chicago Press and Tribune*, August 30, 1860, p. 2.

7. Cape York Institute, "Land and Housing," http://www.cyi.org.au/landhousing .aspx.

8. Cabré and Módenes (2004).

9. Lee Kuan Yew (2000): 105.

10. French et al. (2009).

11. See for example Dean (1954).

12. Akerlof and Kranton (2010).

13. Freeman (2000) and Freeman et al. (2008).

14. Buchele et al. (2009).

15. Subsidizing small businesses is analogous in a way to subsidizing early childhood education, in that it helps people approach the economy on an even footing. Careful evaluation of early childhood education programs has helped us see better which such programs work and which do not work. See Heckman and Carneiro (2003).

16. Phelps and Tilman (2010).

17. Dodd-Frank Act, H.R. 4173-37, 2010, Section 622. In its first annual report, the Financial Stability Oversight Council concluded that "the concentration limit will reduce moral hazard, increase financial stability, and improve efficiency and competition within the U.S. financial system." http://www.treasury.gov/initiatives/fsoc/ Pages/annual-report.aspx 127.

18. U.S. Financial Stability Oversight Council (2011): Figures 1–4, pp. 24–25.

19. French et al. (2009).

Chapter 30. The Great Illusion, Then and Now

1. Angell (1910): 29–30.

2. Goldman Sachs agreed in 2010 to a settlement with the SEC, which had Goldman pay a $550 million penalty.

3. Countrywide agreed to pay settlements according to agreements with numerous state attorneys general. http://countrywidesettlementinfo.com/.

4. Nietzsche (1968 [1901]) wrote: "Man as a species is not progressing. Higher types are indeed attained, but they do not last. The level of the species is *not* raised" (Section 684, p. 365). "The influence of 'external circumstances' is overestimated by Darwin to a ridiculous extent: the essential thing in the life process is precisely the tremendous shaping, form-creating force working from within which *utilizes* and *exploits* 'external circumstances'" (Section 647, p. 344).

5. Angell (1910): vii–viii.

6. Ibid., p. viii.

7. Angell (1933): 53.

8. Owings (1984): 56.

9. Martel (2008): 8.

10. Angell (1933) refers to "the Japanese adventure" and the "semi-mystic nationalism" of Hitlerism (p. 296). He justifies the new edition of his 1910 book as follows: "The problem is not merely to show that 'war does not pay' (is not, that is to say, either advantageous to our country, a satisfaction of our pride in it, or necessary to the assertion of its rights), but to show why the policies which we pursue and which we believe do pay, must lead to war" (p. 5). His idealized policies, "that organization [of nations] be based on clear political and diplomatic obligation" (p. 54), sound like a proposal to create what eventually became the European Union.

11. Moody (1933): 91.

12. Montesquieu (1773): Volume 1, pp. 54–55.

13. Lorenz (1966). The dove example appears on p. 232.

14. De Waal (1990): 234.

15. Pinker (2011): Kindle edition, locations 15155, 15295.

16. Hirschman (1977).

17. Russett and Oneal (2001).

18. Cronin (1999) and Anderson (1991).

19. Acemoglu and Yared (2010) present a case for reverse causality—that shifting political currents may raise the level of militarism in a country, and this then appears to have the effect of diminishing that country's foreign trade. Kupchan (2010: 400) argues from consideration of a number of case studies of stable peace breaking out that economic integration does not seem to promote the early phases of development of stable peace, when unilateral accommodation and reciprocal restraint are first attempted. But economic integration does advance it in later phases, when trust is gradually built.

20. Gartzke et al. (2001).

Epilogue: Finance, Power, and Human Values

1. If one searches on the parallel phrase "poverty and weakness" only some eight hundred titles come up.

2. Akerlof (1976). See also Mailath et al. (2000) and Scoville (2006). Much of this literature has focused on racial discrimination, though the theoretical principles apply more broadly to other forms as well; for a literature survey see Arrow (1998).

3. A ProQuest search for "Social Register" shows a massive downtrend since the 1930s in newspaper articles mentioning the phrase. Broad (1996) documented that the *Social Register* (http://www.socialregisteronline.com/) shows a strong continuity with prominent families from the long past.

4. http://www.burkespeerage.com. An attempt was made to start a new Almanach de Gotha in the twenty-first century, replacing the French language with English. See http://www.almanachdegotha.org/.

5. Quoted in Fraser (2009): 41.

6. "Social Register Drops Notables: Page and a Half Devoted to Roosevelts," *New York Times*, November 21, 1941, p. 19.

7. Members of the Roosevelt family were not mentioned on the short list of the very richest Americans in their time, but one of them, Betsey Cushing Roosevelt Whitney, the former wife of Franklin D. Roosevelt's son James (since remarried into more wealth and then widowed), made it onto the first Forbes 400 list in 1982. She was ranked 92.

8. Pogrebin (2011).

9. Calhoun (2012): 12.

10. Unger (1996).

11. Nietzsche (1968 [1901]): 366.

12. Nietzsche (1968 [1901]: 354) in places sounds like a modern neuroscientist. He wrote: "Affects are a construction of the intellect, an invention of causes that do not exist. . . . Frequent rushes of blood to the brain accompanied by a choking sensation are interpreted as 'anger': persons and things that rouse us to anger are means of relieving our physiological condition."

13. As summarized by Samuel Bowles and Herbert Gintis (2011: 20), "In experiments we commonly observe that people sacrifice their own payoffs in order to cooperate with others, to reward the cooperation of others, and to punish free-riding, even when they cannot expect to gain from acting this way." See also Gintis et al. (2005) and Fehr (2009).

14. Smith (1761).

15. Gelman and Bloom (2000).

16. Smith (1761): 191, 193.

17. "Death of a Drug Lord," CNN, December 5, 1993.

18. Griffiths (2003).

References

Acemoglu, Daron, and Pierre Yared. 2010. "Political Limits to Globalization." *American Economic Review* 100(2):83–88.

Acharya, Viral, Thomas Cooley, Matthew Richardson, and Ingo Walter. 2010. "Manufacturing Tail Risk: A Perspective on the Financial Crisis of 2007–9." *Foundations and Trends in Finance* 4:247–325.

Acharya, Viral, Matthew Richardson, Stijn van Nieuwerburgh, and Lawrene J. White. 2011. *Guaranteed to Fail: Fannie Mae, Freddie Mac, and the Debacle of Mortgage Finance.* Princeton, NJ: Princeton University Press.

Adelino, Manuel, Antoinette Schoar, and Felipe Severino. 2011. "Credit Supply and House Prices: Evidence from Mortgage Market Segmentation." Unpublished paper, Tuck School, Dartmouth College.

Akerlof, George A. 1970. "The Market for 'Lemons': Quality Uncertainty and the Market Mechanism." *Quarterly Journal of Economics* 84(3):488–500.

———. 1976. "The Economics of Caste and of the Rat Race and Other Woeful Tales." *Quarterly Journal of Economics* 90(4):599–617.

Akerlof, George A., and Rachel E. Kranton. 2010. *Identity Economics: How Our Identities Shape Our Work, Wages, and Well-Being.* Princeton, NJ: Princeton University Press.

Akerlof, George A., and Paul M. Romer. 1994. "Looting: The Economic Underworld of Bankruptcy for Profit." National Bureau of Economic Research Working Paper R1869.

Akerlof, George A., and Robert J. Shiller. 2009. *Animal Spirits: How Human Psychology Drives the Economy and Why It Matters for Global Capitalism.* Princeton, NJ: Princeton University Press.

Allen, Noelle. 1993. *Confessions of a Tax Accountant.* Cupertino, CA: Canyon View Institute.

Anderson, Benedict. 1991. *Imagined Communities: Reflections on the Origin and Spread of Nationalism*. London: Verso.

Angell, Norman. 1910. *The Great Illusion: A Study of the Relation of Military Power in Nations to Their Economic and Social Advantage*. New York: G. P. Putnam's Sons.

———. 1933. *The Great Illusion 1933*. New York: G. P. Putnam's Sons.

Aristotle. 1977. *Politics*, trans. Benjamin Jowett. New York: Forgotten Books.

Arnett, Jeffrey. 1994. "Sensation Seeking: A New Conceptualization and a New Scale." *Personality and Individual Differences* 16(2):289–96.

Arrow, Kenneth. 1964. "The Role of Securities in the Optimal Allocation of Risk Bearing." *Review of Economic Studies* 31:91–96.

———. 1998. "What Has Economics to Say about Racial Discrimination?" *Journal of Economic Perspectives* 12(2):91–100.

Athanasoulis, Stefano G., and Robert J. Shiller. 2001. "World Income Components: Measuring and Exploiting Risk-Sharing Opportunities." *American Economic Review* 91(4):1031–54.

Bachelier, Louis. 1900. "Théorie de la Spéculation." *Annales Scientifiques de l'École Normale Supérieure, 3e Série* 17:21–86.

Bagehot, Walter. 1896. *Lombard Street: A Description of the Money Market*, Tenth Edition, London: Kegan Paul, Trench, Trubner & Co. Ltd.

Banerjee, Abhijit V., and Esther Duflo. 2010. "Giving Credit Where It Is Due." Unpublished paper, Department of Economics, Massachusetts Institute of Technology.

Barnett, Barry J., and Oliver Mahul. 2007. "Weather Index Insurance for Agriculture and Rural Areas in Lower-Income Countries." *American Journal of Agricultural Economics* 5:1241–47.

Barr, Michael S. 2004. "Banking the Poor." *Yale Journal of Regulation* 21:121–237.

Barro, Robert J. 1974. "Are Government Bonds Net Wealth?" *Journal of Political Economy* 82(6):1095–117.

Bartels, Larry M. 2005. *Economic Inequality and Political Representation*. Princeton, NJ: Princeton University Press.

Bebchuk, Lucian, and Jesse Fried. 2006. *Pay without Performance: The Unfilled Promise of Executive Compensation*. Cambridge, MA: Harvard University Press.

Becker, Jasper. 1997. *Hungry Ghosts: Mao's Secret Famine*. New York: Free Press.

Berg, Joyce, Robert Forsythe, Forrest Nelson, and Thomas Rietz. 2008. "Results from a Dozen Years of Election Futures Markets Research." In Vernon Smith, ed., *Handbook of Experimental Economic Results*, Volume 1, 742–52. Amsterdam: North-Holland.

Berger, Helge, and Albrecht Ritschl. 1995. "Germany and the Political Economy of the Marshall Plan 1947–52: A Re-Revisionist View." In Barry J. Eichengreen, ed., *Europe's Post-War Recovery*, 199–245. Cambridge: Press Syndicate of the University of Cambridge.

Berk, Jonathan B., and Richard C. Green. 2004. "Mutual Fund Flows and Performance in Rational Markets." *Journal of Political Economy* 112(6):1269–95.

Berle, Adolf A., and Gardiner C. Means. 1932. *The Modern Corporation and Private Property*. New York: Commerce Clearing House.

Bernasek, Anna. 2010. *The Economics of Integrity*. New York: HarperCollins.

Bhagwati, Jagdish, and T. N. Srinivasan. 1994. *India's Economic Reforms*. Delhi: Ministry of Finance.

Black, Fischer. 1986. "Noise." *Journal of Finance* 41(3):529–43.

Black, Fischer, and Myron Scholes. 1973. "The Pricing of Options and Corporate Liabilities." *Journal of Political Economy* 81(3):637–54.

Blank, Rebecca M., and Michael S. Barr, eds. 2009. *Insufficient Funds: Savings, Assets, Credit and Banking among Low-Income Households*. New York: Russell Sage Foundation.

Bloom, Paul. 2004. *Descartes' Baby: How the Science of Child Development Explains What Makes Us Human*. New York: Basic Books.

Bodnaruk, Andriy, and Andrei Simonov. 2011. "Do Financial Experts Make Better Investment Decisions?" Unpublished paper, Department of Economics, University of Notre Dame.

Bogle, John C. 2009. *Enough: True Measures of Money, Business, and Life*. New York: Wiley.

Boness, A. J. 1964. "Elements of a Theory of Stock Option Value." *Journal of Political Economy* 72:163–75.

Bowles, Samuel, and Herbert Gintis. 2011. *A Cooperative Species: Human Reciprocity and Its Evolution*. Princeton, NJ: Princeton University Press.

Brickley, James A. 1983. "Shareholder Wealth, Information Signalling and the Specially Designated Dividend." *Journal of Financial Economics* 12:187–209.

Brischoux, F., S. Chakraborty, D. Brierley, and M. Ungless. 2009. "Phasic Excitation of Dopamine Neurons in Ventral VTA by Noxious Stimuli." *Proceedings of the National Academy of Sciences of the USA* 106(12):4894–99.

Broad, David B. 1996. "The Social Register: Directory of America's Upper Class." *Sociological Spectrum* 16(2):173–81.

Brosnan, Sarah. 2009. "Responses to Inequity in Non-Human Primates." In Paul Glimcher, Colin Camerer, Ernst Fehr, and Russell Poldrack, eds., *Neuroeconomics: Decision Making and the Brain*, 285–302. Amsterdam: Elsevier.

Buchele, Robert, Douglas Kruse, Loren Rodgers, and Adria Scharf. 2009. "Show Me the Money: Does Shared Capitalism Share the Wealth?" National Bureau of Economic Research Working Paper 14830.

Bucks, Brian K., Arthur B. Kennickell, Traci L. Mach, and Kevin B. Moore. 2009. "Changes in U.S. Family Finances from 2004 to 2007: Evidence from the Survey of Consumer Finances." *Federal Reserve Bulletin* February: A1–A56.

Buettner, Russ. 2011. "Reaping Millions in Nonprofit Care for Disabled." *New York Times*, August 2, http://www.nytimes.com/2011/08/02/nyregion/for-executives-at-group-homes-generous-pay-and-little-oversight.html?pagewanted=all.

Buffett, Warren. 2010. "My Philanthropic Pledge." *Fortune*, July 5, 86–87.

Buonomano, Dean. 2011. *Brain Bugs: How the Brain's Flaws Shape Our Lives*. New York: W. W. Norton.

Burman, Leonard, Robert Shiller, Gregory Leiserson, and Jeffrey Rohaly. 2007. "The Rising Tide Tax System: Indexing the Tax System for Changes in Inequality." Unpublished paper, Department of Economics, Syracuse University, http://www.newfinancialorder.com/burman-nyu-030807.pdf.

Bush, Vannevar. 1945. *Science: The Endless Frontier.* Washington, DC: U.S. Government Printing Office.

Cabré, Anna, and Juan Antonio Módenes. 2004. "Homeownership and Social Inequality in Spain." In *Home Ownership and Social Inequality in a Comparative Perspective,* 233–54. Stanford, CA: Stanford University Press.

Calhoun, Craig. 2012. "Shared Responsibility." In Jacob Hacker and Ann O'Leary, eds., *Shared Responsibilities, Shared Values,* 8–16. New York: Oxford University Press.

Campbell, John Y., and Robert J. Shiller. 1988a. "The Dividend-Price Ratio and Expectations of Future Dividends and Discount Factors." *Review of Financial Studies* 1(3):195–228.

———. 1988b. "Stock Prices, Earnings and Expected Dividends." *Journal of Finance* 43(3):661–76.

Caplin, Andrew, Sewin Chan, Charles Freeman, and Joseph Tracy. 1997. *Housing Market Partnerships: A New Approach to a Market at Crossroads.* Cambridge, MA: MIT Press.

Carnegie, Andrew. 1889. "Wealth." *North American Review* 148(391):653–64.

———. 1901. *The Gospel of Wealth and Other Timely Essays.* New York: Century.

Castor, Belmiro V. J. 2002. *Brazil Is Not for Amateurs: Patterns of Governance in the Land of "Jeitinho,"* trans. A. W. McEachern. Bloomington, IN: Xlibris.

Center on Philanthropy at Indiana University. 2011. *Giving USA 2011: The Annual Report on Philanthropy for the Year 2010—Executive Summary.* Giving USA Foundation, http://big.assets.huffingtonpost.com/GivingUSA_2011_ExecSummary_Print-1.pdf.

Chen, Shaohua, and Martin Ravallion. 2007. *Absolute Poverty Measures for the Developing World, 1981–2004.* Washington, DC: World Bank, Development Research Group.

Chevalier, Judith, and Glenn Ellison. 1999. "Are Some Mutual Fund Managers Better Than Others? Cross-Sectional Patterns in Behavior and Performance." *Journal of Political Economy* 54(3):875–99.

Čihák, Martin. 2006. *How Do Central Banks Write on Financial Stability?* Working Paper WP/06/163. Washington, DC: International Monetary Fund.

Cochrane, John. 1991. "Volatility Tests and Efficient Markets: A Review Essay." *Journal of Monetary Economics* 27:463–85.

Cohen, Randolph, Christopher Polk, and Tuomo Vuolteenaho. 2003. "The Value Spread." *Journal of Finance* 58:609–42.

Conant, Charles A. 1904. *Wall Street and the Country: A Study of Recent Financial Tendencies.* New York: G. P. Putnam's Sons.

Cronin, Bruce. 1999. *Community under Anarchy: Transnational Identity and the Evolution of Cooperation.* New York: Columbia University Press.

Davis, Ed L. 1917. "The Refunding Mortgage: A [sic] Amortizing Method for Small Mortgage Loans." *Bankers' Magazine* 95(3):323–26.

Davis, John E. 2006. *Shared Equity Ownership: The Changing Landscape of Resale-Restricted, Owner-Occupied Homes.* Montclair, NJ: National Housing Institute.

Dean, Lois R. 1954. "Union Activity and Dual Loyalty." *Industrial and Labor Relations Review* 7(4):526–36.

De Lazowski. 1788. "Observations Made in a Tour in Swisserland [sic]." *Columbian Magazine* 2(12):688–93.

Della Vigna, Stefano, John A. List, and Ulrike Malmendier. 2011. "Testing for Altruism and Social Pressure." Unpublished paper, Department of Economics, University of California at Berkeley.

De Waal, Frans. 1990. *Peacemaking among Primates*. Cambridge, MA: Harvard University Press.

Diamond, Douglas, and Philip Dybvig. 1983. "Bank Runs, Deposit Insurance, and Liquidity." *Journal of Political Economy* 91(3):401–19.

Dixit, Avinash K., and Robert S. Pindyck. 1994. *Investment under Uncertainty*. Princeton, NJ: Princeton University Press.

Djilas, Milovan. 1982 [1957]. *The New Class: An Analysis of the Communist System*. New York: Harcourt Brace Jovanovich.

Douglas, William O. 1940. *Democracy and Finance*. New Haven, CT: Yale University Press.

Duflo, Esther. 2011. "Balancing Growth with Equity: The View from Development." Paper presented at the Jackson Hole Symposium, Federal Reserve Bank of Kansas City, August 1, http://www.kansascityfed.org/publicat/sympos/2011/2011.Duflo.Paper.pdf.

Dugan, Ianthe Jeanne. 2005. "Sharpe Point: Risk Gauge Misused." *Wall Street Journal*, August 31, C1.

Dugan, Ianthe Jeanne, Thomas M. Burton, and Carrick Mollenkamp. 2002. "Portrait of a Loss: Chicago Art Institute Learns Tough Lesson about Hedge Funds." *Wall Street Journal*, February 1, A1.

Edwards, George W. 1938. *The Evolution of Finance Capitalism*. New York: Longmans, Green.

Esterbrook, Frank H., and Daniel R. Fischel. 1985. "Limited Liability and the Corporation." *University of Chicago Law Review* 52(1):89–117.

Fabozzi, Frank J., and Franco Modigliani. 1992. *Mortgage and Mortgage-Backed Securities Markets*. Cambridge, MA: Harvard Business School Press.

Fabozzi, Frank J., Robert J. Shiller, and Radu Tunaru. 2010. "Hedging Real-Estate Risk." *Journal of Portfolio Management*, Special Real Estate Issue 35(5):92–103.

Fair, Ray C., and Robert J. Shiller. 1990. "Comparing Information in Forecasts from Econometric Models." *American Economic Review* 80(3):375–89.

Falke, Armin. 2004. "Charitable Giving as a Gift Exchange: Evidence from a Field Experiment." IZA Discussion Paper 1148. University of Bonn.

Fama, Eugene F. 1965. "Random Walks in Stock Market Prices." *Financial Analysts Journal* 21(5):55–59.

Fama, Eugene F., and Kenneth French. 2005. "Financing Decisions: Who Issues Stock?" *Journal of Financial Economics* 76(3):549–74.

Fehr, Ernst. 2009. "Social Preferences and the Brain." In Paul Glimcher, Colin Camerer, Ernst Fehr, and Russell Poldrack, eds., *Neuroeconomics: Decision Making and the Brain*, 215–30. Amsterdam: Elsevier.

Festinger, Leon. 1954. "A Theory of Social Comparison Processes." *Human Relations* 7:117–40.

———. 1957. *A Theory of Cognitive Dissonance*. Stanford, CA: Stanford University Press.

Fiorillo, Christopher D., Philippe N. Tobler, and Wolfram Schultz. 2003. "Discrete

Coding of Reward Probability and Uncertainty by Dopamine Neurons." *Science* 299(5614):1898–902.

Fisher, Irving. 1933. "The Debt Deflation Theory of Great Depressions." *Econometrica* 1(4):337–57.

Fliessbach, K., B. Weber, P. Trautner, T. Dohmen, U. Sunde, C. E. Elger, and A. Falk. 2007. "Social Comparison Affects Reward-Related Brain Activity in the Human Ventral Striatum." *Science* 318(5854):1305–8.

Frank, Robert H. 2011. *The Darwin Economy: Liberty, Competition, and the Common Good.* Princeton, NJ: Princeton University Press.

Franklin, Benjamin. 1787. "Information for Those Who Wish to Remove to America." *The American Museum or, Repository of Ancient and Modern Fugitive Pieces &c.* 2:211–16.

Fraser, Steve. 2009. *Wall Street: America's Dream Palace.* New Haven, CT: Yale University Press.

Freeman, Richard B. 2000. "Work-Sharing to Full Employment: Serious Option or Populist Fallacy?" In Richard B. Freeman and Peter Gottschalk, eds., *Generating Jobs: How to Increase Demand for Less-Skilled Workers,* 195–222. New York: Russell Sage Foundation.

Freeman, Richard, Douglas Kruse, and Joseph Blasi. 2008. "Worker Responses to Shirking under Shared Capitalism." National Bureau of Economic Research Working Paper 14227.

French, Kenneth R. 2008. "The Cost of Active Investing." *Journal of Finance* 3(4):1537–73.

French, Kenneth R., et al. 2009. *The Squam Lake Report: Fixing the Financial System.* Princeton, NJ: Princeton University Press.

Freud, Sigmund. 1952 [1930]. *Civilization and Its Discontents,* trans. Joan Reviere. The Major Works of Sigmund Freud. Chicago: William Benton / Encyclopaedia Britannica.

Friedman, Milton (with Rose D. Friedman). 1962. *Capitalism and Freedom.* Chicago: University of Chicago Press.

Friedman, Milton, and Simon Kuznets. 1945. *Income from Independent Professional Practice.* New York: National Bureau of Economic Research.

Gale, David., and Lloyd S. Shapley. 1962. "College Admissions and the Stability of Marriage." *American Mathematical Society Monthly* 69(1):9–15.

Gartner, John D. 2005. *The Hypomanic Edge: The Link between (a Little) Craziness and (a Lot of) Success in America.* New York: Simon and Schuster.

Gartzke, Erik, Quan Li, and Charles Boehmer. 2001. "Investing in Peace: Economic Interdependence and International Conflict." *International Organization* 55(2):391–438.

Geanakoplos, John. 2009. "The Leverage Cycle." In *NBER Macroeconomics Annual 2009,* 1–65. Cambridge, MA: National Bureau of Economic Research.

———. 2010. "Solving the Present Crisis and Managing the Leverage Cycle." Working Paper 1751. New Haven, CT: Cowles Foundation for Research in Economics, Yale University.

Gelman, Susan, and Paul Bloom. 2000. "Young Children Are Sensitive to How an Object Was Created When Deciding What to Name It." *Cognition* 76(2):91–103.

Gilpin, William J., and Henry E. Wallace. 1905. *Clearing House of New York City; New York Clearing House Association, 1854–1905*. New York: M. King.

Gintis, Herbert, Samuel Bowles, Robert Boyd, and Ernst Fehr. 2005. *Moral Sentiments and Material Interests: The Foundations of Cooperation in Economic Life*. Cambridge, MA: MIT Press.

Glezer, Laurie, Xiong Jiang, and Maximilian Riesenhuber. 2009. "Evidence for Highly Selective Neuronal Tuning to Whole Words in the 'Visual Word Form Area.'" *Neuron* 62(2):199–204.

Glick, Reuven, and Kevin J. Lansing. 2010. "Global Household Leverage, House Prices, and Consumption." *FRBSF Economic Letter* 2010-01, http://www.frbsf.org/publications/economics/letter/2010/el2010-01.html.

Glimcher, Paul. 2011. *Foundations of Neuroeconomic Analysis*. New York: Oxford University Press.

Goetzmann, William, Roger Ibbotson, Matthew Spiegel, and Ivo Welch. 2002. "Sharpening Sharpe Ratios." National Bureau of Economic Research Working Paper 9116.

Gollier, Christian. 2008. "Intergenerational Risk-Sharing and Risk-Taking of a Pension Fund." *Journal of Public Economics* 92:1463–85.

Gorton, Gary. 2010. *Slapped by the Invisible Hand: The Panic of 2007*. Oxford: Oxford University Press.

———. 2011. "Review [of books by Michael Lewis and Gregory Zuckerman]." *Journal of Economic Literature* 49:450–53.

Gorton, Gary, and Guillermo Ordoñez. 2012. "Collateral Crises." Unpublished paper, Department of Finance, Yale University.

Gorton, Gary, and Andrew Winton. 1995. "Bank Capital Regulation in General Equilibrium." National Bureau of Economic Research Working Paper w5244.

Graetz, Michael J. 1979. "Implementing a Progressive Consumption Tax." *Harvard Law Review* 92(8):1575–1661.

Granick, David. 1960. *The Red Executive: A Study of the Organization Man in Russian Industry*. Garden City, NY: Doubleday.

Griffiths, John C. 2003. *Hostage: The History, Facts & Reasoning behind Political Hostage Taking*. London: Andre Deutsch.

Grinblatt, Mark, Matti Keloharju, and Juhani Linnainmaa. 2011. "IQ and Stock Market Participation." *Journal of Finance* 66(6):2121–64.

Gross, L. 1982. *The Art of Selling Intangibles: How to Make Your Million($) by Investing Other People's Money*. New York: New York Institute of Finance.

Grossman, Sanford, and Joseph Stiglitz. 1980. "On the Impossibility of Informationally Efficient Markets." *American Economic Review* 70:393–408.

Gruber, Martin J. 1996. "Another Puzzle: The Growth in Actively Managed Funds." *Journal of Finance* 51(3):783–810.

Hacker, Jacob, and Paul Pierson. 2010. *Winner-Take-All Politics: How Washington Made the Rich Richer—and Turned Its Back on the Middle Class*. New York: Simon and Schuster.

Hansmann, Henry. 1990. "Why Do Universities Have Endowments?" *Journal of Legal Studies* 19:3–42.

Hansmann, Henry, Daniel Kessler, and Mark McClellan. 2003. "Ownership Form and Trapped Capital in the Hospital Industry." In Edward Glaeser, ed., *The Governance of Not-for-Profit Organizations*, 45–70. Chicago: University of Chicago Press.

Harbough, William T. 1998. "The Prestige Motive for Making Charitable Transfers." *American Economic Review* 88(2):277–88.

Harriss, C. Lowell. 1951. *History and Policies of the Home Owners' Loan Corporation*. New York: National Bureau of Economic Research.

Hayek, F. A. 1944. *The Road to Serfdom*. London: Routledge.

———. 1945. "The Use of Knowledge in Society." *American Economic Review* 35(4):519–30.

Heckman, James J., and Pedro Carneiro. 2003. "Human Capital Policy." In James J. Heckman and Alan B. Krueger, *Inequality in America: What Role for Human Capital Policies?*, 77–239. Cambridge, MA: MIT Press.

Hellman, Thomas, and Manju Puri. 2002. "Venture Capital and the Professionalization of Start-Up Firms: Empirical Evidence." *Journal of Finance* 57(1):169–97.

Hertzberg, Andrew. 2011. "Exponential Individuals, Hyperbolic Households." Unpublished paper, Graduate School of Business, Columbia University.

Higgins, Benjamin. 1943. "Problems of Planning Public Work." In Seymour E. Harris, ed., *Postwar Economic Problems*, 187–205. New York: McGraw-Hill.

Hill, Claire A. 1997. "Securitization: A Low-Cost Sweetener for Lemons." *Journal of Applied Corporate Finance* 10(1):64–71.

Hill, Rowland. 1837. *Post Office Reform*. London: William Clowes & Sons.

Hirschman, Albert O. 1977. *The Passions and the Interests*. Princeton, NJ: Princeton University Press.

Horesh, Ronnie. 2000. "Injecting Incentives into the Solution of Social Problems: Social Policy Bonds." *Economic Affairs* 20(3):39–42.

Iacocca, Lee (with William Novak). 1984. *Iacocca: An Autobiography*. New York: Bantam Dell.

Jaffee, Dwight, Howard Kunreuther, and Erwann Michel-Kerjan. 2008. "Long-Term Care Insurance (LTI) for Addressing Catastrophe Risk." National Bureau of Economic Research Working Paper 14210.

Jayachandran, Seema, and Michael Kremer. 2006. "Odious Debt." *American Economic Review* 96(1):82–92.

Jayadev, Arjun, and Samuel Bowles. 2006. "Guard Labor." *Journal of Development Economics* 79:328–48.

Jeon, Yoong-Deok, and Young-Yong Kim. 2000. "Land Reform, Income Redistribution, and Agricultural Production in Korea." *Economic Development and Cultural Change* 48(2):253–68.

Joseph, Jane E., Xun Liu, Yang Jiang, Donald Lynam, and Thomas H. Kelly. 2008. "Neural Correlates of Emotional Reactivity in Sensation Seeking." *Psychological Science* 20(2):215–23.

Jung, Jeeman, and Robert J. Shiller. 2005. "A Simple Test of Samuelson's Dictum for the Stock Market." *Economic Inquiry* 43(2):263–92.

Kahneman, Daniel, and Amos Tversky. 1979. "Prospect Theory: An Analysis of Decision under Risk." *Econometrica* 47(2):263–92.

Kamstra, Mark, and Robert J. Shiller. 2010. "Trills Instead of T-Bills: It's Time to Replace Part of Government Debt with Shares in GDP." *The Economists' Voice* 7(3), Article 5, http://www.bepress.com/ev/vol7/iss3/art5.

Kaplan, Steven N., and Antoinette Schoar. 2005. "Private Equity Performance: Returns, Persistence, and Capital Flows." *Journal of Finance* 60(4):1791–823.

Karlan, Dean, and Margaret A. McConnell. 2009. "Hey Look at Me: The Effect of Giving Circles on Giving." Unpublished paper, Yale University.

Karlan, Dean, and Jonathan Zinman. 2011. "Microcredit in Theory and Practice: Using Randomized Credit Scoring for Impact Evaluation." *Science* 332(6035):1278–84.

Kasper, Rob. 1980. "Jerry Rubin Goes Wall Street, but Still Can't Tie a Tie." *Baltimore Sun*, August 19, B1.

Kat, Harry, and Faye Menexe. 2003. "Persistence in Hedge Fund Performance: The True Value of a Track Record." *Journal of Alternative Investments* 5(4):66–72.

Kaufman, Henry. 2005. *On Money and Markets: A Wall Street Memoir*. New York: McGraw-Hill.

Kendall, Maurice. 1953. "The Analysis of Economic Time Series I." *Journal of the Royal Statistical Society, Series A* 116:11–25.

Keynes, John Maynard. 1936. *The General Theory of Employment, Interest and Money*. London: Macmillan.

———. 1937. "The General Theory of Employment." *Quarterly Journal of Economics* 51(2):209–23.

Khurana, Rakesh. 2004. *Searching for a Corporate Savior: The Irrational Quest for Charismatic CEOs*. Princeton, NJ: Princeton University Press.

Kleiner, Morris M., and Alan B. Krueger. 2009. "Analyzing the Extent and Influence of Occupational Licensing on the Labor Market." National Bureau of Economic Research Working Paper 14979.

Kremer, Michael, and Rachel Glennerster. 2004. *Strong Medicine: Creating Incentives for Pharmaceutical Research on Neglected Diseases*. Princeton, NJ: Princeton University Press.

Kroszner, Randall, and Robert J. Shiller. 2011. *Reforming the U.S. Financial Markets: Reflections before and beyond Dodd-Frank*. Alvin Hansen Symposium Series on Public Policy, Harvard University. Cambridge, MA: MIT Press.

Krueger, Alan B. 2003. "Inequality: Too Much of a Good Thing." In James J. Heckman and Alan B. Krueger, *Inequality in America: What Role for Human Capital Policies?*, 1–75. Cambridge, MA: MIT Press.

———. 2007. *What Makes a Terrorist: Economics and the Roots of Terrorism*. Princeton, NJ: Princeton University Press.

Kunreuther, Howard, and Michael Useem. 2010. *Learning from Catastrophes: Strategies for Reaction and Response*. Philadelphia: Wharton School.

Kupchan, Charles A. 2010. *How Enemies Become Friends: The Sources of Stable Peace*. Princeton, NJ: Princeton University Press.

Labuszewski, John W., John E. Nyttoff, Richard Co, and Paul E. Peterson. 2010. *The CME Group Risk Management Handbook*. Hoboken, NJ: Wiley.

Laird, John E. 2009. "Toward Cognitive Robotics." Unpublished paper, Department of Computer Science and Engineering, University of Michigan.

Lakoff, George, and Mark Johnson. 2003. *Metaphors We Live By*. Chicago: University of Chicago Press.

Lederer, Emil. 1915. "Zur Soziologie des Weltkriegs." *Archiv für Sozialwissenschaft und Sozialpolitik* 39:357–384. Translated as "On the Sociology of World War," *European Journal of Sociology* 47:241–68, 2006.

Lederman, Leon M. 2004. *Symmetry and the Beautiful Universe*. New York: Lederman and Hill.

Lee Kuan Yew. 2000. *From Third World to First: The Singapore Story 1965–2000*. New York: HarperCollins.

LeRoy, Stephen F., and Richard Porter. 1981. "The Present-Value Relation: Tests Based on Implied Variance Bounds." *Econometrica* 49(3):555–74.

Lessig, Lawrence. 2011. *Republic, Lost: How Money Corrupts Congress—and a Plan to Stop It*. New York: Twelve / Hachette Book Group.

Levine, Ross. 1997. "Financial Development and Economic Growth: Views and Agenda." *Journal of Economic Literature* 35(2):688–726.

Levitt, Arthur (with Paula Dwyer). 2003. *Take on the Street: How to Fight for Your Financial Future*. New York: Vintage.

Levy, Frank, and Richard J. Murnane. 2005. *The New Division of Labor: How Computers Are Creating the Next Job Market*. Princeton, NJ: Princeton University Press.

Lewis, Michael. 2010. *The Big Short: Inside the Doomsday Machine*. New York: W. W. Norton.

Li, Haitao, Rui Zhao, and Xiaoyan Zhang. 2008. "Investing in Talents: Manager Characteristics and Hedge Fund Performances." Unpublished paper, Department of Finance, University of Michigan.

Li, Zhisui. 1994. *The Private Life of Chairman Mao: The Memoirs of Mao's Personal Physician*. New York: Random House.

List, John A., and David Lucking-Reiley. 2002. "The Effects of Seed Money and Refunds on Charitable Giving: Experimental Evidence from a University Capital Campaign." *Journal of Political Economy* 110:215–33.

Locke, John. 1841 [1690]. *An Essay Concerning Human Understanding*. London: Thomas Tegg.

Long, Charles H. 1983. *Alpha: The Myths of Creation*. Oxford: Oxford University Press.

Lorenz, Konrad. 1966. *On Aggression*. New York: Bantam.

Luthar, Suniya S., and Shawn Latendresse. 2005. "Children of the Affluent: Challenges to Well-Being." *Current Directions in Psychological Science* 14(1):49–53.

Mac Cormack, Earl. 1985. *A Cognitive Theory of Metaphor*. Cambridge, MA: MIT Press.

Mailath, George, Larry Samuelson, and Avner Shaked. 2000. "Endogenous Inequality in Integrated Labor Markets with Two-Sided Search." *American Economic Review* 90(1):46–72.

Malmendier, Ulrike. 2005. "Roman Shares." In William Goetzmann and K. Geert Rouwenhorst, eds., *The Origins of Value: The Financial Innovations That Created Modern Capital Markets*, 31–42. New York: Oxford University Press.

Marcus, Alan J. 1984. "Deregulation and Bank Financial Policy." *Journal of Banking and Finance* 8(4):557–65.

Markopolos, Harry. 2011. *No One Would Listen: A True Financial Thriller.* New York: Wiley.

Martel, Gordon. 2008. *Origins of the First World War.* New York: Pearson Longman.

Martin, Sarah B., D. Jeff Covell, Jane E. Joseph, Himachandra Chebrolu, Charles D. Smith, Thomas H. Kelly, Yang Jiang, and Brian T. Gold. 2007. "Human Experience Seeking Correlates with Hippocampus Volume: Convergent Evidence from Manual Tracing and Voxel-Based Morphometry." *Neuropsychologia* 45:2874–81.

Marx, Karl. 1906. *Capital: A Critique of Political Economy.* New York: Modern Library.

Marx, Karl, and Friedrich Engels. 1906 [1848]. *Manifesto of the Communist Party.* Chicago: Charles H. Kerr & Co.

Mayer, Colin. 1990. "Financial Systems, Corporate Finance, and Economic Development." In R. Glenn Hubbard, ed., *Asymmetric Information, Corporate Finance, and Investment,* 307–32. Chicago: University of Chicago Press.

Melamed, Leo. 2009. *For Crying Out Loud: From Open Outcry to Electronic Screen.* Hoboken, NJ: Wiley.

Mian, Atif, and Amir Sufi. 2010. "Household Leverage and the Recession of 2007 to 2009." *IMF Economic Review* 58:74–117.

Mian, Atif, Amir Sufi, and Francesco Trebbi. 2011. "Foreclosures, House Prices, and the Real Economy." National Bureau of Economic Research Working Paper 16685.

Milgrom, Paul, and Nancy Stokey. 1982. "Information, Trade and Common Knowledge." *Journal of Economic Theory* 26:17–27.

Miller, John Perry. 1991. *Creating Academic Settings: High Craft and Low Cunning: Memoirs.* New Haven, CT: J. Simeon.

Miller, Joseph S. 2008. *The Wicked Wine of Democracy: A Memoir.* Seattle: University of Washington Press.

Miller, Merton H., and Franco Modigliani. 1961. "Dividend Policy, Growth, and the Valuation of Shares." *Journal of Business* 34:411–33.

Mishkin, Frederick. 1996. "Understanding Financial Crises: A Developing Country Perspective." National Bureau of Economic Research Working Paper 5600.

Modigliani, Franco, and Merton H. Miller. 1963. "Corporate Income Taxes and the Cost of Capital: A Correction." *American Economic Review* 53:433–43.

Mongelli, Lorena, and Dan Mangan. 2009. "The SEC Watchdog Who Missed Madoff; Don't Blame Me: Cheung." *New York Post,* January 7, http://www.nypost.com/p/news/business/item_IbjeXQwwTt0whXl6ojz3oJ.

Montague, Read. 2007. *Your Brain Is (Almost) Perfect: How We Make Decisions.* New York: Penguin Plume.

Montesquieu, Charles de Secondat. 1773 [1748]. *The Spirit of Laws,* Tenth Edition, trans. Thomas Nugent. London: S. Crowder, C. Ware, and T. Payne.

Moody, John L. 1933. *The Long Road Home.* New York: Macmillan.

Morrison, Alan D., and William J. Wilhelm, Jr. 2008. "The Demise of Investment-Banking Partnerships: Theory and Evidence." *Journal of Finance* 63(1):311–50.

Moss, David. 2004. *When All Else Fails: Government as the Ultimate Risk Manager.* Cambridge, MA: Harvard University Press.

Myers, Stewart. 1984. "The Capital Structure Puzzle." *Journal of Finance* 39:575–92.

National Commission on the Causes of the Financial and Economic Crisis in the United States (U.S. Financial Crisis Inquiry Commission). 2011. *Financial Crisis Inquiry Report*. Washington, DC: U.S. Government Printing Office, http://www.gpoaccess .gov/fcic/fcic.pdf.

Newcomb, Simon. 1879. "The Standard of Value." *North American Review* 129:223–38.

Nietzsche, Friedrich. 1968 [1901]. *The Will to Power*, trans. Walter Kaufmann and R. J. Hollingdale. New York: Vintage.

Nordenflycht, Andrew von. 2008. "The Demise of the Professional Partnership? The Emergence and Diffusion of Publicly-Traded Professional Service Firms." Unpublished paper, Beedie School of Business, Simon Fraser University.

O'Leary, Ann. 2012. "Risk Sharing When Work and Family Clash: The Need for Government and Employer Innovation." In Jacob Hacker and Ann O'Leary, eds., *Shared Responsibility, Shared Risk*, Chapter 9. New York: Oxford University Press.

O'Reilly, Randy, D. C. Noelle, Jon Cohen, and Todd Braver. 2002. "Prefrontal Cortex and Dynamic Categorization Tasks: Representational Organization and Neuromodulatory Control. *Cerebral Cortex* 12:246–57.

Owings, W. A. Dolph. 1984. *The Sarajevo Trial*. Chapel Hill, NC: Documentary.

Park, Sun Young. 2011. "The Safeness of AAA-Rated Subprime MBSs." Unpublished paper, Korea Advanced Institute of Science and Technology.

Patoine, Brenda. 2011. "Desperately Seeking Sensation: Fear, Reward, and the Human Need for Novelty: Neuroscience Begins to Shine Light on the Neural Basis of Sensation-Seeking," Dana Foundation, http://www.dana.org/media/detail.aspx?id=23620.

Pharoah, Cathy. 2009. *Family Foundation Philanthropy 2009: UK, Germany, Italy, US*. London: Alliance Publishing Trust.

Phelps, Edmund. 2007. *Rewarding Work: How to Restore Participation and Self-Support to Free Enterprise*. Cambridge, MA: Harvard University Press.

Phelps, Edmund, and Leo M. Tilman. 2010. "Wanted: A First National Bank of Innovation." *Harvard Business Review*, January–February, 1–2.

Philippon, Thomas, and Ariell Reshef. 2008. "Wages and Human Capital in the U.S. Financial Industry: 1909–2006." Unpublished paper, Department of Finance, New York University.

Pinker, Steven. 2011. *The Better Angels of Our Nature: Why Violence Has Declined*. New York: Viking Adult.

Pogrebin, Robin. 2011. "Resisting Renaming of Miami Museum." *New York Times*, December 6, C1.

Post, David. 2005. "Altruism, Happiness and Health: It's Good to Be Good." *International Journal of Behavioral Medicine* 12(2):66–77.

Prante, Gerald. 2007. "Most Americans Don't Itemize on Their Tax Returns." Tax Foundation, July 23, http://www.taxfoundation.org/news/show/22499.html.

Proust, Marcel. 2002 [1913]. *Swann's Way*, trans. Lydia Davis. New York: Penguin.

Pulvermüller, Friedemann. 2002. *The Neuroscience of Language*. Cambridge: Cambridge University Press.

Rajan, Raghuram. 2010. *Fault Lines: How Hidden Fractures Still Threaten the World Economy*. Princeton, NJ: Princeton University Press.

Rajan, Raghuram, and Luigi Zingales. 2004. *Saving Capitalism from the Capitalists: Unleashing the Power of Financial Markets to Create Wealth and Spread Opportunity.* Princeton, NJ: Princeton University Press.

Redleaf, Andrew, and Richard Vigilante. 2010. *Panic: The Betrayal of Capitalism by Wall Street and Washington.* Minneapolis: Vigilante.

Rhodes, Gillian. 2006. "The Evolutionary Psychology of Facial Beauty." *Annual Review of Psychology* 57:199–226.

Ross, Lee. 1977. "The Intuitive Psychologist and His Shortcomings: Distortions in the Attribution Process." *Advances in Experimental Social Psychology* 10:173–220.

Ross, Stephen A. 1976. "Options and Efficiency." *Quarterly Journal of Economics* 90(1):75–89.

Roth, Alvin E., Tayfun Sonmez, and M. Utku Unver. 2005. "Pairwise Kidney Exchange." *Journal of Economic Theory* 125(2):151–88.

Russett, Bruce, and John Oneal. 2001. *Triangulating Peace: Democracy, Interdependence and International Organizations.* New York: W. W. Norton.

Saint-Exupéry, Antoine de. 2000 [1943]. *The Little Prince,* trans. Richard Howard. Orlando, FL: Harcourt.

Salacuse, Jeswald W. 2003. "Corporate Governance, Culture and Convergence: Corporations American Style or with a European Touch?" *Law and Business Review of the Americas* 9:33–62, http://heinonline.org/HOL/Page?handle=hein.journals/lbramrca9&div=11&g_sent=1&collection=journals.

Sala-i-Martin, Xavier. 2006. "The World Distribution of Income: Falling Poverty and . . . Convergence, Period." *Quarterly Journal of Economics* 121(2):351–97.

Sargent, Frederic O. 1961. "Feudalism to Family Farms in France." *Agricultural History* 35(4):193–201.

Scharlach, Andrew E., and Amanda J. Lehning. 2012. "The Government's Role in Aging and Long-Term Care." In Jacob Hacker and Ann O'Leary, eds., *Shared Responsibility, Shared Risk,* Chapter 12. New York: Oxford University Press.

Schultz, Wolfram. 1998. "Predictive Reward Signal of Dopamine Neurons." *Journal of Neurophysiology* 80(1):1–27.

Schultz, Wolfram, Peter Dayan, and P. Read Montague. 1997. "A Neural Substrate for Prediction and Reward." *Science* 275(5306):593–99.

Schumpeter, Joseph A. 1962 [1950]. *Capitalism, Socialism and Democracy,* Third Edition. New York: Harper Torchbooks.

Schwed, Fred. 1940. *Where Are the Customers' Yachts? A Good Hard Look at Wall Street.* New York: Simon and Schuster.

Scoville, James G. 2006. "Labor Market Underpinnings of a Caste Economy." *American Journal of Economics and Sociology* 55(4):385–94.

Seavoy, Ronald E. 1972. "Laws to Encourage Manufacturing: New York Policy and the 1811 General Incorporation Statute." *Business History Review* 46(1):85–95.

Shapley, Lloyd, and Herbert Scarf. 1974. "On Cores and Indivisibility." *Journal of Mathematical Economics* 1(1):23–37.

Shefrin, Hersh. 2007. *Behavioral Corporate Finance: Decisions That Create Value.* Boston: McGraw-Hill.

Shefrin, Hersh, and Meir Statman. 1993. "Behavioral Aspects of the Design and Marketing of Financial Products." *Financial Management* 22(2):123–34.

Shiller, Robert J. 1981. "Do Stock Prices Move Too Much to Be Justified by Subsequent Changes in Dividends?" *American Economic Review* 71(3):421–36.

———. 1994. *Macro Markets: Creating Institutions to Manage Society's Largest Economic Risks*. Oxford: Oxford University Press.

———. 1997. "Public Resistance to Indexation: A Puzzle." *Brookings Papers on Economic Activity* 1:159–211.

———. 2003. *The New Financial Order: Risk in the 21st Century*. Princeton, NJ: Princeton University Press.

———. 2005a. "The Invention of Inflation-Indexed Bonds in Early America." In William N. Goetzmann and K. Geert Rouwenhorst, eds., *The Origins of Value: The Financial Innovations That Created Modern Capital Markets*, 239–48. New York: Oxford University Press.

———. 2005b. *Irrational Exuberance*, Second Edition. Princeton, NJ: Princeton University Press.

———. 2008. *The Subprime Solution: How Today's Global Financial Crisis Happened and What to Do about It*. Princeton, NJ: Princeton University Press.

———. 2009. *The Case for a Basket: A New Way of Showing the True Value of Money*. London: Policy Exchange.

———. 2012a. "Give People Shares of GDP." *Harvard Business Review* 90(1/2):50–51.

———. 2012b. "Irving Fisher, Debt Deflation and Crises." *Journal of the History of Economic Thought*, forthcoming.

Shiller, Robert J., Maxim Boycko, and Vladimir Korobov. 1991. "Popular Attitudes towards Free Markets: The Soviet Union and the United States Compared." *American Economic Review* 81(3):385–400.

Shiller, Robert J., Rafal M. Wojakowski, M. Shahid Ebrahim, and Mark B. Shackleton. 2011. "Continuous Workout Mortgages." Discussion Paper 1794. New Haven, CT: Cowles Foundation for Research in Economics, Yale University.

Shleifer, Andrei. 2000. *Inefficient Markets: An Introduction to Behavioral Finance*. Oxford: Oxford University Press.

Shubik, Martin. 2009. *A Proposal for a Federal Employment Reserve Authority*. Economics Policy Note 09-5. New York: Levy Economics Institute.

Simmons, Joseph P., and Nathan Novemsky. 2009. "From Loss Aversion to Loss Acceptance: Context Effects on Loss Aversion in Risky Choice." Working Paper. New Haven, CT: Yale School of Management.

Small, Deborah A., George Loewenstein, and Paul Slovic. 2007. "Sympathy and Callousness: The Impact of Deliberative Thought on Donations to Identifiable and Statistical Victims." *Organizational Behavior and Human Decision Processes* 102(2):143–53.

Smith, Adam. 1761. *The Theory of Moral Sentiments*, Second Edition. London: A. Millar in the Strand.

———. 1776. *An Inquiry into the Nature and Causes of the Wealth of Nations*. London: Ward, Lock & Bowden & Co.

Sprenkle, Case. 1964. "Warrant Prices as Indicators of Expectations and Preferences."

In Paul Cootner, ed., *The Random Character of Stock Market Prices*, 412–74. Cambridge, MA: MIT Press.

Stanley, Thomas J. 1991. *Selling to the Affluent*. New York: McGraw-Hill.

Stark, Oded, and Ita Falk. 1998. "Transfers, Empathy Formation, and Reverse Transfers." *American Economic Review* 88(2):271–76.

Stigler, George A. 1971. "The Theory of Economic Regulation." *Bell Journal of Economics and Management Science* 2(1):3–21.

Stratmann, Thomas. 1991. "What Do Campaign Contributions Buy? Deciphering Causal Effects of Money and Votes." *Southern Economic Journal* 57(3):606–20.

Summers, Lawrence H. 1986. "Does the Stock Market Rationally Reflect Fundamental Values?" *Journal of Finance* 41(3):28–30.

Swafford, Jan. 1996. *Charles Ives: A Life with Music*. New York: W. W. Norton.

Tarbell, Ida M. 1904. *The History of the Standard Oil Company*. New York: McClure, Phillips.

Tarlow, Steve. 2010. "Estate Tax Sends Elderly Racing to the Grave." newsytype.com, November 2, http://www.newsytype.com/3257-estate-tax/.

Tetlock, Philip E. 2006. *Expert Political Judgment: How Good Is It? How Can We Know?* Princeton, NJ: Princeton University Press.

Thaler, Richard H., and Cass R. Sunstein. 2008. *Nudge: Improving Decisions about Health, Wealth and Happiness*. New Haven, CT: Yale University Press.

Thomsen, Jens, and Verner Anderson. 2007. "Longevity Bonds: A Financial Market Instrument to Manage Longevity Risk." *Monetary Review* 46(4):29–44.

Thoreau, Henry David. 2008 [1863]. *Life without Principle*. Forgotten Books, http://www.forgottenbooks.org/.

Toppe, Christopher M., Arthur D. Kirsch, and Jocabel Michel. 2001. *Giving and Volunteering in the United States: Findings from a National Survey*. Washington, DC: Independent Sector, http://www.cpanda.org/pdfs/gv/GV01Report.pdf.

Townsend, Robert M. 1994. "Risk and Insurance in Village India." *Econometrica* 62(3):539–91.

Tufano, Peter, and Daniel Schneider. 2009. "Using Financial Innovation to Support Savers: From Coercion to Excitement." In Rebecca M. Blank and Michael S. Barr, eds., *Insufficient Funds: Savings, Assets, Credit and Banking among Low-Income Households*, 149–90. New York: Russell Sage Foundation.

Unger, Peter. 1996. *Living High and Letting Die: Our Illusion of Innocence*. New York: Oxford University Press.

United Nations. 1948. *The Universal Declaration of Human Rights*. http://www.un.org/en/documents/udhr/.

U.S. Commodities Futures Trading Commission and Securities and Exchange Commission. 2010. "Findings Regarding the Market Events of May 6, 2010: Report to the Joint Advisory Committee on Emerging Regulatory Issues." http://www.sec.gov/news/studies/2010/marketevents-report.pdf.

U.S. Congressional Budget Office. 2011. "Trends in the Distribution of Household Income between 1979 and 2007." http://www.cbo.gov/ftpdocs/124xx/doc12485/WebSummary.pdf.

U.S. Financial Stability Oversight Council. 2011. *Study & Recommendations Regarding*

Concentration Limits on Large Financial Companies. Washington, DC. http://www
.treasury.gov/initiatives/Documents/Study%20on%20Concentration%20Limits%20
on%20Large%20Firms%2001-17-11.pdf.

U.S. National Commission on Fiscal Responsibility and Reform. 2010. *The Moment of Truth.* Washington, DC.

Van Veen, Vincent, Marie K. Krug, Jonathan W. Schooler, and Cameron S. Carter. 2009. "Neural Activity Predicts Attitude Change in Cognitive Dissonance." *Nature Neuroscience* 12(11):1469–74.

Veblen, Thorstein. 1899. *The Theory of the Leisure Class: An Economic Study of the Evolution of Institutions.* London: Macmillan.

Vickery, Thomas J., Marvin M. Chun, and Daeyeol Lee. 2011. "Ubiquity and Specificity of Reinforcement Signals throughout the Human Brain." *Neuron* 72(1):166–77.

Visser, Jelle. 2003. "Unions and Unionism around the World." In John T. Addison and Claus Schnabel, eds., *International Handbook of Trade Unions,* 366–96. Cheltenham, UK: Edward Elgar.

Vuolteenaho, Tuomo. 2002. "What Drives Firm-Level Stock Returns?" *Journal of Finance* 57:233–64.

Weber, Max. 2010 [1905]. *The Protestant Ethic and the Spirit of Capitalism.* New York: CreateSpace.

Weller, Christian, and Amy Helburn. 2012. "Public Policy Options to Build Wealth for America's Middle Class." In Jacob Hacker and Ann O'Leary, eds., *Shared Responsibility, Shared Risk,* Chapter 7. New York: Oxford University Press.

Weyl, Hermann. 1952. *Symmetry.* Princeton, NJ: Princeton University Press.

Whitman, Walt. 1892. *Leaves of Grass.* Project Gutenberg Ebook, http://www.gutenberg
.org/files/1322/1322-h/1322-h.htm.

Wittgenstein, Ludwig. 1953. *Philosophical Investigations.* Oxford: Blackwell.

Wolfers, Justin, and Eric Zitzewitz. 2004. "Prediction Markets." *Journal of Economic Perspectives* 18(2):107–26.

Woodward, Bob. 2001. *Maestro: Greenspan's Fed and the American Boom.* New York: Simon and Schuster.

Working, Holbrook. 1934. "A Random-Difference Series for Use in the Analysis of Time Series." *Journal of the American Statistical Association* 29(185):11–24.

Yavlinsky, Grigory. 2011. *Realpolitik: The Hidden Cause of the Great Recession (And How to Avert the Next One),* trans. Antonina W. Bouis. New Haven, CT: Yale University Press.

Yunus, Muhammad. 2003. *Banker to the Poor: Micro-Lending and the Battle against World Poverty.* New York: Public Affairs.

Zuckerman, Gregory. 2009. *The Greatest Trade Ever: The Behind-the-Scenes Story of How John Paulson Defied Wall Street and Made Financial History.* New York: Crown Business.

Zuckerman, Marvin, Sybil B. Eysenck, and H. J. Eysenck. 1978. "Sensation Seeking in England and in America: Cross-Cultural, Age, and Sex Comparisons." *Journal of Consulting and Clinical Psychology* 46:139–49.

Index